14 - 120 - 1370

SANDERS A. KAHN, Ph.D., A.S.A., S.R.A., is President of Sanders A. Kahn Associates, Inc., Appraisers and Realtors, and Adjunct Professor and Supervisor of Undergraduate Real Estate Education at the Bernard M. Baruch School of Business and Public Administration, The City College of the City University of New York. He is Governor of Region I, American Society of Appraisers, and National Education Chairman and Associate Chairman of the Board of Examiners of that Society.

FREDERICK E. CASE, D.B.A., M.A.I., is Professor of Real Estate and Urban Land Economics, Graduate School of Business Administration, University of California, Los Angeles. He was formerly Director of the Real Estate Research Program at the University of California, Los Angeles, and has taught real estate at Indiana University and the University of Florida. In addition to working with private businesses in highest and best land-use studies, he writes regularly for leading professional and academic journals. Professor Case has been cited by the American Institute of Real Estate Appraisers for his outstanding contribution to the literature of appraisal.

ALFRED SCHIMMEL, M.S.Ed., A.S.A., is a Senior Representative for the New York State Housing Finance Agency. He was previously employed as Principal Appraiser for the New York State Banking Department and as a Tax Assessor for the City of New York. Mr. Schimmel is Lecturer in Real Estate Valuation and Appraisal at the Bernard M. Baruch School of Business and Public Administration, The City College of the City University of New York. He is a Senior Member and President of the Greater New York Chapter of the American Society of Appraisers.

REAL ESTATE APPRAISAL AND INVESTMENT

By

SANDERS A. KAHN

SANDERS A. KAHN ASSOCIATES, INC., AND
BERNARD M. BARUCH SCHOOL OF BUSINESS AND
PUBLIC ADMINISTRATION, THE CITY COLLEGE OF THE
CITY UNIVERSITY OF NEW YORK

FREDERICK E. CASE

UNIVERSITY OF CALIFORNIA
LOS ANGELES

ALFRED SCHIMMEL

NEW YORK STATE BANKING DEPARTMENT

THE RONALD PRESS COMPANY • NEW YORK

Library of Congress Catalog Card Number: 63–17624

PRINTED IN THE UNITED STATES OF AMERICA

Preface

This book presents a thorough treatment of all aspects of real estate appraising and, in addition, has specialized sections on real estate investment and analysis.

In recent years, the rate of investing in properties and the problems of establishing value for them have created theoretical and practical problems which have not been dealt with adequately in real estate appraising and investing literature. Today, it is imperative that a more realistic treatment be given to the subject. The purposes of this book are to restate the theoretical base which underlies real estate valuation and investment and to indicate how it can be applied to a variety of practical situations. A number of illustrations are presented to show how some of the more complex items are treated; mathematical tools needed to solve the problems are explained and supported by the necessary tables.

The debts which the authors owe to the many persons who have contributed materials, comments, or suggestions about the book are too numerous to be detailed here. In every instance where credit could be given to a particular person or organization, it has been given. We would be remiss if we did not acknowledge the intellectual debt which we owe to persons like Frederick Babcock, Henry Babcock, Arthur M. Weimer, Ernest M. Fisher, Richard U. Ratcliff, Leo Grebler, Henry Hoagland, and Herbert B. Dorau, who were the pioneer scholars in the field. Nor can we ignore the many lessons which were shared with us by such successful practitioners. However, we must emphasize that we take full responsibility for the materials which are presented, and we feel that this is a modern and complete presentation on the subject of real estate valuation and investment.

The individual authors assume primary responsibility for specific chapters which best represent their specialized knowledge, but all chapters have been mutually edited.

Sanders A. Kahn
Frederick E. Case
Alfred Schimmel

June, 1963

Acknowledgments

Many real estate investors and appraisers have similarly influenced the authors over the past years. Among these are Leon W. Ellwood, formerly Chief Appraiser, New York Life Insurance Co.; John Mannion, Chief Appraiser, The Chase Manhattan Bank; Earl P. Marshall, Chairman, Board of Directors, Marshall & Stevens; John O. Johnsen, Appraisal Officer, Dry Dock Savings Bank; Sam R. Jackson, Assistant Mortgage Officer, The Seamen's Bank for Savings; Eugene Eichenberg, President, American Shopping Centers; Harry B. Helmsley, President, Helmsley-Spear; Commissioner Walter S. Fried, Housing and Redevelopment Board, City of New York; Lester Eisner, Jr., Administrator, Housing and Home Finance Agency, Department of Urban Renewal; Hyman Adelsberg, Leonard Marx, and John J. O'Connor, Equitable Life Assurance Co.; George E. Fuller, formerly Real Estate Officer, Urban Renewal Division, Housing and Home Finance Agency, Region I; Edward S. Backnick, Jr., Vice-President, Lincoln Savings Bank, Brooklyn, New York; Edwin G. Picken and John Westney, Vice-Presidents, The Bank for Savings in the City of New York; Edgar C. Egerton, Vice-President, The Seamen's Bank for Savings of New York; William Nodyne, Mortgage Officer, The Seamen's Bank for Savings; Julian M. Bond, Assistant Mortgage Officer, East River Savings Bank of New York; Robert V. Tishman, President, Tishman Realty and Construction Co.; Larry Smith, President, Larry Smith & Co., Seattle; John A. Kervick, Treasurer, State of New Jersey; James Felt, Chairman, City Planning Commission, City of New York; Paul T. O'Keefe, Commissioner of Real Estate, City of New York; Frederick Stafford, Philadelphia; Frederick W. Kirch, Philadelphia; the noted architect Victor Gruen; Laurence M. Fist, Los Angeles County Assessor's Office; Robert S. Fuller, San Fernando Valley Savings & Loan; Jerre L. Hewitt, Glendale Federal Savings and Loan; George Hamilton Jones, American Institute of Real Estate Appraisers, Los Angeles; Belden Morgan, Federal Housing Administration, southern California; Laurence Sando, American Institute of Real Estate Appraisers, Los Angeles; Wynne Savage, Real Estate Commissioner, California; Robert L. Reeves, United California Bank; Roy C. Seeley, Charles B. Shattuck, Kurt Shelger, and Robert R. Stone, American Institute of Real Estate Appraisers, Los Angeles; James E. Tweedt, Union Bank; Frederick D. Unger, Capital Co.; Stephan Whittlesey and Dr. Thurston Ross, American Institute of Real Estate Appraisers, Los Angeles.

Special credit should be given to Joseph A. Coyle, Principal Real Estate Appraiser, Real Estate Bureau, New York State Insurance Department, who has, for many years, aided in the development of certain of the materials found in the text.

Contents

Part I. INTRODUCTION: BASIC APPRAISAL FACTORS

Part II. VALUATION TECHNIQUES

Part III. SPECIFIC ASSIGNMENTS

Part IV. INVESTMENT ANALYSIS

APPENDIXES

Part I

INTRODUCTION: BASIC
APPRAISAL FACTORS

1

The Appraisal Profession

The appraisal profession has grown in the past three decades to rank as the most skilled of the realty activities. It has become common practice for both newcomers and professionals to rely on appraisers to help make realty decisions. In the past, almost every realty investor and broker considered himself an appraiser. Today, these same people make regular use of appraisal services. Many realty firms have their own staff appraisers, while others regularly call upon the services of other realty firms having this type of personnel.

ASSIGNMENTS AVAILABLE

Assignments in the appraisal field encompass almost every type of realty activity. Some of the most common uses of appraisal experts are included in the list enumerated below.

1. Land utilization
2. Sale or purchase
3. Lease
4. Options—right to renew lease or purchase
5. Mortgage loans
6. Insurance
7. Income tax
8. Condemnation
9. Realty-tax assessments
10. Urban-renewal projects
11. Estate tax
12. Utility-rate fixing
13. Corporate realty—mergers, stock issues, liquidation, bankruptcy
14. Foreclosure

✓ **Land Utilization.** Property owners often are concerned as to the proper use of their land. For instance, one might believe his farm at the outskirts of a town may be suitable for a shopping center, a home subdivision, or industrial or commercial use.

Other owners may want to know what size office building or apartment house to build. Still others may want to consider the economic feasibility of demolishing or altering an existing building to provide a new or improved use for the land.

All of these types of problems are often analyzed by appraisers.

Sale or Purchase. Both property owners and prospective buyers will often obtain an appraisal of realty. The potential seller will usually employ his appraiser before placing the realty on the market. He wants to know what price is obtainable. Often the seller is acting as a trustee, corporate officer, one member of a partnership, or another person in some sort of fiduciary position who wants an offer for the realty analyzed by an appraiser to guide and protect him before finalization of a sale.

A buyer of realty will often call upon an appraiser to advise him if the "deal" he is negotiating is consistent with the market. He may also require the appraiser to give more than an appraised value, by asking about future physical maintenance for the building and about future realty-tax and financing problems. In this way, the appraiser also acts as a consultant.

Lease. Often an appraiser will be hired by an owner, prospective tenant, or other interested party to rental values. Sometimes this will be related to a contemplated lease. At other times the need will be to establish proper rentals for rent-control regulations or possibly to determine a new use for a building.

Options—Right To Renew Lease or Purchase. Leases are sometimes written for long periods of time, specifying that at regular periods of five, ten, twenty, or twenty-five years the rental is to be modified as a result of rental values current at those times. These leases usually specify that the rental will be set by one or more appraisers.

Sometimes the lease will give the tenant the option to purchase the realty. Often, the option will be based on a specific price. In other cases, it will be established by appraisals.

Mortgage Loans. Almost every mortgage loan on realty is based on at least one and usually two or more appraisals. Many lending institutions have their own staff make an appraisal, but before finalizing a loan they usually will have an independent appraiser deliver his opinion of value in a written appraisal report.

Insurance. Before insuring their realty, many owners will have an appraiser find the "insurable value." Often this is a requirement of the mortgagee.

Income Tax. Income-tax liability has become a major factor influencing realty use and investment. Appraisers are often called upon to determine the value of the component parts of realty, i.e., land, buildings, specialized building equipment.

Another type of appraisal necessary for income-tax purposes is to set the appraised value of a parcel of realty for the year 1913. This was the date of inauguration of the federal income-tax law, and some long-time owners of realty must establish the value of their realty as of that date. This ranks among the most interesting types of assignments.

Condemnation. Under the rights of eminent domain, any levels of government or its agency may take title to private property by giving the former property owner "just compensation." The determination of this compensation is made by the employment of appraisal experts. Often, both the property owner and the condemning authority will employ appraisers.

Realty-Tax Assessments. A large portion of the budget of cities, townships, villages, counties, schools, and other local governmental agencies is obtained by placing a tax on the value of "non-exempt" realty. Exempt realty is realty owned for public purposes of a non-profit nature, such as religious, governmental, educational, and charitable purposes.

Assessors are employed to set the values from which assessed values are established. The assessor usually has appraisal skills or employs private appraisal firms or his own staff to do this work. At intervals, firms are employed to set values for an entire community.

Property owners sometimes believe that their taxes are too high and utilize appraisal services to protest their taxes.

Urban-Renewal Projects. Vast projects are now under way in hundreds of large and small communities to improve obsolete areas. This activity is under the joint auspices of local communities and the Federal Government Housing and Home Finance Agency's Urban Renewal Administration. In addition to condemnation appraisals for this work, there are also "reuse" appraisals. The reuse appraisal suggests future uses and resale prices for the realty after existing buildings are demolished. Appraisers are also employed to prepare marketability and feasibility studies to determine if the project is economically proper.

Estate Tax. Upon the death of a realty owner, estate and inheritance taxes, by both federal and state governments, may be levied. These governmental departments often have staff appraisers and employ independent appraisers. Estate executors will also have properties appraised.

Utility-Rate Fixing. One method of determining rates that public utilities may charge is based upon the land, property, and equipment used by the utility to provide the service. Appraisers will often be employed to establish either current or past values of the realty.

Corporate Realty—Mergers, Stock Issues, Liquidation, Bankruptcy. There has been a large amount of mergers and acquisitions of large and small business corporations. Usually the book value of the realty held by corporations bears little relationship to current market value. The business managers will often solve this problem by employing appraisers. A similar need will exist if the business is to be liquidated or if a public issue of stock is being offered or if the business organization becomes bankrupt.

Foreclosure. Mortgagees, taxing authorities, and other creditors of property owners have the remedy of property foreclosure when their liens are in arrears. In many states, appraisals are ordered to determine the value of the realty at the time of the foreclosure. The appraisal will often determine if the claim against the property owner has been satisfied by transference of the realty to the creditor.

Others. This list of appraisal assignments is not complete. Appraisals are often required in connection with marital and family legal quarrels. There are unlimited matters in litigation trying to determine rights of people to realty.

In future chapters, appraisal methods for most of the enumerated types of appraisals will be discussed in detail.

QUALIFICATIONS OF APPRAISERS

A real estate appraiser is an expert in realty. He determines everything about the realty influencing its uses and the factors affecting them and then rates the property by stating its value in exchange for dollars.

Education. The appraiser must have various qualities that make him capable of carrying out his assignments. His basic skills must include strength in mathematics, as he will have to compute areas of odd-shaped land and buildings. He will also utilize various interest and annuity tables. Most appraisers use slide rules and automatic calculators to speed their work.

Economic geography and urban land economics are two other areas of formal schooling that will prove basic to the appraiser. He must understand why communities prosper, why cities develop, and the order of their growth. Neighborhood factors are studied carefully in every appraisal. This often involves a training in sociology, civics, and government.

The appraiser must often give consideration to financial statements of business organizations, and his accounting training will prove valuable here.

Marketing research and statistics education will help in the analysis of governmental statistics affecting local communities and regions.

In addition to basic courses in general real estate and realty appraising and valuation, college and high-school training for realty appraisers would include the following:

1. City planning
2. Sociology

3. Urban land economics
4. Economic geography
5. Marketing research
6. Statistics
7. Geometry
8. Algebra
9. Commercial mathematics
10. Accountancy
11. Geology
12. Civil engineering
13. Investment principles
14. Government (local)

General Experience. Rarely does anybody directly become a real estate appraiser. Clients would not hire a novice to act as an expert. We usually find that the appraiser must have about ten years of realty experience before people are willing to be guided by his opinion of value. At the end of that period, he will usually be an expert on a particular type of realty such as houses, office buildings, stores, theaters, industrial realty, or one of the numerous other types of realty. He will also usually be skilled in some geographic area, either a neighborhood, community, county, or general area.

Another type of skill obtained by experience may be involved in handling a particular realty function. In this way, he may know renting, management, financing, or selling.

Knowledge of Market Sales, Leases, Mortgages. Since most appraisers are hired to give an opinion as to market value, it appears obvious that this type of knowledge is of prime value.

An appraiser may gain the appropriate experience in several ways. He may be a buyer or seller of realty on a regular basis. He deals in it as an investor, speculator, or operator. Since he buys and sells, he knows the market and knows why buyers and sellers consider particular deals favorable.

He may work for a financial institution making mortgages on realty. Here again, he is acting as a dealer. This time, he is a conservative investor.

He may also gain his market experience working for a large industrial corporation that has bought or rented office buildings, warehouses, and industrial properties for its use. Sometimes, the company has rented the space or engaged in sales leaseback transactions. The same experience is more often gained with a large chain retail organization such as a food market, oil company, variety store, apparel store, or any of numerous others.

However, most appraisers gain their market background as real estate brokers. They have negotiated sales, leases, and mortgages, know the problems of properties, and understand negotiations. Unfortunately, too often the broker's skill at brokerage is developed at the expense of a cold objective attitude so necessary to the appraiser. The rare broker who can take a disinterested approach and who has the training required for appraising can usually become an outstanding appraiser. He knows the market, for he is a living part of it. Other appraisers must act as market reporters.

Knowledge of Operation and Management. A management agent has firsthand knowledge about investment properties. He knows the rentals being obtained in the properties he manages and in competing properties, and he knows the detailed operating costs for all items of expenses. He usually has broken down these costs into approximate units, so he knows, for instance, that operating costs in a large air-conditioned fireproof office building in a large northeastern city may approximate $1.25 per square foot. He also knows each component cost in this total.

The management agent will also be acquainted with costs of alterations to buildings, local realty-tax problems, and all insurance matters affecting realty.

Knowledge of Cost and Engineering. Some appraisers have a background in engineering. This gives them a fine ability to gauge the suitability of buildings for various uses. The engineer or builder will also have clear knowledge of building materials and methods. He will understand the condition, the structure, and the operating equipment. The engineer's or builder's ability to compute the construction cost of a building is obvious. However, determining construction cost is only one method of arriving at value. As we have learned from economic theory, the cost of creating an asset does not necessarily equal its economic or market value.

EMPLOYMENT OPPORTUNITIES

Many realty firms are established with appraisal departments, and some firms almost only handle appraisals. Firms that exclusively deal in appraisals are very few in number. Usually, these firms are engaged in community revaluation for assessment purposes. The typical realty firm has no special appraisal staff and makes only a modest sum from appraisal activities. Even most of the very large realty firms usually only have one or two members of the staff spending an appreciable amount of their time doing appraisal work.

Institutions. Banks, insurance companies, and organizations making mortgage investments usually employ appraisers on their staffs, which include some of the most skilled appraisers in the country, for millions of dollars may be invested by some of these institutions. Often these institutions will also have appraisal trainees who usually get started by inspecting properties on which the institution has outstanding mortgages and by reviewing property files.

Governmental Agencies. There are probably more appraisers with various governmental agencies than with any other class of employers or appraisers.

Local governments have appraisers preparing realty assessed valuations. They also may have to use appraisers before selling community-owned realty or in buying or renting city-occupied realty. In some communities, a city may have an appraiser on its staff in connection with urban renewal, public housing, and city-sponsored realty financing and condemnation.

State and county governments may also have realty-tax assessments made by appraisers on their staffs. They also have appraisers in the banking and insurance departments. Mortgage investments and properties used by these institutions are reviewed by the state to determine if prudent investments are being made. The state itself may invest state funds, particularly employee pension funds in mortgages. It is guided by its appraisal staff.

The federal government has various agencies utilizing staff appraisers. Among these have been the Housing and Home Finance Agency and its components: the Urban Renewal Administration, Federal Housing Administration, Public Housing Administration, and College Housing Administration. The Veterans Administration has been engaged in appraising since World War II. The General Services Administration is involved in acquiring properties to be occupied by the federal government. It also disposes of these properties. Governmental appraisers are utilized on both occasions. The United States Corps of Engineers and numerous other agencies dealing with such matters as roads, small business loans, income taxes, estate taxes, and conservation lands all employ appraisers.

Business Firms. Industrial organizations and chain retailers have large realty departments which include appraisers. These firms need valuations when renting, buying, or selling plants, warehouses, stores, offices, or other properties.

Realty Investment Firms. Some large investors have need of appraisal skill before buying or selling realty. This is particularly true when they are making exceptionally large purchases or buying in areas distant from their normal operation. Investment companies that are on one of the stock exchanges may feel a particular need for this sort of prudent operation.

Clients of Appraisal Firms. Financial institutions often employ independent appraisers to make an appraisal before a mortgage loan is granted. This is often done even though an appraiser on the institution's staff has also made his appraisal. This is part of a series of precautionary steps to assure prudent lending practices. Insurance firms also often want appraisers to value realty damaged by fire and other hazards.

Private Persons. Private owners and their agents often employ appraisers. They require appraisal services for almost every reason for which appraisers are needed. Usually, the owner will not directly order the appraiser. In connection with a mortgage appraisal, a mortgage broker may be the one who commissions the appraiser. In connection with income-tax appraisals, it will be a tax consultant, while a condemnation attorney will be involved if the owner is having his realty condemned. Another attorney may be involved in a question of estate taxes, and still another where the owner wants his realty taxes reviewed by the courts.

Public Agencies. All levels of government employ appraisal firms, in connection with such matters as condemnation, realty taxes, income taxes, estate taxes, property purchases, sales and leases, mortgage placements, insurance matters, and other specialized activities.

Professional Societies. Of the practitioners of all the various types of realty activities, the appraiser has the best claim to professional status. This is due to the need for an objective attitude, long years of experience, and highly specialized skills. He is generally in command of a body of techniques that serve him to reach fair opinions of value. In most cases, he has a high level of college education.

Several appraisal societies have been formed. These organizations have done much to foster the improvement of appraisal techniques and to create a finer group of appraisers. They publish professional journals, sponsor education courses and seminars, and have regular meetings. All of this has resulted in better appraisers with an enhanced position in the public esteem.

AMERICAN INSTITUTE OF REAL ESTATE APPRAISERS. This organization has reached a high level of development. It sponsors appraisal courses annually and has published several texts as well as the *Appraisal Journal* and *The Appraiser,* two fine publications. This organization has also given educational courses on many college campuses.

AMERICAN SOCIETY OF APPRAISERS. This organization includes in its membership all types of appraisers. In addition to realtors, it has engineering valuators, appraisers for public-utility rate making, fine-arts appraisers, insurance appraisers, and security valuators, among others. It publishes the *Appraisal and Valuation Manual,* which is a most elaborate publication, and *Technical Valuation,* a professional journal. It has also published some text materials and offered courses.

SOCIETY OF REAL ESTATE APPRAISERS. This organization is oriented to the appraisal of houses, but its membership includes people making all types of realty appraisals. It is a well-organized group and publishes the *Residential Appraiser*. It also has sponsored educational courses and seminars throughout the country. It was formerly called "Society of Residential Appraisers."

The requirements for all of these societies vary; but, in general, they are based on many years of experience, proof of appraisal skill by examinations, submission of appraisals, and specialization in the field.

OTHERS. In addition to these groups, there are special groups such as the American Right of Way Association, which is concerned with condemnation matters, and the International Association of Assessing Officers. There are also local appraisal societies for states and counties and a very fine appraisal society in Canada as well.

2

The Appraisal Assignment

The role an appraiser should play once he has accepted an appraisal assignment has been discussed in the literature of the field many times, but two principal alternatives are involved: (1) Should the appraiser consider only the valuation problem involved and feel that he has completed his assignment once he has established a value estimate; or (2) should he also include recommendations for actions to be taken as the result of his value estimate? This problem is often faced when an appraiser has been asked to estimate the value of a property for someone contemplating its purchase or use for business purposes. For the professional appraiser the answer is quite clear: An appraisal assignment is undertaken for the purpose of establishing all factors which may influence the value of a property and, after due weighing of the influence of each, to arrive at a single dollar statement representing his considered opinion of the value. If a business-policy recommendation were included, the appraiser would have to broaden his assignment to include an evaluation of the buyer and his business problems so that the appraiser would be well beyond any considerations of property value, which is his sole responsibility.

THE APPRAISER'S RESPONSIBILITIES

An appraisal assignment does not permit the weighing of many known factors and the arrival at a precise and accurate statement; rather, it involves an estimation of the influence on value of economic, sociological, political, and geographic factors. These are social sciences and, therefore, cannot be precise, because not enough is known about persons and groups of persons, who are the central concern of the social sciences. For this reason, if for no other, the appraiser has a sufficiently difficult task to accomplish in weighing these factors without adding to his burden that of recommending business policy.

An appraisal assignment cannot be treated casually, however, even though the process is somewhat inexact. The value of the report rests on the degree to which the appraiser has used good judgment in applying basic economic theory in an organized manner to the observations he has made, the data he has collected, and the problem of value which he is considering. For example, an appraiser may estimate the market value of a property at $35,000 yet the property may be sold shortly thereafter for $20,000. Was the appraiser wrong? Was he incompetent? Or, in a condemnation case involving the taking of private property, the appraiser may set the value at $116,000, the opposing appraiser may set the value at $97,000, and the jury may award $100,000. Are both appraisers wrong? Or is the second appraiser more correct than the first? The degree to which an appraiser can be charged with incompetence in performing his assignment is directly related to the amount of informed and intelligent judgment which he has used in reaching his decision. In the first instance the buyer and seller may have acted in a capricious manner. In the second instance one of the appraisers may have placed more emphasis on his judgment than on his data; or the jury may have been swayed by the arguments of the lawyers rather than by an informed consideration of the factors influencing the property's value.

The appraiser should proceed in his appraisal assignment in such a way that he gives due consideration to all factors which might influence value. Mathematical tables, depreciation tables, engineering formulas, and field data are only incidental tools used by the appraiser to reinforce his judgment and experience. None of these tools make value, they are merely devices for organizing information so that proper weight can be given to all value influences. When an appraiser has used an organized approach to establish his value estimate, when he has been efficient in the collection and analysis of all possible data relating to the value estimate, when he has reduced his area of unsupported judgment to a minimum, then he has properly fulfilled his appraisal assignment.

KINDS OF APPRAISAL ASSIGNMENTS

An appraisal is basically an estimation of the kinds and quality of rights represented in the property. The rights to use, to change, to modify, to exploit, and to possess all apply to a property to some degree, and the extent to which these rights can be exercised to achieve a particular purpose determines their value. It is well to remember that the majority of persons asking for appraisals are less well informed about property and property-value influences than is the professional appraiser, so the appraiser must explain fully and clearly what he did and why he did it. If the parties to the transaction are not satisfied with the results; their eventual solution may be to take their problems to court. Under the private-property system, all problems of property rights which cannot be solved in any other way are ultimately referred to the courts. The professional appraiser must keep this eventuality in mind at all times and make sure that he has carried out his assignment so that he can explain and defend his conclusions in the courts.

A frequent assignment which an appraiser receives involves the transfer of interests or rights. Estimates of fee interests are needed when property is being bought, sold, or exchanged. Use interests are involved when a property is being leased, an easement is being granted, crops are to be grown, or natural resources are to be extracted from another person's land.

A second important body of interests has to be valued when one person has a lien interest in the property of another as the result of the creation of some form of monetary debt. Such assignments involve value estimates for loan purposes, court judgments, or property, inheritance, or gift taxes.

A third type of assignment involves estimating losses suffered and the amount of indemnity to be awarded. This problem arises in connection with the taking of private land for public purposes when either the entire property is taken or only part of it is taken, when a property owner's rights or use has been impaired as the result of condemnation action, or in the case of losses suffered from fire, windstorm, or other events which have been insured against.

A fourth important body of assignments relates to business problems in which the valuation of property rights is an incident in a larger business problem. Property valuation is often involved in various types of rate-making cases, particularly in connection with public utilities, when businesses are bought or sold, or when a property is treated as an investment vehicle and expected to perform chiefly as an investment.

THE APPRAISAL PROCESS

The process the appraiser follows in completing his appraisal assignment can be likened to the scientific method of solving almost any type of problem (Fig. 1). The first step is to analyze the problem and then state clearly and specifically what has to be done. The second step is to determine what information is needed to solve the problem and involves planning the process for gathering this information. The third step is to gather the data, analyze them, and classify them so they can be considered in the solution of the problem. The fourth step is to draw conclusions about the solution of the problem in the light of the facts, the problem to be solved, and the theory which is applicable. A final step is to review carefully the entire process to ensure that all essential facts have been considered and treated properly, that no errors have been made in calculations, and finally to make a definite statement of conclusions reached. The application of this method to an appraisal assignment is discussed in the following paragraphs.

Purpose. A clear statement of the purpose of the appraisal and the problems to be solved in the light of the purpose is a very necessary first step in any appraisal process. Failure to develop a clear statement of what

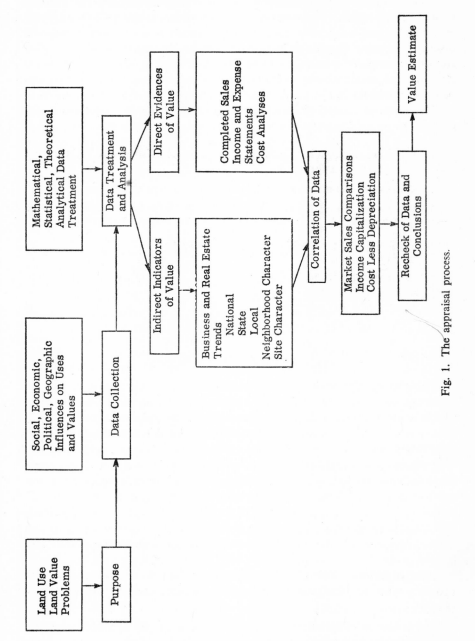

Fig. 1. The appraisal process.

is to be done creates a situation similar to one in which several persons would agree to take a trip together, each driving his own car, but without agreeing as to their destination. The purpose of the appraisal should be discussed at some length with the client, and the final decision as to purpose should be reduced to writing and agreed to by both parties. When this is done there is assurance that there is a meeting of the minds as to what is to be done, misunderstandings are eliminated, and future conflict is avoided.

The purpose should be defined so that the appraiser understands the following:

1. What are the legal description, physical characteristics, and rights of the property to be appraised?

2. What value definition will govern the work to be done?

3. What time period is involved? As of what date is the appraisal to be made?

4. What data will be needed? What conclusions are to be drawn? What type of report is to be submitted?

5. What specific problem is to be solved? For example, is the purpose to determine how much money can be loaned with the property as security? In this case the appraisal estimate will focus on the long-range value trends which are likely to prevail during the time the loan is in force.

   Is the purpose to determine what should be paid for a single-family home? Then all the amenities of the home should be examined and compared with other homes which have sold, so that a market value can be placed on the desired property.

   Is the purpose to determine what the state should pay for property which it is taking for public-use purposes? Consideration must be given to what would be paid for similar properties if a forced sale were not involved.

   Is insurance being placed on the property? What will be the cost of restoring the property owner to his original position if he suffers catastrophes insured against in the policy?

   Is the problem one of establishing a basis for collecting taxes? What share of the tax burden should this property be expected to carry as compared to other properties in the same use, price, and size category?

Identification. The physical boundaries and exact location of the property must be fixed prior to the start of the appraisal in order to ensure that the correct property has been considered. Properties should be identified by legal description which may involve government survey, lot and block number, metes and bounds, monuments, or geodetic survey. Normally this information is provided in the property deed or in the tax records. Identification by mail address or a general description by reference to known land markets may be used in extreme cases, but their use is hazardous because of their inexactness and high possibility of errors.

The legal identification should then be supplemented with a brief description of the site and the improvements to it. For example: how large is the site? Are there improvements on it in the form of landscaping, drives, or walks? What kinds of buildings have been placed on the site—single-family homes, apartment houses, stores, office buildings? Approximately how large are they? How old? What do they look like generally?

Date. Value is directly influenced by time, so every appraisal must be related to a given date. The date permits establishment of the time period to be covered by data collection; it will be useful later as a reference point when the report is being read, and it will establish clearly whether the estimate related to the past, the present, or the future. An appraiser could be embarrassed by his failure to put a date on his estimate, if that estimate is used a year or five years or ten years later. In condemnation cases the trials may be held several months to several years after the appraisal has been made, so dates are particularly important in these instances.

Interests Involved. Previous paragraphs have already indicated that a property is basically a "bundle of rights" and that value is directly proportional to the quantity and quality of rights residing in the property. For example, a single parcel may have mineral rights, use rights, improvement rights, lease rights, lien rights, equity rights, and remainder rights, each held by a different party. For this reason every appraisal should recite the type of rights to be appraised. When there has been no statement as to what rights are involved, the appraiser is justified in stating that the appraisal involves a free and clear title, with no encumbrances or clouds on the title considered.

Rights are the key to value because they set the limits within which the property may be used. The appraiser must always remember that land and improvements are only the vehicles through which value is created and that their capacities to produce value or to have value are defined by the rights relating to them.

Value Defined. Once the purpose has been stated explicitly, the appraiser can summarize his objectives by a proper value definition. In each instance the definition should be given in full by the appraiser, because, as we shall see in later chapters, there are many ways of defining value and there is little agreement as to what any single definition of value may include. For example, there is continuing confusion as to what is to be done when the purpose of the appraisal is to establish market value. Some appraisers interpret this to mean market price; others define it in terms of long-run historical trends; others, in terms of anticipated future trends.

The definition provides the clues as to which data are to be emphasized and provides the authority for the appraiser's conclusions.

By giving a single clear definition, the appraiser is in a position to give a single dollar amount. The definition sets the framework within which the single dollar estimate is placed. Otherwise the appraiser may be open to criticism if he gives a single dollar amount not related to any particular value definition, because the final price the property sells for, is mortgaged for, is insured for, etc., will depend upon the financial positions of the buyers and sellers, the availability of substitutable properties, the conditions of the market, the availability and costs of money, and many other factors.

Preliminary Survey. The purpose of the previous steps is to provide clues as to the kinds and amounts of data needed as a basis for the value estimate; however, before proceeding to collect the data, the appraiser must decide what kinds of work need to be done, how much, how long it will take, and how much other assistance will be required. The process of collecting data can be endless, and much time will be wasted if it is done in an unplanned and unorganized manner. The purpose of the preliminary survey is to avoid useless data collection, unnecessary expenditures of money, and avoidable wastes of time.

The first step in the preliminary survey is to collect the general background data needed for the purpose of analyzing the economic climate within which values are being set. National, regional, community, and neighborhood business and economic trends, political atmosphere, and social trends are all studied in relation to the problem to be solved. These steps are somewhat complex and are described in following chapters. Many of these data are maintained in the appraisers files, so little field work will be involved at this point. However, a great deal of field work will be involved when the appraiser follows through in collecting information on the property site and the improvements on it.

Some of the data may be highly technical in nature, so the appraiser will normally rely on the services of other experts. Engineers are often used in construction analysis. Surveyors establish boundaries and contours. Title searchers examine public records. Economists provide economic background analyses. Agricultural experts render reports on soil conditions and fertility, water flows, and similar factors. The use of such experts is a necessary step if the appraiser is to have accurate data bearing on his appraisal problems.

An effective means of organizing the data-collection and -analysis process is to

1. List the types of data needed
2. List the possible sources from which the data may be secured
3. List the number and kinds of personnel needed in the data program

4. Set time schedules for collecting and processing the data
5. Estimate the costs of the data program
6. Plan the time needed for the report preparation
7. Establish the costs and fees involved in the appraisal assignment and secure a written commitment from the client for the payment of the fee
8. Set the completion date and the form of reporting

Planning and Executing the Appraisal. When the preliminary survey has been completed and the client gives permission to proceed on the assignment, the actual appraisal work begins. One of the most effective means of beginning is to prepare a preliminary but complete outline of the report, including tentative lists of tables, charts, diagrams, and maps which will be needed and the headings for the principal parts and subparts of the report. As the data are collected, they can be fitted into this outline readily so that final report writing is facilitated.

Once this outline is completed, the work of filling in the report begins. Duties and time schedules are assigned to the field staff. Data files in the offices are combed for information already collected and applicable to the assignment. As the data develop, they are applied to the value-estimation problem, usually by means of one or all three of the approaches to value which are identified as the comparative sales approach, the income capitalization approach, and the cost to replace, or summation, approach.

CLIENT RELATIONS AND FEE SETTING

Some appraisers have great difficulty in establishing and maintaining effective relations with their clients and in setting proper fees for their services. Usually these difficulties arise because the client has been properly informed neither on what the appraiser will do nor on the manner in which the fee is calculated. The appraiser is not hired as an advocate for a particular value estimate which the client wishes to have substantiated or established; he is hired to render the best possible impartial decision in the light of the purpose of the appraisal. In order to make sure that this is clearly understood, professional appraisers will not accept an assignment until the terms of employment have been put in written form and signed by the client. In cases of misunderstanding, the dispute can then be settled by reference to the written agreement.

The fees cannot be established merely on the basis of the estimate arrived at. The appraiser must use every effort to remain the impartial judge of what is to be done and what is concluded. Suggestions which have been advanced for the proper method of setting a fee include the following criteria:

1. How much time will be spent in developing the report?
2. What actual cash outlays will be involved in doing the work?

3. How difficult are the problems to be solved, and how much experience and expert assistance might be needed in their solution?
4. What additional testimony, conferences, or other appearances will be required?
5. Will the final report be useful, and to what degree will it be relied upon?
6. What ability and experience will the appraiser have to bring to bear upon the assignment?[1]

There are, however, other peripheral matters which some appraisers would include as important considerations in setting the fee. For example, the client may live at some distance, he may insist on unusual or difficult working conditions, or he may in other ways increase the difficulty of completing the assignment. Fees will also be somewhat related to the magnitude of the property being appraised. Appraisal fees tend to become standardized for certain types of work, or certain fees become customary so that clients expect the appraiser to govern his fees accordingly. Many appraisers fail to consider the overhead including library and staff which they must maintain to render effective services so that a set amount may be added to each assignment to cover these overhead costs. When a long and difficult assignment is undertaken, these latter considerations are often as important as the basic ones previously mentioned.

The importance of maintaining an impartial attitude toward an assignment cannot be sufficiently emphasized, and the dangers of setting a fee which is contingent upon the values estimated must always be recognized. The temptation of contingent fee setting must never be yielded to. It is equally important that appraisers do not bid against the fee prices set by other appraisers, because the final fee may not be sufficient to permit the undertaking of a proper appraising process. However, once the fee is set, the entire appraisal assignment should be completed as agreed upon, whether the fee was correctly estimated or not. If the appraiser makes too low an estimate and finds the fee will not cover his expenses, he must still complete the assignment as agreed upon.

None of these methods are completely satisfactory. Surely a fee based on any of these criteria would be too low in case of very low-value property and could be too high in case of multimillion dollar properties. Any percentage rate must be adjustable on a diminishing scale. Nor should any appraiser set his fee on any one of these bases without adjustments for all the previously stated factors.

Perhaps the best principle to govern fee estimating is that, if value estimates are set by consideration of all the factors which influence value, then similarly the fee should be set by consideration of all factors which influence the cost of doing an efficient and acceptable appraisal.

[1] Berkley W. Duck, "Determining Professional Fees," *The Appraisal Journal* (October 1958), 537–541.

3

The Theoretical Basis
for Appraising

A theoretical understanding of appraising is as necessary prior to making an appraisal as is knowledge of astronomy and mathematics prior to navigating a jet plane on an international flight. Once the decision has been made to undertake the flight, the maps must be selected, possible routes studied, weather and atmospheric conditions checked, and instruments selected which will be used to check the plane's progress as it moves swiftly toward its destination. As the same route continues to be flown, checkpoints can be established, radio and radar controls can be introduced, and navigation can be reduced to a routine which requires little understanding of navigational theory until the routine is interrupted by bad weather, motor failures, or other unexpected events which require a drastic change in the flight plan. These same types of conditions prevail in appraising.

NEED FOR THEORY

Once the decision has been made to undertake an appraisal, theory not only provides a basis for explaining why a particular procedure must be used, but also for deciding what has to be done, how it shall be done, in what sequence, and what data and other tools are needed to make an intelligent value estimate. There are many instances in which the appraisal process has been reduced to a routine because of the large number of times a particular problem has been solved. This is largely true in FHA and VA appraisals, appraisals for mortgage lending, for sales, and in many other instances. However, when any variation occurs in the routine because of a lack of data, unavailability of the necessary tools for completing the appraisal, or for any of a variety of other reasons, recourse must be had to appraisal theory before an estimate can be made.

Thus we see that an understanding of theory is an important foundation for the practice of appraising because it provides the necessary frame of reference as well as a systematic approach to what are often exceedingly complex business and economic decisions. This complexity can be appreciated when we realize that a property may be offered for sale at a price of $125,000, sold for $100,000 cash, valued at $85,000 for long-term mortgage-loan purposes, transferred to the state for $90,000 in the case of condemnation, insured for $115,000, and assigned a $60,000 value for tax purposes. This price complexity would only be compounded if the property happened to be an important historical monument which the community judged to be priceless or if the improvements represented an early and important architectural milestone of international fame.

A framework of theory must be accepted, therefore, as a necessary tool in the kit of any professional appraiser or investor. In order for it to become a familiar and useful tool, it is important to decide: (1) What do we mean by appraising or valuation? (2) What do we mean by value? (3) What important concepts can be accepted from history to guide us in our present value estimating? (4) What are the modern concepts of value theory? (5) What limitations do we face when we attempt to apply economic theories of value in an appraisal problem?

WHAT IS APPRAISING?

We have justified the development of a framework of appraising theory because it is a useful tool in the appraising process; therefore, we must have a clear understanding of the nature of appraising. It is interesting to note that the terms *appraising, valuing,* and *valuation* have come to have the same meaning in the appraisal field. Agreement is almost universal that the terms are interchangeable.

Current literature makes no distinction between *appraising, valuing,* and *valuation,* and all refer to "an act or process of estimating value." *Appraising* has also been defined as an educated guess, as a science in which conclusions are reached from a consideration of facts, as an opinion, and as a process of establishing value. May has even defined *appraising* as "an adventure in economic research." In every instance there is the implication that appraising is actually a continuing development involving the orderly progression from a known to an unknown quantity. Schmutz has summarized the task of appraising as basically "an orderly process which should result in the discovery of the conclusions which logically flow from the facts." In principle, then, an appraiser might be called an economic sleuth who reaches conclusions relating to the value of a property from an examination of a variety of pieces of evidence.

By establishing appraising as a process we imply that we are moving in an orderly manner toward a predetermined goal so in appraising we know that our process must be guided by the goal which has been selected. A goal gives direction to the process making it possible to be selective in the data collected and the methods used to process the data. For example, when the goal is that of establishing a value estimate for tax purposes, the processes used in establishing the final estimate must take into account the laws regulating tax appraising. By contrast, a market estimate will require thorough analysis of all factors influencing market price and a weighing of the impact of these factors on the property we are valuing.

The failure to define clearly and specifically the goal toward which the appraisal is moving not only results in lost motion in collecting and processing data but can produce a final estimate which is difficult to explain or defend. For example, the goal may be described as that of estimating "market value." Such a goal fails to indicate what markets, where, and at what period of time, so any of a number of processes might be used to establish value. On the other hand, a statement that the purpose is to establish the price which an informed buyer would pay as of December 1, 1961, for an apartment house similar to that of the subject property indicates clearly the data needed and the processes most applicable to the processing of the data. An orderly process is an important element in appraising, therefore, because it helps us organize our observations of the many factors which will influence our final estimate.

Appraising is totally concerned with value estimating, which, in turn, relies on the principles of economics, a social science developed over the centuries from the distilled observations of many students and scholars. A social science is not an exact science but one which at best can suggest principles or tendencies which seem to be present when certain phenomena are present. For example, economics tells us that when there are many buyers for a single property the price will probably be high. It does not tell us how many buyers must be present or what the final price will be. Using this simple economic principle as a guide, an appraiser must then observe the actions of the various buyers, search for the reasons why each is buying, establish the price limits within which each will buy and the reasons why each buyer selects a particular price, and from these observations finally reach a conclusion as to the value of the property. The more complete the observations, the more applicable they are to the purpose of the appraisal, and the more accurate will be the final estimate. Babcock has summed up the need for organized observing in these words: "Methods of valuation serve only to break down the complex structure and thereby permit the valuator's judgment to play upon more phases of the problem and take into account the manner in which the various elements operate in creating value."[1]

Having a goal and an organized method of observing is not enough, however, since we are searching for reasons for particular values being found within certain dollar ranges. We must understand the basic causes

[1] Frederick M. Babcock, *The Valuation of Real Estate* (New York: McGraw-Hill Book Co., Inc., 1932), p. 160.

which have produced a particular dollar effect. For these reasons, conclusions drawn from the observations are influenced by the body of theory evolved from economics. Facts developed from observations are often incomplete, inadequate, inconsistent, and inapplicable to the problem at hand. For instance, using our previous example of estimating the warranted purchase price for an apartment house as giving us the purpose of our appraisal, we may find that after collecting all of the data we have no information on what has been paid in the preceding year for the kind of apartment house which we are valuing; however, economic theory would suggest that if no other apartment houses of the type in which we are interested has been built since one year ago, and if buyers have continued to seek this type of property, and if the terms of purchase have not changed significantly so that purchases can still be financed as they were in the past, then the price today should not be less than it was a year ago and may, in fact, be higher. In any case, the basic theory suggests that the price would not, except under very unusual circumstances, be lower. If we finally decide on a higher price than any paid a year ago, we can defend and explain our conclusions, and our decision cannot be challenged easily except by the introduction of another theory which is more applicable.

It is obvious at this point that the final decision with respect to value cannot be exact, nor can it be expressed easily as a single dogmatic statement. Rather, all valuation is a process of estimating, and the final decision is to a degree inexact. The final decision must be inexact, if for no other reason than that it is really a prediction of the future. To continue with our example: When we finally decide on the price which should be paid for the apartment house, we are predicting that this is the price at which the owner will sell. The owner may be completely illogical and unpredictable and sell the property at a price which is extremely remote from the one we predict. The final estimate is not a prediction of what the owner will do, nor is it a recommendation that the property be purchased at that price. The final statement merely indicates that, in the light of all applicable theory and fact, an informed buyer would be warranted in offering to buy at that price. The buyer may choose to ignore this price because of personal reasons about which the appraiser would have no knowledge. The appraisal assignment has been completed when the estimate has been given. The decision to act on the estimate is a business problem with which the appraiser would not normally be concerned.

In summary, then, we can say that a value estimate is the best clue to action which should be taken, because it takes into account all of the economic, social, political, and physical or geographic factors which might influence the value of the property. However, because the final result is an estimate, the client must make the final decision as to whether to use the estimate in reaching his decision about buying. The estimate should not be discarded or heavily discounted because it is an estimate, however, since it has been based on observations of the basic economic forces which influence value.

We have seen that appraising is basically a process, related to a purpose and relying on observations and economic theory, which produces an estimate. It does not create value but merely observes the forces which do create value. It does not recommend action but provides a basis on which action decisions may be made. Although the final estimate is by custom given as a single dollar amount, the final estimate represents an average of the final range within which the single dollar amount is placed. In more particular terms, appraising may be defined as an estimate, expressed as a single dollar amount, of the scarcity and utility, i.e., economic nature, of a specific property at a specified time and place, assuming a specific use, i.e., purpose.

WHAT IS VALUE?

The previous definition excludes any specific mention of value, although the term *value* was used frequently in describing the function of appraising. Value is the central concern of appraising, as it is the central concern of economics, and the purpose of any appraisal is typically to seek an "economic" value. However, because the value definition derives from the purpose, there have been as many concepts of value developed as there are purposes. Some writers have argued that the first step in any appraisal is to define value in order that the purposes and processes may be defined. The difficulty in this approach is that value has come to have many meanings over the years, so any particular named value may have different meanings depending upon the purpose and process. It simply seems more logical to decide what has to be done, to determine the best method of doing it, and then to select a value definition which most appropriately fits in order that there may be no mistake as to which theory is most applicable to the appraising problem, what data are needed, and how the data should be treated to arrive at a single value estimate.

A summary review of some of the more frequently used definitions will indicate the divergence of opinion which exists with respect to defining value. The American Institute of Real Estate Appraisers (AIREA), for example, in its *Terminology Handbook* defines value as (1) "the amount which the potential purchaser will pay for the possession of a thing desired," (2) "the ratio of exchange, one commodity for another," (3) "the power of acquiring commodities in exchange, generally with a comparison of utilities," and (4) "relation of an object to unsatisfied needs." Here we find that definitions emphasize the buyer's viewpoint, or a basically subjective calculation. Definitions (2) and (3) take an opposite viewpoint and suggest that value is related to the market place and exchange.

The AIREA, as well as May, the courts, the FHA and VA, and Wendt, tends to emphasize the definition which says that value is "the highest price in terms of dollars which a property will bring if exposed for sale in the open market allowing a reasonable time to find a purchaser who buys with knowledge of all the uses to which the property is adapted and for which it is capable of being used."[2] This definition has obscure origins in the economists' concept of the perfect market, without providing sufficient guidance to the appraiser who must make an estimate for properties for which no markets exist, such as churches, hospitals, and similar special-purpose properties; it fails to recognize the inexpertness and lack of knowledge with which typical buyers and sellers enter the real estate markets; and it implies the ability to collect a wealth of data on property uses which is rarely found in a typical appraisal situation.

The definition does have some utility if it is further qualified to include the prices paid by both buyers and sellers who enter the market freely and without undue compulsion and if it also recognizes that a reasonable time is allowed for buyers and sellers to become informed as to what is happening in the market place. Fortunately, the definition is sufficiently broad to permit its use with almost any appraisal. Less fortunately, the definition provides minimum clues as to the real purpose of the appraisal or the processes to be used, until the appraiser spends several paragraphs defining the kinds of buyers, sellers, markets, and properties he is observing.

Some definitions such as that by Schmutz emphasize some of the elements of cost as a part of value by defining value as the "relationship between desirous persons and things desired, the amount of sacrifice to be made to gain control of the right of use of a thing." This type of definition, of course, fails to indicate that money and economics are important elements, in that the "relationship between desirous persons and things desired" might imply almost anything. In the context of his writings, however, Schmutz does develop this idea, and any appraiser using this definition in a particular appraisal problem would also have to develop many additional qualifications and limitations.

Babcock, and to a degree Schmutz, has also insisted that value of property is present only because of what the property will be used for in the future. For example, I would not relate my value estimate to the revenue derived from ticket sales in the theater which I planned to buy in order to remove it and build a new office building. My value estimate would be related to the future income to be derived from the office building. For these and similar reasons Babcock defines value as "expectation of future productivity" or "the present worth of future benefits." This definition, of course, is of little use to an appraiser involved with a single-family property,

[2] Paul F. Wendt, *Real Estate Appraisal* (New York: Holt, Rinehart & Winston, Inc., 1956), pp. 1–22.

or any property, from which the future string of benefits will be exclusively in the form of amenities and not money.

The divergences of opinion existing with respect to value definitions and the confusion which arises from using the same definition to cover several different situations can be traced to three fundamental causes. In the first instance, appraisers often assume that any monetary statement about value is value and therefore assume that price is synonymous with value. This is not necessarily the case, because money is simply a convenient device for expressing in a single statement some observations with respect to value. Under a barter system, for example, a lot might be judged to be equal to 10 horses, 100 bushels of wheat, a dozen pairs of shoes, and so on. If each of these items is expressed in dollars, business transactions are facilitated, but the dollar amounts in which property values may be expressed give no necessary clue to the value of a property. Price may be synonymous with value, but only when the processes used in developing the price agree with the purpose of the appraisal.

Confusion may arise in the second place because one definition may put emphasis on how a particular individual reaches his estimate of value whereas another definition will emphasize an estimate which reflects an average of several decisions made in the market place. For example, I may rely on Babcock's definition of value and estimate what I will pay for an apartment house in the light of the income which the apartment may be expected to produce. This approach may have little or no meaning when I go to the market place, because all of the transactions may have been completed by persons who were considering amenities and the prestige factors of being a property owner. Thus "market value" in this instance has no relationship to "income value" and my use of Babcock's definition has made it difficult for me to participate in the market.

Finally, it is apparent in all of the definitions that differing assumptions have been made about the reasons for undertaking appraisal estimates. Some assume value is related to the process of exchanging economic goods with various degrees of utility to the owners, some assume free-will choices in entering the market place, others believe that futurity is the only influence on value, and, finally, the majority believe that value is a conclusion derived from observing the results of numerous individual transactions.

Perhaps we can approach the task of defining value a little more easily if we recognize that all of the various definitions can be fitted into one or more of the following categories of assumptions about value:

1. Value is derived from a relationship which develops in the market place as a result of completed or contemplated transactions
2. Value is related to a particular purpose for entering the market or to a particular use for a property

3. Value assumes a particular type of market condition such as fully informed buyers and sellers acting without compulsion
4. Value anticipates a flow into the future of benefits which can be acquired at the present time

Thus, we see that definitions of value tend to reflect particular situations in which economic factors are given only partial, if any, weight. For this reason, the inexactness of these definitions and their inapplicability in many cases to problems which involve an evaluation of economic factors and forces reduce or eliminate the utility of these definitions for the typical appraisal situation.

TYPES OF VALUE

It is imperative, then, to develop a value definition which will be universally useful in appraising situations, which incorporates the best ideas found in the various other definitions, and which recognizes the economic base of all appraising. If the value definition is to be universally applicable, it must therefore be treated as an expression, usually in monetary terms, of the relationships between the scarcity (or availability) and the utility (or demand) of a property, as found in completed transactions in the market place for properties capable of being put to the same use, with the transactions organized by prices paid as of a particular time and date on terms which are known.

In the light of this definition, there can be no value if the relationship cannot be put in measurable terms, preferably of money, if the property or its use is so unique that nothing comparable has ever existed, or if the transactions cannot be related to finished bargaining processes or calculated conclusions based on market observations.

The assumptions underlying this definition are (1) all appraisals involve transfers of rights; (2) prices paid in the market for similar properties provide a base below which the rights will not be transferred; (3) persons in the market place have individually reached their own decisions about the value of the rights to themselves, if any; (4) the range of prices within which the majority of transactions are completed provides a range within which a reasonably accurate value estimate can be made; (5) the final estimate will be established within the ranges of the market in the light of the purpose of the appraisal being made.

This does not complete the definition, however, because it is still, as Justice Brandeis has said, "a word of many meanings," and for appraisal purposes it must be a word of specific meaning. For appraisal purposes this universal definition can then be qualified by an adjective which reflects the specific purpose of the appraisal. For example, we might have the following value definitions:

1. *Market value*—an estimate reflecting prices actually paid for various types of properties
2. *Insured value*—an estimate reflecting amounts agreed upon for maximum indemnification for particular types of losses
3. *Tax value*—an estimate of the amount for which a property should be valued for purposes of distributing equitably the costs of government
4. *Loan value*—an estimate of the dollar value of the property pledged as security for the repayment of a loan
5. *Economic value*—estimates based on the market place, in which primary consideration has been given to scarcity (supply), utility (demand), and futurity (future benefits)
6. *Condemnation value*—an estimate arrived at for compensation for property taken according to the laws governing the taking
7. *Asking value*—an estimate of the amount which might be asked in the light of similar askings for similar types of properties
8. *Caprice value*—an estimate derived from observing completed transactions involving a large degree of amenities or other personal and unpredictable factors
9. *Cost value*—an estimate derived from costs actually paid to bring properties into being

This list does not by any means exhaust the various types of values which might be considered, but it does indicate how the general definition of value provides a base from which can be developed a more accurate and workable definition in the light of the purpose, processes, and data of a particular appraisal problem.

History of Value Concepts.[3] Value has been discussed by philosophers and economists since the times of the early Greeks, and each generation has arrived at a slightly different concept of value in the light of economic, political, and other events transpiring at the time. Fortunately, or perhaps unfortunately, some of the conclusions with respect to value of each generation have carried over into succeeding generations, thus building misconceptions about value as well as adding a few significant insights. A brief review of some of the more important mainstreams will provide a guide for selecting and rejecting previous thinking on value.

VALUE AND COST. One of the earliest concepts of value revolved around the costs of creating goods. In these early times there was little exchange in the market place; man-made products were always in short supply, and human labor was the chief means of producing goods. Under such conditions it was assumed that the human effort gave the goods value, so value was related to the costs of the human effort involved.

[3] Cf. Edmund Whittaker, *Schools and Streams of Economic Thought* (Chicago: Rand McNally & Co., 1960). References to basic texts will be found in this excellent text.

In A.D. 301 Diocletian codified several laws including one involving *"verum pretium,"* or just price, which was assumed to be the customary cost of production or labor involved. Under law, the seller had the right of recovery in the case of sale for under half of the "true" price. In 1227 Thomas Aquinas, a member of the Scholastic school of thinking, also argued that value should equal the cost of labor involved. This cost would include creating, changing, or transporting an article. Human labor was an important cost because all human labor was assumed to be preparation for salvation. As a result he believed that labor could be classified by its contribution toward salvation, that the status of labor would set the cost, and that the duty of the law was to fix value according to labor.

In the mid-eighteenth century the school of Physiocrats introduced other concepts about value, one of their important ideas being that the value of a product consisted of the original materials plus the subsistence of those who put the materials in finished form and marketed them. They also had a concept of "natural order" which reflected some of the ideas of elementary exchange and which would finally act as a means of setting values in proper relationship to each other. Adam Smith made perhaps the most significant contribution to this stream of thinking in 1776 in his *Wealth of Nations,* wherein he suggested that the wealth of a nation was related to its labor potential and that value was related to the costs of acquisition or the trouble or work needed to acquire the wealth.

In the same period, Ricardo, who is better know for his contributions to rent theory, spoke of exchange value but emphasized a "natural" value derived basically from the quantity of labor required to obtain an article. Others had some contributions to make to the cost mainstream, for example, J. S. Mill synthesized and summarized the existent ideas of value, laying stress on the cost of labor as a significant influence on value. Karl Marx reached perhaps the ultimate in this stream by placing major emphasis on the labor theory of value.

VALUE AND EXCHANGE. The relationship of value to the market place and the exchanges completed there tended to develop as business and commerce spread throughout the various European nations. However, even in the early Greek period, Aristotle suggested that value might be subjective and based on a particular person's estimate of the worth of the article and that in exchange value would be set by such calculations on the part of each person. Thus, in a crude way, exchanges in the market place tended to set value scales.

Perhaps the strongest statements with respect to value and exchange were made by the Mercantilists, who were at their height from approximately the sixteenth to the eighteenth century. This school believed that a nation was only as strong as the gold which it accumulated, that gold was obtained from the sale of goods, and that, therefore, value related to the ability of an article to be exchanged for gold. This emphasis on gold and value is strongly reminiscent of some of the thinking existing in our economy today.

To a degree, the Physiocrats must also be mentioned in the exchange school of value because at an early date they introduced the idea that, in some way, wealth was related to exchange value and that things exchanged for each other were assumed to have equal value. They tended to equate price and value.

The Austrian school tended to emphasize the subjective considerations involved in establishing value, in that the value of a good was related to the personal gain or well-being achieved because of it or the personal wants which would remain unsatisfied without it. The most effective spokesman for this group was Böhm-Bawerk, who pointed out that exchange values were derived from the subjective individual valuations, the upper limits of exchange value being set by the most eager buyer and the most effective seller and the lower limits by the least effective seller and the most eager buyer.

Perhaps the clearest understanding of the relationships between the market and value were offered by Alfred Marshall late in the nineteenth century. He felt that value represented an equilibrium between "demand" prices (subjective) and "supply prices" (cost). The supply prices tended to reflect the seller's costs and the marginal utility of money to them, the marginal supply being the price sufficient to induce labor and capital to offer their services, the costs of supply reflecting principally the costs of labor. Demand was assumed to be a schedule representing the price offerings of potential buyers, with demand being influenced by the degree to which each successive unit satisfied demand. Value then tended to represent an equilibrium point for demand and supply which, over time, would correspond to the costs of supply and, in the short run, reflect the weight of demand.

Market or exchange value is gaining increasing importance today because of the increasing number of instances in which private property is being taken for public use and the number of instances in which law has defined the value to be sought as "market value." Usually the "market value" is taken to include willing buyers and sellers, full knowledge and lack of compulsion on the part of the buyers and sellers.

VALUE AND INCOME. The relating of property values to income was somewhat late in developing, although it had been applied to other forms of investment at earlier dates. Böhm-Bawerk had introduced the idea that present goods possess a higher value than future goods but did not proceed further in this line of reasoning. Marshall, in developing his ideas of marginal values, discussed the possibilities that a product which had reached an advanced age was more likely to be valued for the income it would produce than for the costs of its original creation. Irving Fisher brought this thought to fruition by taking the Austrian ideas of measuring the value of capital goods by their discounted income potential and developed the necessary mathematical concepts to make the ideas useful in valuation. Thus, he developed the details of the discounting process and explored the roles played by rates and risk. Frederick Babcock, in the 1930's, applied this concept to hundreds of properties, argued rather effectively for the idea that the value of a property is the present worth of future benefits, and showed the particular mathematical techniques needed to apply the concept to all types of income-producing properties.

VALUE TODAY. From these various streams of thought has developed the present-day practice of establishing value, whenever data and purpose permit, by use of a market-comparison process, capitalization of net income and estimation of the cost to reproduce minus existing depreciation. It is assumed that each of the three approaches would produce the same value estimate in perfect markets; unfortunately, markets are not perfect, data are never complete, and analysis problems involve many unknowns. Thus, the principal value of the three approaches lies in the need for an appraiser to consider all possible influences on his value estimate while pursuing each of the approaches. Use of the three approaches also permits the appraiser to narrow his range of estimates. The final value estimate must be related to the purpose of the appraisal and usually one approach must be given priority because of the purpose or the data available.

BASIC VALUE PRINCIPLES

The constant attention which problems relating to value have been given over the centuries has resulted in development of a body of principles which tend to become operative whenever particular types of causes and effects are present. These principles become particularly important whenever decisions must be made for allocating scarce resources among competing demands. As our population increases and the quantity of land to be used decreases, it becomes increasingly important to understand how and why land is devoted to a particular use.

In the American business scene we prefer to allow the problem of allocation to be solved primarily through the operation of the price system. It is assumed that, if buyers and sellers are given maximum freedom to enter markets, the competition for land through price offerings will result in the maximum economic allocation of land uses. The imperfections of the markets sometimes result in uneconomic allocations, but, if this tendency continues, some measure of government control is normally introduced to overcome such imperfections.

Price is assumed to be the rationing agent for land placed in the market. Because the demand for land uses is somewhat volatile, depending upon business conditions and future expectations, and because supply is somewhat static or increased only slowly because of the costs, time, and effort required to put land to productive uses, changes in price will,

1. In the short run, allocate uses by changing as the number of bids for land relative to the supply of land available rises
2. In the long run, allocate uses by causing the supply of land to increase relative to the number of bids as a result of the higher prices being bid in the shorter run
3. Eventually, cause the majority of land in an area to be devoted to highest and best use as the more profitable uses become satisfied, prices drop, and less valuable uses are introduced

Personal Maximization. The ability of the price mechanism to operate in this manner is based upon the observation that the majority of persons will seek to maximize their economic well-being. The decision as to what constitutes well-being will depend upon the number of goods available to any single individual and upon the manner in which he chooses to distribute these goods to acquire other goods in satisfying his needs. Unfortunately, few persons have consistently accurate foresight, nor can they always anticipate what their needs will be, so that many times persons find they have used their economic goods unwisely and that their wants remain partially or completely unsatisfied. Some individuals also feel that the satisfaction of their economic wants must be modified to a degree in order that non-economic wants may be met. For this reason, many actions in the markets are based as much on non-economic as on economic factors. For example, it is consistently pointed out that the average American could satisfy his transportation needs by purchasing a smaller, plainer, and cheaper car, but the larger, flashier, more expensive cars continue to be sold simply because of such non-economic considerations as pride of ownership and the desire to keep up with the neighbors. If the head of the family miscalculates his ability to pay for the bigger car, the family loses its transportation. This chance for loss modifies the final decision as to how big and expensive the new car should be. For this reason, the chance for loss tends to modify the profit-seeking motive.

In the development of land, these factors explain much of the action which takes place in the market. For example, as a city grows rapidly, the supply of homes available is insufficient and the new families entering the market bid higher and higher prices in order to have shelter. Builders observe these rising prices and find their potential profit margins sufficient to entice them to build new homes. However, market information may be incomplete and inexact so that builders are uncertain as to how many homes to build and in what price ranges. Some builders will be cautious in their actions and build only the homes in price brackets which will ensure immediate sales. Others, however, impelled by a desire to become large-scale builders and to be known as community developers, may build more homes and more higher-priced homes than can be fully substantiated from examination of the market. In fact, if unusual conditions such as wars or inflation prevail, the government may curtail the actions of the builders by restricting the prices which can be charged and even the amounts and kinds of materials which can be put in the homes. In time, the supply will begin to satisfy the demand, prices will change to reflect these new relationships, and the community will have sufficient homes to meet the demand.

Other factors will operate also to affect prices and the demand for, and the supply of, land, and observations of these forces and the ones already discussed have given rise to a number of principles to be considered in appraising.

Diminishing Returns. Bare, raw land usually has little or no economic value and cannot be used to satisfy demand until capital, labor, and management skill have been used to transform the land. Thus, raw land cannot be used for home construction until sewage disposal, streets and curbs, water, and utilities are brought to the sites. The total costs of doing this are legion, but they divide basically into fixed costs (those whose amounts are not related to the amount of improvements being worked on), variable costs (those whose amounts are directly related to the amount of improvements being made), and marginal costs (those related to putting the last possible unit of land into production). If the improved land can be sold, the residual amount left after paying all of the costs will represent the value of doing the improving and its anticipation determines whether the project should be undertaken.

Ricardo's idea was that all costs except those of acquiring the land would be calculated and, if these costs were less than the potential sales prices, the excess would determine the value of land. Today, however, a developer knows that land is available for a particular use for a particular price, and he therefore includes land as one of the costs. The residue is profit which is his payment for taking the risks of supplying needs in an uncertain and unpredictable market.

The calculations involved in deciding whether an investment should be made in developing land give rise to the principle of diminishing returns, which is illustrated in Table 1 and explained in the following comments.

Let us assume that there is a vacant parcel in an urban area. The builder has purchased one acre of urban land for $1,000 and has asked

TABLE 1

ILLUSTRATION OF THE PRINCIPLE OF DIMINISHING RETURNS

Potential Land Use	Item	Fixed		Costs — Variable				Returns	Net		
		Total Cost	Cost Per House	Labor, Materials, Capital, Mgmt. Total	Per House	Total Added by each New House	Additional per House for Each Added House	Total Gross	Total Net	Per House	Added For Each New House
1 house	1 acre	$1,000	$1,000	$ 4,000	$4,000	0		$10,000	$ 5,000	$5,000	
2 houses	1 acre	1,000	500	8,000	4,000	$4,000	$2,000	20,000	11,000	5,500	$6,000
3 houses	1 acre	1,000	333	11,000	3,667	3,000	1,000	30,000	18,000	6,000	7,000
4 houses	1 acre	1,000	250	15,000	3,750	4,000	1,000	40,000	24,000	6,000	6,000
5 houses	1 acre	1,000	200	20,000	4,000	5,000	1,000	50,000	29,000	5,800	5,000

how many houses should be put on this acre. Your appraising experience indicates that a proper house would sell for $10,000 including the land. Your costs figures show that labor, materials, capital costs, and management would cost $4,000 for the first house; would increase to $8,000 if two houses were built, because more men and materials would be needed; would rise to $11,000 if three were built, because of the need for more mechanical construction equipment; and would eventually equal $20,000 if five homes were built. It is apparent that, per house, both the land costs and the variable costs drop as more homes are built, and that the additional variable costs per home remain relatively steady if more than two homes are built. Thus we see that savings are introduced as we add more houses per unit built but that over-all costs rise steadily.

In order to decide the number of houses to be built, we must next examine the effects on returns. For each home sold, a gross income of $10,000 will be earned. The first home sold will yield a total profit of $5,000; the second, a profit of $11,000; and each additional home increases the total profits made. Our desire, however, is to maximize our returns per dollar of costs or investment. When the net returns are allocated to each unit, we find that building two homes brings a net return per house of $5,500; three homes, a net per house of $6,000; four houses, $6,000; and five houses, only $5,800. If we wish to maximize our return per unit of cost, it seems clear that building three homes will give the highest net return per house built. The last-column analysis confirms this conclusion by indicating that adding one more house to one already built brings in an additional $6,000, adding a third house brings in an additional $7,000, and so on.

In summary, we would be wise in recommending that the developer place only three homes on each acre and buy more acreage for similar developments because this will maximize his returns on his costs and investments. If he builds five houses simply because they will return $29,000, he must be reminded that he could earn the same net return per house and have far less risk, fewer managerial worries, and fewer costs if he simply purchased additional acreage and put one house on each acre, i.e., engaged in extensive use.

The principle involved here can be stated simply by saying that, as additional increments of labor, capital, materials, and management are added to a single parcel of land, i.e., as the use is intensified, the net return from each new improvement added to the land will tend to increase and then decrease. The developer may, if he wishes, continue to add units until the last unit added provides a return just equal to the costs of adding the unit. Beyond this point additional improvements would be uneconomic.

The marginal unit thus determines the total size of the investment which should be made. The diminishing returns per unit added indicate the point at which the improvement should be halted for maximum profits. If the builder were in a market in which land was scarce and if he wanted to improve this particular site, his added profits would indicate how much additional he could afford to pay for the land over the original estimated $1,000 under varying improvement assumptions.

Proportionality. From the diminishing-returns concept we derive a concept of proportionality which says that for any given parcel of land there is a combination of capital, materials, labor, and management which will yield the highest return. For example, an appraiser may be asked if an apartment house should provide garages for the tenants. If the added costs of this service can be recovered in additional rent, then perhaps they should be added, if the added rent does not provide a competitive disadvantage.

Highest and Best Use. Diminishing returns also tell us any parcel of land should be examined for all possible uses and that use should be selected which will yield the highest return in relation to costs and other factors. If a property is developed to this use, it should then bring the highest return in the market. Any use less than highest and best will produce a proportionately smaller return per dollar invested and so will cause a lowering of market value.

Competition. Any experienced investor or appraiser has the ability to evaluate vacant or improved land in terms of the principle of diminishing returns. This process is constant, so any site or property which has not been developed to its highest and best use will immediately attract the attention of these persons, and bidding will begin for acquisition of this property. If the property has been developed to its highest and best use and the net returns per unit of investment are high as compared to those on other properties, the bidding for the site will be even more spirited and additional improvements of this type will be constructed. For this reason, it is stated that each site, in time, tends to be developed to its highest and best use and that when it is thus developed the returns cannot be excessive without attracting competing uses or competitive bidding which will cause the market return to become equal to that for similar types of investments.

Market Price. Market price tends to be the best single indicator of the degree to which supply and demand are in balance with respect to a particular type of property use in a particular type of market because of the extremely local character of typical real estate markets. In active markets where rising population and income create a heavy demand for properties, prices will serve to allocate the property uses among the various demand units until additional units are supplied in response to the higher profits being made on existing units.

Monopoly Price and Location. Any particular location tends to command a higher price than any other location when the density of population surrounding it increases and income continues or rises. Location is important because properties cannot be moved to places where they are needed but must be erected in those places. If the need for a particular type of property declines because the population decreases or the ability to use property on the part of the population declines, the value of the property declines. However, a complete monopoly price is not possible, because other sites almost equally accessible will often serve as reasonable substitutes when the price of the monopoly site is so high as to warrant the added costs of the less convenient location. For example, a drug chain may want to locate at an intersection where there are heavy flows of pedestrian traffic, but it might find all four corners of the intersection unavailable. It might, therefore, decide to move several feet away from the intersection, where prices might be less, and then use the difference between what it would have had to pay for the ideal corner and what it actually paid to maintain a heavy advertising program designed to maintain the same flow of customers into the store as would have prevailed at the ideal corner.

The impact of location may also be illustrated in the previous example in that the heavy flows of pedestrian traffic, representing potential buying power, suggest that the highest and best use would be for some type of retail sales operation as compared to an apartment-house use, an industrial use, or a warehousing use. Location is the first factor to be studied in establishing the highest and best use for a property.

Rights. The value of a property is directly related to the rights which exist in the property. The greater the number of rights and the fewer restrictions existing with respect to exercising these rights, the more likelihood there is that values will be higher. In the example of the drugstore, for instance, if there were strong zoning ordinances or building codes prohibiting the use of the corner for retail purposes, the site would have no value in terms of its highest and best use and less value if the other uses were permitted. A property with a cloud on the title or heavily encumbered with liens has less value than a similar type of property without these encumbrances.

Time. Value is a dynamic concept which changes with time, primarily because changes in supply-demand relationships, population movements, tastes and fashions, business conditions, and a variety of other things are all parts of our dynamic private-enterprise economy. For this reason, value estimates must always be related to a specific time period. For example, what would be the value of a property developed for use as a stable in our present era? If it were in a park or some other place where horses could be kept, it might have some value, but basically it is probably less valuable than if it were used for storing automobiles or airplanes.

Substitution. The value of a property tends to be set by the values of properties devoted to similar uses whenever location is not the single most important consideration. This is really another aspect of the monopoly-price principle. Actually, no site has a complete monopoly, because a variety of sites can usually be devoted to the same use. Monopoly, if it exists, exists in the minds of the buyers or the sellers who are so enamored of a particular site that they would not accept a substitute location. For this reason, homes of a particular style, size, and use potential on the east side of town may easily have the same value as similar homes located several miles away on the west side of town, if all other factors are the same. The differences between the two groups of houses will develop only when locational advantages begin to develop in the minds of the buyers and sellers. This substitution of one property for another may be in terms of structures, uses, or earnings. An investor who wants a particular return on his money, for example, will usually accept any property which will provide this return, if the risks of investment are also equal. In the same way, a manufacturer will accept any industrial building which suits his needs and will rarely feel that only one particular building will be satisfactory.

Homogeneity. When properties in an area are devoted to approximately the same types of uses or to diverse but compatible uses, values will tend to be higher. Absolute uniformity in style or use may, however, have an unfavorable effect on value. One of the more serious complaints leveled against tract housing is that the homes look too much alike.

Futurity. In the majority of cases the value of a property is more likely to be influenced by the future benefits to be derived from future uses than by anything that has happened in the past. The past is of interest chiefly to the degree to which that which has happened in the past can be expected to continue into the future. The few exceptions to this rule are historical sites or properties which are to be preserved in their original forms for the benefit of posterity, and even here the benefits derive primarily from the lessons which they can teach future generations. These future benefits are measured in terms of the time period and the place involved and the quality and quantity of possessive rights acquired.

Contract vs. Economic Rent. The value of a property, as we have seen, tends to be set by the anticipated net returns which it will yield, and experienced persons allow this to guide them when estimating property values. However, a property may be encumbered with a lease contract calling for net rents under or over economic rent. In this case, the value of the property tends to be set by the terms of the lease contract or by the additional costs of having the lease removed.

When contract rent coincides with economic rent, it may be capitalized to reflect the value of the land. If the owner of the property were fortunate enough to have some income left after paying the rent and the costs of operating the property, he would treat this as profit earned by his superior business ability or luck and not treat it as additional rent from the land. Economists who believe that rent is a residue would say that in this situation it is apparent that contract rent and economic rent are not equal and that the additional return would have to be capitalized and the result added to the value derived from the capitalization of the contract rent.

NON-ECONOMIC LIMITATIONS ON VALUE PRINCIPLES

Although economic principles provide the basic explanation for the values of properties, there are other influences which act to mitigate or change the impact of economic forces. These include political, social, and locational factors.

Political factors are perhaps the most important modifiers of economic forces because, as was indicated previously, property has value in proportion to the quantity and quality of rights it possesses and the quantity and quality of these rights can only be established in the courts or by reference to existing law. If a right is disputed, the dispute can only be settled in the courts. Unfortunately, the courts have come to recognize many shades of value and have established no fixed guides for measuring these shades. At times the courts may even minimize important economic factors because the law does not permit their recognition. This often happens in condemnation cases where the proof of value must conform to what the law requires even though this may eliminate many important and valid economic evidences. However, as the number of condemnation cases increases and as the courts begin to define their position more clearly in the light of the exposure which they are receiving to the thoughts of appraisers and economists, the appraisers' position is becoming a little easier to support.

Custom and tradition often operate to mitigate the influences of economic forces. For example, rents for particular types of uses tend to be fixed at certain levels through custom, and these rents must be used in an appraisal situation. Certain types of architecture, or sizes, may become customary even though they cannot be justified economically. If the general market expects a particular type of architecture and will pay additional money to secure it, this is an item of value which the appraiser must consider.

Property, as a physical product, also has certain important characteristics which influence its value. The immobility of property has already been mentioned. Property often has a long physical life, and the costs of removing or altering a property are usually high, so an uneconomic property may continue to be used and have some value simply because the costs of remodeling or removing it are too high in relation to the added increments of value which would result. Finally, a property's value is directly proportional to the public facilities available to it. Streets, sidewalks, utilities, water, sewage disposal, parks, post offices, and similar types of public uses tend to increase property values when they are adjacent to, or easily accessible to, a property.

4

The Economics of Realty:

Population and Land Values

Do sharp increases in population automatically result in equally great increases in land values? The evidence of the 1950's and early 1960's would suggest that there is a positive correlation between population increases and density and land values. However, an equally important body of evidence indicates that this correlation is not always a positive one. For example, Thomas Malthus argued as early as the eighteenth century that population was increasing more rapidly than the ability of the earth to support it and that we would be unable to accommodate future population on the existing land. Underlying the Malthusian assumption is the idea that this increasing population would prevent the economic exploitation of land resources so that economic levels would be so low that land could not have a value. Population trends in countries like India and China seem to support his argument, because increasing population in these countries has resulted chiefly in more poverty and more intensive but less effective land uses.

Many economists take issue with the Malthusian school and argue that, as the demand for land increases because of population pressures, new ways will be developed to use land more intensively. For example, someone has suggested that, if necessary, the entire population of the world could almost be accommodated in an area equal to the nation of Germany, if the density were about equal to that found in a city such as Paris. The assumptions underlying this argument are that, as it becomes profitable to devote land to a particular use, land will be put to this use, and that, as profitable uses change, the uses to which land is put will change.

These arguments are important to the appraiser because he must decide to what degree a particular type of use is adaptable to a particular site and what effect this use will have on his final value estimate. In the light of the arguments which have been advanced about the effect of population on land uses, the appraiser may assume that population changes will cause changes in land uses and values but that the changes may or may not be proportionate. Correlation between population and land uses is most likely to be close when population changes coincide with changes in economic conditions. Thus the increases in land values which accompanied population increases in the 1950's occurred primarily because there were equally great increases in business activity, employment, and family income. During the Depression years, population increases had minimum effect on land values. The purpose of this chapter is to explore the relationship between land values, interests in land, and land uses.

INTERESTS IN LAND

Interests are acquired in land for many reasons including the return which can be earned, the legal rights involved, the physical qualities of the land, and many others, but for the appraiser the most significant involve recognition of land as a means for satisfying any of a number of types of use needs. The degree to which a particular use can be satisfied is a factor in determining the highest and best use potential for land, and the type of use to be satisfied determines the earning potential or economic value of the property.

Space. In a scale of values reflecting the various interests in land, the use of the land as space or room for activities would carry the lowest rating. In the most elementary sense, all human activities must originate from land-based activities, therefore any land has some value for this purpose. Land as space becomes more valuable as the needs for a particular parcel of land increase and bidding for the use of the space causes prices to rise. For example, a department store must rest on land in order to be built, and, for this purpose, almost any parcel of land will be satisfactory. However, some parcels of land are found in the centers of high population density where large profits can be made from selling goods in a department-store type of operation. Those parcels have value according to the amount of such space available and the amount of profits to be derived from such uses. A basic principle of land use is, therefore, that land as a platform for activities has minimum value which tends to increase as the kinds of profitable activities which can be accommodated on that space increase. Present population booms suggest that land as space will tend to have increasing value.

Nature. The next consideration which would influence the value of land would be the kinds of natural interests associated with a particular parcel of land. Thus, space located in a pleasant climate, with enough but minimum rainfall and no bad weather conditions, and quantities of water, minerals, and other natural resources would tend to have more value than a parcel less abundantly endowed. One of the important explanations of the growing flood of persons moving to the southwestern part of the United States is the desirability of land in those areas not only for homes and business but for climatic reasons. This flood will tend to slow and eventually stop when natural conditions such as limited water supplies prevent the land from accommodating further population increases.

One of the more important natural considerations which give land value is that derived from recreational uses. In the United States the majority of our mountainous areas, which would normally have only limited appeal for other interests, are ideally suited for recreational purposes. Rivers and other natural waterways, particularly important in the early days of the nation, are still vital today as channels of communication and cheap transportation. For this reason land adjacent to natural resources which facilitate recreation, transportation, or communication has higher value than land not so situated.

Finally, land becomes important when it contains a natural resource which has an economic value. In the rating of land with natural resources, that with the most valuable mineral or other deposits will rank either high or low depending upon the types of minerals, or other resources, their accessibility, and their availability to the places where they are needed. Land equipped with, or adjacent to, natural resources thus tends to have more value than land not so endowed.

Consumption Good. Land has always had value as a means of directly satisfying human wants through the production of food and the supplying of shelter. As urban areas grow, the importance of land for agricultural purposes increases; however, improved technology has been making it possible to secure almost the same amount of food from increasingly smaller portions of land, so agricultural land values generally have not increased as rapidly as have population and the demand for food. Nevertheless, some agricultural land produces food more easily and is therefore more valuable than immediately adjacent but less fertile land. The ability of land to satisfy wants directly is sometimes obstructed by other interests, and its value in this respect is decreased. In many areas of the world, for example, land has been divided into smaller and smaller parcels among succeeding generations until the existing parcels cannot be worked efficiently and have only limited productivity. The value of land as a consumption good is directly proportional to the state of economic advancement and to the technological status of the area in which the land is located. The southern United States, which has depended on human labor to produce crops, has suffered as the western states have found ways of producing these same crops more abundantly and cheaply with the use of fertilizers and farm machinery. As technological processes continue to unlock the fertility of land at lower and lower cost, land which can take advantage of these advances will increase in value while other land decreases in value.

Factor of Production. Land tends to have increasingly higher values as it can be adapted for a variety of interests, particularly when one of the interests finds land valuable as a factor of production. For example, agricultural land has value for the crops grown on it; if, however, these crops can then be used to produce additional products of higher value, the land has more value. Under these conditions the value of land as a factor of production is directly proportional to the costs of the other factors of labor, capital, and management needed to make land productive as compared to the income which can be produced from applying all of these factors.

Stated in its simplest terms, this principle means that land which can be combined with labor, capital, and management to produce more income will have more value than land which cannot be so combined. For this reason some land will always have limited value because no amount of labor, capital, or management can be used to increase the productivity of the land, either physically or in an economic sense.

Situation. Location, or situation, is one of the first and most important considerations influencing urban land values and is an indirect but very important consideration in non-urban uses. Within a city, land located near concentrations of population and economic activity has more value than land farther from these factors. Outside the city, land used for agricultural purposes and close to the urban food markets has more value than land farther away. It is axiomatic that an urban area can develop neither rapidly nor on any significant scale unless it is supported by a fertile hinterland. For this reason it is not surprising to find many of the richest agricultural counties in the United States located near important urban centers. In general, therefore, it may be assumed that land endowed with any of the other interests has an even higher value when the situation is favorable. The corollary of this is that some situations are so poor that no amount of additional capital, labor, or management nor any quantity of the other interests will make the land more valuable.

Property Rights. Some appraisers would argue that property rights are the paramount interests in determining value because rights determine the degree to which the other interests can be exploited. However, property rights are subject to differing interpretations and unfavorable rights can often be exchanged for more favorable rights or even changed completely through proper court actions. For example, the development of a property in a favorable situation may be impeded by the existence of remainder interests but negotiation may result in the acquisition of the remainder interests. On the other hand, a poor situation could not be remedied so easily. Nevertheless, rights remain more important than the previously listed interests because they determine the degree to which the other interests can be exploited. Other factors remaining unchanged, the parcel which has the greatest quantity and quality of rights will have the greatest value.

Capital. Land probably has its greatest value when it can be combined with other factors of production to produce additional goods. Analysis of the other interests and a clear definition of the rights represented in a parcel provide the foundation upon which the use of land as a capital good may be built. In the majority of cases land is important as an economic good only because it is a means to another end, the production of money or amenity income. For this reason the highest land values are always found at the centers of growing population in expanding economies. Usually such land is found in the central business districts of the major metropolitan areas.

Figure 2 roughly summarizes the relationships presented in the preceding paragraphs. In general, the chart also suggests that, as we move from wild, undeveloped hinterland toward the center of a vigorous metropolitan area, land values increase and land uses tend to move from the surface of the earth upward into the air.

TABLE 2

GRADATIONS OF LAND USES IN URBAN AREAS

Order of Use	Major Cities	Small Cities
1	Office—major buildings	Retail—Women's wear, variety stores
2	Retail—women's wear, variety stores	Retail—other shopping goods, recreational
3	Retail—other shoppers' goods	Offices
4	Offices—secondary showrooms	Civic center Retail—necessity goods
5	Apartment houses—luxury	Apartment houses
6	Recreational—theatrical	Residential—high-price houses
7	Town Houses—luxury	Shopping centers, industrial, one-family houses
8	Offices—civic-center	
9	Loft—Showroom	Highway uses—truck terminals
10	Apartment house—middle class	Recreational
11	Retail—necessity goods, Shopping centers	
12 ⎱	Industrial—distribution, manufacturing	
13 ⎰	Residential—high-priced houses	
14	Tenement	
15	Highway—truck terminal, golf driving, etc.	
16	Residential—one-family, low-price	
17	Agricultural	

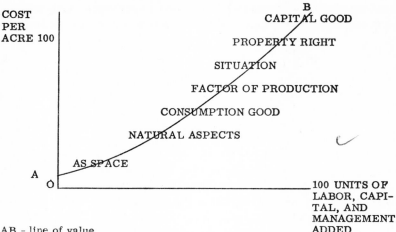

AB - line of value

Fig. 2. Interest in land and land values.

The Appraiser and Land Interests. The typical appraisal assignment usually requires an estimate of the impact on value of the interests of space, situation, rights, and the factor of production. In order to establish value the appraiser poses his questions in somewhat this order: (1) How much space is present? This represents the maximum physical use potential. (2) Where is the space located? This represents the maximum economic potential. (3) What rights are represented? This represents the framework within which the physical and economic potentials can be exploited. (4) What type of income can be produced, in what quantities, and for how long? Which indicates in a single dollar sum the value of the particular site as compared to other sites.

USE OF THE INTERESTS IN LAND

For the appraiser the interests in land are most easily valued when they are regrouped as either agricultural interests or urban interests. The methods of establishing value are somewhat alike, with one important difference. In agricultural valuation the qualities of the soil or the interests of nature and consumption goods are paramount as modified by the situation interest. Good climate, fertile soil, and proximity to markets produce the most valuable agricultural land. In urban valuation the interests of situation, property rights, and capital become paramount. Location in a thriving urban community where a maximum of rights are reserved to the individual so that high money and amenity income can be derived produces the highest land values.

Principles of Valuing Agricultural Interests. Agricultural developments represent the extensive use of space more than do urban developments. For this reason agricultural valuations start with an analysis of the kinds of soil found in the parcel and an estimation of the types of crops which can be grown. These crops can be produced directly from the soil in the form of valuable minerals, ores, oil, and similar items; they can be corn, wheat, vegetables, and food products; they can be cotton, soy beans, and similar crops which are ingredients of other products; or they can be food crops for raising marketable animals.

The decision as to which of these various uses should be undertaken is then made by reference to the markets for these items, and the costs of getting the products to the markets. The potential income from market sales modified by the costs of producing and marketing the products then provides the basis for estimating value. Thus the income capitalization and costs of production methods become paramount in estimating value, and the market-sales-comparison method is a check on these methods.

Principles of Valuing Urban Interests. The emphasis in this text is on the valuation problems arising from analyzing urban interests, which are fully discussed in the other chapters; the purpose here is to indicate the basic foundation upon which the complex framework of valuation is erected. Urban land has value either because there are amenities or because money income is to be derived from the use of the properties. Amenities are the intangible benefits associated with using or owning a property and are most often found in single-family homes. The attachment which members of a family develop for the home in which their parents lived and in which they are now living, as well as the satisfactions derived from living in a particular neighborhood or next to certain neighbors, are amenities. They are subjective in nature and have a value attached to them which does not easily translate into market price. The appraiser usually, therefore, either ignores amenities or assigns them minimum value, unless there is a strong tendency in the market place for accepting values which include these amenities.

Approximately one-third of the residential market and all of the business- or commercial-property market, and the industrial- and manufacturing-property markets, are concerned with the income-producing potentials of the property. Valuation of these properties is based upon a capitalization of the net income remaining after all of the expenses of earning the gross income have been deducted from it. If amenities cannot be translated into either income or expenses, they are not included. Whereas the income approach cannot include amenity considerations, the valuation of income properties does include consideration of the market and cost approaches so that, to the degree to which the market reflects amenities, amenities may be considered eventually in the income-capitalization approach. Because both amenity and income properties rely on all three approaches in value estimates, there are basic economic principles common to both.

Economics of Urban Land Uses. Because urban areas are dynamic and in a constant state of change, any given parcel of land will often grow through a variety of use changes. Usually zoning laws, private contracts and deed restrictions, and the family cycle will cause a given use to prevail for any period up to a quarter of a century, after which another type of use will enter. In new, rapidly growing cities the use cycle will be very rapid. The use cycle also varies for commerce and business, industry and manufacturing, primarily in response to changing business conditions. In all properties the principle of change is an important one and should not be overlooked or forgotten.

MULTIPLE USE. Because the principle of change is so important, any site or any improvement to the site which can be easily adapted for multiple uses is more valuable than a site of limited or specialized use. For example, a single-family home which can be adapted easily for various kinds of family activities or sizes has more value than one which cannot. A non-residential site which can be used for retail stores, office buildings, loft buildings, or some combination of these uses will tend to have more value than one restricted to only one of these uses. Industrial sites with improvements adaptable to a variety of manufacturing needs and supplied with utilities, transportation, and other necessary facilities which will accommodate these various needs will tend to have more value than one with limited use capacities.

PLOTTAGE. Flexibility and value are further enhanced if a single site can be combined with other sites to produce higher net income. The tendency in retail centers, for instance, is to find sites which will permit combining a variety of retail services into a single shopping center with ample parking. The individual site is becoming less valuable as this trend develops. The value of a planned industrial park with accommodations for a variety of complementary manufacturing activities is proportionately greater than that of a single site which could accommodate only one activity. Under these conditions the combined value of the sites is typically greater than the value of a series of isolated sites which cannot be combined. The principle underlying these trends is that value is adversely or positively affected by the degree to which single parcels can be combined to produce more net income.

EXTENSIVE VS. INTENSIVE USES. The costs of putting urban land into productive uses have been rising steadily as property taxes, costs of labor and materials, and interest on borrowed money has risen. Furthermore, the number of urban sites adaptable to the various use interests has been steadily declining with our nation's mounting population pressure and rapid urbanization. The choice for many urban developers lies not so much in determining which site to develop as in what combinations of labor, capital, and management should be devoted to a particular site to produce net income. Under these conditions the site which can produce the highest net income in relation to the costs needed to bring the site into productivity will have the highest value. In simpler terms, the higher the net income produced, proportionate to the intensity of development, the higher will be the value of the site. This principle must, however, be applied together with that of diminishing returns, which latter implies that increasing intensity of use can be carried only to a particular point beyond which greater intensity will yield smaller portions of net income.

NET INCOME. For the investor or property owner an urban site is valuable chiefly because of the net income it will produce. Few owners or investors are greatly concerned about the type of use interest which will produce this net, as long as the use interest produces quality, quantity, and stability of income. This principle is simple and easy to understand and basic to all property value: The value of a site which can be used to produce net income is directly proportional to the amount of net income the site can produce.

NET INCOME AND COST. Net income represents the residue of gross income remaining after the costs of earning that gross income have been deducted. Fluctuations in the costs of earning represent the most important threat to the net return. For this reason, if there are two urban sites which will produce the same net income but one of the sites will produce this income with a smaller gross and a smaller proportion of expenses, this one will have the greatest value. For example, if a site could be used to develop either a parking lot or an office building, and if the net from either use were the same, the lot would be most appropriately developed as a parking lot, because less capital investment is required and the operating expenses with respect to the gross income will be the lowest, and thus the parking lot will represent the highest and best use.

These principles are common to all urban value-estimation problems; however, there are additional influences on value, depending upon the final decision as to the type of use interest selected for development on the site. These use interests divide into the broad categories of residential, commercial-business, industrial, public, and central business districts. The special requirements for these areas are presented in Chapter 6.

SCALE OF URBAN LAND USES

The specific uses to which urban land is put provide an indirect indication of land values when general gradations are sought. An idea of such gradations is given in Table 2. The uses which provide the highest values in an urban area are listed first; the lowest values, last. Differences which occur between some of the largest cities and some of the smallest are also indicated.

It can be seen that retail is typically the best use of the land. Only in a few cities can office buildings compete for the use of this quality land. Among retail uses, the highest are uses such as ladies' apparel, ladies' accessories, jewelry, variety stores, and candy. These type uses can sell large quantities of goods in relatively small stores, owing to the lack of bulk and to the regular turnover of these type goods. This is particularly true of popular-price merchandise. These stores require heavy pedestrian flow, and thus they pay for the best location in town.

In the largest cities, we find town houses and luxury apartment houses bidding high for the use of land convenient to offices, shopping, and theaters and having choice views and prestige appeal.

There will be variations from the suggested land uses dependent upon special attractions to the community. As an example of this, a suburban area may include several communities. One of these towns may attract very wealthy inhabitants. In this community, the best home area, possibly on a lake or hill, may represent the highest or one of the highest land uses in that town.

INDICATORS OF URBAN LAND USES

Many analytical methods are used by economists, researchers, and statisticians to determine the economic well-being of a community, neighborhood, or region. Most of these are helpful, but often the appraiser finds himself out of his element when trying to relate this information to his assignment.

One of the best gauges to local property is the investment of private capital in realty projects. This can be easily seen by the appraiser in his inspection. He should look for new buildings constructed for profit motives to be used for homes, apartments, retail stores, offices, banks, and other land-use purposes. He should also look for stores with new fronts and fixtures; business buildings with new lobbies, electrical systems, elevators, and air-conditioning installations; and similar improvements to residential realty. Where this type of investment is not taking place, the area is stagnating. The appraiser should attempt to find the reason for the distress.

Incidentally, public investment in housing, schools, and civic buildings, while encouraging, is no substitute for private investment. The reasons for this investment factor are obvious. In normal times, private capital is always seeking to be invested. In an area that can be developed with rentals attractive to an investor, he will build. The degree of its attraction will vary. In some areas, builders will only use vacant land. In other areas, they will buy land with obsolete residential or business buildings and demolish them for new improvements. In some cases, where the neighborhood is extremely desirable, investors will buy land having major structures that are not obsolete. They will then demolish them and replace them with uses of the land that are more intense. New York's Park and Madison avenues since 1947 have had some of their most fashionable apartment houses and hotels replaced by new office buildings.

5

City and Economic
Background Analysis

Some of the most difficult and complex appraisal problems arise in the valuation of urban properties, and their solution is possible only if the appraiser understands the impact of urban environment on property values. The purpose of this chapter is to examine some of the more relevant theories on city growth and structure, in order to determine how they can be used to establish value estimates. As we have seen from previous chapters, a parcel has value only if it is adequately supported by its environment. For example, property values can be sustained only if an urban area has employment, business activity of all types, transportation, utilities, effective city government and services, and a dynamic and growing business base.

MODERN CITIES, THEIR ORIGINS AND GROWTH

Although cities have been in existence since the earliest recorded time, the appraiser is primarily concerned with modern cities, and these cities can be explained most accurately in terms of economic activities. Almost all American cities can be explained in terms of economic origins, and their growth and stability are directly related to the strength of their economic base. The appraiser is interested in the nature of the economic base as a means of determining the kinds of land uses which will prove to be most profitable, the relationships between land values and city growth, and the degree to which economic growth will maintain property values.

Economic Origins. At the present time there are nine major types of economic activity which lead to the formation and growth of urban areas: (1) trade and commerce, (2) mining and extraction, (3) finance, (4) recreation, (5) government activities, (6) manufacturing, (7) agriculture, (8) education, and (9) retirement. The importance of many of these activities in the economic base of a city can be determined most easily from a study of employment. Normally, employment data are reported by the U.S. Department of Commerce, state departments of commerce, and local chambers of commerce, not only for the current year but also for at least

53

the previous decade. Employment figures will provide the clues as to which types of economic activity should be given the greatest weight in an analysis of a city's economic base.

The significance of the economic base as an explanation for the origin of a city can be appreciated by a review of various cities throughout the United States which have been influenced by a major type of economic activity as is indicated by the distribution of employment. For example, trade and commerce have played a large role in the growth of New York, Chicago, St. Louis, and Pittsburgh. In each instance the city was located at an important transportation junction or center—rivers, lakes, a seaport, railroads, overland highways. Mining and extraction have influenced the growth of such cities as Denver and Leadville in Colorado, southern and eastern cities in the coal belts, western cities in the forest belts, and mid-western cities in the iron-ore belts. Finance has been important in New York and San Francisco, which have become the "bankers" for the eastern and western regions of the United States. Recreation has accounted for much of the growth in Miami, Sun Valley, and Los Angeles. Government activities explain the origin of Washington, D.C., whose location was decided by political compromise and whose existence today is due to the centralization of federal-government activities in that city.

Manufacturing has, of course, been important in almost all American cities; however, these types of activities are most often associated with cities like Pittsburgh, Detroit, and Gary. West-coast cities such as Los Angeles and San Diego have been coming to the fore in recent years because of their manufacture of rockets, space missiles, and other accouterments of the new "space age."

Agriculture is an important economic activity even in our modern industrial age because food is vital to the well-being of urban populations. Urban centers surrounded by rich agricultural hinterlands enjoy more growth and stability than cities without such hinterlands. For example, many midwestern cities such as Des Moines and Chicago were located in order to serve as central marketing places for agricultural products.

The complexities of modern city living are requiring increasingly higher levels of educational attainment, and the support of education takes increasing proportions of the tax dollar. Many of our large educational institutions were located originally in small communities, but the growth of enrolments has stimulated these small communities into unexpected growth. For example, there are Indiana University, at Bloomington, Indiana; The Ohio State University, in Columbus, Ohio; Stanford University, at Palo Alto, California; and Harvard University, in Cambridge, Massachusetts.

Finally, there is the growing number of retired persons who are seeking communities which will meet their special needs. Although this influence is still new and therefore rather unevaluated, we see communities such as

Youngstown, Arizona; Palm Beach, Florida; and Phoenix, Arizona, enjoying a considerable growth by catering to the needs of retired persons.

Non-economic Growth Origins. Economic influences are not the only explanation of modern cities, nor can economic influences serve by themselves as an adequate stimulus to city growth. Economic influences are supplemented, complemented, directed, or even halted by political, social, or geographic influences.

If economic growth is not directed into desirable land-use patterns through good community planning, zoning, and property-tax policies, the property values will suffer. A hostile city council which does not want manufacturing in a community can devise numerous zoning and building regulations which will make property development prohibitive in cost. A planning commission which permits incompatible land uses to exist side by side discourages the improvement and expansion of these uses and the introduction of new developments. Cities which are pursuing active programs of urban redevelopment often stimulate business by creating new sites for manufacturing and commercial activities which might have moved elsewhere or which were never planned for growth.

The social influences in the form of numbers and rates of growth of population are fundamental to any form of urban growth. A basic truism is that people make value. The amount of value which they make will be discovered from an examination of the characteristics of the people, including not only their number but also their age, family composition, cultural interests, educational background, and work qualifications and interests.

Geographic influences are the final factors which can modify economic influences. For example, weather, climate, topography, rivers, lakes, and soil all determine the kinds of developments which will be possible in an urban area. Geography provides the basic physical environment within which properties are used and value created.

The methods of making a detailed analysis of these non-economic factors are described in another chapter, but these factors are mentioned at this point primarily to emphasize their ability to modify and shape the basic economic influences which essentially determine whether a city will grow.

THE ECONOMIC BASE

The *economic base* of a metropolitan area may be defined as the sum of all income-producing activities which maintain and stimulate its growth. Many theoretical attempts have been made to isolate and measure the economic bases of urban areas, but the interrelationships of urban economies with each other and with the national economy have prevented the precise types of measurements which many analysts would prefer. The underlying assumption is that an urban area produces goods and services which it sells for income from which must be deducted the expenses incurred in producing the goods and services. If the income is produced from diverse sources by activities which are basic to economic survival, at a cost which is in excess of the expenses of production, the growth potential is assured. As the diversity of the sources decreases and they are related to the more ephemeral types of activities at increasingly higher costs, the economic growth potential is less assured and property values are likely to suffer. For example, the economic base of Detroit is built around the manufacture of automobiles; when automobiles are selling well, Detroit prospers; when strikes or poor sales develop in the industry, unemployment rises, population moves from area, property values decline, and the Detroit urban area tends to stagnate.

There is no simple consistently effective and accurate method of analyzing the economic base of a community. Rather, the appraiser must evaluate several factors and, in the light of his business experience and judgment, decide what impact they will have on property values.

Employment. The single most important measure of the economic base is employment. The percentage of population employed, the length of the average work week, and the average rates of pay indicate how much family income will be available in the area for the purchase of housing, consumer goods, and other items which contribute to business growth. A review of employment over previous years will provide clues to the fluctuations which have occurred in employment and to the degree to which they might occur in the future. A further breakdown in employment, according to types of industries, will indicate the degree to which the local economy is geared to a single industry or to an unstable type of business or industrial activity. For example, Sun Valley, Idaho, is geared primarily to winter-sports activities. When summer arrives, employment based on winter sports almost disappears. Furthermore, spending for recreation is directly related to the prosperity of individual families and is likely to decrease when family income drops. On the other hand, employment in the steel industry might be more desirable than dependence on recreation. An even better base would be one related to employment in steel, autos, consumer goods, government, and recreation industries.

Income. One of the more effective measures of economic prosperity at the national level is the gross national product, which measures in dollar amounts the total of goods and services produced. Unfortunately, such a measure is not available at the local level; however, personal income serves almost as well. Personal income is a reflection of the total of consumer spending which is likely to occur, and its continued rise reflects a sound economic base; therefore, a measure of personal income can be used as a single measure of the economic strength of a community.

Industry. Not all employment adds to the strength of the economic base. For instance, barbershops, food stores, cleaners, and restaurants exist to service persons employed in other industries, and the strength of these service industries is directly related to the strength of the basic industries. For this reason, employment and income must be related to the type of activity from which they are derived. Any economic activity which serves markets beyond the boundaries of the urban area is classified as a basic industry and one which will strengthen the economic base. Any economic activity which serves only the local markets is a service industry and adds little to the strength of the economic base. Some efforts have been made to classify industries as basic or service, but only a few lend themselves to this approach. A retail store exists, in most instances, to serve those employed in basic industries; however, when the retail store is of a large size and is part of a shopping center which attracts shoppers from miles beyond the economic limits of the local market, retailing can be accepted as a basic industry. Such industrial dual personalities limit the use of service vs. basic-industry types of analyses.

The Role of Existing Facilities. Economic activities must be supported by certain types of physical facilities. Steel requires mills and blast furnaces; automobiles and airplanes, various types of shaping and forming machines. Often the existence of such facilities gives rise to additional peripheral but important activities which can use such facilities. Impetus was given to airplane manufacturing on the west coast by the existence of war-created facilities for airplane manufacturing. The existence of plane-manufacturing facilities, in turn, gave rise to missile production. The existence of the marine-engine industry along the Great Lakes led to the location of automobile manufacturing in this area so that the supply of engines could be assured. Modern, up-to-date, adaptable manufacturing facilities are therefore important for the maintenance and growth of basic industrial activities.

PATTERNS OF URBAN LAND USE

The locations of various types of land uses within a city are not determined in a random manner but in response to certain types of basic influences. A knowledge of the role of these influences is important to the appraiser when he is faced with valuing a particular location. Knowledge of the economic base provides clues to the degree to which property values will be maintained or increase or decline; knowledge of locational influences gives these same clues with respect to a particular location or site.

Another influence on locations of activities in a city stems from family living habits. A family survives on the employment of the principal wage earner, therefore the family locates so that the wage earner can reach his place of employment. The children must be educated, so school facilities must be available. The entire family must be clothed, fed, treated when sick or injured, and entertained, therefore the family must be able to reach facilities which provide the appropriate goods or services. Usually, of course, the family locates first and, as the number of families increases, these facilities appear. If such facilities fail to appear, population increases in the area will probably not occur. Actually these linkages develop together, each dependent on the rate of increase of the other, so if one fails to develop all others are adversely affected. The particular factors which cause certain types of locational uses to develop are discussed in the following paragraphs.

Residential Locations. Residential locations, whether for homes or multiple units, are enhanced when they are in the direction of city growth and well supplied with shopping, employment, school, religious, and recreational facilities. Utilities and public transportation should be available on continuous- and reliable-service bases at average costs. The area should be protected from the nuisances and hazards of industrial or commercial areas but should be easily reachable from these and other areas of the city along non-congested traffic routes. The prevailing climate should be highly conducive to pleasant family living.

Values are further improved if the population is relatively homogeneous in family size, age, education, employment, and recreational and cultural interests. Additional dividends will be present if the neighbors work together to maintain the appearance of their properties and to provide interesting and varied neighborhood activities.

Property taxes, as well as special assessments for other types of public services, should be equitable. Public services such as police and fire protection should be available with minimum delay and on continuous-service basis.

Office and Commercial Locations. Population is again an important determinant of the location of office and commercial locations, since population provides the markets for the commercial activities and the labor for the office activities. The necessity for linkage between business firms and between firms and their clients requires that the location be accessible to public transportation and highways and roads and that it be well supplied with communication facilities. The general appearance of the area must be such that clients will be willing to visit the area, will find sufficient parking, and will prefer to patronize the area when they have business to transact.

Local ordinances on conducting business, zoning and building-code regulations, the supply of utilities, and public services play as important a role in making the area attractive as they do in the case of residential districts.

Industrial Locations. The locational needs for industry are considerably less flexible than those for residential, commercial, and business uses. Industry must have transportation facilities readily accessible at reasonable cost and on a dependable-service basis. Industry also has great need of a high volume of power, water, and sewage-disposal facilities. When industrial activity involves such nuisances as smoke, odors, and noise, the location must be such that other locational use areas are not bothered by these. When large numbers of workers are employed, they should be able to reach the area over high-speed roads which do not require transit through quiet residential or congested business areas. Community planning will do much to facilitate the solution of nuisance problems in locating industry. Finally, the tax policy of the community with respect to encouraging or discouraging the location of industrial activity is important because many communities may expect industry to carry more than its share of the public tax load.

Government-Service Locations. Many of the larger communities are beginning to follow the practice of redeveloping their central business district to serve as the seat for local and regional governmental activities. Such locations place these services at the center of the area to be served and also help to maintain the desirability of the central business district through programs of constant rehabilitation and modernization. However, as population shifts in an urban area, government-service areas can be expected to shift to meet these needs and few other considerations will be as important as the single one of providing maximum service to an optimum number of the population needing such services.

LAWS OF NEIGHBORHOOD GROWTH

The first and most important law of neighborhood growth is that no neighborhood will remain in the same state of use for any considerable period of time. Reliable research is lacking on this point, but general observation indicates that any particular use will prevail in a single location for approximately a quarter of a century, after which the use will either decline, become more important, or give way to another type of use. The rate of change and the direction the change takes will be determined by the nature of the economic background of the urban area.

Gresham's Law of Neighborhoods. In recent years a theory has been advanced that the entrance of less desirable uses into an area will eventually cause the better uses to move elsewhere. For example, as a residential area becomes older, many homes are offered for rent, some homes are converted to rooming houses, and generally home ownership gives way to renting and the area enters a new use phase as an apartment area. The ability of Gresham's law to operate in an area is in inverse proportion to the interest which the property owners and users have in preventing lower uses from entering the area.

Intensive Use. As a city grows and its economic base becomes strengthened, the intensity of land uses in the central area tends to increase as the new population seeks to locate nearer to existing activities. Extensive land uses in an urban area are usually possible only when the city is in its early stages of growth or when large amounts of land are available on the edges of the urban area. Appraisers will find this tendency important when estimating future highest and best use potentials for urban parcels. Intensity of use normally creates higher land values.

Economic Specialization. As use intensity rises and population increases, individual locations tend to develop increasing specialization of uses. For example, in the early stages of growth a central location may be used for retail sales, office uses, or warehousing. As growth continues, the area may then develop into a strict office-building use, and, if population pressures continue, a particular office-building area may then be devoted to a particular type of office use. For this reason it is common to see areas in large urban centers with concentrations of office buildings occupied by insurance companies, by financial firms, or by advertising agencies.

PRACTICAL MEASURES OF LOCATION

It should be apparent from the preceding discussion that certain items must be examined carefully in evaluating the impact of an area on property values. A minimum checklist or program for data colletcion should include the following:

1. Population—number, rate of increase, family size, ages
2. Income—total personal, family, average wage rates, purchasing power
3. Employment—total employed, sources of employment, fluctuations in employment
4. Transportation—types, costs, service, major arteries
5. Land use—existing, planned, average values by uses
6. City growth—rate of land absorption, direction of growth, types of uses, total areas occupied by each use
7. Geography—climate, topography, natural and man-made barriers
8. Market—number and dollar volume of sales, average prices
9. Political—land planning, zoning, building codes, land-use restrictions
10. Industrial activity—markets served, total volume of sales, diversity
11. Consumer markets—total purchases by principal types of goods and services

BUSINESS AND REAL ESTATE CYCLES

The majority of land-use decisions and prices are set by actions in the market place. In the short run, when demand exceeds supply, market prices rise or, when demand is less than supply, the prices drop until supply and demand are equated. If prices do not equate supply and demand in the short run and prices continue to be high, the new construction takes place in response to the high prices until equation occurs. Prices also serve as an influence on whether or not areas will develop. For example, an area may be zoned for retail uses but, unless there is a demand for retail services sufficient to warrant the construction of retail facilities, the area will not develop into retail uses. An area may be planned for large-size residential lot development, but, if the costs of such development are prohibitive, the area will not develop or pressures will develop for a change in the regulations.

Another important influence on market prices and the economic base is the general state of business conditions. The strength of real estate markets is derived from the strength of business generally, and it is rare that real estate markets can enjoy prosperity while business conditions are in a depressed state. For this reason, decisions about trends in real estate markets and locational developments must rest on conclusions about the state of business conditions and trends. For example, many persons firmly believe that real estate markets tend to follow an eighteen-year cycle with values fluctuating according to this cycle, but this condition rarely prevails. Rather, the real estate cycle is definitely linked to the business cycles, and a study of business-cycle trends will yield more clues to possible real estate market performance than will reliance on the eighteen-year theory.

MARKET INDICATORS

In any market a number of indicators are available by which an appraiser can measure market activity and estimate its impact on value trends. Many real estate transactions must be recorded, and information on these provides clues to what is happening. Other indicators are reported by lending institutions, chambers of commerce, local utility companies, and others, so the appraiser need not do the actual data collection himself. Among the more important and easily secured indicators are

Property Prices. Many local real estate boards and multiple-listing boards summarize the activities of their members on a monthly basis. Such summaries give clues to prices and sales terms for various types of properties.

Deeds Recorded. In the majority of communities, every exchange of ownership must be indicated by means of a deed which is made a part of the public record. The total number of deeds recorded and their value are another source of information on market activity and prices.

Building Permits. Building permits are announcements of intention to construct and estimates of the costs of such construction, so they are reasonably accurate measures of future events. However, their validity is weakened by the degree to which intentions are not carried out.

Subdividing and Developing. Many communities require that intention to develop five or more parcels as a single unit must be made a matter of public record. The lag between plans to subdivide and the actual start of the work will vary from six to twelve months; therefore subdivision recordings are an excellent reflection of what builders anticipate about future market conditions. The locations of the planned subdivisions also provide clues as to which urban areas will be growing.

Loan Recordings. Eighty per cent or more of all real estate sales must be supported by mortgage financing. Large numbers and high volumes of mortgage recordings reflect lenders' optimism about the future of real estate markets. As lenders become more reluctant to lend and loan activity declines, market changes are to be expected.

Vacancy Factors. Only a limited number of urban areas have measures of vacancy; however, when these are available, they provide important clues as to the degree to which supply and demand are being equated.

THE USE OF BUSINESS ANALYSTS

An increasing number of business analysts' services are becoming available today and may be purchased by anyone who will pay the subscription price. In addition, professional journals such as *Sales Management* provide all types of market information to their subscribers. Governmental agencies such as the Department of Commerce, the Federal Reserve Board, and the Department of Labor publish inexpensive or even free reports on their business-analysis studies. For these reasons, an appraiser need not undertake detailed studies of economic background, or business and real estate market analyses. Careful study of published reports to determine what types of information are offered, the reliability of the information, its timeliness, and its applicability to real estate appraisal problems will soon permit the appraiser to develop a valuable file of economic information which will permit him to undertake area analyses largely in his own office.

6

Location, Neighborhood, and Site

Appraisers often say, somewhat jokingly, that three things influence value: (1) location, (2) location, (3) and location. This statement would be much more accurate if the three factors were listed as (1) location, (2) neighborhood, and (3) site. Although these three factors are often referred to interchangeably, they cannot be assumed to be equivalent for appraisal purposes; rather, they must be analyzed in different ways. However, all of these terms are similar in that they relate to geographic and economic influences on value.

Location is the broadest term and is defined as the geographic area within which a property use might take place without suffering loss because of the lack of a particular factor necessary to that use. For example, an industry might locate anywhere within an area of several hundred square miles because within this area it could service its markets efficiently and obtain at approximately the same level of costs all the labor, materials, machinery, and financing it would need for its operations. Analysis for location is, therefore, broad in nature and generally focuses on population, over-all employment, income, and similar items (see Table 3).

A *neighborhood* is defined more specifically as a geographic area within which there is a high degree of use similarity between contiguous parcels. In an economic sense, a neighborhood would be defined as an area within which approximately the same prices prevail for properties which permit approximately the same types of uses. For this reason, a neighborhood is smaller in geographic area than a location, and, normally, several neighborhoods will be found within a particular location.

A *site* is defined as a single parcel with a combination of geographic and economic characteristics which distinguish it clearly from any other parcel. The term *parcel* implies that the sites may vary in size, with the limits set by the point at which there is a sufficiently distinct change in the geographic, legal, or economic characteristics to have significant impact on the use characteristics of the parcel. For example, a corner parcel, as such, is limited to the point where a higher price will no longer be paid for additional footage to gain the advantages assumed to be found in a corner parcel.

TABLE 3

LAND ANALYSIS

Commercial Business (including shopping centers and central business districts)	Industrial	Public Use
Market		
What is the volume of consumer purchases?	What is the volume of industrial activity in sales, employment, value added?	What is the density of population?
What percentage of family income is spent for what items?	What kinds of industries?	What are the age and income characteristics of the population?
Who does the shopping, husband or wife?	What markets are served by industry?	What special needs do they have?
When is the shopping done?		
Location		
Near dense population?	Location of work force?	Population—age, numbers, ethnic needs?
Availability to the population?	Transportation—air, rail, bus, highway availability?	Kinds of properties to be serviced?
What services are already offered?	Utilities—availability and costs?	Existing facilities?
Income and shopping habits of surrounding population?	Relation to principal markets?	Acceptance by adjacent neighbors?
Transportation, traffic arteries, and accessibility of location?	Community acceptance and cooperation?	Availability of utilities?
Delineation of the trading area?	Presently developed sites?	
Competing locations?	Adjacent to supporting industries?	
Existing similar-type facilities?		
Growth potential?		
Zoning and planning requirements?		
Public-utility connections?		
Current volumes of retailing, advertising, sales-tax receipts?		
Appearance?		
Other Factors		
Parking?	Soil and subsoil and bearing qualities?	Parking?
Accessibility?	Utility connections?	Soil, subsoil, drainage?
Contouring? Drainage?	Parking—employees, clients?	Utility connections?
Expansion potential?	Freedom from hazards of adjoining uses?	Access to streets?
Utility connections?	Room for expansion?	Character of surrounding property uses vs. accessibility to site?
Taxes?	Taxes?	Public transportation?
Shape and size of site?	Zoning and use restrictions?	
Zoning, other use restrictions?		
Tenant potential?		
Foot and auto traffic?		

TABLE 3—*Continued*

Commercial Business (including shopping centers and central business districts)	Industrial	Public Use
	Trackage to site? Access to transportation networks? Sewage, sanitary and plant waste disposal?	
Gross vs. net usable area? Age and condition? Sizes per unit? Adaptability? Costs of operation and maintenance? Appearance and modernness? Accessibility from parking areas? Traffic flow and potential tenant arrangement? Parking? Gross size and physical characteristics?	Degree of efficiency in plant use? Expansion potential? Adaptability of uses? Accessibility of various areas on buildings? Dockage and shipping facilities? Light, heat, air conditioning, and other influences on work efficiency? Gross size and physical characteristics?	Building to site ratio? Use efficiency and adaptability? Age and condition? Gross size and physical characteristics?

The appraiser will consistently face some difficult conceptual problems when he attempts to set the boundaries for each of these items. In most instances he will determine boundaries according to the availability of data. Location, for example, may be defined according to state, county, or city boundaries. Neighborhood may be defined according to census tract boundaries or economic areas prepared for other types of analyses. Sites are defined by the legal definitions of the parcels involved.

LOCATIONAL ANALYSIS

As is true in any appraisal assignment, locational analysis begins with a consideration of the reasons for undertaking the analysis. For example, if the purpose is to appraise land for a particular type of manufacturing activity, the first requirement is that the needs of the manufacturer be defined in terms of labor, transportation, markets, raw materials, power, utilities, and taxes. These needs are usually sufficiently broad in character for a wide geographic area to be defined within which the availability and costs of these items are equivalent.

The first step in locational analysis is a thorough economic analysis in terms of the market, economic background, and real estate and business trends of the area. Normally, highest property values will be found in areas with active markets, diverse and strong economic backgrounds, and active and slightly rising business and real estate market trends (see Table 3).

A second step is to relate the findings to the purpose of the appraisal. An appraisal for estimating the warranted investment in a large apartment house would be concerned with such locational characteristics as general population growth for the area, percentage of population usually interested in renting, average wage levels as clues to rents which would be paid, stability of employment as an indication of tenant stability, and credit problems. In contrast, an appraisal to determine the purchase price of an industrial site would emphasize the work skills of the population, union strength and its impact on wage rates, availability and costs of transportation and utilities, and accessibility to markets as compared to accessibility of raw materials needed to make the finished products.

A final step is to arrange in order the qualities of the location, neighborhood, and site insofar as they will affect the value of the property being appraised and to translate these into a range of values within which the value of the subject parcel is most likely to be found. As the analyses move from a consideration of the location to the neighborhood and finally to a specific site, the value range is finally narrowed to a single dollar amount.

NEIGHBORHOOD ANALYSIS

The operations of the market and the limitations introduced by planning and zoning combine to divide any urban area into a series of districts within which approximately the same types of uses prevail. The rationale underlying these groupings is that compatibility of uses produces more efficiency among individual users and over-all higher property values in the area. Thus an area of single-family homes is more likely to be a pleasant place in which to live, and for a longer period of time, if almost all of the properties in the area are used for family residential purposes.

For a number of reasons, an area can rarely be devoted completely to a single use. Industrial areas must have restaurants, service stations, and other facilities for their employees. Residential areas must have shopping, recreation, and other facilities nearby. For these reasons, complete homogeneity does not necessarily produce the highest values. Within the area the highest values with respect to particular use will be found in the central part. On the borders of an area, where differing uses are found in adjoining areas, the values will probably be lowest. For example, the home sites for single-family-housing use on the border of a residential area immediately across the street from industrial land uses have less value than the similar types of sites located several blocks away in the center of residential land uses.

What Is a Neighborhood? A neighborhood has already been defined as an area in which the same types of land uses tend to prevail, and the possible difficulties in the bounding of such an area, particularly when differing uses exist in close proximity to each other, have been mentioned. In the majority of urban areas, zoning serves as the simplest means of establishing various types of use districts, particularly if the zoning is efficiently enforced. Traffic arteries, railroads, streams and rivers, valleys, hills, and other natural and artificial barriers often supplement zoning controls so that subareas of use can be defined within a particular type of neighborhood. Population per square mile and family income and size are further clues to possible boundaries. Property prices, ages, and sizes as reflected in current Bureau of the Census reports or in market transactions also aid in determining uses and boundaries of any particular area of the city.

The number and types of neighborhoods are direct reflections of the economic base of a city. A strong and growing base will produce equally strong and diversified land-use districts. A weak base will produce poorly defined and weak land-use districts. If the urban area is growing, new use districts will spring up and the older districts in the core of the city will tend to change, as is indicated in other chapters. If the economic base is rather stable, the patterns of land uses will tend to stagnate and the same types of uses will continue to prevail in each of the districts for much longer periods of time than is common in a dynamic urban area.

The Single-Family-Home Neighborhood. The evaluation of the impact of the single-family-home neighborhood on the values of the properties located in it is fundamental to almost any other type of area analysis. Neighborhoods with high property values can support strong commercial areas and are an indication of strong industrial and commercial areas. In addition, many of the items which are analyzed for single-family-home neighborhoods must also be analyzed for the other areas. Population and family income, for example, are basic to the analysis of all other districts.

Property values in a single-family-home neighborhood are more likely to be maintained if the neighborhood is located so as to benefit from future city growth because population increases and the constant demand for properties maintains property values. Neighborhoods are dynamic in nature, moving through a series of life cycles whose length and character are directly related to such changes occurring in the total urban area as were discussed in previous chapters.

An important influence on the neighborhood life cycle is the degree to which the area is protected against blighting influences. A single-family-home neighborhood tends to have the highest property values when the amenities associated with family living are present in the greatest quantities.

If zoning regulations are enforced so that industrial and other non-residential uses are prohibited from entering the area, property values will be maintained. Similarly—if building codes are enforced so that properties must be maintained; if city planning provides parks and harmonious combinations of residential and non-residential uses; if private deed restrictions produce reasonable uniformity in architecture and building sizes; if there are hills, valleys, lakes, rivers, streams, and similar natural barriers to halt objectionable uses from encroaching; and, if freeways, highways, parks, plantings, and other artificial barriers are also created to halt adverse uses —the entire neighborhood benefits, single-family residential uses will continue to prevail, and property values will be maintained.

The age of a neighborhood does not provide an automatic clue to property values but does assist in estimating how long existing values might prevail. Newer neighborhoods are much more likely to have higher or rising values than are older neighborhoods. However, very new neighborhoods are still in a process of development, and, until they have existed for a few years, the exact trend in their property values is not likely to be clearly apparent. A neighborhood in mid-life, usually the tenth to fifteenth year after the last houses have been constructed, will usually have the highest and most stable values which will prevail during the life cycle of the area. Changing land uses in the neighborhood may produce higher land values at a later date but will not produce the highest over-all single-family-home values.

Similarity in architecture and in building size and age, quality of construction, and improvements made to the site also contribute to higher property values. Absolute homogeneity of construction, however, produces a monotony which rarely adds to land values. Perhaps the most common criticism leveled against tract construction is the monotony produced by the sameness of properties. Extreme heterogeneity, in which large and small, old and new properties are mixed indiscriminately, will have an equally unwholesome influence on property values.

Although the private automobile is increasingly supplanting public transportation systems, the presence of fast, frequent low-cost public transportation invariably adds to property values. Few families can afford two cars, so, if the wife uses the car, the husband must have transportation to work. If the husband uses the car, the children must have public transportation to school and the wife needs access to shopping, recreation, and similar types of activities. One of the more important causes of the resurgence of population to the central areas of cities is the accessibility of theaters, restaurants, churches, and shopping because of frequent, nearby public transportation.

Property-tax burdens and special assessments for schools, lighting, sewage, and other items are becoming increasingly heavy on the single-family home. Urban areas with little industry or commercial activity must rely almost completely on property taxes from single-family homes, so home construction in such areas is often slow and property values relatively low because of these tax burdens. Low taxes and assessments must, however, be balanced against the quantity and quality of public services offered. Property values will be highest in areas where the levels of taxes and assessments are directly proportional to the quantity and quality of public services offered.

The mushrooming suburban areas have often preceded the introduction of adequate water, gas, electricity, and sewage-disposal facilities. Sometimes one or more of these services may be supplied by small private concerns at rather high prices. Price, quality, and dependability of these services are all interrelated. An area which is supplied with utilities on a dependable basis, with high quality of service and moderate prices, will usually have the highest single-family-home values.

The addition of multiple suburbs to existing urban areas has also resulted in the creation of numerous small political entities which are unable to provide many of the services usually associated with city living. Perhaps the most neglected of these services are police and fire protection. Adequate services in these two categories reduce insurance rates and prevent the entrance of many types of deteriorating influences. When both police and fire protection are available on a very few minutes call, property values will tend to be higher.

Some irregularity of topography, particularly when it produces some views as well as privacy between homes, is most often desired in single-family-home neighborhoods. Hills and irregular topography do produce higher construction costs, so the higher-priced homes are most often found where such conditions prevail. Flat land permits lower construction costs but also produces greater monotony, so the lowest values are usually found here. The influence of topography on values is largely dependent upon the local community traditions and customs.

Residential neighborhoods are adversely affected by any type of activity which adds hazards to life or produces obnoxious odors, noises, lights, or activity. For these reasons single-family homes will have the lowest values when they are immediately adjacent to, or affected by, the presence of high-speed traffic, airports, industrial activity, railroads, ravines, gullies, pools, drainage canals, sewage-treatment plants, or similar hazards and nuisances.

Apartment-House Neighborhoods. Apartment-house locations need approximately the same conditions as do single-family-home areas for maximum property-value maintenance. Apartment areas can, however, be located closer to the central districts of urban areas, on or along major traffic arteries, or close to commercial or business districts and still have high property values. The siting of the properties and the provisions for open or green areas around the apartments will have almost as much influence on property values as location.

Transportation facilities and accessibility to shopping, work, and recreation tend to play more important roles in property values than is true in single-family-home districts. Taxes and assessments also play a somewhat less important role because they can be spread over a larger base.

Non-residential Locations. OFFICE-BUILDING AREAS. Office buildings provide space for the administrative activities necessary to support business activity, so they normally are located near the business interests they serve. For this reason, professional buildings for lawyers and accountants are located near the banks, warehouses, and retail establishments which house the executives who need legal and financial services. Large office complexes are found in large urban areas because they house the regional offices for the various businesses and industries located in the urban area. Improved transportation and communication facilities are tending to free companies from the need of having offices in special locations, so many offices are now being constructed where climate and employment forces are favorable. For example, jet planes make possible the location of some office and manufacturing centers in the southern or far-western areas of the country where climate is more equitable, because their speed still permits four- or five-hour delivery to some of the most distant consumers in the United States.

However, in spite of recent advances in communication and transportation, office-building areas which are properly located to service a maximum of business and industrial activities will also have the highest property values. In addition, such areas need to be reasonably available to public transportation, both local and nationwide. Property taxes and assessments are also strong influences on values because of the degree to which they are translated into higher or lower rents. Some cities have recognized this fact and follow a deliberate policy of giving tax advantages to businesses and industries which they are seeking to attract.

The appearance of office-building areas is given a high rating by tenants who are interested in presenting the best possible image of their business activities. Modern, attractively designed office areas therefore have higher values than others not as well designed. In the larger cities, where the very tall office buildings are constructed, local building regulations tend to dictate the appearance of the buildings. New York City, for example, is faced constantly with the problem of regulating the shape of office buildings so that the buildings can be operated profitably but still maintain an outward appearance in harmony with the development of the rest of the city.

A great deal of discussion has been generated in recent years about the desirability of central vs. outlying office districts. Some firms have moved far out in the suburbs and have created their own office complexes. Others feel that, the nearer they are to the central area, the more effective is their performance. The question cannot be settled except by reference to the needs of the individual tenants. Some firms must have constant daily contact with a variety of other businesses and are required to locate in central business districts; others are not. In all cases, office properties will tend to have higher values when they are located in a complex of other offices, whether the complex is in the central district or in the suburbs.

Non-Residential locations include:

COMMERCIAL DISTRICTS: SHOPPING CENTERS, CENTRAL BUSINESS AREAS. The same arguments about the desirability of outlying vs. central locations have been present in the field of commercial retail locations. There is no question but that central business districts are changing in their functions and the bulk of retail activities is moving to the suburbs. On the other hand, there are many types of retailing activities which continue to thrive in the central business district. In all cases there are certain characteristics common to retailing districts which must be present if the properties in them are to have maximum value.

Retail districts exist to serve population, so a district which can serve a maximum amount of population will have the greatest value. The districts should be readily accessible to both public and private transportation; the services offered should be geared to the economic status and shopping habits of the surrounding markets; duplication of existing facilities and unwise competition from similar facilities should be avoided; the over-all development of the district should be planned so that each property in it supplements or complements the others; and zoning and planning regulations and service facilities such as utilities should be favorable to maximum growth.

The site is an important part of locational considerations because the site should be large enough to permit the offering of the proper combination of services, the construction of stores of the most economic size, and the provision of ample parking and growth potential.

From the consumer viewpoint the most effective commercial district is one which is easily reached, pleasant to shop in, equipped with a maximum variety of retail services, and organized to offer a maximum range of price, style, and model choices. Such centers will maximize locational advantages and enjoy the highest property values.

INDUSTRIAL LOCATIONS. Industrial activity usually generates some combination of noise, odors, heavy traffic, and similar phenomena which have a decided negative effect on other types of property uses. For this reason, industrial districts should have well-defined boundaries and locations which are not likely to seriously affect other uses. To the degree to which particular industries can eliminate or modify these hazards, they can locate nearer to the central districts of urban areas.

More important to industrial locations, however, are the location and availability of the work skills which they need, the markets they will serve, and the transportation facilities which can be used to bring in raw materials and deliver finished products. Other factors which influence industrial location choices are the kinds, quality, and quantity of utility facilities available. For example, industry places heavy demand on power companies, sewage-disposal facilities, and water companies. Communities which make these services sufficiently available and provide the right setting for industry are able to develop diverse and strong economic bases which not only support relatively high industrial land values but other property values as well. Many industries must also locate so that they can be serviced by varieties of complementary facilities. The construction of automobiles and airplanes requires the existence of motor manufacturers, body makers, accessory manufacturers, and many other types of smaller supporting manufacturing activities.

The highest industrial land values will therefore be found where the development of the area has been carefully planned and controlled so that complementary industrial complexes can work together in harmony in supplying maximum markets at minimum prices.

PUBLIC-USE AREAS. Public-use areas are those devoted to city administrative centers, courts, public-welfare activities, libraries, concert halls, and similar activities and institutions which receive their principal support from tax funds. The typical appraiser will rarely be faced with the problem of valuing such property, but he will be faced constantly with the problem of estimating the impact of such facilities on the other types of land uses. A properly designed and planned public-use area will increase the values of all other types of properties. The homeowner will find it convenient for paying taxes and dealing with zoning and planning problems affecting his property. The businessman will find it convenient for securing permits. The industrialist will find is valuable in securing his permits and working with city officials in the operation of his activities.

A public-use area maximizes property values when it is located to service a maximum number and variety of population. The broader and more extensive the services which can be offered in such an area, the more the surrounding properties will benefit. If the center is designed to fit in harmoniously with surrounding uses, the benefits in increased land values are even greater. The actual location will be influenced, as are those for other uses, by the availability of utilities, public transportation, accessibility by private automobile, and parking.

SITE ANALYSIS

Site analysis requires detailed analysis of the factors that are considered by the builder in considering the qualities of a specific parcel of land within an area. He will be interested in the physical qualities of the site, both natural and man-made. The soil-bearing qualities and drainage qualities will affect the cost of creating a new project. Obviously, the land topography will affect cost of construction and actual use of the land. Two extreme examples would be sheer cliffs rising from a highway or a ravine below the road. Rocky conditions or swamp areas will also indicate extreme land-development problems.

In choosing a site for a supermarket, a store chain will be concerned with the ability of a woman shopper to enter the road from the parking lot and to exit from the road to the lot. The speed at which the traffic moves on the highway, the amount of frontage, and the topography will affect choices that the shopper makes as to where to spend her grocery dollars. Similarly, a traffic light, bus stop, or high school may make an adjacent site suitable for a gas station, newsstand, or soda fountain, respectively.

The site is also affected by neighboring site layout. A home site will be adversely affected by an abutting supermarket parking lot. An overhead, or even underground, utility easement may limit the flexibility of site layout and desirability.

A site will also be affected by legal restrictions on its use. A current example of this is the severe quantity of construction controls in urban renewal redevelopment projects. Redevelopment companies are often restricted from attaining the highest economic use from a site.

Dimensions and shape of the site will affect its desirability and potential use. Sometimes, it becomes necessary to acquire additional land in order to create an economically sound project.

The availability and location of utilities can also materially affect property values. These utilities usually include water, sewers, gas, and electric service.

In site analysis, the appraiser is determining specific qualifications of a site to contribute to the creation of a suitable economic project.

CONCLUSIONS

The processes of analyzing neighborhoods are still based largely on a combination of data collection and guesswork, and the quality of the evaluation of the material is related directly to the appraiser's judgment and experience. For example, there is no effective method of rating precisely the quality of zoning in a neighborhood, the homogeneity or heterogeneity of architecture, and similar items. The FHA has attempted to develop numerical ratings for neighborhoods, but their chief value lies in the degree to which important factors are emphasized and in the consistency with which these factors must be considered by FHA appraisers. The principal purpose of neighborhood analysis is to develop comparisons between areas. Mathematical precision is not particularly important. It is quite clear that a great deal of research will have to be devoted to the impact which various factors will have on property values in a neighborhood. Until that is done, neighborhood analysis must remain a guesswork science in which the experience and judgment of the appraiser play the largest roles.

7

Methods of Approaching Value

The fact that any value statement is only a form of "educated guessing" requires that all possible factors be considered which might influence value and that all possible methods be used in relating these factors to the purpose of the appraisal. The classic appraisal approaches to value have been through market sales comparisons, the capitalization of income, and the cost to reproduce. Many appraisers firmly believe that all three of these approaches should be used in every appraisal assignment except those where they are obviously not applicable. Other appraisers feel that only one or two of the three approaches are really necessary in typical appraisal assignments and that the three would be used only rarely. Investors often find that the detail and work involved in using the three classic approaches are too much for their purposes, so they often use an income multiplier, equity net return, or free and clear net return method of estimating investment values. The purpose of this chapter is to examine the rationale of these various ideas; later chapters give the details of using them.

THE CLASSIC APPROACHES

The use of three approaches is based on the assumption that in perfect markets the use of any one of the three would produce the same value estimate as any of the other approaches; therefore, in any market the three tend to approach each other. Any differences between the three presumably can be traced to aberrations in the market place, which can be isolated and compensated for in the appraisal process. Furthermore, the use of three approaches should serve to narrow the range within which an estimate must be made, and inadequacies in one approach can be overcome through the use of the other approaches. Perhaps the most effective argument for using the three approaches is that appraising is only estimating and subject to personal bias, data errors, incomplete data, and many other things, so any means which can offset these should be used.

There may be times, however, when a single approach may be the only approach or the best one. These occasions are determined primarily by the purpose for which the appraisal is undertaken and the kind of value definition governing the appraisal assignment. For example, fire insurance companies base their payment of compensation on the costs of restoring the policyholder to his previous position. Under these circumstances, the income-capitalization method would have no value and the sales-comparison approach only limited value. It is also true that in any appraisal assignment the purpose of the appraisal will tend to make one approach more significant than another even when the three approaches are used. The appraisal of a home for loan purposes usually dictates that primary emphasis be given to the sales approach and that the cost and income approaches be used only as checks on the market comparisons. There are also times when there are no data or very invalid or poor data are available for one of the approaches so that only two of the approaches are possible. This situation often arises in the appraisal of special-purpose buildings, such as hospitals, schools, and public buildings, for which there is little or no market.

The Cost-To-Reproduce Approach. The reproduction-cost approach consists of estimating the value of the land, adding to it the cost of reproducing the various improvements found on the land, and subtracting losses in value which reflect the differences between new properties of this type and the present condition of the property being appraised. Cost to reproduce implies that cost estimates will be based on the creation of an equally desirable substitute rather than an exact duplication of the existing structure. The techniques of this approach are given in detail in a later chapter.

The assumption underlying the cost approach is that no one would want to pay more for a used property than he would pay for a similar new property, if he could afford to wait while he built the new property on available vacant land. There is an additional assumption from economics that, because of the operation of the law of competition, excess profits will have been removed from the cost operation so that, over the long run, reproduction cost and sales prices will be the same; therefore, the reproduction-cost approach serves the same purposes as the comparative sales approach. On a more practical basis, the cost approach furnishes the investor with an estimate of the minimum investment he would have to make if he were to construct a new property. When used to compare the alternatives of buying or building, it requires the additional consideration of the possibility of appreciation or depreciation of capital value in an existing structure and a basis for deciding whether there would be any financial advantages in building a new structure. In a period of rapidly rising building costs and minimum losses in value in existing structures, the cost approach permits an estimation of the range of uncertainty which might be expected if construction were undertaken.

The costs are established by reference to the market place; therefore, many persons argue that the cost approach is only a form of the market approach. The principal difference between the approaches is that the comparative-sales approach emphasizes the property as a single unit of value in exchange, whereas the cost approach examines the various components which together make the single unit so that the investor can determine which factors have influenced value the most. In other instances, the purpose of the appraisal may require that exact replica or historical costs be used, in which case there would be no necessary relationship between costs and the current market place, although costs would be based on historical markets. Rate making based on historical investment cost is an example of this. There may also be a need to anticipate the future so that cost estimates reflecting what is anticipated would be of more importance than current market costs.

The cost approach also includes estimates of the costs of waiting while invested capital is being used to create a property, as well as of the costs arising because the money invested in the construction cannot be used in alternative, perhaps likewise profitable, forms of investment. Thus, the cost approach indicates rather clearly the various direct and indirect outlays which together have been or must be considered in reproducing a new property. An investor may decide that the indirect costs are much too high and that the purchase of an existing structure would avoid such costs.

The reproduction-cost approach is not an easy approach to use and is subject to wide error in the hands of someone who is not familiar with construction methods and materials. The degree of error can, to some extent, be reduced through the use of engineers, architects, builders, contractors, and others in developing cost estimates. Various engineering companies, also, publish manuals in which various methods of estimating costs are explained and the amounts for these given. Such services may give costs in terms of square feet, cubic feet, major components such as foundation, walls, roofs, heating, plumbing, etc., or the amount of materials and labor involved. Some services also base costs on a moving index related to various types of properties.

One of the more difficult problems faced in the cost approach is that of estimating the amount of depreciation or value deficiency which has occurred in an existing structure. Some appraisers believe that depreciation is basically a lump-sum amount to be deducted which is determined by comparing the cost of building a structure and the price for which an identical or closely similar structure sells in the market place. Others break down depreciation according to the types of depreciation—i.e., physical, which arises from wear and tear and age; economic, caused by changes in the surrounding environment, or economy; and functional, caused by changes in the market place in terms of style. Some rather elaborate formulas have been devised for estimating depreciation, but none have proved adequate for the problem of quantifying the depreciation estimate.

The cost approach has often been criticized because it fails to include such factors as amenities, which make up a large part of the value of residential properties; because of the large amounts of judgment involved in estimating depreciation; and because of the errors which can be introduced when costs are being estimated by inexperienced appraisers. Furthermore, many errors may be introduced when an attempt is being made to estimate the costs of reproducing an existing structure in which many costly items of construction may be hidden from view and inaccessible during the property inspection. An additional, very telling criticism of the approach is that it often fails to reflect losses which might arise because the improvement is not a proper one for the site or the location.

In the hands of an experienced appraiser, the cost approach may be an effective approach, and he will be able to discover and evaluate some of the weaknesses previously mentioned when he checks the approach against the other approaches. Moreover, there are many instances, as in special-purpose properties, when the cost approach, limited as it is, is the only applicable approach.

The Sales-Comparison Method. As is implied in its name, the sales-comparison approach involves searching the market place for properties comparable to the one being appraised and making comparisons on the basis of terms of sale, conditions in the market place at the time of the sale, and the degree of comparability to the subject property. Very great difficulties are often encountered in finding properties sufficiently like the subject property to permit comparisons.

The effectiveness of the approach lies in a large measure in the ability of the appraiser to make price adjustments sufficiently accurate to reflect property differences. For example, suppose that two properties are exactly alike except for architectural style. How much, if any, allowance should be made for this? This type of problem is often encountered in tract house appraising. In some cases differences can be reconciled by estimating the costs of remedying these differences. An overenthusiastic homeowner may have placed a marble-front fireplace in a home when normally only stone would be used. The differences in cost in the two facings provide some clue to possible differences in price. In these cases the principles of diminishing returns and contribution play a large role.

The sales-comparison approach acts as a lower limit on value because it represents the price which must be paid if the property is to be acquired. Furthermore, the approach has a great deal of appeal because it is easily understood and is a method commonly used by all types of appraisers. Theoretically, the approach is sound because it represents the considered judgment of many buyers in transactions which have been completed and does not rest on the estimates of a single appraiser.

The approach does have some serious weaknesses which must always be kept in mind if the final estimate is to be accurate. In the first place, very few properties are really sufficiently similar to permit accurate comparisons. For this reason the approach may be very inaccurate if large adjustments have to be made because of location, property characteristics, sale terms, or other items. In some cases, the market may be so stable, or the kind of property being appraised may be so unique, that no market information is available, or that which is available is unusable because it is outdated. Finally, the sales-comparison approach rests on the securing of actual sales prices and terms and of asking or offered terms and prices, and buyers and sellers may not be willing to disclose this information.

The Income-Capitalization Approach. The income-capitalization approach is more properly identified as the net-income-capitalization approach, because the amount capitalized is the remainder after charges have been made against gross income for the costs of earning the gross income. Because land is assumed to be a non-wasting asset, the net income earned by it is capitalized by dividing it by the interest rate desired as a return on the investment. Buildings, however, do depreciate, so the capitalization rate, as contrasted to the interest rate, provides for a return on, and a return of, the investment. The method by which the investment is recovered depends upon the type of mathematical formula used in the capitalization process. (This is explained in detail in Chapter 12.)

The process of capitalization is simple in concept but complicated in use because of the numerous mathematical formulas which have been developed for use with the method. The assumptions underlying the method are (1) a net income stream will be earned over the future; (2) this income stream may be in equal, increasing, or decreasing annual amounts; (3) the investor will want to earn a profit on his investment, in this case interest on whatever capital he invests; (4) the investor will also want to receive from income an amount which represents a return of the capital he invests; (5) any income to be received in the future has less value than income to be received immediately—therefore, the amount which will be paid for future income will be less than that paid for more immediate income; (6) the return on the investment and the return of the investment are expressed in percentages of value which are then translated into a single capitalization figure which, divided into the net income, represents the value of the future stream of income.

The income-capitalization method forces the appraiser to consider those factors which may affect the value of the property during the period of proposed ownership so that points of weakness in the investment will be uncovered. In addition, the investor knows what may happen if during the investment his earnings drop, expenses rise, or other events occur which are at variance with his original assumptions. If expenses rise, he knows he must increase his gross income or suffer a loss of earnings, in which case he may have to extend the period of his investment if he cannot increase his gross income. In this way each element affecting value can be watched by the investor and assessed for its possible effect on his value estimate.

Although the income-capitalization method works very well with business, commercial, and investment properties, it is of limited value in estimating the values of dwellings, special-use properties, or properties where value is affected in a large degree by amenities. Inexperienced persons are also tempted to give undue weight to the approach because the various mathematical techniques used give it an air of spurious accuracy. In fact, the mathematical techniques needed in the approach are not often understood by the typical investor and are shunned for this reason. Even experienced appraisers who understand these techniques may use them in their own calculations but will rarely attempt to explain them to their clients. The weaknesses of the approach can be appreciated from a quick perusal of the many variables which must be dealt with in estimating gross income, exenses, and capitalization rates. As the need for projecting income further into the future develops, the accuracy of the method is open to additional doubts.

The income-capitalization method is particularly effective when rents or income have been guaranteed by a lease signed by a strong tenant who pays all expenses or when records are available on the costs which will be incurred over the life of the investment. As the strength of the tenant lessens, as less is known about operating expenses, the accuracy of the method declines.

OTHER METHODS OF APPROACHING VALUE

Occasions often arise when a quick estimate of value is required as a preliminary to later and more extensive investigations. There are also investment situations which do not require the involved types of analyses usually associated with the classic approaches to value. These briefer analyses should not be called "appraisals," because they are not, but they are valuable tools for business decision making.

Income Multipliers. Some investors determine the warranted investment by examining the relationships found in the market place between gross income and sales price for a group of comparable properties. The ratio thus developed is then applied as a crude measure of the warranted investment price of properties. For example, properties may be selling for $100,000 and earn monthly gross incomes of $1,000. The ratio between sales price and monthly income is 100 to 1. If a property being considered for purchase had a gross income of $1,200 monthly, the assumed warranted price would be $120,000. Such ratios might also be developed between gross annual earnings and sale price or between net monthly or annual earnings and sale price.

These gross multipliers are never more than crude measures of warranted price, because of the variations which any experienced investor or appraiser knows regularly exist in expense to gross income ratios of properties. There are also many problems inherent in the selection of comparable properties, because of lack of comparability among properties in terms of sales, and physical and economic factors. Basically, the approach is a market approach, and all the precautions surrounding the use of the market approach should be observed in the use of multipliers.

Return on Equity. Many experienced investors use the "leverage" device as a means of increasing the returns on their equities. With this device, the investor seeks to reach a balance between the use of his money and borrowed money which will pay him the greatest net return on his capital. To the normal operating expenses are added the costs of using borrowed money, and the total is then deducted from gross income. The resulting net income is then expressed as a percentage of the capital which the investor has placed in the property. The assumption underlying this approach is that, although the dollar amounts of earnings are smaller, the percentage rate of earnings is higher because of the smaller equity invested. For instance, a property purchased for $100,000 might earn $10,000 annually before income taxes were deducted. If the investor has invested $75,000 of his own money and is paying 6 per cent interest on the remaining $25,000, he must deduct approximately $1,500 interest in the first year from his $10,000, leaving $8,500, which represents an 11⅓ per cent return on his $75,000. On the other hand, if he had borrowed $75,000, he would have paid $4,500 in interest and he would be earning only $5,500, but this would represent a return of almost 22 per cent on his capital of $25,000.

In many cases, professional investors would also deduct an additional percentage for return of the capital investment. If the amortization were 2 per cent per year, for example, then the return on investment would be reduced to 9⅓ per cent and 20 per cent, respectively.

This practice was followed during the early speculative days of the 1920's, and many investors lost all of their capital because the high payments on mortgages actually exceeded the net earnings of their properties. This is one of the dangers of this type of investing. However, the approach does permit spreading a given amount of capital among a number of different properties so that the chance of loss is reduced.

AN EVALUATION

The assumption that each of the three approaches to a value estimate will yield results of approximate equivalence is based on a type of economic condition which prevails only in the thinking of the neoclassical economists. However, the insistence among some appraisal theorists that the majority of appraisals require the use of the three approaches and that the three will produce approximately the same estimates has produced some amazingly complex and unrealistic appraisal estimates. Unfortunately, the large number of variables which must be dealt with in any value estimates gives the appraiser wide latitude in "forcing" his three approaches into some proximity of amounts. If the cost approach seems out of line, adjustments which are rationally, if not economically, defensible can be made. The extent to which comparability can be produced in the market approach is readily apparent in the majority of reports where the appraiser explains that his judgment forces him to make "a 10 per cent upward adjustment for time, 15 per cent downward adjustment for appearance," etc. Consciously or subconsciously, the appraiser who thinks the three approaches should produce approximately the same value estimates can reach his objective in spite of his data or his economic reasoning.

The real danger of the three-approach concept lies in the degree to which it is reduced to a formula into which various data are inserted at appropriate points, after which a final answer is produced. Inexperienced or poorly educated or trained appraisers are thus tempted to use this "ritualistic" approach to estimating in every situation. Although their final estimates may be only very poor guesses, the fitting of the data into an apparently soundly designed system of analysis produces a report which appears to be based on sound judgment.

Some appraisal theorists have observed the difficulties and inadequacies of the three-approach system and have argued forcefully for the acceptance of only one system. One group, for example, argues that the income-capitalization approach is the soundest, and they cite not only the arguments about real estate representing a bundle of future income streams but also European preference for this system. They, of course, are forced to yield, although reluctantly, in the appraisal of amenity or special-use properties. They also overlook the degree to which leaseholds rather than freeholds predominate in the European scheme of property holding.

An increasing number of appraisal theorists are emphasizing the comparative-sales approach, asserting that all transactions must be completed in the market place and that, therefore, estimates must finally be based on the market place. Complete reliance on this method is founded on a bit of circuitous reasoning that says an individual should look to the market for the estimate of the value of his property but that the market price is established by the bids of numerous individuals making their own estimates. This is a form of chicken-and-egg reasoning—which comes first?

Obviously, a great deal of work needs to be done in developing theoretical models which reveal the relationships and the impact of the various factors which determine value. These models have to be refined so that they will fit various appraisal situations and types of properties. Current appraisal writings tend to be repetitious in their analysis of the use of the three approaches and merely perpetuate the present incomplete doctrine without advancing the theory. Until models and doctrine are improved the appraiser should consider the following when attempting to make an appraisal estimate:

1. The purpose: Why was the appraisal desired? How will the estimate be used?
2. The data: Are they complete, reliable, and valid in terms of the purpose?
3. The logic: Do the conclusions flow naturally from the data, or have they been forced in order to fit preconceived notions?
4. The economic theory: Are the conclusions based on sound economic theory which has been properly interpreted and applied?

Bibliography—Part I

AMERICAN INSTITUTE OF REAL ESTATE APPRAISERS. *The Appraisal of Real Estate.* Chicago: American Institute of Real Estate Appraisers, 1960. Chapters 4–7.

BABCOCK, FREDERICK M. *Valuation of Real Estate.* New York: McGraw-Hill Book Co., Inc., 1932.

BARLOWE, RALEIGH. *Land Resource Economics.* Englewood Cliffs, N.J.: Prentice-Hall, Inc., 1958.

BONBRIGHT, JAMES C. *Valuation of Property.* New York: McGraw-Hill Book Co., Inc., 1937. Volume I. Chapters 2–5.

CASE, FREDERICK E. *Modern Real Estate Practice.* Englewood Cliffs, N.J.: Allyn & Bacon, Inc., 1956, Chapters 3–4, 10–11.

DORAU, HERBERT B., and ALBERT G. HINMAN. *Urban Land Economics.* New York: The Macmillan Co., 1928.

ELY, RICHARD T., and EDWIN W. MOREHOUSE. *Elements of Land Economics.* New York: The Macmillan Co., 1924.

FISHER, ERNEST M., and ROBERT M. FISHER. *Urban Real Estate.* New York: Holt, Rinehart & Winston, Inc., 1954. Chapters 12–14.

GALLION, ARTHUR B. *The Urban Pattern.* Princeton, N.J.: D. Van Nostrand Co., Inc., 1950.

HOAGLAND, HENRY E., and LEO D. STONE. *Real Estate Finance.* Homewood, Ill.: Richard D. Irwin, Inc., 1961. Chapter 18.

HOOVER, EDGAR M. *Location of Economic Activity.* New York: McGraw-Hill Book Co., Inc., 1948. Chapter 8.

HUSBAND, WILLIAM H., and FRANK R. ANDERSON. *Real Estate.* Homewood, Ill.: Richard D. Irwin, Inc., 1960. Chapters 3, 11–12.

LAND ECONOMIC INSTITUTE. *Modern Land Policy.* Urbana: University of Illinois Press, 1961. Chapter 9.

MARTIN, PRESTON. *Real Estate Principles and Practices.* New York: The Macmillan Co., 1957. Chapter 2.

MAY, ARTHUR A. *The Valuation of Residential Real Estate.* Englewood Cliffs, N.J.: Prentice-Hall, Inc., 1953. Chapter 1.

NELSON, RICHARD L. *The Selection of Retail Locations.* New York: F. W. Dodge Corp., 1958.

NELSON, RICHARD L., and FREDERICK T. ASCHMAN. *Real Estate and City Planning.* Englewood Cliffs, N.J.: Prentice-Hall, Inc., 1957. Chapters 2–4.

NORTH, NELSON L., and ALFRED A. RING. *Real Estate Principles and Practices.* Englewood Cliffs, N.J.: Prentice-Hall, Inc., 1960. Chapter 24.

SCHMUTZ, GEORGE L. *Appraisal Process.* Manhattan Beach, Calif.: Published by the author, 1959. Chapters 1–3.

WEIMER, ARTHUR M., and HOMER HOYT. *Principles of Real Estate* (4th ed.). New York: The Ronald Press Co., 1960. Chapters 18–19.

WENDT, PAUL F. *Real Estate Appraisal.* New York: Holt, Rinehart & Winston, Inc., 1956. Chapters 1–2.

WHITTAKER, EDMUND. *Schools and Streams of Economic Thought.* Chicago: Rand McNally & Co., 1960.

Part II

VALUATION TECHNIQUES

8

Comparative-Sales Approach

One of the most important tools available to the real estate appraiser is the *comparative-sales approach* to value, which is sometimes referred to as the *market approach, market-comparison approach,* or *sales-comparison approach.* The nomenclature is of no significance; the technique remains the same regardless of what it is called.

THE FOUNDATIONS OF THE APPROACH

The technique is based on the *principle of substitution,* which states that the cost of acquisition of an equally desirable substitute property, without undue delay, ordinarily sets the upper limit of value. The cost of acquisition may refer either to the price which must be paid for an already existing substitute, or comparable property, or to the cost of acquiring a plot of land and building an equally desirable structure thereon. In the latter instance, the principle has significance in the cost approach to value. In the former, it has significance in the comparative-sales approach. It follows that a prudent investor will, in the absence of unusual pressures of time or utility, pay no more for a parcel of real estate than he would have to pay to obtain a comparable parcel. Therefore, the prices that are paid for similar or comparable properties should, at any given time, reflect the market value of a property under appraisal.

The validity of the technique is widely recognized in the valuation of commodities such as wheat, potatoes, copper, common stocks of a single company, etc., all of which are characterized by high degrees of similarity and mobility. National and international markets have been organized to trade in these commodities, and daily changes in the prices are published for all those who are interested in their sale or purchase.

Owing to the non-homogeneous nature of real estate parcels and the lack of any but strictly local markets for the sale of real estate, value cannot be obtained from daily "market quotations" nor even from the sale of one or more similar parcels of real estate. Each market appraisal of a parcel of real estate is a separate problem requiring an analysis of location, physical condition, income, available financing, and other relevant factors in addition to sales of comparable properties.

The chief problems facing the appraiser are the establishment of criteria to determine comparability and the setting of dollar values on the different features which characterize comparable properties. Residential land may vary with locational features, topography, or soil conditions. Buildings may vary with age, condition, or type. For example, if property A, which sold for $20,000 within the past year, is a five-year-old ranch-type one-family dwelling containing seven rooms in good physical condition and is located two blocks from a school, on a gently sloping lot, with a southwest exposure, what should be the sales price of property B, which is ten years old, also in good condition, but located six blocks from the school, on a level lot, with a northwest exposure? If we assume both properties are sufficiently alike to be called comparable, there are still sufficient differences in features to require an appraiser to take these differences into consideration in his estimation of market value for property B.

The existence of these and other problems in connection with the use of the comparative-sales approach does not mean that it has only limited value in the appraisal process. A careful analysis of comparable sales will yield important data that can be used in the other approaches to value. Certainly, any process that purports to measure market prices and costs must concern itself with the actions of buyers and sellers as revealed by their market behavior. Economists have long observed that potential buyers and sellers are influenced by current prices and that, therefore, current prices are serviceable guides for estimating value. Thus, the appraiser must be familiar with current sales as a first step in estimating how and to what degree social and economic trends may operate to vary current expectations.

COMPARATIVE-SALES-APPROACH PROCEDURE

When the comparative-sales approach is used in estimating the value of vacant and improved properties, the first step is to limit the period of time and the area in which the sales have occurred.

Establishing a Time Period. While there are no set rules as to how long a period of time should be considered, it is obvious that sales made close to the date of appraisal should be given the most consideration. Sales dating back over a long period of time, while helpful as a guide to value trends, may encompass different economic levels, and this may cause them to have doubtful value in current market conditions. If there are sufficient sales (three to five) within a one-year period, then heavy, if not exclusive, weight should be given to these sales. It may be necessary to go back in time as much as five or ten years, but this can be done safely only if there have been no radical swings in the economic climate over that period. Limited time periods avoid the necessity of making "time adjustments" which cannot be readily substantiated. In general, the limitation on time should be governed by the sales data available during a comparable "economic" time, in order to warrant a conclusion of value.

Determining the Market Area. As with time, so with area: A larger area is apt to be more helpful in establishing trends, values, and historical facts; however, there is no particular advantage in including a larger area unless it contains reasonably comparable properties. If the appraisal is of a large luxury-type apartment house on a main residential street, consideration of sales on intersecting side streets improved with smaller apartment houses is not likely to produce significant conclusions. If the appraisal is of a retail property on a main shopping street, sales made on side streets are usually of little help.

Unless the period is almost exactly that for which value is to be found, and unless the locations are comparable to the property under appraisal, all sales must be adjusted for any differences. Such adjustments are largely the result of a subjective analysis, so different appraisers may differ widely, with their differences increasing as the area is expanded. This is an added reason for narrowing the field of study. To the extent that adjustments are needed in the sales analysis, the validity of the entire approach is brought into question.

Finding Data. Having decided upon the time and area limits of his investigation, the appraiser next proceeds to gather his sales data. Sales data may include not only actual transfers of property but also leases, asking prices, and bona fide offers to purchase. The data may be obtained from several sources. Of prime importance are the records which the appraiser may have in his own office. He may have acted as a broker or a consultant in several transactions, and, if this is so, he is fortunate in that he has available not only the actual prices paid but also the background material as to the motives or special considerations surrounding the sales. As a broker, he may be aware of the asking prices or upper-limit bid prices of his clients. Bid and asking prices in real estate play a role similar to bid and asking prices on stock and commodity exchanges. The former represent the floor of values, while the latter represent the ceiling.

A second source of data is the official records of deeds and leases available in county clerks' offices or assessors' offices. Deeds are required by federal law to carry Internal Revenue stamps on the basis of 55¢ for each $500 cash consideration exclusive of existing mortgages. Purchase money mortgages which a seller takes back are subject to the stamp tax on the same basis as the cash payment. Since many deeds recite the amount of existing mortgages, it becomes a simple matter to calculate the total purchase price by adding the existing mortgage amount to the amount indicated by the Internal Revenue stamps. Thus, a recorded deed with $11 in stamps reciting an existing mortgage of $20,000 indicates a total purchase price of $30,000 ($11 ÷ .55 × $500 = $10,000 [equity above existing mortgage] + $20,000 = $30,000). Caution must be exercised in the use of recorded deeds. Frequently, stamps in excess of, or less than, the amount required are placed on the deed. This may be done to mislead a subsequent buyer or to conceal the actual price paid. At other times, the appraiser may find no stamps on the deed; they may be placed on the instrument after it has been recorded and returned by the county office. Still another difficulty is the failure of the deed to recite the amount of an existing mortgage or to indicate by how much it may have been reduced since it was originally placed on the property. Sometimes a property-purchase contract is sold or assigned before title passes. The original buyer is paid a profit by the ultimate purchaser. This profit does not appear in the record, since only the contractual price is paid to the seller. All of these possibilities merely make the appraiser's task more difficult and force him to seek other sources of information.

A third source of sales data is the brokers or salesmen who were involved in the transaction. Friendship and personal contact, where they do not involve a breach of confidence, may enable the appraiser to obtain his data.

A fourth source may be either of the principals to the sale who are willing to divulge not only the price paid but also any unusual circumstances surrounding the transaction.

A fifth source consists of published records of transactions distributed by private service organizations in the field or by local real estate boards who keep a record of real estate sales.

Finally, newspapers may be a source of information, although this source is usually not too reliable and must be double-checked for details.

The problem of obtaining a list of sales is not too difficult. The next step, however, requires additional information and a good deal of judgment. In any list of sales that is obtained, many will be regarded as not significant or not valid for use in the comparative-sales approach. Those sales that seem to be of use must first be verified as to actual price and financing arrangements, motivations, relative position of the parties involved, and the absence or presence of any unusual circumstances.

THE TREATMENT OF MARKET DATA

Prior to the analysis and interpretation of the valid sales data, the appraiser will find it necessary to discard several items for any one of a number of reasons. The determination of whether a sale is a valid one or not is primarily a process of elimination. The starting point is an assumption that all recorded sales in the area are worthy of consideration except those that were made under one or more of the following conditions:

1. The parties to the sale were related individuals or interrelated corporations.
2. Either party was under some compulsion to enter into the transaction.
3. The sale was made to liquidate assets for estate-tax purposes.
4. The sale was made from an income-tax rather than a real estate standpoint.
5. The sale was a foreclosure.
6. The sale was made to protect or expand a business location.
7. The sale was conditioned upon exceptional terms, either all cash or little or no cash; in either case, it was not made under "ordinary circumstances."
8. Special business and/or financial consideration entered into the picture.
9. The sale was not at "arm's length," for any reason at all.

It is probable that an appraiser may find other reasons for rejecting a sale. Regardless of the reason, if the appraiser is dubious about the validity of any sale or lease, he should discard it from his list of transactions and concentrate on the remaining items.

Analyzing Data. Having discarded the invalid sales and verified those that seem bona fide, the appraiser must next analyze his sales to determine the degree of comparability that exists between his subject property and each of his valid sales. This is an important step. Too many factors of non-comparability in any of the sales may require so much subjective adjustment that the appraiser may conclude that what he originally thought was a comparable sale may not be so on closer examination. Some of the factors which would require adjustments include the following items:

1. Terms of the sale
2. Existing and potential financing
3. Character of the tenancy
4. Expense-income ratio
5. Gross rent and leases in force
6. Adequacy and condition of mechanical equipment
7. Layout and functional utility
8. Type and quality of construction
9. Age and condition of building
10. Size, shape, and location of plot
11. Zoning
12. Neighborhood changes during period studied
13. Differences in time in an era of changing price levels
14. Sale included other assets such as furniture or fixtures

As has already been pointed out, the greater the number of adjustments needed, the further away is the validity of the sale. It should always be borne in mind that the purpose of a sales analysis is to develop comparable standards, units, or denominators for application to a specific property under appraisal. However, experience indicates that most appraisers face the problem of selecting a few sales of varying degrees of comparability and applying their judgment, experience, and knowledge of the real estate market to these sales to develop significant measuring rods. If sales which lend themselves to relative easy adjustments do not exist, the appraiser would be wiser to abandon this approach in favor of an approach where the data is more consistent. Sales data, as well as other data, must be of sufficient quantity and quality to give the value conclusion a solid base.

Modifying Data. The amount of modification needed in sales analysis will vary with the type of property under appraisal. Several sales of vacant land in a given area made within a relatively short period of time will probably give the highest degree of comparability. For example, if the property under appraisal is a residential lot 100×100, in a given area, and a sales search reveals the data in Table 4, the sales require no modifi-

TABLE 4

LIST OF COMPARABLE SALES

Sale	Date	Size of Lot	Area	Sales Price	Unit Sq. Ft. Price
1	1962	75 × 100	7,500	$ 9,000	$1.20
2	1962	100 × 100	10,000	12,000	1.20
3	1962	125 × 100	12,500	16,000	1.28
4	1962	150 × 100	15,000	16,500	1.10

cation relating to time, location, or physical condition and the appraiser would have no difficulty in establishing an estimating zone ranging from $1.10 to $1.28 per square foot for the subject plot. Having established this zone, sometimes referred to as a "zone of reasonableness," the appraiser is required to exercise his judgment in selecting a square-foot value for the subject property. It is considered poor practice to derive a mathematical average, for to do so is to reduce the appraiser's function to that of a calculating machine. The appraiser is paid for exercising his judgment, and his selection of a unit value factor should be on the basis of where the greatest degree of comparability exists within his developed data. If the appraiser selects $1.20 as his value estimate, then the subject property, containing 10,000 square feet, would have an estimated value of $12,000.

Where modifications or adjustments of sales data are necessary, the appraiser should use only those sales which lend themselves to a recognized objective measurement. This means that time, location, and physical and possibly financial differences are the practical limits. Time adjustments based on the relative level of real estate prices as compared to stable assessed valuations, or to the consumer price index in an area, may be utilized. A knowledge of expert opinion, of past sales, or of rental levels may be utilized to measure the relative values of similarly developed areas. Local practice relative to land increments for corner, key-lot, depth, and plottage differences may be followed to measure physical differences in plots.

Costs of adding finished basements, attics, or garages may be taken as a measure for value differences between buildings. Knowledge of discounting practices for second mortgages may be utilized in adjusting sales where liberal terms are a part of the sale. An example of the procedure to be followed in making these adjustments is given below.

The property under appraisal is a 100 × 100 inside plot in an elevator-apartment-house area. An examination of comparable sales in the area reveals five sales ranging in dates from 1960 to 1962. Table 5 is a tabulation of these sales with necessary adjustments.

The square-foot values range from \$3.25 to \$4.03. If the appraiser adopts \$3.50 as the indicated square-foot factor for the subject plot, its value would be 11,000 × \$3.50 = \$38,500.00.

Land-value factors may also be developed on the basis of front foot or unit foot values. It is only necessary to translate the plot areas into these units of measure by means of the value increments in local use. Examples of this technique are found in the chapter dealing with special land-valuation problems.

In addition to the development of unit land values from sales of vacant land, sales data may be utilized by the appraiser to develop value standards for improved properties. These standards may be expressed as gross income multipliers, earnings-price ratios, value per room or apartment, value per square or cubic foot, or value per theater seat, hospital bed. etc.

CENTRAL POSITION OF COMPARATIVE-SALES APPROACH

The opportunity afforded to the appraiser to derive comparable value yardsticks, so vital for the proper formation of a value estimate, places the sales approach in the central position of the appraisal process. The use of a gross rent capitalization rate or gross income multiplier as a measure of value is nearly always based on an examination of comparable sales. If the appraiser states that a property has a value of six or seven times the gross rent, he can only justify his conclusion by reference to sales of comparable properties that have revealed such a relationship. If he uses a net-income-capitalization rate, he is in effect saying that a well-informed purchaser could be found to buy the property at that rate of return. Reference to actual sales to buttress his selection of the rate is the most

TABLE 5
ADJUSTMENT OF SALES DATA

	Sale 1	Sale 2	Sale 3	Sale 4	Sale 5
Date	1960	1960	1961	1962	1962
Size of plot	100 × 100	100 × 150	75 × 100 (corner)	100 × 100	150 × 100 (corner)
Sales price	$30,000	$42,000	$38,000	$45,000	$60,000
Terms	All cash	All cash	All cash	$15,00 cash $30,000 PM mortgage	All cash
Adjusted price	$30,000	$42,000	$38,000	5 yrs. @ 6% interest $37,500[a]	$60,000
Area of plot	10,000 sq. ft.	15,000 sq. ft.	7,500 sq. ft.	10,000 sq. ft.	15,000 sq. ft.
Adjusted area[b]	11,000	16,500	9,900	11,000	18,150
Time adjustments	+10%	+10%	+5%	0	0
Location adjustment	0	0	0	−5%	+5%
Physical Adjustment	+5,000[c]	+10,000[d]	0	0	0
Modified sales price	$38,000	$56,200	$39,900	$35,725	$63,000
Derived price per sq. ft.	$3.45	$3.47	$4.03	$3.25	$3.47

[a] Mortgage discount of 25% as per current local market.

[b] Area adjustments made on the basis of 50% corner-lot increment, 10% key-lot increment, and 10% plottage increment.

[c] Cost of demolishing existing building on plot.

[d] Cost of removal of rock on plot.

convincing evidence he brings to bear. In effect, a value estimate by the income approach is merely the reverse side of the market coin.

As in the income approach, sales data play a significant role in the cost approach to value. While reproduction cost new ordinarily sets the upper limit of value, at any given time the value of a parcel of real estate may vary widely from its cost. This is due to the ravages of depreciation that create declines in value. Since the measure of depreciation is the difference between reproduction cost new and current market value, an analysis of comparable market values acts to solve the ever vexing problem of determining the amount of depreciation. Thus the use of pseudoscientific mathematical formulas for calculating depreciation can be avoided. If a new one-family ranch-type property will cost $20,000 in a specific location and ten-year-old similar properties will command $18,000 in the market, the measure of depreciation for the older properties is $2,000 in spite of their age. This would hold true even if the ranch houses were fifteen or twenty years old. Similarly, if new apartment-house properties can be constructed for $3,000 per room and comparable older buildings of the same type can be purchased for $2,500 per room, then again the depreciation problem is solved without the necessity of making tenuous mathematical calculations. The other important aspect of relationship between the sales and cost approaches lies in the use of the sales data to produce the first step in the cost approach, namely, the estimate of land value. The technique for arriving at this step was previously illustrated in this chapter.

INHERENT DIFFICULTIES IN THE USE OF THE COMPARATIVE-SALES APPROACH

While the sales approach would seem to recommend itself as the most logical and most objective approach to value, several inherent difficulties must be considered, the chief of which lies in the all too frequent problem of insufficient valid sales or, even more unfortunate, a condition where no sales exist. If such problem presents itself, the appraiser will have no choice but to turn to either or both of the other approaches to value.

Another difficulty, as has already been indicated, is the need for making numerous adjustments to sales that might be considered as comparable. All too frequently, these adjustments are based on subjective evaluations of the differences between properties or locations. The validity of these adjustments is almost impossible to prove to an impartial observer, and, therefore, doubt may be cast on the value estimate based on the various adjustment ratings that have been made.

A further difficulty presents itself when the appraiser finds he cannot verify either the motives or the relative knowledge of either buyer or seller, or both. Almost very sale represents both a "good buy" and a "good sale," because each party feels that he has had the advantage in the bargaining process. The future action of social or economic forces will confirm one or the other opinion. If the appraiser feels that either party may not have been aware of the future trends, one of the cardinal requirements of a normal market-value transaction has been violated, and the sale must be discarded as not valid evidence. Unfortunately, there has not yet been developed a method whereby the degree of knowledge of mental processes can be accurately measured.

One final difficulty, all too frequent in the real estate market, must be noted. Most sales of income property are usually made subject to mortgage financing. The size and terms of the mortgage influence the price at which the property can be sold. Therefore, it is possible, in many cases, that the total of the mortgage and the equity payment may not equal the value of the property. Any deviation from the norm in either financing or equity positions can create distorted market prices.

If a property is mortgaged for more than its value, the seller may accept a nominal equity payment. The prospective purchaser may be counting on improved income, reduced operating expenses, leniency from the mortgagee in deferring amortization, etc. This has happened in the sales of "608" housing developments in many parts of the country.

On the other hand, where properties are mortgaged at far less than the conventional percentage of their value and the sellers are reluctant to take back a purchase-money mortgage, or other secondary financing is not available, they may accept a cash payment from purchasers, which when added to the existing mortgage would not equal the value of the property. Other financing and equity relationships such as the presence of a long-term low-rate mortgage about to mature, or a long-term low-rate mortgage with many years to maturity, will affect the price. The former condition will probably cause the price to fall below market value in the face of the need to refinance at a higher rate; the latter may act in reverse to reflect the favorable terms.

KEEPING MARKET-DATA FILES

The appraiser who wishes to obtain the best results in his work should keep a file of the sales within his area. These may be kept on cards or forms of the appraiser's own design. Where possible, the following data should be included on the cards.

1. Date of the sale
2. Price paid
3. Terms of the sale
4. Indication of length of time property was on the market
5. Size of the plot
6. Location of the plot (corner, key, inside, exposure, etc.)
7. Size and layout of the building or buildings
8. Type of building
9. Age of the building
10. Physical condition of the building
11. Cubic contents or area
12. Special features (favorable or unfavorable)
13. Gross income (if applicable)
14. Operating-expense ratio (if applicable)
15. Level of real estate taxes
16. Gross income multiplier (actual or implied)
17. Indicated price per unit (room, square foot, cubic foot, seat, etc.)
18. Indicated land value per unit foot
19. Earnings-price ratio (if applicable)
20. Names of grantor and grantee

The cards may be filed and cross-indexed according to type of property and location, and only those sales cards which have been verified as reflecting bona fide sales should be kept in the "live" file. Notes as to any extraordinary circumstances accompanying the sale may be placed on the back of the card for future reference.

In addition to compiling actual sales data, the appraiser should keep a record of an important type of market data that is frequently ignored, namely, bid and asking prices for various types of properties. If bona fide offers to buy and sell can be obtained, the appraiser is afforded an opportunity to bring his value evidence to a current level. The "size" of the market becomes more easily recognizable by a consideration of these bids and offers. Trends of current attitudes relating to rates of return, gross income multipliers, unit land values, desired locations, etc., are made apparent by bids. The bids, as in the market transactions of all other commodities, provide the floor, while the offers provide the ceiling, of value.

In addition to compiling lists of sales, bids, and asking prices, the appraiser should try to devise for himself a consistent system of relating sales to varying time and location trends. It will help to develop a chart showing the trend of either the cost of living or the purchasing power of the dollar. There is sufficient similarity in the real estate price trend, especially in well-developed areas, to provide significant time adjustments for sales made over a period of years. He should also devise a scale of relative location ratings and trends. In this manner, individual streets and locations within a homogeneous area may be rated, as well as various areas within a city or town. The 100 per cent location should be identified, and all other locations then can be rated with relation to the 100 per cent location. Experienced judgment, expert opinions, and close observation of market conditions are the prerequisites for a valid location-rating system. A high degree of correlation between sales prices and rental levels will usually indicate the accuracy of the location ratings. Needless to say, the appraiser must be quick to notice any preference changes by renters and purchasers and to reflect these changed attitudes on his relative location value chart.

AN EVALUATION OF THE COMPARATIVE-SALES APPROACH

The comparative-sales approach, for all its inherent difficulties, remains a bulwark for the formulation of the appraiser's value estimate. Proof of value, presented to clients or courts, based on reasonable comparisons is most likely to be given the greatest credence. Since market value involves a meeting of the minds of potential and actual buyers and sellers, it is only by an objective examination of the level of the market that valid conclusions may be drawn. Slide-rule accuracy is not a requirement of the appraisal process. It is sufficient if the appraiser can establish a documented value estimate within a reasonable range based on prices that result from a bargaining process that fits the framework of the definition of market value. The properties used in his analysis should be similar to the one under appraisal, or, where dissimilarities exist, they must be subject to reasonable and logical adjustments.

9

Capitalization-of-Income Approach—

Part 1: A Description of

the Approach

BASIC PRINCIPLES

Investors in real estate, who are primarily interested in the income-producing possibilities of their investment, are mainly guided by the capitalization-of-income approach to value. The prices they are willing to pay for property will depend upon the returns they can anticipate from their capital investment. A property that will yield a net return of $8,000 on an investment of $100,000 is said to show an 8 per cent return. If an investment of only $80,000 is required to purchase the same property, the return will be 10 per cent. Conversely, a property with an $8,000 net income capitalized at 8 per cent will be worth $100,000, and at 10 per cent will be worth $80,000.

The usual problem facing the appraiser is the estimation of the income and rate of return that will attract a typical investor to a piece of real estate. A further consideration that presents itself is an estimate of the value of the property at some future time when the investor may be ready and willing to sell. In some respects the appraisal of a parcel of income-producing property is similar to the valuation of common stocks. Investors in common stocks are attracted by dividend returns and resale possibilities. The amount they are willing to pay for any particular stock is determined by the rate of return they can receive on their capital investment and the possibility of enhanced capital value at any time they decide to sell. However, since both returns and enhanced capital values cannot be determined with any degree of certainty, in most cases, at the time of the original investment, they are said to be anticipatory. Whether or not they materialize in accord with the investor's expectations cannot be determined until the property has been held for a period of time and a resale has been made. The significant item is the *anticipation* of both returns and resale value. It is on the basis of these anticipations that investors make decisions to commit capital to an investment.

Investments in real estate are subject to their own characteristic market conditions and anticipated rates of return. The real estate appraiser is an expert who, on the basis of his training, knowledge, and experience, is capable of estimating the market value of a parcel of income-producing property. Decisions to buy, sell, or lend on real estate are vitally affected by the appraiser's analysis and conclusions. The appraiser makes a step-by-step study of all the economic and social factors that influence (1) the amount of net income to be received, immediately and in the future, for net incomes are subject to change; (2) the duration of the income; and (3) the rates of return desired by investors and the possibilities for enhanced value in the future. By applying to the results of his study a mathematical capitalization technique, he is able to arrive at an estimate of market value that reflects the economic value of the property. Thus economic value and capitalized value become synonymous.

Basic Steps. Prior to the use of a mathematical capitalization technique, the appraiser must prepare several preliminary estimates: (1) He must estimate the amount of the expected future gross income from the property. (2) He must estimate the possible rent loss due to vacancies and bad debts. (3) He must estimate the amount of the expected operating expenses and capital charges that the property will bear during the time that the gross income is being received. (4) By deducting the expenses and charges from the gross income, he will arrive at an estimate of the net income. (5) He must estimate the probable duration of this net-income stream. This estimate may be conditioned by the economic life of the building or by a consideration of the time that typical investors would tend to hold the property before offering it for resale. (6) He must select the capitalization or discount rate to be used for the property under appraisal. (7) He must choose a capitalization technique to process the net income in accordance with the facts and assumptions that the particular property presents.

It may be observed from the above that the judgment of the appraiser is a key factor in the use of the capitalization-of-income approach. Judgment applies to all aspects of the problem: the estimate of future annual net income, the capitalization rate, the duration of the income stream, and the reversionary value of the property at the end of the economic life of the building or at the time of resale.

While these judgment factors present obstacles in the path of the appraiser, these obstacles are not entirely insurmountable. A skillful and experienced appraiser, making full use of all the available data regarding the property, can arrive at a conclusion that will meet the requirements of an estimate of market value.

IMPORTANCE IN PLANNING NEW PROJECTS

The capitalization-of-income approach is useful not only in the valuation of existing properties but also in the planning of new projects. The new project may be either a rehabilitation of an existing building or the acquisition of a plot of land as a site for new construction or the demolition of an existing building and its replacement with a new structure. In these situations the builder or investor will only proceed if it can be demonstrated either that the property to be brought into being will bring an adequate return on his investment or that he will be able to sell the newly created project at a profit.

In each of the above-mentioned projects, the appraiser may be called upon to demonstrate whether or not the economic value to be created is sufficient to warrant proceeding with the new project. This can be accomplished by use of the income approach.

An example will illustrate. Park Avenue in New York City, north of Grand Central Terminal, was up until the end of World War II the site of some of the finest multistory apartment residences in New York City. Unfortunately for the owners, these properties were nearly all subject to rent-control laws. As taxes and costs of operations increased after the war, the net returns became smaller and smaller. Beginning in 1946 and continuing through the fifties, farsighted investors saw the possibilities of tearing down the apartment houses and replacing them with office buildings to meet the needs of business firms seeking to expand and modernize their office space. The success of the first ventures led others to emulate the practice of acquisition, demolition, and replacement. Competition for available sites and strong demand for space in the modern air-conditioned office buildings led to a rapid increase in land values and an office-building boom in what was once a fine residential area.

A builder purchased for $1,200,000 a corner plot in this area containing 12,500 square feet. It was then improved with a twenty-five-year-old fifteen-story apartment house containing 45 apartments and 256 rooms, plus 4 stores on the ground floor. The total gross rent at the time of acquisition was $155,000 per annum, subject to rent control. Operating expenses, including taxes, but before depreciation, came to $110,000 per annum. The net income of $45,000 was insufficient to provide a 4 per cent return on the land value, leaving no return for the capital invested in the building. The building was in good physical shape but, owing to the "legislative obsolescence" occasioned by rent control, was clearly no longer the highest and best use for the location.

An appraiser, if called upon to evaluate the wisdom and prospects of a new office building on this site, could proceed as follows: After studying the site and the area, he would assume that the proper improvement was a new twenty-one-story office building. The building could be constructed at a cost of $5,000,000 and would contain about 240,000 gross square feet, with a rentable area of 204,000 square feet. By examining comparable rentals in the new postwar office buildings, he might assign a gross rental to the property of $1,170,000 and an effective gross rental, after a five per cent vacancy allowance, of $1,111,500. Operating expenses, including real estate taxes, but before provision for capital recapture, could be estimated at $487,500. This estimate would be based on the experience of comparable and competing buildings in the area. Therefore, a net return of $624,000 would be available for return on and of the capital investment. If 8 per cent, including provision for capital recapture, were selected as a capitalization rate, the indicated economic value would be $7,800,000 ($624,000 ÷ .08). After subtraction of the cost of the new building from the total value, an indicated improved land value of $2,800,000 appears. While it is not always possible to equate the cost of a building with its value, appraisers are generally agreed that, when a building is new and improves the land to its highest and best use, then cost and value will be equal. Since the new office building meets the requirement, we may assume that the cost and value will be equal.

Inasmuch as the property was purchased for $1,200,000, it is obvious that it would be economically wise for the builder to proceed with the new development. A potential capital-value increase of $1,600,000 is available to him if he should desire to sell the property. If he decided to keep the property as an investment and if a mortgage was obtained representing two-thirds of the value of the property with a combined interest and amortization rate of 8 per cent, the cash return on his equity investment would be almost 21 per cent.

The facts in the above illustration may be summarized as follows:

Purchase price of existing property		$1,200,000
Cost and development of new building		5,000,000
Total project cost		$6,200,000
Gross rent	$1,170,000	
Less vacancy allowance (5%)	58,500	
Effective gross income	$1,111,500	
Operating expenses	487,500	
Net income	$ 624,000	

Value of property capitalized at 8%	$7,800,000
(624,000 ÷ .08)	
Cost of building	5,000,000
Residual value of land	$2,800,000
Cost of land as existing	1,200,000[1]
Potential capital gain	$1,600,000
Available mortgage ($7,800,000 × ⅔)	$5,200,000
Annual interest and amortization charges	416,000
Net income before interest and amortization	$ 624,000
Interest and amortization charges	416,000
Net return to equity	$ 208,000
Equity in property ($6,200,000 — $5,200,000)	$1,000,000
Return on equity	20.8%

Similar economic analyses may be applied to other proposed building projects to determine whether or not they are feasible at any given time. Experienced builders and investors will not proceed without an analysis of the economic potentialities of a project. This economic analysis is nothing more or less than a capitalization-of-income appraisal, and its value conclusions will determine whether or not the project will be created.

ESTIMATING GROSS INCOME

We have seen that the first step in the income approach is the estimate of gross income for the property under appraisal. *Gross income,* or "gross potential," may be defined as the total receipts obtainable from a property during a given period of time, or as the total amount of rent realizable through the rental schedule. *Effective gross income* is the estimated potential rent receivable, less allowances made for anticipated vacancies and collection losses.

Units of Measure. The need to establish original estimates or to reconstruct existing rent schedules requires the development of a set of standard reference units for each type of property. These are developed to make the available comparative data more meaningful. Each property type usually has a standard unit of measure by which appraisers can express and analyze not only the amount of rent but also the amount of operating expenses. Apartment-house properties are generally rated in terms of

[1] For practical purposes, the entire cost of the existing land and apartment building may be classified as a land purchase. Since the building is obsolete and will be demolished as soon as possible, the usual practice is to ascribe the entire purchase price to the land and, for appraisal purposes, to include in the land price the cost of demolishing the building. In the illustration cited above, the cost of the demolition has been included in the development costs.

rental rooms. Retail-store rentals may be expressed in terms of front-foot or square-foot values. Industrial- and loft-building rentals are calculated on the basis of so much per gross square foot of area. Office-building rentals are generally considered on a net rentable square feet basis. Motion picture theater rental values may be estimated on a per-seat or percentage of ticket revenue basis. Estimates of garage rentals may be made either by gross square feet or by the amount of rental received per car times the capacity of the garage. Gasoline service stations are frequently rated by the gallonage sold times a stated rent per gallon. Appraisers must be familiar with the general practices in their area and guide themselves accordingly.

The reference units, once established, require further study and analysis in order to differentiate between various quality levels within specific property types. An attempt, for example, to compare apartment-house room rentals even within a single neighborhood or within adjoining buildings may lead to serious errors unless these qualitative differences are taken into account. Some of the more important factors to bear in mind, as they relate to this type of property are

1. Size of the rooms
2. Age of the building
3. Number of rooms per apartment
4. Appointments (interior finish, kitchen, bath)
5. Layout and exposures
6. Location of apartment (upper or lower floor)
7. Air conditioning
8. Prestige address
9. Surroundings
10. Services received

It should be noted that there frequently is a wide divergence as to what constitutes a rental room. What one builder or owner will call a 2½- or 3½-room apartment for renting purposes may only be considered a 2- or 3-room unit by another builder or by a lending institution. Thus, an attempt to make an income estimate on the basis of so many dollars per rentable room often leads to an inaccurate estimate. The appraiser must list each unit with its scheduled rent and then arrive at a total figure for the building. For purposes of comparison, it would probably be more fruitful if the appraiser developed a scale of comparable rents based upon a gross square foot area for several buildings. The scale can be classified so that each similar type of apartment building has a separate schedule. In this way, room-count estimates can be checked against square-foot estimates and the appraiser can be alerted to any possible errors in his income projections. This procedure has proved very valuable in an analysis of postwar air-conditioned luxury apartment houses in New York City.

The qualitative factors that apply to retail-store, loft, industrial, office, and other building types must similarly be analyzed. These include, in the main, location and neighborhood, services received, appointments, functional adaptability, age of buildings, size of floor space, percentage rentals, participation clauses, existing competition for trade, air conditioning, etc.

After establishing his units, the appraiser should proceed to a study of the major factors affecting the gross income potentialities of the property under appraisal. These factors are the quantity, quality, and durability of the income stream.

Quantity of the Income Stream. The quantity of the income stream is dependent upon the actual existing rental levels in the property under appraisal; competitive rental levels; supply and demand for similar space; leases in effect, if any; and rent-control regulations, if applicable.

If the appraiser is satisfied that the property is under competent management, he may consider using the actual existing rental as the starting point in his analysis. He must, however, be mindful of the fact that periods of economic distress force rental rates down. Boom periods and periods where abnormal scarcity occurs will reflect in above-average rentals. Rent-control regulations will tend to keep rentals below their economic level and will tend to reflect rent levels of an earlier depressed period.

Though starting with the current rent schedule, the appraiser must look beyond the existing rentals. He must establish a gross rent estimate that will reflect his best judgment as to the rent potential for the future period that will be encompassed by the capitalization technique he will select. By limiting his projection period to a realistic time in the future, the appraiser may avoid some of the pitfalls of gross-income estimation. L. W. Ellwood, formerly chief appraiser of the New York Life Insurance Company, recommends that, in the absence of special conditions, a ten-year income projection would seem to be adequate in most cases.[2]

Comparable Rents. The income estimate should give consideration to comparable rents in competitive buildings. The comparable rents will indicate the possibilities of obtaining increased rentals or will indicate that the existing rents may be subject to competitive pressures that will cause them to decline.

Comparable rentals are also a good guide for the appraiser in establishing a rent schedule for a proposed project. Let us assume that an appraisal has been ordered for a proposed multistoried apartment house which will

[2] L. W. Ellwood, *Ellwood Tables for Real Estate Appraising and Financing* (Ridgewood, N.J.: published by the author, 1959), p. 8.

contain thirty 2-room and thirty 3-room units. An examination of three somewhat similar buildings in the area reveals the following:

Building A .... 32 apartments—108 rooms .... gross rent $37,000
Building B .... 40 apartments—216 rooms .... gross rent 63,200
Building C .... 80 apartments—160 rooms .... gross rent 64,000

An analysis of these rentals reveals the following data:

	Property A	Property B	Property C
Average No. of rooms per unit	3.38	5.40	2.00
Average annual room rent	$342.00	$292.00	$400.00

The property to be appraised has thirty 2-room apartments and thirty 3-room apartments. Comparable property C affords a good basis for estimating the rental value of the 2-room units ($400 per annum per room). Comparable property A provides a starting point for estimating the rental for the 3-room units. This building averages 3.38 rooms per apartment renting at $342 per room per annum. Because of the higher average number of rooms, this rental is probably lower than that which might be obtained from 3-room units. Usually, the fewer rooms per unit, the higher the rent per room and vice versa, as is confirmed by the data on comparables B and C. Accordingly, a fair estimate of the rental for the 3-room apartments would probably average $360 per room per annum.

In setting up the potential rent schedule for the subject property, the appraiser could make this estimate:

Thirty 2-room units @ $400 per room per annum $24,000
Thirty 3-room units @ $360 per room per annum   32,400
    Gross potential rent $56,400

Supply-and-Demand Factors. Supply-and-demand factors play an important role in the gross income estimate. A neighborhood, location, or particular building that is in great demand due to social prestige or business potential will be able to command high rentals. If the appraiser feels that the trend in the area is, on the evidence, up, he could reflect this condition in his income projection. Conversely, adverse conditions will cause him to consider revising the present rent schedule downward. However, areas in a growth stage have the tendency to attract builders and investors, and the possibility of increased amounts of competitive space being created must always be kept in mind. A careful examination of the potential building sites, the availability of capital, equity and mortgage, and building costs in relation to rentals must be made in order to determine the possibility of creating additional units of space that will result in a condition of oversupply. An oversupply of space, even in a growing area, will almost certainly result in a weakening of the rental rate structure, or in increased vacancies, or both.

Leases. Existing leases, while giving some stability and certainty to the gross-income estimate, must nevertheless be carefully examined. If an appraisal of a retail-store property is being made, the following items should be carefully checked and verified:

1. The date when the lease was made
2. The date when the lease terminates
3. The stated rentals
4. Rent graduations, if any
5. Percentage provisions, if any
6. Options to renew or purchase
7. Tenant obligations (heat, electricity, water, insurance, etc.)
8. Tenant participations (taxes, fire insurance, repairs, etc.)
9. Cancellation clauses, if any
10. Special incentives offered by owner, such as free rent periods, etc.
11. Miscellaneous (competition, volume required, subordinations, etc.)

Leases in some of the newer office buildings contain escalator clauses, whereby the owner is protected against increases in taxes and operating expenses during the term of the tenants' leases. The leases generally provide that any increases in these items are to be prorated among the tenants. This has the effect of providing a guaranteed net income to the owner once the building is fully rented.

In many new apartment houses, leases frequently provide for concessions to tenants during the first term of the lease. These concessions may have been granted initially to induce the tenants to rent the apartments. Experience has shown that, after the initial term of the lease, the concessions are no longer granted and that in some cases the rents have even been increased. This is particularly true where the rent levels in the area have continued to rise.

Rent Controls. Rent-control regulations, while rapidly disappearing in most parts of the country, still play an important role in some areas. In appraising properties subject to these controls, it is unrealistic to assign rental values to space that do not take cognizance of the existing laws. However, experience has shown that, even in areas of tight rent regulations, many buildings have managed to increase their gross rents from year to year owing to increased services and tenant turnovers. A careful study must be made of the average yearly increased rental expectancies in an area before settling upon a potential rental for a property of this type.

Other Considerations. In addition to anticipation of rental increases or declines due to the factors previously mentioned, other considerations must not be overlooked.

Space which is occupied by owners, or relatives of owners, is sometimes listed at a low figure or is entirely omitted in the rent schedule presented to the appraiser. In these cases he must assign to this space a rental value which is comparable to that of similar space in the building or the area.

Frequently the appraiser will be confronted with a property where there are existing long-term leases to responsible tenants. At the same time he feels that the rents are too high for the space and services offered. Some appraisers proceed to stabilize these rentals downward, or separate the income into a "normal" and an "excess" rental. They will then use one capitalization rate for the normal rental and another rate (higher) for the "excess" rental. Sometimes this practice is questionable. If the tenants are really responsible and capable of meeting their obligations at all, then they will continue to pay the lease rental until the expiration of the term. For this reason it seems incorrect to always assume that a reduced rental will be forthcoming or that there is any more risk in obtaining the "excess" rental than there is in receiving the "normal" rental. This is particularly so where the income projection does not exceed, in terms of years, the length of time still remaining in the leases.

Quality and Duration of the Income. After completing his quantitative analysis, the appraiser must turn his attention to those factors relating to the quality and duration of the gross income. The quality, or degree of certainty, of receipt of the income will depend primarily on the financial rating of the tenant or tenants and the competitive position of the building. The durability of the income will depend on the general economic trends, the trends in the area in which the property is located, and the length of the leases in effect.

These factors of quality and durability should not directly affect the appraiser's estimate of the gross income in the initial phases of the income approach. They will, however, exert an important influence upon his selection of both a capitalization method and a rate. Thus a high income projection which carries with it a high degree of risk in its realization will call for the use of a high capitalization rate to reflect that risk. On the other hand, a conservative approach which seems certain of realization calls for a low rate to reflect the lack of risk. In some respects this compensating feature may be called the "law of compensating errors."

Gross rent levels have shown over the years a tendency to respond to changes in the general price levels and the value of the dollar. A study must be made of these trends and their implications. The economic period in which the appraisal is called for becomes of great significance. If the appraisal is made at the peak of a boom, the appraiser should bear in mind the facts that booms do not last for more than a few years at a time in our economy and that caution in his income projection is called for. Conversely, if the appraisal is made during a depressed period, he must remember that this too will pass. A knowledge of the ebb and flow of the business cycle thus becomes of extreme importance. Without such knowledge, the appraiser's income projection becomes even more hazardous than it normally would be.

Importance of the Gross Income Estimate. The importance of an accurate gross income estimate cannot be overemphasized, since it is essentially the first step in the capitalization process. Even a minor variance in this estimate substantially alters the value conclusion, assuming no other errors in the intermediate processing. This may be illustrated by an example involving the use of the land residual technique.

	Assumption 1	Assumption 2
Estimated gross income	$ 20,000	$ 22,000
Vacancy allowance (5%)	1,000	1,100
Effective gross income	19,000	20,900
Operating expenses	9,000	9,000
Net income	10,000	11,900
Building cost	100,000	100,000
Building charges (6% + 2%)	8,000	8,000
Net income available to land	2,000	3,900
Land value at 6%	33,333	65,000

Thus an increase of 10 per cent in the gross income estimate resulted in an approximate increase of 100 per cent in the land-value estimate.

VACANCY AND COLLECTION LOSSES

While there are no uniform rules to guide an appraiser in setting up deductions from the potential gross income in order to arrive at an effective gross income estimate, experience has shown that some percentage deductions usually should be made. In each case the appraiser's judgment must prevail depending upon

1. Present and past experience of the property
2. Competitive conditions (rent levels in the subject and other buildings)
3. The estimate of future area trends (population and economy)
4. Lease durations
5. Tenant credit ratings

A normal allowance of 5 to 10 per cent is frequently set up for vacancies, but different types of buildings demand greater or lesser percentages.

In some cases, no allowance for vacancies may be justified. This is true where space is occupied by AAA tenants under long-term leases in office, industrial or store buildings. It is also true in rent-controlled apartment houses located in good areas, where the rental level is considerably below the economic level. On the other hand, high-rental buildings that cater primarily to single and unattached transients probably require more than the normal allowance. The same would apply to any building located in an area of transition or decline, especially if the building suffered from inadequate maintenance or obsolescence or both.

OPERATING EXPENSES

The next step in the income approach is the estimate of operating expenses for the period of time that the gross income will be received. Operating-expense estimates involve either a reconstruction of an owner's submitted figures or an original estimate, depending upon the nature of the appraisal problem. This estimate, when subtracted from the effective gross income, will produce the net income stream that will be translated into a value estimate by means of a capitalization rate and technique.

Operating expenses may be defined as the annual costs necessary to obtain and maintain income. These can be classified as general operating costs, fixed charges, and reserves for replacements.

General operating costs include such items as wages and benefits of building employees, fuel, utility services, painting and decorating, repairs, management and leasing charges, and miscellaneous items. Fixed charges include real estate and water taxes and insurances. These are annually recurring costs. Reserves for replacements must be provided for those items of building equipment that wear out more than once during the lifetime of the building. While these are not annual charges, it would distort the picture if the total expenditure for one or more of these items were allowed only in the year in which the actual replacement expense was made. Therefore, the practice is to provide a prorated annual amount, based on the cost of the item and its expected life, as an additional charge against the gross income.

Establishing a proper operating-expense statement involves knowledge of the local customs and practices as they relate to the operation of various buildings. The item of wages to employees should take into consideration union wage schedules, if any are applicable or customary in the community. Payments for unemployment insurance, old-age benefits, and fringe benefits such as hospitalization and health insurance, vacation pay, and welfare and pension funds should also be included where they apply.

The fuel item, whatever the source of energy, and air conditioning must be considered from the points of view of the type of heating system in the building and of the division of costs between owner and tenant. In retail-store property and factories it is quite common for the tenants rather than the landlord to assume these costs. The number of exposures to which a building is subject, the degree of insulation, the type of construction, and the general climatic conditions will all affect the expenses that have to be borne for this item.

Charges for electricity may include lighting the halls, lobby, and in some cases apartments or other tenant space. Operation of the elevator or elevators (where present), the boiler, air-conditioning system, and laundry rooms is another item that may have to be accounted for. Here again, it is important to know who pays for what. There are some office buildings where the owner pays for the electricity consumed on a wholesale basis and charges each tenant for his proportionate share on a retail basis. In these cases, the item for electricity, instead of being an expense item, may turn out to be an additional source of income for the owner.

Charges for gas and water consumpton require the same careful analysis as is given to the electricity item. New apartment-house buildings in some communities, include free utilities to the tenants as an added attraction for rental purposes. This, of course, must be checked by the appraiser.

Painting and decorating charges cover the cost of redecorating both tenant and public spaces. Even though painting may only take place once every two or three years, or less often, depending upon lease terms, an annual prorated charge should be established. Here, as in most of the other items of expense, the appraiser must acquaint himself with the relative responsibility of owner and tenant for this expense.

Repairs will include carpentry, plumbing, and electrical, elevator, boiler, and refrigerator and range maintenance. In some properties such as stores and garages owners are only responsible for exterior repairs, while the tenant bears the brunt of the interior repairs. A careful reading of the leases, where they exist, is mandatory to determine the obligation of each party.

Management and leasing commissions are usually established by local custom and often real estate board rates as a percentage of gross income collected. Sometimes the appraiser may discover that competent management is available at less than the established rates. In these cases this fact should be reflected in his expense item.

Miscellaneous items may include building and janitor supplies; legal and accounting fees; advertising charges; exterminator charges; rubbish- and ash-removal fees, where necessary; and any other items which do not fit the major classifications of operating expenses.

Reserves should be set up, where necessary, for ranges, refrigerators, and boiler, elevator, and roof replacements, and other items which usually must be replaced before the end of the economic life of the building. In rent-controlled apartment buildings, where regulations permit an increased rental for the replacement of some of these items, the appraiser could consider omitting a replacement-reserve charge if the rent increase pays, as it usually does, for the new equipment in a few years.

Real estate taxes should be taken at their existing level with due consideration of the trend of assessment levels and tax rates. It is a rare community that has not or will not witness a continuing rise in the level of real estate taxes. Where revaluation programs are contemplated, this must be taken into consideration. In the event that the property to be appraised is new and has not been assessed at the time of the appraisal, the appraiser would do well to make a study of the tax burdens on comparable properties, as assessors are most conscious of the need for tax equality for similar properties. Water and sewer charges, where fixed on a frontage basis, usually do not vary from year to year. Other taxes such as sales taxes, excise taxes, and utility taxes on resale of electricity, while often small in amount, should not be ignored.

The insurance item usually includes premiums for fire and extended-coverage insurance, public-liability insurance, and workmen's compensation insurance. Other insurance payments, covering boiler damage, water damage, or loss of rent, are sometimes found, and, if applicable to the property, they should be included. An illustration of the construction of an operating-expense statement follows:

For the purpose of our illustration, let us assume that the appraiser has been assigned to appraise a proposed twelve-story and penthouse luxury-type apartment house located in a large city of the northeastern section of the country. The building, on a plot 150 × 100, will have an area of 122,000 square feet and approximately 1,200,000 cubic feet. There will be one hundred fifty-four apartments and 420 rentable rooms. The layout is as follows: forty-six 2-room apartments, thirty-two 2½- room apartments, forty-five 3-room apartments, twenty-eight 3½-room apartments, and three 5-room apartments. The superintendent will occupy one of the 3-room units. Effective gross income is estimated at $300,000. The building will have two self-service elevators and twenty-four-hour doorman service. There will be eight in help consisting of the superintendent, three doormen, two porters, one handy man, and one relief man. The building will be heated by #6 oil and air-conditioning units, located under the windows, will be in each bedroom and living room. The operating statement may be developed in the following manner:

Wages and Benefits. The building will be operated under local union contracts and the payroll amount is calculated in the following manner:

1. a. Superintendent	$ 87.50 weekly
b. 3 doormen @ $71.56 each	214.68 weekly
c. 2 porters @ $71.56 each	143.12 weekly
d. 1 handy man @ $75.56	75.56 weekly
e. 1 relief man @ $71.56	71.56 weekly
Weekly total	$ 592.42
(Add provision for vacations, overtime and paid holidays—3 weeks)	× 55
Base payroll	$32,583.10
2. Welfare benefits ($81 per man p.a.)	$ 648.00
3. State and federal unemployment insurance (3% on limit of $3,000 per man)	720.00
4. State non-occupation disability ($16 per man per annum)	128.00
5. Social security payments (3⅝% on limit up to $4,800)	1,392.00
6. Pension Payments ($3 per man per week)	1,248.00
Total	$36,719.10, say, $37,000

Heat. Buildings of this type and in the stated locality usually will require one gallon of #6 fuel oil for heat and hot water for every 12 cubic feet of space in the building. An alternate method of calculating heat costs would be to allow between $.005 and $.006 per cubic foot of space. Using the first method, the heating cost is 1,200,000/12 cubic feet × $.0685 per gallon = $6,850.00.

Insurance. The usual insurance coverage would include fire and extended coverage, public liability, and workmen's compensation. They may be calculated as follows:

1. Fire and extended coverage:	
Estimated reproduction cost of building	$1,700,000
Less exclusions (foundation and excavation)	75,000
Insurable value	$1,625,000
Co-insurance clause	.80
Amount of insurance required	$1,300,000
Rate for building and area (.078 per $100)	× .078 per C
Subtotal	$ 1,014
Term Rate (4 premiums for 5-year coverage)	.8
Total	$ 891.20

2. Public Liability:
Liability area .... 122,000 square feet
Rate .... $ 0.49 per 100 square feet

                                                    $599.48
Limits modifier 2.03 (1,000,000–2,000,000) .... × $ 599.48
Total liability charge $1,216.94

3. Workmen's compensation:
Base payroll ($30,383) × $2.20 per $100 .... $ 668.42

The total of all insurance charges comes to $2,776.56, which may be considered as $2,800 for the projected expenses.

Maintenance. Those items of building equipment that are subject to frequent repair or overhauling must have allowances made for their maintenance on a yearly basis. It is assumed that some form of contract service will be provided in accord with the character of the building and the need to keep all equipment in tiptop condition.

1. *Elevators.* A contract calling for complete service of each elevator could be obtained for approximately $1,200 per car. Therefore, for two cars the total amount would be approximately .... $2,400.

2. *Air-conditioning units.* Annual maintenance contracts are available at an average cost of $9 per unit. Since there are 266 units (420 rooms— 154 kitchens) @ $9, the amount would be .... $2,394.

3. *Refrigerators.* Units could be serviced @ $2 each, since there 154 units the total cost would be .... $ 308.

Total maintenance charges would come to .... $5,102.
Use .... $5,100.

Light and Power. Tenants will pay for their consumption of gas and electricity. The owner will pay the charges for these items:

1. Operation of elevators @ $500 per car per annum $1,000
2. Hall Lighting @ $100 per floor per annum 1,200
3. Lobby, basement, boiler, supt. apt., etc. 1,000

          Total light and power $3,200

Repairs and Supplies. With the amount of maintenance previously charged, an estimate of $5 per room should suffice for plumbing, electrical, carpentry and masonry repairs that might be expected in the forseeable future.

Therefore, 420 rooms @ $5 per room total $2,100.

Painting and Decorating. Painting of tenant space will be done every three years; public spaces, once every five years. An analysis of the charges reveals the following:

1. 420 rooms @ $45 per room × ⅓ .... $6,300 annually
2. Halls—$200 per floor × 12 × ⅙ ....   580 annually
3. Lobby and other areas (1,500 × ⅕) ....   300 annually

      Total $7,180
      Take $7,200

Water and Sewer Tax. Water and sewer charges in this property are based on frontage, rather than meter, and can be expected to be constant. An inquiry at the municipal water department resulted in an estimate of $2,000 for this building.

Management. Management charges are based on the recommended real estate board rates for the neighborhood, with due consideration for the willingness of competent management firms to take on the job at a possible lower rate. In this case, it was determined that a competent management firm could be obtained for 3 per cent of the effective gross rent roll, or a total of $9,000. This figure would be in accord with the recommended real estate board rates.

Reserves. Reserves should be set up for relatively short-lived items such as refrigerators, ranges, and air-conditioning units.

Item	Cost	Estimated Life	Annual Charge
1. Refrigerators (154)	$18,480	10 years	$1,848
2. Ranges (154)	10,780	10 years	1,078
3. Air conditioners (266)	45,000	10 years	4,500
Total			$7,426
Take			$7,500

Miscellaneous. An amount of $1,500 is estimated as the yearly charge for covering a series of minor charges such as legal and accounting fees, advertising, telephone, uniform cleaning, exterminating, license fees and permits, holiday expenditures, etc.

Real Estate Taxes. By comparing the tax burden on similar properties in the area, the appraiser can arrive at an estimated figure for the property. In this case it was revealed that similar properties were taxed at approximately 21 per cent of their effective gross income. This would indicate a tax burden of $63,000. However, since the trend of the tax rate in this community is steadily increasing, it would be prudent to increase the allowance for real estate taxes to $64,000.

A summary of the operating expenses follows.

Item	Annual Charge
1. Wage and benefits	$ 37,000
2. Heat	6,850
3. Insurances	2,800
4. Light and power	3,200
5. Maintenance	5,100
6. Repairs and supplies	2,100
7. Painting and decorating	7,200
8. Water and sewer taxes	2,000
9. Management	9,000
10. Reserves	7,500
11. Miscellaneous	1,500
12. Real estate taxes	64,000
Total operating and taxes	$148,250

It will be noted that the total operating expenses including real estate taxes amount to approximately 49 per cent of the effective gross income. This figure compares favorably with the experience of other properties of the same types which have been in existence for a few years.

In addition to the consideration of all the services and charges that must be borne in return for the rent to be collected, and the examination of leases to determine the degree of responsibility of tenant and owner for these charges, the appraiser should be informed about items that often appear in owner-submitted statements that do not properly belong there for appraisal purposes. The process of eliminating these items or revising the remaining valid charges is known as "reconstruction" of the operating expense statement.

Reconstruction of the statement as submitted by owners is a common experience for appraisers. The statements are usually prepared by accountants, for income-tax purposes, and include items that are not considered as real estate operating-expense charges. Income-tax payments, mortgage and amortization charges, salaries to corporate officers, depreciation charges, payments for capital improvements, and special local assessments (if not prorated over a long period) are examples of expense items that must be eliminated from the annual operating-expense estimate. Mortgage interest and amortization charges are omitted because appraisals are generally made on a "free and clear" basis, and the endless variety of financing arrangements would make comparison a hopeless task. The financial factors are provided for in the establishment of the capitalization rate, as will be observed when this aspect of the income approach is discussed. Further, the inclusion of mortgage and amortization payments would result in "equity" appraisals, whereas the prime function remains that of estimating a market value for the entire property. The practice of including depreciation charges which represent some percentage of a cost-equated value is erroneous on two counts. First, it assumes that cost is equivalent to value, and, second, the practice involves an assumption of value, where the problem in appraisal practice is to find the very value that is assumed. Depreciation factors, like those of the mortgage, are best relegated to the selection of the over-all capitalization rate.

Fuel, insurance, and real estate tax items, where the books are kept on a cash basis, are sometimes paid in one year for more than an annual period. In these cases, the outlays must be prorated to reflect the normal annual charge.

While often including these items which must either be eliminated or prorated, owners frequently neglect to provide for certain expenses which properly belong in the expense statement. Management fees, where the owner acts as manager, and a reserve for replacements would be in this category. The value of rental space for a superintendent or janitor should also be included, but only if the space has also been included in the gross income estimate. In the event that it is not included in the gross income, the general rule is to omit it from the expenses.

On page 118 is an example of the reconstruction of an operating-expense statement. The owner submitted the statement, prepared by his accountant, to the appraiser. The property is a six-story self-service-elevator apartment house, constructed in 1952. It contains 54 apartments and 156 rentable rooms. Room sizes average 280 square feet. The building contains 43,680 square feet and 510,000 cubic feet. The plot is an inside one and contains 11,000 square feet. The gross rent roll totals $70,500 per annum.

Since the appraiser's figures are estimates, they should be evened out. An examination of the reconstruction of the statement reveals that the principal changes that the appraiser has made consist of several eliminations of items such as depreciation of the building, interest on the mortgage, amortization of the mortgage, and corporation franchise tax. The item for officers' salaries and wages was modified downward to reflect a normal wage cost for a building of this type. At the same time, the item for employees' benefits was increased to reflect the upward trend in pension and unemployment-insurance costs. The superintendent of the building is a union member and receives the benefits that accompany union membership. The superintendent is the only employee, and hence the item for salaries and wages obviously includes some payments to corporation officers, which do not belong in the operating expense statement.

The item for painting and decorating was scaled down. It was found that an inordinate amount of painting was done for the year, owing to a large number of tenant turnovers. Since painting is usually done every three years for tenant spaces and every five years for public space such as halls, lobby, etc., and a complete painting of the entire building would cost about $6,000 dollars, a normal annual charge of $2,000 seems correct.

STATEMENT OF INCOME AND EXPENSES, JANUARY 1–DECEMBER 31, 1962

Item	Owner's Figures	Appraiser's Estimate
Gross income	$70,500.00	$70,500
Allowance for vacancies	–	3,750 (5%)
Effective gross income	70,500.00	$66,750
Expenses:		
Officers' salaries and wages	5,209.11	$ 3,000
Employees' benefits	308.60	360
Fuel	2,331.60	2,400
Painting and decorating	3,394.80	2,000
Insurance	1,237.22	1,250
Repairs	1,411.00	1,500
Supplies	349.23	350
Light and power	817.80	820
Reserves	–	1,200
Management	2,000.00	2,000
Real estate taxes	16,800.00	17,000
Water and sewer tax	275.00	275
Depreciation—building	9,810.00	–
Interest on mortgage	11,000.00	–
Corporation franchise tax	107.43	–
Legal and accounting fees	200.00	200
Amortization of mortgage	600.00	–
Miscellaneous	200.00	200
Totals	$56,051.79	$32,555
Net income	$14,448.21	$34,195

The real estate tax item was increased slightly, primarily to account for an increased tax rate that was anticipated. No increase in the assessed valuation was anticipated, as several similar buildings in the area were assessed in the same proportion. The real estate tax item, it may be observed, already takes about 25 per cent of the gross rent, almost a maximum figure for property of this type.

The owner did not include in his statement an item for reserves, while the appraiser did, in accordance with standard appraisal practice. All other items were found to be substantially correct and were merely rounded off.

OPERATING-EXPENSE UNITS OF MEASURE

Just as the appraiser develops units to measure the gross income of various properties, so he correspondingly develops units for the estimation of the operating expenses. The reference units should correspond in each case. If rents from apartment properties are expressed in terms of annual rent per room, operating expenses may similarly be expressed as an annual charge per room. A further refinement is usually made by the description of the gross square-foot area of the room. In office buildings the expenses may be expressed in terms of an annual amount per net rentable area, and loft-building expenses are stated in terms of gross square feet, etc. The development of these units has great value in the establishment of standards for comparison. These standards enable the appraiser to establish "bench marks" to assist in the analysis of submitted operating statements or in the creation of original estimates. A word of caution must be expressed about the use of these standards. An appraiser cannot afford to allow his standard figures to become outdated. Individual expense items will change, owing to variations in price levels and to fluctuations of the dollar. Inflation, which pushes the costs of goods and services to new highs, will have the same effect on the cost of operating a building. In addition, some expenses such as repairs will normally tend to increase as the building gets older and its components begin to wear out. Other items may decrease with the passing of time. The amount for management will tend to decrease as the gross rent declines.

By and large, the trend of operating expenses for most buildings has tended to increase year by year. Where the appraiser does not find this to be true, he should be alert to the possibility that a good deal of deferred maintenance exists, and he should adjust his figures to reflect normal maintenance charges. Some new office buildings equipped with autotronic elevators have been able to reduce the normal wage expense, but at an increased capital investment. The conversion of manually operated elevators to self-service elevators has the same effect in apartment-house properties. The appraiser must be familiar with new technological building advances that are available to owners and management in their desire to keep the operating expenses as low as possible.

Standards. The standards, or "bench marks," which the appraiser develops are generally considered as average figures for separate building classifications. Estimates for a six-story self-service-elevator apartment house, are applied only to similar apartment houses with similar room sizes and dates of construction. They are not used for walk-up apartments or for luxury-type apartment properties. Operating-expense estimates for office buildings with autotronic elevators are not to be applied to the older office buildings with manually operated elevators. Similar distinctions must be made for loft buildings and, in fact, for practically every type of building where it is necessary to make an operating-expense estimate. It must be borne in mind that standard operating expenses are average figures based on the experience of a selected number of properties. As averages they may not exactly fit any specific property and, thus, should be used with that fact in mind.

Another method of expressing operating standards is by ratios of expenses to income. The ratios may be expressed as percentages of the total gross income or of the effective gross. Here too the basis of the expense ratios must always be clear in order to develop effective comparative techniques. Still another method of expense ratios involves an analysis of individual operating expense items as a percentage of the total operating costs.

The careful preparations of the income and expense estimates are the preliminary steps toward the estimate of the net income. It is net income that is all important in the capitalization-of-income approach. Net income may be defined as the total income remaining after provision for vacancies and operating expenses, but prior to an allowance for recapture of capital. The estimate of net income is a mechanical mathematical computation—effective gross income less operating expenses. However, the reliability of the net income estimate depends upon the accuracy and judgment used in the income and expense estimates. The final step is the selection of a capitalization rate and technique by which the net income is translated into an estimate of value.

10

Capitalization-of-Income Approach—
Part 2: Selection of a
Capitalization Rate

BASIC PRINCIPLES

The procedure whereby the market value of a parcel of real estate may be estimated from an analysis of the quantity, quality, and duration of the net returns is known as *capitalization*. Capitalization is thus a means by which appraisers express their opinions of the amount of money a typical investor would be justified in spending for ownership of a parcel of income-producing property.

Investment in real estate, like investment in other income-producing property, involves several basic factors. The first is the amount and certainty of a return on the investment. The second is the possibility of recapturing the principal amount invested. A third consideration is the ease or difficulty of managing the investment and collecting the income. The prime consideration for the investor is the yeld or income that can be obtained consistent with the safety of the principal. An investment will produce a yield under any of the following conditions:

1. When the total income for the term of the investment will exceed the original capital investment
2. When, in the absence of income, the resale value will exceed the original capital investment
3. When the sum of the total income to be received and the resale value will exceed the original capital investment

The yield is usually expressed as an annual rate of profit per dollar of capital investment. It can only be computed precisely when the following factors are known:

1. The original cost of the investment
2. The amount and duration of the annual income
3. The amount of money that will be realized at the time of resale, sometimes referred to as the amount of the reversion

Thus, while the actual yield on an investment cannot be determined until the property is sold, the appraiser's chief function lies in estimating the original justified cost. The original cost becomes synonymous with the estimate of market value and reflects his opinion of the amount to be paid in order to realize an expected yield, or return, on the investment. This investment or market value thus bears a direct ratio to the yield, and the ratio is expressed as a capitalization rate.

The capitalization rate is determined by the characteristics of the property to be appraised. The rate, therefore, is an *expected,* or anticipated, rate of return necessary to attract capital to the investment compared with all other forms of investment opportunities. In this respect it also measures the quality, quantity, and possible duration of the income stream.

An investment of $100 that produces a net income of $10 annually, with no assumption of increase or decrease in the initial capital outlay at the time of resale, has a capitalization rate of 10 per cent. Conversely, and under the same assumptions, $10 of annual net income capitalized at 10 per cent warrant an investment of $100. Thus the capital value of any investment, where the resale value remains constant, may be expressed as $V = I/R$, where $V =$ the capital value, $I =$ the annual net income, and $R =$ the capitalization rate necessary to attract investors.

Most appraisal problems are concerned with solving the equation for V. Where V and I are known, the rate can be determined by $R = I/V$. The latter equation becomes important when one desires to analyze comparable properties that have been sold in order to determine the rate at which they attracted investors in the market place.

The key factors in the capitalization process require estimates of the total future income including the reversion, the duration of the term of ownership, and the selection of the capitalization rate. Another factor is the assumption made by the appraiser as to the method by which the original investment will be returned to the investor. Current appraisal practice usually provides for either a periodic return of capital investment or a lump-sum return at the time of resale. The selection of one or the other of these methods will determine the capitalization technique to be used. A full explanation of these techniques will be found in a succeeding chapter.

COMPARING INVESTMENT PROPERTY

Real estate as a medium for investment dollars is in competition with other types of investments that seek capital. This competition is with government bonds, industrial bonds, stocks, mortgages, etc. In addition to these outlets for investment capital, the investor has a choice between various types of properties should he choose real estate as his field. He may choose apartment houses, taxpayers, office buildings, hotels, or any other type of income-producing property. Each of these investment opportunities will demand a capitalization rate which is consistent with the characteristics of the specific property. The rate that is finally selected by the appraiser cannot be a mere expression of his opinion. It must be based on money market and financing conditions available plus an analysis of equity yields that will attract potential investors. This requires a good deal of analysis of comparable properties and investment media so that a capitalization rate, when adopted, bears some relationship to actual market behavior.

Investment opportunities are usually considered by investors with several factors in mind. The more important of these include

1. Security of the principal invested
2. Rate of return on the principal invested
3. Certainty of the returns
4. Possibility of capital appreciation
5. Relative ease of liquidation of the investment
6. Relative burden of managing the investment
7. Possibility of obtaining favorable financing or refinancing
8. Neighborhood trends, if real property, in which it is located
9. Possibility of producing income-tax-free income

On the basis of these factors, it is possible to set up a method by which investments may be graded according to their desirability. It will probably be difficult to find any single property that combines all the most desirable features of an ideal investment, that is, absolute security of principal, ready marketability, adequacy and certainty of returns, good location, tax-free income, good financing, possibility of capital appreciation, etc. However as the particular type of property approaches most closely these favorable features, the rate of capitalization will be lower. A low capitalization rate produces a high value of each dollar of income, while a high rate produces a low value. Thus $1,000 capitalized at 5 per cent produce a capital value of $20,000, while the same $1,000 capitalized at 10 per cent produce a capital value of $10,000.

When comparing alternate investment properties the appraiser is concerned with evaluating each dollar of income produced. In other words he is analyzing not $10,000 of income from an apartment house against $15,000 of income from a taxpayer but, rather, each $1 of net income from each type of property.

As has already been indicated, the capitalization rate selected by an appraiser is determined by comparison. To a large degree the behavior of investors in the market place, where such data is available and of sufficient quantity, provides the most compelling evidence of the comparative value of alternate investment media. Where the data are lacking, or are not clear, as frequently happens, the appraiser is obliged to place himself in the position of a "typical investor" and make his rate selection on the same basis as if he himself were to purchase the property.

The rate of return necessary to attract investors to the purchase of a fee under a long-term lease with a large office building in a leasehold in a desirable location may be as low as 5½ to 6 per cent in today's market. Investment in the leasehold will probably command an 8 to 10 per cent return, as the certainty of the returns is not as well established as in the fee position. In addition, the possibility of a default may bring on the loss of the investment in the building. Apartment-house properties, in good locations, would probably attract investors on the basis of 8 to 10 per cent on equity capital, but, in cases where increased rental possibilities exist, lower returns are acceptable and these properties (usually under rent control) have been sold to show a return as low as 4 per cent. In these cases, the possibilities of increased rentals and capital appreciation are the main factors, and the actual rate of return is anticipated to be much higher. Single retail-store properties occupied by AAA tenants can attract investors on a 7.5 to 9 per cent basis, while local retail property with neighborhood merchants as tenants would need 10 to 12 per cent returns. Subdivision investment may require 25 to 35 per cent returns. The variations in returns needed to attract investors run through the entire field of investment opportunities and depend upon the risks and opportunities involved.

CHOOSING THE CAPITALIZATION RATE

In choosing a capitalization rate, appraisers have used several different methods. Regardless of the method chosen, it should be remembered that the rate must be based on a consideration of the characteristics of the real estate market and that, when so considered, the rate may then be produced mathematically. The characteristics of the real estate market that must be considered are

1. The rate of return demanded by equity investors for various types of property
2. The available ratio of mortgage money to value
3. The interest and amortization rates current in the mortgage market
4. The number of years in which net income may be expected to continue
5. The provisions for recapture of the investment, mortgage, and equity
6. The possibility of increase or decrease in market value of the property during the period of time that the property is held

The test of the validity of a capitalization rate may be made by reference to the extent that all of these significant market factors have been included in the selection process.

Band-of-Investment Technique. A technique that permits the appraiser to consider the above-mentioned market factors is known as the *band of investment* technique. It is a synthesis of the mortgage, equity, and recapture features of the real estate investment market. There are several different methods of applying this technique, each involving certain basic assumptions. The simplest procedure can be followed when the financial structure of a piece of property consists of an interest-bearing mortgage, no amortization, and a return to equity. For example, assume that a parcel of real estate which produces a net income of $7,800 per annum, before provision for depreciation, can be purchased with a first mortgage covering 70 per cent of the value of the property. Interest on the mortgage will be at the rate of 6 per cent. The equity portion, or 30 per cent of the value of the property, requires a 12 per cent return. The capitalization rate would be determined in the following manner:

Net to First mortgage—
 70% of the value of the property @ 6% equals 4.2% of value
Net to equity—
 30% of the value of the property @ 12% equals 3.6% of value
    Net income   equals 7.8% of value
   ∴ capitalization rate   equals 7.8%

The value of the property becomes $7,800/.078, or $100,000. With a value of $100,000, the first mortgage would be $70,000 and, with interest at 6 per cent would require $4,200 of the net income for mortgage charges. The equity of $30,000, at 12 per cent return, would require $3,600. The total of mortgage and equity charges would amount to $7,800, which is exactly the amount of net income available.

It should be noted that this method assumes no amortization of the mortgage and, further, that the value of the property will remain constant so that, when it is resold, the owner can realize the full amount of his original investment; hence there is no depreciation.

Where secondary financing is involved, the procedure is the same. Let us assume a first mortgage of 60 per cent of the value of the property, with interest at 6%, and a second mortgage of 20 per cent of the value of the property, also with interest at 6 per cent, and a 20 per cent equity requiring a 15 per cent return. Since the equity is thinner and the risk greater, a higher rate of return is called for. The calculations for the capitalization rate would be as follows:

Net to First mortgage—
 60% of the value of the property @   6% equals 3.6% of value
Net to Second mortgage—
 20% of the value of the property @   6% equals 1.2% of value

Net to equity—
    20% of the value of the property @ 15% equals 3.0% of value
              Total net income   equals 7.8% of value
    ∴ total capitalization rate   equals 7.8%

An alternate way of computing the capitalization rate by this method is by use of "mortgage coefficients," as is suggested by Ellwood in his tables. In this way the capitalization rate can be determined as follows:

1. Subtract the mortgage interest rate from the equity yield rate and call the difference the "mortgage coefficient."
2. Multiply the mortgage coefficient by the ratio of mortgage to purchase price.
3. Subtract the product of this multiplication from the equity yield; the result will be the composite rate.[1]

Using the facts in our first illustration, the rate would be calculated in the following manner:

Mortgage coefficient equals .12 minus .06, or .06
Ratio of mortgage to purchase price equals 70%
Mortgage ratio (70%) times mortgage coefficient (.06) equals .042
Equity yield equals .12
Capitalization Rate equals .12 minus .042, or .078

Since most properties are purchased with mortgages that require interest and amortization payments, the typical investor is primarily interested in the return on his equity after these payments. A band-of-investment method that takes into consideration the level of mortgage money investment, the rates of mortgage interest and amortization, and the rate of return required on equity investment provides an alternate approach to the selection of a capitalization rate. Assume that a mortgage of two-thirds of the value of a property is available at 6 per cent interest with amortization that will provide full payout in twenty years; equity money requires 12 per cent and the net income is $19,472. The rate may be calculated as follows:

Mortgage—two-thirds (66⅔%) of value @ .08604[2] = .05736
Equity—one-third (33⅓%) of value @.12   = .040
           capitalization rate   .09736
Value of the property—$19,472/.09736 = $200,000

This band-of-investment method assumes that the amortization payments will equal the depreciation in the value of the property over a twenty-year period and that, at the end of that period, the reversion value of the

---

[1] L. W. Ellwood, *Ellwood Tables for Real Estate Appraising and Financing* (Ridgewood, N.J.: published by the author, 1959), p. 67.
[2] Annual requirement per $1 of loan for mortgage with interest at 6 per cent and providing for full amortization in twenty years.

property will be exactly equal to the original equity payment. This is generally an unwarranted assumption, for most properties do not suffer depreciation according to an amortization schedule, nor do they depreciate by two-thirds of their value over a twenty-year period.

A third band-of-investment method, developed by L. W. Ellwood, takes into consideration not only the mortgage level and payments and the equity yield but also the forecast for market-value depreciation or appreciation over a period of time considered to be a normal term of ownership. In a set of valuable tables, these factors have been precalculated for many typical investment situations. For example, A property having a net income before mortgage payments of $8,690 is available for purchase. A mortgage of two-thirds of the value of the property at 5.5 per cent interest with full payout in twenty years is available. The investor desires 12 per cent on his equity and will probably hold the property for ten years, after which he will resell it. He anticipates that, at the end of that ten-year period, the market value of the property will be 90 per cent of the current value, that is, it will have depreciated by 10 per cent. The capitalization rate can now be determined quickly by reference to Ellwood's tables.

The Basic rate before depreciation or appreciation, on the basis of the above-mentioned factors, is   .0812.[3]

The sinking fund at 12 per cent necessary to provide for 100 per cent depreciation in ten years is .057; since only 10 per cent depreciation will be suffered, the sinking fund factor to be added to the basic rate is .057 $\times$ .10 or .0057.

The overall capitalization rate is .0869.

The value of the property is $8,690/.0869, or $100.000.

In the event that the appraiser had anticipated a 10 per cent appreciation in market value after ten years, the sinking-fund rate would be *subtracted* from the basic rate to produce an over-all capitalization rate.

In the absence of the precalculated Ellwood tables, the basic capitalization rate can be calculated by using the following formula:

$$\text{Basic rate} = m \left(f - p \, \frac{1}{s_{\overline{n}|}} \right) + y \times e$$

where

m = Ratio of maximum available mortgage to value
f = annual requirement for interest and amortization of the mortgage
p = percentage of mortgage paid off at the end of the income-projection period
$\dfrac{1}{s_{\overline{n}|}}$ = sinking-fund factor at the equity rate of return
y = equity yield rate necessary to attract a purchaser
e = ratio of equity investment to value

[3] Ellwood, *op. cit.*, Table 1; see Fig. 3.

Interest Rate Annual Requirement (f) Coverage, Min. Rate		4¾% .07764 .05176	5% .07920 .05280	5¼% .08088 .05392	5½% .08256 .05504	5¾% .08436 .05624	6% .08604 .05736	$\frac{1}{s_{\overline{n}}}$
Projection	Balance(b)	.830277	.834519	.838135	.841804	.844831	.848599	+ Dep. — App.
	Equity Yield	Basic Rate before Depreciation or Appreciation						
	4% .04	.0442	.0458	.0474	.0490	.0505	.0521	.1846
	5% .05	.0480	.0496	.0511	.0526	.0542	.0558	.1810
	6% .06	.0518	.0533	.0548	.0564	.0580	.0595	.1774
	7% .07	.0555	.0570	.0586	.0601	.0616	.0632	.1739
	8% .08	.0592	.0607	.0622	.0638	.0653	.0669	.1705
5 Years	9% .09	.0629	.0644	.0660	.0675	.0690	.0706	.1671
n = 5	10% .10	.0666	.0681	.0696	.0712	.0727	.0742	.1638
	11% .11	.0703	.0718	.0733	.0748	.0764	.0779	.1606
	12% .12	.0740	.0755	.0770	.0785	.0800	.0815	.1574
	13% .13	.0777	.0792	.0806	.0822	.0836	.0852	.1543
	14% .14	.0817	.0828	.0843	.0858	.0873	.0888	.1513
	15% .15	.0850	.0865	.0880	.0894	.0910	.0924	.1483
	Balance(b)	.615155	.622146	.627803	.633664	.638118	.644382	+ Dep. — App.
	Equity Yield	Basic Rate before Depreciation or Appreciation						
	4% .04	.0438	.0452	.0466	.0481	.0495	.0510	.0833
	5% .05	.0481	.0495	.0509	.0523	.0538	.0552	.0795
	6% .06	.0524	.0538	.0552	.0566	.0580	.0594	.0759
	7% .07	.0566	.0580	.0594	.0608	.0622	.0636	.0724
	8% .08	.0608	.0621	.0635	.0649	.0663	.0677	.0690
10 Years	9% .09	.0649	.0663	.0676	.0690	.0704	.0719	.0658
n = 10	10% .10	.0690	.0704	.0718	.0731	.0745	.0759	.0628
	11% .11	.0732	.0744	.0758	.0772	.0785	.0799	.0598
	12% .12	.0772	.0785	.0798	.0812	.0826	.0839	.0570
	13% .13	.0812	.0825	.0838	.0852	.0865	.0879	.0543
	14% .14	.0852	.0865	.0878	.0891	.0905	.0918	.0517
	15% .15	.0892	.0904	.0918	.0930	.0944	.0958	.0493

Fig. 3. Capitalization rates, assuming two-thirds of purchase price to be

Using the facts cited in the previous illustration calculate the basic rate under the formula as follows:

Basic rate = .67 (.08256 — .366 × .057) + .33 × .12
Basic rate = .67 (.08256 — .020862) + .04
Basic rate = .0412 + .04 = .0812

To find the over-all capitalization rate, it merely becomes necessary to add the depreciation component of .0057, and the over-all rate becomes .0869, just as it appears in the Ellwood tables. Since the Ellwood tables are based on an assumed two-thirds mortgage financing, the appraiser will find the

Interest Rate Annual Requirement (f) Coverage, Min. Rate		4¾% .07764 .05176	5% .07920 .05280	5¼% .08088 .05392	5½% .08256 .05504	5¾% .08436 .05624	6% .08604 .05736	$\frac{1}{s_{\overline{n}|}}$
Projection	Balance(b)	.342493	.349597	.354491	.359815	.362740	.368924	+ Dep. — App.
	Equity Yield	Basic Rate before Depreciation or Appreciation						
	4% .04	.0432	.0445	.0458	.0471	.0484	.0497	.0500
	5% .05	.0482	.0494	.0507	.0520	.0532	.0546	.0464
	6% .06	.0530	.0542	.0555	.0568	.0580	.0594	.0430
	7% .07	.0577	.0590	.0602	.0615	.0627	.0640	.0398
	8% .08	.0624	.0636	.0648	.0660	.0673	.0686	.0368
15 Years	9% .09	.0669	.0681	.0693	.0706	.0718	.0731	.0341
n = 15	10% .10	.0714	.0726	.0738	.0750	.0762	.0775	.0315
	11% .11	.0758	.0769	.0781	.0794	.0806	.0818	.0291
	12% .12	.0800	.0812	.0824	.0836	.0849	.0861	.0268
	13% .13	.0843	.0854	.0866	.0878	.0891	.0904	.0248
	14% .14	.0885	.0896	.0908	.0920	.0933	.0945	.0228
	15% .15	.0925	.0938	.0949	.0961	.0974	.0986	.0210
	Balance(b)	none	none	none	none	none	none	+ Dep. — App.
	Equity Yield	Basic Rate before Depreciation or Appreciation						
	4% .04	.0428	.0438	.0449	.0460	.0472	.0484	.0336
	5% .05	.0483	.0494	.0504	.0516	.0528	.0539	.0303
	6% .06	.0537	.0547	.0558	.0570	.0582	.0593	.0272
	7% .07	.0589	.0599	.0610	.0622	.0634	.0645	.0244
	8% .08	.0639	.0650	.0661	.0672	.0684	.0695	.0219
20 Years	9% .09	.0688	.0698	.0710	.0720	.0732	.0744	.0196
n = 20	10% .10	.0735	.0746	.0756	.0768	.0780	.0791	.0175
	11% .11	.0781	.0792	.0802	.0814	.0826	.0837	.0156
	12% .12	.0826	.0836	.0847	.0858	.0870	.0882	.0139
	13% .13	.0869	.0880	.0891	.0902	.0914	.0925	.0124
	14% .14	.0912	.0922	.0933	.0944	.0956	.0968	.0110
	15% .15	.0953	.0964	.0974	.0986	.0998	.1009	.0098

financed by mortgage (twenty years' amortization: 4¾ per cent to 6 per cent).

above-described formula suitable for any combination of mortgage and equity financing ratios.

The chief value of Ellwood's method lies in its recognition of the typical investment factors of the real estate market. It considers mortgage payments, equity returns, duration of ownership, and possibilities for capital appreciation or depreciation. It recognizes that property values do not decline according to any schedule. It provides for possible appreciation in value, a condition often overlooked but just as possible as depreciation. It substitutes a typical term of ownership, based on extensive research and experience, for an atypical concept of economic life within which the capital investment is recouped. It recognizes that capital recapture is ordinarily made by resale and not by scheduled straight-line or sinking-fund provi-sions. The need for an accurate forecast of future reversionary value forces the appraiser to study the social, economic, and political factors affecting the property.

The Summation Technique. A popular method used by appraisers to select a capitalization rate is known as the *summation* method. This method builds a capitalization rate by adding several component rates together. The starting point in this method is the selection of a base, or "safe," rate of return. This "safe" rate is sometimes called a "pure interest" rate. Most appraisers use either the going rate on long-term United States government bonds or the rate paid by banks on savings accounts. Since this rate will vary from time to time, the appraiser must be aware of the going rates at the time he is making an appraisal. The current rate may be taken as 3.75 to 4 per cent.

To the base rate are added component rates, which attempt to evaluate the risks and hazards attendant upon ownership of a particular piece of property, including a rate for non-liquidity, which is basically a penalty rate due to the relative difficulty in converting real estate to cash. This difficulty can be a serious problem in a falling market, and, as the type of property is characterized by increased difficulty of marketability, the rate will be greater. This rate may range from .5 to 3 per cent.

In addition to the rate for non-liquidity, there is usually added a rate for management. This should not be confused with the management fee charged for running the property, but it is, instead, analogous to the service charge that lending institutions impose for managing their mortgage port-folios. It is an added penalty due to the work involved in managing the investment and reinvestment of the funds received from the property. This rate varies from .5 to 1 per cent.

A final additive to the base rate is known as the risk rate and is thought of as a compensation for all the special hazards that accompany investment in real estate. The safer the investment, the lower the amount added for risk. This rate can vary from 1.5 to 12.5 per cent.

An examination of the possible range of rates available to the appraiser under this method reveals the following:

Component	Safest (Minimum) Rate	Riskiest (Maximum) Rate
Base rate	3.75%	4.0%
Non-liquidity	.50%	3.0%
Management	.50%	1.0%
Risk	1.50%	12.5%
Composite rate	6.25%	20.5%

The degree of subjective selection and the ease of manipulation, especially of the risk-rate feature, are serious handicaps to the use of this method. Its reliance on factors divorced from the money market, except the base rate, has led many appraisers to condemn its use. Several variations of the summation method exist in the appraisal field. Most of these include the four components mentioned above but add another factor for market conditions. It has been observed that, where the additional market factor is added, a reduction is made in the other components so that the total rate is somewhat similar. An interesting variation of the summation method is a procedure whereby the total rate is conceived as consisting of only two components. The first is a base rate usually taken as the rate for conservative first mortgage loans, to which is added an equity risk rate which usually ranges from 1 to 2.5 per cent for top-grade properties.

Analytic Technique. In addition to the band-of-investment and summation methods, appraisers also make use of an analysis of comparable sales to determine capitalization rates. It should be observed that this method and the band-of-investment method are intimately related. If investors are guided by the considerations of the band-of-investment method and express their opinions of value by purchasing properties on that basis, each sale so consummated is the raw material for the comparative analysis method. With the sale at hand and the known facts about the property, net income, mortgage, etc., the appraiser is able to analyze the sale to determine over-all rates of return, equity rates, mortgage rates, and terms.

The simplest type of sales analysis is one whereby the over-all rate is found by dividing the net income ratio by the indicated gross income multiplier. Thus, if a property with a gross income of $50,000 sold for $300,000, or at a gross income multiplier of 6, and had a net income of $30,000, its net income ratio would be 30,000/50,000, or .6. Dividing .6 by 6, produces an over-all rate of 10 per cent. It should be observed that the same over-all rate of return can be derived by dividing the net income, $30,000, by the sales price, $300,000.

A further analysis of this sale may be made in order to determine the equity rate. If $200,000 was the amount of mortgage with interest and amortization payments of $17,000, the equity of $100,000 was receiving $13,000, or 13 per cent. If several valid sales of this type are available, the appraiser is in a good position to substantiate his choice of over-all capitalization rates, mortgage rates, and equity rates. This of course leads once more to the recurring appraisal problem. When valid sales are available, no other method is really necessary. In the absence of sales, or when they are uncertain, the appraiser must assume the conditions upon which they would take place. In this instance, the band-of-investment method stands in the place of comparable sales.

EVALUATION OF THE CAPITALIZATION APPROACH

The chief virtue of the capitalization approach lies in the opportunity it affords the appraiser to judge the level of the real estate market. The appraiser is not merely a recorder of sales prices. He must have a standard to measure whether the level of prices is too high or too low. The capitalization process can create an independent standard of value and thus make comparisons between properties more meaningful.

The capitalization process allows the appraiser to substantiate mathematically the reasoning of the real estate market and to interpret the actions of buyers and sellers. In this respect, its value as an element in the process of correlation is tremendous.

New construction projects can be tested by capitalization of income, and the wisdom of embarking on any new project can thus be weighed. In the absence of sales or cost data, it provides an independent approach to the value of property.

The chief difficulties in the use of this approach have already been indicated. They include the needs for accurate income estimation, estimation of the duration of the income stream, estimation of the reversion value of the property, and selection of a capitalization rate. To the extent that all the elements save the reversionary factor can be established by existing market conditions, the capitalization approach is valuable. The estimate of reversionary value will always be a forecast. But forecasting is an integral part of every business venture, and, while it requires intensive study of trends and conditions surrounding the property, the appraiser should not feel that the need for such a forecast forecloses its use.

SOME PRACTICAL SUGGESTIONS

In order to make the maximum use of the capitalization approach, appraisers must keep well informed about the money market as it affects real estate. The levels of mortgage interest and equity rates are constantly changing, and all too frequently appraisers continue to use a rate of 6 or 7 per cent when conditions call for a higher or lower rate. Similarly, some appraisers tend to use the same rate for all kinds of properties, regardless of their risk or appreciation possibilities. This should be avoided. Each class of property in each neighborhood must be studied so that the capitalization rate used will properly measure its investment characteristics.

There is also a tendency to capitalize income streams into perpetuity or for long imagined economic life-spans. This is a mistake. Most properties are never held for such periods of time. The appraiser should use a duration span that is consistent with market facts. To this end, a continuing study of typical ownership spans should be made. Only in those cases where income is subject to long-term leases should the income spans exceed the typical term of ownership. By adoption of a typical span, comparison is made easier.

The appraiser should be aware of the fact that investors are frequently more interested in the possibilities of market appreciation than in annual dollar income. Where such possibilities are clearly indicated, they should be reflected in the capitalization rate, and the reasons should be clearly stated.

Finally, the appraiser should learn to use the capitalization approach as a means of indicating to his clients the yield possibilities that exist under various assumptions. Investment yields, whether in the form of annual income or equity capital appreciation, are the prime motivating factors in real estate investing. By indicating the various yield possibilities under assumptions of rising, falling, or static market values, the appraiser can render a greater and more meaningful service to his clients.

11

Mathematics Used in

Capitalization Approach

The average annual income received from a parcel of investment property may be thought of as an annuity. An annuity is a series of periodical payments, usually but not necessarily equal in amount, and usually made at equal periods of time, such as quarterly, semiannually, or annually. These annuity payments must be translated into value. This is done by the capitalization process, which is basically a discounting process. Each year's income to be received has a present worth which is less than its face value in an amount equal to the loss of interest during the time until it is collected.

Thus the discounting of future net incomes is based on compound interest functions. The value of a series of future annual payments to be received from income-producing property will depend upon such factors as the rate of interest to be used, the duration of the payments, and the assumptions relating to the recapture of the capital. Each annual income payment consists of two elements. The first is interest on the capital invested and the second is a partial return of that capital, known as recapture.

Only in those cases where income is to be treated as being received in perpetuity, as where land is under a perpetual or ninety-nine-year lease at a uniform annual rental, may consideration of capital recapture be ignored. This is so because perpetual incomes do not involve the return of capital, as the principal is never exhausted. In these cases, a simple interest return rather than a compound interest one will satisfy the requirements of the investment. The valuation of such a perpetuity is accomplished by direct capitalization, that is, value = net income/interest rate.

The vast majority of properties to be appraised are not considered as being perpetuities. They are improved with buildings which have limited economic lives, and provision must be made for recapturing the capital originally invested in these structures. Capital recapture may be treated in two ways. The first procedure usually assigns a perpetual value to the land and then makes an annual provision out of net income for recapture of building capital by one of three different methods: (1) the straight-line method, (2) the sinking-fund method, or (3) the Inwood annuity method.

134

Basic to this procedure is the concept that a property consists of two component parts: land, which is permanent and stable in value, and the building, which is a wasting asset subject to loss in value owing to depreciation and obsolescence. The annual provision for recapture of the capital in the building component is based on the estimate of the economic life of the structure.

The second procedure, while recognizing the land and building components, tends to regard *both* elements as subject to depreciation, or even appreciation, over a given period of time. Capital recapture, of both land and building, is provided for partly through the annual net income and partly by the reversionary value to be realized at some future time when a resale is to be made. The duration of the income is tied not to an estimate of economic life but to a typical period of ownership as revealed by experience and research.

Since each of the methods of handling income and recapture involves different assumptions, different values may be arrived at even when applied to the same net income. This chapter will deal with the basic mathematics and methods used to process a net income stream into a capital-value estimate.

DISCOUNT TABLES

The Amount of 1. Before embarking upon an explanation of the various methods of translating net income into capital value, it is necessary to consider briefly the theory behind the various discount tables that are used in appraisal practice.

For convenience of computation and use, all discount tables are constructed on the basis of a $1 income.

The more important tables are entitled "the amount of 1," "the amount of 1 per annum," "the present value of 1," and "the present value of 1 per annum." This may be $1, 1 ruble, or any other monetary unit.

The basic table from which all others may be constructed is the table entitled "the amount of 1." This table is based on the fact that a single investment of $1 left at compound interest will accumulate to a sum found by solving the equation $S = (1 + i)^n$, in which

$S =$ the amount to which 1 will grow at compound interest
$1 = $1 of invested capital
$i =$ the effective interest rate or yield for one interest-earning period
$n =$ the number of interest-earning periods for a year, a month, a quarter, or a half-year.

This will be recognized as the simple compound interest table. If $1 is invested at 5 per cent per annum for five years, it will amount to $(1 + .05)^5$ $= $1.2763. This may be computed as $(1 + .05)^5 = $1.05 \times $1.05 \times$

$1.05 \times $1.05 \times $1.05 = $1.2763, and the process by which it grows to $1.2763 may be illustrated in the following manner:

Original investment	$1.00
Interest @ 5%, first year	.05
Accumulation at end of first year	$1.05
Interest @ 5%, second year	.0525
Accumulation at end of second year	$1.1025
Interest @ 5%, third year	.0551
Accumulation at end of third year	$1.1576
Interest @ 5%, fourth year	.0579
Accumulation at end of fourth year	$1.2155
Interest @ 5%, fifth year	.0608
Accumulation at end of fifth year	$1.2763

If reference is made to the 5 per cent table under "the amount of 1," in the Appendix, opposite the fifth year, the figure will be found to be 1.2763. Since the table is computed, as was previously stated, on the basis of $1, if the amount of any other figure is desired, the figure taken from the table is multiplied by the other. The amount of $1,000 at 5 per cent for five years would be $1,000 × 1.2763, or $1,276.30. The table gives the amount of 1 at the end of the year, after interest has been added. If the amount of 1 at the beginning of the fifth year is desired, take the figure opposite four years in the table, or 1.2155.

In appraisal practice, this table may be used to calculate the amount for which a vacant plot would have to be sold in order to earn 5 per cent on the initial investment. If $10,000 were paid five years ago for the plot, it would have to be sold for $10,000 × 1.2763 or $12,763 in order to realize a 5 per cent return on the initial investment. This calculation does not take into consideration any taxes or other expenses that may have been paid during the term of ownership, other than interest on the original investment.

Present Value of 1. The second table to which we turn our attention is known as "the present value of 1" and is commonly referred to as the table for calculating a reversion. The present value of 1 is simply the sum which must be set aside, and allowed to accumulate at a given rate of interest, so that the initial investment plus the interest will amount to 1 at the end of the period. We have seen previously that $1 invested at 5 per cent compound interest for five years will amount to $1.2763 at the end of that time. Therefore the present value of the right to receive $1.2763 five years hence with interest at 5 per cent is $1, which is merely $1.2763 divided by the factor 1.2763. The same answer may be obtained by multiplying $1.2763 by the reciprocal of 1.2763, which is .7835. The reciprocal of any number is the quotient produced by dividing 1 by the number. Any amount multiplied by the reciprocal of a number will give the same result as if we divide the amount by the number. The reciprocal of 5 is $\frac{1}{5}$, or .20, and $100 \times .20 = 20$, and $100/5 = 20$.

If the present value of $1.2763 due five years hence is $1, the present value of $1 becomes $1/1.2763$, or .7835. The mathematical formula for this table is simply the reciprocal of the formula for "the amount of 1." It may be expressed as $1/(1 + i)^n$.

This table has widespread application in appraisal procedure. It is used to calculate the present value of a leased fee that will revert to the lessor after a given number of years; it is used to calculate the present value of land at some time in the future when the buildings shall have ceased to have any value; and it is used to calculate the present value of land and buildings which may be sold in the future, where the future value will be estimated at some percentage of current market value. The simplest application would be a situation requiring the present valuation of a parcel of vacant land which will be worth $100,000 ten years hence. If the investment in this parcel should return 6 per cent, how much could an investor afford to pay for this parcel today? By examination of the table under the 6 per cent heading for ten years, the factor for $1 will be found to be .5584. Therefore, the present value of $100,000 to be received ten years hence is $100,000 \times .5584$, or $55,840.

Another use for this table arises when it is desired to give effect to, and deduct from value, the amount of a contemplated expenditure. If the appraiser concludes that a complete overhaul of an electrical system would be required in three years at a cost of $10,000, he would apply a deferment factor at a rate of interest, say, 6 per cent, to the $10,000 to produce the current value of the anticipated expenditure. In this case it would be $10,000 \times .8396$, or $8,396.

The Present Value of 1 per Annum. This is probably the best known and most widely used table in appraisal work. It is commonly referred to as the Inwood table. It is used to determine the present value of an income stream or annuity at a given rate of interest over a period of time. The factors in this table give the investment value today of the right to receive $1 each year for a period of years so calculated that the $1 received each year will pay interest on the investment and will provide also for an amount each year which in the aggregate will return the original investment at the end of the period.

Since an annuity is nothing more than a series of income payments, each of which is one period farther removed from its previous payment, in effect the factors in the table are the total of a series of reversion payments. The factor at any given rate of interest for any number of years is established by adding the yearly reversion factors for the period of years. This may be illustrated by the computation of the value of the right to receive $1 per annum for five years at 5 per cent.

P.V. of 1 to be received at the end of 1 year @ 5% = .9524
P.V. of 1 to be received at the end of 2 years @ 5% = .9070
P.V. of 1 to be received at the end of 3 years @ 5% = .8638
P.V. of 1 to be received at the end of 4 years @ 5% = .8227
P.V. of 1 to be received at the end of 5 years @ 5% = .7835

The present value of $1 per annum for five years at 5 per cent will be the sum of these reversionary values—4.3294.

This figure is the same as will be found by examining the table entitled "the present value of 1 per annum" under the 5 per cent heading at the five-year period. Thus the present value of an ordinary annuity of $1 per period for any number of periods is represented by a progression: $1/(1 + i) + 1/(1 + i)^2 + 1/(1 + i)^3 + 1/(1 + i)^4 + 1/(1 + i)^5$, etc., to the end of the series. This progression may also be expressed mathematically by the formula $1/1 — (1 + i)^n/i$.

Let us examine what happens to an investor who pays $4,329.40 for the right to receive an annual income of $1,000 with interest at 5% ($1,000 per annum $\times$ 4.3294), where the original investment is $4,329.40:

End of	Payment	Interest on Outstanding Capital	Return of Capital	Capital Remaining
1st year	$1,000	$216.47	$ 783.57	$3,545.83
2d year	1,000	177.29	822.71	2,723.12
3d year	1,000	136.16	863.84	1,859.28
4th year	1,000	92.96	907.04	952.24
5th year	1,000	47.61	952.39	–
Total	$5,000	$670.39	$4,329.55[1]	

The investor has received a total of $5,000 from which he has repaid his original investment and has received $670.39 interest allocated to the capital remaining for each of the five years.

The table for "the present value of 1 per annum" may be used in all cases where an income stream is to be valued. The use of this table for valuing annual income payments, plus the use of the table "the present value of 1" (reversion), is the basis for most methods of capitalizing income. Some appraisers may question the use of annuity tables for income streams that are not fixed, such as those under a lease. However, as Ellwood has pointed out:

[1] The slight discrepancy is due to the fact that, for purposes of calculation, the figures were not carried out beyond a reasonable point of accuracy.

The fact is that any series of payments collected at even intervals of time is an annuity of one kind or another. The payments *do not* [original emphasis] have to be equal in amount. Only the time intervals between payments have to be equal. Thus, it is preposterous to question the propriety of treating any income stream as an annuity. For this would rule out the valuation of every income stream where the income is expected to be collected monthly, quarterly, semi-annually or annually. The ordinary annuity is just one of several types. In addition, we have the fluctuating annuity as in multiple tenancy, landlord service properties where earnings fluctuate from year to year because of variations in rents, occupancy and expenses. We have the increasing annuity as represented by the equity income in a net lease constant curtailment mortgage combination. We have the cyclical annuity in some sandwich lease situations. We have deferred annuities in step up leases. We have declining annuities in constant curtailment mortgages purchased at discount and in mortgage portfolio servicing accounts.

These are all variations of the ordinary annuity and in every case correct valuation is determined by application of the reciprocal of the basic formula $(1 + i)^n$ to each installment. . . . The point here is that the question of propriety is not whether the income stream has the characteristics of an annuity. Instead it is whether the arithmetic employed in its valuation fits the type of annuity presented by the problem.[2]

The Instalment Needed To Amortize 1. A table giving the appropriate factors to be used in determining the periodic instalment needed to amortize a level payment mortgage over a period of years with interest on the remaining balances after each period is known as an amortization table. The factors in this table are merely the reciprocals of the factors found in "the present value of 1 per annum" tables. In effect a mortgage loan represents an ordinary annuity for the lender. In return for the loan he obtains the right to receive a series of level payments from the mortgagor that will return the mortgage principal with interest on the outstanding balance over a stated term of years. The total amount of the mortgage merely represents the value of an annuity at a rate of interest for a term of years. Therefore, if the present value of $10,000 per annum at 6 per cent for fifteen years is $10,000 × 9.712, or $97,120, a mortgage loan of $97,120 could be completely amortized over a fifteen-year period by annual payments of $10,000, calculated as follows: $97,120 × 1/9.712, or $97,120 × .102963.

Out of the total of $10,000 paid during the first period, $5,827.20 will represent 6 per cent on the principal, and $4,172.80 will represent the first payment on the principal. By treating the first principal payment as an amount to be deposited in a sinking fund and multiplying this amount by a factor for the "amount of 1 per annum," it is possible to determine the balance of the mortgage paid off at any time in the future. Thus, at the end of five years, the amount of mortgage paid off will be $4,172.80 × 5.637, or $23,522.07, leaving a balance of $73,597.93.

[2] L. W. Ellwood, *Ellwood Tables For Real Estate Appraising and Financing* (Ridgewood, N.J.: published by the author, 1959), pp. 177–178.

In addition to being able to determine the periodic amount necessary to pay off a mortgage loan, a factor of importance in most real estate investments, the derivation of a proper capitalization rate in some situations depends to a degree on the amount of the mortgage balance. This is so because all mortgage principal payments that have been made represent a return of purchase capital where there has been no offsetting decrease in the market value of the property during the period of time over which the property is held.

The Amount of 1 per Annum. If, instead of investing $1 and letting that accumulate for several years, we invest $1 at the end of each year, we will at the end of the period receive the amount of 1 per annum. A table giving these amounts for various periods at different rates of interest is known as "the amount of 1 per annum." This table starts with 1 and proceeds from top to bottom by adding the corresponding factor from the "amount of 1" table. Thus, in the example used for illustrative purposes in the discussion of the amount of 1, we used a 5 per cent rate and the factors for the end of each year were

    1st year—1.05
    2d year—1.1025
    3d year—1.1576
    4th year—1.2155
    5th year—1.2763

The corresponding factors in the "amount of 1 per annum" table for each year are

    1st year—1
    2d year—2.05 (1 + 1.05)
    3d year—3.1525 (1.1025 + 2.05)
    4th year—4.3101 (1.1576 + 3.1525)
    5th year—5.5256 (1.2155 + 4.3101)

The reason for this progression is that each dollar invested will earn interest as long as it remains invested. Thus, at the end of the period, the accumulation is equal to the number of dollars invested plus the amount of interest earned by each dollar. The formula for this table may be expressed mathematically as $(1 + i)^n - 1/i$.

While this table is not used as frequently as the others in appraisal practice, it has value for the solution of several types of appraisal problems. If an investment is made in vacant land and held for five years with annual tax payments of $200 per year, it may be necessary to compute the value of the tax payments to be added to the compound amount of the original investment, if interest is to be earned at, say, 5 per cent. In our previous example illustrating the compound amount of a $10,000 land investment, we found that, at the end of five years, the compound amount would become $12,763 ($10,000 × 1.2763). To this amount we would then have to add $200 × 5.5256, or $1,105.12, as the amount of the annual tax payments. Therefore, for the investor to realize 5 per cent on his original investment of $10,000, he would have to receive $12,763 + $1,105.12, or $13,868.12, at the time of resale.

The Sinking-Fund Table. The final table we will consider is the sinking-fund table. This table indicates the annual amount that must be set aside to accumulate to a definite sum at a given rate of interest. The table itself is merely the reciprocal of the table for "the amount of 1 per annum." Thus, if $1 deposited annually at 5 per cent will amount in five years to $5.5256, the annual deposit required to accumulate $1 in five years is $1 divided by 5.5256 = 1/5.5256 = .180975.

The mathematical expression for this table is $i/(1 + i)^n - 1$.

The sinking-fund table has wide application in appraisal practice. It is the basic table used for computing the depreciation or appreciation component in the capitalization rate. It is also the basis used for determining the amount to be set aside to recapture a building investment in building residual problems or leasehold valuations. Thus, if an investor leases land on a twenty-one-year basis with the provision that he construct a $100,000 building on the property, and at the end of the term of the lease the building becomes the property of the lessor, the investor must earn interest on his investment but must also set aside each year out of his earnings enough to recapture the building cost over the period of the lease. If he sets up a sinking fund that will earn 4 per cent on his money, the amount to be set aside annually can be determined by the table. From the table, we find that .03128 set aside each year at 4 per cent for twenty-one years will amount to $1. Therefore $100,000 × .03128, or $3,128 per annum, must be set aside in a sinking fund out of annual earnings.

RECAPTURE OF CAPITAL

At the outset of this chapter it was pointed out that the majority of appraisal problems involve considerations of an interest return on original investment plus provisions for recapture of the capital in the investment. In those cases where land was considered to have a perpetual constant value, only the building capital component was required to be recaptured. One method of processing income into capital value under these assumptions is known as the building residual technique. In this technique, the land value is usually derived from comparable sales, and out of the entire net income a portion is deducted to represent interest on this land value. The balance of the net income is allocated or "residual" to the building and forms the basis for estimating building value. This building income, in turn, is allocated to interest on the building value and recapture of the building value. A full explanation of the residual techniques will be found in the next chapter. At this time we turn our attention to the various methods used and the mathematics involved in treating building values and building recapture, sometimes referred to as provision for future depreciation.

Straight-Line Method. Let us assume a property with a net income before recapture of $10,000 per annum. The land value has been determined by comparative sales to be worth $30,000. Interest on land and building is calculated at 6 per cent per annum. The building is assigned an economic life of thirty years. The portion of the net income allocated to the building is found as follows:

Total net income	$10,000
Interest on land value—$30,000 × 6% (perpetual)	1,800
Net income residual to building	$ 8,200

Since the building has been assigned an economic life of thirty years, it is necessary to provide for the recapture of building capital at the rate of 3⅓ per cent per year under the straight-line depreciation method. Thus the net income allocated to the building represents 6 per cent interest on and 3⅓ per cent recapture of the building's capital value. The total capitalization rate for the building is thus 9⅓ per cent. The capital value of the building may now be computed as follows:

Net income residual to building—$8,200
Capitalization rate—9⅓%
Building value—$8,200/.0933 = $87,889, say, $88,000
Total value of the property is $88,000 + $30,000 = $118,000

The straight-line method of providing for building recapture involves a basic assumption. That is that the income each year in this property will decline in equal amounts equal to the interest on the amount annually recaptured. Since 3⅓ per cent of $87,889 amounts to $2,926.66, and 6 per cent interest on this amount is $175.60, the annual income decline is equal to this amount. This has the effect of equating the straight-line depreciation method with a constant declining annuity, and the formula for determining the rate of decline is $R \times D / R + D$, where R = interest rate and D = annual rate of depreciation.

In the example cited above, the rate of decline amounts to .06 × .033/ .06 + .033 = .0198/.093 = 2.13% per year.

Unless the income is assumed to decline in this fashion, the method should not be used. If the income remains constant for the thirty-year period, the rate of the return will be not 6 per cent but over 8.5 per cent. This can be verified by examination of the Inwood-table factor for thirty years at 8.5 per cent. A second assumption is that the building value is at its peak at the time of the appraisal and that it loses value in a straight-line manner consistent with the decline in income.

Since very few properties have characteristics that meet these assumptions, it is surprising that so many appraisers continue to use this method of capitalization.

Sinking-Fund Method. Another method for providing for recapture of capital is known as the sinking-fund method. Under this method, it is assumed that, out of the net income residual to the building, an appropriate amount will be taken out annually which when placed in a sinking fund at a safe rate of interest will return the entire building investment in one lump sum at the end of the building's economic life. Therefore, the annual amounts to be taken out for recapture will be less than under the straight-line method, since each year's amount will be earning compound interest at the rate provided by the sinking fund.

In appraising the value of a building with a residual net income of $8,200 and an estimated life of thirty years with interest on the investment at 6 per cent and a 3.5 per cent sinking-fund rate, this method will develop the following results:

Net income to building = $8,200
Interest on building value = .06
Sinking-fund factor—30 yrs. @ 3.5% = .01937
Composite capitalization rate = .07937
Value of building $8,200/.07937 = $103,314

It should be noted that the same income projection under the straight-line method produces a capitalization rate of .0933 and a value of $87,889. The reason for the difference is in the amounts deducted annually for recapture and hence in the amount of income decline assumed in both methods. Since a smaller amount is being recaptured each year under the sinking-fund method, the assumption is that the income decline will also be smaller.

This method also assumes a pattern of declining income and value, although not to the same degree as in the straight-line method, and it suffers from the same objections that apply to the latter method.

It may be noted in passing that building valuation using the sinking-fund method will produce the same results as valuation by use of Hoskold tables. The factors found in the Hoskold tables are merely reciprocals of the capitalization rates obtained by adding interest rates and sinking-fund rates.

Annuity Method. The annuity method of providing for building capital recapture treats the net income residual to the building as an annuity which may be processed into a value estimate by multiplying the net income by the appropriate factor found in the "present value of 1 per annum" table, sometimes referred to as the Inwood table.

Let us return to the property illustrated under the straight-line recapture method. The net income to the building was $8,200. Using a 6 per cent interest rate for a thirty-year period, one would calculate the building value as follows:

Net income to building = $8,200
Annuity factor—30 years @ 6% = 13.765
Value of building—$8,200 × 13.765 = $112,873

While this method assumes that the income will remain constant over the economic life of the property, there is an implied assumption that the building value is constantly decreasing, but at a rate which is slow in the early years and more rapid in later life. The slow decrease in value in the early years, with the consequent lower recapture provisions, operates to produce the high building value under this method.

Because of the constant income feature of this method, appraisers tend to apply it to those properties which are assured of constant income streams. Commercial buildings leased to national chains and well-secured ground leases are examples of properties which will produce income streams consistent with these long-term constant income projections. However, as has previously been pointed out, income streams do not necessarily have to be constant to be treated as annuities.

The chief objection to the use of this method of building valuation lies in the assumption that the income stream, remaining constant over an estimated building economic life-span, will suddenly disappear during the next year. This is contrary to the experience of nearly all properties. The one possible type of appraisal situation where this may be true is in the case of a long-term leasehold held by a gasoline company where the appraiser, at the time of the appraisal, is convinced that, at the expiration of the lease, it will not be renewed, because of some change in traffic patterns that will render the location unsuitable for gasoline stations. In that event, the building income and building value may cease at the expiration of the lease.

REVERSIONARY VALUE OF REAL ESTATE

We have already pointed out that appraisal practice tends to place great emphasis upon the economic life of a building as the time span over which the income should be capitalized Implicit in all the previously discussed methods of capital recapture is the thought that building value, and hence building *income,* ceases at the end of the projected life-span. Is it practical to assume that income and value will decrease at a constant rate? Experience indicates that these assumptions are usually without foundation.

Is it not more realistic to assume that properties will be held for average periods of ownership and that recapture of capital will be mainly accomplished by resale rather than by periodic instalments? Recapture is accomplished in two ways. It can be provided for out of income which permits amortization of existing mortgages at a faster pace than the decline in the market value of the property. Secondly, it may accrue to the owner when he sells his property. If the total of the income and reversion exceeds his investment, he has recaptured his capital and enjoyed a yield. If either the income or reversion alone exceeds his investment, he has recaptured his capital and enjoyed a yield.

By treating land and building as a unit and capitalizing the total net income for a period of years consistent with typical investment market patterns, rather than with theoretical economic lives, and providing for an estimate of reversionary value for both land and building in the capitalization rate that reflects the appraisers best judgment of future trends, we will put the capitalization process on firmer ground. In the previous chapter, we pointed out how the selection of a capitalization rate which took the foregoing factors of income and reversion into consideration met the requirements of capitalization theory. In the next chapter we will discuss the residual techniques that appraisers use in processing income into value.

12

Capitalization Techniques—Residual

The derivation of capital value for an income-producing parcel of real estate may be accomplished by one of several capitalization techniques. These techniques are known as the *residual techniques*. They include the *land residual, building residual,* and *property residual* techniques.

The term *residual* refers to something remaining after all deductions have been made. In the appraisal process, it may refer to (1) the net income remaining to the land after all building charges have been deducted, (2) the net income remaining to the building after all land charges have been deducted, or (3) the net income remaining to the property as a whole.

Most valuation problems can be handled satisfactorily by the use of the property residual technique, which treats the land and building as a single entity. However, it sometimes is necessary or desirable to find a separate value for the land or the building, and in these instances either the land residual or the building residual technique can be utilized.

The land residual technique can be used to check on the reasonableness of an asking price for a plot that is the contemplated site for a new income-producing building. In this application, the appraiser reenacts the thinking of the builder. A parcel is offered at a given price. After determination of the highest and best possible use of the plot, the cost of the improvement is estimated. Further estimates of gross income and operating expenses are made. From the total net income remaining, all charges to the building —including provisions for interest on, and recapture of, the capital invested —are made. The amount of income remaining is then said to be residual to the land. By capitalization of this residual net income attributable to the land, a capital land value is determined. If the land value equals or exceeds the asking price, the project is economically feasible.

An alternate method of accomplishing the same purpose requires that the entire value of the property be determined by the capitalization process and that the value of the proposed building be subtracted from this value. The land value is then the difference between total value and building value, where building value and cost are equal.

Appraisals for real property taxes and for condemnation awards almost always require the use of residual techniques. In these cases, land values, as if unimproved, are required to be established, and to them is added the value of the improvements to produce either the total assessed value or the value for condemnation.

Building residual problems are usually encountered where the vacant or unimproved land would have a greater market value than is indicated by the income being produced by an existing structure. In these cases, the building either is not the most profitable type for the location or suffers from a great deal of obsolescence. In either case, it may still produce net income exceeding that needed for the capital requirements of the market value of the land alone. If this is so, redevelopment of the land may prove to be premature and unprofitable. On the other hand, if the net income is insufficient to meet the land charges, it is a signal that redevelopment is imperative. In each instance, the building value is calculated on a residual basis, and its value is only equal to the amount which it adds to the land value. When a negative building value is indicated, as frequently occurs in areas undergoing changes and rapid land value increases, demolition of the building and redevelopment are indicated.

In determining the capital value of a parcel of real estate, each of the techniques will produce approximately the same answer, if the interest and recapture assumptions remain constant for each procedure. The correct technique is the one that permits the most dependable basic assumptions to be processed.

LAND RESIDUAL TECHNIQUE

The land residual technique is well suited to land value estimation under the following conditions:

1. The building is new or in its early life.
2. A proper ratio exists between land and building values.
3. The building represents the highest and best use of the land.
4. The land value cannot be determined from an analysis of comparable sales.
5. Prices are relatively static.
6. A starting point is needed for assessment or for dealing with similar valuation problems.
7. Land value under retail stores is to be estimated when there are no comparable vacant-land sales.

In the land residual technique, the appraiser starts with an assumption of building value. The building value is assumed to be equal to the cost of the structure. Since this is most nearly the case when the building is new or fairly new, the use of this technique should be restricted to these conditions. The building need not be in existence. Frequently, a hypothetical new building is conceived, and, in fact, as has already been pointed out, it is in these hypothetical or proposed new building situations that the land residual technique finds its greatest application. From the total net income of the property are deducted the charges attributable to the building. The remainder is residual to the land and forms the basis for determining land value.

The following example will illustrate the technique. A new one-story taxpayer with an area of 8,000 square feet and costing $119,250 produces a gross income of $32,000 per annum. Operating expenses including real estate taxes amount to $12,400. Net income to the entire property is $19,600. Assume a forty-year-economic life for the building, an 8 per cent capitalization rate, and the use of the Inwood annuity procedure to recapture the capital investment.

Assumed building value = $119,250
Total net income = ... $ 19,600
Inwood factor—8%—40 yrs. = 11.925
Building charges $119,250/11.925 = ... $ 10,000

Net income residual to land = ... $ 9,600
Land value = $9,600/.08 = $120,000
Total value of property—building value (assumed) $119,250
land value (calculated) 120,000

Total $239,250

It should be noted that, in this example, an annual charge of $10,000 against the net income will provide an 8 per cent return on the capital invested in the building, plus complete return of the investment over a forty-year period. Further, this technique assumes that, at the end of the forty-year period, the building value will be zero, and that the land value will remain constant at $120,000.

Proof:
P.W. of $19,600 per annum @ 8% for 40 years = $19,600 × 11.925 = $233,730
P.W. of $120,000 due 40 years hence @ 8% = $120,000 × .046 = ... 5,520

Total value = ... $239,250

In those cases where it is necessary to determine a land value for tax-assessment purposes, the appraiser or assessor must process the net income before real estate taxes have been deducted, since the amount of real estate taxes will be calculated on the capitalized value to be found. In the example cited above, assume that the tax rate in the area is $4 per $100 of assessed value, or 4 per cent. Further, assume assessments are made on a basis of 80 per cent of value; therefore, the effective tax rate is 3.2 per cent. The total net income from the property before taxes is now $27,256. The valuation procedure is as follows:

Assumed building value = $119,250
Total net income before taxes = $27,256
Building charges:
   (a) 119,250/11.925 = 10,000 (as before)
   (b) R.E. taxes—119,250 × .032 (effective tax rate) =................ $ 3,816
   Total building charges = ...   13,816

Net income residual to land = ... $13,440
Land value = $13,440/.112 (.08 + .032) = $120,000

The land residual technique enjoys wide popularity among appraisers, both as a means to determine land values in the absence of sales data and also as a check against indicated values where sales are available. Unfortunately, the inherent difficulties in this technique are frequently overlooked. It demands great skill and knowledge in the various preliminary estimates. In an earlier chapter it was pointed out that in some instances a 10 per cent variation in the gross income estimates by two appraisers could ultimately lead to almost a 100 per cent difference in the land value estimate, even if all other estimates were consistent. The great sensitivity of this technique, not only in the gross income estimates but also in the expense and rate selection aspects, has led some authorities to look with disfavor upon its use.

BUILDING RESIDUAL TECHNIQUE

The building residual technique is a means of determining building values under the following conditions:

1. The value of the land can readily be estimated by sales or by use of the hypothetical-building land residual technique.
2. The building is an improper improvement.
3. The building is in late or middle life, with obvious deficiencies due to deterioration or obsolescence.

Ordinarilly, in a well-planned and well-executed building project where the building represents the highest and best use of the land, the building's value will approximate its cost and make possible the use of the land residual technique. As a building gets older, what was once a proper improvement may no longer be so. Neighborhood changes, population shifts, obsolescence and deterioration factors all combine to create differences between current value and current replacement cost. The value of the building often is equal only to the capitalized value of the income it contributes over and above the income that the land would produce if developed to its highest and best use. For this reason the building residual method is utilized where older buildings are under appraisal. To do otherwise would be to distort the underlying land values.

As with the land residual technique, two procedures are possible in this technique. The first would be to make a composite appraisal of the property as a whole and subtract from that total the land value as indicated by comparable sales. The difference would be the residual building value. The second method is to follow the same procedure as in the land residual technique but with the land and building positions reversed. In the land residual technique, we assumed a building value and calculated a land value on the basis of the residual land income. In the building residual technique, we assume a land value and calculate a building value on the basis of the residual building income.

The following example will illustrate the use of the building residual technique. The property under appraisal is a thirty-year-old apartment house producing a net income of $10,000 per annum after taxes. Sales and leases in the area indicate that the land value may be estimated at $50,000. A capitalization rate of 8 per cent is proper, and the building is estimated to have a future economic life of twenty-five years. The straight-line method of capital recapture is used in this case.

Assumed land value = $50,000
Total net income = $10,000
Land charges—$50,000 × 8% =   4,000
                                                            ─────────
Net income residual to building $ 6,000
Building rate:
  (a) 8% interest on investment
  (b) 4% recapture rate (25-year life)
    ────
    12%
Building value—$6,000/.12 = $50,000
Total value of property—land value (assumed) $ 50,000
                building value (calculated)   50,000
                      Total $100,000

In this example, the reproduction cost new of the building is estimated at $300,000, but its economic value is only $50,000. The virtue of the building residual technique is that it enables the appraiser to make a more accurate estimate of economic value than would be possible if he relied solely on reproduction cost new estimates with deductions from some standard depreciation scale. At some time in the future, if land values should rise and/or if the net income should drop below a point where it cannot produce an adequate return on the land, the building, even if structurally sound, would have no economic value.

One of the chief virtues of the building residual method is its ability to demonstrate the amount of depreciation that exists in an older structure, without the necessity of resorting to tables or schedules which are incapable of proof. As for new structures, the building residual method may indicate whether or not the building is an over- or underimprovement and whether or not it has come into being with some aspects of built-in depreciation. In these cases, the building value will not be equal to its cost, and the difference between cost and value can be calculated by the building residual technique.

PROPERTY RESIDUAL TECHNIQUE

The capitalization technique that will serve the appraiser best in most cases is the property residual technique. Most appraisal problems involve properties where land value estimates are difficult to support and the buildings are of sufficient age to carry some degree of depreciation. In these cases, the use of the property residual technique is highly recommended. In addition to these properties, those which involve the valuation of long-term leased properties are also best handled by the property residual method.

The basic theory of this technique stands in opposition to the theory of the land and building residual techniques. It is based on the thought that the income from a property cannot be logically split into land returns and building returns. The property is approached as a single unit, both land and building being wedded together with no logical reason for making separate allocations. This is the way most investors look upon properties, with little or no consideration given to separate land returns and separate building returns. From a practical point of view, this concept seems logical, and, except for special-purpose appraisals where separate land and building values are required, it would appear that the property residual technique is to be preferred.

Either of two methods may be used in this technique. The first is actually the direct capitalization of the total net income into perpetuity. Thus, if a property yields $10,000 in annual net income and is capitalized at 8 per cent, the value will be $125,000 ($10,000/.08). In this method, the reversionary value and the income are assumed to be constant into perpetuity, and the rate is derived from an analysis of sales of comparable property. While this is the simplest method, it does not meet the realities of the market. It has already been pointed out that most properties are held for a finite term of years; they are then sold, and a reversionary value is realized at the time of the sale.

In order to meet the requirements of the real estate market, the property residual method that seems most suitable is one that would value the income stream for a term of years and value the reversion at the end of that period. The basic formula for property residual valuation in this method is: Value = P.W. of income stream + P.W. of reversion.

Since the reversionary value involves both land and building value at the time of resale, it is difficult to make an accurate dollar-amount estimate of this figure. Instead, the appraiser makes an estimate of the percentage decrease or increase in the reversionary value, depending upon his estimate of the prospects for the property. In the example cited above, where the property was producing $10,000 net income per annum and the capitalization rate was 8 per cent, a further estimate of the duration of ownership and reversionary value at that time is needed. If the appraiser adopts a ten-year period of ownership and assumes a 10 per cent decline in the value of the property at the end of that time, he is predicting a reversionary value of 90 per cent of current value. Using the property residual formula cited in the previous paragraph, the mathematics of the valuation would be as follows:

1. V (value) = P.W. of $10,000 p.a. @ 8% for 10 years + P.W. of R (reversion) × .90
2. V = $10,000 × 6.71 (P.W. of 1 per annum for 10 years @ 8%) + .463 V (reversion at 8% due in 10 years) × .90
3. V = $67,100 + .4167 V
4. V − .4167 V = $67,100
5. .5833 V = $67,100
   V = $67,100/.5833 = $115,035

It should be noted that the value of the income stream in this example is 58⅓ per cent of the total value of the property. If the duration of the stream were twenty years instead of ten years, it would become almost 81 per cent, and for forty years it would become approximately 96 per cent. Any further projection would tend to produce a result similar to the one obtained by direct capitalization. The chief virtue of this method of property residual valuation is that it is consistent with market behavior and does not assume perpetual ownership or constant value, both rare phenomena.

CONCLUSION

In considering which technique to use, it has been found that the property residual technique is most satisfactory. Once a property valuation has been arrived at, if it is required to make a separate valuation of land or building, a mathematical subtraction of either of the known elements will produce the unknown. Thus, if the land value is known, the building value is obtained by subtracting the land from the total and vice versa. It is interesting to note that, before either the land residual or the building residual technique can be used, either element must first be known; therefore, the procedure suggested above is feasible in place of separate land or building residual techniques.

A great deal of unnecessary complexity has been introduced in the appraisal field by the use of various methods of providing for recapture of the investment. Land and building residual techniques can be applied using straight-line, sinking-fund, Hoskold annuity, or Inwood annuity methods. To be consistent, the method chosen by the appraiser should conform to the assumptions of income behavior (constant, declining, increasing), how recapture of the investment is to be made (piecemeal or in a lump sum), and the rate of interest required on the investment. We have not considered the variations in value possible in the land and building residual techniques using the different recapture assumptions, since we feel that for all practical purposes they would confuse rather than clarify. Nor have we considered increasing or declining income streams. Experience has shown that most properties never experience increases or decreases in income that fit a predictable pattern. Most appraisers use stabilized income streams which are considered as constant. Ellwood has shown that no significant error is introduced by treating average annual income as an ordinary annuity in a comparatively short-term projection.[1] This is so, even where the year-to-year variations have proven fairly substantial.

The property residual technique is sufficiently elastic to meet any given appraisal problem. It is the preferred technique.

[1] L. W. Ellwood, *Ellwood Tables For Real Estate Appraising and Financing* (Ridgewood, N.J.: published by the author, 1959), pp. 196, 197.

13

Cost Approach

In the search for value evidence, appraisers have always placed much emphasis on the cost approach. The basic steps in this approach involve consideration of

1. The estimate of value of land regarded as vacant
2. The estimate of reproduction cost new at the time of the appraisal
3. The estimate of accrued depreciation
4. The addition of the land value and the depreciated reproduction cost to form a value estimate

BASIS FOR USE

At any given time, costs may or may not equal value, depending upon whether the costs are warranted and whether the building, when erected, meets the test of sound economic use. However, the thought that market values in the long run will tend to equal "normal" costs of production, is a central theme in the use of this approach. Further, since the accuracy of value estimates derived from the market or income approaches depends a great deal upon subjective judgment factors, the use of the cost approach serves primarily as a check upon the other approaches. In addition, the concept that the cost of acquiring a substitute property, without undue delay, ordinarily sets the upper limit of value is generally conceded to be a valid one in the appraisal field. The last statement will be recognized as the principle of substitution. Frequently, through the favorable circumstances that may attach themselves to a specific piece of property, the market value will exceed the reproduction cost new. A parcel leased to a strong tenant at a rental that exceeds the economic rent is one example. Rezoning of an area, by a municipality, creating a monopoly use for a gas station is another example. In fact, any set of circumstances that tends to create conditions of imperfect competition will create value-cost differentials. Appraisers, by and large, find that such cases are but a fraction of the situations that confront them. The typical appraisal assignment is one where the market value of the property is at a figure somewhat less than the reproduction cost new. The difference between reproduction cost and market value is known as *accrued depreciation*. This chapter deals with the techniques involved in determining reproduction cost. The succeeding chapter will discuss the techniques for estimating accrued depreciation.

It should be kept in mind that cost data, like market and income data, are only means to a single end—the estimate of market value. Several factors have led appraisers to give great weight to the cost approach. The need for standardized mass valuations by tax assessors and by VA and FHA appraisers has led to a general acceptance of this method because of the belief that reproduction costs could thereby be determined with relative ease. The acceptance by the courts, in most states, of this approach as a reliable index of value has also aided in its acceptance by appraisers. Further, the inherent difficulties of both the income approach and the market approach, as has already been pointed out, has commended the cost approach as the most promising for many appraisers. Unfortunately, the many pitfalls that await the appraiser in the use of this technique seem to have been forgotten. One factor of great importance is the possibility of combining the cost and income approaches in the planning and appraisal of a new realty project. By relation of the net income to costs, an over-all capitalization rate can be determined and correlated with the rate selected by the appraiser in his income approach. Since the latter rate is usually selected on the basis of money market conditions and investor expectations, the different basis for each rate affords an opportunity for objective cross-checking. If the rates, as derived, vary to a great degree, the need for review of the work is self-evident. If, after review, the income valuation cannot justify a cost expenditure, obsolescence is indicated and the project may have to be abandoned or a less costly one substituted. On the other hand, if the income valuation exceeds the cost estimate, it is probably a signal that the land value estimate is too low. This can be particularly important in urban-renewal appraisals where municipal bodies seek expert appraisal advice on the resale value of land earmarked for renewal projects. Finally, an estimate of project costs will determine to a large degree the rental levels necessary to support the venture or, in the case of non-investment properties, the prices required to make the project profitable. If costs are too high relative to prices and rents obtainable in the market, an abandonment of the project may be indicated. If, on the other hand, current prices and rents are favorable relative to costs, the project will probably be undertaken.

In addition to using the cost approach as an aid in estimating market value, the appraiser may employ this method of valuation for specific purposes not related to market value. Appraisals for fire insurance are usually made on the basis of reproduction cost less depreciation. Other uses are for tax-assessment proceedings, where reproduction cost less depreciation is recognized as the upper limit of value; for allocation of purchase price to land and building in order to set up a basis for income-tax depreciation allowances; for determining going concern value; and for setting up a proper value in mergers and acquisitions. Our prime consideration in this chapter is of the use of the cost approach for determining market value.

SOURCES OF DATA

Land Value. As has already been indicated, the first step in the cost approach is the estimate of land value. It is interesting to note that the determination of land value either is based on an analysis of comparable sales, leases, bids, or offers or it is by recourse to a land residual technique. In either case it is apparent that there is an integral relationship between the cost approach and the other approaches, at least in this very first step. As we shall see later on, this relationship also exists in some of the other steps that make up the cost approach. Wherever possible, the use of comparable sales as a measure of value is preferred. The technique of determining land value by the sales-comparison or income approach has been described in the respective chapters dealing with these subjects, and they should be consulted for a full explanation of the suggested procedure.

Building Values. The cost approach equates building values with building costs. In determining costs, the appraiser must first fix in his mind just what building costs he is seeking. Every appraisal presents its own problems. Is he seeking the cost of a new, substantially identical replica? Or an equally depreciated substitute property? Or the most advantageous new and modern substitute? It would seem that for all practical purposes the appraiser is seeking the cost of a new and modern substitute property that will fulfil the function of the subject property. Just what this new and modern substitute is will depend largely upon the appraiser's own judgment.

After selection of the type of building, another problem presents itself. Whose costs shall be used? It is well known that cost estimates will vary among several different builders, each of whom is prepared to build the building according to the architect's specifications. These variations may range from 10 per cent to 20 per cent or even more. There is no such thing as a one and only cost to build a given structure. Recognition of this fact has led appraisers to rely heavily on construction cost services which can only approximate costs for typical structures in both the residential and non-residential field. The reliance on various published construction cost services is dictated frequently by the need for speed and the economics of appraisal assignments. Appraisal fees usually do not permit the appraiser to spend the time needed for detailed cost analysis and, fortunately, in most cases, the cost services provide estimates that are within reasonable ranges and serve the purpose for the appraisal. A list of some of the well-known cost services follows:

1. Dow Service Building Cost Calculator
2. Boeckh's Manual of Appraisals; Building Costs
3. Wenzlick Construction Cost Manual
4. Marshall and Stevens Valuation Quarterly
5. J. Cleminshaw Manual
6. Joint Committee Report (Chicago chapter of American Institute of Architects and Appraisers, Division of Chicago Real Estate Board)
7. Society of Residential Appraisers Manual

The general purpose of each of these services is basically the same. They are designed to reduce the construction costs of various types of buildings to average unit costs, either on a square-foot or cubic-foot basis. Some are more detailed than others, breaking down the costs into the various building components such as excavation, foundation, basic structure, roof, walls, utilities, elevators, etc. In each case, instructions are given for modifying the basic average costs to fit the characteristics of buildings that vary in some measure from the prototypes that were used in computing the original costs. In addition to providing the cost data for the various types of buildings, these services usually supply a cost index and local cost modifiers for areas other than the home area from which the costs are obtained. This latter feature of the services is designed to enable the appraiser to keep his cost figures up-to-date.

Direct and Indirect Costs. Before embarking on an explanation of the details of cost estimating by appraisers, it would be well to consider all the elements that make up construction costs. When appraisers consider these costs, they include not only the direct costs of the materials and labor to put them in place but also the indirect costs that must be borne as a part of the building project. Some of the more important indirect costs include

1. Preliminary expenses (consultation fees, surveys, permits)
2. Professional fees (architects, engineers, legal)
3. Taxes during construction
4. Financing charges
5. Interest on equity capital used during construction
6. Administrative and overhead costs
7. Development costs (advertising, leasing, etc.)

The total of these indirect costs will vary from job to job, but it has been found that they will usually amount to 15 per cent to 18 per cent of the total direct costs. One of the difficulties facing appraisers is the inability to convince builders that the indirect items are just as much a part of the costs as the labor and materials that are expended. Therefore, in obtaining data relative to building costs from on-the-job builders, it is recommended that inquires be made about net field costs, which will represent the sum total of the various subcontracts, and then the indirect costs.

COSTING METHODS

Quantity-Survey Method. Construction costs may be accurately determined by calculating the quantity and costs of materials, supplies, equipment, and labor involved. This is known as the *quantity-survey* method. This method necessitates complete familiarity with current prices of materials, the handling of labor, construction, and job conditions. For an appraiser to use this method means that he is endeavoring to use the detailed procedures that each subcontractor goes through before submitting a bid to the general contractor. While it is true that this method of cost estimating is the ideal one, it is obvious that such a detailed procedure is practicable only for those experienced in, and actively connected with, building construction. Further, it is an expensive and time-consuming process, and most appraisers do not have the training to undertake such a cost breakdown. For most actual appraisal assignments, the use of this method is not recommended. The appraiser is not undertaking to build the structure, he is trying to arrive at a practical result, a reasonable estimate of value. The quantity-survey method is useful as the basis for the derivation of less cumbersome and more practical methods of cost estimating. It forms the yardstick by which all other methods can be measured for their accuracy.

Subcontract Method. The builder or general contractor seldom makes a quantity survey or estimates costs other than those for work he does himself. He depends largely upon the bids from subcontractors for various parts of the work. The subcontractors, however, make a detailed estimate of labor, material, and overhead costs before submitting their bids. Many subcontractors depend upon experience with similar work for a guide and frequently do little more than guess at costs of their work. This is true of dwellings and, to a lesser extent, of larger structures.

Perhaps the most practical method of estimating construction costs is through an analysis of subcontract figures. By the obtaining of a complete statement of costs for all types of work included in a number of similar buildings, comparisons readily can be made and the "normal" cost of a typical class of building determined.

A schedule of all items which enter into the costs of a building should be established, and actual prices for the various parts of the work should be included. The cost of each portion of the building should be compared with the same portion of other typical buildings of the same class. In this way, large differences, if any, can be investigated and modified. The subcontract figures for several typical buildings should give a very close approximation of average costs. From these figures, the appraiser can develop usable reproduction costs for his appraisal work. An example of a subcontract breakdown will be found in Table 6.

TABLE 6

SUBCONTRACT COSTS—TYPICAL NEW YORK CITY SIX-STORY SELF-SERVICE-ELEVATOR APARTMENT HOUSE—600,000 CUBIC FEET, INSIDE PLOT 150 × 100

Item	Cost (Rounded)
DIRECT COSTS	
Excavation	$ 22,000
Foundation	25,000
Brickwork	100,000
Electrical	25,000
Plumbing	50,000
Heating	27,500
Steel	45,000
Oil burner	5,000
Hall and kitchen tile	20,000
Lumber	32,000
Plastering	40,000
Hardware	2,500
Sash and glass	6,500
Kitchen equipment	13,000
Concrete arches and flatwork	28,500
Elevator	14,000
Roofing	7,000
Doors and bucks	3,000
Air conditioning	20,000
Sprinklers	4,000
Millwork	20,000
Carpentry	30,000
Tile and terrazzo	15,000
Painting	15,000
Common labor	9,000
Insulation	1,500
Architect and surveyor	7,500
Supervision	10,000
Builder's fee	25,000
Miscellaneous	25,000
Total direct cost	$648,000
INDIRECT COSTS	
Taxes during construction	$ 2,500
Interest on land	4,500
Interest on working capital	6,000
Mortgage charges	17,000
Insurance	3,000
Legal	2,000
Misc. development (adv., leasing, etc.)	5,000
Total Indirect Costs	$40,000

Total Cost: $688,000 = $1.15 per cu. ft.

Unit-in-Place Method. A method slightly less time-consuming than the quantity-survey method but requiring a good deal of experience and knowledge and producing fairly good results is the *unit-in-place* method. In this method, cost factors are developed by the appraiser to represent the cost of a square foot of exterior or interior wall surface, floor, roof, etc., in place. In effect, the wall, floor, or roof is constructed on paper. If the cost of a square foot of exterior wall were to be calculated, the appraiser would estimate the number of bricks, the amount of mortar, lath, plaster, labor, overhead, profit, etc., required to construct the unit and would determine the cost of each component in place. The unit cost multiplied by the total net wall area, plus the cost of openings, windows and doors, would give the total cost of the exterior wall in place. By repeating the process for the floor and roof areas, one would account for the major components of the building cost. Separate calculations for heating, plumbing, and electrical installations are made, as well as allowances for porches, detached garages, driveways, sidewalks, landscaping, and any other items of outside construction that may be encountered.

The accuracy of this method depends a great deal on the appraiser's ability to maintain an accurate file of current labor and material prices and on his ability to recognize the ingredients of a square foot of surface of construction and to know whether or not the surface or unit involved in the appraisal fits the cost factor he is about to apply.

As has been pointed out previously, this method is not as time-consuming as the quantity-survey method, but it still requires, in most cases, enough time and painstaking care to make it economically unfeasible for the average appraisal. Residential properties lend themselves to the development of unit-in-place factors that can be applied rather quickly with accurate results. One large insurance company has developed such factors for the use of its appraisal staff, on the basis of the wide experience it has had in estimating costs of residential properties.

Unit-in-place estimating may be illustrated by the following example:

Property. Six-story office building. Fireproof and air-conditioned, containing 28,300 square feet—344,500 cubic feet.

Excavation. 270 cubic yards @ $1.50 .... $ 405
Foundation. 5,100 cubic feet @ $1.83 9,333
Floors. gross area 28,300 square feet

Steel	$ 2.15 per square foot
Arches	1.40 per square foot
Asphalt tile	0.25 per square foot
Pan ceilings	1.10 per square foot
Electrical	1.70 per square foot
Heat & Vent. (AC)	2.85 per square foot
Plumbing	1.00 per square foot

                      $10.45 × 28,300 295,735

Walls. gross area 22,050 square feet

Brick facing	1.40 square foot
Backup block	0.75 square foot
Furring & lath	0.25 square foot
Plastering	0.30 square foot
Painting	0.08 square foot

2.78 × 22,050	61,299
Partitions. 1,750 linear feet @ $15	26,250
Elevators. 2 @ $30,000	60,000
Subtotal (field cost)	$453,022
Profit, overhead, administration, fees, insurance, taxes, financing, etc. (22%)	$ 99,665
Total cost	$552,687,

or $19.50 per square foot

Square-Foot and Cubic-Foot Factors. By far the most widely used methods for estimating building costs are the *square-foot-* and *cubic-foot-factor* methods. Both are the same in that they make use of a number of typical buildings in each class they purport to represent, average out their known costs, and then divide the average cost for the group by either the square-foot area or the cubic contents of the typical building. The result is a square- or cubic-foot factor that is applied to similar buildings that are being appraised.

The square-foot factor is generally preferred for modest residential buildings, industrial buildings, taxpayers, garages, and other relatively simple structures. The cubic-foot factor is generally preferred for large and expensive residential buildings, apartment houses, office buildings, hotels, theaters, lofts, etc.

To a large extent the use of either the square-foot or the cubic-foot factor will depend on local custom or tradition in expressing price units, the availability of source data for one or both methods, and the type of building.

The square-foot method requires the appraiser to calculate the area of the building by multiplying the frontage by the depth for each story above ground. When the area has been determined, it is multiplied by an appropriate square-foot cost factor to produce an estimate of the reproduction cost of the building. This cost factor is generally applied only to the area of the building above ground and not to any basement or cellar space. The cost of basement or cellar space is reflected in the square-foot factor.

The cubic-foot method requires the appraiser to obtain the cubic contents of the building, usually from the plans. The basis for calculating the cubic contents of a building is the standard adopted by the American Institute of Architects and by the building industry. By this standard, the cubic contents of a building may be computed by multiplying the area of the building, measured from the outside of the exterior walls, by the height of the building. The height of a building is measured from a point 6 inches below the lowest floor to the top of the roof, if it is level; in case of pitched roofs, to the average height. The portions of the buildings having different areas and heights should be calculated separately or proper deductions made. The lowest floor may be the cellar, subbasement, pit, etc. Included in the calculations are all pits, roof structures, extensions, or other inclosed appendages. Footings, steps, parapet walls, cornices, belt courses, open courts, or buildings not connected with the main structure are not included. The last item should be calculated separately.

Once the cubic contents of a building are obtained, then, as in the square-foot method, a cubic cost factor is applied to produce an estimate of reproduction cost.

Segregated Costs. Another method available to appraisers is known as the *segregated-cost* method. In this method, the component parts of a building are priced either on a square-foot or cubic-foot basis, and a total is arrived at. An example of this method[1] follows:

Industrial one story—masonry

Factory   7,000–9,000 square feet

Production area, 9 offices, public and private conveniences, no basement.
Base building—7,150 square feet—100,100 cubic feet

Base Costs

Item	Costs	Unit Costs		% of Total
		Sq. Ft.	Cu. Ft.	
Structure & finish	$33,650	$4.71	.336¢	74.8
Heating & ventilating	5,250	.73	.052	11.7
Plumbing	2,500	.35	.025	5.5
Electrical	3,600	.50	.036	8.0
Total	$45,000	$6.29	.449	100.0

A variation of segregated costs as applied by the *Marshall and Stevens Valuation Quarterly* is based on giving separate consideration to each of the major component parts of a building. The only measurements normally needed in this method are the linear feet of exterior wall and the total floor area. Costs based on linear feet are applied to the foundation and exterior wall. Costs based on floor area are applied to the roof, floor, ceiling, interior construction, heating, and electrical items. To these costs

[1] Joint Committee on Building Costs of Chicago Chapter American Institute of Architects and Appraisers, Division of Chicago Real Estate Board. Building Cost Manual (New York: John Wiley & Sons, Inc., 1957), Item 10-1-2-A.

are added lump sums for plumbing, built-in appliances, and fireplaces. The components of each of the segregated items are as follows:

1. *Foundation.* Includes foundation and excavation costs
2. *Floor costs.* Includes allowances for girders, posts, piers, floor joists, subfloor, and flooring
3. *Roof costs.* Includes allowances for roofing, sheathing, ceiling joist, rafters, and bracing
4. *Exterior wall.* Includes allowance for basic wall, outside wall cover, interior facing, finish, windows, doors
5. *Ceiling costs.* Includes allowances for lath, plaster, paper, paint, etc.
6. *Interior construction and fixtures.* Includes allowances for interior partitions, doors, closets, and cabinet work
7. *Electrical cost.* Includes switching, wiring, and fixtures for average lighting and appliance outlets
8. *Heating costs.* Includes allowances for heating unit and distribution system
9. *Lump-sum plumbing.* Includes allowances for fixtures, roughing in, installation, and a normal amount of water and gas connecting piping
10. *Lump-sum fireplace.* Includes allowance for foundation, masonry, reinforcing, and flashing

An example of the application of this method of cost estimating is given in Fig. 4. The property is a conventional, one-story residential building of good-quality construction.

Trended or Index Costs. In determining building costs, appraisers will frequently attempt to take known historical costs for various types of buildings and project them into a current cost estimate by means of a published construction cost index. There are several such published cost indexes available, and they all have in common an effort to relate current costs to a base period. Thus, if 1926 is used as a base period at 100 and the current cost index stands at 270, the percentage increase is 170 per cent. A building which had a cost of $10,000 in 1926 is thus rated at $27,000 today. A partial list of some of the better-known cost indexes and their component parts is given below.

Index	Base Year	Component Parts
1. Engineering News Record Building Cost Index	1913	2,500 lb. structural steel shapes 6 lb. cement (Chicago) 1,084 board feet (pine or fir—20 cities) 58.38 hours skilled labor (20 cities)
2. American Appraisal Co.	1913	Four types of construction in 20 cities (no mechanical or plumbing elements)

Index	Base Year	Component Parts
3. Austin	1926	Repricing one-story frame monitor-type industrial building
4. Marshall & Stevens	1926	Replacement costs of four definite type buildings: a. Fireproofed structural-steel frame b. Reinforced-concrete frame c. Masonry-bearing walls d. Wood or open steel frame
5. Boeckh	1926–29	Repricing of labor, material, overhead, etc., of 10 major building types based on nine basic materials and classes of labor.
6. Dow	1941	Several items of building materials, 9 skilled labor trades, common labor, labor productivity, and market conditions

Each index involves a current repricing of the several components, and the derivation of a base cost factor which then must further be modified for specific localities. Of all the methods for cost estimation available to appraisers, the index method is certainly the least reliable when applied to any specific building. The index numbers at best represent a composite of their ingredients, which are not buildings but selected building materials and wage rates for certain building-trades mechanics. Changes in building techniques and conditions and in labor productivity are rarely considered, and, if they are considered, the weight given to these changes is hardly ever indicated. The chief value of the index method lies in the indication of trends, and their use for specific buildings will frequently result in gross errors. The authors of these indexes have never intended them to be used in cost estimation for specific buildings. That they have been used and abused by appraisers is due primarily to the simplicity involved. An appraiser need only know a past cost, and, by taking that figure and applying an index number to it, he could arrive at a current cost figure. This technique requires no careful area or cube calculations; it is quick and simple, and dangerous.

Costs per Unit of Use. Another technique sometimes used by appraisers is to estimate building costs on the basis of the unit of use. Thus a building cost may be expressed in terms of the cost per room, which may range from $3,600 to $4,000 for six-story apartment houses and from $4,500 to $6,000 for luxury, high-rise apartments. In the case of theaters, it could be expressed as $500 per theater seat; for small hotels it could be expressed as $8,500 to $15,000 per room; large hotels, as $10,000 to $20,000 per room; small motels (10 to 60 rooms), as $5,000 to $8,000 per room; and grand motels (61 to 250 rooms), as $8,000 to $15,000 per

Item	Units	Quality	Quantity	Unit Cost	Ext.
Foundation—Concrete, Frame, and Stucco	Linear Ft. of Wall	Good	190	$2.50	$ 475
Exterior Wall—Stucco	Linear Ft. of Wall	Good	190	19.54	3,713
Roof—Shakes	Sq. Ft. of Wall	Avg.	1,600	1.12	
Floor—Hardwood	Sq. Ft. of Wall	Good	1,600	1.33	
Ceiling—Acoustical Plaster	Sq. Ft. of Wall	Good	1,600	.48	
Interior Construction— Conventional	Sq. Ft. of Wall	Good	1,600	2.24	
Heating—Forced Air, Gas	Sq. Ft. of Wall	Good	1,600	.40	
Electrical—Flexible Conduit	Sq. Ft. of Wall	Avg.	1,600	.55	
Total Floor Area Cost			1,600	$6.12	$ 9,792
Plumbing—Ten Fixtures	Each	Good	10	$160	1,600
Built-in Appliances— Garbage Disposal	Each	Good	1	100	100
Exhaust Fan	Each	Good	1	45	45
Fireplace—Single, One Story	Each	Good	1	375	375
Porch—Concrete with Steps— Shake	Sq. Ft. of Porch	Good	100	$3.63	363
Garage—Frame & Stucco Type (Foundation)	Linear Ft. of Wall	Good	80	1.15	92
(Wall)—Stucco	Linear Ft. of Wall	Good	80	7.56	605
(Floor and Roof)—Shakes	Sq. Ft. of Floor	Avg.	400	1.39	556
Total Base Cost					$17,716
Replacement Cost—Local Multiplier 1.05 × Total Base Cost					$18,602

Fig. 4. Segregated Cost Appraisal Form. (Adapted from Marshall & Stevens Segregated Cost Appraisal Form for use with *Residential Cost Handbook*. Published by Marshall & Stevens Co., Los Angeles, Calif., p. B-2, 2/60.)

room. These cost estimates are based on comparisons with known building costs of similar buildings and thus are merely another way of translating total costs into simple unit costs. Only, in this method, the unit has become a broad spatial-use unit rather than a square- or cubic-foot unit. At most, it should only be used as a rough guide, in a way that architects may indicate rough costs to a client. At worst, this method can lead to gross errors depending upon the variations and characteristics of the prototype and subject buildings.

Some Practical Considerations. Appraisers are aware that what buildings *should* cost and what they *will* cost are frequently at variance.

Many variable factors enter into construction costs in addition to the less variable labor and material costs. Some of these factors include site topography, excavation and foundation conditions, nearness to sources of supply of materials and equipment and labor, competitive conditions, etc. As has previously been pointed out, several qualified builders can be found to construct a building according to specifications at a cost figure that may vary as much as 20 per cent from high to low bid. This would seem to indicate that there is no such thing as a one and only cost to build a given structure. At best then, even the most careful detailed estimates can only be approximations. For practical purposes, the appraiser should adopt a standard or typical structure in each building class with which he is concerned in his assignments. More than one typical building may be necessary in each class, depending on the type of materials used in construction. This building or buildings should be his bench mark for comparisons. The cost of these buildings may be calculated by either the unit-in-place, segregated-cost, or square- and cubic-foot method. Even more desirable would be a submission of these typical buildings to a few builders in the area, with specifications, with a request for them to price the buildings on a quantity-survey basis. From this quantity analysis, the desired units may be calculated and adopted for appraisal purposes. This, then, is the first step, the adoption of standard building types and their cost analysis into convenient units that can be applied to comparable buildings. Most appraisers will use a square-foot or cubic-foot unit as their basis for comparison.

Application of Unit Cost Factors. Since the use of unit cost factors or any other cost-estimating method is dependent upon an analysis of costs of similar buildings, it may be observed that many of the difficulties that appear in the comparative-sales approach are also present in the cost approach. It is necessary not only to select the proper comparative properties but also to make adjustments for differences and to weigh the significance of the adjustments. Factors of size, height, quality of construction, presence or absence of amenities, and special conditions are among the most common items that require careful scrutiny.

The difficulties surrounding the use of derived standard units may be illustrated by an examination of their application to dwellings and apartment houses. A cost factor that is based upon average construction by operative builders obviously cannot be applied to a dwelling with superior specifications, which would have a higher factor.

Various sizes of houses will require different factors. A house having 24,000 cubic feet will invariably have a higher cube factor than one with identical specifications and equipment but with 30,000 cubic feet content. A house with 9-foot ceilings will have a lower cube factor than one of equal area and specifications but with 8-foot ceilings. In both cases, the extra cubic content involves construction which is cheaper than the average cubic cost of a smaller building.

Many inaccuracies in the application of cubic-foot factors to dwellings are caused by variation of roof pitches and shapes, that is, volume of attic space. A building with a hip roof may cost the same as one with the same dimensions having a gable roof, and yet there may be hundreds of cubic feet less in the former type. Similarly, a roof with a 9-foot rise may add a great deal more cubage to a house than would a roof with a 6-foot rise, but the difference in cost would be very slight—only a fraction of the average cubic-factor cost. The factor for a house with a flat roof is not comparable to that for one with a pitched roof, and, other things being equal, the factor will be higher for the flat-roof house. These conditions must be considered in applying a cost factor.

Accurate cost data may have been obtained for a basementless, one-story, frame dwelling. In the appraisal of a similar building with a basement, a higher square-foot factor would have to be employed, since the square-foot area does not include basement space and the extra cost must be reflected in the factor to be used. However, if a cubic cost factor is being used, a lower factor must be employed, as the space in the basement is relatively unfinished and cheaper. The addition of cubage of lower cost reduces the over-all cube factor.

If cost data are available for a rectangular dwelling of a given area, it would be necessary to apply a higher factor to an L-shaped building of the same area. The L-shaped dwelling would be more costly owing to greater wall perimeter, greater foundation area, additional corner detail, more difficult roof framing, possibly more interior partitioning, and possibly greater cost of heating installation.

In using unit foot factors, care must be taken to obtain accurate costs for "extras" that will modify the costs for similar buildings. Extra baths, fireplaces, garages, etc., should be calculated as in-place units, and their costs should be broken down to the appropriate square-foot or cubic-foot factor to be added or subtracted for the building under appraisal.

The use of factors for apartment houses requires the same careful consideration. A factor for an apartment house with 9-foot ceilings cannot be used for one with 10-foot ceilings. The latter factor would be much lower than the former even if the specifications were the same. The size of the apartments will affect the factor. An apartment house with seventy apartments and 180 rooms, having the same cube and area content as one with sixty apartments and 200 rooms, will cost more owing to the additional plumbing and tile costs for the extra baths and kitchens. Other elements adding to the cost are higher partitioning costs, higher millwork and trim costs, greater electrical costs, greater equipment expenditures (refrigerators and ranges), and possibly higher elevator costs, if the layout is such as to require an additional elevator installation.

What has been said of the examples cited applies generally to all buildings. All conditions which do not conform to the typical building must be weighed in applying a factor.

CONCLUSION

The chief virtue of the cost approach is in the role it plays in conjunction with the other approaches in the appraisal of existing buildings and the planning of new projects. It provides, in the latter case, that a measure of the minimum expenditure that must be borne in order to realize an economic value is the *cost* of the land plus the *cost* of the building. On completion, a new project may exceed these costs in value under certain conditions, or it may be worth less than cost if demand and market conditions have become adverse. As for existing buildings, the cost approach provides a practical guide to the upper limit of value, if the buildings are capable of being readily reproduced and the site is available.

The chief weakness of the cost approach stems from the fact that appraisers are seeking value rather than cost. Aside from the fact that cost estimates are at best approximations, even the best estimates are subject to further market considerations before they can be accepted as evidence of market value. Further, at any given date, abnormal market conditions may serve to modify costs as value indicators. Supply and demand factors are rarely in balance, which, combined with the necessity of making depreciation allowances, usually creates an imbalance between costs and values. This is not only so with the vast majority of older properties which form the bulk of appraisal practice, but it is also true of many newly constructed buildings. In our next chapter, we will turn our attention to the elements of depreciation and the role they play in the cost approach.

14

Depreciation

From the appraiser's point of view, the estimate of reproduction costs of buildings does not present insurmountable problems. The previous chapters has indicated several possible approaches to cost estimation. The value of a building will approximate its reproduction cost, if two conditions are met: First, the property must be new or practically new; second, demand for this property must be large enough to cause it to be replaced, if it should be destroyed. If a specific property cannot meet either or both of these two conditions, its value will be less than reproduction cost new. The difference between reproduction cost new and current market value is known as *accrued depreciation*. It is *accrued* because the depreciating factors have been at work from the time the building was constructed to the date of the appraisal.

NECESSITY FOR DEPRECIATION ESTIMATE

We have already noted that the largest number of appraisal assignments concern properties that are worth something less than their reproduction cost new. The appraiser is therefore required to estimate the amount by which the cost must be reduced, in order to arrive at a value estimate. This is an essential part of the cost approach. The value of a building may be simply expressed as an equation:

$$\text{Current reproduction cost} - \text{depreciation} = \text{value}$$

If value can be determined more readily by either the market approach or the income approach, the cost approach will generally be unnecessary and inappropriate. The estimate for depreciation will then become a subsidiary matter, not germane to the main problem of estimating value.

However, in a number of cases, sufficient sales or income data will be lacking, requiring the appraiser to fall back upon the cost approach for his value evidence. In these cases it must be recognized that differences exist between cost and value, differences due to several causes which acting together create the effect of depreciation. It is this effect on property value which leads potential buyers and investors to pay less than the reproduction cost for a piece of property.

CAUSES OF DEPRECIATION

Physical Deterioration. Depreciation is an economic effect caused by either physical deterioration, functional obsolescence, economic obsolescence, or a combination of these. Physical deterioration, sometimes referred to as physical depreciation, commonly accounts for only a minor part of the total depreciation in a building. New buildings that are not subject to any physical defects may suffer considerably from the other causes of depreciation. Most buildings, as they age, suffer some value-reducing effects upon their physical qualities, resulting from ordinary use, disintegration, and action of the elements. The degree to which a building is subject to deterioration depends mainly upon the quality of the materials and labor that were put into it, and the degree of maintenance. Deterioration may be normal or minor in a well-constructed building, but, in a poorly constructed one, the normal deterioration will occur much more rapidly, and serious faults in walls, foundations, roof, or floor construction will appear to create great losses in value.

The effects of deterioration may be accelerated by lack of proper maintenance, the presence of adverse chemical elements in the atmosphere, biological hazards such as termites, and any other special hazard or extraordinary condition surrounding the property. Deterioration will be revealed by lumber that swells, shrinks, cracks, warps, or rots as time goes by. It will be revealed by leaking roofs, internal water damage, corroded plumbing lines, cracked plaster, broken steps, and a whole host of physical deficiencies—some easily discernible and others not so—all of which make the property undesirable to potential buyers.

Functional Obsolescence. In spite of the many value-destroying conditions attendant upon physical deterioration, most properties suffer their greatest loss in value from the effects of obsolescence. In its broadest sense, obsolescence is a loss in value for reasons other than physical deterioration. The test of obsolescence is whether or not local demand is sufficiently strong to warrant the cost of reconstruction of a property if it were to be destroyed and then rebuilt with the same design and quality of construction. If market conditions do not warrant such rebuilding, the property is subject to some form of value-reducing obsolescence.

Obsolescence is usually divided into functional absolescence and economic obsolescence. *Functional obsolescence* is the loss in value arising from decreased utility, inadequacy, overcapacity, or changes in architectural style which are inherent in the structure itself. The building may be an overimprovement or an underimprovement; the equipment may be obsolete; the rooms, too small; the ceilings, too high; the light, inadequate; or the architectural plan, style, and design may be poor. Thus, all those items inherent in the structure itself which are not deteriorating but are responsible for a decreased demand or value of a property may be classified as functional obsolescence. Technological improvements creating a similar falloff in demand and utility may also be classified as causes of functional obsolescence.

Economic Obsolescence. *Economic obsolescence* is a loss in value resulting from conditions, outside the building, which adversely affect its character and degree of utilization. It may arise from many factors, the most important of which are listed below:

1. Population movements either reduce the total number of persons interested in owning or renting property, or result in the substitution of persons on a low economic level for persons on a higher level as potential buyers
2. Changes in the consumption habits of the general populace (Amusement and luxury trades are vulnerable to these changes, which make their production facilities either inadequate or overadequate; motion-picture theaters are a prime example of property subject to such obsolescence.)
3. Growth of industrial and commercial areas that, in the absence of adequate zoning, encroach upon residential areas to the detriment of the residential properties
4. Presence of special nuisances and hazards such as excessive noise, smoke, and traffic
5. Proximity to airfields with their noise and danger potentials
6. Deterioration in the quality and accessibility of schools, shopping, and community facilities
7. Deterioration or breakdown in public transportation facilities
8. Excessive level of real estate taxes and assessments
9. Adverse legislation (Rent control is a form of "legislative" obsolescence, artificially holding down the rentals and, hence, the values of controlled properties. A repeal of protective tariffs would adversely affect communities dependent upon protected industries.)

All the factors creating economic or functional obsolescence are easily recognized as elements in lessening demand for properties afflicted with them. The smaller demand is reflected in decreased prices and rentals which the properties can command in competition with newer or similar properties in more desirable neighborhoods. The appraiser's task is to measure the dollar effect of the obsolescence and subtract it from the reproduction cost new to arrive at a market value estimate. If the equation for value was previously "Reproduction cost — deterioration = value," it may now be expanded to read, "Reproduction cost — deterioration — obsolescence = value."

One feature of depreciation should be noted. There is frequently a close interrelationship between obsolescence and deterioration. Decreased rentals from obsolete buildings may preclude proper maintenance and repairs, which in turn may lead to even greater undesirability for the property. Functional deficiencies may lead people to move to more modern quarters, leaving the older properties to be filled by new population groups of a lower economic level who are not able, or do not care, to maintain the properties as they should be maintained. But, regardless of the conditions that cause depreciation to take its toll of the value of real estate, once the process has begun, it is difficult to arrest, and it only becomes a matter of time before the building is torn down. In fact, most buildings do not fall down by deterioration; they are torn down by obsolescence.

INSPECTING THE PROPERTY

Most of the conditions that create differences between cost and value having been identified, the fundamental problem remains. It is simply to determine a method whereby all of these adverse social, physical, and economic factors can be quantified into a dollar amount to be deducted from reproduction cost new. In order to do this with a reasonable degree of accuracy, the appraiser must place himself in the position of the potential buyers and evaluate the property from their point of view. The first step in this procedure is to make a thorough inspection of the building and its surroundings.

A physical inspection of the building should be carried out in a planned fashion with a checklist of items to be observed. The inspection of a residential building might start with a survey of the neighborhood, to determine whether the location will meet the requirements of the average user or investor. In considering residential properties, the appraiser should check the convenience of transportation and shopping facilities; location and reputation of schools; absence of excessive traffic noise, smoke, or unpleasant odors; recreation facilities; police and fire protection available; and whether or not adequate zoning protection is provided.

After inspection of the neighborhood, the plot should be examined to determine whether the size is satisfactory to potential buyers. Consideration should also be given to drainage topography, ease of access to garage, condition of lawns and view.

The appraiser may next turn his attention to the exterior details of the building to determine if it is as good as, or better than, typical properties offered for sale in the area, and how it compares with new dwellings. The conditions of porches, terraces, garage, gutters, storm sash, windows, screens, siding, roofing, chimney, exterior paint, doors, etc., should be noted carefully.

In examining interior construction and detail, the chief consideration should also be to determine whether the property will afford living conditions and amenities sufficient to the needs of typical buyers or renters. Here the factors to be observed are the size of the rooms; number of closets; access to, and number of, bathrooms; sufficiency of storage space; arrangement of kitchen space; adequacy of light and air; and number of electrical outlets.

After notation of the above items, the interior is examined to see if the plaster is free of excessive cracks and stains caused by leaking roofs and sidewalls; if the windows move freely; if the fireplace, if any, works properly; if the basement is dry and will resist moisture penetration; if the heating and mechanical equipment are in good working order; if there is adequate insulation in the walls, floor, ceiling, and roof. In addition to these items, the floor finish, sink top, kitchen range, bathroom fixtures, painting or papering, and exposed joists and beams should be examined to determine whether they are in acceptable condition.

The detailed physical inspection indicated above is necessary for the appraiser to make realistic depreciation deductions for the property. If deficiencies show up in the inspection, an estimate of the cost to cure the faults provides a good guide to the dollar amount of depreciation to be charged against the property. In this respect, physical deterioration lends itself to a closer estimate than does economic or functional obsolescence. So many of the items that make up obsolescence do not lend themselves to be cured that it becomes more difficult to estimate their effect on the ultimate market value of the property. For this reason, it is preferable to make separate estimates of physical deterioration and obsolescence.

METHODS OF MEASUREMENT

Since the reason for measuring depreciation is to make a deduction from reproduction cost in order to arrive at an estimate of market value, it follows that no method of depreciation estimating is valid unless it is consistent with the values expressed in the market place for comparable properties. This points up an interesting paradox. The ultimate measure of depreciation is found in the prices paid by investors for similar properties and in the comparison of these prices with prices paid for similar new properties. But this kind of analysis is simply part of the sales approach. If value can be found by this approach, or even by the income approach, no purpose is served by trying to measure depreciation and obsolescence. Why then do appraisers concern themselves with this problem at all? Primarily because, as has been previously indicated, there is no choice. The sales and income data are frequently insufficient for the appraisal problem, and some method must be found to make a value estimate. Secondly, the estimate of reproduction cost new less depreciation becomes a correlating and sustaining element in an appraisal based on sales and income data where those data are recognized as highly subjective and open to criticism.

Most of the methods used to measure depreciation may be classified as either mathematical or non-mathematical processes. The mathematical methods have been adopted from the accounting profession, whose fundamental purpose in depreciation calculation is to charge off the costs of physical assets over the years they are in use. Thus the purpose of the accountants and that of the appraisers are completely dissimilar. One profession is interested in original costs and their recovery; the other is interested in estimating current market value.

Straight-Line Method. The simplest and most commonly used method of measuring depreciation is known as the *straight-line method*. This method assumes a constant decline in the value of property. The rate of decline is expressed as a percentage of reproduction cost and is found by dividing the property's estimated economic life in years into the estimated cumulative depreciation in per cent at the end of its economic life. If the total estimated cumulative depreciation is estimated at 100 per cent and the estimated economic life is estimated at fifty years, the rate of depreciation is 2 per cent per annum (Depreciation rate $(R) = 100\%/50 = 2\%$ per annum). The use of this method requires a knowledge of estimated economic lives of typical properties, which can be acquired either from personal experience or by using tables of life expectancies. The most widely used table is that found in Bulletin "F," prepared and published by the Bureau of Internal Revenue in 1948 and revised in 1962. The table in the earlier publication[1] (reproduced here as Table 7) sets forth reasonable composite rates of depreciation, including equipment, that may be used to compute straight-line depreciation for income-tax purposes.

Where building equipment is set up separately for depreciation purposes, the Bureau suggests that the composite rate not be used but that the appropriate rate be determined by reference to a table of useful lives, such as Table 8, which is for buildings of standard or sound construction.

It should be noted that the higher rates depicted in Table 7 are due primarily to the fact that they include items of building equipment which have a shorter life than the building itself. Schedules for the average useful life, in years, of equipment items are also presented in Bulletin "F."

The revision of Bulletin "F," entitled *Depreciation Guidelines and Rules,*[2] was issued by the Treasury Department in July, 1962. Under the new rules,

---

[1] *Income Tax Depreciation and Obsolescence Estimated Useful Lives and Depreciation Rates,* U.S. Treasury Department, Bureau of Internal Revenue Bulletin "F" (Washington, D.C.: Government Printing Office, 1948).

[2] *Depreciation Guidelines and Rules,* U.S. Treasury Department, Internal Revenue Service, Publication No. 456 (July 1962), published by Government Printing Office, Washington, D.C.

TABLE 7
Composite Rates of Depreciation (per cent), by Type of Construction

Building	Good	Average	Cheap
Apartments	2½	2½	3
Banks	2	2	2½
Dwellings	2	2½	3
Factories	2¼	2½	3
Farm buildings	2	2	2½
Garages	2	2½	3
Grain elevators	1½	2	2½
Hotels	2½	2½	3
Loft buildings	2	2	3
Machine shops	2	2½	3
Office buildings	2	2½	3
Stores	2	2	2½
Theaters	2½	3	3½
Warehouses	1½	2	2½

TABLE 8
Total Life (years)

Apartments	50	Hotels	50
Banks	67	Loft buildings	67
Dwellings	60	Machine shops	60
Factories	50	Office buildings	67
Farm buildings	60	Stores	67
Garages	60	Theaters	50
Grain elevators	75	Warehouses	75

TABLE 9
Useful Lives for Building Types (years)

Apartments	40	Loft buildings	50
Banks	50	Machine shops	45
Dwellings	45	Office buildings	45
Factories	45	Stores	50
Garages	45	Theaters	40
Grain elevators	60	Warehouses	60
Hotels	40		

most of the building equipment is included under the over-all-useful-life, or composite, rate, and the new composite rates show reductions in useful lives for six of the categories found in Table 8. The new revised rules with composite useful lives are indicated in Table 9.

The application of this method is fairly simple: Assume a ten-year-old building with a current reproduction cost of $20,000 and an estimated economic life of fifty years. The rate of depreciation is 100%/50, or 2 per cent per annum. Total accrued depreciation is 2 per cent × 10 years, or 20 per cent. The value of the building is calculated as $20,000 — $4,000 (20 per cent of $20,000), or $16,000.

A variation of the straight-line method is known as *broken-line* depreciation calculation. Under this method, the procedure is to depreciate the building at one rate for a given number of years and then to use another rate, higher or lower, for the balance of the economic life. If a 1½ per cent rate is used for the first twenty years and a 2⅓ per cent rate is used for the next thirty years, a cumulative total of 100 per cent for the fifty-year period will be arrived at. The use of lower or higher rates will usually depend upon the appraiser's judgment based on his observations of the depreciation behavior of various types of buildings.

A further variant of the straight-line method substitutes the "effective" age for the physical age in calculating the depreciation deduction. A property may have been built twenty years ago, but on examination the appraiser notes that, owing to good care and maintenance, it is as good as a ten-year-old property of the same type in the area. If the rate of depreciation, as indicated in the example previously presented, is taken as 2 per cent per annum, the twenty-year-old property is given an effective age of ten and the total depreciation is calculated at 20 per cent, just as it would be for a ten-year-old building. Conversely, if the building had been poorly maintained, it is possible that the appraiser would see fit to give it an effective age of thirty years, with a consequent increased depreciation deduction.

Declining Balance Method. The *declining balance* method, or *reducing balance* method, assumes no finite economic life to a piece of property. Throughout its interminable lifetime, the property is assumed to decline in value each year by a fixed percentage of the reproduction cost less accumulated depreciation. To illustrate: Assume that a $20,000 building is depreciating at the rate of 2 per cent each year.

At the end of the first year depreciation is	$400.00 ($20,000 × .02)
Capital balance becomes	$19,600
At the end of the second year depreciation is	$392.00 ($19,600 × .02)
Capital balance becomes	$19,218
At the end of the third year depreciation is	$384.36 ($19,218 × .02)
Capital balance becomes	$18,833.64

The depreciated value of a property after any given period of time can be calculated by the formula

$$\text{Per cent condition} = (1 - r)^n$$

in which

r = the rate of depreciation per annum

n = the age of the property

The declining balance method is chiefly used as an accounting device for income-tax purposes, as liberalized rates of depreciation are provided under recent federal tax statutes to encourage building construction. Few, appraisers use this method in their appraisal work, and those that do usually confine its use to commercial and industrial buildings.

Other Mathematical Methods. Several other mathematical methods of calculating depreciation are known to appraisers. In one method, called the *sum-of-the-year's-digits* method, the depreciation rate for a given year is a fraction whose numerator is the actual age of the building and whose denominator is computed by adding the numbers 1 to 50, if the building is expected to have a total service life of 50 years. For purposes of illustration, assume a building with an expected economic life of 5 years. The sum of the digits 1, 2, 3, 4, and 5 is 15—the denominator. For the first year the depreciation rate is $\frac{1}{15}$; for the second year it is $\frac{2}{15}$; for the third year it is $\frac{3}{15}$; for the fourth year it is $\frac{4}{15}$; and for the fifth year it is $\frac{5}{15}$. At the end of the fifth year, $\frac{15}{15}$, or 100 per cent, depreciation has been accounted for. Sometimes the procedure is reversed and the numerator in each year is taken to be equal to the remaining life expectancy.

Other methods such as the sinking-fund and annuity methods, in which accrued depreciation increases more rapidly as the property ages, are of more interest to accountants than to appraisers. Neither of these methods, nor the sum-of-the-year's digits method, is ever used with any frequency by appraisers in applying the cost approach.

Non-mathematical Methods. Mathematical methods lend themselves to ease in calculating accrued depreciation. However, central to their use is the concept of a relationship between the age of a building and its market value. Experience has indicated that this basic idea is fallacious and extremely dangerous to use. In addition, many buildings whose ages have long since exceeded the expected service lives are still standing and are performing a useful and valuable function. A study of over 1,000 residential buildings, undertaken by the city of Somerville, Massachusetts, in 1950,[3] clearly indicated the fallacy of accepting mathematical methods for calculating accrued depreciation. By comparing the market value of these properties each year for thirty- to forty-year periods, it was demonstrated conclusively that there was no relationship between age and rate of depreciation.

A method of calculating depreciation widely advocated and used by appraisers is known as the *cost to cure,* or *observed condition,* method.

[3] Charles R. Brunelle, *A Study of Depreciation,* published by the *Review* of the Society of Residential Appraisers, Chicago, December 1950.

In this method, the appraiser is required to carefully inspect the property and to prepare separate estimates of the following:

1. Physical deterioration—curable
2. Physical deterioration—incurable
3. Functional obsolescence—curable
4. Functional obsolescence—incurable
5. Economic obsolescence

The difference between a curable and an incurable factor lies chiefly in the economic feasibility of undertaking to cure one or more of these depreciating factors. The estimate of "physical deterioration—curable" is derived from a physical inspection of the property and a listing of the costs of those items that need repair or replacement. The costs of making the repairs and replacements are equated with the discounts which buyers place on properties when comparing them with new or other properties in the area.

The estimate of "physical deterioration—incurable" is based on those items that are not generally economically replaceable during the life of the building. These usually include the foundation and framework of the building. The usual procedure is to allocate an amount for depreciation equal to the ratio of the effective age of the building over its normal economic life to the reproduction cost new of these items. For example, in a building with an effective age of ten years and a normal service life of fifty years, a reproduction cost new of $200,000 is established; the foundation and framework amount to 50 per cent of the cost, or $100,000; the amount for "physical depreciation—incurable" would be $10/50 \times \$100,000$, or $20,000.

The estimate of "functional obsolescence—curable" is based on the cost of removing all deficiencies in the plan, style, or equipment of the building which cause it to lose value. They include such items as modernizing kitchens, bath, and electrical systems and installation of air conditioning. The cost of replacing all the outmoded items is totaled to an estimate of "functional obsolescence—curable."

The estimate of "functional obsolescence—incurable" is usually based on the value loss arising from deficiencies in the building which are not economic to replace. Such items as small bedrooms, inadequate closets, poor bathroom layout, and excessive ceiling heights, are examples of this type of deficiency. The presence of these items usually leads to a rental loss when the property is compared with newer properties that are free from them. By capitalizing the rental loss into capital value, the amount of "functional obsolescence—incurable" may be estimated. By way of illustration: If apartment houses in a certain area are selling at five times the gross rent roll, and the property under appraisal is suffering a rental loss of

$1,000 per annum owing to its functional deficiencies that are not curable, the amount of functional obsolescence could be calculated at 5 × $1,000, or $5,000. Functional obsolescence is not characteristic of older buildings solely. Frequently, builders and architects will plan a building to maximize the number of rooms or other rentable units. In doing so, they may skimp on closet space or create poor layouts which translate themselves into unanticipated rent reductions or concessions in order to fill the building with tenants.

The estimate of "economic obsolescence" is based on the loss of value due to neighborhood or extrinsic factors surrounding the property. This loss can also be measured by capitalizing the loss in rents due solely to these factors, if the property were considered cured of the physical and functionally obsolete factors. Thus, if the property cited above would bring a rent roll of $10,000 per annum in a better neighborhood, but commands a rent roll now of only $8,000, then, assuming that properties are being sold on a basis of five times the gross rent roll, economic obsolescence would total 5 × $2,000, or $10,000. This total would include obsolescence of the entire property, land and building. Therefore, the appraiser would have to allocate the loss in value in accord with the ratio of land and building value to total value in the area for this type of property. This is necessary, owing to the fact that the land value has already been determined, as the first step in the cost approach, by comparison with the value of land used for the same purpose in other neighborhoods. Theoretically, the lower land unit values due to economic obsolescence are reflected in the land sales and, therefore, the penalty for obsolescence has already been taken. If we were then to take the capitalized value of the rent loss and charge it to the property as a whole, we would in effect be penalizing the land twice. If we determine that the land ratio is 1 to 5 in this area, that is, 20 per cent of the value is in the land, and that the total economic obsolescence is $10,000, we may attribute $2,000 to the land and $8,000 to the building. Only the $8,000 item would be included in our calculations.

After making all the separate estimates, the appraiser adds them up to arrive at a total estimate of accrued depreciation which he will deduct from the reproduction cost to give an estimate of the market value of the building.

PROBLEMS OF MEASURING DEPRECIATION

Some of the problems of measuring depreciation have already been indicated. An attempt to make deductions for deterioration and obsolescence shifts the basis of value from the market reactions of buyers to an "intrinsic worth" of the property. But real estate in and of itself does not have value. Appraisals can only be significant if they respect market action. Thus we come to a dead end. The significant measurement of depreciation can only be found in the market place, which leads the appraiser back to the sales-comparison approach.

Another problem presents itself in the case of buildings whose age is greater than indicated by normal life-expectancy tables. In static, residential areas such as those found in certain parts of New England, building ages bear no relationship to value, and in fact they can increase in value with age.

Usual Methods Used by Realty Appraisers. Most appraisers use either of two methods. The first combines the use of scheduled tables of depreciation, usually on a straight-line basis, with a close observation of the property. Thus, the appraiser thinks of properties in terms of "effective" or "comparative" age rather than chronological age. In this way, a building, no matter how old, can be given an "appraisal age." This method is undoubtedly more accurate than a sole dependence upon schedules of depreciation.

The second method attempts to measure depreciation by the cost to cure physical deficiencies, as one aspect of the problem, and to add the loss in rental value due to obsolescent factors, as a further deduction. This is a more time-consuming and more persuasive method and may be more accurate than the first method, if great care and skill are exercised.

Some Practical Suggestions. In the appraisal of older buildings, the problem of measuring depreciation accurately and convincingly is apt to prove to be an insurmountable obstacle. Wherever possible, the sales or income approach should be relied upon. If the cost approach must be used, as with institutional or specialty buildings, separate estimates should be made for physical deterioration and for obsolescence, based upon observation and inspection. Since these buildings ordinarily do not sell, the prime consideration to their owners is the cost of replacing the function. What appraiser is capable of making an estimate of depreciation for a 200-year-old church? It may very well be that depreciation should not even be considered in those properties where use and not market value is the dominant factor.

If scheduled depreciation tables are used, different schedules should be applied to buildings with different locations, structural characteristics, uses, and different conditions of maintenance.

It must be recognized that the amount of depreciation attaching to a property may vary from 0 to 100 per cent regardless of age, and that ultimately depreciation estimates can only be tested by actions of buyers and sellers.

15

Re-examining the Approaches and Writing the Report

The discussion of the three approaches to value should not obscure the fact that essentially they should be considered as interrelated components of a single process designed to produce a value conclusion for a specific purpose. Each approach contains diverse elements which if woven into an over-all picture will produce a correlated estimate of value.

Appraisers have, in the past, tended to regard the appraisal process from the point of view of three separate approaches or of one or two approaches. Many appraisers have paid "lip service" to the concept of three approaches, with frequent fanciful results. Others, like Babcock or McMichael, have maintained that one or perhaps two approaches would suffice for any particular appraisal problem.

Only recently have appraisers come to recognize that the soundest approach to a correlated value estimate is a unified approach that reflects the prices at which property changes hands, the ability and willingness of buyers and tenants to pay the costs of creating and operating real estate, the rate and terms of mortgage money, and the potential yield from competitive investment opportunities.

CORRELATING THE APPROACHES

Methods Used. The problem of correlation is twofold. On the one hand, it involves a re-examination of the specific data pertinent to each approach as an entity; on the other, it requires a logical coordination of the data derived from all the approaches.

We have observed that each approach presents difficult problems for the appraiser. The sales-comparison approach, in theory the best, is limited by the heterogeneous nature of real estate as a commodity, the imperfect market conditions, and the frequent need for making subjective value adjustments, even where market data are available. The cost approach, well suited for new properties with no depreciation and with known costs, is seriously limited in its application to the bulk of older properties by the problems arising in measuring depreciation. The income approach involves sensitive estimates of an income stream, both in amount and duration; determination of a capitalization rate; a reversion estimate; and provision for recapture of investment.

How to analyze and interpret all the often contradictory data flowing from each of the three approaches and organize them into a unified conclusion is the prime challenge facing the appraiser. So much is tenuous and subjective in appraisal procedure that it requires expert judgment and specific knowledge to produce a logical and convincing value estimate.

Most of the difficulties encountered by appraisers arise from the attempt to treat each of the three approaches as an independent road to a value estimate. Frequently, three separate estimates will be derived. In an effort to reconcile the differences, a "zone of reasonableness" is established. At one end is the low value estimate, and at the other is the high estimate. The appraiser then proceeds to review his data, his mathematics, his emphasis, etc., in an effort to narrow the zone as much as possible. This technique, which has become known as "forcing an equivalence," is unfortunate. In actual practice, the appraiser has decided to lean on one of the three available approaches, and most of the revisions take place in the other approaches so that the desired result is reached. A slight change in the capitalization rate, in the depreciation estimate, or in the adjustments of sales prices of comparable properties is often the method used to correlate the estimates.

To some extent, much of this procedure can be avoided if only one approach is relied upon. But in this case, some room for doubt exists if the appraiser gave serious thought to all the aspects of the appraisal problem. If the income approach is relied upon as the sole criterion, does the result exceed an amount for which the property could readily be reproduced? If the market approach is the one method used, does the result indicate a justified or warranted value? Or is it merely a reflection of a temporary market condition? If the cost approach is the method, does cost really reflect value? Is there built-in obsolescence that has not been accounted for?

Basis for Correlation. In order to evaluate the data derived in each of the three approaches, the appraiser must rely upon his specific knowledge and his judgment. The starting point depends upon the purpose of the appraisal and the type of property. The purpose of the appraisal will indicate the type of ownership that can be expected, the nature of the benefits to be derived from ownership, and the applicable value concept.

Most appraisals are market-value appraisals. Therefore, the appraiser must be thoroughly familiar with the sales, offers, and bids that are current in the market. He must know the breadth of the market, and the financing available for the prospective purchasers. He must know the average exposure the property must have before a sale can be made, and on what terms. He must know the discounts and premium factors that typical buyers consider. He must be familiar with the areas in which activity is greatest, and what the prevaling trends of values are. He must be familiar with current replacement costs, with expected equity rates of return, and with average lengths of ownership. The accumulation of these facts is a continuous process and represents the real stock in trade of the appraiser.

The acquisition of specific knowledge, gained by experience and study, acts to limit the areas where judgment is relied upon. The use of judgment should be reserved for the selection of the facts and comparisons that will affect the valuation result. Anyone can give an opinion of value; but few can give an opinion that will stand the test of logic and knowledge.

Suggested Procedure. We have already indicated that the starting point in testing the reliability of the approach rests with a consideration of the purpose of the appraisal. The appraisal of one-family homes requires a knowledge of prices paid and replacement costs. Where there is an active market without undue pressure to buy or sell, and where prices and costs are in line, then undoubtedly the sales-comparison approach will provide the greatest reliability. The relatively large size of the residential market enables the appraiser to place great weight on this approach. However, there are very few other properties which enjoy such an active market with significant comparatives, and, hence, value evidence from the other approaches must be brought into play.

Appraisals that are made for other than "market value," such as fire-insurance appraisals, going-concern-value appraisals, owner-occupied or institutional appraisals will rely heavily on the cost approach. It is the appraisal of investment properties that affords an opportunity for a *correlated* estimate in the true sense of the word.

Such a correlated estimate would proceed first with an estimate of the physical value of the property, land and building. Land value would be determined on the basis of comparable sales, and the building value, on the basis of reproduction cost minus depreciation based on observed cost to cure procedures. A capitaliaztion rate based on physical value could be obtained by dividing the estimated average net income for the projected term of ownership by the physical value. The next step would involve a study of sales of competitive and comparative properties. Gross income multipliers and net-to-gross income ratios would then be studied for these properties. By division of the net income ratio by the gross income multiplier, a capitalization rate could be obtained for each of the properties in the analysis. A high, a low, and a composite rate should be indicated. By selection of a rate within the range, one that is consistent not only with the sales but also with the physical value, a correlation is established for two of the methods. The final step would be an income valuation based on the correlated rate with an analysis to show prospective yields that would attract an investor to the property.

A procedure that follows the outline described above will result in a situation that has been described as follows:

When appraised value is reasonably close to the ceiling represented by a well document physical summation and, at the same time is not only supported by sales but is also shown by analysis to provide for investment yields that will attract purchase capital at time of appraisal, we have a correlated appraisal. We also have a value from which there can be little divergence without resorting to false premise.[1]

It is interesting to note that, for income properties, the selection of a proper capitalization rate determined by the market factors makes possible a correlated appraisal.

The Unified Approach. The re-examination of the approaches does not mean a procedure whereby the data will be "forced" into a mold. All too frequently, the necessary information relating to sales, costs, depreciation, equity rates, etc., is simply not available to enable the appraiser to produce an integrated appraisal. In those cases, he must work with what he has, relying on both the information and the knowledge of his own that seems most appropriate to the appraisal problem at hand.

Where, however, sufficient information is available, the preferred approach is the unified approach suggested at the beginning of this chapter. It is this approach that truly reflects the market in all its aspects—sales, costs, mortgage terms and rates, and investment yields.

WRITING THE APPRAISAL REPORT

After the three approaches are correlated and a value has been arrived at, the appraiser may write his draft of the appraisal report. An appraisal report is basically a business report; therefore, it should conform to all the tenets of good business-report writing. However, it is also a technical report whose form and content are dictated by the requirements of the appraisal assignment. Any type of report, whether business or technical, must be well written and conform to the practices of good writing and grammar usage. However, it is not the purpose of this chapter to explore these matters. The purpose is to emphasize those aspects of good business and technical writing which must be considered in the preparation of a professional-quality appraisal report.

[1] L. W. Ellwood, *Ellwood Tables For Real Estate Appraising and Financing* (Ridgewood, N.J.: published by the author, 1959), p. 50.

The Qualities of Any Good Report. THE THREE C's. An appraisal report is basically a business report devoted to explaining the processes and data used in reaching a single conclusion. For this reason, the first requirement for such a report is that it be *clearly* written so that the reader can follow each step leading from tentative hypotheses to final conclusion. As each new idea is introduced, the reader should understand why it was introduced, what it contributes to the final conclusion, and where it fits in with the other materials presented. The need for clarity must not be confused with verbosity. A huge collection of words does not produce clarity; therefore, a report should contain a minimum of words. The typical report reader does not have the time to read through a great deal of extraneous material before he gets to the heart of the report, so *conciseness* is a second important characteristic of a good report. Finally, the reader should be able to reconstruct each step of the process which leads to the final conclusion, in order that he may judge for himself the reasonableness of the conclusion. If important data or steps in reasoning are omitted, the reader will challenge the validity of the conclusions; therefore, the final requirement for a report is that it be *complete*.

LOGICAL ORGANIZATION. An often repeated admonition to speakers is that they must tell their audience what they are going to say, say what they have to say, and then summarize what they have said. This applies particularly to the appraisal report. Previous chapters have emphasized the need for identifying immediately the purpose of an appraisal, and this same precept applies to the appraisal report. The reason for undertaking the report should be presented first, followed by a brief summary of the principal findings. The main body of data and reasoning used in reaching the value estimate follow next, and a final statement as to what was decided should conclude the report.

The main body of material can be presented basically in two ways. In the first, or inductive, method the various data relating to the appraisal are first presented in detail and then the reader is led through these data to the final conclusion. In the second, or deductive, method the principal conclusions about the factors influencing the value estimate are presented and then supported with summaries of the more pertinent data. Any other materials are placed at the rear of the report, to be referred to by the reader if he so desires. Neither of these methods can be considered to be superior to the other: The method used must be fitted to the type of reader using the report.

OBJECTIVITY. An appraisal estimate is based to a large degree upon the personal experience and judgment of the appraiser, but this fact should not be allowed to intrude upon the reader throughout the report. A report should normally be written with a very minimum use of any type of personal pronoun. Data and descriptive matter, particularly, should be presented in a straightforward reportorial style of writing which moves smoothly into the conclusion. At the end of the report, when the appraiser finally must indicate that it is on his judgment that the conclusion is based, the personal pronoun may be introduced sparingly and naturally. For example, many reports are dotted with the phrase "in your appraiser's judgment. . . ." Such references should be minimized or eliminated, and the conclusion should read, "in my judgment. . . ."

Technical Terminology. The experienced appraiser rarely realizes the degree to which obscure technical terminology exists in the field of appraising, and so he is prone to use such words or phrases as "depreciation," "economic life," "highest and best use," "capital recovery," and others, without explaining their meaning. Even experienced real estate investors or brokers may not understand fully the implications of these words; therefore, good report-writing procedure requires that the first time a technical term is introduced it should be fully defined. This procedure should probably be followed even in reports to be read by technically competent persons, because of the degree to which there is divergence of opinion within the appraising fraternity as to the meaning of many commonly used technical words. Perhaps the most outstanding example is the word "value."

Non-verbal Communication. Written words are perhaps the most difficult type of communication used and probably require the greatest amount of time and space of any means of communication in the presentation of an idea. For example, a full page might be used to describe the boundaries and streets within a neighborhood, when this same information could be conveyed more accurately, easily, and completely by means of a map. For this reason an appraisal report should be well supported by graphs, charts, tables of figures, pictures, maps, and plots plans, rather than volumes of words. These devices are particularly effective in supporting involved or difficult word descriptions or analyses. A great deal might be written about the contents of a statement of income and expenses in the appraisal of an apartment house, but a well-prepared financial-type statement would make the words more meaningful.

Steps in Report Preparation. A very effective device for producing a top-quality report is to plan the work carefully before a single word of the final draft is written. The first step in the planning is to define carefully the purpose of the report; a second step is to plan how the problem of proving the value estimate should be solved; a third step is to assemble in the form of tables, charts, and graphs all data which will lead to the solution of the problem; and a final step is to prepare a detailed outline with the first sentence of each paragraph already written. Then, and only then, will the report writing proceed quickly and naturally, resulting in a clear, concise, complete report.

TYPES OF APPRAISAL REPORTS

The American Institute of Real Estate Appraisers has required the submission of what they term "demonstration" reports as a part of their admission requirements for many years, so their admissions committee has had to develop suggestions as to what it believes should be included in such reports. Their latest suggestions on report writing provide an effective guide for any appraiser. Most appraisers would protest that the requirements for a demonstration report are much more inclusive than those for the typical assignment and they are probably correct. However, an appraiser must always anticipate that he may have need to refer to any of his finished reports at any time for purposes of court testimony, conferences with clients, or the preparation of other reports. For this reason, the elements of a demonstration report should always be included in the appraiser's work sheets from which the finished report is written, even though the final report may consist of only a single page. In this way, the appraiser can reconstruct easily and quickly the steps which led to any value estimate he may have made.

Format and Size. In contrast to the rather complete, narrative-type report which the Institute expects (and which will be discussed in later paragraphs) are the many briefer types of reports which are rather widely used. For example agencies such as the Federal Housing Administration, banks, savings and loan associations, and insurance companies that need a high volume of reports as a basis for their lending operations have developed brief standard forms which they expect the appraiser to complete. Nothing more in the form of a report is expected of the appraiser. Some appraisers follow the practice of submitting only their conclusions in the form of a letter inviting the client to discuss any of the details or supporting data at any time he wishes. Other appraisers may go a bit further and submit a short report which contains the conclusions and some of the more pertinent data. The extensive narrative reports comparable to the demonstration reports required by the Institute are normally prepared for more expensive properties or when the client has special need for such a report.

The format and length of the report are determined by what the client needs and asks for. The size of a report has nothing to do with either the validity of the conclusions or the quality of the work completed in making the estimate. The final estimate is not more accurate or worthwhile because it is supported by a lengthy report. The data on which the estimates are based and the experience and judgment which the appraiser brings to bear on the estimate are the elements which give the estimate validity. The purpose of the report is to convince the reader that these elements were a vital part of the process which led to the final conclusion on value.

The Narrative Report. The narrative type of report recommended by the American Institute of Real Estate Appraisers consists of four basic sections (1) the introductory materials, (2) the descriptive information, (3) the analytical processes, and (4) judgment matters and conclusion. A typical outline follows:

Table of Contents For A Complete Narrative Report

EXHIBITS

A. Maps of the City and Area—Population Centers, Use, Occupancy
B. Economic Data Tables
C. Photographs of the Area
D. Leases and other Pertinent Legal Items

INTRODUCTORY MATERIALS. The first page of a narrative report is usually a title page which identifies the type of property, its street address, the date of the report, the person for whom the report was prepared, and the name and address of the appraiser who is submitting the report.

The second page is the letter of transmittal, which indicates the authority for undertaking the appraisal, a legal description of the property and rights to be appraised, the purpose, the definition of value used, the conclusion about the dollar amount, the date to which the appraisal applies, and the appraiser's signature.

The table of contents follows next, indicating the pages on which the principal parts of the report begin.

A summary page then follows, in which are set forth important data identifying the property and stating its tax value, the value estimates according to each of the three approaches to value, and the final value estimate reached. Some appraisers use this page to summarize in a single sentence what will be found in each of the major sections of the report.

An appraiser may prefer to follow the summary page with statements on assumptions and limiting conditions which prevailed in the estimating process, and his qualifications. Others prefer to place these materials in the addenda materials. In any case they should be included.

The assumptions and limiting conditions statement usually indicates such things as

1. The title is assumed to be free and clear.
2. The legal description as furnished is correct, as are other data gathered from sources assumed to be reliable.
3. Any sketches or diagrams furnished are for purposes of visualization only.
4. The report is for the exclusive use of the client unless he indicates otherwise.
5. Court testimony or other appearances are not required in connection with the report unless arrangements have been made for these.
6. No warranty is given as to matters which could be established by survey of the property.
7. The Institute particularly urges that a statement of caution be included about using the separate valuations for land and building which are used in some of the approaches to value.

A person reading the report is always interested in knowing what the qualifications of the appraiser are, because experience and judgment are essential in the appraisal estimate. For this reason, a page should be included, preferably in the introductory section, which sets forth the types of experience and education which qualified the appraiser.

DESCRIPTIVE INFORMATION. An appraiser may collect a great deal of descriptive material in order to estimate the impact of environment on the subject property, but only a sufficient amount of this material should be included in the report to make the final conclusion sound reasonable. Among the descriptive materials included are

1. Additional and complete legal designation of the property
2. The purpose of the report and a full definition of the value term used
3. The quantity and quality of rights being appraised
4. A brief history of the ownership and use of the property
5. Economic background information on the nation, region, state, and urban area insofar as these are applicable
6. Detailed statements on the neighborhood characteristics
7. Conclusions with respect to the highest and best use of the property, based upon description of the zoning, deed restrictions, covenants, easements, assessments, taxes, and other legal limitations which might affect the use of the property
8. Detailed descriptions of the size of the property and its physical and functional characteristics including both the site and any improvements or buildings on the site

ANALYTIC PROCESSES. With the presentation of descriptive matters completed, the appraiser is ready to use these items in reaching conclusions about the value. He, therefore, presents the cost approach, setting forth analyses of the land value, the improvements values, and his conclusion as to the summarized value under the cost approach. Next he presents the comparative-sales approach, setting forth analyses of comparable properties, market conditions and terms, and the impact of these conclusions on the subject property. Finally, he presents the income-capitalization approach, indicating his analyses of the gross income, the deductions made from gross income, the allocation of net earnings to buildings and land, capitalization rates, and methods by which he used the capitalization rates to establish a value estimate.

JUDGMENT MATTERS. The appraiser must present his final estimate as a single dollar amount; therefore, he must now review his appraisal efforts and use his best judgment in correlating the estimates established by the three approaches into a single dollar estimate. There may be rare occasions when the appraiser can present his final estimate as a range of values, but normally he cannot escape the need for using his best judgment in establishing a single dollar amount.

The appraiser must indicate that he has been impartial in his conclusions, basing his estimate entirely on the data and his experience. It is recommended that a certification be used to the effect that he personally inspected the property; that he has no personal interest in the property, nor is his remuneration based upon his reaching a particular conclusion, nor is it related to the amount he finally estimates; that his statements of fact are correct according to the best of his knowledge and the limiting conditions set forth; and, finally, if he is a member of a professional organization, that the appraisal was completed according to the standards and ethics of the organization of which he is a member. This certification may stand alone in the report or it may be included as a part of the letter of transmittal.

ADDENDA. A value estimate is always based upon a review of a great deal of data and information, and, as the report is prepared, many drawings, diagrams, and photos may be assembled. These items often have no direct bearing on the actual estimate but would be of great assistance to the reader in following the main body of the report. For this reason the addendum usually includes additional tables of supporting data, maps, photographs, plot and floor plans, and résumés of leases, deeds, contracts, and other items which influenced the appraiser in reaching his final conclusions on value.

THE APPRAISAL PLANT

The majority of professional appraisers find the maintenance of a plant or library a necessary part of their daily operations. Such plants include old reports, market data, property information, economic and business information, reference materials on technical matters, and maps. The size of the plant and the kinds of materials maintained relate to the kinds of work in which he is most frequently engaged. The maintenance of these items in usable condition is costly, so such plants are kept at a minimum. Normally, the bulk of the items will consist of cross-classified old reports which permit access to data which will aid in the preparation of new reports, maps, and ownership information.

The necessity of maintaining a large plant is considerably reduced if the appraiser has easy access to a public library, technical libraries, and public records. In the absence of such access, the plant will also include trade journals on technical appraisal matters; books on appraising, real estate economics, and related subject areas; market and sales data; and the most useful business market letters and analyses.

AN EVALUATION OF APPRAISAL REPORTS

The most important characteristic of a competent professional appraiser is his ability to reach sound value judgments from an orderly consideration of factual materials. The principal means available to such an appraiser for demonstrating his competence is through his reports. If he fails to prepare his reports so that a reader can follow the chain of reasoning leading from observations to conclusions, the reputation of the appraiser suffers and the reader remains unconvinced. The appraiser must learn to lead the reader slowly from the statement of what had to be done, through the various data which provided insight into possible conclusions, to the final conclusions which the judgment of the appraiser indicated were warranted.

Many appraisal reports include pages filled with population, employment, and other economic statistics. No comment and analysis indicates how this information was utilized to aid the appraiser in forming an opinion of value.

Similarly, appraisers often list property sales and rentals without any indication of how they relate to the value of the subject realty. Unfortunately, this information is often included merely to demonstrate that the appraiser assembled data. Often a thorough analysis of the listed sales by the reader will show that they were not closely comparable to the subject realty or the value indicated by the appraiser.

In effect, every time an appraiser writes a conclusion, he should be prepared to say, "Here are the data which I considered before reaching a conclusion. These are the various conclusions which I might have reached from viewing the data. This is the conclusion which I accepted, and this is why I believe it to be the best one." If an appraiser does this, he educates his clients on the complexities of the appraisal process and the contribution which an experienced appraiser makes. In return, the client can say, "I understand what he did and why he did it, and I believe his conclusions to be the best in the light of my problem and the data available for solving it."

Although an appraisal report is prepared for a specific client, it may receive rather wide reading. This is particularly true when the client is a corporate organization or a government agency. Many of these readers will be keenly interested in the conclusions but will not have the necessary appraisal background to follow complex details. These readers will, however, be experienced business managers, lawyers, engineers, and others of equal competence who can pierce through a meaningless jumble of words to detect bluffing, inadequate presentation or treatment of data, and faulty logic. The opinions of such persons determine the esteem in which an appraiser is held; perhaps too many appraisers have ignored this fact in their report-writing practices.

It must also be understood that almost any experienced appraiser, when reading the report of another appraiser, with whom he has little sympathy, can find numerous points to attack. When the writer knows that his report is to be subjected to extremely critical review, he will be well advised to submit the briefest report possible, consistent with good practice. Generally, appraisals offered in court as testimony should be extremely brief, so as to prevent the opposing attorney from harassing the appraiser during his testimony.

Bibliography—Part II

AIMSTREET, WILLIAM C. "Writing Letters and Reports," *Appraisal Journal*, XXVII (April, 1959), 198–202.

AMERICAN INSTITUTE OF REAL ESTATE APPRAISERS. *The Appraisal of Real Estate* (3d ed.). Chicago: American Institute of Real Estate Appraisers, 1960. Chapters 14, 16–17, 19, 21–22.

BABCOCK, F. M. "How Much Off for Depreciation?" in *Appraisal and Valuation Manual*, volume II. Washington, D.C.: American Society of Appraisers, 1957.

BABCOCK, FREDERICK M. *Valuation of Real Estate*. New York: McGraw-Hill Book Co., Inc., 1932. Chapter 27.

BLOOM, GEORGE F. "Practice of MAI's Regarding the Appraisal Plant," *The Appraisal Journal*, XXI (July, 1953), 394–396.

BONBRIGHT, JAMES C. *Valuation of Property*. New York: McGraw-Hill Book Co., Inc., 1937. Volume I. Chapters 9–11.

CHAPMAN, FRED L. "Developing Rent Schedules," *The Appraisal Journal*, X, No. 1 (January, 1942).

CHURCH, BYRON. "Are Appraisers Talking to Themselves?" *The Appraisal Journal*, XXVI (July, 1958), 393–396.

ELLWOOD, L. W. *Ellwood Tables for Real Estate Appraising and Financing*. Ridgewood, N.J.: Published by the author, 1959. Chapter 1 and pages 171–222.

FENTON, HENRY R. "The Logis-stics of Appraising," *The Appraisal Journal*, XXVIII (April, 1960), 190–192.

HERTZMAN, IRVING L. "Construction Cost Indexes," *The Appraisal Journal*, XVIII, No. 1 (January, 1950).

JOHNSON, E. HOLLAND. "Cost Data in Appraising," *The Appraisal Journal*, IX, No. 3 (July, 1941).

KAHN, SANDERS A. "How Good Is the Comparative Sales Approach?" in *Appraisal and Valuation Manual*, volume III. Washington, D.C.: American Society of Appraisers, 1958.

KAHN, SANDERS A. "Valuation of Urban Land," in *Appraisal and Valuation Manual*, volume IV. Washington, D.C.: American Society of Appraisers, 1959.

KNISKERN, PHILIP W. *Real Estate Appraisal and Valuation*. New York: The Ronald Press Co., 1933. Chapters 18, 20–22.

LOUIE, CHARLES F. "Depreciation and the Cost Approach," *The Appraisal Journal*, XXIX, No. 4 (October, 1961).

MCMICHAEL, STANLEY L. *McMichael's Appraising Manual* (4th ed.). Englewood Cliffs, N.J.: Prentice-Hall, Inc., 1951. Chapters 4, 6, 15.

MARSTON, A., R. WINFREY, and J. C. HEMPSTEAD. *Engineering Valuation and Depreciation*. New York: McGraw-Hill Book Co., Inc., 1953. Chapters 5, 9, 11.

MATTHEWS, MYRON L. "Construction Costs for Valuation Purposes," in *Appraisal and Valuation Manual*, volume V. Washington, D.C.: American Society of Appraisers, 1960.

RATCLIFF, RICHARD U. "Net Income Can't Be Split," *The Appraisal Journal*, XVIII, No. 2 (April, 1950).

SCHMUTZ, GEORGE L. *The Appraisal Process.* Manhattan Beach, Calif.: Published by the author, 1953. Chapter 23.

SCHMUTZ, GEORGE L. "Some Annuity Computations," *The Appraisal Journal*, XX, No. 4 (October, 1952).

UNITED STATES TREASURY DEPARTMENT, INTERNAL REVENUE SERVICE. *Depreciation Guidelines and Rules.* Publication No. 456 (July, 1962). Washington, D.C.: Government Printing Office.

WENDT, PAUL F. *Real Estate Appraisal.* New York: Holt, Rinehart & Winston, Inc., 1956. Chapters 6, 8.

WHITE, JOHN R. "Selection of the Capitalization Rate," *The Appraisal Journal*, XVII, No. 4 (October, 1949).

Part III

SPECIFIC ASSIGNMENTS

Part III

SPECIAL ASSIGNMENTS

16

Valuation for Realty-Tax Purposes

THEORY OF THE PROPERTY TAX

The property-tax system in the United States evolved from the English rating system used in colonial times. Under this system, properties were rated for taxation according to their annual estimated earnings. The schedules of standard rates for various types of property were set by legislative action, and, so long as the tax base remained farmland, the established schedules proved fairly satisfactory.

With the growth of the country and, specifically, with the growth of urban centers and urban real estate values, with varying real estate values dependent upon location, the concept of property taxation underwent a fundamental change. The rating system was replaced by the ad valorem concept of the property tax. The tax no longer became a measure of an individual's ability to pay, but the property itself became the object of taxation, with its value as the tax base. Along with this shift in concept, there arose the corollary idea that all property within a taxing district should be valued uniformly and taxed according to a uniform rate.

This new concept transformed the property tax into a tax on capital values and required that each taxing jurisdiction set up administrative procedures that would ensure both the proper level of value for all types of properties within the jurisdiction and their uniform assessment. Since the determination of the relative value of all properties on the tax rolls is the prime function of the local assessment officers, without consideration of the owner's ability to pay or the benefits he receives from the community, the assessment function in the last analysis rests on appraisal principles and techniques.

ASSESSING

The Law. The function of the assessor is to locate, list, and value all taxable property according to a uniform standard, so that each taxpayer will share the cost of government in proportion to the value of his property. The appraisal of real estate, which is the technical aspect of the assessment function, is basic to all other assessment functions.

Assessors are bound, in their performance of duties, by a considerable volume of specific law that deals with uniformity of appraisals, exemptions, and other aspects of the assessing process. The laws, in turn, are subject to changes in interpretation by judicial decisions in the many cases that come before the courts. While assessors are free to determine values in the first instance, these values are, in turn, subject to review by various administrative and judicial bodies. Boards of review may change values of specific properties. Equalization boards may alter the relationships between the values of groups of properties. A taxpayer usually has the right of appeal not only to local Boards of Review but also to the courts. He may engage the services of expert appraisers to help his case. He may, generally, appeal his assessment on any of three general grounds: overvaluation, inequality, or illegality. The majority of appeals are taken on the grounds of overvaluation, a condition that usually requires the services of an appraiser who will testify to a value differing from the assessor's estimate. The limitations and reviews of the assessor's work do not lessen his responsibility for arriving at accurate and equalized values. Indeed, they emphasize the need for accurate appraisals that can only be produced by sound methods, in order that the values derived therefrom will survive the most critical review.

The law, in general, usually requires the assessor to determine the "full value," the "fair market value," the "full cash value," or "market value." Regardless of the terminology in use, the definitions by the legislatures, state constitutions, and courts have been vague at best. Attempts by the courts to define the terms usually involve a consideration of the action that willing buyers and willing sellers would arrive at under ordinary circumstances. The difficulty, in turn, of defining "willing buyer" or "willing seller" under ordinary circumstances does nothing to mitigate the inherent difficulty of valuing real estate.

This difficulty stems primarily, as we have pointed out in an earlier chapter, from the fact that the value base is not a tangible thing which can be measured physically, but depends upon the relationship of such a thing to the economy. The relationship is hard to determine. Since the law and the courts are not specific in defining the goal, and the concept of value is the subject of differences of opinion among economists and appraisers, the inherent difficulties of assessing well are greater than the public appreciates. Anyone can ascribe a value to any parcel of real estate, but to ascribe a good figure may be very difficult.

Out of the magnitude of cases reviewing real property valuations that have reached the courts, there emerge a number of guiding principles that affect the work of the assessors. Some of the more important concepts that have emerged from the judicial interpretations of assessment law are

1. A presumption that the assessor's value is correct until proved otherwise and that, if it can be proved that the assessment is equalized with similar properties in the taxing district, it will not be disturbed

2. That assessors must show that they have considered all factors of value in making their assessments

3. That the courts will approve a standard method of taxing property but will not approve the use of a formula to the extent that it precludes other obvious value factors

4. That, even though the taxpayer is contesting the correctness of the assessor's value, he should not be compelled to produce evidence that may aid the assessor's case, and that, therefore, the assessor should develop such evidence from his own sources

5. That, if capitalized income results in a value higher than reproduction cost new less depreciation, the latter figure will be accepted as closer to market value

6. That, in considering income, the assessor must be careful to distinguish between income arising out of the property itself and income developed from a business conducted on the property

7. That prices paid in any sale that shows an element of distress, compulsion, or unusual financing will rarely be considered to be conclusive of market value

8. That, in addition to the three standard yardsticks of value: sales, income, and cost, the court will place a good deal of weight on prior decisions regarding the value of property (The weight given to prior court decisions will however, not effect the general principle that an opinion of value for one year is not binding for subsequent years. The principle of "res adjudicata" does not generally apply; each assessment must be separately fixed as of the legal status date for each succeeding year.)

The principles that have emerged from the various court decisions indicate that the courts will generally be satisfied if the assessor can prove that he has taken all elements of value into consideration and that any individual property valuation has been arrived at in a standard manner to produce an equalized assessment roll. The assessor is thus required to do two things: He must establish the market value of each parcel in his district, and he must equalize the tax burden. From a theoretical point of view, if each parcel were assessed at a figure representing its market value, the problem of equalization would be solved at the same time. However, since we have already pointed out the difficulties of arriving at market value, we can see that the assessor, faced with the task of producing an assessment roll with thousands of property valuations, must look to some practical method of accomplishing his task.

Concept of Value for Assessment Purposes. For all practical purposes, while the assessor pays "lip service" to the concept of market value, as ordinarily understood by real estate appraisers, he in effect, is using "constructive" market value. According to the publication *Assessment Principles and Terminology,* published by the then National and now International Association of Assessment Officers, "constructive" market value may be defined as "an approximation of market value arrived at through the application of reasonable rules and procedures of appraisal, such as corner influence and depth rules, building classification and cost schedules and physical depreciation schedules."[1]

The courts have generally recognized the practical necessity of arriving at this type of value for assessment purposes. However, since the statutes usually specify market value as the basis, the values found on the basis of "constructive" market value are usually defined as evidence of value, not as value itself.

In use of standard procedures, the absence of an active market presents no obstacle to estimating property values. The chief virtue of the method lies in the fact that it makes equalization possible. Equalization is required by all assessment jurisdictions and is the fundamental concept in the theory of property taxation.

Within the framework of the concept of "constructive" market value, assessors have adopted appraising methods to determine the value of real property for assessment purposes. Sales analysis, replacement cost, and capitalization of income thus find their way into assessment appraisals. Heavy reliance is placed on the comparative process whereby results obtained from properties where the data are available are used to determine the value of all similar property within the taxing district.

While all three methods of determining value are used, not all are applied to every type of property. Sales analysis is used primarily for land values; reproduction cost less depreciation is applied to most building values; while the income approach is confined to investment property. In actual practice it has been observed that the reproduction cost less depreciation method is in most common use for the majority of properties on the assessment rolls, because this method lends itself most readily to the use of standard rules, formulas, and schedules as well as to the requirements of quick mass appraisal needs. While this procedure can operate fairly satisfactorily in homogeneous areas with similar structures, it is most unsatisfactory in those areas where economic factors play a strong role in accentuating the value differences between individual parcels. The unique features of each parcel of real estate are apt to be most important where values are high, and it is here that standard procedures may often create results contrary to those sought, that is, an equalization of the tax burden.

ASSESSMENT PROCEDURE

Land Valuation. Most assessing officers are required to appraise the properties under their jurisdiction in two stages. The first stage is the determination of land values for each parcel, as if unimproved, and the second

[1] *Assessment Principles and Terminology,* (Chicago: International Association of Assessing Officers, 1937) p. 137.

is the determination of the land value with the improvements thereon. The difference between the land value as vacant land and the land value as improved is generally recognized to be the building value. Thus, for all practical purposes, the total assessed value is the sum of land value plus estimated building value.

In approaching the problem of land valuation, the assessor first establishes a system of land classification. The land-classification system is based on use. The broad classifications of urban land uses are residential, commercial, industrial, recreational, and institutional. Within each broad use classification, there may be several subclassifications. Thus, residential may be separated into one-family, two-family, and multifamily categories, while commercial may be divided into retail, wholesale, and office categories.

In addition to establishing his classification system, which will govern the general level of values, he then adopts procedures for specific value analysis, establishing value units and modifications for variables.

Just as in every individual appraisal assignment, one of the first steps is to identify the property. The assessor, therefore, must be equipped with an adequate set of tax maps which will correctly identify each parcel to be valued. These maps must show every parcel of property in true relation to its size, shape, and location. In addition, a satisfactory system of legal identification must be on the map. In most urban tax districts, a system of identifying properties by sections of the city, specific blocks within the section, and specific lot numbers in the block will serve the identification purposes. The tax maps usually indicate streets, existing or proposed; railroads; rivers; and other factors affecting property values. While zoning restrictions are ordinarily not shown on tax maps, they are available on supplementary maps, and frequently assessors will pencil in the existing zoning for each block. The use of a pencil makes it simple to record any subsequent changes in the zoning law without cluttering up the map with too many changes.

In addition to the tax maps, the assessor will have at his disposal a land value map where he can place the relative unit land values for every block in his area. To use a means of recording the land value for each parcel, he will probably have an assessment record card for each property, which he will use as his work record.

All land values are expressed in terms of land units. The most frequent unit is the *unit foot,* or *front foot,* which is a level rectangular strip of land lying perpendicular to the street, with a frontage of 1 foot and a specified depth. This unit foot is usually designated as a strip in the center of the block, free from all location and plottage influences. Other units of value that may be used are the *square foot* or the *acre,* depending upon local usage and the characteristics of the land.

Assessors use the unit foot values for two reasons. First, they permit the establishment of common denominators of value, permitting, in turn, value comparisons between groups of parcels. Second, they allow individual parcel value modifications to be made for size, location, topography, non-standard shape, and depth.

Equipped with maps, records, units, and value modification factors, the assessor must then proceed to establish his unit land values in accord with conventional appraisal methods. This requires data on sales and income of a sufficient number of properties, and their verification, as a basis for his opinion of value for each appropriate unit in each block and for value comparisons. Since conventional appraisal methods for land valuation are used, and as we have explained the procedure in previous chapters, it will not be repeated here. However, it is necessary to point out a prime difficulty that arises in land assessment owing to the use of conventional appraisal procedures. Basic to all land valuation theory is the idea that land shall be valued at its highest and best use. In those areas where land use is mixed, or where changes in use are taking place, special problems exist. It is obvious that not every parcel will be developed to the highest and best use. To do so would probably create an oversupply of residential or retail space that would act to destroy all values. Some parcels may be improved to their best use potentials but only at some date in the future and, hence, should not carry the same value as similar parcels which are already so improved. Other parcels will never see their potentialities realized. The ordinary appraiser concerned only with a single parcel can weigh its potentialities in the light of all present conditions. The assessor-appraiser must be concerned not only with the value of thousands of individual parcels but also with the administrative problem of equalizing land values for similar parcels in the same tax district. The application of unit land values to parcels of the same size and shape, in accord with the legal requirement to assess them as if unimproved, may produce equalized mathematical answers at variance with the economic values these parcels possess.

Valuation of Improvements. Improvements to land vary endlessly. In addition to the infinite variety of buildings that may be found in an assessing district, there are such improvements as tanks, docks, paving, fences, some forms of industrial equipment, and railroad and public utility property. In the large urban areas, the problem of improvement valuation becomes the most time-consuming function.

In order to meet the problem of improvement valuation, which will be referred to from now on as *building valuation,* most assessors use the reproduction cost less depreciation method of valuation. Although, as has been pointed out previously, this method of building valuation has serious deficiencies, it is defended by assesors as necessary for the mass appraisal task they face, and as one that promotes the greatest uniformity.

As with land valuation, the assessment of buildings first requires the establishment of a classification system. The classification system will list buildings according to their uses and their construction types. Design establishes uses, and the kind of materials used establishes construction types. Construction types may be further subdivided into classes for each different kind of contruction, and these, in turn, may be classified according to the quality of construction.

The number of use classifications for a tax district will vary with the sizes and uses that are found in the district. In most jurisdictions, the predominant use type will, of course, be the residential building.

Construction types usually fall into four principal categories. These are

1. Wood-frame construction
2. Masonry construction
3. Reinforced-concrete-frame construction
4. Steel-frame construction

Where buildings are of mixed construction such as frame and brick, assessors frequently use a separate classification for these types.

Since assessors must make wholesale, equalized building valuations, they seek the most economical and timesaving methods consistent with standard appraisal practice. Usually, each building is described on an appropriate property card, and a picture, if the funds are available, is desirable. The basic data as to use type, construction type, date of construction, cost of construction, alteration or rehabilitation record, area or cube contents, layout, etc., are all vital points of information that should be part of the record.

The value units most commonly used by assessors are the cubic-foot or square-foot reproduction costs. These costs, in most instances, are supplied either by the assessor's files or by standard assessment cost manuals supplied by state or county agencies. There are several appraisal firms that specialize in developing these manuals for assessing officers. Among the more prominent are Marshall and Stevens, the Cleminshaw Company, the Cole-Layer-Trumble Company, Roy Wenzlick and Company, Valuation Associates, Inc., Doane Appraisal Service, E. T. Wilkins and Associates, J. L. Jacobs and Company, and the E. H. Boeckh Company.

Each basic building type will be assigned a unit value, and then modifications will be made for individual buildings. The most common modifications will be those for size and shape, with further additions or subtractions necessitated by the presence or absence of special features and equipment. In rare instances, assessors will make unit-in-place computations for special buildings, and in almost no case will they use the quantity-survey method. Once the reproduction cost new is established, a deduction for depreciation will be taken from some empirical schedule or table that is in use by the assessor. In some cases, different depreciation tables may be used for different classes of buildings. The value of the building found by this method is then added to the land value to give the total assessed value. In many cases, where properties are assessed at a percentage of full value, the final step is to multiply the property value estimate by the percentage factor in use.

As in standard appraisal practice, the chief criticism of this method of determining building value stems from the use of the depreciation tables which frequently give a distorted picture of the building's economic value. Another problem arises when old buildings that have outlived their usefulness are still carried on the assessment rolls at some percentage of their reproduction cost. In many cases, especially where buildings of this type are in the process of being removed to make way for the highest and best use of the land on similar plots in the area, these buildings really have a negative value equal to the cost of demolishing them less salvage value. It seems incongruous to assess land according to its highest and best use and in addition to add a building value when clearly the owner would be better off by removing the structure. If this procedure were to be followed where it applies, the assessed value of some properties might appear on the assessment rolls as follows:

Land value: $50,000
Land with improvements: $45,000

This type of assessment would at least be consistent with the prices that builders and investors are willing to pay for land that is ripe for redevelopment. They usually will pay more, all other things being equal, for cleared land than for land encumbered by a worthless building that needs to be demolished.

While the cost approach to assessed valuation is the most common procedure in use, many assessors, especially in the big cities, where investment properties abound, make use of the income approach. The income approach is used primarily as a check on the other approaches. The technique used by most assessors in the income approach is to develop a set of standards to be applied to the various types of investment properties under their jurisdiction. Standard gross income capitalization multipliers, standard operating expenses, and standard capitalization rates are integral parts of the procedure. In developing standards, assessors, on the basis of a wide sampling of properties, attempt to develop "normal" or average factors which, for equalization purposes, are then applied to all properties of a given type to determine the assessed valuation. This use of standards produces a bench mark against which any individual property may be measured. Where a specific property reveals characteristics dissimilar to those that comprise the average, the necessary modifications will then be made. The need for the use of income appraisals arises out of the fact that private appraisers, who are commonly employed by owners to contest the assessments, make use of this approach to value. Thus, use of the income approach by assessors in these cases improves the chances of having the values upheld if the assessments are contested before review boards or the courts. As was earlier pointed out, the courts generally require that *all* factors of value be considered in making assessments. In addition, the courts will generally take the lower estimate of value, regardless of whether it was derived from the cost approach or the income approach.

REVIEW PROCEDURE

In the last analysis, an assessed valuation of a parcel of real estate is a matter of opinion. Just as in the case where ordinary appraisals are made, there is room for difference of opinion. Since tax payments and capital values are at stake in assessments, it is natural and consistent with the philosophy of democratic society that some form of machinery should be established to resolve differences of opinion between assessors and tax-payers.

While the courts stand as the final arbiters of value, court procedures are frequently too time-consuming or expensive for many property owners. In addition, there is nothing in the training of judges that makes them especially competent to establish property values. As a result, review boards and equalization boards have generally been established for the purpose of hearing and deciding assessment grievances and effecting equalized tax levies. Usually a taxpayer must exhaust his legal remedies for relief through these review agencies before the courts will entertain his complaint.

Taxpayers are generally given a specified time after the assessed values are made public to make their complaints. The complaints must be made in writing and must specify the grounds upon which they are made. Failure to make the complaint within the required time or to specify the grounds on which the complaint is based is usually fatal to the taxpayer's cause.

In acting on the taxpayer's complaint, the review agency usually relies on the assessor to supply it with all the data upon which the original assessment was made. In some cases, it may even solicit the assessor's opinion as to whether or not an adjustment should be made. In the absence of a patent error, most assessors are loath to recommend a reduction in value, for to do so is to admit that their judgment was faulty in the first instance. However, where the taxpayer can produce data which was not available to the assessor, he will, if he thinks it of sufficient importance, recommend the adjustment. In those cases where the assessor is not in attendance during the review hearings, the board will act in the light of any new data presented. Most review agencies have the right to take testimony under oath, summon witnesses, and require the production of papers, records, and taxpayer's books. Ordinarily the boards of review act solely on the case at hand, but, where they are convinced that a wholesale revaluation is necessary, they are empowered to make one.

Most hearings before review agencies are informal hearings. The taxpayer himself, or his legal representative, may appear to plead his case. Only in cases involving substantial amounts is an effort made to produce independent appraisers or appraisals to substantiate the grievance claims. The use of appraisers is largely confined to those cases which ultimately reach the courts.

After a review agency has met and heard the complaints, it, generally, renders its decisions within a short space of time. Any owner who is dissatisfied with the decision of the review board is then free to pursue his grievance to the courts, within a specified legal time limit. When a property valuation is contested in the courts, the general procedure is for both parties to produce expert appraisal witnesses to testify as to value. In some jurisdictions, the assessor who made the original assessment may be called on to testify; in others, the taxing jurisdiction relies solely on the testimony of outside appraisal witnesses to sustain the assessor's value. The use of independent appraisers to give testimony to assist the court in reaching its decision has generally produced unfortunate results. The appraiser for the taxpayer invariably testifies to a value below the assessment; the appraiser for the municipality testifies to a value at or above the assessed value; and the judge, recognizing the "advocate" character of what should be impartial testimony, is frequently confused or annoyed. This has resulted in a general expectation by the courts that the testimony presented will be at great variance, with the result that appraisal testimony has come into low repute. This has thrown the burden of decision upon the court, which frequently tends to regard the property value as lying between the high and low figures presented. While it is true that the value may be between the high and low figures, it does not mean that it is exactly in the middle as some jurists have concluded. It may be at any point between the high and low estimates.

The appraiser who testifies in court must be prepared to prove his right to be qualified as an expert, and to demonstrate the methods by which he arrived at his value estimate. He will be examined and cross-examined by the opposing attorneys, who will attempt to elicit from the appraiser evidence either to prove or to disprove the value estimate. Appraisal fees are usually set in advance and are dependent upon the complexity of the property, the amount of work required, and the time to be spent in court. The written appraisals made by both appraisers are usually entered as evidence and made a permanent part of the records. Appraisers who have a reputation for being "low value" or "pessimistic" are generally sought after by property owners, while the taxing authorities seek out their opposites. It is interesting to note that the "low value" appraisers may often be sought out by municipalities in condemnation cases, while owners of properties to be condemned will employ the "high value" appraisers. Many appraisal firms which specialize in all types of appraisal assignments frequently have two or more appraisers on their staff; one will be the "pessimist," the other the "optimist."

Court decisions relating to assessed values are subject to appeal to the higher courts of the states, an expensive procedure which only the largest taxpayers may profitably exercise. The bulk of the property owners, owning small residential or investment properties, must rely on the review agencies. Attempts to improve review procedures have led to several suggested improvements. One suggestion involves the appointment of "court appraisers" whose sole function would be to advise the courts regarding property values and whose sole loyalty would be to the courts in the interest of justice. Another proposal would eliminate the courts entirely as a factor in the review process and substitute an independent board of appraisers appointed by the mayor of a city or the governor of a state, after approval by the various professional appraisal societies. This latter method of selection is similar to the selection of judges in some areas, where prior approval is solicited by the bar associations before final designation is made by the selecting official.

SPECIAL ASSESSMENT PROBLEMS

Assessors face three special types of problems. The first stems from the lack of a clear definition of value. The second, from the general inadequacies of appraising methods. The third, from the close relationship of the level of assessed values with the fiscal requirements of taxing jurisdictions.

The first problem will probably never be solved. It involves the solution of the fundamental problem in economics—the nature of value. The second problem offers some hope of alleviation as appraisers continue to refine their techniques and improve their methods of valuation. For assessors this means constant attention to, and close alliance with, the professional appraisers. It means that improved methods of administration and training must be provided for assessing officers. It means that adequate salaries must be paid to attract and hold competent men, and that assessors should be full-time professional employees with adequate educational and experiential backgrounds.

It is to the third problem that we now turn our attention. During the postwar period, the general level of property assessments has lagged behind the rise in property values and market prices. As the population has grown, and with it the demand for more and more services to be supplied by local governments, the government agencies have found it increasingly difficult to get the necessary revenues to provide the services. Real estate will continue to provide the bulk of local revenue for many years to come, in spite of the imposition of new forms of taxation. Borrowing capacity is generally tied to real estate values, and limits on the tax rate are almost always a part of the local government financial picture.

Most jurisdictions in the United States today are assessing real estate at less than the statutory limit. This is due to the failure of assessors to keep pace with rising market conditions. Faced with a problem of assessing at statutory limits, usually full value, and of producing a uniform tax roll, the assessors have found it more convenient to pay more attention to uniformity than to full value. There has also been a fear of adverse public reaction to the raising of the general level of assessments. The public, through habit, has been taught that assessments are never made at full value and has come to feel it has a vested interest in low assessments. In addition, low assessments make it more difficult for individual property owners to complain about inequalities, as they too are the recipients of a hidden "tax exemption."

The requirements for more revenue, and the action of county and state governing bodies concerned with equalization of the tax burden throughout the various jurisdictions, have forced more and more communities to abandon their low assessments. They have decided on revaluation programs conducted either by the local assessing officials or by private appraisal firms. Private appraisal firms have been favored in these revaluation undertakings for two main reasons: Firstly, either the local officials were inadequate to the task or it was considered poor politics to raise assessments. Secondly, the use of a professional appraisal firm tended to give the revaluation project a degree of prestige and authority it might not have received if done by local officials. As a result, the number of such firms engaged in these projects has grown by leaps and bounds. All of the firms listed previously in connection with assessment manuals are engaged in this type of work. The community, usually, has several firms bidding for the contract to do the work according to its specifications. The time required to complete such a revaluation project will vary in accordance with the size of the community. One concern estimates that it would take six months to a year to revalue a city of 100,000 population, with the longer time period preferred.

The revaluation of a community involves the preparation of adequate tax maps where they are non-existent or unsatisfactory. It involves the preparation of property cards, photographs, measurements, and classification schedules for all the improvements in the area. It requires the gathering of all appraisal data relating to sales, cost, and income. It requires the preparation of separate land value maps and of cost and depreciation schedules to be applied to the individual properties. These schedules are ordinarily incorporated into a manual which is left with the assessor with instructions for keeping it up-to-date and for defending the assessments. Training is generally given to the local assessor so that he may understand the appraisal methods used and apply them to subsequent new construction. Taxpayers are generally informed of their new assessments, and an informal review is offered them in order to correct any individual errors. If appeals are made to state authorities against proposed assessments, the appraisal firm is expected to defend the new assessments. Assistance in defense may also be required for the first year or two after the new valuations take effect.

OTHER PROBLEMS

The discussion of the aforementioned problems does not exhaust all the problems that arise from the general property tax. Some of them fall into the realm of public policy and economics and are merely listed below:

1. Should improvements be exempt from taxation and the full burden fall upon the land only?
2. Should tax policies be used to affect land uses and redevelopment of urban areas?
3. Should there be a limit on the amount of money to be raised from real estate taxes?
4. What relations exist between costs and services needed by different types of land uses, and should there be differential taxation of different land uses?
5. What role should computing machines play in the assessment process without affecting the assessor's judgment?
6. Should assessments be averaged over a period of years rather than be made annually or biannually?

CONCLUSION

In concluding the discussion about real property taxation, it seems appropriate to point out one factor that has an important bearing on the value of real estate. An increase in real estate taxes, all other things remaining equal, acts to reduce the capital value of the property. A decrease will raise the value. A property with a net income of $20,000 after taxes may sell for $200,000 in the market, or on a 10 per cent basis. If the taxes are increased by $1,000, the property, on the same 10 per cent basis, is now worth only $190,000. This problem arises frequently when existing property is assessed at a fraction of the required level and then sold at a figure considerably above the assessment. The assessor, on the basis of the sale, may raise the assessed valuation. If this is done, the new owner finds himself in the position of having lost part of his capital value. The property is now worth the selling price less the capitalized value of the tax increase. The assessor, if he is not to overassess the property, must include his effective tax rate in his capitalization rate just as if he were making an assessment on a new building. Appraisers, who appraise property where the possibility of tax increases exists owing to sales based on their appraisals, would be exercising prudent caution if they too gave consideration to a changing tax picture.

17

Condemnation Appraising

The rapid increases in population and the expansion of cities in the last two decades have created a constantly increasing demand for parks, roads, and other varieties of public facilities. The acquisition of the land needed for these improvements has required increasing use of the power of eminent domain, which permits governments and public authorities to take private property by paying just compensation. In these cases, all private rights are extinguished, since the property owners share in the compensation which is paid, even when these rights include mortgage lien interests, easements, leases, or any other form of private right.

The power of eminent domain is exercised through the right of condemnation, which means that the public authority taking the property must follow a legally defined procedure in the taking. Normally, the public authority will try to secure a negotiated sale with the property owner, but, if this fails, it may then condemn the property through court action and take it.

THE NATURE OF CONDEMNATION

Condemning authorities include not only state, federal, municipal, and county governments but also special school, sewer, and road authorities, as well as, public-utility companies and numerous agencies. There are many examples of one of these agencies being given rights to take municipal property and even to wipe out an entire community to provide a dam, seaway, or hydroelectric plant. Recently, for example, one such agency modified a treaty with an Indian nation in New York State and took some of its land. This right was even upheld by the United States Supreme Court.

In general, this is as it should be; the projects are developed for the public welfare, and, without the right of condemnation, one or a few property owners could force the agencies to pay prices far beyond the worth of the realty. Even worse, the owners could refuse to sell at any price. Since the law requires that the owners be paid full value, they suffer no financial loss if the condemnation is properly executed. However, they may lose in other ways because they will not be paid for special sentimental value that the property holds for them, nor are they usually paid for moving expenses.

A businessman may suffer serious loss because he is not paid for the good will that his business has established at its location.

Note that, to qualify for compensation under eminent domain, the property must be "taken." A zoning resolution may damage a property and not give the owner the right of just compensation, for the power is a "police power." Enforcement of building codes may require an owner to demolish a building at his own expense and without compensation. Only when eminent domain is involved is the owner compensated.

REASON FOR TAKING

Property may be taken by local communities for schools, streets, fire-houses, municipal offices, libraries, parks, and all the other real estate needed to provide local governmental services to the townspeople. Recently, this power has been expanded to include urban-renewal projects. This last item will be covered in a complete chapter owing to its uniqueness and magnitude.

Counties condemn property for courts, airports, highways, parks, beaches, administration office buildings, and other purposes directly involved with county business.

States and the federal government condemn property for all of the above reasons and also for armories and other military purposes including missile-launching sites. Property may also be acquired for universities, conservation of resources, and numerous other operations of constantly expanding state and federal governments.

The state and federal highway programs have taken on gigantic proportions and probably involve the most extensive acquisition of private property by government. Often such a program involves acquisition by special agencies such as the state highway or thruway authority or by a municipality which needs the property for a bridge, tunnel, or arterial road.

Property is also acquired by organizations such as the St. Lawrence Seaway, a port authority (airports, bridges, tunnels, truck and bus terminals, and docking facilities), and the Tennessee Valley Authority.

There are also takings by public-utility companies for natural-gas-transmission pipelines, electric power lines, and telephone poles, railroads, ferries, street cars and bus lines, etc. Even though public-utility companies are privately owned, they may be given condemnation rights because public welfare requires that this be done.

CONDEMNATION LAW

All of our states and the federal government have special laws involving condemnation of property. Court decisions interpreting the laws form a basis for current decisions. It is impossible to present the legal facts covering each of the points under condemnation, as they vary from state to state. This chapter will deal with prevailing systems. Those readers interested in state-by-state decisions will find excellent source materials in the Bibliography at the end of Part III.

SPECIAL PROBLEMS OF VALUATION

Although, in general, appraisals for condemnation are market-value appraisals and follow the same methodology, there are several specialized problems. Some of these are of an ethical nature, and others are involved in the system of appraising.

Partial Takings. When an entire property is taken, the market value is found by the standard appraising techniques. The courts usually place a marked emphasis on the comparative-sales approach, even to the extent of accepting "comparatives" that differ widely in terms of time of sale, location, and physical characteristics.

The real problem occurs when only a portion of a property is taken, because the property owner must be compensated for the value of the property taken and the possible loss of value to the property that is left to him. It is obvious, if a road is cut through a property, it not only may damage the owner by the loss of the property for the road but also may divide the remaining realty in a manner that prevents its future use. In Fig. 5, the road has been cut through a lot, eliminating any street access to part B, because the road (part C) is below grade. At the same time, part A is rendered almost useless owing to a size and shape which makes it uneconomical for almost any logical building project. As a matter of fact, a local zoning ordinance may prevent any use being made of it. This is an extreme example of severance damage, but, to some extent, there usually is some severance damage connected with partial takings.

In order to determine whether severance damages are involved, the courts have set up three criteria: (1) physical contiguity, (2) continuity of use, and (3) continuity of ownership. *Physical contiguity* means that any parcels for which severance damages are claimed must have either platted property boundaries or natural physical boundaries which are contiguous. *Continuity of use* means that parcels under the same ownership must be used as a unit in such a way that removal of a portion of the property would damage the remaining property to a degree greater than the proportion of that property to the whole property. *Continuity of ownership* means that the parcels must be under one ownership but need not be contiguous if they are devoted to the same use. For example, parcels may be separated by public ways, yet they may be considered as contiguous, if they are under one ownership and devoted to the same use.

Severance damages may be computed by estimating (1) the difference between the fair market value of the property before and after the taking; (2) the value of the part taken, treated as a separate unit, plus damages to the remainder; (3) the value of the part taken, treated as part of the whole, plus damages to the remainder; and (4) damages to the remainder, included in the value of the part taken.[1]

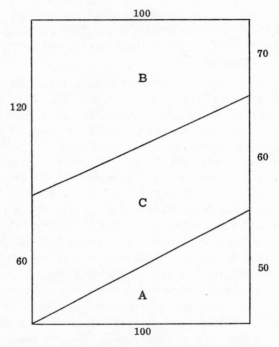

Fig. 5. Example of severance damage. (See text for explanation.)

In preparing a report on partial taking, the appraiser first appraises the whole property, as it existed before the taking. He may then place a value on the remainder after the taking. The difference between the two values constitutes the amount of damages suffered by the owner, and it is this amount of money that he should be paid by the condemning authority.

In the example shown in Fig. 5, assume that this is a parcel of land, 100 × 180 feet, in a good residential section of a fine suburban community. The appraiser checks land sales in the area and finds that this site could be readily sold for the construction of a new home for about $8,400.

The portion taken (C) is 60 × 111.8 feet, with an area of 6,000 square feet. The 60-foot right of way is about 12 feet below the grade of part B

[1] William H. Crouch, "The Meaning of Just Compensation," *Condemnation Appraisal Practice* (Chicago: American Institute of Real Estate Appraisers, 1961), p. 6.

and is a restricted-access road. This renders *B* valueless to the present owner, as it is now "land-locked." In the computation of value after the taking, the value of *B* is nominal, say, $100.

The direct taking (*C*) has no remaining value to the owner, as he has no property rights to this road, which is now owned by the condemning authority. His only remaining substantial realty is part *A*. This has 100 front feet on the usable street. For the purposes of this example, we will assume that the remaining size permits future construction (although this is actually unlikely). By the use of depth tables and triangular value tables, it is found that its remaining value is $2,400.

Severance damages would be computed as follows:

1. *Valuation before taking:*
   Area of part *A* 50′ × 100′/2 .... 2,500 square feet
   Area of part *B* 70′ × 100′ + 100′ × 50′/2 .... 9,500 square feet
   Area of part *C* (part taken) .... 6,000 square feet

   Total area before taking 100′ × 180′ .... 18,000 square feet
   Value of entire area before taking $8,400

2. *Valuation after taking:*
   Part *A*
   Value of road frontage of 100′ $2,400

   Computed as follows:
      Value of property with 100′ depth.............. $6,000
      Value of property with 50′ depth................ $4,000
      Value of triangle with varying depth where
        perpendicular is 50′ $4,000 × .60 .... $2,400

   Part *B*
   "Landlocked," with only nominal value 100

3. *Loss of value due to taking:*
   Value before taking $8,400
   Value remaining after taking (parts *A* & *B*) 2,500

   Loss of property due to taking $5,900

Loss of Value. Various factors which would reduce the value of remainders are the following:

1. Size of parcel too small for any high-type use
2. Shape prevents high-type use
3. Shape causes a waste of a portion of remaining land (irregular and narrow strips)
4. Separation of remainder from railroad, waterfront, highway, or other desirable locational feature
5. New adjacent use obnoxious, noisy, or dangerous (sewerage plant, airport, missile range)
6. Change of grade of highway

7. Any of the above or any other factor which can be shown to reduce its value (This can be shown by reduced rental value or lower sales prices available.)

Sometimes, as a result of a partial taking, the remainder of the property is "landlocked"—it has no direct access to any street or highway. A property having no land access would only have air access and, therefore, limited value. Since the property became landlocked as a direct result of the action of the condemning authority, the authority will have to pay the owner for his damage. In most cases, the condemning agency will try to prevent this occurrence by finding some method of giving the owner good and valuable access.

Consequential Damages. In the above example of partial taking, the cause of damage to the remainder was based upon a severance of the property taken from the whole. Not only was there a loss of the portion taken, but the remainder also was damaged. This was proved by the before-and-after method. Consequential damages are often difficult to distinguish from severance damages. The basic difference is that consequential damages normally are not compensable under eminent domain unless some of the property is actually taken. A new road improvement which changes the grade may be installed, making access difficult to property owners, but most states would not give damages to a property owner in this case unless part of his realty was taken. The basic theory is that owners have no inherent right to the streets. Other types of consequential damages are moving costs, loss of good will and business profits, and damages from inability to find a new location, most of which are not compensable under eminent domain. However, if a road or bridge is built in a manner that causes flooding of neighboring realty and a loss in value, the owner usually has a cause of action.

Condemnation Value. Value in condemnation is normally considered to be market value. The owner must be put in a financial position equivalent to his condition before the taking. The statutes of the various states rarely use the term *market value* or *fair market value.* They usually use terminology such as *actual value* or *true value,* which is difficult to translate into proper economic terms. Nor is there agreement on the definition of *market value.* One of the most succinct definitions was stated by a West Virginia court: "Market value is the price for which land can be sold by a person desirous of selling to a person willing to buy, neither acting under compulsion, and both exercising intelligent judgment." Usually, it is understood that the property will have to be offered for sale for a reasonable time.

Most states also consider "normal times." If there is a limited and depressed market at the time of the taking or if the market is unusually active, the courts believe that those values are temporary and are not applicable. Of course, this creates the problem of determining what is "normal."

The property that is taken cannot be valued at its value to the taking authority. It must be the value to prudent buyers and sellers. Nor can the property be valued in the light of the improvements which are planned by the condemning authority. Obviously, the new improvement may create higher value. For example, this might occur if a new, large state-university campus were to be created on agricultural land or in a tiny community. The value must not be placed in contemplation of this improvement. An exception to this rule would occur, however, if the university announced the taking of a tract of land, started to build the college, and then subsequently condemned adjacent land for expansion of the original plan. It is obvious that the additional land might have had a market-value increase based on the adjacent college campus. The university would have to pay the new value.

It is also possible for the remainder of a property having a partial taking to be damaged by a new but dangerous or nuisance-creating installation of the condemning authority. Conversely, the remainder may benefit from the creation of a project that would give special advantages to the remainder. If so, some states permit this offset against the condemnation award or, at least, the portion of the award affecting the remainder.

COST AS A MEASURE OF VALUE. The cost appraisal technique is not ordinarily given much consideration in court if there is an active sales market. When there is a complete taking, the cost of a building on a parcel of land will usually be reflected in the sales price. However, many courts insist that, in giving a total value, the appraiser must also place separate values on the land and improvements. This requirement is based upon the court's attempt at uniformity of awards. When the building is a special-purpose structure not usually marketed and not readily subject to a capitalization-of-income approach, some courts add the depreciated value of the structure to the land value. This sounds equitable, but often the structure has become completely obsolete and is inadequate as an improvement to the land. The courts have often given full land value for the land as a site for the highest and best use and then added a value for the structure. Proper appraisal technique would usually value the "improvement" as a negative factor which reduces the value to a purchaser by its demolition cost and the problems inherent in demolition. Fortunately, most of these type properties fall under the heading of churches, cultural monuments, and other properties of semipublic organizations. A property of this sort valued by one of the authors was the world-renowned Carnegie Hall.

When there is a partial taking of a structure, the damage to the remaining improvements partially destroyed is often a function of the cost approach.

CAPITALIZATION-OF-INCOME APPROACH. Courts and condemnation commissioners attempt to avoid this approach, since it can involve the use of too many "judgment" factors. For example, changing the capitalization rate one or two points will effect a tremendous change in values. Also, a miscalculation of gross rentals or major expense items will seriously modify the values. However, it is unfortunate that more credence is not given this method, as it actually conforms to the thinking of buyers in the market. Investors want to know how much money the property will pay them on their investment. In the hands of a skilled appraiser, this method is as reliable as any other.

HIGHEST AND BEST USE. Buyers will also purchase a property on the basis of changes that they plan to effect. They will, therefore, hope to expand or change the existing operation and then resell at a price in excess of their total costs. To the professional buyer, the price that he pays is not the market price. He believes that he will resell at a higher price because the typical seller may not understand the full potential of the property.

Courts allow the valuation of a property in its highest and best use rather than the existing use at the time of the taking. However, the contemplated use may not be fanciful or speculative. It must be reasonably certain of taking place, on the basis of a current need for the use. To demonstrate the need, the owner must show that it is consistent with surrounding property development and with the pattern of land use in comparable areas.

After showing the new use, its cost, and the income and expense computations, the appraiser will then use a land residual technique to demonstrate the land value under the new structure. He should give the entrepreneur an extra profit for creating the new combination. Usually, the appraiser must believe that the site is not only proper for the improvement but uniquely appropriate, owing to physical qualities, zoning, or the fact that few other properties are obtainable for that use.

Expert Testimony. The job of the expert appraiser is not only to appraise a property but also to testify in court in such a manner that the judge, jury, or condemnation commissioners will accept his judgment.

He should not be an advocate for the side that employs him but should do everything possible to convince the decision makers that his appraisal is accurate and that he did everything possible to come to a fair, unbiased, and sound conclusion of value. The following rules will help to create this result:

1. Never take an assignment for which your qualifications are weak.
2. Never merely give the lawyer or owner, who employs you, a value which he wants to hear but which you can't support in court.

3. If your value is partially based upon the statements of other experts, be certain that they too are qualified and honorable. (If a soils engineer tells you that the subject property is suitable for the construction of light-industrial buildings without expensive land preparation and he later is not believed by the judge, your value will be much too high.)

4. Never testify as to value without being fully prepared. This is one type of appraisal where you will be challenged aggressively. Know all the sales, locational factors, capitalization rates, special assessments, zoning, deed restrictions, and new plans for the area. Be familiar with all street names and new highways to be constructed.

5. Watch your courtroom appearance and dress to be certain that you always project the feeling that you are a qualified realty expert.

6. Be truthful, unbiased, and sincere. Remember, you want to produce an appraisal that you believe to be a credit to your reputation. You will defeat that purpose by any factual distortions, huckster techniques, or display of smart-aleck attitudes.

7. The opposing attorney will attempt to discredit you by numerous techniques. He may attack your ability, integrity, or knowledge of the facts. He may also pose questions in a harmless manner and be quite pleasant, but, at all times, he is an advocate opposed to your attorney, and he will not try to help you, even if you are socially acquainted. Treat him with respect and caution. Don't answer any question until you are sure you understand it.

8. Don't be afraid to give an answer in cross-examination that seems to refute your appraisal. Your attorney will have the opportunity to clarify the point on a redirect examination.

9. Don't argue with the opposing attorney.

10. Always remember that every appraisal is only your opinion and is subject to criticism. The opposing attorney will usually succeed in showing up some of the weak points. Don't get angry or give evidence of insecurity. You should always feel free to say, "Yes, sir, that is my opinion."

11. If you have actually made an error in computation, admit it and try to correct it. Do so with care. Decide if that error actually changes your value. Remember, you may have used other approaches to value.

12. Never take an assignment with the fee contingent upon the amount of the award. When you admit to this type of employment in court, you will be disqualified as a witness.

13. Keep good worksheets and guides for your testimony, but memorize as much of the appraisal as possible. You should be thoroughly conversant with the valuation of the property and able to talk about it readily.

14. Be sure that you visit the property several times before testifying. Take many photographs. Be able to locate it on various maps of the area. Also have the same acquaintanceship with all comparable sales.

SETTING A FEE

More stress must be placed upon the setting of a fee for condemnation appraising than for other appraisal purposes. For one thing, the contingent fee problem is more prevalent. This is due to the fact that attorneys sometimes set their fees as a percentage of an award and incorrectly suggest that similar arrangements be made with the appraiser. More often, the owner favors such an arrangement because he is reluctant to pay a large fee when he doesn't know if he will win his case. The appraiser must be paid a fixed fee. Most appraisers will charge a fee for the appraisal and then make a charge for each day that they appear in court or are on call for appearance. The fee may be $500 to $5,000 for an appraisal, plus a per diem court fee of between $100 and $200. Of course, fees for home appraisals or other small properties will be lower. In the event that the lawyer is inclined to demand more than one or two preparatory conferences, an additional fee equivalent to court rates should be charged.

ETHICAL PROBLEMS

The basic problem with condemnation appraising is involved with ethics and the very legal foundation of the system. The appraiser should not be an advocate, yet he is being paid by one of the litigants, who obviously expects that the appraiser will be worth his fee. The judge, in turn, listens to experts on either side of the case. He is not an expert, yet he must make the decision as to value. Sometimes, it becomes obvious to him that he cannot rely on the experts. A recent case in New Jersey involved two experts for a governmental agency who testified to a value of $1,500 while the owner's experts valued the identical realty at $200,000 and $250,000. In other words, the difference alone between the opinions of the owner's experts was about thirty-three times the total value found by the governmental experts.

Such disparities are not common, yet variations of 100 to 500 per cent occur with some degree of regularity. They are often based upon faulty legal or engineering guidance given to the appraisers, who are often abused as much as the courts.

Possibly a better system would involve the employment of three experts by the court, which could choose the experts from a panel who have been qualified by an examination and their experience in appraising the specific types of property in litigation. To prevent political pressures, the panel would be given assignments under a system of automatic rotation. The judge would then give legal instructions to the appraisers and also give them the benefit of other expert opinions, for example, on soil adaptability to specific uses.

The present system, at times, does work properly. Most appraisers resist any pressures and refuse to set values they cannot support. Also, most litigants and attorneys do not make improper suggestions to appraisers.

Owing to the necessity in some jurisdictions, the problem of setting separate land and building values occurs. Often, when there are two appraisers for each side, the judge will combine the higher land value with the higher building value of the experts for the condemning agency, and the lower building value with the lower land value found by the owner's two experts. He will then proceed to set a value somewhere between these two numbers. This is in complete contradiction with the codes of ethics of the various professional societies and with the statements made in the individual appraisals.

In general, property owners obtain an award that is not injurious to their interests and sometimes is most generous. There have been notable exceptions. Since property is being involuntarily surrendered, it is not only against our law but contrary to our philosophy of government to injure any group of citizens by not giving them full compensation for the property taken.

18

Urban-Renewal Appraising

The urban-renewal programs of the federal government have produced some of the most stimulating and controversial assignments, as well as the most rapidly increasing volume, ever received by appraisers. The assignments are of two kinds, one of which involves valuing existing land and improvement for taking under the power of condemnation, and the second of which requires establishing values based on anticipated reuse of the properties once the existing improvements have been removed. In the first type of assignment, the appraiser is the condemning authority's expert, guiding the community and the federal agencies in their decisions as to the appropriate acquisition prices for their properties to be included in their programs. As such, the appraiser should expect to appear in court as an expert witness. In the second type of assignment, the appraiser must consider the best use of the cleared sites either as individual units or as parts of a larger redevelopment plan. In this chapter the principles, problems, and techniques involved in such appraisals are discussed.

THE EMPLOYMENT OF APPRAISERS

Urban-renewal appraisal assignments can emanate from various sources:

1. The director and commissioners of the local community renewal agency may employ one acquisition and reuse appraiser. They will usually ask for guidance from the regional federal urban-renewal office in this selection because they will feel that federal governmental approval will be somewhat easier to secure if they use an appraiser in whom the federal urban-renewal office has confidence.

2. The regional federal urban-renewal office may prepare a list of qualified urban-renewal appraisers from which the local community's choice can be made.

3. The regional federal urban-renewal office until recently would choose the second reuse appraiser and one acquisition appraiser from their list of qualified appraisers. However, the local community now makes this choice.

4. A group of citizens and property owners in a proposed urban-renewal site may wish to approve the project. They may employ an appraiser to determine if the area really requires governmental action.

5. A prospective developer of an urban-renewal project may employ the appraiser to guide him in submitting a price for the land.

6. Condemnation of property for urban renewal will also usually mean that appraisers are hired by property owners and lawyers for property owners, to act as experts in actions taking their property. Such an appraiser will be testifying for the property owner and against the condemning authority.

REUSE APPRAISAL PROCEDURES

Reuse Appraisals. There are actually two reuse appraisals made. The first of these is made at the inception of the project when the appraiser looks at the community and a suggested urban-renewal area and determines if the area is suitable for new development. He must ignore the existing buildings, which are presumably slums, and determine if the land would be valuable for other types of uses if it were cleared of the existing improvements. In considering the problem, he must do many things:

1. Examine neighboring land uses to determine their influence upon, and compatibility with, the redevelopment area
2. Study street, road, and highway patterns and chart access to the area
3. Examine topography of the area and neighboring portions of the community (He will also consider bearing qualities of the soil, flooding conditions, and utilities serving the site.)
4. Analyze public transportation facilities, because they will be of major consideration in close-in sectors of large cities and of lesser importance in small communities and outlying sectors of large cities

In addition, he may very likely have to make a thorough study of the economic factors directly and indirectly affecting the community and the neighborhood. These will include a complete population analysis; studies of the employment and income of the population, of uses of realty, and of economic trends; and a complete market and feasibility study. Recently, the federal government has asked that a market and feasibility study be made separate from the first reuse appraisal and at an early date.

Coordination of Appraiser and Planner. The reuse appraiser will work in conjunction with the planning department of the community and the city planning consultant, since all will be concerned with providing a good redevelopment use for the urban-renewal area. For example, the redevelopment plan must not be destructive to the community but should create an area which is so attractive to developers and so well priced that it will attract some of the best business and residential use from the community. However, it is important that, in the process, a new slum not be created by such movements, since this would be a waste of the urban-renewal program; rather, the redevelopment area must be planned so that it will be an asset to the community. It should, therefore, complement and build upon other land uses in the community and not compete with them.

Land-Use Controls. The appraiser and market and planning consultants will find it necessary to consider the intensity of development, which will include land coverage, parking and loading ratios, heights of buildings, amounts of units of buildings, and people using buildings. Finally, the appraiser and market consultant will recommend types of uses and the boundaries of the project and give an estimate of resale price of the land.

It must be understood that the resale price will always be tied together with conditions of land-use controls. The appraiser and planner will recommend specific intensities of land development. If the developer erects substantially more units of buildings on the land than contemplated, he is expected to pay a higher price for the added use he is obtaining from the land.

The second reuse appraisal is more conclusive as to the resale price. Here, the appraiser's primary objective is to find a proper market price for a project that has been analyzed and approved. This does not mean that the second reuse appraiser must automatically concur with previous findings. He may not even agree that the project is marketable, or that the uses assigned are marketable, either in the quantities or in the specific sites designated. If he does not agree with the proposal, he must then suggest prices which he believes will encourage the planned development of the land while avoiding hidden "speculative" profit, but the appraiser, in doing this, will fix a value for the project site by site and use by use. Often, a redevelopment area may have from five to twenty uses or more, and some projects have exceeded 100 acres, thus requiring a high degree of multiplicity of uses.

URBAN-RENEWAL USES

Land uses in urban-renewal areas can run the entire gamut of possible urban uses including streets; schools; apartments (often of several varieties and price ranges); private houses; offices; industrial; retail; motels; cultural; recreational; parks; museums; federal, state, county, and city buildings; and parking. Recently, all but one of these uses was programed for a large project in Syracuse, New York.

One immediate problem faced by the appraiser is to set the reuse price for property being purchased by the community for governmental use. Since he is not able to set prices for these uses from the market place, he must appraise them as though they would be utilized by the most obvious and appropriate private use compatible with the redevelopment plan as a whole. Usually, this use will be similar to adjacent uses planned for the redevelopment area.

MARKET-PLACE THINKING

The biggest problem of the reuse appraiser is to implant firmly in his mind one basic question, "Will a developer do the things I'm recommending, and will he pay the land price as appraised?" Many projects are planned which will never "take," because no mortgage financing will be available and no developer knows how to put them together. Such projects are highly speculative, and the appraiser errs who includes speculative uses in his assignment. Many realtors and appraisers have projects that they would like to see created, but urban-renewal projects are not proper media for the appraiser to use for such purposes. His uses must be practical and obviously possible in the eyes of the typical project developer. He must be able to show an obvious demand by presenting information indicating that a market exists at the rentals he is stating in his report.

The uses that the appraiser recommends should generate activities for the area. Usually, the existing trends affecting an urban-renewal area are bad. The object of having urban renewal is to change the trends. This is one of the most difficult feats in urban land economics. Only by means of a dramatic and large undertaking can this be accomplished. The appraiser must, therefore, try to find the method that will attract those people to the area who would consider it an appropriate location for new capital investment.

ESTIMATING REUSE VALUE

In estimating reuse value, the appraiser is faced with the difficult problem of estimating values for several acres of land for which no comparable market sales may have been made in many years. Faced with this problem, the appraiser will have to search through the entire community and find instances in which sales were completed for parcels which were put to the same uses as those contemplated in the reuse project.

Example of Reuse Method. As an example of the problems and processes involved in reuse appraising, consider a community in which the second reuse appraisal indicated a need for low-rise office buildings.[1] The appraiser carefully studied the city and found a number of two-story office buildings which had been built recently for tenancy by branch offices of insurance companies, business-machine companies, and similar types of business service organizations. He then computed the ratio of building space per square foot to per square foot of land occupied and related these to the purchase prices of the sites. From this he computed the land cost per square foot of office building constructed and was able to establish the range of prices within which the developers of office buildings would be

[1] This is an actual appraisal completed by one of the authors.

willing to buy land in the reuse area for such types of office-building construction. Final prices were decided on the basis of locational advantages of the reuse site compared to the other sites. In addition, all developers who purchased sites in the reuse area were required to conform to the area's over-all plan with respect to parking ratios, loading ratios, and building heights.

An example involving hypothetical figures will help to clarify the advantages and the use of this method:

Sale 1—64 Action Street. Size: 200 feet × 100 feet. Area: 20,000 square feet. Sales price 11/10/61: $28,000. Existing on the land at time of the sale was an old brick building which cost $2,000 for the buyer to demolish. Therefore, the property cost $30,000 for the buyer to use as a site for a new office building. He paid $30,000 ÷ 20,000 feet, or $1.50 per square foot. He then erected a new office building with its own parking area and with landscaped areas. The building contained a gross building area of 30,000 square feet. The price of the land, therefore, equaled $1.00 per square foot of building area.

Assuming that other sales were similar, we can see that builders will pay for an office-building site a price that will equal $1 for each square foot of office building that can be erected on the land.

In this example, assume that the office-building site in the urban-renewal area contains 100,000 square feet. Also assume that the planned controls for the area limit building height to two stories and land coverage to 25 per cent. This would permit a building of 50,000 square feet.

$$25,000 \text{ square feet} \times 2 \text{ stories} = 50,000 \text{ square feet}$$

Based on the controls and the comparative sales, it can be seen that the reuse value is 50,000 square feet × $1 per square foot of building area, or $50,000.

This value will translate into fifty cents per square foot of land area. Naturally, this will be the value only if the appraiser considers the future use of the land to be exactly equivalent to the land use in his comparative-sales analysis. The value may be modified by any differences in the sites.

The same process was repeated for each use such as store, motel, public parking, and other commercial uses. In this way, a complete value schedule for the urban-renewal area was developed and was translated into a value per square foot of land. It was then only necessary to multiply this value by the number of square feet in each site to find the value of each site.

The advantage of this method is that it utilizes actual sales per use unit. It gives the appraiser a double-check on his judgment and his comparative-sales analysis, by giving him another check on market conditions. If builders in one community are paying higher prices than typical for land for certain uses, it may be due to several causes. First of all, general land costs may be higher. It may also be due to a large demand for good locations for the particular use. If this is so, the appraiser may have a particularly profitable project for a developer, and his land valuation will reflect it. He will then also expect higher rental schedules for the project.

Comparative Sales. Another method of setting the land values is to make comparisons between sales of similar properties and to adjust by lump-sum differentials for variations between the urban-renewal site and comparative-sales sites. These differentials would be caused by variations in land-preparation costs, operating costs, and location (translated into, or from, rental value).

Residual Approach. The standard land residual system of appraising can be applied as a check on the other methods. The appraiser has estimated the types of improvements and their costs. He will also estimate income and expenses for the project. Then he will follow the method by figuring a market return on the investment on the buildings. The residual income will then be available to the land and will be capitalized according to local realty investment market conditions. The resulting amount will be the value of the land after being improved. A proper allowance should be made for the entrepreneurial profit and the time discounting factor.

This method is an excellent tool in the hands of the appraiser who knows all local market conditions. However, it is not to be used by mere system-type appraisers, even though it can be computed on a site or per-acre or per-square-foot basis.

Other Factors. Some consideration must be given to the possibility that the entire urban-renewal area will be purchased by one developer. In that event, some markdown in value may be considered by the appraiser, owing to the wholesale-type acquisition, speculative feature, and extra length of time holding realty before it becomes income-producing.

An important indication of too low valuation occurs if the resale value of the cleared land is below value of the slum land before redevelopment. Under most conditions, an urban-renewal project will eradicate slum conditions and make the land available to better realty activities. If so, future land value should be higher. Naturally, every project will have building controls that restrict land coverage, height, and other conditions of intensity of development, but there usually are certain construction economies geared to such types of buildings that will often compensate for the controls in whole or in part.

In the second reuse appraisal, the appraiser is expected to show the amount of construction in each site. He computes this in units such as motel units, apartments, rooms, square feet of office space, stores, number of car spaces in parking lots, etc. He must compute the capital that will be invested in each site. He must be prepared to suggest how the area is to be marketed and possibly even to recommend specific developers. This is actually a consultation feature rather than an appraisal function, but, in much of his assignment, the appraiser is actually acting as a consultant.

THE MARKET AND FEASIBILITY CONSULTANT

Mention has been made of separate market and feasibility reports under Urban Renewal Administration contracts, which evaluate the urban-renewal project's feasibility. The market and feasibility consultant must study the economic trend of the community and neighborhood and determine the potentiality of the land to support new realty enterprises. This assignment will include a supported opinion of the consultant covering each of the following factors:

1. Suggested boundaries of the urban-renewal area or areas
2. Time necessary to have the area absorbed by the demand for new projects
3. Specific land uses and quantities of land to be allocated to each use
4. General feasibility of the project

Usually, these projects are assigned to appraisers with more than ordinary knowledge of urban-land economics and the real estate investment market. Although much information covering population, income, retail sales, and housing supply and demand statistics is included in these reports, this is included as a tool to supplement and assist the judgment and decision-making role of the realty expert.

ACQUISITION APPRAISING FOR REDEVELOPMENT

In addition to reuse appraisals, acquisition appraisals are also made. These are typical condemnation appraisal assignments, but usually many individual properties are condemned. A typical assignment may cover from 50 to 500 parcels. Most of the properties will be of poor quality and obsolete, but the appraiser may find some high-grade realty included in his area, which will present some of his most difficult appraisal problems. Obviously, since urban-renewal areas are large, he may also have to appraise all types of realty including special-purpose realty such as churches, clubhouses, theaters, and bowling alleys.

Usually two acquisition appraisals are made (or one made in two parts). In the first one, or the first portion of the assignment, the property owner will still have title to the realty. He may be reluctant to give information on rental income and operating expenses. If the appraiser cannot induce the owner to give him the information, he must make his own estimates. A further problem will occur if he is refused permission to inspect the interior of the premises. He must then utilize skill in either talking his way in or making estimates. In the final appraisal, however, he will be able to see the realty and have the rental schedule, as the condemning authorities will then have title. He will then be able to properly testify about these matters.

PROBLEMS OF THE APPRAISER

In reuse appraising, the appraiser will sometimes find certain pressures made upon him. He may be asked to prepare a valuation that merely supports a price previously agreed to by a developer and the urban-renewal director. This price is usually very low, and the community is willing to mark the value down sharply to solve its immediate problem. Since the federal government assumes most of this markdown, the community often feels that this is good business. The problem of the appraiser is obvious in this case. Needless to say, if the federal authorities believe he is a party to this type of arrangement, his appraisals will not be recognized. He will also be destroying local realty values, and the realtors will condemn his activities.

The appraiser may also be confronted with a difficulty in the person of the planning consultant. The consultant may also attempt to win the appraiser to his point of view, particularly when there is a conflict of opinion concerning a proper use of the land. The planner may want certain uses in the area. The appraiser may not be able to justify these uses, on the basis of his findings that a developer could not profitably undertake such uses. These may be difficult questions, but, when both men are experienced and of good will, these problems can be amicably resolved.

QUALIFICATIONS OF REUSE APPRAISERS

The reuse appraiser is actually a combination of urban land economist, city planner, and real estate broker. He must blend these abilities as he studies the effect of the proposed project on the community.

In his abilities must be included a strong understanding of realty statistics, so that he knows what they can and cannot do. He must know that these statistics are not the major basis for realty investment. He must be able to interpret them.

The reuse appraiser must have an honest interest in cities and a desire and ability to understand their problems. He must know how cities develop and what effect specific projects have on their development.

His realty knowledge should consist of actual dealings in city property. He should have negotiated sales, leases, and mortgages. His appraisal experience should include work for investors, mortgagees, and people with estate problems. He must be conversant with investment realty and sales of land for apartment houses and business buildings. This experience gives him specific knowledge of transactions in the market place and an acquaintanceship with the needs and thinking of developers. He can obtain these from the market place, as a participant, and then he will not merely be a reporter of values as told to him by others.

He must also have independent integrity so that he will resist all improper pressures. His personality must be stable. There are too many "prima donnas" in realty. He must believe neither that only he has the right answers nor that he is the only one trying to do a proper job.

Whatever position he takes, he must be able to explain it to civic associations and public officials. Often they will have contrary opinions due to special interests that exist in the town. He must not scorn them for attempting to protect these interests. However, usually, if the appraiser has done a proper job, any opposition will be misguided. Typical opposition will be from local merchants if the urban-renewal area includes new stores. They will usually state that there is now too much competition from the shopping centers. The appraiser must convince them that it may be proper to include more central-business-district stores to enlarge the trading area. An expansion of store presentation of merchandise will usually also expand the trading area for the central business district.

The appraiser's opinions will be respected if he has a reputation for having the enumerated qualifications. Not only will the local realtors, banks, merchants, and political officials trust him, but developers will be more interested in projects that he has stated to be feasible.

One last feature is a must. The appraiser should not associate himself with local political factions, because he will appear to be an advocate of special interests rather than an impartial observer.

Urban-renewal appraising is probably the most important activity for appraisal skills. The volume of assignments has even now caused the appointment of some men with few qualifications for the work. The appraisal profession owes itself and this country an effective performance in every assignment that is undertaken.

19

Mortgage Loan Appraising—
Income Property

The continued importance of credit in the purchase and sale of real property is attested by the fact that mortgage debt has risen from $35.5 billion on all properties in 1939 to $223.1 billion at the end of 1961.[1] In fact, the general levels of business activity, new construction, and home sales are all dependent upon a continued flow of mortgage funds. As a result, the United States has one of the most highly organized and effective mortgage lending systems, the effectiveness of which rests on the activities of the key institutional lenders—insurance companies, savings banks, commercial banks, and savings and loan associations—who regularly supply the great bulk of all mortgage funds loaned. A key part of this mortgage lending system is the loan appraisal, which differs slightly from institutional lender to institutional lender but is basically the same in almost all circumstances.

TYPES OF MORTGAGE LENDERS

The institutional lenders are chartered by state or federal agencies and are limited in the total volume of mortgage lending they can do, in the terms on which they can make mortgage loans, and, most importantly, in their methods of appraising and the amount of money which they can loan on any particular appraised value. On the other hand, the non-institutional lenders are usually free to carry on their mortgage lending as they see fit, but still within rather broad limits.

Insurance Companies. Insurance companies, as a group, comprise an extremely varied type of mortgage lending activity, including, as they do, some small but also some of the largest financial institutions in the country. They make a wide variety of loans on urban and rural properties but, because of the large amounts of funds which they have available for mortgage lending, are usually most interested in furnishing mortgage funds for

---

[1] *Economic Report of the President,* January, 1962 (Washington, D.C.: Government Printing Office, 1962) Table B-50, p. 267.

the large office buildings, industrial plants, shopping centers, and other types of major properties. They do, however, make a considerable volume of loans on single-family homes, but usually only those which represent the best-quality security.

Although insurance companies are chartered by state aegncies, they can be found making mortgage loans throughout the country, through their branch offices or loan correspondents and brokers. Their loans may include FHA-insured, VA-guaranteed, and conventional loans (loans not guaranteed by a government agency).

Savings Banks. Savings banks are concentrated in the northeastern United States and are organized primarily to collect local savings and to lend these savings locally. They can make FHA and VA loans almost anywhere in the country, but they usually restrict their conventional lending to their home-office region. Usually, their lending is limited to single-family home loans, although some of the larger banks will lend on other types of properties. Many make individual six-figure loans. The average size of their mortgage loans tends to be somewhat below that of insurance companies.

Commercial Banks. Commercial banks are interested primarily in making short-term business loans; therefore, they sometimes restrict their mortgage lending to their depositors, as they may make only FHA or VA loans. They do serve as an excellent source of short-term construction loans, even though they tend not to maintain a large portfolio of permanent mortgage loans. Some commercial banks may even serve as correspondents for other mortgage lenders such as life insurance companies or pension funds, and their trust departments are often searching for good mortgage loans in which to invest estate and trust funds.

Savings and Loan Associations. Savings and loan associations are also organized primarily to collect local savings, but the bulk of their mortgage lending is limited to one- to four-family homes. All of the associations may lend a small portion of their assets for larger-income properties, but usually only the larger associations will invest funds in these income properties. Associations tend to favor conventional loans, but many can and do make government-insured and -guaranteed loans in all parts of the nation.

Savings and loan associations are permitted to make higher-percentage loan-to-value mortgages than other institutional lenders, but they also insist on amortized repayment of both principal and interest, a practice which they are credited with originating. In this way they maintain a constant flow of funds from the mortgagees.

Pension and Welfare Funds. Of growing importance as sources of mortgage loans are the pension and welfare funds administered by companies and unions. These funds may be administered by a specially created investment department or by commercial banks or insurance companies. Recently, savings banks were also permitted to act in this capacity. In some cases the funds may be administered by a state agency which is under the control of the state treasurer or comptroller.

The mortgage lending policies of the funds vary, with some funds preferring only government-guaranteed or -insured loans and others any type of quality loans. For example, one of the funds recently made a loan of $40 million on a large office building, one of the largest mortgage loans ever placed by a single institution.

Non-institutional Lenders. Many non-institutional lenders prefer to limit their mortgage lending to unusual types of loans, often those with high risks, because of the better returns possible with such loans and because the demand for such loans is quite strong in an expanding ecoonmy. Such lenders may be individuals, estates, real estate brokers, or non-profit and semipublic institutions.

LENDING POLICIES

Although each institution will have its own lending policy which reflects the thinking of its mortgage department, officers, and loan committees, there are certain policies rather generally common to all mortgage lenders.

First of all, even if a profit would result, every effort is made to prevent the creation of a loan which would have any likelihood of default. The reason is obvious. Mortgage lending is a service operation, and it is necessary that each loan be trouble-free to the mortgagee. Interest rates of almost any size do not produce sufficient income to the institution to pay for the administrative action involved in dealing with troublesome or delinquent loans.

The success of a mortgage department is measured by a low record of foreclosures, and a foreclosure is usually considered to be evidence of error on the part of a lending officer, or error in the lending procedure. Furthermore, all mortgage lending actions are subject to review by the institutions' officers and regulating agencies who would be quick to challenge any consistently bad foreclosure record.

Fee Appraisals. Some mortgage lenders have their own appraisal staffs, but many employ real estate appraisal firms to appraise realty before mortgages are made. Some institutions will have independent appraisals made for all mortgages, and others will have them only when a mortgage exceeds a given size. Even when the institution uses an independent appraiser, it will normally have the realty reviewed by its own staff, which will usually include one or many professional appraisers, in addition to mortgage supervisors. If the staff appraiser considers the work of the fee appraiser suitable, he may then recommend future assignments to the fee appraiser.

Independent fee appraisers are used for the purpose of supplying the added opinion of an appraiser who is neither directly responsible to the lending officer nor dependent upon him for a weekly salary. The independent appraiser, if possible, will do a complete appraisal, utilizing the best and most appropriate techniques to arrive at an opinion of value. He will then submit a complete report, sufficiently detailed, to explain how he arrived at his valuation, but not necessarily a detailed explanation of each of his value judgments. As an appraisal expert, or more properly as a realty expert, he is hired for his expert opinion—not to present a detailed analysis defending such opinion. Naturally, the expert must later document this opinion if a problem arises. He will have in his appraisal files work sheets which support his opinions. The crux of his problem is never to give a value which is not supportable in the market place.

The fee appraiser is usually employed by the lending institution on an assignment-to-assignment basis. The institution will have a list of appraisers whom it considers expert in a locality or in certain types of realty. A few institutions may rely on a single appraiser to handle all assignments, but this is somewhat unusual.

Regulatory agencies play a key role in setting mortgage lending appraisal policy, because they regularly analyze the mortgage portfolios of institutions subject to their jurisdiction. Any appraisals which were the basis for mortgages which the regulating authority questions will be critically examined. If the appraisal is not supportable, then the lending institution and the appraiser will both be in a vulnerable position; the lending institution's portfolio will receive a poor rating, and the appraiser will not be given further assignments.

This emphasizes a critical issue in this field. Some aggressive mortgage officers who have excessive funds to lend may sometimes be tempted to make loans that cannot be considered prudent. If the appraiser happens to value a property below an amount sufficient to justify a loan, there may be conflict between the lender and the fee appraiser. However, in most cases, the lender will realize that the independent appraiser's opinion must govern. The appraiser, if necessary, will show the lending officer how the value was determined and why a higher value would be insupportable. Usually, in actual practice, a mortgage officer will ask an appraiser neither to change his value nor to reach a particular value when the appraisal is being assigned.

Appraisal Fees. Fees are set by actual time, effort, and knowledge that must be applied to each assignment. Consideration is also given to the size of the realty. Some professional societies suggest that the fee should never be contingent upon the final value. The belief is that appraisers would be prone to raise their values in order to obtain a larger fee. A quick arithmetic calculation should prove that the slight additional fee involved ($10 or less per $10,000) would not be a temptation to any reputable member of the appraisal profession. In this connection, many real estate boards recommend fees based upon final value.

Mortgage Safety Features. Mortgage lenders will take every precaution to make prudent loans, which means that they are always concerned with the ability of the borrower to meet the contract obligations. On an investment property, this means that the income must be high enough to pay all charges against the realty, the full interest and amortization charges, and a surplus sufficient to give the owner a satisfactory return. The lender is not directly concerned as to whether or not the owner has a surplus as such, but he wants to be sure that there is an adequate surplus to protect the mortgage, in case income declines or expenses increase. This is a safety feature covering the "margin for error." Usually, lenders calculate that net income free and clear must be from 150 per cent to 250 per cent of debt charges. For example, assume that a mortgage is being processed for $100,000 and has annual debt charges of $8,500 including 6 per cent interest rate. Also assume that net income before the payment of debt service is $17,000. This means that the income is twice as large as the debt-service charge ($17,000 ÷ $8,500 = 2, or 200%).

Under certain conditions, lenders may relax this measurement standard. If the property to be mortgaged is occupied by a tenant that is well rated and subject to a lease that extends for several years beyond the mortgage term, they may not apply this formula to the same degree. Also, if the mortgage calls for very heavy amortization payments, it would not be necessary to have the high ratio, for two reasons: First, it is obvious that the very heavy amortization would make it more difficult to apply the ratio, and, second, if the loan is being repaid more quickly, the loan is less hazardous than a similar mortgage loan with slower payout provisions.

A special adaptation of the ratio is applied by many lenders to shopping-center loans. They often add up all the rental income from national tenants rated AA–A1. They then take complete operating charges, taxes, and insurance and debt charges on the desired loan and deduct these from income. If the AA–A1 income is not as large or larger than the charges, they will not make a loan on those terms. This obviously doesn't mean they will reduce the interest-amortization rates. They will insist that the amount of the loan application be reduced to bring income and expenses in line. It is important to note that rent from small chains and independent tenants will not be computed in this measurement. This does not mean that a shopping center with all national tenants will qualify for a loan where income and expenses are at a one-to-one ratio. No income would be available to the owner, and the appraisal would not justify the loan. Obviously, under almost all circumstances, the capitalization approach to value would prevent this loan from being made.

Loan-Value Ratio. Most institutional mortgagees are restricted to making a mortgage loan that is considerably below the value of the realty. In most cases, investment realty loans cannot exceed 66⅔[2] per cent of appraised value. Special legislation has sometimes permitted loans to be 80 per cent and even ninety per cent of appraised value, but these are usually government-insured or -guaranteed loans on one- and two-family dwellings.

The 66⅔ per cent standard is based on the assumption that the mortgage should, in case of foreclosure, be able to sell the realty without loss. This works well if the following conditions prevail:

1. If the original valuation was well prepared, by a skilled appraiser
2. If no economic catastrophe took place either nationally or in the neighborhood or community
3. If much time passed since the loan was made and an effective amortization schedule reduced the amount of the loan

The loan-value ratio, or percentage, is an excellent investment safety standard but sometimes acts to interfere with good investment opportunities. Furthermore, by giving the same treatment to top-grade loans as to mediocre loans, it fails to differentiate between various types of loan risks. For example, a mortgage officer may wish to exceed this ratio when a well-located property is under lease to a prime tenant for twenty-five years. It it obvious that, if this realty is appraised at $150,000, he can lend only $100,000. The tenant is paying an annual net rental of $11,250. With that set of conditions, a loan of $120,000, with constant payments of $10,200 including 5½ per cent interest, will pay out the loan in about nineteen years and three months. This will give a rental surplus of $1,050 above debt charges. When the mortgage is completely paid out, there will be nearly a six-year obligation under the lease. By all investment standards, this is a very prudent loan.

Compare the safety of the above loan with a mortgage on a home or a store property occupied by small merchants. It should be obvious that, if all types of loans have the same ratio applied to them, the weaker loans are being favored.

The summation approach to value is an additional harsh check against prime credit loans. If the land and building costs on a new building are added together, the result will often be below the market value of the realty.

---

[2] Legislation now permits 75 per cent and 80 per cent conventional loans in some states by savings banks and insurance companies, but these ratios are seldom used.

This approach to value gives no consideration to the low risk of the realty based on the high quality of rental obligation. If the theory prevails that cost sets the upper limit value of a new building, then, under the loan-value-ratio formula, it is even difficult to make a 66⅔ per cent loan on prime credit realty.

However, the capitalization-of-income approach reflects the willingness of buyers to accept a lower rate of return when a long-term lease with a national tenant is involved; and, in most cases of this type, the income approach will be considered to more properly reflect market value. Furthermore, the comparative-sales approach will provide additional checks on the use of the income-capitalization approach, by showing prices actually being paid for these investments.

As in most types of appraisals, the summation approach can actually distort the valuation process. This will be discussed further at the end of this chapter.

The Mortgage Appraisal. In preparing investment property mortgage appraisals, the appraiser will try to place himself in the position of an investor. He will be concerned with the current market value and the reasonably expected performance of the realty during the term of the mortgage period. He will analyze income to determine its present amount and consider what will happen in the future. He will examine all expense items and then trend them for expected changes. He will place particular stress on real estate taxes as an item that can be expected to rise constantly. But he will not merely generalize. In a few communities, there may be no necessity to expand schools because of land use, so this type of community might not be vulnerable to major tax increases. A suburban community may have large shopping centers and industrial parks which provide a very adequate tax base so that the tax liability may be lower than in a neighboring suburban town with mainly one-family homes.

The appraiser will spend a good deal of his time thinking about the location. He will attempt to determine if its future trend is up or down. Will it attract more people of high spending power? He will ask what rate of return an investor will want when buying this property.

Although a proper appraisal will be made on a free and clear basis, no skilled appraiser will fail to consider the return on cash investment. In most property purchases, the buyer computes his return on his cash investment after computing debt charges on a typical mortgage, available in the market. The appraiser must also employ this check against his formal approach.

The mortgage appraisal report will include all of the standard parts found in any good appraisal. Since location is so important in investment realty, a good description of surrounding realty will be included, including an area map which shows transportation, shopping, parks, major realty developments, educational, civic, cultural, and religious activities. The appraiser will often include many photographs in color in an attempt to give a picture of the entire neighborhood.

Finally, the appraiser will relate his opinion of value to a specific date and purpose. Some institutions are very particular as to the choice of words here. Although typically an appraiser will state the value to be "market value," some institutions want the report to simply say "value." They do not want any limiting conditions. For this reason, the appraiser must determine the lender's policy on this matter before preparing an appraisal.

The appraisal will usually include the summation approach and the capitalization-of-income approach as well as the comparative-sales approach. However, not only will the comparative-sales approach be used to support the other two approaches, but the comparative land sales will help to justify the land value in the summation approach, and the sales of other properties will be used to determine the market capitalization rate.

Special Problems of Mortgage Loan Appraising. Most mortgage appraisals require that the values be broken down to show separate land and building values. Many leading authorities do not agree that the parts can be distinguished once land and structure have been joined together. As an example, consider the builder-investor who purchases a piece of land at the junction of two major roads, for $25,000. He contacts a major oil company, and they agree to take a twenty-five-year lease on a new station that the builder erects for $35,000. His total cash investment is $60,000. The rental that is agreed to is $7,000 per annum, net, with the tenant paying an average of $0.015 per gallon on all gasoline sales over 475,000 gallons per annum. Immediately after completion, the builder sells the realty for $93,000, to an investor who is happy to obtain 7.5 per cent on his money free and clear. It is evident that the builder has sold the realty for about $33,000 over his cost. The problem in allocating value to the land or building is apparent. Obviously, the value has been increased, because the owner has combined the land and building with a proper occupancy. (This does not imply that the tenant is overpaying.)

In economics, it is sometimes stated that, in addition to land, labor, and capital, one factor of production is the entrepreneur or management. Possibly this is an example. In studying this example, some might be under the impression that the difference is a "builder's profit." That item goes to the contractor and has been figured in the $35,000 cost. The party referred to as a "builder" in this example actually employs a contractor in the same manner as is available to anyone who plans to build. The builder-investor is actually an entrepreneur, and the extra $33,000 that the builder-investor can obtain on a resale is his only compensation for his efforts in putting this transaction together. It is reasonable to assume, therefore, that this sum represents entrepreneurial profit or wages.[3]

Another problem in mortgage lending is not the direct concern of the appraiser, but it will influence the investment. This is the question of the loan-value ratios mentioned previously. It would seem logical to vary them in connection with types of realty investments so that properties with leases of fifteen years or more, which are to be paid by national credit tenants, could be made eligible for 75–80 per cent loans instead of for the normal 66⅔ per cent. Some lending institutions are allowed to make 80 per cent and even 90 per cent loans on houses in some states, but these ratios were introduced primarily in order to stimulate home ownership. Surely, if this legislation is considered proper, laws also should be passed that will give lending institutions opportunities for high loan-value ratios on all low-risk properties.

[3] Sanders A. Kahn, "The Entrepreneur: The Missing Factor," *The Appraisal Journal* (in press).

20

FHA and VA Single-Family-Home Appraisals

The residential appraising activities of the Federal Housing Administration (FHA) and the Veterans Administration (VA) are placed under two important constraints which influence the nature of the work. In the first place, the appraisal procedures of each agency must be basically the same and use approximately the same valuation standards, except for certain regional differences, because of the mass of appraisals which are completed and the fact that both are national agencies. In the second place, the appraisal methods must be fairly simple and clear but still take into account that the value must reflect a reasonably long trend because the properties will be security for rather long-term (i.e., up to thirty years, or perhaps more) loans.

The need for standard appraisal policies and procedures has been met by the publication of various manuals, of which the most important is the FHA *Underwriting Manual,*[1] which gives the procedures, policies, and theory on which all FHA appraisals are based. These are followed to a degree by the VA. Each agency uses standard appraisal forms which are furnished to each appraiser, and each item on the forms must be completed. The particular construction requirements and cost figures which are to be used are also furnished the appraiser, but they reflect local needs and trends.

FHA AND VA LOAN PROGRAMS

The purpose of FHA and VA appraisals is to determine the degree to which the property being pledged as security for the loan will continue to maintain a market value which is in excess of the remaining amount of the loan. However, FHA appraisals tend to place more emphasis on future long-term values so that there will be sound loans on sound property. The VA's approach is that of a sponsor seeking a "reasonable value" for its ward, the veteran.

[1] Washington, D.C.: Government Printing Office.

The FHA *Underwriting Manual* emphasizes that the value sought refers to "a price which a purchaser is warranted in paying for a property rather than a price for which a property may be sold, and is defined as: the price which typical buyers would be warranted in paying for the property for long-term use or investment, if they were well informed, acted intelligently, voluntarily and without necessity."[2] This definition reflects the FHA assumption that buyers and sellers purchase properties primarily for future benefits which are then translated into current prices. By contrast, the VA philosophy reflects the requirements of its enabling legislation which emphasizes a value estimate based on current prices. This difference between FHA and VA is based on the fact that FHA value relates to prices which "buyers are warranted in paying" whereas VA value will tend to reflect prices which buyers are actually paying. However, their final value estimates under either policy are not likely to vary widely during periods of relative stability in real estate markets. During periods of housing shortages, premium prices for immediate acquisitions are more likely to influence VA appraisals.

The FHA has a unique risk-rating system which affects part of the appraisal system. Under this system, methods are established for rating on a numerical scale the economic background of the city in which the property is located, the neighborhood, the site, the property, the borrower, and the mortgage pattern. An unsatisfactory rating in any of these categories is sufficient reason for refusing to insure a loan. The appraiser is required to provide an evaluation for the neighborhood, on which the numerical rating is based, and actual ratings for the site. He is guided in his rating process by a detailed comparative analysis with other neighborhoods and other properties, as is outlined in the *Underwriting Manual*.

A substantial proportion of both FHA and VA appraising is concerned with tract construction and involves value estimating from blueprints. Neither agency insures a tract, as such, but only individual properties in the tract. For this reason each property and site must be evaluated independently, but the process is facilitated when similar floor plans are being used. The remainder of the FHA and VA appraisals are concerned with scattered, individual homes. The actual appraisals may be done for the FHA by staff or fee appraisers and for the VA by fee appraisers selected from a panel of approved appraisers. In all cases, the appraisers must take a series of courses which instruct them in the policies and procedures of the respective agencies.

A final important difference between FHA and VA estimates is that the buyer using the FHA plan may pay more for the property than is indicated by the appraisal, while the VA buyer is not permitted to pay more than is indicated by the appraisal. Under these conditions, it is important that all

2 P. 1005.

similar types of properties be treated in a uniform manner, so both agencies will exercise more than usual care to produce uniform appraisals.

THE APPRAISAL PROCESS

The FHA, through its innovation of the risk-rating procedure, and its thorough, analytical approach to the entire valuation process of residential properties, has contributed greatly to the advance of appraisal technique in the last twenty-five years. Its basic procedures have been adopted by most leading lending institutions and are familiar to any experienced appraiser. The appraisal begins with an analysis of the neighborhood and then continues through a checklist of fifty or more items which ends with a numerical rating of the location. After evaluating the neighborhood, the appraiser makes a detailed architectural and functional analysis of the main building, subordinate buildings, other site improvements, the site, prevailing market prices and rentals and the general state of supply and demand for homes in the area, and finally the degree of marketability the subject property will probably enjoy.

Great emphasis is placed on the sales-comparison method, and the agencies will often supply their appraisers with information on recent sales and recent appraisals. The appraiser is expected to use his own judgment in establishing the comparability of the properties. The comparable properties are then used to establish the range within which the value of the subject property will be found.

After the market-price estimate has been established, the appraiser estimates the replacement cost of building the subject property, on the basis of unit cost figures and comparable land prices. The replacement cost new is then used as the upper limit of value and will be the figure used if the market price exceeds this amount.

The FHA (but not the VA) then uses a final check on value by means of a gross rent multiplier developed by the agency from a review of rents and sales prices. In some instances, the appraiser may have to establish his own multipliers. The usual lack of valid rental data in a single-family-home area usually limits the validity of this approach so that its chief function is that of providing an additional check on the other two approaches. It would rarely serve as either an upper or a lower limit in a value estimate.

The FHA appraisal report is completed with ratings applied to forms known as *rating grids* for analyzing the physical-security and site-desirability features of the subject property. On each grid each item must be checked in either the reject column or column 1, 2, 3, 4, or 5. The location of the check mark determines the value given to each item. These values are totaled by the appraiser to obtain the total category rating. A reject rating of any feature in the grid results in the agency determining whether the total, or checks in a reject column, is sufficient for refusing the loan application. The appraiser is also given the opportunity of making any additional remarks about the area or the comparable properties which would aid the reviewing officer in determining his concurrence with the appraiser's conclusions. Pictures of the subject property and the area, and plot plans to scale, are attached to each completed form. The VA does not follow the FHA grid rating system but has its own appraisal forms; however, there are few basic differences in the field methods.

Once the appraisal forms have been completed and submitted, they are sent to the respective agencies for a series of reviews and, if necessary, revisions for completeness, accuracy, and consistency. The major problem of the reviewing officers is to see that all pertinent agency regulations, standards, and requirements have been complied with and that comparable value estimates have been made for comparable properties. Appraisals by the FHA and VA for the same properties may or may not be the same, because the agencies are not required by law to check with each other; their purposes are different; but they may attempt to maintain liaison between their appraisers. Furthermore, the FHA maintains a staff of appraisers which is supplemented with fee appraisers whenever there are temporary periods of extra heavy work, whereas the VA operates completely with fee appraisers. In each local office of each agency there is one officer who is assigned the responsibility for seeing that local appraisal policies and procedures are proper and in conformity with national policy.

LOCATION ANALYSIS

The emphasis which the FHA places on location analysis provides interesting insights into the thoroughness with which the agency undertakes all phases of value and mortgage loan analysis. These instructions, as presented in the FHA *Underwriting Manual,* provide a model which any appraiser would do well to follow. The rating schedule shown in Fig. 6 is only a bare skeleton of the items which they name.

Among the more important principles emphasized by the FHA are the importance of location with respect to the direction of city growth, the difference between new and old neighborhoods, the value of having younger families who are likely to continue to reside in a neighborhood, the importance of good planning, the impact of homogeneity in promoting value, and the rate of buildup in the area.

Adverse Factors. Locations are expected to be protected from inharmonious uses by properly drawn and enforced zoning regulations and protective covenants. The geographic location of the neighborhood and the character of the neighborhood structures are supposed to enhance the quality of family living. For example, natural and artificial barriers to inhar-

Site-desirability features	Reject	1	2	3	4	5	Rating
Protection against inharmonious land uses		4	8	12	16	20	
Physical and social attractiveness		4	8	12	16	20	
Adequacy of civic, social and, commercial centers		4	8	12	16	20	
Adequacy of transportation		4	8	12	16	20	
Sufficiency of utilities and services		2	4	6	8	10	
Level of taxes and special assessments		2	4	6	8	10	
Rating of site desirability							
Relative marketability		16	12	8	4	0	
Rating of location	Rate of site desirability minus adjustment for relative marketability						

Fig. 6. FHA site-rating grid.

monious encroachments, street layouts which discourage heavy through traffic, and areas dedicated by law or usage to residential uses are given great weight.

The physical and social attractiveness of an area is determined by the environmental appearance of the neighborhood and the degree to which family health, safety, and recreation are affected. Such potential dangers as rough or steep topography, subsidence, floodings, oil or gasoline storage, and similar items are all considered. These analyses are supplemented with consideration of landscaping, neighborhood design, architectural appearances, and compatibility of the neighborhood occupants.

Convenience. The ability of a neighborhood to maintain property values and the amenities of family living, in addition to the above attributes, is determined by consideration of the quality and accessibility of schools, shopping centers, churches, recreation centers, and theaters. The presence or absence of adequate transportation to work, shopping, and other areas of the city is also considered, but it is rated by comparison with availability of such facilities in all areas of the city. Adequacy is measured in terms of diversity, cost, quality, frequency, distance from the area to boarding points, and travel time to various destinations.

Utilities and Services. Sufficiency of utilities and services such as police and fire protection, garbage disposal, street improvements, and similar items is measured in a large degree by the attitudes of the persons in the neighborhood. Thus, a neighborhood may require the use of septic tanks for sewage disposal but not be rated down if the homeowners considered this to be acceptable. Cost and quality of service are rated on the degree to which they are comparable to other areas.

Taxes. Taxes and special assessments are rated according to the burden they place on the areas as compared to other similar areas. Special attention is given to the nature, amount, and the duration of the special assessments, particularly when they are unusually high or obligate the homeowner under special bond issues.

The rating is summarized in a final numerical value which includes some estimate of the comparability of a neighborhood to other neighborhoods. For example: will the properties share in any market increases or declines because they are in a particular area? Is the demand for properties in this area strong?

ANALYSIS OF PROPERTY

To determine eligibility for an FHA-insured loan, a number of property analyses have to be made. These include detailed architectural and cost analyses for properties to be constructed and unit cost and physical security analyses for existing properties. The analysis of physical security shown in Fig. 7 summarizes the more important property features which are of concern to the FHA in all of these analyses.

Visual Appeal. The analysis of visual appeal is based not on the appraiser's preferences but on his judgment as to the degree to which the property will appeal to the general buying public. Some of the items which the FHA *Underwriting Manual* states will add to the appeal are simplicity or "freedom from complexity, intricacy and elaborateness," harmony derived from well-proportioned elements, and "good taste" or "freedom from ostentation, and by restraint in design." Also considered are the integrity of the exterior design, the wisdom exercised in fitting the house to the site, and the functional qualities of the interior. Each of these items is expected to add to the marketability of the property.

Layout. The analysis of livability is basically an attempt to measure the degree to which the property will promote family living because of the convenience and comfort arising from the various items listed under this feature. For example, the site is expected to be utilized in a way which promotes both indoor and outdoor living. Interior design is evaluated in terms of the promotion of various family activities. Provisions for closet and storage space, kitchen efficiency, and minimum waste space are given high priorities. Natural light and ventilation might be considered to be a part of livability, but the FHA rating singles these out for special consideration. Its analyses of these items lay stress on the desirability of maximum natural daylight and natural through- or cross-ventilation (i.e., openings located on opposing walls of a room).

								(Serial Number)

Property Address _____

City _____ State _____ Basic Structure_____

Features and Component Elements	Ratings							Remarks
VISUAL APPEAL OF PROPERTY	Rej.	1	2	3	4	5	Rating	
		4	8	12	16	20		
Exterior Design of Structures								
Setting								
Interior Design of Dwelling								
LIVABILITY OF PROPERTY	Rej.	1	2	3	4	5	Rating	
		4	8	12	16	20		
Site Utilization								
Dwelling Space Utilization								
Room Characteristics								
Room Orientation								
Circulation								
Privacy								
Closet and Storage Space								
Kitchen Efficiency								
Service Facilities								
Insulation								
NATURAL LIGHT AND VENTILATION	Rej.	1	2	3	4	5	Rating	
		2	4	6	8	10		
Natural Light								
Natural Ventilation								

Fig. 7. Federal Housing Administration ex-
Housing Administration, *Underwriting Manual*,

Features and Component Elements	Ratings							Remarks
STRUCTURAL QUALITY	Rej.	1	2	3	4	5	Rating	
		4	8	12	16	20		
Foundations								
Wall Construction								
Partitions								
Floor Construction								
Ceiling Construction								
Roof Construction								
RESISTANCE TO ELEMENTS AND USE	Rej.	1	2	3	4	5	Rating	
		2	4	6	8	10		
Lot Improvements								
Building Exteriors								
Building Interiors								
SUITABILITY OF MECHANICAL EQUIPMENT	Rej.	1	2	3	4	5	Rating	
		4	8	12	16	20		
Plumbing System								
Heating System								
Electric System								
Supplementary Equipment								
RATING OF PHYSICAL SECURITY								

Date prepared_____ Signed _____
        Construction Examiner Staff Fee Per diem

Date reviewed_____ Signed _____
        Chief Architect   Deputy for Chief Architect

panded grid rating of physical security (Federal
Washington, D.C.: Government Printing Office).

Structural Analysis. Structural quality analysis does not require an engineering background to be accomplished, but it is facilitated if the appraiser has knowledge of the more common types of construction materials and methods. The purpose of the analysis is to determine whether proper types and qualities of materials have been assembled in a workmanlike manner and have produced a structure which will be sound and also find market acceptance. Details of structural analysis are provided by means of manuals reflecting regional building practices. These manuals set forth the standards commonly advertised as FHA minimum property standards.

Analysis of resistance to elements and use center in the ability of the structure to meet local weather conditions and typical family use. Localities subject to unusual fire hazards or insect and pest damage require special attention to these risks. Under this rating, appraisers are also expected to pay some attention to potentials, maintenance expenses, or hazards. Older properties, for example, are given closer attention in this regard.

Mechanical equipment is rated on its ability to contribute to family comfort. This means that attention is paid to kinds of equipment which are installed, then ease of use, economy of operation, and costs of maintenance. The ratings reflect the desires of the market, particularly insofar as these desires can be judged from an examination of the kinds of equipment being placed in new homes.

The expanded grid form shown in Fig. 7 is used by placing X's in the appropriate grids and putting supporting remarks in the right column. The numerical total is then used as a guide by the reviewing officers.

An appraiser cannot make an accurate estimate of residential values unless he knows something about residential construction. In FHA appraising, particularly, this type of knowledge is required. Included also is an understanding of basic building vocabulary and architectural types. These are subjects which would require volumes of writing to be covered successfully. Figure 8 identifies some of the more common parts of a house and some of the more prevalent architectural types.

ANALYSIS OF THE BORROWER

Since its creation in 1934, the FHA has developed a number of criteria by which it estimates the eligibility of a mortgagor for a loan. The purpose of the analysis is to determine whether the borrower has a sufficient motivation for purchasing a home to make him want to repay the loan on schedule and whether he has sufficient income and assets to avoid defaulting. Each feature in the grid shown in Fig. 9 receives an independent evaluation. Then the total numerical rating must exceed 50 or the application is denied.

THE COMPONENT PARTS OF A HOME

KEY TO CONSTRUCTION DETAILS

1. Window Head Frame
2. Wall Sheathing, Diagonal
3. Verge Board
4. Gutter
5. Window Jamb Trimmer
6. Wood Joist
7. Window Sill Frame
8. Cripple Stud
9. Wall Siding
10. Window Shutters
11. Corner Bracing 45°
12. Corner Studs, Double
13. Sole Plate
14. Box Sill
15. Basement Areaway
16. Basement Sash
17. Grade Line
18. Gravel Fill
19. Ridge Board
20. Collar Beam
21. Roof Rafters
22. Interior Studs
23. Interior Studs
24. Cross Bracing
25. Plaster Base, Lath
26. Gable Studs
27. Interior Window Trim
28. Plaster Walls
29. Cross Bridging
30. Second Floor Joists
31. Arch Framing
32. Insulation, Batts
33. Dining Nook
34. Interior Door Trim
35. Plaster Base, Rock Lath
36. Finish Floor
37. Floor Lining Felt
38. Sub-Flooring, Diagonally
39. Sill Plate
40. Termite Shield
41. Girder
42. Plate Anchor Bolt
43. Post
44. Foundation Wall
45. Frame Partition
46. Tarred Felt Joint Cover
47. Drain Tile
48. Footing
49. Flue Liner Tops
50. Chimney Cap
51. Brick Chimney
52. Flashing
53. Flashing & Counter Spaced 1" x 4" Sheathing (Wood Shingles)
54. Tight Roof Sheathing (All Other Coverings)
55. Ceiling Joists
56. Exterior Wall Plates
57. Lookouts
58. Furring Strips
59. Stair Rail & Balusters

60. Stair Landing Newel
61. Finish Flooring Over Felt Over Sub-flooring on Wood Joists
62. Book Shelves
63. Picture Mould
64. Mantel and Trim
65. Damper Control
66. Ash Dump
67. Base Top Mould
68. Baseboards
69. Shoe Mould
70. Hearth
71. Plaster Ceiling
72. Boiler or Furnace
73. Cleanout Door
74. Basement Concrete Floor
75. Cinder Fill
76. Roof Cover (Shingles)
77. Roofing Felts
78. Soffit of Cornice
79. Facia of Cornice
80. Vert. Board & Batten Siding
81. Fire Stops
82. Ribbon Plate
83. Stair Wall Partition
84. Stair Rail or Easing
85. Starting Newel
86. Main Stair Treads & Risers
87. Basement Stair Rail & Post
88. Wall Stair Stringer
89. Face Stringer & Moulds
90. Starting Riser & Tread
91. First Floor Joists
92. Basement Stair Treads & Risers
93. Basement Stair Newel
94. Facia Board
95. Basement Post
96. Facia Board
97. Cornice Bed Mould
98. Leader Head or Conductor Head
99. Bit Course
100. Porch Rafter
101. Porch Ceiling Joists
102. Porch Ceiling Soffit
103. Porch Roof Beam
104. Porch Beam Facia
105. Entrance Door Trim
106. Leader, Downspout or Conductor
107. Porch Trellis
108. Porch Column
109. Porch Column Base
110. Concrete Porch Floor
111. Concrete Stoop
112. Entrance Door Sill
113. Stoop Foundation

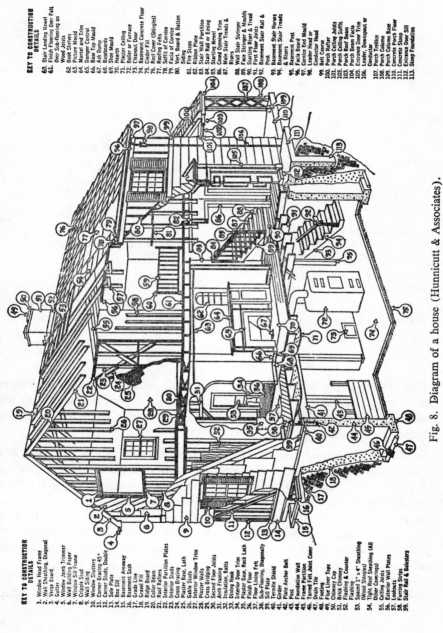

Fig. 8. Diagram of a house (Hunnicutt & Associates).

FEATURES	REJECT	1	2	3	4	5	RATING FACTORS	TOTALS
Credit Characteristics of Mortgagor		4	3	2	1	0	$X =$	
Motivating Interest in Ownership of the Property		4	3	2	1	0	$X3 =$	
Importance of Monetary Interest to Mortgagor		4	3	2	1	0	$X =$	
Adequacy of Available Assets for Transaction		4	3	2	1	0	$X2 =$	
Stability of Effective Income		4	3	2	1	0	$X =$	
Adequacy of Effective Income for Total Obligations		4	3	2	1	0	$X =$	
Order of Assignment of Rating Factors: 6-4-3-2				TOTAL DEDUCTIONS				

RATING OF MORTGAGOR — Maximum possible rating 100 minus Total Deductions

Fig. 9. Rating of mortgagor.

Each of the items is given careful attention, because FHA lending experience has shown that default is usually the result of several causes, each of which by itself might not lead to default, but whose total impact is disastrous.

Buyer Financial Condition. In evaluating the motivation of a borrower, the FHA considers such items as how well the mortgagor has met previous financial obligations, whether he has serious personal defects which would lead to financial instability, the size of his family and the ages of its members, the number of years of his married life, his ability to manage his finances consistently so that he always meets his obligations, and whether he has selected a property which will meet a maximum number of his family's needs.

Ability to pay is related to assets which the mortgagor already has available to meet his initial down payment and loan costs, relationships between his effective income, the mortgage obligation he is assuming, and other financial obligations already assumed. Among assets which would be counted favorably would be ownerships in fee of the lot on which construction is planned and contribution of personal labor in the construction process. The greater the net worth which the mortgagor plans to invest, the greater is assumed to be his ability and interest in repaying.

THE RATING OF MORTGAGE RISK

The final rating of importance to FHA is the mortgage-pattern grid, which summarizes all of the previous ratings (Fig. 10). The purpose of this summary is to provide a basis for selling the mortgage terms which

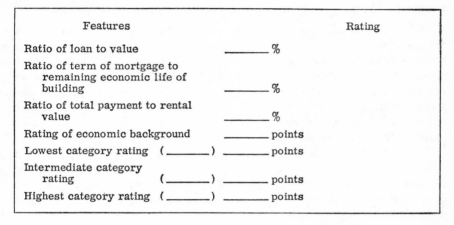

Features		Rating
Ratio of loan to value	_____ %	
Ratio of term of mortgage to remaining economic life of building	_____ %	
Ratio of total payment to rental value	_____ %	
Rating of economic background	_____ points	
Lowest category rating (_____)	_____ points	
Intermediate category rating (_____)	_____ points	
Highest category rating (_____)	_____ points	

Fig. 10. Rating of mortgage pattern (amenity-income case).

would be approved. For example, a high ratio of loan to value request might have to be offset by a mortgage term well short of the remaining economic life of the building. Or a long-term mortgage request might have to be supported by a high economic-background rating. The ratings for the first three items are directly related to percentage amounts as established by FHA policy and legislation, so, for example, a request for a loan equal to 100 per cent of appraised value would be rejected because it would be ineligible under the enabling legislation. The final three ratings deal with points assigned to the property, location, and mortgagor categories. When one or more of these three is given a very low rating, its importance is examined with respect to possible impact on the loan request. The most desirable situation would be one in which all three categories receive high ratings.

FHA AND VA MANUALS

Both the FHA and the VA have various manuals for the use of their appraisers. None of these are generally available to other appraisers, except the FHA *Underwriting Manual,* mentioned previously. In it are found detailed explanations of appraisal procedures and the use of the rating grids. The FHA also issues a manual of *Minimum Property Standards,*[3] with modifications to reflect regional differences, which indicates what is expected in terms of structural design, materials, and workmanship. The agencies also have unit cost handbooks for each of the local areas in which they operate. These give the unit costs to be used in their cost approach and are renewed periodically in order to conform to local cost trends. The FHA also furnishes each appraiser with ratings for the area in which he is working, to be used as bench marks in rating individual properties.

The Place of FHA and VA Appraising. Today the FHA and the VA are faced constantly with the problems of producing a large volume of reasonably uniform appraising at a relatively low cost. The necessity for consistency in reporting cases is one of the biggest problems confronting the agencies. Both FHA and VA appraisers must therefore adapt themselves strictly to agency policy and procedures to attain the desired high degree of consistency between appraisers and must subordinate their own individual opinions to the agency viewpoint.

The problems which the FHA and the VA face in setting standards for volume appraising are similar to those faced by any organization engaged in mass appraising. Certainly these organizations have contributed a great deal to both appraising theory and techniques through their procedures manuals and rating systems.

Many of the appraisal problems of the FHA and VA arise because of the intense political interest in their programs. There is some reason to believe that such political overtones often dictate the manner in which standards are set. For example, Congress has been quite clear in stating the objectives of the VA program, and this has dictated much of the appraisal process and standards, while the FHA is criticized sometimes by groups interested in securing adoption of new materials or construction methods. At all times, appraisers who participate in, or rely on, the FHA and VA appraisal systems must recognize the legislative restraints placed on these organizations.

Over the years, the FHA has constantly pioneered to improve construction standards and has had significant influence on the building industry. Many states, counties, and local communities have adopted standards pioneered by the FHA and have included them in their own building codes and ordinances.

---

[3] Federal Housing Administration, *Minimum Property Standards* (Washington, D.C.: Government Printing Office).

21

Building Analysis—Dwellings

In analyzing a building, the appraiser will probably make one or more inspections before developing an opinion as to value. His first inspection will probably be a cursory outside observation in connection with his preliminary survey, and his second will be a more thorough examination of the interior and the equipment. Before proceeding to his examination, he should equip himself with a checklist of items to be examined, a flashlight, a pocketknife, a carpenter's rule, paper, and a pencil. He should devise a rating schedule for faults that he may find. The schedule should provide a method of classifying these faults into minor, medium, and serious and major categories. In this way, the appraiser may put himself in the place of the typical buyer and rate the building for its desirability as compared with other buildings of the same type that are available for purchase. The inspection of the building should include the style, the exterior, the basic structure, the interior design and construction, and the utilities. To illustrate the procedure to be followed, let us consider the inspection of a one-family wood-frame and wood-siding type of residence.

STYLE

The architectural style and design of a building should be related to the site. Frontage is important. Narrow lots make for narrow, inconvenient houses, like those in cities where residential buildings are built wall to wall, or in suburbs where houses are too close to each other for privacy. A confusion of styles and materials can result in an architectural monstrosity. Generally speaking, the style should be consistent with the other houses in the immediate vicinity, so as to enhance its marketability. It should take advantage of its site characteristics. Thus, if it is basically designed to blend with wooded slope, it should not be put on a level lot devoid of trees. If constructed on a hillside lot, the land should be terraced to avoid erosion. Landscaping is important: A house with attractive plantings and healthy, mature trees may be far more valuable than the same house in an ordinary setting.

Style, design, and site must be considered in relation to the prevailing attitudes of the market. If public taste rejects the style or design, no matter how excellent it may be, the house will lose value. Because of their suitability to local climatic conditions, the various adaptations of Spanish and California styles are popular in the South and the West. The Cape Cod type is still popular in the East. The most striking trend in recent years has been represented by the appeal of the modified ranch and split-level types with most of the living space on a single floor. However, the rising cost of construction has led to a revival of the two-story type as a means of effecting lower building cost.

THE EXTERIOR

The inspection of the outside of a shingle or clapboard house should begin with the exterior walls and corners. By standing a foot or two from each of the walls, the appraiser can look for spaces in the joints between boards, broken and warped shingles, etc. Much that might be overlooked from a distance may be revealed with the line of sight nearly parallel to the wall. A few linear yards of siding separation, requiring calking, is only a medium fault, but, if there are general gaping and looseness, the fault may be considered serious.

Shingles used for siding are usually wood, composition, or plywood. While wood shingles are more expensive than composition, they may be expected to last longer. High-grade cedar shingles may last twenty-forty years. Plywood shingles are usually water resistant and are generally considered satisfactory. Composition shingles do not make for as good an appearance as wood or plywood and are better suited to roofs for that reason.

Any severe protuberance or bulging in the walls, with bending or breaking of the siding, must be regarded as a major fault indicative of a basic structural unsoundness.

In the case of an outside chimney, any separation developing between the masonry and the wall is a serious defect and may mean that the house is going out of plumb. If the chimney is snug against the house but open joints are visible, this may be considered as a minor defect readily correctible by repointing. A light outside chimney on a wooden support is both unsightly and dangerous and becomes a serious defect.

Paint. Wooden houses normally require outside repainting at about five-year intervals, subject to considerable variation. Since the appraiser has no way of knowing how long a fresh coat of paint will last, the presence of old paint is not too revealing. Of much greater importance is the manner in which the old paint is failing. Paint should "chalk" or powder not blister or peel ("flaking"). When flaking occurs soon after a repainting, it is usually a sign of intra-wall condensation. Discolorations or vertical streaks sometimes point to the same difficulty. If moisture damage is also found in the attic and cellar, exterior paint trouble is a conclusive symptom of condensation, becomes a major fault, and affects the marketability of the house.

Roof and Chimney. A well-laid shingle roof in good condition appears as a perfect mosaic when viewed from the ground. A roof nearing the end of its useful life is ragged all over, with numerous broken, warped, and upturned shingles. A roof in poor condition may be rated as a serious fault. In general, the steeper the roof, the longer the life of the shingles. Appraisers may conservatively estimate the life of a roof at fifteen years.

Where the roof is of multilayer material or built up on a flat or slightly pitched deck, the appraiser will have to go up on the roof to inspect it. He should then look for bare spots in the mineral surfacing, separations and breaks in the felt, and corroded flashing at parapet walls and vents.

The chimney should be inspected in relation to the roof for correct design and freedom from leaks. If it is going out of plumb, it will have to be rebuilt sooner or later, and, therefore, it may be rated as a medium fault. Whenever a chimney passes through or adjoins a roof, copper flashing is necessary to prevent leaks. Other materials that are used include heavily galvanized sheet iron, roof rolling, and hot tar or plastic roof cement. Copper is superior to any of these. Tar and cement are seals, not flashing, and require periodic renewal. The presence of any material save copper may be considered a medium fault.

Copper or aluminum gutters and leaders are preferable to galvanized iron, but the latter, if periodically painted, should last as long as the roof. If rust spots and holes appear in galvanized gutters and leaders, they are considered medium faults. Wooden gutters, unless lined with metal or sealed with tar, may develop leaks which will admit water to the walls. Leaders or rainspouts should discharge into buried tile drains to drain off the water, but surface drainage is also common. Stone or concrete splash blocks under leader outlets are frequently used to prevent surface erosion and to keep roof drainage water out of cellars.

THE BASIC STRUCTURE

Attic. If the house has a gable or sloping roof, the appraiser may note, in the attic, that the roof is supported by rafters—2 × 6's or 2 × 8's or even larger ones, depending upon the span and the local building code. These rafters are placed edgeways at 16- or 24-inch intervals and converge at the peak. A steep roof should have horizontal "collar" beams on every other set of rafters about halfway up, for added strength.

Two- by four-inch instead of 2- by 6-inch rafters, except in a very small house, will allow the ridge to sag under a snow load. This is a serious fault. It is also serious if, despite rafter size, there is appreciable deflection. If any of the rafters look suspicious, insert the blade of a knife into them at intervals of a few feet. It should not penetrate more than ⅛ inch. Decaying and deformed rafters will require reframing and probably re-roofing.

If the house has wood shingles, they should be visible from the attic. The shingles should be laid on nailing strips or lath set far enough apart so that half or more of the roof surface will show nothing between the shingles and the rafters. Only in the coldest climates should wood shingles be laid on solid sheathing, and even then there should be no building paper under them. Wood shingles need air. Under asphalt or composition shingles should be found building paper and sheathing. The sheathing is usually laid over the rafters and is usually of solid boards, although ply-wood may be used. The plywood should not be less than ⅜ inch in thick-ness, otherwise it is a medium fault. Plywood is found in the more recently built homes. The sheathing boards are mostly square edged, and there will be spaces where the building paper is visible. If the roofing can be seen through these spaces, it indicates a lack of paper and is a medium fault.

The triangular wall sections at the end of the attic, the gables, are usually places where the wall construction can be studied from the inside. The studs, 2 × 4 or 2 × 6 inches, ordinarily 16 inches apart, should be examined in a manner similar to the rafters. Outside the studs there should be sheathing and building paper, as are on the roof (unless it is wood-shingled). Diagonal sheathing adds more strength to the house, but frequently the gables are sheathed horizontally while the rest of the house is sheathed diagonally. Lack of building paper creates a medium fault, while lack of paper and sheathing, found only in very old houses, is a serious fault, as fuel consumption is apt to be very high.

If the inspection is made on a cold day and the house is heated, look for moisture on any exposed paper surfaces and on the sheathing itself. If enough water has been deposited to run down the slope, it is a serious fault; the attic needs more ventilation than it is getting. Next inspect the plates, the horizontal timbers on which the lower ends of the rafters rest. There should be two visible nails on each side of each rafter; in fact, there should be an abundance of nails wherever the appraiser looks, as nailing is a primary factor in the ability of a building to withstand high winds. Skimpy nailing is a serious fault.

Fire hazards are the next item for which to look. If a chimney goes up through the attic, there should be a space of about 2 inches at the floor all around, which may or may not be filled with incombustible material. There should also be a small marginal gap where the chimney intersects the roof. If the space around the chimney is not filled, it may be possible to see some distance down. If, as in some rare instances, the joists are found built into the chimney and supported by it, it is a major violation of sound building practice. The house and chimney should be structurally independent, each self-supporting, and, further, the presence of any combustible material in masonry is a major fire hazard.

A finished attic presents special problems, as much of the checking described above may not be possible. However, if the house is otherwise well built and in good condition, this inability to make the structural inspection may not be too significant. Another problem arises with finished attics, namely, the practice of insulating them on the rafters. This involves a special hazard.

The practice of insulation requires an answer to the questions: Where is it insulated? What materials were used? How were they installed?

Insulation. Among the most widely used insulating materials are fiber insulating boards, which may be used as wall sheathing or plaster base and thus perform a structural function in giving the house extra rigidity; blankets or batts of mineral wool or equivalent materials (plant fibers, cotton, etc.) or loose fills of the same substances, which provide only insulation but, for a given thickness, do this more effectively than the insulating boards.

In general, a well-insulated house should have insulation of one type or another throughout the walls, in the attic, and in the floor over any unheated area. Complete absence of insulation is a serious fault. If the attic alone is insulated, but not the walls, it is also a serious fault. If the walls are insulated, but not the attic, it is a medium fault. A rough check of the insulation may be made on a winter day by laying a hand alternately on an inside wall and a shaded adjacent outside wall. The two surfaces should feel practically alike even at freezing temperatures. If there is a sharp contrast, it is a serious fault. On a very hot day in the summer the inside temperature of a well-insulated, two-story suburban house with full cellar and attic should not exceed 65° F. in the cellar, 75° on the first floor, and 85° on the second floor—if the windows are kept closed all day.

The amount of insulation called for depends on climate. In the most parts of the United States that enjoy mild temperatures, insulating board $^{25}/_{32}$ inch thick installed as sheathing will provide sufficient insulation, but 3 inches of mineral wool or other soft insulation between the studs will ensure lower fuel bills and more comfort in summer and winter. In colder areas, anything less than the above-described insulation is a serious fault.

Unfortunately, insulation may indirectly cause trouble in a house. Condensation, which occurs whenever relatively warm air laden with water vapor comes up against a relatively cold surface, can precipitate a large quantity of water in a house, especially in the northern areas of the country. Insulation has aggravated the problem of condensation, which existed prior to insulation. The good, tight construction of modern houses makes it harder to get rid of water vapor, and the relative decline in the size of houses creates a correspondingly greater vapor pressure per unit area of walls and ceilings. Much of the better insulation is provided with self-contained vapor barriers, or a separate vapor barrier may be installed. A double coat of aluminum paint on the inside of insulated walls and ceilings is an example of such a separate vapor barrier.

Cellar. A cellar should have a concrete floor, absence of which is a medium fault. A floor drain is a desirable convenience, even if the cellar is perfectly dry. Completely dry cellars under *all* conditions are rarities. When the ground is waterlogged after a thaw or heavy rains, seepage of a small amount of water, no more than enough to wet a floor, is not a fault.

A cellar is most apt to take in water by seepage when the house is located in a hollow, against a bank, below a road, on filled land, or in any other situation where hydrostatic pressure can build up against one or more walls. When a cellar is exposed to underground waters, drains should have been laid in gravel or crushed stone against the outside walls when the house was built. If the cellar floods, there will be water marks on the walls. This is a serious fault. The installation of an automatic sump pump will remedy this condition. Even a perfectly watertight cellar may be wet from the condensation which occurs during the summer on hot, humid days, and this should not be confused with seepage. It is not a fault of the house but a matter of earth and air temperatures.

The cellar, if partly or wholly unfinished, frequently permits the appraiser to learn more about the building than the attic.

The foundation walls in a modern house will be poured concrete, or in small houses with shallow cellars, concrete blocks. Thickness, which should be a minimum of 8 inches in small houses, can be measured at cellar windows. The presence of severe cracks indicates uneven settling or poor material and is a serious fault.

Concrete walls should rest on footings about twice as wide as the walls are thick. If the floor is paved, it will not be possible to determine the presence or absence of footings. If the building is new, the builder can supply the information. The foundation should extend at least 6 inches below the frost line. If you can walk upright in a cellar, they probably do; if you can't, it is a medium defect.

Frame inspection begins with the sills, the horizontal timbers which lie on the foundation walls. Sills should be anchored to the foundation with bolts, two at each corner and 8 feet apart along the walls. The bolts are ordinarily not visible, but in a new house the builder can also supply the relevant information.

The first-floor joists rest on the sill, sometimes partly on the sill and partly on the top of the foundation wall, or, if the sill is high, against it.

They should not be set into the masonry where they can absorb moisture, as this is a medium fault, except where the joist (or other beam) is creosoted and a small space is left around the sides.

The joists rest on girders or main horizontal beams, which may be steel or, if wood, may be built up of three or four thicknesses of 2 × 6 inches, 2 × 8 inches, or larger, depending upon the span. The girders may be supported on hollow steel columns filled with concrete ("Lally columns"), on wooden columns about 8 × 8 inches, or on interior masonry or concrete walls.

Any wood posts set into concrete tend to rot at the base and may offer entrance to termites. This is a medium fault. In any event, wood posts are inferior to steel ones. The best foundation for wood or steel posts, is a concrete footing raised a few inches above the floor.

All accessible framing members should be examined for rot, bad cracks, and sag. If any of them have been deeply notched or cut to pass pipes, they should be reinforced and supported. The joists, which must be no smaller than 2 × 6 inches, are normally spaced on 16-inch centers and should be X-bridged in the middle of the span. Absence of bridging, except where the span is under 10 feet, is a serious fault as it indicates careless construction.

In some old houses, signs of shoring where weakness began to develop may be noticed. There may be a plank, for example, under the joists supported by posts. This is a serious fault and requires further inspection of all the joists and girders. If general decay or weakness of the framing is indicated, it is a major fault.

Before leaving the cellar, one should examine the floors from below. A modern floor consists of a subfloor, building paper, and the finish floor. Absence of a subfloor (rare in a modern house, but common in older ones) is a serious fault. The subfloor should be laid diagonally to add strength to the building and to give a choice of direction for the finish floor.

A house may have a full cellar, partial cellar, or no cellar at all. Where there is a partial cellar, the rest of the house will usually have an air space underneath, or such a space may underlie the entire house. When high enough to admit a man stooping, crawling, or wriggling on his belly, such an underfloor area is called a crawl space. Since it is not as deeply excavated as a cellar, or not excavated at all, a crawl space is less likely to be wet, but it may be dirty, damp, unventilated, and too difficult to get into.

The minimum height for a crawl space should be about 4 feet. A common type with 18 inches or less under the beams, no ventilation, boulders obscuring the view of some parts, hot-air ducts blocking access, and a dirt floor littered with wood debris is a serious fault. Crawl spaces may involve serious problems. Even where the water table is well below the surface, moisture may be drawn up by capillary action and evaporate from the ground surface into the house. Since this is a 24-hour process, the resulting damage may not be confined to the crawl space but may extend right up to the roof by water vapor rising in walls, partitions, and shafts.

Rot and Termites. The condition of the cellar, crawl space, and foundation is closely linked to the protection of the house against rot and termites. A house dry underneath and within, with monolithic foundations and no wood in contact with the earth, is not subject to rot or termite attack. Damage of this sort is always the result of poor construction or neglect.

Rot, which is caused by decaying fungi, is more serious than termites, and destroys more houses. Termites come out of the ground and normally obtain water, without which they cannot live, through clay tunnels which they build along the foundation walls or, if the construction permits, inside them. These are about the size of a lead pencil—or larger—irregular in shape, and flattened against the wall. If there are no visible tunnels inside or outside the walls, or if the foundations are poured concrete (or of hollow blocks with a solid concrete block coping) and no part of the frame or siding is in contact with the ground, there are probably no termites. If termites have invaded a house, they can be detected and eradicted before they do serious damage. Since their eradication calls for expert assistance and recurrence may be possible, a house that shows evidence of termite invasion has a serious fault.

INTERIOR DESIGN AND CONSTRUCTION

Good design has as its objective the integration of the areas given over to living, dining, food preparation, sleeping, hygiene, and storage into a logical whole. Sleeping areas must be isolated from noisy areas, and halls and corridors must be arranged for no confusion in circulation. The living room in any house should be protected as far as possible from through traffic. If the living room is used as a passageway, it is a medium fault. Bedrooms arranged in series so that one must be gone through to enter the other constitute either a medium or serious fault.

General poor design, which can take many forms, is always a serious or major fault. The single most important item is inadequate room sizes. Theoretically, under the FHA Minimum Property Standards, a three-bedroom house could be put together into about 750 square feet of area, but good design would probably demand almost twice that amount of space.

Closet Space. Within the envelope encompassed by the house, a number of other features act to add or detract from its value. There must be adequate closet and storage space. There should be a coat closet, preferably at the entrance of the house, or at least in some place convenient to the living room. A shelved closet on each floor with at least 16 square feet of shelf space is also essential. Each bedroom should have a closet at least 4 feet wide and 20 inches deep at a minimum, and ceiling high. Walk-in closets are highly desirable. Lack of adequate closet space is a serious fault.

Interior Walls. In spite of the many new wall finishes developed in recent years, plaster probably remains the most common and one of the best. In an old house, the absence of cracks in the plaster is a good sign. In a new house, slight cracking is normal during the first year or two. Severe cracking extending over an entire wall surface and through the plaster is usually structural in origin and due to excessive or uneven frame shrinkage, uneven settling, and weak framing, all of which are serious faults. Other types of cracks are caused by poor bonding between the plaster and its backing, or by defects in the plaster itself. If widespread, they constitute a serious fault. Bulging caused by expansion and loosening of the surface is also serious, if it requires replastering throughout the entire house.

In one type of "dry wall" construction, gypsum board nailed to the frame is utilized. The joints are then filled, taped, and "sprickled" with plaster. If the joints are not readily visible, it is a satisfactory job. On papered dry walls, if the joints can be felt, it is a serious fault, for in time they will probably show through the wall.

Fireplace. Fireplaces serve a decorative function, although they may be socially useful as well. In most modern designs, the living room has a built-in fireplace, absence of which rates as a fault only if the typical prospective purchasers demand its presence. Fireplaces that look as if they have been used a great deal probably draw well. Modern fireplaces have fire-clay flues running all the way to the top; if this is lacking, it is a serious fault. In the absence of a flue, and if the mortar in the joints is crumbling, a fire hazard exists and constitutes a major fault.

Doors and Windows. An outside door should have a threshold and metal weatherstripping. Windows should also be weatherstripped. Lack of weatherstripping is a minor fault except in mild climates, where it is not a fault.

In a new house, general sticking of doors and windows indicates green lumber, sloppy workmanship, foundation settling, or frame trouble and is a serious fault. In an old house, provided the timbers are in good shape, it is not as serious and may only be the result of a long wet spell. Door and window defects are usually accompanied by plaster cracking and wrinkling of wallpaper. Rotted window sills usually require an expensive replacement job and may be considered a serious fault.

Floors and Stairs. Oak is the accepted material for wood floors, although even pine floors have been known to last for 100 years or more.

In some modern houses, vinyl asbestos, pure vinyl, rubber, cork, or linoleum may be found along with hardwood flooring. Flooring materials should be selected to fill the needs of each area of the house.

Modern floors are usually laid with 2- to 3¼-inch strips, but there is a current trend toward traditional wide-board flooring in some higher-priced homes, the boards running in widths up to 10 inches. While this makes for a more decorative floor, especially with pine, it increases the likelihood of board separation if the lumber has not been thoroughly seasoned. If any of the tongues are exposed, it is a medium fault, and if, in addition, the edges are chipped, it is a serious fault.

Sagging floors may be the result of joists or beams acquiring a permanent bend or deflection with age. Or they may be due to rotting or shrinking of joists, or even foundation trouble. If the floor feels spongy, it is a serious fault.

For appearance and stability, stairs may be rated the same way as floors. In addition, they should be examined as household hazards. The horizontal boards are called treads; the vertical ones, risers. Treads should be at least 9 inches from the riser to the edge, and risers should not be over 8 inches. If the stairs feel steep, the risers should be measured, and, if over 8 inches, may be classed as a serious fault. The handrail should be firm, and, if the width of the stairs is below 31 inches, it creates a problem of getting furniture up and down. This is a medium fault.

Kitchens. The modern trend in kitchens is toward large areas, with complete enclosure from the other areas of the house. A good typical kitchen may be about 15 × 13 feet, with the equipment lining three walls to make a U-shaped working area. The sequence of appliances, typically, will be range, counter space, sink (with or without garbage-disposal unit underneath), dishwasher or double sink, counter space, refrigerator, broom closet. Total counter space will be about 20 square feet, exclusive of work surfaces afforded by the range and dishwasher top. Cupboard shelf space above may be 35–40 square feet, with another 30 square feet below, to which will be added drawer space of about 20 square feet.

Using the work and storage areas as outlined above as a good standard, half or less may be called a serious fault, three-fourths or less a medium one. Other faults may be awkward heights for work surfaces, inconvenient or inefficient arrangement (range next to refrigerator), inadequate or poorly placed window space, inadequate ventilation, absence of linoleum or equivalent floor covering, or worn linoleum. These are all minor or medium faults, depending upon the preferences of the women of the typical families who may be expected to occupy these houses.

Baths and Lavatories. In a two-story house, a toilet-lavatory or "powder room" on the first floor is desirable, and, in the $20,000 range, its absence may be classed as a serious fault. Improper ventilation, either by windows or blower exhaust fans, is a medium fault. The bathtub should be built in; the leg type is completely out of style. The absence of a shower is a minor fault. In a two-bathroom house, a combination of tub shower and stall shower is good. Showers should be of ceramic tile; prefabricated metal ones have relatively short lives and are rated as medium faults. Wash basins should not be under 20 × 17 inches, and medicine chests should be at least 22 × 16 inches. If they are smaller, it is a minor fault. For bathroom floors, ceramic or rubber tile is best. Wooden floors are medium faults, and they should be covered. Tile around a built-in bathtub with shower, or as a splashboard in back of a basin, is now so common that its absence may be rated as a medium fault, and ceramic tile is better than metal or plastic.

UTILITIES

Heating Plant. The rating of heating systems is very complicated. Individual preferences as to the types of heating systems vary widely. There are many types of acceptable heating systems such as hot water, forced circulation; warm air, forced circulation; hot water, gravity; steam and warm air, gravity, if new. Inferior systems include old-fashioned hot-air systems of the gravity type; warm air, gravity, pipeless; and oil-fired or gas-fired floor furnace. The latter two systems are only acceptable in small one-story houses.

Other considerations are the type of fuel or heat source for the system and the type of house. There are four principal sources of heat: oil, gas, coal, and electricity. The choice of a fuel, which should not be confused with the type of system, depends upon the kind that is most readily available and least expensive in the area.

The type of house, small or compact, large or rambling, with a basement or crawl space, or even concrete slab, will dictate to some extent the type of system that is proper and suitable.

Heating systems vary in speed of warmup and in steadiness and evenness of heat distribution throughout a house. There are also other considerations. In cold climates, a hot-water system requires draining if the house is left during the winter. If the system is oil- or gas-fired and left on during temporary unoccupancy, the consequences of electrical failure or burner breakdown will be more serious than with air systems, since the boiler and radiators may be damaged. Warm air, oil fired, is often noisier than hot water, because the ducts conduct sounds as well as they do the air. Steam and hot-water systems may be used to furnish hot water for the faucets. Radiant heating may be very good, but defects may be excessively difficult to remedy. Warm-air ducts in a crawl space tend to keep it dry and minimize decay, but they may also take up most of the space.

The use of gas-fired furnaces and boilers is increasing. Gas is fully automatic, requires no fuel delivery by vehicle, and, other things being equal, probably makes for the quietest and best of all heating plants. The cost is somewhat higher than for oil or coal, except where low-cost natural gas is available. The furnace space required with gas is small, and no space is required for fuel storage.

Where electricity is available for 2¢ or less per kilowatt hour, the annual fuel bill may be competitive with the other heat sources. In electrical systems, the air is heated by heating elements and then discharged into the room. The heating may come from panels in the walls or ceilings or by circulating air drawn in at ceiling height, forced downwards over an electrically heated element, and discharged as warm air at the baseboard. Another system of electrical heating is by means of a "heat pump," whereby heat is extracted from either the ground or outside air and, with the use of a compressor, fans, liquid refrigerant, and ducts for circulating, air may heat a house in the winter or cool it in the summer.

The rating of a heating system must be on the basis of one that avoids cold or overheated rooms, high fuel bills, or high maintenance. If the system is being inspected on a very cold day, and the house is occupied and heated, a check of the thermostat may reveal something of the adequacy of the system. If the temperature of the house is much below the setting, something is wrong somewhere, unless the owner says he likes it that way. From the kind of house it is, rambling or compact, the number of doors and windows, the amount of insulation, the site itself (sheltered or open) a rough judgment may be formed. An examination of the fuel bills may be indicative of its efficiency. If there is any doubt about the heating capacity, it may be listed as a medium or serious fault.

An explanation of the construction and means of operation of various heating systems used in residential construction will be found in the Appendix.

Hot Water. Except in houses lacking modern equipment throughout and priced accordingly, the absence of automatic hot water is a serious fault. The water heater may be combined with the house-heating system, if the latter utilizes steam or hot water. The hot water in the boiler that heats the house transfers heat to a coil connected with a storage tank, which is, in turn, connected to the cold-water supply and the hot-water faucets, or a tankless water heater may be used.

If the heating plant is of the hot-air type, coal-fired, a water-heating coil may be located in the firebox, but it tends to interfere with the fire and may not supply enough hot water. When the fire is allowed to go out in the spring, the system ceases to function, and a small auxiliary stove must be provided to supply hot water. Automatic gas and electric heaters are extremely convenient. Gas is faster but requires a vent. Electric heaters should have a tempering tank, which allows the water to come up to cellar temperature before entering the heater. The water heater should be of 50–80 gallons' capacity for a family of four in a two-bathroom house. A 30-gallon tank is a medium fault. A safety valve should be on, or close to, the tank; its absence is a minor fault.

Plumbing. Modern plumbing needs are moving in the direction of installing 1-inch pipe connections instead of the standard ¾-inch, for greater supply and quieter operation of the water system. They also call for first-line fittings, faucets and other devices whose finish will be trouble-free for at least twenty years.

During an inspection of the plumbing system, the appraiser may make certain tests. If the faucets are turned on and off abruptly, a jarring noise as the valves close is indicative of a faucet defect or "water hammer." "Water hammer" may be caused by a lack of air chambers in the supply lines. Sometimes the air chambers may be there but may have become waterlogged. Air chambers serve to bring the flow to a gradual stop, thus avoiding the recoil which in time will cause leaks. Absence of air chambers, or waterlogging, is easily remediable and hence may be rated as only a minor fault.

Low pressure at the faucets is more serious. Sometimes pressure in the mains is low. Flow may be passable on the first floor and feeble on the second. If the house has its own water supply, look at the gauge which is mounted on the pressure tank or on the pump. It should read between 20 and 50 pounds. If it does and the water lines are of galvanized iron, low pressure at the faucet means the pipes are clogged or undersized. This rates as a serious fault.

Brass or copper lines are better than galvanized ones, both for water supply and for hot-water-heating systems. If the water lines are copper, at least ¾-inch pipe (outside dimensions) from the pressure tank or from the point of entrance to the point where the line branches is better than smaller pipes. If the water lines are galvanized, the main pipe should be at least 1⅛ inches in diameter and the branches at least ⅞ inch. If the main pipe is ⅞ inch, it is a minor fault. The sewer pipes should be provided with cleanouts, with large plugs which may be taken out so that obstructions can be reached and removed. Their absence is a minor fault.

Electrical System. In general, there should be an electrical outlet on each wall of a room, two or more on long walls, and a wall switch for each ceiling fixture. If there is no ceiling fixture, there should be a switch to control one of the wall outlets. Inadequate outlets and switches constitute a medium fault.

In the cellar will be found a switchboard with a main switch fused for 30 amperes, 115 volts, if electric power is used only for lighting, refrigeration, furnace motors, etc. If electric power is also used for cooking or water heating, the board will be rated at 60 amperes and a range switch fused for 50 amperes. An ampere is a unit of measure of electric current, indicating the rate of flow of electricity as gallons per minute indicates the rate of flow of water. This arrangement is standard for any high-priced home. The main circuit will divide into fused branches (15 or 20 amperes each). Separate cutouts in metal boxes should be provided for the oil burner, dishwasher, if any, and water pump. If there is an electric water heater, it will have a switch and double fuse box of its own (20 amperes at 230 volts).

In all likelihood the house will be wired with conductors in conduits or armored cable (BX), or, if of recent construction, with an equivalent non-metallic cable. Inspect for rust all the visible BX runs. If one is badly rusted, it is a medium fault. Normally, the cable in walls and ceilings is all right even when the cellar circuits show deterioration, but not necessarily so in a house with serious condensation trouble. This is a further reason for checking on condensation troubles. The BX cables should not run across the lower edges of joists but should pass through holes in the joists. If across the edges, they constitute a minor fault.

EVALUATION

There are many more things that an appraiser may not know about a house without tearing it apart. But if he has made his inspection in the manner described above, he will have spotted about 90 per cent of the deficiencies. This inspection should take about one and one-half to two hours of his time, especially if he has prepared in advance with a checklist of the items to be inspected.

The next problem is to reduce the inspection to a mathematical basis. The various faults may be assigned a demerit rating. Minor would be 1, medium 2, serious 3, and major 4. By addition of all the demerits under each section, a total will be obtained. Starting with a new house that is almost fault-free, one may make comparisons for similar houses in the area. The new house and its price is given a 100 per cent rating. The older homes are then rated somewhere below, depending upon the inspection and the faults found. The comparisons will be more meaningful if the houses are divided into general types as to age, design, type of construction, and reproduction cost new. One method of rating may be to allocate one percentage-point penalty for each single demerit. Thus a house with 20 demerits would rate as worth 80 per cent of a new 100 per cent house. A house with 80 to 90 demerits would generally be unmarketable unless the owner were ready to give it away. The appraiser may devise his own rating system to suit the type of properties with which he is accustomed to dealing.

MASONRY HOUSES

Almost all of the faults of a wood house may exist in masonry houses, plus some that are peculiar to masonry construction itself. While wooden houses far outnumber masonry ones, there is undoubtedly a growing demand for brick houses, and, in some built-up sections of cities, wood construction is prohibited. Masonry itself does not make a masonry house. Houses advertised as "all brick" or "brick all the way around" frequently are conventional wood-frame structures with nominal 4-inch (one-brick thickness) veneer walls, supported vertically by the same foundation on which the sill and studs rest. No matter how much masonry veneer there is, when it has no function other than to cover a wood frame, it is not a masonry house, properly speaking. For that, the masonry must carry a significant load. Thus a "solid brick" house will have 8-inch walls supporting the floor joists and roof trusses. Masonry load-bearing walls can be distinguished by thickness, but there are numerous combinations of materials: brick, concrete blocks, stone, hollow tile, cast concrete, stucco, etc. Since both materials and construction may change from floor to floor, except when the house is new or the original plans are available, the task of evaluating a masonry house is harder than with a wood-frame house.

Masonry Faults. The two basic types of masonry used for house construction are

1. *Monolithic, or cast-in-place, concrete.* Concrete is cement plus an aggregate (sand and stone) plus water, making a mixture that can be poured or worked briefly and which then hardens and gains strength over a long period. Properly mixed, cured and reinforced with metal when necessary, concrete constitutes the strongest and most serviceable of all masonry constructions, although for aesthetic reasons it may not be the preferred one.

2. *Built-up, or unit, masonry* consists of separate pieces (brick, stone, concrete blocks, etc.) joined together by mortar. Unit masonry utilizes a variety of materials in a variety of combinations and is characterized at its best by unit shape (except in the case of rubble masonry, where uniformity is not sought), regularity of assembly, and strong, well-compacted joints.

Common faults of concrete are cracking, chipping, crumbling, a poor mixture (evidenced by stones at the surface of a wall), and softness (resulting from freezing, premature drying, defective or insufficient cement, etc.). Built-up masonry walls may crack under stress like monolithic walls. Units may be broken or malformed. Joints may be incompletely filled or poorly finished. The mortar may be weak. Where the units are placed in horizontal layers, the layers (or courses) may be uneven, or individual units may be out of plumb. If any of these faults are found on a large scale, it may be rated as a serious fault. If there are severe cracks, or if an entire wall is out of plumb, it is a major fault.

Joints should be tooled, or formed into a V-shape or concavity. Tooled joints are more likely to be watertight, because the tooling presses the mortar, after it has shrunk in the early stages of setting, back into close contact with the masonry units. Untooled joints are a medium fault.

If there are many projections that are not calked or flashed to prevent water from getting into a masonry wall, it is a serious fault.

All exterior masonry walls should have furring strips and air space between the inside of the wall and the interior finish of the house. Furring strips are commonly wood, usually 1 $\times$ 2 inches and spaced 16–24 inches apart. Plastering directly on masonry is poor practice, as rain may get through to stain the plaster, and plaster may crack from expansion and contraction of the masonry. Since so little of a masonry house may be seen from the inside, it must be judged almost entirely by the condition of the exterior walls. Inside, however, stains caused by moisture, peeling paint, and other evidences of widespread water penetration may be rated as a major fault, especially if the water damage is present in spite of furring. The presence or absence of air space may be verified by knocking on the walls. The sound will be drummy and hollow in the middle of the voids between the furring strips, and will rise to a higher pitch over the strips.

Roofs of masonry houses may be of masonry (slate, tile) or relatively light asphalt, or even wood shingles. Another rigid material, intermediate between masonry and asphalt, is cement asbestos. Any of these materials is acceptable, but framing design must take the weight of the heavy ones into account. Those features of framing that were covered in the discussion of wood-frame houses apply equally as well here—especially the features of frame strength, such as size and spacing of roof rafters. A few broken or loose tiles or shingles constitute a medium fault; widespread breakage and irregularity, a serious one.

As was previously indicated, the evaluation of masonry houses can be accomplished in the same manner as with wood-frame houses. Many of the faults described as applying to the wood-frame house will be present in masonry houses as well, and a rating scale will be equally appropriate for both types.

CONCLUSION: THE APPRAISER'S ROLE

Most of the faults discussed in the previous paragraphs are to be found in houses of some age and use. New houses, unless faulty in design, are usually free from the physical faults found in old ones. One of the chief difficulties new-home builders find is the unwillingness of appraisers to give full credit for the extra cost of quality and good design in new houses. Appraisers can play a decisive role in the creation of better housing standards for the American public if they are familiar with the elements of good design, the requirements of good living, and the characteristics of good construction.

In today's market, five out of six houses are constructed and planned for an unknown purchaser. As a result, nothing is planned or built in that cannot be financed under a mortgage. The mortgage lender depends upon the appraiser to fix the size of the mortgage by his appraisal, and, where mortgages constitute, as they do, the predominant part of the purchase price, the appraisal invariably sets the price. The appraiser's function thus transcends the concept of merely indicating the price at which a house could be sold. In the new-home field, he becomes a true evaluator and practically sets the price. Both the lender and the buyer are making a long-term investment and thus are interested in long-term value.

Architectural styles and designs are constantly changing. The appraiser must be familiar with the new architectural designs that will meet modern living conditions. Houses designed for backyard living, for servantless living, for big overhangs to minimize heat gain and lessen the need for repainting are examples of the modern trend. They must be given their full value and not be penalized owing to prejudices based on older styles and designs.

Air conditioning and adequate wiring are among the two most easily recognized new requirements for the modern house, yet many appraisers fail to penalize new-house construction where these factors are lacking.

Adequate room sizes, adequate storage space, adequate labor-saving devices, and adequate bath facilities are among the most desirable features sought by prospective homeowners. Where they do not exist, as in the case in a good many of the new houses built today, their lack should be penalized.

Appraisers can encourage good quality of materials. Builders are aware that in too many cases they can get by with the same credit for cheap hardware, second-line fittings, inadequate hot-water heaters, and poor switches and outlets, instead of first-line and first-quality material. It is all too true that builders are influenced more by what they think the appraiser will accept as value compared to cost than by what the prospective buyer, who frequently is unqualified to judge, will accept. Thus items of design and material that get overappraised, in relation to cost, get put into buildings, while those that get underappraised get left out, no matter how desirable.

As the American standard of living continues to rise, appraisers must familiarize themselves with those social and economic factors that are creating changing designs, changing construction, changing materials, and the changing market. If they do so, they can play a significant role in the creation of better standards of housing and more stable values.

22

Appraising Lease Interests

When an owner enters into a contract with a second party to lease his property for a stated period of time, he, in effect, creates a leased fee or lessor's interest with two separate interests in the real estate. In return for the lease, permitting the tenant to occupy and use his property, he receives an annual rental stipulated in the lease contract and he retains the right to repossess the property at the termination of the lease. The value of the rental payments plus the value of the property at the end of the lease, known as the reversion, constitute his interest in the property. This leased fee may be sold or mortgaged, subject to the rights of the tenant, and the value of this leased fee will determine the price it will bring in the market, or the amount of loan that can be obtained from a lending institution.

The second interest created by the leasing of the property belongs to the tenants. It is referred to as the *leasehold estate,* or *lessee's interest.* Since the lessee is obligated under the terms of the lease to pay a contract rent, his interest in the property can only have value if the agreed-upon rent is less than the economic rent justified by the land value and if he constructs an improvement on the land. In some instances, where the tenant leases property that is already improved, his interest in the property would exist if the income from the property were in excess of the rental necessary to pay an adequate return on both the land and building value.

From a theoretical point of view, the total value of the leased fee and the leasehold estate cannot exceed the value of the property if it were not subject to a lease. It is possible, however, that the value of each of the separate interests may not equal the value of the unencumbered fee. This condition might arise if the lessor were to prohibit the lessee from demolishing an inadequate structure and replacing it with one that would improve the land to its highest and best use, or if the term remaining in the lease is of short duration, making it uneconomic for the tenant to put up an adequate structure.

When a tenant has a leasehold estate of value, he, in turn, may sublet his interest. By doing so, he creates what is known as a "sandwich" lease, and the value of the property becomes divided into three interests: the lessor's, the prime lessee's, and the sublessee's.

CREATION OF LEASE INTERESTS

Leases may be made at fair market rentals, at rentals below the going rate, or at rentals above the market rate. Since changing conditions affect the value of real estate, leases made prior to the current period may prove to be at rentals above or below the current market figures. If values have risen since the lease was originally made, there generally will be a gap between economic rent and contract rent in the tenant's favor. If values have declined, the reverse will generally be true. In the first instance, lease-hold value will have been created; in the second case, leased fee value will have been enhanced, or a negative leasehold value created. If the gap between contract rent and economic rent becomes too great in the lessor's favor, the lessee may default or try to arrange a renegotiation of the terms. Of course, if the lessee is a strong tenant such as a national chain, he may either be obliged to meet the contract rent or make a lump-sum payment to be relieved of his obligation.

The basic principle in the valuation of lease interests is similar to the principle of capitalized income valuation. The value of lessors' and lessees' interests is determined by capitalizing the present value of the income they receive plus the reversionary value of the land, or land and building, at the expiration of the lease term. Ordinarily, it is the lessor who receives the reversionary value of the property. But some leases provide for payments to the lessee by the lessor for any improvements made by the lessee that revert to the lessor. Thus the value of the lessor's interest may be said to consist of the following:

1. The present value of the reasonably expected income for the term of the lease
2. The present worth of the property at the end of the lease (land and sometimes building)

The lessee's interest would then consist of the following:

1. The present value of the building, if constructed by him
2. The present value of expected excess rentals (net gains) for the term of the lease
3. Improvement adjustments, if any, in his favor

TYPES OF LEASES

Net Leases. The valuation of lease interests depends primarily upon the terms of the lease. The appraiser must be thoroughly familiar with the terms before he can proceed in his valuation process. Since there are various forms of leaseholds with varying rights and obligations for owners and tenants, we shall turn our attention to some of the more common types found in the real estate market.

NINETY-NINE-YEAR LEASE. From the owner's standpoint this type of lease offers many advantages. Basically it is a well-secured long-term investment on a net basis. This type of lease is usually made on large pieces of valuable land. Owners may be large estates confronted with a problem in distribution, or the sale of the property may be impossible owing to will restrictions. Even assuming that the property could be sold, an outlet for the safe investment of the money at a fair return would have to be found, which is not always possible. Where the property has been in an owner's possession for a long time, sentimental reasons may impede a sale, or the matter of the income tax may intrude. Upon the sale the government is paid by way of a capital-gains tax on the difference between the property's original value and the sale price. That may be a considerable amount. If a long-term lease is made, the capital-gains-tax feature is eliminated and the owner only pays on the income received.

From the tenant's standpoint, the first consideration is that he practically owns the land but instead of paying cash for it he pays only the agreed interest rate on its value, in the form of annual rent. The next benefit is the increment in rental value which may accrue to the leasehold interest.

If the property to be leased on a ninety-nine-year basis consists of land with old improvements, the owner generally will seek some protection for his interest. The tenant will generally be required to purchase the old improvements for cash and to agree to erect a new building or to spend substantial amounts to improve the existing buildings.

Under this type of lease, the landlord receives a net rental, and the tenant pays, in addition to the rent, the taxes, water rates, insurance, and operating expenses. In fact, the tenant pays all charges and expenses, and the only offset to the owner's return is the income tax on the rent he receives.

Since these leases are most common on high-value land in central locations, the rents tend to be fixed at 5 or 6 per cent of the fair market value of the land. Some leases are straight, that is, the rental is the same for the entire term. Other leases are graduated, with rental increases every five, ten, or twenty years; still others are reappraised leases, where the rentals are fixed only for the first period of the lease and, therafter, at stated intervals, the rental is determined by arbitration. Reappraised leases are not generally favored by tenants, as it is more difficult to obtain financing for improvements with this type of lease. The threat of a large unpredictable increase in ground rents may be a discouraging factor to prospective lenders, whose loans are usually in a subordinate position to the ground lease. To a lesser degree, this objection applies to graduated leases also, except where the initial rent was made below the market value in order to encourage the improvement of the land.

TWENTY-ONE-YEAR LEASE. A type of long-term lease characteristic of New York real estate is the twenty-one-year lease. It is known as a ground lease, and basically it is what its name indicates—a lease on the land. The main difference between this lease and the ninety-nine-year lease is that, under the ground lease, where there are improvements, the tenant purchases the existing improvements but is not obliged to erect a new building. If there are no improvements, or if the improvements are obsolete, the tenant may at his option erect a new structure.

The twenty-one-year lease usually gives the tenant one to three options to renew for additional terms of twenty-one years each. The rent paid is also net, the tenant paying all other charges. There may or may not be step-up provisions for the rentals. The renewal options provide that one or two years prior to the expiration of the original term the tenant must signify his intention to exercise his renewal privilege. The renewal options may specify that the rent be set at a percentage of the market value at the time of renewal, or at a predetermined figure, but, in any event, the rental in the renewal period is hardly ever set at a figure below the amount paid in the preceding term.

An exception to this general rule will occur where sales-leaseback transactions have been entered into. In these cases, particularly where insurance companies are involved, the initial rental is set at a figure sufficient to completely amortize the initial investment by the company, with interest on the outstanding balances during the first term of the lease. The renewal options then call for sharply reduced rentals for the succeeding terms. But sales leaseback transactions are more in the nature of financial arrangements, between insurance companies and substantial tenants, than they are real estate transactions. In these cases, the credit rating of the tenants, the former owners, is at least as important as the value of the property as security for the lease.

LONG-TERM NET LEASE. There is a type of long-term net lease that differs from the two preceding leases in two major respects: First, the tenant leases the property mainly for his own occupancy, and, second, the tenant neither purchases the existing improvements nor is he obligated to make any. In these leases, the financial responsibility of the tenant is of prime importance. The long-term lease is for twenty years or longer and calls for a net rental. If it carries any options for renewal, the rental to be paid on renewal is usually stated, and, in those cases where reappraisal is provided, the valuation is on both land and building. The Woolworth Company has made many such types of leases.

Generally, owners who make these types of leases consider the financial responsibility of the tenant first and then the income. Such leases are usually made to tenants who intend to occupy all or the greater portion of the space.

The leases described above have several points in common:

1. The landlord has no problem of management—the tenant has relieved him of his burden. The landlord simply receives his monthly or quarterly rental, and his obligation lies in paying the interest and amortization on his mortgage, if any.

2. All are net leases. The tenant pays all charges of every description.

3. The landlord is not obligated to make any repairs. In case of fire or other casualty-causing damage or destruction of the building, the tenant is obligated to repair or rebuild, and, if the insurance proceeds are insufficient, the tenant makes up the dificiency. Rent does not cease for any reason.

Gross Leases. Under this type of lease, the owner assumes the burden of management. The tenant pays the agreed rent; the landlord does the rest. Generally, there are four types of gross leases:

1. The lease with a tax-participation clause
2. The lease with an excess-tax-participation and operating-expense clause
3. The lease with no tax clause
4. The percentage lease

Under Type 1, where the tenant occupies part of the property, he pays in addition to his rental the proportionate share of the real estate taxes on the entire property. For example, say, the entire property contains an area of 100,000 square feet. A tenant occupying 50,000 feet would pay one-half of the real estate tax.

Under Type 2, the liability of the tenant or tenants is to pay in addition to the rent any increase in real estate taxes, and operating expenses such as labor costs and cleaning expenses, that may occur after a certain period. If the tenant occupies only part of the property, he pays his proportionate share. This type of lease is very common in many of the new postwar office buildings and in some of the new one-tenant store properties built for national chains. This type of lease has the effect of creating a floor under the income received by the owner, once the building is fully rented, and transforms the gross lease into a modified net lease.

Under Type 3, the tenant has no liability outside of paying the agreed rent.

Under Type 4, the tenant pays as rent a certain agreed percentage of the total sales made on the premises. Some percentage leases carry "minimum guaranties," that is, the tenant is obligated in any event, regardless of the amount of sales, to pay the landlord a stipulated minimum rent. Some leases carry "maximum guaranties," that is, the landlord's top rent is fixed —he can only share up to a certain volume. A few leases may also call for a percentage of the profits of the enterprise.

Gross leases may be made for any length of time and may include as many varying terms and conditions as the landlord and tenants see fit to include. The above-described leases are the most common types in use at this time.

VALUATION PROCEDURE

We have already indicated the basic valuation principles to be used in appraising various lease interests. In essence, they are mathematical computations of present value of income received, or implied, plus the present value of any reversion flowing to any of the interested parties. It is also possible to compute the value of a lease interest by first determining the total value of the property as if unencumbered by leases, and then subtracting either the leased fee interest or leasehold interest, depending upon which is known. Thus, if a property has a fee value of $150,000 and a leased fee value of $125,000, the leasehold estate is worth $25,000.

The following are examples of some types of leased property situations and suggested methods of appraisal:

Example I: Ninety-nine-Year Net Ground Lease. A leases to B for ninety-nine years at $100,000 per annum. B is to construct new building costing $5,000,000. What is the value of A's interest (leased fee), if capitalization rate is at 6 per cent and reversionary value of land is estimated at $1,600,000?

Procedure:

Present value of $100,000 @ 6% p.a. for 99 yrs—
$100,000 × 16.615 = ... $1,661,500
Present value of reversion due in 99 years @ 6%—
$1,600,000 × .0031 = ... 4,960
Total value of leased fee = ... $1,666,460

It should be observed that in ninety-nine-year net ground leases, the reversion value becomes insignificant and the income may be treated as a perpetuity. Thus $100,000 capitalized at 6 per cent in perpetuity is worth $1,666,667, which is practically the same as the amount found by use of the annuity tables.

Example II: Twenty-one-Year Net Lease—Graduated Income. A leases B land for twenty-one years—terms: $5,000 net for the first five years, $5,500 net for the second five years, $6,000 net for the balance of the term. Capitalization rate at 6 per cent. Reversionary value assumed to be $100,000.

Procedure:

P.V. of $5,000 p.a. for 5 years @ 6% = 5,000 × 4.212 = $21,060
P.V. of $5,500 p.a. for 5 years @ 6% = 5,500 × 3.148 = 17,314
         deferred 5 yrs.
P.V. of $6,000 p.a. for 11 years @ 6% = 6,000 × 4.404 = 26,424
         deferred 10 yrs.
P.V. of reversion—$100,000 due 21 years, hence @ 6% = 29,420

Total value of leased fee = $94,218

In treating graduated income streams, it should be observed that the value of each succeeding block of income is deferred by the number of years preceding the right to receive that income. Thus, the second block of $5,500 is to be received for five years, but its receipt is deferred five years. The value of this block of income could be calculated as the present value of $5,500 at 6 per cent for five years, which would be equal to $5,500 × 4.212, or $23,166, and then this total could be deferred or treated as a reversion for five years. It would then be worth $23,166 × .7473 (present value of reversion at 6 per cent due five years hence), or $17,314, which is the same figure found in the second computation. In order to save time, the same result is obtained by subtracting the factor representing the value of the last year of the first block of income from the factor representing the value of the last year of the second block of income, and applying the difference between the two factors to the rent reserved in the second block. This procedure can be carried out for each succeeding block of income where the rent changes. The appraiser will find it helpful to diagram the various income streams in order to clarify the problem. The diagram below illustrates the treatment of the income stream in example II.

		6,000 × 4.404	
	5,500		
5,000 × 4.212	× 3.148 (7.360 — 4.212)	(11.764 — 7.360)	

Years	1	5	10	21
Factor @ 6%	–	4.212	7.360	11.764

A word about the reversionary value—Since it is impossible to estimate accurately the reversionary value of land for many years in the future, appraisers make their estimates on one of the following assumptions:

1. Land Value at the time of the reversion will be equal to land value today.
2. Land value at the time of the reversion may be taken at the capitalized value of the last year's income into perpetuity.

Frequently a reversionary rate may be used that is higher than the rate applied to the income stream. This has the effect of compensating for the uncertainty of the future land estimate. When leases are of sufficient duration, the effect of the reversion on the total value will be negligible, while on short-term leases the effect is greater, but so is the possibility of a more accurate forecast.

In the above-cited example, if the current value of the land as unencumbered by the lease is $100,000, then B has a leasehold estate worth $5,782, determined by subtracting $94,218, the value of the leased fee, from $100,000. This can be demonstrated mathematically if we assume that B could sublet the property at 6 per cent of its current value, or $6,000 per annum for twenty-one years, to C. In that case, B would have the right to receive $1,000 a year for five years ($6,000 — $5,000) and then $500 a year for the next five years. During the last eleven years, he would be getting $6,000 from C, paying $6,000 to A, and reaping no benefit. The value of B's leasehold estate would be $1,000 p.a. × 4.212 = $4,212.

$$500 \text{ p.a.} \times 3.148 = \underline{\quad 1,574}$$

Total value of B's leasehold estate = $5,786

The slight discrepancy in values is due to the use of only three decimal places in the factors.

Example III. An insurance company leases a plot to a building corporation for sixty-six years. The net rental is $45,000 per annum for the first three years (during construction) and $185,000 per annum for the next sixty-three years. The building corporation is required to construct a building with a value of $15 million. At the end of the lease term, the building is to become the property of the insurance company in return for a payment of $1 million. The reversionary value of the land and building is estimated at $7.5 million. With the capitalization rate at 5 per cent and the reversion rate at 8 per cent, what is the value of the leased fee?

Procedure:

P.V. of $45,000 p.a. for 3 years @ 5% = $45,000 × 2.723 = $ 122,535
P.V. of $185,000 p.a. for 63 years deferred 3 years @ 5% =
$185,000 × 16.478 = 3,048,430
P.V. of reversion @ 8% due 66 years hence = $7,500,000 ×
.0062 = 46,500
$3,217,465
Less P.V. of payment to lessee—$1,000,000 deferred 66 years @
5% = $1,000,000 × .0399 = $ 39,900
Total value of leased fee = $3,177,565

In this example, the reversionary value is calculated at 8 per cent to reflect its speculative character, but the reversion payment to the lessee is calculated at 5 per cent, owing to its firm contract price. The present value of this payment is deducted from the leased fee value, based on income and reversion, to reflect the payment that will be made sixty-six years hence.

Example IV. A leases a vacant plot to B for $10,000 per year for fifty years. B erects a building with an anticipated economic life of fifty years, at a cost of $200,000. B's net income after all charges (ground rent, operating expenses, taxes, etc.) is $20,000 per annum. The reversion is assumed to be $250,000 (land only). Using a 5 per cent rate for A's interest and a 7 per cent rate for B's interest, what is the value of the leased fee and the leasehold estate?

Procedure:

Leased Fee (A)—
P.V. of $10,000 p.a. @ 5% for 50 years = $10,000 × 18.256 = $182,560
P.V. of reversion due 50 years hence @ 5% = $250,000 ×
.0872 =   21,800
Leased fee value   = $204,360

Leasehold estate (B)—
P.V. of $20,000 p.a. for 50 years @ 7% = $20,000 × 13.801 = $276,020

It should be noted that the leasehold estate in this example exceeds the value of the building by $76,020. This figure is in effect the value of the excess rentals accruing to the lessee. This can be demonstrated by the following:

Value of the building = $200,000
Amount required for interest and recapture of the building cost @ 7% for 50 years = $200,000 ÷ 13.801 = $14,492
Excess income = $5,508
P.V. of excess income at 7% for 50 years = $5,508 × 13.801 = $76,016, or $76,020.

If the appraiser feels that the excess income is speculative, he may use a higher rate. At 8 per cent it would be worth $67,379 ($55,084 × 12.233), and at 10 per cent it would amount to $54,612 ($5,508 × 9.915).

The fact that a higher rate was used for the leasehold estate than for the leased fee is indicative of the relative position both interests have toward the income produced by the property. The owner's position may be compared to that of a first mortgagee, while the tenant is in the same position as an equity holder. Since the ground rent has a prior claim on the net income, it is more secure and may be capitalized at a lower rate than the income remaining to the tenant. Another factor that might justify a lower rate on the leased fee is the possibility of an increase in land value at the expiration of the lease. If this happens, the owner, not the tenant, reaps the benefit. In this respect, the owner reaps the benefits of a mortgage holder as far as security of income is concerned and of an equity holder as far as capital appreciation is involved.

Example V: Advance Rent Contract. A leases land to B for twenty-one years at $12,000 net, payable in advance. Reversionary land value is estimated at $200,000; capitalization rate, 6 per cent; what is the value of the leased fee?

Procedure:

```
Advance payment                                           = $ 12,000
P.V. of $12,000 p.a. @ 6% for 20 years = $12,000 × 11.47 =   137,640
P.V. of reversion = $200,000 @ 6% due 21 years $200,000 × .2942
                                                          =    58,840
                                                            ─────────
         Value of leased fee                              = $208,480
```

The value of payments made in advance may be calculated either by adding the initial advance payment to the present value of the remaining payments or by multiplying the rent by a factor that will represent one year less than the lease term plus one. In the example above, the value of the advance payments of the rent could have been obtained by adding one to the twenty-year factor $(1 + 11.47 = 12.47)$ and multiplying that factor by the income. In both cases, the value of the rental payments would amount to $149,640.

Example VI: Sandwich Lease Calculation. Land was leased thirty years ago for a term of ninety-nine years at $15,000 per annum. The lessee built a building and sublet to a nationwide shoe chain for $20,000 per annum. The present economic rental is $26,000 per year. The present value of the property on the basis of an economic appraisal is land, $200,000 and building, $200,000. Assuming a 5½ per cent rate for the leased fee and a 10 per cent rate for the subtenant's interest, what is the value of the leased fee, the sandwich leasehold, and the subleasehold's interest, with reversion (land only) at $200,000?

```
Leased fee value—
   P.V. of $15,000 for 69 years @ 5½% = $15,000 × 17.730 = $265,950
   P.V. of reversion due 69 years hence @ 5½% = $200,000 ×
                                                .0249 =       4,980
                                                           ─────────
      Value of leased fee                               = $270,930

Subleasehold interest (user)—
   P.V. of $6,000 p.a. @ 10% for 69 years = 6,000 × 9.986 = $ 59,916
                                                           ─────────
   Leased fee and user's interest                       = $330,846
   Value of property                  = $400,000
   Value of leased fee and user's interest =  330,846
                                            ─────────
   Value of sandwich leasehold        = $ 69,514
```

If it were desired to know the actual rate of return the sandwich lease-hold was receiving in this example, it could be calculated in the following manner:

Leasehold value $69,514 ÷ 5,000 (income) = 13.831

By inspection of the annuity tables, we find the factor 13.831 to lie between 7 per cent and 7½ per cent for sixty-nine years. The 7 per cent factor is 14.152 and the 7½ per cent factor is 13.243. By interpolation it will be found that the actual rate is 7.2 per cent.

Occasionally, an appraiser will be called upon to give his client some advice as to the course of action he should pursue with his property. The next two examples are indicative of the type of problems that might arise.

Example VII. Land now worth $100,000 is leased to a national chain at a net rent of $15,000 per annum. If the owner offered to sell the land and the lease for $140,000, would it pay the tenant to buy? If so, how much would he save, if the capitalization rate is 5 per cent?

Value of Leased Fee—
 P.V. of $15,000 p.a. for 10 years @ 5% = $15,000 × 7.722 = $115,830
 P.V. of reversion $100,000 deferred 10 years @ 5% = $100,000
             × .6139 = 61,390

Value of leased fee   = $177,220
Offering price (land and lease)   = 140,000
Savings   = $ 37,220

The tenant could realize the above savings by buying at the offering price.

Example VIII. A is offered $180,000 for a plot of land on Retail Street. He can also lease the property to a good tenant at a net rental of $12,000 per annum against a rental of 5 per cent of the gross sales volume for a period of forty years, provided A constructs a building for the tenant. The following assumptions are made:

1. The fair net rental of the property on completion is $18,000 per annum.
2. The gross sales volume of the tenant is estimated to be $500,000 per annum for the first five years, and after that it will average $400,000 per annum.
3. The building will cost and be worth $120,000, and its economic life will expire with the end of the lease.
4. Six per cent is a fair rate of return for this type of investment.
5. Eight per cent is a fair rate of interest to use in valuing excess rental income.
6. Six per cent is a fair rate of interest to be used in valuing the land reversion of $180,000.

Based on these assumptions, should the owner be advised to sell or lease the property.

Procedure:

Presumed Investment = $300,000 (land, $180,000; building, $120,000)

	Economic Rent	Expectations	Excess Rent
5 years	$18,000	$25,000	$7,000
35 years	$18,000	$20,000	$2,000

Process:

Economic rent = P.V. of $18,000 p.a. @ 6% for 40 years = $18,000 ×
$$15.046 = \$270,828$$
Reversion = $180,000 deferred 40 years @ 6% = $180,000 × .0972 = $ $17,496$
Excess rent = P.V. of $7,000 p.a. @ 8% for 5 years = $7,000 ×
$$3.993 = 27,951$$
Excess rent = P.V. of $2,000 p.a. for 35 years deferred 5 years @
$$8\% \ \$2,000 \times 7.932 \ (11.925 - 3.993) = 15,864$$
Total value of leased fee = $\overline{\$332,139}$

The advice to the owner is to lease, as the lease creates a capital value in excess of the capital investment. It is worthwhile noting that this excess capital value is sometimes referred to as intangible value or a third element of value in addition to land and building value. It is marketable, and, in the absence of competing plots of land for similar developments, the value will ultimately become part of the land value, should the expected rentals materialize.

23

Special Land-Valuation Problems

The general techniques of land valuation have been discussed in earlier chapters dealing with the comparative-sales approach and the land residual technique. In most appraisal problems, the task facing the appraiser involves the determination of comparable units of value indicated by sales and income data, and the subsequent application of these units to a specific property under appraisement.

The use of this comparative process requires that like be compared to like. This calls for the development of a set of value-determining factors and a method of measuring the effects these factors have upon different areas and different parcels within these areas. Some of the more important value-determining factors affecting different areas include

1. Population trends in the area
2. Income level of the neighborhood population
3. Density of the neighborhood population
4. Pressure of social, educational, and recreational facilities
5. Accessibility to public utilities (transportation, electricity, gas, water, sewers, etc.)
6. Zoning and private restrictions
7. Climate and view
8. Character of public improvements (streets, sidewalks, sewers)
9. Level of taxation

As for individual parcels within an area, the chief value-determining factors include

1. Location
2. Size
3. Shape
4. Utility
5. Frontage
6. Character of the soil

These lists by no means exhaust all the possible factors of land value, but for practical purposes they will serve to indicate those which most commonly require the attention of the appraiser. The mere listing of these factors serves only to present another problem. It is relatively simple for most appraisers to recognize that land in one area is more valuable than land in another area, or that some individual parcels are more valuable than others, on the basis of these value factors. The problem of measuring the value differences remains. The usual procedures by which appraisers have attempted to measure value differences consist either in establishing a rating method or in the use of standard rules common to an area. Rating methods depend to a large degree upon individual subjective weighting that does not find general agreement and is therefore considered impractical. The standard rules include corner-influence rules, depth factors, plottage factors, and others which have general acceptance in the community and therefore lend themselves to greater use by appraisers.

The use of standard rules does not relieve the appraiser of the necessity of using his judgment in establishing his basic unit land value, nor does it require him to adhere to his rules where common sense and experience tell him that they are inappropriate. It does enable him to break down the problem of appraising complex properties into a step-by-step procedure, and it does permit the narrowing of opinions by different appraisers, especially where the rules have the sanction of the courts. Since so much appraisal work winds up as court testimony, the latter aspect is of no small importance.

The measurement of relative land value levels within a community is accomplished by analysis of the sales and income data that appear in the market. Once these have been determined, the appraiser can turn his attention to specific properties within these areas for which he has assignments. Since it is unlikely that he will find many cases of exact comparability, he must reduce the already established values to a common denominator or yardstick before he can apply them to properties for which he has assignments. These common denominators are generally known as unit land values and may vary according to the type of property being appraised.

UNIT LAND VALUES

The value of most commodities is measured by multiplying the number of units by a unit price. Wheat is valued by a price per bushel; cotton, by the bale; and cloth, by the yard. With land, the first problem is to find an appropriate unit of measurement. The units will vary with the location and use of property. In rural areas, the acre is the customary unit. The acre may also be used in large, unimproved urban tracts, and, when such acreage is developed into streets and lots, each acre will produce about fifteen 20- × 100-foot or twelve 25- × 100-foot lots. The acre has a clearly defined size but may be indefinite in shape.

In intensively developed urban areas, value depends largely on shape and frontage. The urban units are thus well defined as to area and shape.

The most common unit of measure used for urban property is known as the *unit foot*. It is a rectangular strip lying perpendicular to the street, with a frontage of one foot and running for a standard depth in any particular area. It is also referred to as *front-foot value*. The standard depth will vary from area to area but 100 feet is probably the most common depth used. It is also possible to have varying depth standards within an area, to conform with different uses. The *unit foot value* represents the value of one foot of street frontage at the standard depth of an inside lot of normal size on the level with the grade of the street. This unit foot value is subject to modification when the value of any particular lot is derived from it. The value is modified if the lot is above grade or below grade or if the lot is so narrow as to preclude its appropriate improvement. The unit foot value does *not* include the increments because of corner location, key influence, or plottage.

Not all urban land is appraised on the basis of unit foot values. Many parcels are appraised on a square-foot basis. The square foot, like the acre, has a definite area but may have an indefinite shape. Where square-foot values are used, the assumption is that frontage and shape, within limits, are not as important as size. Thus the square-foot unit is used in the valuation of industrial property or other types where street frontage is not of much importance. It is also used in high-value, congested areas with narrow streets and irregular plots, as in the financial district in New York City.

In choosing between a square foot and a unit foot, the appraiser should be guided by zoning laws; usage, both present and contemplated; and by the custom of usage in the market place. In areas where there is mixed usage, the predominant use should serve as a guide, except where evidence exists that this use will soon give way to a higher and better use. There has been a growing trend to restrict the use of unit foot values to retail and some residential properties, and to use the square foot with most other types.

SPECIAL FACTORS AND INCREMENTS

Value differences may exist between parcels of land devoted to similar uses, owing to location (corner vs. inside), size (long vs. short lots), and shape (rectangular vs. triangular or polygonal). The problem facing the appraiser is to secure good appraisals of various comparable parcels throughout his area and then to "rectify" the appraisals of those pracels which vary from the standard size and shape. The process of rectification permits the appraiser to analyze the value, found by sales and income, of various parcels in order to break that value down to a common unit value that he will be using. Once the indicated unit value is determined, the appraisal of any other comparable parcel can be made by a simple arithmetic process.

CORNER INFLUENCE

A corner lot is a standard lot located at the intersection of two streets. As such it has the advantage of double street frontage and in most cases is more valuable than a lot of the same size which has only single street frontage. The chief advantages that accrue to a corner lot over an inside lot are

1. Greater building-area potential due to zoning and building laws
2. Accessibility to greater flows of pedestrian and automobile traffic
3. Increased light and air
4. Greater show-window and advertising space
5. Greater facility of entrance and egress

The added value that accrues to a corner lot as a result of the aforementioned advantages is usually shown either in higher sales prices per unit foot or in increased rentals. This added value is known as *corner influence.* Variations in the value of corner sites depend upon the value of the advantages enumerated above as well as upon general economic factors. Generally, the amount of corner influence is greater in areas of high land value and decreases as land value decreases. It will also vary with the widths and values of the intersecting streets. Corner influence is greatest in high-volume retail areas and decreases in importance in approximately the following order: financial, office, hotel, apartment, ordinary retail, wholesale, industrial, residential, and undeveloped or rural areas.

While most appraisers are in general agreement that corner lots usually have an added value over inside lots, they differ as to the amount and extent of corner influence. A further difference of opinion exists as to whether any corner-influence value accrues in single-family residential areas.

Amount of Corner Influence. Although several formulas have been developed in an effort to determine the added amount of value accruing to a corner lot, they all have one element in common because they are empirical rules which have been developed primarily as aids to the equitable assessment of real estate. The rules fall into three main classifications:

1. Those rules based solely on the main-street values to which an added percentage is then allocated for corner influence
2. Those rules based on both side- and main-street unit foot values which require the computation of corner influence as a percentage of base value, the percentage varying with the ratio of main- to side-street values

3. Those rules based on side-street values which involve adding together the value of the corner lot as if it were an inside lot on the main street and an inside lot on the side street

The first rule is generally applied by New York City appraisers who tend to use a 50 per cent increment to the value of the corner lot along the more valuable street. However, they will vary the added percentage in accordance with the widths and values of the intersecting streets. One hundred per cent corner influence may be used where the intersecting streets are both wide and valuable. The corner of 42d Street and 5th Avenue would be an example where 100 per cent corner influence would be used. On the other hand, 40 per cent or less may be used where streets are narrow or are in strictly residential areas.

The second and third rules are in use in other parts of the country. Some have been published as tables with variations to be used for different classifications of property. The Bernard rule developed for Baltimore and the Zangerle rule used in Cleveland are outstanding examples. The appraiser must be familiar with the rule in general use in his area, so that he may conform his calculations to the general practice.

Extent of Corner Influence. While there is general agreement that a corner lot, particularly in a retail district, is normally more valuable than an inside lot, there is disagreement as to whether the second or third lots from the corner are also more valuable than inside lots. Some appraisers maintain that corner influence only extends from the corner to the first lot line. Others maintain that it extends a certain distance from the corner, up to 100 feet. The same disagreement exists where corner lots are greater than the standard depth in the area. Many appraisers make use of a "key" lot increment where the corner lot is too narrow for development to its highest and best use. The key lot is so called because of its strategic value to the owner of the corner. In some communities, appraisers generally assign a 10 per cent increment to the key lot, with adjustments above and below this figure. Thus, where higher corner-influence percentages are used, a higher key lot increment will also be used, and vice versa.

Where the corner is large enough for proper development, the general practice is to assign corner influence only to that portion of the corner lot that reaps the benefit of corner location. This is frequently taken as the width of a standard lot.

As far as depth is concerned, the most common arbitrary rule is to assign corner influence to a distance which equals the standard depth in the area. For lots of less than standard depth, a depth rule factor is applied to the corner influence, while, for lots of greater depth, the portion beyond the standard is ignored as far as corner influence is concerned.

Regardless of the rule or formula used, it is recognized that no one of the varied procedures in use is considered satisfactory by appraisers. Even where they have adopted a procedure, they recognize that it must occasionally be abandoned where conditions peculiar to any particular corner do not fit into the pattern. The problem of assigning corner-influence values is one that must constantly be reviewed in the light of valid market transactions and rental conditions. Theoretically, it is possible to construct a table of values based on sales and rents, but, unfortunately, the problem of the extent of the corner-influence zone will remain a subjective factor.

Use of Corner Influence. To return to the fundamental purpose of developing corner-influence rules, it should be remembered that they are merely devices to enable the appraiser to formulate unit foot values to be applied to properties under appraisal. The use of a simple example will illustrate how these rules can be applied in practice. Suppose an appraiser is making a sales search in order to develop unit land values. A sale of a corner parcel of land in a retail area is discovered. The plot (Fig. 11) is 25 feet on the main street and 100 feet in depth along the side street. The lot sold for $37,500.

If land is valued in the area on the basis of front-foot values, it becomes necessary to arrive at an equivalent number of unit front feet for the corner plot. Assume that this is an area in which an arbitrary corner-influence factor (50 percent) is applied to corner-lot values. The procedure is as follows:

Number of front feet in the lot, if an inside lot   =   25.0′
Corner-influence factor = 50% × 25.0′   =   12.5′

Total number of equivalent front feet in plot   =   37.5′
Unit front-foot value = selling price ($37,500)/equivalent
front feet (37.5) = **$1,000 per front foot**

Thus, this sale reveals that the indicated front-foot value was $1,000. By analysis of several other sales of plots in the area, corner or inside, a range of values can be developed within which will fall the figure the appraiser chooses to adopt for his subject property.

DEPTH TABLES

The most valuable part of a lot is the street frontage. Thereafter, as the distance from the street increases, the value decreases. Further, if a parcel of land having a standard frontage and depth for an area becomes enlarged by the addition of increased depth, it will normally have an increased value but the increase will not be in proportion to the increase in depth. At the same time, if the parcel contains less than the standard

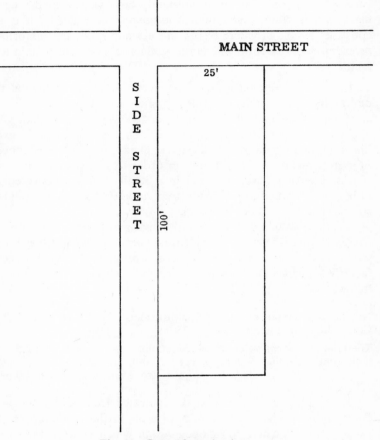

Fig. 11. Corner-lot valuation.

depth, it will normally have a decreased value but the decreased value will not be in proportion to the decrease in depth. This phenomenon is known as depth influence and has been generally recognized by appraisers on the basis of both common sense and experience. Street frontage is generally recognized to be of greatest importance in high-class retail areas and of least importance in industrial or rural areas. Further, street frontage is more important in large cities with heavy pedestrian and vehicular traffic than in small towns. As in the case with corner influence, there have been

developed over the years many different tables to measure the depth influence for different cities. Depth tables simply show the relationships between various depths and depth influence as a percentage figure. This figure, when multiplied by the front-foot value of a standard lot, gives the
front-foot value of an inside lot having a depth equal to the depth of any
lot which is more or less than the standard depth. Examples of several
depth tables in use are given in Table 10.

TABLE 10
DEPTH FACTORS (IN PER CENT) FOR SELECTED DEPTHS AND SELECTED DEPTH RULES
(STANDARD DEPTH = 100 FEET)

Depth in Feet	Hoffman-Neill	Davies	Somers	Jerrett
5	17.3	12.5	14.4	9.5
10	26.0	21.7	25.0	18.2
25	44.4	41.7	47.9	40.0
50	66.7	65.6	72.5	66.7
75	84.5	84.1	88.3	85.7
100	100.0	100.0	100.0	100.0
125	114.0	113.9	109.1	111.1
150	126.8	126.4	115.0	120.0
200	150.0	149.2	122.0	133.3

In order to appraise an inside rectangular lot fronting on the street, it
is necessary to

1. Find the appropriate depth factor in the depth table
2. Multiply this depth factor by the width of the lot to obtain an adjusted
   width
3. Multiply the adjusted width by the unit foot value

Thus a lot 25 × 50 feet on a street with a unit value of $300 per front
foot would be valued as follows, using a Hoffman-Neill factor:

$$25' \times 66.7 \times \$300 = \$5,000$$

An examination of the selected tables will show that a 25- × 50-foot
lot which has only 50 per cent of the area of a standard lot is given an
equivalent value of ⅔ of a standard lot. At the same time, a lot of 25 × 150
feet which has an area of 150 per cent of a standard lot is only given an
equivalent value of 126.8 per cent. This is in accordance with the theory
of depth influence mentioned previously.

In certain areas, land will be valued on a square-foot basis. To convert a front-foot depth table into equivalent factors for square feet, it is only
necessary to multiply the front-foot depth factor by 100 and then to divide
by the actual depth of the lot. For example, the depth factor for 50 feet is

66.7 in the Hoffman-Neill rule. Multiplying by 100 gives 6,670 and dividing by 50 amounts to 1.333. Thus a 25- × 50-foot lot has an equivalent area of 1,667 square feet (25 × 50 × 1.33), which when multiplied by $3 a square foot equals $5,000.

Several other depth tables are in use throughout the country. The striking thing about them is the close similarity in the factors assigned to the various depths. Tables can also be constructed with standard depths exceeding 100 feet. The construction of a depth table would be a simple statistical problem if sufficient sales data were available. It would merely involve a comparison of values of lots of standard and non-standard depths. The earliest rules such as the Hoffman-Neill and Davies rules were indeed based on hundreds of sales of vacant land. However, the sales were made under conditions that no longer exist today. Zoning regulations and increased lot requirements have acted to cast serious doubt upon the advisability of continuing to rely on these and other depth rules. Even if the tables are converted to square-foot factors in accordance with the growing practice of buyers to purchase on the basis of square footage rather than frontage, it is questionable whether they are concerned more with depth than with total area.

Deviations from Depth Tables. Appraisers who recognize the existence of depth tables and make use of them are usually aware of the necessity to deviate from them where circumstances warrant. In a retail district, where satisfactory store depths need not exceed 50 feet, a plot of 50 feet in depth will probably be worth more than 66.7 per cent of a standard lot. In a factory district, on the other hand, a 50-foot depth will probably not be worth 66.7 per cent of a standard lot, and lots in excess of 100 feet will probably be worth more than the depth influence ascribed to them under the tables. In apartment-house and office areas, with the growing emphasis on open land space, lots of less than standard depth will probably be worth less than is indicated on the depth tables. In fact it has been suggested that the depth tables, based as they are in most cases on 100-foot depth, are no longer adequate for apartment and office-building areas. A new standard depth of 125 or 150 feet has been suggested.

Use of Depth Tables. Just as with corner-influence rules, depth tables may be utilized to assist the appraiser in analyzing several sales in order to arrive at a usable land value factor. The task is to arrive at an equivalent unit foot value for those parcels which deviate from the normal depth in the area. If a parcel of 25 × 75 feet were sold for $4,225, its equivalent unit lot value would be arrived at in the following manner, using the Hoffman-Neill rule:

$$25' \times 84.5\% \text{ (H.-N. factor for } 75') = 21.125 \text{ equivalent front feet}$$
$$\$4,225/21.125 = \$200 \text{ per front foot}$$

Thus, a front-foot value of $200 is indicated for a foot of standard depth.

Another use to which the depth tables can be put is for modification of corner influence. As has already been indicated, many appraisers make it a practice to modify their corner-influence factor when the depth of the lot is less than standard in the area. A corner lot of 25 × 50 feet is then subject to two value modifications. First, the frontage is modified by the depth rule used, and then the added increment for the corner location is likewise modified by the same depth rule.

Modification #1 (Hoffman-Neill table) 25′ × 66.7%   = 16.67 eq. fr. ft.
Modification #2 (Hoffman-Neill table) Corner influence—
                         50% = 12.5′ × 66.7% =   8.33 eq. fr. ft.
Total equivalent front footage of corner parcel   = 25.00′

When unit foot values are developed through sales and income and the parcel under appraisement varies from the standard depth, the appraiser merely uses the table commonly in use in his area to assist himself in arriving at his estimate of land value. This aspect of the work is pure arithmetic. The true skill and ability of the appraiser lies in his being able to utilize his knowledge and experience in order to determine what the unit values are.

PLOTTAGE

The question of comparative values of large and small plots has been the subject of much discussion and disagreement among appraisers. The added value inherent in the combined common ownership of two or more contiguous lots is known as *plottage value*. This added value is due to

1. Greater utility
2. Larger building and rental opportunity
3. Economy in operation
4. Costs of assembling

Plottage value is largely a result of the increased potentialities of a combined plot. The amount of plottage increment usually varies with the size of the plot, availability of land, intensity of development, and difficulty of assemblage.

Methods of Computation. While general recognition of plottage value exists, the problem of measurement, like many other aspects of land valuation, remains in the realm of controversy. In many areas, appraisers and assessors use a formula or percentage increment for lots that exceed the width of standard lots. In some cases, a plottage increment is added for every 500 additional square feet in a plot; in other cases, only when the area of the plot reaches a minimum of two standard lots will the plottage increment be applied. Another aspect of the problem of measurement involves the treatment of land of varying values. Some appraisers will apply plottage increment percentages or formulas on a uniform basis, regardless of unit land values; others will use different percentages for different unit values.

To determine the percentages suitable for plottage increments, and to substitute mathematical analysis and experienced judgment for mere unsubstantiated opinions and formulas, no matter how long in use, the appraiser should analyse several typical commercial and residential building plots from the point of view of the potential investor and builder. Floor layouts for plots of varying sizes could then be studied in light of the existing building and zoning regulations.

If a 25- $\times$ 100-foot lot is worth $50,000 and the one next to it is also worth $50,000, it can be readily observed that the two lots, if combined, would be worth more than $100,000. If two 25-foot buildings were to be constructed on each of the separate plots, their total cost would exceed the cost of a 50-foot building of the same type. In addition, a 50-foot building would, after allowance for stairs, elevators, outside walls, and public halls, produce a greater net rentable area. The advantages of a larger building would also be revealed in decreased operating costs. A builder, contemplating an improvement for these parcels, could then afford to pay for the combined plots an amount equal to the savings in construction costs plus the capitalized value of the increased net returns. If the total savings came to $5,000 per lot, he could afford to pay $55,000 per lot for each parcel. This would indicate a plottage increment of 10 per cent per lot.

As unit lot values increase, it is possible that the percentage for plottage will decrease. In the example cited above, if the unit lot values were $100,000 per lot and the savings per lot remained at $5,000, the plottage increment would reduce to 5 per cent. From a builder's viewpoint, the added amount he could afford to pay for plottage would tend to decrease as land became more valuable.

Studies of plottage increments seem to indicate that, when a parcel exceeds 10,000 square feet in area, very little plottage value accrues to the parcel. Where a parcel containing 10,000 square feet, the equivalent of four standard 25- $\times$ 100-foot lots, would have a plottage increment of 10 per cent, a similar parcel of 20,000 square feet would have a plottage increment of only 12 per cent, and a parcel of 50,000 square feet would command a plottage increment of 15 per cent.

If a series of studies were carried out by an appraiser, or by appraisers in a joint effort, a pattern or formula could probably be evolved that would correspond with the economic realities of the real estate market in the area.

As conditions changed relative to zoning and building-code requirements, the formulas could be revised and brought up to date. In this way, a greater degree of acceptance among appraisers regarding plottage increments could be obtained.

Application of Plottage Factor. A plottage formula, where its use is justified, is merely another tool available to the appraiser in his analysis of parcels of known or indicated value. The prime function of reducing these parcels to a unit foot or unit lot value must not be overlooked. Thus, if an inside lot of 100 × 100 feet has sold for $44,000, the derivation of a unit lot value is a simple matter. The parcel is equal to 4 separate lots in area. If we assume that 10 per cent is the proper plottage increment, the combined parcel is equivalent to 4.4 separate unit lots. By dividing $44,000 by 4.4 unit lots, a unit lot value of $10,000 is obtained. This unit factor can then be used as a basis for the valuation of comparable parcels.

Adverse Plottage. Just as a plottage increment is recognized by appraisers, there is a further recognition that plots of less than standard size may be subject to a value decrement. In an area where large improvements exist and are warranted, single standard-size lots, standing between the larger improvements, may be subject to value decrements. The decrease in value arises from the knowledge that buildings erected on small plots will have proportionately less rentable area and would cost proportionately more to build than structures on the standard plot sizes in the area. The problem of adverse plottage has received even less study than has been applied to plottage increment. This has probably been because the possibility of combining several smaller uneconomic lots into a single economic one exists and, by this combination, the factor of adverse plottage would be removed. However, it is in those areas where that possibility is foreclosed by the nature of the existing improvements that adverse plottage must be considered. The suggestion advanced for analysis and study of plottage increment could be followed for adverse plottage and workable formulas could be developed. Separate studies for residential and non-residential land should be undertaken. The few studies that have been made do not reveal any areas of agreement, except that some penalty should be assigned to the smaller parcels.

Another aspect of adverse plottage that should be considered is usually found in residential areas. If zoning regulations call for a minimum frontage and several parcels in the area exceed the minimum but are not large enough to be divided into two separate building lots, a question arises as to the value of the "excess frontage." If a 40-foot frontage is the required minimum and land is worth $100 per front foot, what value should an appraiser ascribe to a parcel with a 70-foot frontage? Further, if the land adjacent to this parcel has already been built upon, and 40-foot lots are characteristic in the area, the possibility of acquiring an additional 10 feet to create two building lots no longer exists. It is possible that the increased size of the 70-foot parcel will appeal to some potential buyer who would like to have increased area and enjoy greater privacy and prestige. If so, he might be willing to pay the going rate for the entire parcel. On the other hand, in view of the typical lot size in the area, most potential buyers would probably consider the 30 feet as "surplus" or excess frontage of limited use and calling for added caretaking and inconvenience. The in-increased tax burden would also be a factor to be considered. It is most probable that potential buyers would be unwilling to pay the going rate for the excess land. Where this is true, the appraiser would be required to make two calculations for land value. The first 40 feet could be appraised at the indicated market rate, while the excess 30 feet would be appraised at a lower unit value. The percentage by which the unit value would be reduced depends on the appraiser's judgment based on the usual comparable values that he can find in the market. In any event, this lower unit value may be regarded as a form of adverse plottage.

IRREGULAR SHAPES

Although the vast majority of lots are rectangular in shape, there are many of non-rectangular shape. Such lots are common in the older cities of the East and among the newer subdivisions throughout the country. The assumption made by most appraisers in valuing lots of irregular shape is that they have a tendency to be worth less than a rectangular lot of the same area. This is due to several factors. If a building of conventional shape is to be constructed on an irregular lot, the building area is generally smaller than on a rectangular parcel. If unconventional design is used to accommodate the irregular shape, it usually is more costly and may lack the resale value of conventionally designed buildings. On the other hand, it must be recognized that some of the irregularly shaped lots that have been created by curved street lines may enhance the appearance of residential locations and have a value equal to, if not greater than, that of rectangular lots.

The problem facing the appraiser dealing with irregularly shaped lots is once again one of using appropriate modifying factors to sales of these parcels in order to arrive at a basic unit land value. The most common procedure is to apply a set of mathematical formulas to the irregular parcels in order to break them down to the equivalent standard lot sizes and shapes. An infinite variety of irregular geometrically shaped lots may confront the appraiser. The most common are the triangle, the right trapezoid, the oblique parallelogram, and the lot with curved boundaries.

A brief discussion of the most common methods in use for analysis of these non-rectangular lots follows.

Triangular Lots. For appraisal purposes, triangular lots are of two major types. A triangle with its base on the street is known as a *delta* triangle. A triangle whose base is parallel to the street but whose apex lies on the street is referred to as a *nabla* triangle. Delta triangles are usually appraised by considering them first as rectangles with a frontage equal to the base and a depth equal to the triangle's altitude. From this value, a percentage is taken in accordance with the procedure followed in the area. The usual percentage lies between 60 and 70 per cent of the value ascribed to a rectangle. The value of a nabla triangle is found by taking a percentage of the value of a rectangle having a frontage equal to the base of the triangle and a depth equal to the altitude of the triangle. The proper percentage is simply the difference between 100 per cent and the percentage used for a delta triangle. Thus, if a delta triangle has a percentage factor of 66⅔ per cent of the rectangle value, the nabla triangle would have a percentage factor of 33⅓ per cent. An example is given in Figure 12.

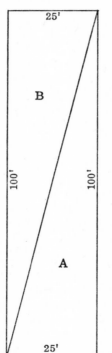

STREET

Fig. 12. Triangular-lot valuation.

Triangle *A* is the delta triangle. If it sold for $8,000, its unit front-foot value could be computed as follows:

$8,000/25' × 66⅔% (delta factor) = $480 per front foot

Conversely, if an appraisal of the triangular parcel were required and $480 per front foot had been determined as the unit value in the area, the value of the triangle would be computed in the following manner:

Value of triangle = 25' × $480 × 66⅔% = $8,000

The value of the nabla triangle *B* would be found in this manner:

Value of triangle = 25' × $480 × 33⅓% = $4,000

Where triangular lots are found on corners or where the altitudes vary in depth from the standard, further modifications for corner and depth influences would be made before applying the triangle percentage factors.

In most cases, appraisers will make a further modification for adverse plottage due to the shape of the triangular lots. This is usually done by reducing the triangle factor. Instead of using a 66⅔ per cent delta factor and a 33⅓ per cent nabla factor, they will use a 60 and 30 per cent factor, respectively. When this is done, the two factors will add up to 90 per cent instead of 100 per cent. The deductions, if they warrant, may be more or less, but, in any event, some consideration should be given to the fact that the two triangles, by themselves, are probably less valuable than if they were part of a rectangular parcel.

Trapezoids. For appraising a trapezoid-shaped lot, there are two general rules in existence. According to one of these, such a lot has a value equal to that of a rectangle having the same frontage and having a depth equal to the average length of the parallel sides of the trapezoid. The other rule averages the *depth factors* of the two parallel sides. Simply stated, it says that a trapezoidal lot whose two parallel sides are perpendicular to the street has a front-foot value equal to the unit foot value times the average of the depth factors for the two parallel sides. A third possibility is to divide the trapezoid into a rectangle and a triangle and apply the rules previously suggested for these shapes. For most lots, there will be only negligible difference in value if either of these methods is used. Only in cases where shallow lots, having one parallel side much shorter than the other, are to be valued, will the use of the first method give a wide variance from the other methods. This method is generally not recommended in these cases.

Oblique Parallelograms. Lots having the shape of a non-rectangular, or oblique, parallelogram have a special rule for their valuation. The rule states that a lot of such shape has a value equal to that of a rectangle having a width equal to the perpendicular distance between the lot's sidelines, and a depth equal to the length of the sidelines. This rule will produce a lower valuation than if the lot were divided into a rectangle and two triangles. This may be attributable to a negative shape factor. The extent of this adverse factor must remain a matter of judgment with the appraiser rather than one dependent upon a mathematical formula.

Curved Boundaries. There is no exact procedure to be followed for the valuation of lots with curved boundaries. The possible variations in shape are limitless. One method that is in use is to divide the actual area into a number of triangles and rectangles which will practically include all of the area of the lot and then to appraise each triangle and rectangle by ordinary rules. Still another method is to obtain an approximate area and then proceed to construct a rectangle or triangle of equal area and comparable shape; from there, either the triangle or the rectangle may be appraised.

OTHER PROBLEMS

There are other special land-valuation problems aside from those arising owing to size and shape irregularities. Merge lines, where a lot extends and faces on parallel streets of different value, and problems involving alley influence are two common examples. Unfortunately, there seem to be as many possible ways of handling these situations as there are appraisers. Many of the methods are purely empirical, and frequently there is no agreement within an area as to the proper method. It would serve no purpose at this point to go into a discussion of these methods. The appraiser should examine the method in most common use in his area, and, if he feels that it fits the picture of the market, he can adapt it for his own purposes.

CONCLUSIONS AND RECOMMENDATIONS

The previous discussion of rules and formulas for the appraisal and analysis of odd-shaped and non-standard lots should not cause the appraiser to lose sight of his basic objective, namely, to find the market value. This holds true whether the task is to analyze sales data to obtain a basis for land value estimates, or to arrive at the value of a particular lot once the units have been established in the appraiser's mind. It must be remembered that the use of any of the rules is only a means to an end and not the end in itself. Where common sense tells the appraiser that the rules do not fit, he can either search for a new rule or appraise the parcel on another basis. The empirical nature of most mathematical rules leaves them open to a great deal of criticism. This fact, plus the recognition that a great deal of disagreement exists among appraisers as to the validity of several of the rules, gives further cause for doubt and distrust. Finally, when it is realized that in many cases the conditions under which the rules were initially worked out no longer exist, there is ground for further skepticism. The rules are probably best suited for tax assessment valuation where quick and equitable appraisals are required. But even in this type of work the appraiser is obliged to depart from his rules where it is plainly evident that they fail to result in market-value appraisals.

To cast doubt upon the validity of the existing methods of handling irregular parcels is not enough. Is there a better way?

The Land Value–Construction Unit Method. The most promising approach to land valuation would seem to be one in which any individual parcel could be related to a unit of construction which represents its highest and best use at the time of the appraisal. Each plot should be carefully analyzed to determine the maximum potential building considering zoning laws, building codes, market conditions, demands for space, etc. An example will illustrate the procedure to be followed.

For the purposes of our example we shall assume that the appraiser is confronted with an irregularly shaped plot containing 12,000 square feet. He determines, upon study of the neighborhood and area, that the highest and best use is a six-story self-service-elevator apartment house. He also knows that the zoning and building codes will only permit 70 per cent coverage of the lot. This means that he will be able to project a maximum of 50,400 square feet of building space (12,000 × .7 × 6). If room sizes in this area call for an over-all average of 300 square feet, he will also be able to project a building with 168 rentable rooms. The land value of the plot can now be related either to total building area—4.2 square feet of building space for each square foot of land—or to maximum rentable room coverage, which in this case would be .014 rentable rooms for each square foot of land area. The appraiser selects the rentable room–square foot relationship and proceeds to investigate further. He finds that properties of this type command an annual rental of $600 per room and that the total of operating expenses and real estate taxes amounts to 40 per cent of the gross income. Finally, he discovers that the market indicates that an over-all capitalization rate of 9 per cent, including recapture provisions, is proper. His calculations would then proceed as follows:

One square foot of land produces .014 rentable rooms
.014 rentable rooms produces $8.40 in gross rental (.014 × $600)

Gross rent	$8.40
Taxes and operating	3.36 (8.40 × .40)
Net income to property	$5.04 per square foot of land

Value of property per square foot of land = $5.04/.09 = $56
Less building cost per square foot of land $42
(300 × .014 × $10 per square foot)
Residual value to land (per square foot) **$14**

The land value of this parcel is now established on the basis of its economic value. The unit value can be applied to other similar parcels in the area, and valid comparisons or adjustments for different areas can be made. The emphasis can now be put on the comparative earning capacity of different plots rather than on their geometric design or depth or corner location. Corner location, for example, can now be analyzed in the light of the extra rentals and coverage that the corner affords the parcel. The use of this approach to land valuation tends to overcome the difficulties inherent in the market approach. It enables the appraiser to develop for his use a set of significant economic relationships that can be substituted for the mathematical formulas that have been described in this chapter. These economic relationships can be applied to land of various uses, making rapid comparisons possible.

A note of caution is in order. While values of land are usually predicated on its highest and best use, this is only correct when it is economic to improve the land to its highest utility. It is obvious that all properties cannot be improved according to their legal, permissible maximum at the same time. To do so would create a situation where overbuilding would be rampant. The succession of land uses must proceed at an orderly pace in harmony with the needs and growth of a community. It follows that land that is improved or ready for improvement can be worth more than similar parcels that are not yet ready. A "time discount" factor is present with the latter parcels, and it requires expert judgment on the appraiser's part to determine how much must be taken. The ability to exercise such judgment is a prime requisite of a good appraiser, and it comes about not only with a knowledge of mathematical formulas but through an ability to adapt formulas and procedures to the requirements of reason and the economic facts of life.

Bibliography—Part III

ALBERT, STERLING H. "Neighborhood Factors Affecting Residential Values," *The Appraisal Journal*, XXVIII (No. 1), 81–89.

AMERICAN INSTITUTE OF REAL ESTATE APPRAISERS. *The Appraisal of Real Estate* (3d ed.). Chicago: American Institute of Real Estate Appraisers, 1960. Chapter 12.

AMERICAN INSTITUTE OF REAL ESTATE APPRAISERS. *Condemnation Appraising.* Chicago: American Institute of Real Estate Appraisers, 1962.

AMERICAN INSTITUTE OF REAL ESTATE APPRAISERS. *Selected Readings in Real Estate Appraisal.* Chicago: American Institute of Real Estate Appraisers, 1953. Sections 9–10, 14.

BLOOM, MAX R. "Fiscal Productivity and the Pure Theory of Urban Renewal," *Land Economics*, XXXVIII, No. 2 (May, 1962).

BONBRIGHT, JAMES C. *The Valuation of Property.* New York: McGraw-Hill Book Co., Inc., 1937. Chapter 17.

BROADBENT, L. "Eminent Domain and Valuation of Land Containing Minerals," *The Appraisal Journal*, XXIX, No. 1 (January, 1961).

BRYANT, WILLIS R. *Mortgage Lending.* New York: McGraw-Hill Book Co., Inc., 1956.

BURBANK, NELSON L., and OSCAR SHAFTEL. *House Construction Details.* New York: Simmons-Boardman Publishing Corp., 1959.

CHERINGTON, HOMER V., and ROBERT H. PEASE. *Mortgage Banking.* New York: McGraw-Hill Book Co., Inc., 1953.

DALGETY, GEORGE L. "The Appraisal of Long Term Leaseholds," *The Appraisal Journal*, XVI, No. 2 (April, 1948).

DIAMOND, T. M., JR. "The Appraiser in Court," *The Residential Appraiser*, XXVII, No. 4 (April, 1961).

DUNN, DOMINICK. "Knowledge of Architecture Valuable to Appraisers," *The Appraisal Journal*, XVII, No. 2 (April, 1949).

FEDERAL HOUSING ADMINISTRATION. *Underwriting Manual.* Washington, D.C.: Government Printing Office, 1955.

HOAGLAND, HENRY E., and LEO D. STONE. *Real Estate Finance.* Homewood, Ill.: Richard D. Irwin, Inc., 1961.

JENSEN, JENS P. *Property Taxation in the United States.* Chicago: University of Chicago Press, 1931.

JOHNSON, L. "Acquisition Appraisals for Urban Renewal," *The Appraisal Journal*, XXIX, No. 2 (April, 1961). Part I.

JOHNSTONE, B. K., *et al. Building or Buying a House.* New York: McGraw-Hill Book Co., Inc., 1945.

KAHN, SANDERS A. "Reuse Appraising," in *Appraisal and Valuation Manual*, volume VI. Washington, D.C.: American Society of Appraisers, 1961.

KAHN, SANDERS A. "Valuation of Urban Land," in *Appraisal and Valuation Manual*, volume IV. Washington, D.C.: American Society of Appraisers, 1959.

KNISKERN, PHILIP W. *Real Estate Appraisal and Valuation.* New York: The Ronald Press Co., 1933. Chapters 16, 27.

KUEHNLE, WALTER R. "Valuation of Real Estate for Ad Valorem Tax Purposes: Part I," *The Appraisal Journal,* XXI, No. 1 (January, 1953).

LEE, H. O., and W. D. LEFORESTIER. *Review and Reduction of Real Property Assessments.* New York: Clark Boardman Co., Ltd., 1960.

MCMICHAEL, STANLEY L. "Appraising Leasehold Estates," *The Appraisal Journal,* XV, No. 4 (October, 1947).

MCMICHAEL, STANLEY L. *McMichael's Appraising Manual* (4th ed.). Englewood Cliffs, N.J.: Prentice-Hall, Inc., 1951. Chapters 35–38.

MCMICHAEL, STANLEY L., and PAUL T. O'KEEFE. *How to Finance Real Estate* (2d ed.). Englewood Cliffs, N.J.: Prentice-Hall, Inc., 1953.

NATIONAL ASSOCIATION OF ASSESSING OFFICERS. *Urban Land Appraisal.* Chicago: International Association of Assessing Officers, 1940.

ORGEL, LEWIS. *Orgel on Valuation Under the Law of Eminent Domain* (2d ed.). Charlottesville, Va.: Michie Co., 1953.

PROUTY, W. L., C. W. COLLINS, and F. H. PROUTY. *Appraisers and Assessors Manual.* New York: McGraw-Hill Book Co., Inc., 1930.

RANDALL, WILLIAM J. "Reflections of a Condemnation Appraiser," *The Residential Appraiser,* XXVII, No. 8 (August, 1961).

RIGHT OF WAY CONSULTANTS, INC. *Just Compensation.* Warrenton, Va.: Published by the authors. Annual with monthly supplements.

ROGERS, RUSSELL R. "Appraising for Condemnation," *The Residential Appraiser,* XXVII, No. 6 (June, 1961).

SCHMUTZ, GEORGE L. *The Appraisal Process.* Manhattan Beach, Calif.: Published by the author, 1953. Chapter 35.

SCHMUTZ, GEORGE L. *Condemnation Appraisal Handbook.* Englewood Cliffs, N.J.: Prentice-Hall, Inc., 1949.

SILVERHERZ, JOSEPH D. *The Assessment of Real Property in the United States.* Special report No. 10. Albany: New York State Tax Commission, 1936. Chapter 15.

SLAYTON, WILLIAM L. "Appraiser's Role in Urban Renewal," *The Appraisal Journal,* XXX, No. 1 (January, 1962).

SMITH, CHARLES E. "Urban Renewal Programs from an Appraiser's Viewpoint," *The Residential Appraiser,* XXVII, No. 6, (June, 1961).

SMITH, WALSTEIN. "Acquisition Appraisal in Urban Renewal," *The Residential Appraiser,* XXVII, No. 3 (March, 1961).

STEUBENS, HERBERT H. "Appraising and Acquisition for Right of Way Purposes," *The Residential Appraiser,* XXVII, No. 5 (May, 1961).

UNITED STATES DEPARTMENT OF AGRICULTURE. *Use and Abuse of Wood in House Construction.* Miscellaneous publication No. 358. Washington, D.C.: Government Printing Office, 1939.

UNITED STATES DEPARTMENT OF AGRICULTURE. *Wood Frame House Construction.* Agricultural handbook No. 73 (February, 1955). Washington, D.C.: Government Printing Office.

WOLTZ, SETH P. "Case Studies in Severance Damages," *The Residential Appraiser,* XXVII, No. 8 (August, 1961).

WRIGHT, HENRY. "Trends in Architecture," *The Appraisal Journal,* XVI (October, 1948).

YOUNG, MELVIN A. "Organization and Installation of a Method for a Tax Equalization Program," in *Appraisal and Valuation Manual,* volume V. Washington, D.C.: American Society of Appraisers, 1960.

Part IV

INVESTMENT ANALYSIS

24

Investment Features of Real Estate

Probably no other economic activity has stirred the imagination of business people as much as has the opportunity to "make a killing" in realty. Many books on this subject written for the novice, sometimes by lucky non-professionals, have become topics of conversation in business offices and parlors. Games of chance based upon rolling dice and moving markers to gain control of choice realty have become perennially popular. Unfortunately, many realty purchases are "investments" similar to rolling dice.

A realty investment cannot prudently be made by an amateur guided by an accountant and a lawyer, for then it is being made by three amateurs. If real estate analysis merely meant looking at income and expense statements, any bookkeeper would be a more competent analyst than the realtors. Similarly, if the basis of analysis were legal clauses in bonds, leases, and mortgages, the attorney would be superior to the realtor. From the point of view of determining the feasibility of a realty investment, the skill of the accountant or the attorney is limited. Basically, they can determine if the income-tax structure is advantageous, if the documents give adequate protection, and if rents and expense items are as represented. But it is precisely at this point that real estate analysis only begins.

Investments are rated on certain basic factors:

1. How safe is the principal? Will it be returned to the investor?
2. How certain is the anticipated yield on the investment?
3. How liquid is the investment? Can it quickly and inexpensively be converted to cash?
4. What are the chances of capital appreciation? Can the investment be sold for a profit?
5. What protection does the investment give the investor from inflationary pressures?
6. What is the tax liability of the realty investment?

In general, real estate as an investment ranks high in all aspects other than in respect to liquidity. However, it is not possible to guide an investor "in general." Each realty investment is different from any other, for there are no two identical realty interests. The authors have prepared a table covering types of realty investments and have attempted to rate each type as to various investment characteristics. It can be seen from Table 11 that various limiting assumptions are necessary to rate realty investments even when the investments are broken down into thirteen specific categories.

SAFETY OF REALTY INVESTMENT

Every investor considers the amount of cash he plans to invest in the realty. He wants to be assured that when he sells the property he will get back his investment. During normal economic eras, he will be able to do so under the following circumstances:

1. He bought the property at market price.
2. Neighborhood and community have not economically decayed since purchase.
3. Property has been maintained in conformity with neighborhood.
4. Income, expenses, and mortgage financing affecting the realty have not become less favorable than at time of purchase.

SAFETY OF YIELD ON INVESTMENT

All investment realty must be based upon annual cash income the property gives to the investor. This is the obvious major reason for investment in most cases, but it does not always mean that, at the time of purchase, the return is similar to what will exist after a few years. Sometimes a property is purchased with a relatively low rate of return but can be greatly improved. This improvement can take place by raising rents, lowering costs, or refinancing. For example, an office building may be rented at a rate of $2.50 per square foot. These rents may be in effect under leases that were made several years in the past, when that rental prevailed in the market. Let us assume that the building contained 40,000 square feet of rentable area and, therefore, had a rent roll of $100,000. Taxes, operating expenses, and mortgage interest and amortization totaled $90,000, leaving the buyer $10,000 per annum, after payment of all charges including mortgage charges on a $200,000 mortgage. The total investment that he made was $200,000 above the existing mortgage, for the price was $400,000.

Now that he owns the realty, he negotiates with the tenants for new leases and is successful in arranging new leases upon the expiration of the old ones, at a new rate of $3.75 per square foot. This increases the rent roll to $150,000. He will now have a net cash flow income of $60,000 instead of $10,000. If he did not have to increase his investment, the rate of return would have risen from 5 per cent to 30 per cent. However, the rent increase was very large and, in many cases, would be obtainable only because the owner installed new improvements, which might include new lighting, air conditioning, heating and elevator modernization, and decoration. Possibly, they required the owner to invest an additional $200,000.

TABLE 11
Rating of Realty Investments

Type of Investment	Safety of Initial Investment	Safety of Annual Earnings	Capital Appreciation	Liquidity	Income-Tax Shelter	Inflationary Protection
Apartment houses (middle income)	E	E	E	E	G	E†
Apartment houses (luxury)	F	F	F	F	G	E†
Office buildings (multitenant, in city)	G	G	G	E	F	E†
Office buildings (one national tenant, suburb)	F	G*	P*	E*	E	N
Office buildings (multitenant, suburb)	P	F	P	P	E	G
Retail property (average tenant, in city)	F	P	N	F	P	F
Retail property (one national tenant, in city)	F	G*	P	E*	P	N‡
Retail property (shopping centers)	F	G	G	G	E	P‡
Retail property (one national tenant, suburb)	G	G*	P*	E*	E	N‡
Loft buildings (multitenant)	G	G	F	F	G	G†
Industrial buildings (one national tenant)	G	G*	P*	E*	E	N
Gas stations (one national tenant, highway)	F	F*	P*	E*	E	P
Gas stations (one national tenant, in city)	E	G*	G	E*	F	P

Code: E—Excellent; G—Good; F—Fair; P—Poor; N—Negative

* Assume rental is at market, lease has many years to run, and purchase price is fair.
† Under free market conditions, otherwise *poor.*
‡ Unless percentage lease, then *excellent.*

His investment would now be $400,000, and his return would be 15 per cent.

The possible changes have not been exhausted. He may have been able to reduce operating costs because elevator and heating-plant modernization gave him an additional $10,000 net cash flow. He may have also decided to refinance the property, owing to the major new improvements and changes in income and expense structure. The old mortgage of $200,000 at 8 per cent interest and amortization might be increased to $400,000 with the interest and amortization charges of $36,000. His net income would now be $50,000 and would be a 25 per cent return on his total cash investment of $200,000 above the $400,000 mortgage. A summary of the investment would be as follows:

Original Investment

$200,000 cash
 200,000 mortgage (total of 8% interest and amortization)
$400,000 realty cost

$100,000 rent roll

$ 16,000 interest and amortization
   60,000 operating costs
   14,000 realty taxes
$ 90,000 total charges against income (before depreciation)

$ 10,000 net cash flow income

Modified Investment

$200,000 cash
 400,000 mortgage, covering additional building improvements
$600,000 realty cost

$150,000 new rent roll

$ 36,000 total of 9% interest amortization on new mortgage
   50,000 operating costs, reduced
   14,000 realty taxes
$100,000 total charges against income (before depreciation)

$ 50,000 net cash flow, after modified rent roll, mortgage, building operating
         costs, and building improvements—25% return on $200,000 cash
         investment

At this point, the tax assessor might increase the assessment due to the changes in the realty. This might reduce the income by $4,000 to $8,000 per annum.

It has been shown from this example, which, incidentally, is not atypical, that the current cash flow does not necessarily indicate future earnings of realty. Last year's income statement is only history. It may or may not indicate future potentials of the realty. No investor should buy realty on its past earning record. The last owners had the benefit of that income. The new owner must look to future earnings only.

It is obvious that the example given with his analysis showed how a property owner improved his income position. Many other examples can be shown to indicate that the future of the realty is not as bright as its past, or as it is being represented to the buyer.

ITEM EVALUATION

Many amateur investors are under the impression that a few items of expense may often be understated in the offering prospectus and that, if they increase the allowance for these expenses, they will be shrewdly dealing for the realty. This is complete naïveté. The items that can be understated in the property offering are usually relatively small items—fuel, repairs, and insurance. They affect the "bottom line," the net cash income flow, to a relatively small degree. This does not mean that they should not be checked. It is only being stated here that their effect on the investment is of minor importance. The items of major significance are rent roll, mortgage, assessed value, taxes, and payroll.

Rent Roll. An investor should consider not only potential rent-roll improvement but also the possible reduction in the rent roll. Sometimes, rents were made above the market owing to temporary shortage of space, poor knowledge of the market by the tenant, or optimism of the tenant as to business potential of the space (retail realty). Sometimes, neighborhoods or communities have declined and tenants will refuse to sign leases calling for the same high rents paid under leases negotiated when the area was better.

Mortgage. The buyer must also consider if the existing mortgage can be refinanced when it comes due. This is of special significance when the mortgage expires within a few years. It also merits serious consideration if the mortgage expires just as a large business tenant's lease is expiring. It is most difficult to get a new mortgage when a significant amount of space is vacant.

Realty Taxes. The assessed value is the basis for realty taxes. The buyer must be sure that assessed value will not be raised after his purchase or by improvements being made. The example shown earlier in this chapter of the fine modifications in a realty investment may very well have been adversely affected by a rise in realty taxes. This may result from the assessor learning of the sale and realizing that he had been underestimating the property value. It is even possible that politics had kept the taxes down for the old owner. It should also be understood that tax rates tend to increase over time.

Payroll. The payroll affecting the realty may be reduced by labor-saving devices but often will be increased owing to a general wage increase. A good building superintendent and staff are greatly responsible for the success of a building and affect operating costs and tenant relations.

Overvaluation of Prime Tenancy. In rating of types of realty on safety of income, long-term leases of prime national tenants have usually been considered the safest income properties. However, buyers sometimes have paid such high prices for these properties that, upon the approach of the termination of the lease, a resale of the realty could not be effected except at a sharp loss. It can, therefore, be seen that safety of income may not be the only basis for investment analysis.

LIQUIDITY OF INVESTMENT

Realty ranks low as a liquid investment. This is because realty cannot be standardized and offered on an exchange similar to a stock exchange. It has been demonstrated that shares in realty syndicates cannot be resold more readily than realty. As a matter of fact, a syndicate shareholder's investment is less liquid than a normal realty investment. Liquidity refers to the resale of the investment at a price reflecting its value at the time of the resale. It also gives consideration to the time it takes to consummate the sale and to the cost of the transfer. In 1949, the author made a survey of the liquidity of one-family houses in a booming community. Despite all those fine market conditions, it was found that the resales required an average of six months. Costs of sales are expensive. The usual home sale costs the seller in excess of 6 per cent, and up to 8 per cent or 9 per cent, if he prepares for the sale with new financing. Investment realty sales are usually much cheaper, generally running no higher than 6 per cent and often as little as 3 per cent. This is due to proportionally lower commissions and legal and title fees on larger sales. The sale of realty is excessively difficult owing to legal factors of property transfer. If we transferred title to shoes as we do to realty, we might all go barefooted.

CAPITAL APPRECIATION

Most investors have always hoped that their investments would prove so advantageous that in a short time they would be able to sell at a large profit. Every farmer secretly hopes that oil, gold, or uranium will be discovered on his land, or, more recently, that it will become a new resort or shopping-center site. All of these windfalls have, at times, given tremendous profits to realty owners. Property increases in value for various reasons:

1. Location becomes more desirable for some economic purpose.
2. A transportation system opens up the property to development.

3. The land yields raw materials.
4. Existing use of the realty can be modified to yield a higher income.
5. A reduction in operating costs can be effected.
6. A large new development is created near the property.
7. General business conditions improve.
8. General inflationary pressures exist.
9. New financing and market conditions provide buyers who accept lower returns on their investment.

Investors attempt to calculate the possibility of these factors affecting potential realty investments. It must be admitted that some very wealthy property owners did not have to be shrewd investors. They were there when the oil started gushing.

INFLATIONARY PRESSURES

Realty has always been considered a fine hedge against inflation. There is little basis for this general assumption. For many years, Dr. Herbert B. Dorau, a noted urban-land economist, has been showing that large amounts of realty, not only do not advance in value faster than the loss of value of the dollar, but in many cases, they lag behind many other commodities in price rises during inflationary eras.

It must be recognized that realty lags behind the economic market owing to its general slow marketability, its lack of standardization, and, most of all, its legal restrictions. Many properties do not proportionally increase in value during inflation, because they are subject to long-term leases at fixed rents. Since rent is payable in dollars, and the dollar income may not be increased under many leases, this type of realty has a poor degree of inflation protection. Other types of property might do better. Apartment-house rents do increase under normal inflationary conditions. However, during extreme scarcity of housing, the government has, at times, refused owners the right to increase rents. There are many properties that do well during inflation. Buyers are also willing to accept lower returns from realty when inflationary trends are in effect. They recognize that the returns will increase when leases are renewed. Realty is also a tangible asset which is desired when money starts to lose value.

INCOME-TAX LIABILITY OF REALTY INVESTMENT

Real estate has special advantages as a tax shelter. Many properties can be sold at a profit, and the investor can usually pay the lower rates under capital-gains provisions of the Internal Revenue laws.

Realty is often subject to heavy depreciation credit for income taxes. The Internal Revenue Service has prepared a schedule of annual depreciation of various types of buildings and equipment. It is often possible to offset the cash flow income by depreciation credit, thereby eliminating normal income-tax payments. After the property is substantially depreciated, it is normally sold, and, at that time, a capital-gains tax will be paid. However, this tax will usually be at a lower rate than the normal income-tax rate, and, furthermore, the owner then will have delayed his tax payment. Under some circumstances, even the capital-gains tax need not be paid. This can be accomplished by donating the property to non-profit institutions. Also, if the owner dies and his estate is small, there will not only not be a capital-gains tax, there might not even be estate and inheritance taxes.

Property most desirable for income-tax purposes will usually be realty that has a high ratio of building and equipment to land value. Land does not receive a depreciation credit from the income-tax authorities, for they do not consider that land depreciates in value.

Specific types of realty with a favorable income-tax position include shopping centers, industrial buildings, and high-rise apartment and office buildings. Poor tax shelter is afforded by one-story retail buildings in the centers of cities.

It must be stated that the income-tax laws have created some uneconomic action by investors. As an extreme but typical example, investors are often willing to pay higher mortgage interest rates to mortgagees in return for lower amortization payments. In other words, they are willing to pay higher rental rates for the use of money. The reason is simple. Internal Revenue considers interest an expense, and amortization, being the return of principal indebtedness, is not deductible from income. Most investors would eagerly pay an additional ½ per cent interest if they could reduce amortization 1 per cent.

LEVERAGE IN REALTY INVESTMENTS

There are many classes of realty investors, in addition to the property owner. Often, the property owner has a relatively small portion of the total investment. A financial institution may make a mortgage investment in the property. It will usually take an interest up to two-thirds of its valuation of the realty. Then a second mortgage investor may take an interest of about one-sixth of the property value, but usually for a short term. At this point, the property owner is left with an interest in the realty which is only one-sixth.

Why do property owners do this? There are usually two reasons: (1) They do not have sufficient funds to own a more substantial portion of the property. (2) They can have a large cash flow return on their investment. This can be accomplished by their surrendering the safer portions to the first mortgage and junior mortgagees. The term *junior mortgagees* is used because, at times, there are third and fourth mortgage interests in the realty, but usually the owner has about a minimum of 10 to 15 per cent interest.

Example of Leverage. To demonstrate the leverage principal for properties owned subject to mortgages, the following example is offered:

A property was purchased, free and clear, for $80,000, and there is a net return, before depreciation, of $10,000, or 12½ per cent.

A $50,000 first mortgage is placed against the realty, with annual payments of $3,750 including interest charges of 5½ per cent. The net cash flow is reduced to $6,250, but now the owner's cash investment is reduced to $30,000. The return is now 20.7 per cent.

If he now obtains $15,000 against a second mortgage and pays $1,650 per annum, including 8 per cent interest, the net cash flow is reduced to $4,600 but he will only have an investment of $15,000 and the return will be over 30 per cent.

These mortgages are not obtained without cost, and this will reduce the return to the investor, for his investment will be somewhat higher than that stated in this example. However, the results will be nearly as effective as shown.

The investor who has $80,000 cash can repeat this same process in the purchase of about five properties, and, instead of being satisfied with a cash flow of $10,000, he will actually have about $23,000. In addition, amortization is the repayment of the mortgage indebtedness, and he will be increasing his portion of the property ownership with each payment. He will also be able to reduce his income-tax liability because the mortgage interest is an expense against his earnings.

Obviously, such a fine situation must also have some negative factors. First of all, it must be understood that the mortgage interest rate on the first mortgage was stated to be 5½ per cent and that on the second mortgage, 8 per cent. Why are these mortgage investors willing to take a lower return than the over-all rate of 12½ per cent available to the realty? The reason is obvious. They are taking the safer portion of the investment.

Property values would have to decline more than 33⅓ per cent before it would be possible for the first mortgage holder to lose any of its money. (Since its mortgage is being decreased by the regular amortization payments, the actual decrease in value would have to be greater.) Even then, only a portion of its investment would be lost. However, a loss in value of 20 per cent would wipe out the property owner completely, and the second mortgagee would lose a little, unless the amortization had reduced the mortgage sufficiently.

Another way of showing this is to indicate that, before mortgage financing, $10,000 a year were available to the owner but that, after the two mortgages were placed against it, debt charges totaled $5,400, leaving only

$4,600 to the owner. Now let us suppose that a combination of the rent loss and an operating increase occurred. A total income loss of $5,000 would leave the property owner with a deficit of $400. He would, therefore, have to pay to own this realty. He would have a negative return on his investment. If he had not mortgaged the realty, his return would still be $5,000 on an $80,000 investment, or over 6 per cent.

The speculative investor can also show that a $5,000 increase in rental return would give the free and clear investor $15,000 net income on an $80,000 investment, or a return of a bit under 19 per cent, while, with the mortgages stated above, the thin equity holder would have a return of $9,600 on an investment of $15,000, or 64 per cent.

The figures given in this example are not indicative of market conditions affecting any particular investment but are offered to indicate clearly potentialities of leverage. Typically, the most skilled professional investors utilize this system. They have even devised additional methods of investing and applying leverage by separating the fee from the leasehold and also trading in leasehold positions.

The novice usually does not understand the economic propriety of higher returns for the more speculative portions of the real estate "pie" that he is being served and is usualy given a lower rate of return than is proper. This has often been the case with real estate syndicates.

RISKS

Real estate varies in risks, on the basis of certain fundamental elements:

1. Type of interest in realty
2. Type of realty
3. Margin of interest
4. Rent-paying ability of occupants
5. Neighborhood factors

Type of Interest. LAND INVESTMENT. The safest realty investment is the ownership of land under a large modern building which is well designed and a proper improvement for the land. This is true, if a ground lease has been given to a good builder who is paying ground rent and did not have the privilege of "mortgaging the fee." Even if the building is not profitable to the builder, it is almost impossible for him to discontinue rent payments on the ground. The building will show some profit and will represent a substantial capital investment that either the builder or the leasehold mortgagee will protect from passing into the hands of the landowner. Therefore, the landowner has the highest degree of safety. The two time periods that will be somewhat hazardous will be the period of construction until the building is rented and the period at the end of the lease. Usually the ground owner protects himself against the first-period mishaps by demanding a temporary security deposit or a completion bond. Since buildings usually do not become obsolete for at least forty years, the status at the end of the lease has less practical significance. If it is obsolete at that time, it is usually because the area has improved, and the building can be modernized or replaced by another building. An example of this is the replacement of first-class apartment houses and hotels of twenty-five-year vintage on Park and Madison avenues in New York City that recently had to be replaced because of the demand for new office buildings for the area. Landowners made large profits at that time. At the same time, in many other cities, fifty- and sixty-year-old structures continued to operate and prosper.

First Mortgage. A prudently placed first mortgage with sufficient amortization payments is another low-risk realty investment. These loans should rarely exceed two-thirds of the value of the realty. The loan-value ratio can be increased if the tenant occupant is of high financial quality or if the ownership is of that type and agrees to guarantee payment of the loan. Similarly, government-guaranteed mortgage loans can be made at a higher ratio to value. It should be understood that, actually, under either the government-guaranteed (or -insured) loans or the high-credit ownership or occupancy loans, the reason for excess lendability is credit not real estate value. The mortgagee can rarely lose in these cases and, therefore, wants to be able to invest additional money in these loans. State regulating agencies allow the government-backed loans to be of a higher loan-value ratio but do not give prime corporate credit loans any special mortgage status.

Fee Interest. The free and clear fee position is the next safest position, as this interest includes the same position as the first mortgagee and the ground fee owner would have if the bundle of rights was separated. However, the fee interest also includes all of the lesser and riskier interests including the leasehold and the equity above the first and junior mortgage holder's normal lending areas.

Leasehold Interest. The leaseholder pays rent to the fee owner. He may have a leasehold subject to only a ground lease. He then pays a ground rent and has his investment in the building. Instead of the above, he may have acquired a leasehold on land and buildings. He did not construct the buildings. In this case, he is paying rent on the land and building and may have no investment other than lease security. In this last case, he earns nothing until sufficient rent is collected to pay all charges including rent to land and building owner. It is obvious that this leaseholder has less chance of earning money than the one who only must pay ground rent.

However, this type of leasehold requires a higher rate of return, as it is more speculative.

FURTHER FRACTIONALIZATION. The leaseholder may also borrow money on a leasehold mortgage, thereby decreasing his earnings. Sometimes, if the leaseholder is still earning a profit, he will subdivide this profit in one of several ways. He may sublease his leasehold to a subleaseholder, who will have to pay him a somewhat higher rental. On other occasions, the leaseholder may want cash but may also want to continue to hold a lease-holder's position. He will accomplish this by selling his leasehold position and agreeing to pay enough rent to the buyer to pay the property owner rent under the master lease and yield a return to the buyer.

The authors recognize that this explanation of fractionalization may confuse the reader. Unfortunately, many "investors" involved have also been confused as to their position. Basically, the degree of risk, at times, defies computation. It should also be stated that some of the largest realty companies participate in these types of transactions.

Type of Realty. Certain types of realty have more safety than others, all other things being equal. The authors frown upon generalizations, for, among any "safe" group, many examples of imprudent investments can be found. It is always assumed that the original purchase was made on a basis consistent with the market. Usually, safe realty investments include middle-income apartment houses, well-rented office buildings, retail property with choice occupancy, and industrial buildings and gas stations with national tenants under long-term leases. Motels, hotels, bowling alleys, theaters, nursing homes, and similar properties are considered risky, because they are not actually realty investments. They involve the operation of a business on realty premises. It is true that the business may be thought of as the renting of bed space, alley space, motel unit space, or theater seat space, any of which can be compared with store, office, or apartment space, nevertheless, it is a highly specialized form of operation. The return should include a realty return, a business-management return, and an entrepreneurial-risk return.

Margin of Interest. In the discussion of leverage, it was demonstrated that the thinner the margin, the higher the return. This was based upon the need to pay the other interests first and the hazard of the thin margin interest being entirely eliminated when property values fall.

Rent-Paying Ability of Occupants. If the tenants are paying rents that are not excessive in the market, and they have the ability to pay market rents, the property is subject to less risk. This not only refers to high-credit business tenancies but also to apartment tenants whose employment record is unmarred either by their own erratic employment habits or their vulnerability due to a bad employment environment.

Neighborhood Factors. Real estate, like people, is affected by environmental factors. Obviously, if the realty is located in an area that is no longer wanted by large numbers of people, or if people with high income are leaving and being replaced by others with small incomes, the property will be adversely affected. It can also be injured if builders have been overly optimistic and have erected more buildings than demanded. Under those circumstances, competition will create lower income, higher costs, and lower occupancy ratios.

SYNDICATION

History. One of the most important factors in the field of real estate investment since about 1948 has been the development of real estate syndicates. This form of investment can be loosely traced back to the investment trust, highly developed in Massachusetts, and to various types of joint realty ventures. Groups of investors have often banded together to purchase realty. However, a new development has taken place. Syndicators assumed responsibility for finding potential realty investments. They asked real estate brokers to submit suitable investment properties to them. The syndicators would then arrange to purchase the realty under a contract covering a relatively long period of time. During the contract period, the syndicators would then chose a form of property ownership of the realty. In the early days of syndication, the syndicator and his staff would themselves merchandise the participation in the syndicate. More recently, they have turned this job over to another group of people, whose job is to find the ultimate syndicate investors. The latter groups and their staffs often have no knowledge of realty and often are considered "security dealers," but they too refer to themselves as syndicators. In the early syndication period, they were paid commissions of 3 to 5 per cent. Now, they earn as much as 10 per cent.

Attraction of Syndicate Investments. Syndicate investments can be most favorable. They allow the small investor to participate in the real estate investment market. Usually, investors with $1,000 to $30,000 become members of syndicates that require from $75,000 to many millions of dollars cash investment. Often the syndicate investments are arranged to include excellent income-tax protection. Investment returns are offered on a basis of from about 9 per cent to about 15 per cent plus the possibility of bonus income and capital gains.

Forms of Syndication. Syndicates are usually set up as corporations with stock ownership or as a limited partnership. Each property has a separate corporation or partnership organization. Under the corporation, the usual corporate advantages of durability, limitation of liability, and orthodoxy or legal organization are factors. The partnership has some of the dangers of partnerships and lacks typical corporate advantages. However, in many cases, there are special income-tax advantages if it can be shown that the partnership is not, in fact, equivalent to a corporation.

Syndication and Syndicate Investors. The syndicator makes his profit in several fashions. Sometimes, he will contract to buy a property for $500,000 cash with a total price of $2,000,000 including a mortgage of $1,500,000. He will then divide the "equity" into 100 shares to be sold at, say, $7,500 each. The price of the realty to the syndicate investors then becomes increased to $2,250,000, and the cash is $750,000. The syndicator then has $250,000 for organizational expenses, temporary financing, legal and accounting costs, selling costs, and profit. This profit may be from $75,000 to about $125,000. He will also usually continue to operate the property for the syndicate at a fee of about 3–5 per cent of rents collected. He often will have some chance of a profit made on a resale, and, also, if the property produces earnings above a specified amount, the syndicator will retain a large percentage of these excess earnings.

Sometimes, the syndicator will not take any immediate profit. The $75,000–$125,000 profit shown above will become part of the syndicate, and the syndicator will retain syndicate shares equivalent to that profit.

Another form of organization is to set up two syndicates. The syndicator and some of his close associates will contract to buy the realty and then they will resell it to another group of syndicate investors that they form. The second group will be the ultimate investors, although the syndicator will often take a small position with the second syndicate. The first syndicate will then pay rent to the second syndicate. This rent will be fixed to yield between 9 and 15 per cent to the investors, sometimes with additional bonuses. Thus, the syndicator and his close associates will be tenants of the syndicate investors. The syndicator will obtain his profit from higher rental collections from occupants of the realty, a share in profits from a future resale, and sometimes a profit during the initial organization of the syndicate.

Problems of Syndication. The original syndicates were able to buy good large investment realty profitably, for there were few investors capable of buying multimillion-dollar properties. With the multiplication of syndicate groups, the competition has become intense, leading to declining returns to investors. It has also led to syndictors buying riskier realty so as to entice investors with the hopes of high annual earnings. They have bought fractional interests, poor leasehold positions, and special-type operations rather than realty investments. Early syndicators were professional real estate investors, or they were guided by realtors such as Harry B. Helmsley, one of the nations most informed realtors. Some of the more recent syndicators have very limited realty knowledge and sometimes have displayed only a limited degree of personal integrity. This has led to the formation of the National Association of Syndicators and to some degree of regulation by the Securities and Exchange Commission and the state authorities. None of these devices as currently constituted give syndication the degree of control needed to allow it to assume its full ultimate status in the field of realty investment.

25

Apartment Houses

TYPES

Apartment houses are generally considered to be multiunit residential dwellings accommodating more than four families in individual self-contained units. Each apartment will have its own food-preparation and storage area as well as a bathroom. The apartment may have a luxurious full-size kitchen with full refrigerator freezer, wall oven, proliferation of cabinets, gas or electric range, sink, dishwasher, exhaust fan, garbage-disposal unit, pantry, dining nook, and service entrance. On the other extreme, it may merely have one unit in a tiny alcove that is known as a pullman kitchenette, where all the services are performed. Apartments may consist of a bathroom, pullman kitchenette, and one room that serves as a combination living room and sleeping room. Other apartments may consist of over fifty rooms and occupy three entire floors in a large apartment house.

SIZES AND STYLES

Apartment houses have been as many as forty stories high, with a multitude of elevators, and constructed of tons of steel, brick, and concrete, or have merely been garden apartments, one, two, or three stories high, with no elevators, and frame constructed with or without some stone or brick veneer.

Apartment houses may be constructed for multifamily occupancy or may be buildings that have been altered from one-family houses, stables, churches, schools, office buildings, and other uses.

TENANCY

Apartment houses may also be erected to fill various types of demands. A common conception of an apartment house is a place in which a young couple start their marriage and remain until their children have all been born and they move to a one-family house. Other housing is also created for the other end of the age range, specifically, to house mature people whose children have been married. Some cities also have housing designed for "one person" families. This person often has left home to make his or her "mark" in the world. Some small units are located near hospitals or colleges, to house interns, nurses, faculty members, or married students. We also have seen tremendous apartment-house developments near military bases to house base-personnel families.

We have often lost track of the fact that apartment houses are possibly the best type of housing for family living. The apartment house provides the most flexible type of housing, as it can provide the exact number of rooms required by a family at any stage of its family size. A move from one apartment to another can be accomplished with less cost and emotional difficulty than from a private house. The apartment house differs from the one-family house by not requiring the labor of the occupant. A superintendent makes the repairs and handles emergencies. In addition to leaving more time to the occupant to relax, it also can give more services and amenities. With an apartment house, it is economically feasible to provide playgrounds, pools, recreation rooms, and even baby sitters and domestic help.

APARTMENT HOUSES AND THE GOVERNMENT

Unfortunately, the family-size apartment of three or four bedrooms is no longer being built in large quantities. The reasons are manifold and are based on the fact that the family-size apartment is in direct competition with the private house. The private house has been given assistance by all levels of government to enable it to outstrip the apartment house.

Local-Government Aids to One-Family Houses. Often the best areas of the community are zoned for one-family houses. Apartment houses, when they are permitted, are often restricted to industrial areas, behind the retail district and in heavy-vehicular-traffic areas. Rarely are any neighborhood amenities or social status available to the resident of the apartment-house district.

It has become almost a universal policy of communities to assess apartment houses at a higher proportion of value than that applied to one-family houses. In this way, the tax per dwelling unit of equivalent value is much higher for the apartment house. This inequity is perpetuated often by political expediency. Considering that the apartment house invariably produces less cost to the community than does the private house, it is against the community interest to discourage apartment houses. Apartment-house communities require less streets, water and sewer lines, playground facilities (owners often provide areas within the development), schools, fire and sanitation service, police protection, and municipal administration than do one-family-home towns.

State Aids to One-Family Houses. State governments have often given special realty-tax exemption to homeowners. This has included benefits to special groups such as veterans and elderly families, but, in some states, a blanket exemption from realty taxes might be given to all homes for the first $5,000 of assessed valuation. If the assessed value represented 40 per cent of market value, the first $12,500 of market value would pay no realty taxes.

Federal Aids to One-Family Houses. The federal government has been a major influence in encouraging home ownership. (1) It has provided both Veterans Administration and Federal Housing Administration lending aids to homes. Its aid has been in enabling people to "buy" homes with little or no cash down payment and has spread the payments over progressively longer periods. This aid has made it expedient for millions to choose houses rather than apartments. The VA loans do not, in any way, apply to rental apartments. As for the FHA, only about 10 per cent of its program has involved private rental housing. In addition, because of the specific FHA rental-housing formula, it is rarely advantageous to build apartment-house units larger than two bedrooms. (2) The federal government has also given many income-tax benefits to homeowners which are not allowed to renters. (3) Indirectly, the federal government has also aided home ownership by its vast highway program.

Governmental Controls on Apartment Houses. Apartment-house investment has also sometimes been discouraged by controls applied against operating procedures. The foremost control is rent control that has been applied by governmental agencies. Realty investors are reluctant to retain capital investments in communities that are prone to be antagonistic to rental-housing private ownership. It is true that the community officials may believe that, during some severe housing shortages, tenants, must be protected against exorbitant price (rent) increases. However, there is a tendency on the part of some politicians to maintain controls beyond the emergency period, for political purposes.

APARTMENT-HOUSE INVESTORS

Investment in apartment-house equities originates with the builder-investor, an experienced builder who considers the apartment house profitable owing to his immediate building profit and the future income or resale profit. Among builder-investors are people who build a small six- to forty-family building and others who build apartment-house developments with several thousand units. These investors build with various types of financing. Usually, they will use standard bank construction loans and long-term realty mortgages. In addition, the builder may obtain the equity funds by forming a syndicate.

Sales Leaseback Transactions. Many builders will sell their property, but they usually will wait three years so as to avoid severely burdensome income taxes. Often, a sales leaseback deal will be arranged, with the buyer being given a return of 8–14 per cent on his investment. The rate of return varies with conditions of the transaction, type of property, economic conditions, and the neighborhood.

If the seller is willing to arrange a sales leaseback for $900,000 with $200,000 cash on a property which is salable for $1,050,000, a buyer may be willing to take a return of 8–9 per cent. The buyer feels relatively safe because the seller is retaining an investment of $150,000 in the realty.

This type of transaction causes an additional problem, which involves the mortgage amortization. It is to be noted that the buyer put in $200,000 cash and, assuming that he bought on an 8 per cent basis, his cash flow income was $16,000 after all charges including interest and amortization on the mortgage. Let us assume that the mortgage had constant payments of 8½ per cent on its $700,000 principal, with interest computed at 5½ per cent. At the end of fifteen years, the balance due on the mortgage would be about $210,000. (At the end of ten years, it would be about $280,000.) A question arises concerning the refinancing of the mortgage. It may be expedient to obtain a new mortgage at the end of ten years. Assume that the mortgage could be increased from the then balance of $280,000 to $600,000. Who would get the $320,000? This must be determined at the time of the original transaction. Both parties have valid economic claims to all or part of this money. The original owner still has a long lease period. He also has retained an investment. If the rent he pays were based on a set return on the buyer's investment, he would pay less rent if the mortgage were not refinanced. But then the buyer would not really be the owner, for the reduced financing charges would give all the benefits to the seller, and the buyer's position could not improve. Usually, it is arranged that both parties obtain some benefit from the refinancing.

Investors who purchase apartment houses outright face the problems of all the ownership risks. They must operate the realty and be subject to increased realty taxes, operating costs, vacancies, and landlord-tenant frictions. Often, they will employ qualified property managers to assume some of these problems.

APARTMENT MODERNIZATION

In many cities, sound old buildings are converted from one-family houses, tenement houses, and non-residential buildings into modern apartment buildings. The structures are made safe, clean, and comfortable and are equipped with modern plumbing, heating, cooking, air conditioning, and elevators. Thousands of these conversions have been made into successful realty investments.

However, William Pain, formerly associated with *Life* magazine, has added a special feature to this field. Mr. Pain has a strong appreciation of architecture and history and has been able to market this to a select group of tenants. He has bought buildings that are, usually, 100 to 135 years old and restored them to the fine standards of housing that they offered during their original years. The fireplaces are restored to their original condition; the brick walls are sandblasted; the courtyards are landscaped; and the result is to bring back the early charm of the structure. Of course, modern comforts—air conditioning, closed-circuit television, modern kitchens, and bathrooms—are installed. A bronze plaque is affixed to each building by the American Society for the Preservation of Future Antiquities, organized by Mr. Pain and his associates. The formula is simple. There are enough people in our large cities to rent the relatively few apartments of this type that are created each year. These tenants feel that they are buying something unique. They have been willing to pay extremely high rents. A large waiting list has developed.

As an example of this kind of investment, one such property restoration will show these results. The property is located in a poor neighborhood consisting of tenements and business properties but within the heart of the city. It is convenient to the theatrical district as well as the commercial center.

The property was purchased for $85,000, and it cost $140,000 to restore the buildings and get them completely rented quickly. It consisted of two tenement buildings and a carriage house built in the 1840's. It was converted into eighteen small apartments with forty rooms. A rent roll of $38,500 was developed, and after a 5 per cent vacancy allowance was set up, the effective income was $36,500.

Expenses are as follows:

Taxes	$ 6,500
Payroll	1,650
Heat	2,400
Light and power	350
Paint	650
Repairs	500
Supplies and misc.	300
Replacement reserve	750
Management	1,450
Insurance	700
Water	300
Total	$15,550

This leaves a net income (free and clear) of approximately $21,000. (Since the property was completely rented upon completion, the current net cash flow is much higher.)

The owners were able to obtain a first mortgage of $130,000 and a second of $30,000, so their cash investment was $65,000. Debt charges are about $15,000, leaving about $6,000 or just under a 10 per cent income, after deducting the vacancy allowance. Actually, during the early years, it might be expected that the return would be about 14 per cent if the building were maintained fully rented.

This entrepreneur is giving the community a unique type of apartment. He is creating for a special market. At this time, he is new in this field. He will be able to improve his investment by subsequent improved buying ability. With reduced construction costs, his entire financial picture will improve significantly.

APARTMENT-HOUSE ANALYSIS

In analyzing an apartment-house investment, it must constantly be remembered that past income statements are only vague shadows of future results and, like all shadows, distorted.

Rental Income. First of all, the rental income must be carefully analyzed. The following means of analysis must be used:

First, define the rental income. Is it based on past rental collection? Is it an analyzed rental based on current rental value? Do the rents include special services, furniture, maid service, linen service? What allowance has been made for vacancies and losses of rent caused by tenant turnover? Who are the tenants? How long have they been in the property? Have they deposited security for rent payments? Did they receive free rent concessions as an inducement to sign a lease? How do the rents compare with rents of comparable apartments? What is the vacancy rate in the building? What vacancies exist in competing buildings?

It becomes obvious that all of this information should be known to the investor.

Since an investor is buying the future productivity of the building, he must analyze the future rent-earning capacity. First, he will list all current rentals. He will determine if this is pure space rental or if the rent requires additional service that costs money to furnish. He will check to see if free-rent concessions were offered. He will then check competitive buildings to find the current market value. The result will be a schedule similar to the one shown in Fig. 13.

Once the schedule of rents is prepared, the total rent is annualized and an allowance for vacancies is deducted. The resultant figure will be the effective gross income.

Rent roll — vacanies = effective gross income

Floor	A 2½		B 3½		C 3½		D 4½		E 4½		F 3½	
	*	**	*	**	*	**	*	**	*	**	*	**
1st	50	52	70	70	68	66	88	90	90	92	Not on lobby floor	
2d	53	55	76	73	69	69	89	93	92	95	70	72
3d	53	55	76	73	73	69	85	95	97	97	73	75
4th	53	55	84	75	73	70	93	95	96	97	70	75
5th	56	57	80	80	77	74	95	98	101	103	75	80
6th	56	57	80	80	77	74	95	98	101	103	75	80

* Current.
** Budget.

Fig. 13. Rent-roll analysis.

The effective gross income is the most important point of analysis. This can be shown by a typical abbreviated statement:

Effective gross income = $115,000
Operating and taxes   =   87,000
Net income   = $ 28,000

A 10 per cent change in effective gross income will be $11,500, which changes the net income 41 per cent. Often, investors will worry about the fuel item, believing that a broker may have understated this item. In the example above, the fuel item was $4,000. A 10 per cent variation in this item would be $400. A 20 per cent variation would be $800. The 20 per cent understatement would change the net income less than 3 per cent, and a 10 per cent variation would result in a 1½ per cent change. This does not mean that the investor should not be concerned with expense analysis. It does show the great importance of income analysis. In the example shown above, the analysis was on a free and clear basis.

Of the expense items, usually real estate taxes, mortgage debt service, and payroll are the most critical, because they are the largest items and are subject to major changes.

Realty Taxes. Real estate taxes have been increasing because of larger municipal budgets for schools and other public services. Typically, investment realty pays a high proportion of these budgets. In analyzing an apartment-house tax schedule, the following must be done. Determine the policy of the community in taxing various types of realty. Inquire when properties were evaluated for tax-assessment purposes. Find out the ratios of assessed value to market value of apartment houses, and the basis of computing market value.

When the property is sold, this will alert the assessor to the price paid. He may then reassess the realty at a higher price. He may also do this if an institution makes a large mortgage loan. The appraiser also must determine if the tax rate is about to change.

Mortgage Financing. The investor will carefully analyze the mortgage for several reasons:

1. He will be concerned with the amount of debt against the realty and when it must be repaid.
2. He will want to know how much cash must be invested in the realty.
3. He will want to know the annual debt charges to be paid out of rent collections.

If the mortgage must be repaid in a short time, he must consider if new financing can be obtained. He will try to determine if refinancing will improve the cash flow or not. If the mortgage was recently placed, it may be an indication of the lender's valuation of the realty.

Mortgage	Loan	Value
$200,000	66⅔%	$300,000
$200,000	60%	$330,000

The above computation shows that an institution that lends up to 66⅔ per cent of value had valued the property at no less than $300,000, while a 60 per cent loan would be a result of a $330,000 valuation.

The investor will also determine if the mortgage includes prepayment privileges so that he may refinance. Refinancing may substantially improve the cash flow on invested capital.

Payroll. Although wages are prone to rise, the investor will analyze the realty for all possibilities. He may find that this item of expense will increase on the basis of higher wage rates or the need for more personnel.

Conversely, he may be able to reduce the payroll if there are excess employees. This is usually not possible without some forms of mechanization. Automatic heating systems, automatic elevators, incinerators, closed-circuit television, and mechanized gardening and cleaning equipment all have the effect of reducing man-hours needed to run a building. Firemen, porters, gardeners, doormen, and their assistants represent the types of employee services that can be reducd or eliminated.

Expense Survey. Julian M. Bond, assistant mortgage officer of the East River Savings Bank, prepared a study for the Graduate School of Banking of the American Bankers Association analyzing income and expense statistics from forty-two Manhattan properties.

He found that, for the period of 1953 to 1957, the operating ratios shown in Table 12 prevailed with computations on a free and clear basis.

TABLE 12

AN EXPENSE SURVEY

	Percentage of Gross Income	Percentage of Total Expenses
Net income	34	–
Total expenses	66	–
Real estate taxes	18	27
Other expenses	48	73
Wages	22	33
Fuel and utilities	8	13
Repairs and maintenance	9	13
Management	3	5
Realty taxes as percentage of net income before taxes	35	

Source: Julian M. Bond, *Effects of Postwar Inflation on Net Income of Urban Properties, 1946–1957* (New York: American Bankers Association, 1959).

The investment history of some of the typical urban apartment properties is shown in Tables 13–15, but it must be remembered that these buildings are operating under rent-control regulations.

CONCLUSIONS

The apartment house remains the most effective housing system, on a basis of functional service, economy, and social needs. Investment in these properties should be encouraged. It is unfortunate that, in recent years, landlord-tenant relationships have become poor in many communities. An investor must beware of communities that consider apartment houses political fodder. The owner must also maintain the property so that he will give his tenants pride in residing in their homes in the apartment house. A landlord-tenant code was designed by the authors: "Owners should maintain property as if they occupied the premises. Tenants should use the building as if they were paying the bills."

TABLE 13

APARTMENT BUILDING (WEST SIDE) LINCOLN SQUARE SECTION—MANHATTAN

(9-story apartment building on plot 97′ × 100′. Fair side-street location. Building constructed 1929; 692,000 cubic feet; 2 elevators [1 converted to automatic operation in 1950]. Fuel—oil, installed 1950. Layout: 52 apartments—183 rooms; 3- and 4-room apartments predominate.)

	1946	1947	1948	1949	1950	1951	1952	1953	1954	1955	1956	1957
Effective rental income	$51,166	$51,375	$55,275	$55,806	$55,941	$58,394	$57,035	$58,323	$61,378	$63,203	$63,877	$65,068
Operating expenses:												
Labor	12,023	12,921	14,080	15,520	16,861	11,124	7,780	7,855	7,969	7,991	8,412	8,852
Fuel	2,545	3,332	3,180	4,108	2,073	2,765	2,840	2,625	2,494	2,878	3,667	4,061
Electricity	1,609	1,459	1,480	1,476	1,490	1,374	1,758	1,308	1,300	1,331	1,557	1,293
Insurance	638	1,321	790	977	1,227	1,513	881	1,332	1,954	1,342	358	1,989
Water	874	807	802	790	770	1,024	1,023	1,023	1,031	1,023	1,035	1,031
Painting	4,282	3,776	3,820	3,974	2,116	7,201	5,377	2,165	3,371	4,514	2,960	4,347
Repairs	976	616	1,012	2,019	1,665	2,221	3,730	1,765	2,357	3,525	924	3,624
Supplies & misc.	1,012	2,090	2,301	3,834	1,904	2,530	1,407	1,570	2,216	1,699	1,753	2,078
Management	1,544	1,618	1,835	2,773	1,678	1,753	1,710	1,768	1,870	1,911	1,926	1,942
Total	25,503	27,940	29,300	35,471	29,784	31,505	26,506	21,411	24,562	26,214	22,592	29,217
Real estate taxes	10,857	10,868	11,287	8,122	9,801	9,982	10,137	10,509	11,655	12,000	12,608	13,120
Total expenses	36,360	38,808	40,587	43,593	39,585	41,487	36,643	31,920	36,217	38,214	35,200	42,337
Net income	14,806	12,567	14,688	12,213	16,356	16,907	20,392	26,403	25,161	24,989	28,677	22,731

Source: Julian M. Bond, *Effects of Postwar Inflation on Net Income of Urban Properties, 1946–1957* (New York: American Bankers Association, 1959), p. 99.

TABLE 14

APARTMENT BUILDING (WEST SIDE) WASHINGTON HEIGHTS SECTION—MANHATTAN

(6-story and basement, semifireproof, on plot 155' × 200'. Constructed 1928; 1,560,000 cubic feet; 2 elevators [1 converted to automatic operation in 1949]. Fuel—oil, installed 1953. Layout: 129 apartments, 454 rooms; 2-, 3-, and 4-room apartments predominate.)

	1946	1947	1948	1949	1950	1951	1952	1953	1954	1955	1956	1957
Effective rental income	$80,412	$80,916	$83,124	$84,732	$84,732	$85,918	$86,495	$90,814	$94,511	$96,383	$97,717	$98,620
Operating expenses:												
Labor	9,048	9,432	9,465	9,660	5,075	5,293	5,205	5,436	5,138	5,970	6,262	5,890
Fuel	5,418	6,638	6,527	6,413	6,874	6,478	7,069	6,215	6,810	7,260	7,680	9,091
Electricity	1,540	1,538	1,503	1,535	1,670	1,665	1,685	1,522	1,607	1,470	1,545	1,632
Insurance	1,803	2,796	1,494	4,206	3,700	1,437	3,791	2,561	937	6,064	2,116	1,734
Water	1,320	1,320	1,320	1,320	1,320	1,760	1,760	1,760	1,760	1,760	1,760	1,760
Painting	2,048	1,863	2,048	2,040	2,142	2,335	2,625	2,160	2,595	2,385	2,042	4,747
Repairs	4,126	4,680	2,847	9,500	2,604	1,835	4,935	4,963	7,584	15,170	7,482	4,380
Supplies & misc.	727	830	694	962	1,210	1,329	1,398	625	656	600	288	625
Management	2,802	2,855	2,907	2,942	2,970	2,994	3,042	3,130	3,236	3,340	3,395	3,456
Total	28,832	31,952	28,805	38,578	27,565	25,126	31,510	28,372	30,323	44,019	32,570	33,315
Real estate taxes	13,536	13,728	14,749	14,651	16,170	15,900	16,317	16,451	18,335	18,263	19,197	20,015
Total expenses	42,368	45,680	43,554	53,229	43,735	41,026	47,827	44,823	48,658	62,282	51,767	53,330
Net income	38,044	35,236	39,570	31,503	40,997	44,892	38,668	45,991	45,853	34,101	45,950	45,290

Source: Julian M. Bond, *Effects of Postwar Inflation on Net Income of Urban Properties, 1946-1957* (New York: American Bankers Association, 1959), p. 101.

TABLE 15

APARTMENT BUILDING (EAST SIDE)—MID-MANHATTAN

(6-story and basement, semifireproof building on corner plot 100′ × 100′.
Constructed 1938; 515,000 cubic feet; 1 automatic elevator. Fuel—oil.
Layout: 7 stores; 43 apartments—141½ rooms; 3-, 4-, and 5-room units.)

	1946	1947	1948	1949	1950	1951	1952	1953	1954	1955	1956	1957
Effective rental income	$49,776	$50,640	$54,890	$56,008	$56,363	$58,986	$63,346	$66,554	$68,226	$70,389	$73,469	$75,796
Operating expenses:												
Labor	8,532	9,552	11,098	11,720	13,064	13,648	13,251	13,934	14,244	14,807	15,757	17,843
Fuel	2,412	2,948	4,336	2,601	2,639	2,651	3,029	2,436	2,927	3,390	3,660	4,759
Electricity	1,149	613	1,086	971	927	1,002	983	834	902	974	1,039	1,114
Insurance	712	651	813	933	1,045	1,289	1,904	787	729	1,601	885	806
Water	528	528	525	495	498	673	385	867	512	938	747	866
Painting	1,900	1,381	1,425	751	2,289	1,399	1,900	1,255	1,285	1,749	2,522	3,541
Repairs	1,624	2,114	1,106	1,119	2,773	901	1,632	1,827	1,626	3,790	1,645	3,209
Supplies & misc.	829	659	945	1,325	1,341	1,116	690	783	711	935	1,003	1,578
Management	1,493	1,518	1,647	1,680	1,690	1,770	1,900	1,995	2,046	2,120	2,215	2,283
Total	19,179	19,964	22,981	21,595	26,266	24,449	25,674	24,718	24,982	30,304	29,473	35,999
Real estate taxes	9,372	9,686	9,867	9,801	10,214	11,036	11,824	12,276	13,896	14,395	15,182	15,829
Total expenses	28,551	29,650	32,848	31,396	36,480	35,485	37,498	36,994	38,878	44,699	44,655	51,828
Net income	21,225	20,990	22,042	24,612	19,883	23,501	25,848	29,560	29,348	25,690	28,814	23,968

Source: Julian M. Bond, *Effects of Postwar Inflation on Net Income of Urban Properties, 1946–1957* (New York: American Bankers Association, 1959), p. 128.

26

Office Buildings

Office buildings fall into two general groups. One is the corporation-built, -owned, and -occupied. The other kind of office building is the competitive rental office building.

CORPORATION-OWNED AND -OCCUPIED BUILDINGS

Many office buildings are owned and occupied by large corporations, banks, and insurance companies. These buildings, at times, come into the real estate investment market but, even then, are bought and sold under special circumstances. They may come on the market in connection with sales leaseback transactions, which are mainly credit investments rather than realty.

At other times, the realty may be placed on the market when it is being vacated by the corporation owing to a change in the corporation's needs or to the obsolescence of the realty. At such a time, a buyer may contemplate demolition and the creation of a new structure. He may also consider changing the structure so that it may be placed in a different use such as a hospital, hotel, consulate, or other unrelated use. On some occasions, the building may be suitable for modernization and may be retained as an office building for multiple occupancy. This usually involves a very expensive alteration including a new lobby and lower façade, new elevators that are usually of the self-service type, rewiring, and complete air conditioning.

This latter type of development will only take place if

1. The price to a purchaser is attractive
2. There is a demand for office space in the area of the building
3. The combined purchase price and alternation cost will assure a profit to the buyer after consideration of income and expense budgets

Corporations that have structures of the types being discussed are insurance companies, banks, utility companies, and national companies such as Seagrams, Lever Brothers, Union Carbide, and The Radio Corporation of America. In most cases, these companies would be better off financially if they became tenants of realty investors. However, often, they hold real estate for other considerations, which include

1. Control over building operation
2. Permanence of occupancy
3. Advertising purposes
4. Desire for the building to be a monument to the company's chief executive
5. Desire to be architecturally creative, on the part of the chief executive or his family

It is obvious that none of these motivations are greatly beneficial economically to the corporation, and at least the first three or four can be achieved by the company as a tenant in the building.

An excellent example of the working of this theory is the fact that many large and small buildings are named for a tenant who signs a long-term lease for about 25 per cent of the space in the structure. Smart leasing brokers have closed many leases based on this inducement. However, it is not this corporation-owned group of office buildings with which we are generally concerned in realty investments.

COMPETITIVE RENTAL BUILDINGS

The main group of office buildings are known as competitive office buildings. They are built by investor-builders for long-term investments or sometimes for resale. Eventually, all or most of them are sold, whether for estate-tax purposes (Empire State Building) or because of changed investment needs. Sometimes, a building will be sold for the profit that is available. Other times, it may be sold at a sacrifice because of a poor market or the need of quick funds by its owner.

TYPES OF OFFICE BUILDINGS

Office buildings comprise several basic types:

1. Governmental buildings
2. Corporation-owned and -occupied buildings
3. Professional buildings
4. Pre-World War II competitive buildings
5. Post-World War II competitive buildings

Both the first and second categories are normally of little interest to the office-building investor.

Professional Buildings. The professional building is one of the most difficult types of realty to analyze. Such a building may consist of as little as five or six suites of offices in a one- or two-story structure with parking. The other extreme may be a high-rise fireproof building of twelve or more stories. The latter structure may include a professional library, a pharmacy, and a private hospital as well as offices for 100 or more doctors and dentists of all types.

The professional medical building has expensive installations of water, gas, electric, and drainage lines. Various types of plumbing facilities are required as well as extensive costs for sound and vibration resistance. Partitions will be numerous, since a doctor will have diagnostic rooms, his office, a laboratory, a waiting room, and a lavatory, all in a compact area. Many of these buildings are created by the venture funds of one or a few doctors creating a building for their offices and as a secondary investment.

Unfortunately, these buildings are not considered to be prime investments. The tenants are stable members of the community, but usually their net worth is not considered to be significant as compared to that of commercial office tenants. In addition, these buildings have considerable competition, one type of which is the existing large house that can be purchased cheaply and shared by two or more doctors after being altered and modernized. The other form of competition is the dual-use building which gives a doctor an opportunity to have an office in one section of his home. The doctor may then have a home and office with little more cost than is required by the home. He also saves travel time and may obtain other economies from this type of operation as well.

Financing of professional buildings is quite difficult. Mortgagees usually consider these buildings to be single-purpose structures. They fear that, if the building loses money, it will be of little value. Often, the location of these buildings is dissimilar from that of recognized commercial-office-building locations. Even when they are in the same areas, it is often difficult to obtain commercial tenants to fill the empty space. A commercial tenant will usually consider the atmosphere to be inappropriate for business.

To change the building will also involve extensive alterations because of the difference in utilities in the two types of buildings.

INVESTMENT HAZARDS. In analyzing a professional building, a prospective investor should be wary of the mortgage financing. If the terms of an existing mortgage are liberal, and the mortgage matures within five or six years, the investor must try to determine the amount and terms of a replacement mortgage.

In analyzing the rents, the questions that must be asked are

1. Does the rent include water? If so, what is the cost of this water? The same questions should be asked about hot water.
2. Does the rent include gas and electricity? If so, what does this cost the building?

3. Did the owner have to build the partitions and special fixtures as an item included in the rent?
4. Does the rent include cleaning service?

After these questions are answered, the true realty rental can be determined. It will also be easier to analyze building expenses for water, fuel, electricity, help, and cleaning charges.

The investor should also consider the vacancy record of the building. Many of these structures have erratic occupancy records. The rent schedule must be analyzed to determine the following:

1. Are comparable rents received for comparable size and quality of space? If not, what is the reason for the variations? Possibly, additional partitions, facilities, and services are being given to the tenants paying high rents.
2. When the tenants signed leases, were special inducements given? Typical inducements include free-rent concessions.
3. Do the leases call for any special tenant benefits? These might include telephone-answering services, furnishings, and other items which tend to reduce net income to the realty.

Of the expense items, water, fuel, electricity, help, and cleaning service have been mentioned as variables dependent on arrangements made with tenants and on the method of operation. The hours of operation will also affect all of these costs. It is most difficult to offer guides to these costs for professional buildings, since there are relatively few buildings of this type in any community. In addition, the range of their sizes, services offered, physical qualities, and tenant agreements makes it difficult to offer typical expenses. Each investment of this type must be individually analyzed without a safe set of guides.

The investor must carefully examine records of past operating costs. He can further check these against specific estimates of combustion engineers for heating and hot-water costs, of utility companies for gas, electricity, and water charges; and the help and cleaning costs can be analyzed by having discussions with building employees and examining payroll records. When cleaning service is contracted for by outside firms, it is necessary to carefully check all bills and the service contracts. This will show the record of payments for direct and additional costs. The contractor should also advise the investor if he contemplates renewing the contract. Discussions with the tenants concerning their satisfaction will often reveal that the cleaning service leaves much to be desired. This may require greater expenses for future cleaning.

A very critical item of expense covers real estate taxes. It can be assumed that municipal costs will force the tax rate higher. It is necessary for the investor to provide for this. However, even more important is the current real estate assessed valuation. Sometimes, this has been set to give an advantage to the property, possibly for political reasons or because the community felt it was necessary to give a temporary inducement to the developers of the project. A property sale will provide the assessor with property-value information which may materially affect the assessed valuation.

Insurance costs should be studied to determine if proper coverage is carried, as well as to check the correctness of this expense item.

As was mentioned previously, the mortgage debt service must be checked not only as applied to the present mortgage but also in connection with any new mortgage that may have to be substituted. Very often, it will be necessary to make interest and amortization payments considerably higher than under existing financing.

In the event that other professional buildings exist in the community, the investor should check occupancy rates and rentals and determine relative competitive positions. It may be necessary to invest more capital to bring the subject realty up to the standard set by the others. This might include extensive modernization, creation of parking facilities, and the addition of other services.

In this discussion of professional buildings, we have only considered medical and dental office buildings. Buildings serving the legal profession are somewhat rare, and their characteristics do not differ materially from commercial buildings. Sometimes, they will include a common-law library, receptionist, and telephone-answering services. They also will locate near courthouses. In almost all other respects, they will be similar to the commercial office buildings. Tenancy in these law buildings will often include a title company and accounting and realty tenants. Many lawyers will locate in the normal rental office buildings.

Competitive Rental–Commercial Office Buildings. Except for occasional low-rise office buildings, the competitive commercial office building of six stories or more will not be found in cities with an economic sphere of influence covering less than about 100,000 of population. Smaller communities may have hybrid buildings, which are often created by banks that occupy the grade floor and rent space to professional and small commercial tenants in five to nine floors above. Typical tenants in these communities can rarely afford the rentals needed to support standard commercial office structures. These tenants can also have their demands met by occupying offices in converted dwellings, small office buildings, and store-type structures.

The commercial rental building will be created for main, regional, or local offices of commercial firms; service organizations such as insurance companies, realtors, and accountants; legal, medical, and dental offices; and some sales- and showrooms.

In larger communities, buildings will be created to serve specific groups. In a city like Chicago or New York, separate office and showroom buildings tend to be centers for such specialized tenants as lawyers; realtors; toy showrooms; shippers; boys' or men's clothiers; buyers' offices; manufacturers of cotton, woolen, or silk textile; securities dealers; insurance agents or companies; produce dealers (with different buildings for different types of products); advertisers; furniture companies; fine-arts dealers; dealers in gifts; and numerous other categories. Furthermore, certain buildings will cater to one type of merchandise within a specific price range.

Buildings which become highly specialized can often retain their economic strength for a longer period than either the age of the structure or the suitability of the neighborhood might indicate. This is due to the benefits of the business being concentrated under one roof. In this way, the firm's customers find it easier to deal with it.

OFFICE-BUILDING LOCATIONS. Office-building construction costs are the same within a community, except for variations in land-preparation costs. However, obtainable rents vary widely, depending on location. At the present time, rentals in New York vary from between $3.50 to $6.50 per square foot in pre-World War II buildings. This variation is for similar types of structures and space. The only major difference is location. In New York City, prime locations in the financial district and the Grand Central area will command the high rentals. This is because the locations have inherent advantages in being close to transportation or market activities. Because of this, the most successful firms locate there, and this gives the area an even greater desirability. Premium rents can be charged. At the same time, less desirable locations attract their tenants by giving lower rents. This attracts the firms of lower financial strength, which then compounds the problem of the area being of low desirability. Therefore, a builder can afford to pay high land costs to choose the best location. A recent sale of a site for a new structure in New York approximated $300 per square foot (about $13 million per acre). At the same time, some locations in New York have new buildings on sites costing about $60 per square foot. Some office buildings in suburban locations are being built on land costing $0.50 to about $5.00 per square foot. Usually, there is considerable difficulty in creating a successful building on all but the first-mentioned type of suburban site. If this statement is difficult to agree with, a simple survey of areas will prove its validity. (Don't include one- or two-story and one- or two-tenant buildings, as these are subject to other considerations, as can be found in other chapters, on one-tenant investments and sales leaseback transactions.)

Pre-World War II Competitive Office Buildings. In most cities, these buildings are found in choice locations. This is a direct result of the logical fact in urban land economics that the most desirable land is developed first. Later on, less desirable locations will be developed. (However, there are some communities where the prime office buildings were erected between 1900 and 1930 in a location that was then choice. In some cases, these locations have lost their desirability for various reasons. This discussion is not intended to cover these situations.)

After analyzing these office-building investments and deciding that the location is still excellent, the next step is to carefully check the office-building rental market. This requires a thorough study of vacancies. If the rate is about 5 per cent or more, it is necessary to be concerned. The size of vacant rental units, the locations in which vacancies exist, the rental rates in the buildings with vacancies, and the physical condition of buildings with vacancies must all be found. All of these situations must be matched against the subject realty. If, after this analysis, the investor believes the vacancy factor will not be a problem, he must examine the tenancy of the building. This should be done in the following manner: A schedule should be prepared covering very floor of the building. A sample covering one floor is shown in Fig. 14.

Unit	Tenant	Size	Rent	Rate	Expiration
900	Monsanto Chemical Co.	2,000	$ 8,000	$4.00	5/1/67
920	Ford Motor Co.	1,500	6,500	4.33	5/1/65
928	Arabian American Oil Co.	4,000	18,000	4.50	5/1/75
930	Johnson Advertising Co.	1,000	3,000	3.00	5/1/68
935	NAM	500	2,500	5.00	5/1/68
938	Goldman & Drazen	500	2,600	5.20	5/1/72
940	Fribourg & Fribourg	800	4,000	5.00	5/1/66
942	Dr. Harvey K. Soloff	500	2,600	5.20	5/1/68
945	Frederick Babcock	500	2,000	4.00	5/1/70
946	Royal Arcanum Society	1,000	4,000	4.00	5/1/65
948	Vacant	1,000	Asking	4.50	—

Fig. 14. Office-building rental schedule (portion covering ninth floor).

The investor will carefully check the schedule for the building to determine if any tenants are paying higher or lower rentals than is proper for their space. His objective is to consider rentals that might exist upon lease expirations.

At the end of the rent schedule, an analysis will show the following information:

	Square Feet	Income	Rate
Total rentable area	285,000	–	–
Rented	278,000	$1,217,000	$4.20
Vacant	7,000	–	–

	1965	1966	1967	1968	1969	1970	1971	1972
Lease expiration (000 sq. ft.)	25.0	27.5	48.0	51.0	37.5	23.5	18.8	46.7
Rent (000 dollars)	105.0	121.0	182.5	193.5	189.3	103.2	92.5	230.0
Rental rate (dollars per sq. ft.)	4.20	4.40	3.85	3.79	5.05	4.38	4.92	4.93

Further information could show the rental rates of the expirations by years of expiration and the number of tenants involved. With all of this information, it is possible to determine the risks involved in renewing tenants and finding replacement tenants. The year 1965 does not appear to be critical to this building, for only a small amount of leases expire then, and the rental rate is below the average. If this space is as good as the average space in the building, it might even be possible to expect a rental increase. In 1969, 1971, and 1972, on the other hand, a much larger total area of space expires, and the rental rate is much higher than the average rate. If these expirations were due five years earlier, the investor might be even more concerned.

POTENTIAL RENT INCREASES. An analysis of an existing office building may sometimes reveal a potential of creating additional rental space. Some outstanding examples have materially increased rentals. It is possible to change floor layouts in a way that may reduce corridor space loss that, at times, has produced an additional 1,000 square feet per floor. Sometimes, the superintendent, employees, and engineer have quarters that might better be used as rental space. These building-service offices can often be placed in the basement or in a portion of the building having low rental value.

Penthouse space is sometimes considered premium office space, particularly when served by an elevator. It is sometimes possible to create this space or to convert poor roof structures to such uses. Some buildings have been constructed with floor heights of 18 feet or more. Some of these buildings have been altered to provide additional floor levels, thereby obtaining additional rental space. In certain buildings, space has been created on levels below the street, for either retail or office purposes.

The student of realty will always consider the potentialities of a building to become more productive. This will include ancillary income in the form of vending machines, special building services for tenants, signs, radio and television towers, and almost all other sources of revenue. Once again, luncheon clubs have become popular, so certain building space can be upgraded for this highly specialized use.

EFFECT OF MAJOR INCOME CHANGES. It is seen that the investor will pay special attention to the income-production phase of realty operation. This is obviously the most important element. A building properly rented can afford some excess costs in operation, but a building well maintained may be a loser. A 5 per cent rent increase will sometimes result in a 50 per cent increase in profit to the owner, as follows:

Cash investment	=	$1,000,000
(over $3,000,000 mortgage)		
Net income	=	$ 70,000
Gross income	= $700,000	
	× 0.05	
5% income increase	$ 35,000 = 50%	
÷ Previous net income	= $ 70,000	

This does not imply that operational costs are of no concern to the owner. A building that gives improper service will lose tenants, while a building that is run extravagantly will become a losing proposition. Before examining costs, we will consider potential improvement of income by modification of the building operation.

An investment in new automatic elevators may reduce costs of building operation at the rate of from $5,500 to $7,500 per car. At the same time, this conversion may cost from $20,000 to $75,000 per car, depending on the type of system installed, present equipment, and the height of building. In a similar fashion, a new heating plant may reduce labor and fuel costs. Insurance costs may also be reduced by installation of certain fire-protection systems.

EXAMPLE OF FINANCIAL STATEMENT. A recent financial statement for a twenty-one-story office building built in the 1920's in a choice location in New York City, with about 330,000 square feet of rentable space, revealed the following:

Basic rent collections =	$5.05	
Store overage =	0.22	
Total collections =	$5.27 =	100%
Expenses		
Operating =	$0.92	
Repairs and maintenance =	0.14	
Taxes and insurance =	1.01	
Management and administration =	0.24	
	$2.31 =	44%
Tenant and building alterations =	$0.14	
	$2.45 =	46%
Net income free and clear =	$2.82 =	54%

This building is in a prime location which results in higher than normal realty taxes due to the high land value. Of course, this also produces higher store rents than normal, and the office rents also benefit.

A further breakdown of expenses follows:

Fixed Charges
    Real estate taxes = $.96
    General insurance =   .048
       (net including employees)

Operating Expenses
    Payroll =   .72
    Payroll surcharges =   .07
    Heat =   .08
    Miscellaneous =   .06

Repair and Maintenance
    Supplies =   .03
    Painting =   .05
    Repairs =   .06

Management and Administration
    Management commissions = .08
    Leasing commissions, averaged = .09
    Legal, accounting, advertising,
       administration, etc. =   .07

These expenses are based on expert management operation but with manually operated elevators. At this writing, the owners have programed the installation of new elevators, and this will result in a much lower cost for labor. The building is almost entirely air-conditioned but with several systems.

Post-World War II Competitive Office Buildings. These buildings vary considerably from their older counterparts. Physically, they usually look different from the exterior. Whereas the earlier buildings had masonry walls, the new buildings have glass and metal skin or exterior curtain walls that are non-load bearing. The new building usually has a wide expanse of windows, so its lines are horizontal bands of glass and metal (or brick). The earlier era of buildings produced vertical lines, with each building seeming to reach into the sky.

The new building gives more natural light, but, since it is air-conditioned, it may often have large floor areas and be lighted by various modern lighting systems.

Economically speaking, the new building was designed for a rental market of single floor occupancy. This gives it great advantages.

1. There is practically no unrentable space within its walls other than elevators and stairs. (It is a trade joke that some owners are about to charge tolls for the use of these facilities—but only during rush hours.) Tenant space even includes lavatories.

2. With large corporations signing long-term leases for their floors, these buildings have become eligible for special financing.

3. The new building is a status symbol as well as a more comfortable place to work and has produced an amazing demand for space. The first major building of this type was created by a major builder, Tishman Realty Construction Corporation, in 1946. It was a glowing success, but the renting was an educating process. Tenants paid from $4.25 to $4.85 per square foot. The highest rents in New York City at that time were between $2.50 and $3.25 per square foot for similar-size units. (They also did not include charges for space as mentioned above.) The building attracted such tenants as Monsanto Chemical Company, Ford Motors, Universal Pictures, Lever Brothers, Electric Boat Company (now General Dynamics), Bankers Trust Company, Cunard Lines, and others of this caliber. However, when the building was finished, the Tishman organization refrained from similar ventures for several years in New York, for they thought they had exhausted the market. They subsequently built several others, but only after successive lucrative ventures by other builders.

These newer buildings require the same type of analysis as the office building thoroughly analyzed in this chapter. However, certain factors must be stressed again. Since these buildings were created in a period of high demand, the rentals must be checked against the current market with a greater degree of skepticism.

Also, many of the buildings were created by builders using new methods and building products. Sometimes, these products have caused additional repairs and maintenance costs. The glass windows usually are subject to greater heating and ventilating costs. Some of the wall facings have become discolored owing to corrosion and rusting of the exterior metals. Also some of the "skin" has created water damage due to expansion and contraction.

Another important factor has been the extremely favorable financing. Some of this financing may have to be replaced. The terms may no longer be as favorable. This may materially reduce its value.

As in shopping centers, office buildings are rated by mortgagees in accordance with the strength of tenancy. It is incumbent upon the investor to follow this principle if he wishes to maintain a secure investment position.

Office-building buyers require assurances that their investments will give them an average cash flow rate of return of 8–12½ per cent for a period of about ten years' ownership. The range of return is dictated by risk, skill that they will have to apply to obtain optimum income, income-tax liability, type of location, tenancy, and financing. They will also have to consider carefully the trend of the area and the eventual resale value of the realty.

27

Sale and Leaseback Investing

A *sales leaseback* transaction is one in which the owner of a property sells the property to another party and, as a part of the transaction, agrees to lease the property for a given period of years. For example, a large company may own a site on which it wishes to erect a plant which it needs for its operations, but it does not want to invest its capital in real estate. The company could sell the land to an investor who would agree to erect the kind of building the company would need. The company, in turn, would agree to rent the building on a long-term lease which the investor could then pledge as collateral for a loan to be used in constructing the building. The investor ends up with a guaranteed income from the lease and full ownership rights to a fully improved property at the end of the lease. The company has a building to use which exactly meets its need; its business capital is not tied up in real property; and all of its costs of using the building can be charged against its operating income. There are, of course, many variations of this which will be discussed in this chapter.

This unique type of financing has been used for many years, but it gained tremendous momentum in the 1940's when, by legislative action, insurance companies were permitted to own real estate for investment purposes. Since they needed large-scale investments which would return an assured income, they immediately turned to investing in large office buildings, retail property, shopping centers, and industrial properties, using the sales leaseback arrangement. Other large investors soon saw the advantages of this form of investment, and its use became widespread.

BENEFITS TO SELLER

The seller gains several advantages:

1. The seller converts its investment in real estate into cash which it can now invest in its normal business operations. Usually, the seller is an industrial or retail concern that can earn higher returns on invested capital than are available in conservative realty investments.
2. The seller may also improve its balance sheet in two ways:
   a. The realty may have been subject to orthodox accounting procedures which "wrote down" its "value" each year by a standard depreciation deduction. This reduced book value may not in any way reflect

the actual market value of the realty assets. A sale in the market place would enable the selling company to improve its position in the eyes of stockholders.

b. The rent payable under the sales leaseback agreement is not treated on the balance sheet with as much force as a normal liability. Therefore, the sale usually increases the assets without a compensating increase in liability.

3. A company can often improve its income-tax position via the sales leaseback route. This is accomplished in several ways. First of all, the entire rent payment is tax-deductible as an expense. While the company owned the property, only mortgage interest and building depreciation were deductible capital charges; amortization of the mortgage (capital investment) is not tax-deductible. This results in a substantial reduction in taxes for a profitable business.

4. A business may create an economic operating basis. Often, the property will be sold at a price of 70–80 per cent of its market value.

Since the rent is based upon the selling price, the rent will then be lower. (Even the rate of return desired by the investor may be lowered when the price is lower than market value.)

For example, if a property is worth $1,000,000, and the selling price is $800,000, the rent may be $56,000 annually, assuming a good tenant. However, if the selling price were set at $1,000,000, the rent might be $75,000, which would represent a higher rate of return on a higher sales price. The additional $200,000 are obtained at a rate of 9½ per cent vs. the 7 per cent rate on the $800,000. It can be seen that the annual property occupancy cost is set at a low basis when the sales price is lower than market value. This helps the selling company to operate more economically.

BENEFITS TO BUYER

The advantages of the sales leaseback to the buyer are also significant:

1. The investor purchases valuable realty combined with the obligation of highly rated corporations. These combine to produce extremely satisfactory investments.

2. The investments are usually in large amounts, resulting in lower investment-management costs.

3. The investor has greater control over its investment than with most other types of investment.

4. At the expiration of the lease and renewal options, the realty usually becomes the property of the investor, free of any encumbrances.

5. The investment term is relatively long, which reduces investment-management costs.

6. Tax advantages are available to the investing buyer, on the basis of the depreciation structure.

PRINCIPLES OF SALES LEASEBACK FINANCING

The principles of the sales leaseback are quite simple. A corporation will sell its realty to a large buyer-investor and simultaneously take back a lease for a long period of years. The rent will be based on the purchase price. The price may be market value, 70–80 per cent of market value, or even higher than market value; for obvious reasons the last type of transaction is often desirable to the seller. The selling company not only will pay a capital-gains tax at the favorable rate for the selling profit, but then it will pay a higher than normal rental on which it will be able to take credit for income taxes at a 52 per cent rate.

The selling corporation retains the use of the realty under a lease term which usually has a total of from 50 to 100 years in periods of 21 or 25 years, with additional renewal options. It, therefore, retains complete and practical control of the realty.

In most cases, the realty is high-grade retail or industrial buildings. However, sales leaseback deals have been made on hotels, office buildings, apartment houses, motels, bowling alleys, shopping centers, and just about every type of income-producing realty.

Investors and Typical Deals. At first, the typical buyer-investors were mainly insurance companies, colleges, non-profit organizations, and similar large funds with special income-tax advantages.

The impetus to insurance companies entering this market started in the 1940's, when Virginia, Connecticut, New York, and other state legislatures passed laws specifying the types of realty investments available to insurance companies. In general, they restricted these investments to 3 or 5 per cent of company assets. The companies usually would buy only choice realty with prime credit corporations on the lease obligation. Sears Roebuck, Allied Stores, Continental Can, S. H. Kress, Safeway Stores, General Electric, General Motors, and some major oil companies were typical of these lessees.

Investors included Yale University, Union College, Metropolitan Life Insurance Company, New York Life Insurance Company, Teachers Insurance and Annuity Society of America, Bankers Trust Company (as trustee), Equitable Life Insurance Company, Mutual Benefit Life Insurance Company, Cornell University, and numerous other, similar institutions.

A typical transaction for this original group would involve a leaseback at $5,000,000 with rental payments at $325,000 (6½ per cent) for thirty years. There might be two additional, equivalent lease terms at rentals of $100,000 or less. Under this system, the investor received interest of 5 per cent and a return of capital just before the end of the lease. Rentals received during the renewal-option periods can be considered a little gravy as compared with mortgage investments. This example assumed that the institution had alternative investments available whereby mortgages could be obtained at 5 per cent interest.

Multiple-Tenant Office Buildings. Many large office buildings with multiple tenants become the subject of sales leaseback investments. An actual example of one such transaction made with a leading life insurance company, affecting a well-located office building, follows:

A group of investors purchased the property at an all-cash price of $8,750,000 and simultaneously sold it to the insurance company for $7,000,000. The investors also had to invest approximately $250,000 additional cash for working capital and organizational cost. They also had to borrow funds from a bank for building modernization.

The lease rental was $525,000 for ten years and $456,000 for about fourteen years. It can be seen that the insurance company's return, on the $7,000,000, was 7½ per cent for the initial period and then was reduced to about 6½ per cent. This income is completely net to the insurance company, with the operating group paying all charges against the realty. However, the insurance company did not consider the rental to be all income. As is usually done, it credited part to interest income and the balance to working off the investment.

The lease called for three twenty-one-year renewal terms at a rental of $210,000 each. At the end of the three renewal terms, the realty became the unencumbered property of the insurance company.

The insurance company received a very advantageous deal that has worked out very well. The tenant-investors have also done very well. Their financing was in a larger amount than is available in normal mortgage financing. In addition, the entire rental payment was tax-deductible. They were also able to use the difference between the original cost and the sales price (about $2,000,000) as a tax base for the leasehold investment. Naturally, they were not entitled to normal building depreciation, as the building was insurance-company property. However, all leasehold improvements could be written off during the term of the original twenty-four-year lease.

Sales Leaseback Combinations. The leaseback investment has also been combined with other forms of financing. One such transaction was developed by Irving Zimmerman of George Ponter, mortgage brokers. It involved the first major postwar office building in New York City, at Park Avenue and 57th Street, built by Tishman Realty and Construction Corporation and described in the chapter on office buildings.

The builders purchased the land at a price of about $1,200,000. They then started to construct a twenty-one-story office building, at a cost reputed to be less than $6,000,000, and secured prime tenants.

On the basis of the fine tenancy, they arranged the following financing:

1. They sold the land to Mutual Benefit Life Insurance Company for $3,000,000, and the leaseback carried a rental of $175,000 per annum for twenty-one years and an option period totaling seventy-five years, at a rental of $33,500 per annum.
2. They obtained a total of $6,000,000 on a twenty-year leasehold mortgage from Mutual Benefit and John Hancock Life. The interest rate was 3¾ per cent. Mutual Benefit took $2,500,000 of this investment for twenty years with no amortization, but the lower ground-lease rental option was conditioned on the repayment of the loan at the end of twenty years. John Hancock lent $3,500,000, with constant payments of 6¾ per cent to pay out in twenty years.

Therefore, the property obtained financing totaling $9,000,000, and the owners had a profit of about $2,000,000 above their cost and still had an income reputed to exceed $450,000.

If the owners had desired, they could have sold their leasehold position for a substantial price. They could also have made another leaseback deal.

An example of the type of transaction available follows:

Price of leasehold above mortgage—$3,000,000. Rent to purchaser—$270,000 for twenty-one years. (After the twenty-one years, rent declines proportionately to ground lease.) Tishman would then have another $3,000,000 profit and continue to have an income from the realty of $180,000 per annum.

Income after original financing = $450,000
Rent on new financing   = 270,000
Remainder   = $180,000

Recent One-Tenant Sales Leaseback. A recent one-tenant sales leaseback of a small size might also indicate the types of deals that are created. This involved a small regional supermarket chain. The building contained 20,000 square feet on a plot of approximately 100,000 square feet and was built by the chain to its exact specifications. The lease was for a twenty-year term at a rental of 8.6 per cent of the purchase price. There were also five, five-year renewal options at 70 per cent of the primary rent—in other words, at approximately 6 percent. After five years, the chain could repurchase the property if the store became unprofitable. Unprofitability was determined to be average sales of $20,000 per week or less for two consecutive years. The insurance company in this transaction figured interest at about 6 per cent and a recapture of its investment during the initial twenty-year lease.

ENTER THE SPECULATIVE STAGE

Now there is a new era of sales leaseback transactions, with pension and welfare funds, syndicates, and individual investors using this form of investment with great advantages to themselves. Special-purpose realty is not usually favorably considered by these types of institutions. However, some other new investors are buying more speculative deals. A popular deal which has entered the scene during the last few years involves leaseback agreements involving bowling alleys, second-rate hotels, motels, nursing homes, and similarly non-realty-type properties. Investors have been led into these transactions with the lure of 12–18 per cent returns on long-term leases. The basic problem is that the appropriate return should be double these rates, owing to the great risk. These are businesses, and, if business becomes poor, the tenant doesn't pay the stated rent, and there is little remedy for the investor. This doesn't imply that all transactions of this type are poor. The problem lies with the difficulty in evaluating both the long-term success of these types of businesses and the ability of the tenants to operate them. Syndicators have gravitated to this type of transaction in order to offer to the public returns of 10 per cent and over.

SALES LEASEBACK AND THE MARKET

Sales leasebacks bring more funds and flexibility into the realty market. They have the over-all effect of increasing realty prices for two reasons:

1. More demand for realty investments is created, with the natural economic result of higher prices.
2. Different interests in realty are marketed to investors on the basis of their specific investment and income-tax needs.

Sometimes these transactions appeal to investors, because of seemingly high returns, which usually would be higher if the investor actually understood the risks involved.

INVESTMENT GUIDES

The investor should analyze the investment in the following manner:

1. Analyze the basic realty. Determine its status as an investment.

    a. Determine its rental productivity, present and future.
    b. Check all annual expenses to determine their stability or their vulnerability to increases or potential reductions.
    c. Consider the resulting market value of this realty.
    d. Determine the shares into which the investment is being divided.

e. Consider the benefits available to these various investment "positions," i.e., income-tax shelter, liquidity, financeability, limitation of risk, and control.

In a sales leaseback where the seller is not a highly rated corporation, the buyer wants the seller to retain a substantial investment in the property. When the property is being sold by one realty investor to another, subject to a leaseback, the buyer wants to be sure that he isn't paying the full price for the realty and still not getting full control. He wants to see a cushion of annual income available to the seller. For example, an apartment house might have the following investment features:

Mortgage		= $240,000
Rentroll	= $50,000	
Operating, mortgage, fixed charges	= 35,000	
Net cash flow after amortization	= $15,000	

A sales leaseback deal with the investor paying $80,000 above the mortgage and receiving $8,000 rental would be an appropriate deal if the property was of a good type. This would give the investor 10 per cent. It can be seen that the seller will still earn $7,000 per annum. This will act as a cushion to the buyer, assuring him that the seller will pay $8,000. He may also require security to guarantee the lease payment.

Another way to make the rental secure is for the buyer to insist that he pays only $60,000 of the price in cash. The balance is given in a purchase-money mortgage which becomes cancelable if the rent is not paid by the seller.

INCOME TAXES

The income-tax feature has become of prime consideration. Income-tax shelter in the sales leaseback can become most favorable to both parties. When the seller sells at a price below his depreciated cost, he may take a loss, but, in many cases, he must amortize this loss over a reasonable-term lease (usually twenty or twenty-five years). This is considered to be part of his leasehold investment. To this he may add capital improvements to the building. The seller may also deduct his full rental payment to the owner as a normal expense. The buyer, for his part, may deduct normal building depreciation from his income. It can be seen that both buyer and seller find tax advantages in the sales leaseback.

CONCLUSIONS

The sales leaseback transaction may act to raise realty prices. It also reduces federal income-tax collections, increases the market for realty, and gives large corporations lower realty occupancy costs based on their credit position.

These investments require a good knowledge of realty and the mathematics of investment. It can be seen that the institutions compute their return on two bases. First, they consider the over-all rate, that is, the ratio of the rental as a percentage of the purchase price. Then they break down that rental into interest and capital return. They figure that the investment is returned during the initial lease term with interest equivalent to mortgage interest on similarly occupied realty. The non-institutional investor must make similar computations. However, his investments will usually carry greater degrees of risk; thus, he should require higher interest and faster capital return.

Typical Over-all Rates on Sales Leasebacks

25-year lease, prime occupant	6– 7½%
25-year lease, $1,000,000–$10,000,000 net worth tenant	8–11%
Multiple-tenant office buildings, apartment houses sold by builders	8–13%
Bowling alleys, motels, nursing homes, and other business-type operations	12–25%[1]

The sales leaseback transaction is a valuable form of financing. It requires great skill in handling by both sides.

[1]These rates should usually be higher, but quoted rates are based on those found in transactions. This is not the rate to the ultimate member of the syndicate. It is the rate available to the syndicate manager or professional investor. The 12 per cent deals are given to large-chain operators, on the basis of their credit and operational skill.

28

Shopping Centers

Shopping centers were introduced in the early 1940's and before by outstanding retailers such as Sears Roebuck that saw the advantages of moving away from the crowded central business district and nearer to the buying population. Since then, the rapid movement of families to the suburbs and their increased mobility through widespread automobile ownership have encouraged an unprecedented increase in shopping centers. However, even though shopping centers have found increasing acceptance by shoppers, they have, in many cases, proven to be poor investments.

SHOPPING-CENTER WEAKNESSES

The weaknesses of shopping centers derive primarily from the fact that too many are being built because of a lack of knowledge about how to locate and plan them. A poorly located and poorly planned center is particularly subject to the weaknesses discussed in the following paragraphs, and a strong center must be constantly alert to avoid them.

Franchise Value. A shopping center can be located on any of a number of sites within a given market area; therefore, the center's owners can negotiate with a number of landowners in order to obtain the lowest possible land prices. In the process the owners have to be careful that they weigh properly the advantages of a site compared to the costs of acquiring it. Unfortunately, tenants are also free to locate in a number of different shopping centers, so they are in a position to negotiate rental terms. When there was only a single central shopping district, the franchise values of the business sites within the district were high, but the prospective tenants had no other choices.

In the typical suburban community today, very few commercial parcels have a sufficiently monopolistic strength to permit charging high rents. Prospective customers can be contacted from locations along a number of traffic thoroughfares. The traffic can easily move to a site occupied by good retail stores, since the automobile is a more flexible form of transportation than bus, railroad, streetcar, subway, or pedestrian traffic.

This lack of franchise value is important as a hazard in shopping-center investment because

1. it places the tenant in the most favorable bargaining position
2. it creates competitive centers
3. it induces developers to overbuild
4. it creates a difficult mortgage financing market

All of these factors are interrelated, but they are direct results of a lack of franchise value, which can be defined as a property location having a high degree of monopolistic retail site value.

Tenant Master in Negotiation. Since several locations are available, the tenant can negotiate with full power. If it is a department store, the "corn field" it chooses may easily be developed as the heart of retail activity for the entire region. Site owners will compete with each other to obtain such tenants, and finally one will offer the most inducements.

Sometimes the inducement given to the department store will be title to a choice piece of land in the center, free of cost, or a long-term lease on the land without rental payments. In other cases, the developer will agree to construct a building on the land and to charge the store such a low rental that the rent will be insufficient to produce a return on capital. Similarly, in dealing with the junior department store, variety store, ladies' wear store, shoe store, and a few other categories of stores, the owner may grant special inducements to chain tenants of prime credit standing in order to ensure that his center will become the prime shopping center in the region.

Neighboring Competitive Centers. As an area develops and one new shopping center develops successfully, other suitable sites will be bought by other developers, who will consider the region logical for additional centers because of the success of the first center. Some competing stores will see what is happening, will want to be represented in the region, and will agree to rent stores if additional centers are built. Some competing centers will be developed because of their proximity to the first center and will then become parasitic centers living off the traffic created by the first.

Developers Induced To Overbuild. Since developers will find it necessary to grant subsidies to many of the prime tenants in the centers, they may soon face substantial financial losses if they can secure only these major tenants. A developer of a regional shopping center that has a major department store and well-rated chain-store tenants who occupy 200,000 to 350,000 square feet of stores will find the project unprofitable owing to the low-rent structure. The developer is in business to earn a substantial income on his project; therefore, he rents to other tenants from whom he must obtain his profit. He will make an effort to charge them enough rent not only to make a good profit on their portion of the center but to produce a profit covering the subsidized large tenants. He will try to build as much of this type of secondary space as possible.

In other words, the small tenants will pay excessive rents and will have severe competition from the low-rent chains and an overabundance of small tenants. Usually, these small tenants will be relegated to inferior locations in the center, so they will be further handicapped! This will often result in their bankruptcy. Thus, the stores that actually produce the developer's income may be doomed from inception in all but the best centers. Incidentally, this also may prove detrimental to the major tenants owing to special loss sales of the failing stores and desperate merchandising methods that lower the good will of the center.

Difficult Mortgage Financing Market. Since shopping centers have relatively low-value land, the mortgages are usually based on the credit of the tenant. Rentals from national credit tenants must carry all expenses and debt service to qualify for mortgages from many lenders. This compounds the excellent bargaining position of this group as tenants in dealing with owners. Of course, in some cases, it has had a reverse effect. The tenants who want percentage leases with no minimum or nominal fixed rentals find that, even if the owner desires to make such leases, he cannot secure mortgage financing and so may not be able to build the center. Also, the mortgagees want unconditional tenant obligations; therefore, the leases must often be amended to make them acceptable to the mortgagees.

Shopping centers usually cannot be started until a mortgage commitment is available. Since it can't be obtained until the prime-tenant leases are finalized, the time for development is extended, which, obviously, increases development costs. The permanent mortgage commitment is important because building loans are usually granted only on the assurance that a permanent lender is obligated to make a mortgage. Without this assurance, the lender of construction money would not be assured that it would be repaid. Typically, the commercial banks that make the building loans are not interested in long-term mortgages.

PLANNING FOR SHOPPING CENTERS

The key to successful shopping-center developments lies in a carefully prepared preliminary market study. Such studies are useful not only to the developer of the center but also for convincing lenders that they should provide mortgage funds and for showing to major tenants who are being sought for the center. Such studies may be prepared by organizations which specialize in such work or by general real estate or research firms.[1] Some studies are prepared as primarily engineering, architectural, land-

---

[1]Some of the more familiar names in the field of specialized shopping-center studies are Larry Smith & Co., Real Estate Research Corp., James Rouse, Sanders A. Kahn Associates, Donald Curtiss, First Research Corp., Real Estate Analysts, Inc., Roy Wenzlick & Co., Amos Parish, and Homer Hoyt.

planning, or statistical reports and fail to give proper consideration to economic and financial matters, so centers built on the basis of such plans often fail.

Basically, a market study will attempt to determine the feasibility of a location on the basis of the following criteria:

Trading Area Served by the Site. This is the geographical area from which the shopping center's customers will be drawn.

ROAD PATTERN. The condition of roads, travel speed on roads, ingress and egress from center, and type of traffic using roads will also be important factors in determining the trading area. It is not enough to count the number of cars on the road. Most cars traveling major interurban routes are not likely prospects for the wares of a shopping center, other than its restaurant and gas station, when located in structures separate from the main structure. Roads leading from the central city through a group of suburban communities are usually the types with traffic significant to a shopping center. In determination of the limits of a trading center, the unit of measurement is travel time, not physical distance. Regional shopping centers usually will have a trading area limited to thirty minutes' travel time. Community shopping centers will have about fifteen-minute limitations, while neighborhood centers will attract customers from a five- to ten-minute area. Obviously, many factors will modify these criteria. These will include location of competing stores, prestige and good will of a store, traditional shopping patterns, special barriers such as toll bridges, tax differentials between two political boundaries, and driving hazards or difficulties.

Computation of the Number of Families in Trading Area. This is not too difficult to accomplish. After the outline of the area is defined, the family units within the area must be counted. Census records, school attendance records, public-utility-company service contracts, building permits, and directories will be available as source material. Aerial photography may also be used, and there is no restriction against driving through the area and counting houses. The latter method has the tremendous advantage of giving the researcher a close-up look at the potential customers. One of the outstanding chain-store realtors[2] has mentioned that he and a team of his staff would choose a location in a community only after a novel device. They would spot themselves in residential areas of the type in which their customers were known to reside and would observe closely the travel routes used by housewives while shopping. They were then able to choose locations at points most convenient to these customers.

[2] Henry Wolfson, formerly vice-president in charge of realty, H. L. Green Co. Personal communication.

Income and Disposable Income. It will be very necessary for the study to show the amount of money earned by the residents of a potential shopping center market area because from these figures will be computed the money which these families will spend for various types of products, and in various types of stores. These will include department stores, variety stores, apparel store, furniture and appliance stores, food stores, restaurants and taverns, hardware stores, drugstores, children's stores, and various others. After the total spending is computed for an area, it must then be divided among the competing centers, on the basis of the size, convenience, quality, attractiveness, and accessibility of each center, as well as the quality and range of goods, reputation, aggressiveness, and price policies of the individual merchants.

Share of Market. Unfortunately, the share of the market that will be secured by each center is not easily predicted. This is due to the dynamic changes in our retailing system, in our suburbs, and in our travel patterns. A drugstore today may compete with a supermarket. A variety store may compete aggressively with a luncheonette. Most of all, a discount store may compete with all. It has become almost impossible to explain why a particular farmers' market, discount house, supermarket, or drugstore will become a major factor in a trading area.

Store Mix. Allocation of space to individual types of merchants is based upon space needed to sell the products, estimated total sales for each category, consideration of price ranges for merchants, and volume of sales per square foot of retail area.

Competing Centers. The market survey will attempt to estimate the competitive effect of other potential shopping-center sites, the potential addition to the market of more families in the trading area, the economic stability of the area, the availability of top-grade merchants for the center, and customer attraction from beyond trading areas.

At the time the subject site is developed, the trading area may be able to support more stores. However, if two or three sites are developed as shopping centers, the results may be an overbuilding of stores either temporarily or for a long period. The survey should include an analysis of all potential sites. Zoning in the area must be studied to help determine future uses.

Potential Additional Population. Not only must present population be analyzed, but consideration must be given to entry of new families into the area. This will be based upon recent population increases, new construction, the vacancy factor, the amount of vacant land, plans announced for new developments, and city planning.

Economic Stability. The study must include employment factors, diversity of employment opportunity, trends in wage rates and unemployment, new business entry into the area, and effects of new governmental policy on the area.

Availability of Merchants. The results of the proper shopping-center development are scored in terms of the roster of tenants desiring to join in merchandising the center. Some centers have many excellent qualities, but the prime merchants in that region may have certain requirements not satisfied by the center. They may also have stores in, or on the borders of, the shopping center. It may also be just beyond the warehouses of a particular chain at the time it is being developed, thus eliminating that chain at the time; all of these factors must receive prime consideration in the survey. Obviously, if a center cannot qualify for the rental requirements of top-caliber tenants, it will not be a successful venture.

Secondary and Tertiary Trading Areas. Although from 75–98 per cent of the sales of a shopping center will be attracted from its primary trading area, additional sales may be attracted from other areas. Regional centers will sometimes attract up to about 25 per cent of their sales from beyond their primary trading area. On the other extreme, a neighborhood center will usually not generate more than 2 per cent of its sales from beyond its trading area. These numbers are logical. The regional center has many stores generating an individual and cumulative pull from a large area and offering a variety of merchandise. A neighborhood center has very few stores, selling only a small number of everyday items, usually stated to be necessities, thus the travel time will be limited.

As extreme examples, department stores in Dallas, Texas, and Allentown, Pennsylvania, have advertised in New York newspapers, and even department stores in Paris, London, and Amsterdam have done so to attract the tourist. On the other hand, many families will buy poultry, eggs, and produce at a farm or roadside stand an hour or more distance from their houses.

TYPES OF CENTERS

There are three basic types of shopping centers usually designated as *regional, community,* and *neighborhood.*

Regional Center. This is the largest type of shopping center. It will generally have 400,000–1,200,000 square feet of stores, with at least 40 stores, most of which will be selling shopping goods rather than convenience or necessity items. The leading stores will be one or more department stores; one or more junior department stores; one or two variety stores; several each of ladies' wear, shoe, men's wear, and furniture stores; and one or more hardware stores, luncheonettes, restaurants, bakeries, jewelry stores, candy stores, fabric stores, toy stores, gift shops, florists, stationers, liquor stores, camera stores, greeting-card stores, bookshops, hobby stores, record stores, barbers, beauty parlors, tailor shops, shoe-repair establishments, banks, and post offices. One or more supermarkets will also be in the center but often in a separate section.

The center will be located on at least one, and often two or three, important roads. It will draw a trading area consisting of several suburban communities and the fringes of one or more large cities, in which will be found a total population of 150,000 or more.

Community Center. This type of center will usually range from about 50,000 square feet to 150,000 square feet. It will have twenty to forty stores, and its main stores will be junior department stores, variety stores, supermarkets, shoe stores, a few apparel shops, and a bank, as well as all of the other types present in the neighborhood shopping center. Such a shopping center will have all of the convenience goods of the neighborhood center and a narrow range of the shopping goods found in regional centers. It will serve a population of 20,000–75,000.

Neighborhood Center. The neighborhood center will range from 10,000 to 50,000 square feet. It will have five to fifteen stores. Its principal stores will be the supermarket and, in the larger cities, a variety store. Its other stores will typically include a drugstore, luncheonette, hardware store, cleaner, tailor, laundromat, bakery, delicatessen, and stationer. These centers serve a population of about 1,500–8,000.

ANALYZING SHOPPING-CENTER INVESTMENTS

An actual shopping center built in the Midwest had the following current figures according to the corporate records:

The location is strategically facing on two roads. It covers 35 acres at the outskirts of a large city where there has been a considerable residential growth.

The center was built with 175,000 square feet of ground-floor stores and another 70,000 square feet of basement and mezzanine.

Cost figures were

Land and improvement	= $	105,000
Parking lot	=	275,000
Buildings	=	2,662,000
Leasehold improvements for tenants	= $	187,000
		$3,229,000

These costs represent about $16 per square foot of ground-floor area for buildings (including tenant improvements), about $1.60 per square foot for parking-lot improvements, and about $0.60 per square foot for land. This will total about $18.20 per square foot.

Operating Statement. It can be seen from Fig. 15 that the total income including fixed, overage, straight percentage rent, and ancillary income will total less than $2.00 per square foot of ground-floor area (without considering the mezzanine and basement space). It is obvious that this rental cannot produce a fair return for capital investment and entrepreneurship. Proper rental income should average $2.50 or more per square foot, on the basis of the cost of this project.

Income		
Guaranteed rental:		
Fixed minimum	$249,060	
Straight percentage (no minimum)	34,953	
Percentage excess	55,189	
Utilities and maintenance	4,156	
Taxes and insurance	1,844	
Other	1,629	
Total income:	$346,800	
Expenses—Operating		
Advertising	$ 3,600	
Leasing commission	959	
Insurance	10,223	
Janitors' salaries	3,930	
Janitors' supplies	27	
Management fee paid local representative	8,596	
Repairs and maintenance:		
Buildings	2,248	
Parking lot	642	
Utilities	5,179	
Taxes:		
Property	$76,863	
State income tax	5,118	81,981
Legal and audit	1,778	
Total cash operating expenses:	$119,100	
Net income free and clear:		$227,700
Capital Charges		
Interest on mortgage	$123,888	
Amortization of mortgages	66,752	
	$190,640	
Net income to equity (before depreciation):		$ 37,000

Fig. 15. Shopping center—1961 operating statement.

Fully rented and without vacancy allowance, the project shows a net income of about $227,000 free and clear. Since the capital investment was $3,229,000, this very speculative investment produces only about 8½ per cent return. It should be understood that this return includes depreciation and does not include a vacancy provision. In addition, $90,000 of $227,000 income is not a firm obligation of tenants but is based on percentage of sales. If business conditions worsen, the return will be reduced.

Actually, the developer obtained very favorable mortgage financing totaling $2,600,000, which represents about 85 per cent of the total project cost and over 90 per cent of the value of the center. This contrasts with a normal mortgage of about 67 per cent of value. The high loan was doubtlessly based on the fact that about 70 per cent of the space and 69 per cent of the income were derived from highly rated tenants.

Operating costs for this center are $119,000, of which real estate taxes constitute $77,000. This is about $0.70 per square foot of ground-floor space for total costs. It breaks down to about $0.45 for realty taxes and $0.25 for general operation.

If an investor were to buy this property today, he would consider it to be a favorable investment only if he could anticipate rental increases and it would be available for purchase at a price of about $300,000 above the present mortgage, which is paid down to about $2,230,000. It can be seen that the developer would suffer a severe loss, but the buyer would expect to earn approximately 12 per cent on his investment.

It would also be possible to obtain a higher price if the seller would consider taking only $150,000 cash and a purchase-money mortgage of about $300,000 for ten years with debt service of about $19,000. This too would give the buyer his 12 per cent return ($18,000 on $150,000 cash). The seller would be getting an additional price of $150,000 but only by retaining a mortgage with unattractive terms.

This example demonstrates that the basic problem is usually in the initial, rental, program. If this center had been properly rented, an additional $90,000–$100,000 would be found in the profit column. The developer would then have a profitable and economic venture. To make matters worse, this center contributes only $3,600 to its own merchandising. A proper budget for a center of this type should be at least $20,000 per annum. The low promotional budget is a direct result of poor rental policy.

An appropriate and complete rental schedule (Fig. 16) for a regional center was developed by Larry Smith and Victor Gruen to cover all elements that must be considered. In the schedule, note that figures are given for square-foot area, fixed rent per square foot, fixed rent in dollars, estimated sales, sales per square foot, appropriate-percentage rents, and total rents. Each of these items is given for all stores that might be in the center. Few people have the skill necessary to make these estimates.

	Rentable Area (sq. ft.)	Guaranteed Rent		Estimated Stabilized Sales		Total Rent	
		Per Sq. Ft.	Total	Per Sq. Ft.	Total	Rate (%)	Total
Food	32,000		$ 51,875		$3,927,500		$ 80,150
Candy & nuts	500	$4.00	2,000	$100	50,000	10	5,000
Delicatessen	1,500	3.25	4,875	85	127,500	6	7,650
Supermarket	30,000	1.50	45,000	125	3,750,000	2% to min.	67,500
Department store	160,000	1.25	200,000	60	9,600,000	1½% over 2½	240,000
Junior department store (of the variety-store type)	60,000	1.25	75,000	50	3,000,000	4% to min.	108,750
Apparel	115,000		276,900		7,261,500	3% over	412,980
Women's specialty	10,000	2.00	20,000	65	650,000	4½	29,250
Women's wear	8,000	2.25	18,000	65	520,000	4½	23,400
Women's wear	3,000	2.50	7,500	60	180,000	6	10,800
Women's wear	2,500	2.50	6,250	60	150,000	6	9,000
Women's wear	3,000	2.50	7,500	60	180,000	6	10,800
Men's quality wear	2,000	2.50	5,000	60	120,000	7	8,400
Men's wear	14,000	2.25	31,500	65	910,000	5	45,500
Men's wear	10,000	2.25	22,500	65	650,000	5	32,500
Men's wear	8,000	2.25	18,000	65	520,000	5	26,000
Apparel store	4,000	2.50	10,000	55	220,000	6	13,200
Children's wear	3,500	2.50	8,750	55	192,500	6	11,550
Women's shoes	8,500	2.50	21,250	65	552,500	6	33,150
Women's shoes	10,000	2.50	25,000	65	650,000	6	39,000
Women's shoes	8,000	2.50	20,000	65	520,000	6	31,200
Family shoes	4,500	2.50	11,250	65	292,500	6	17,550
Men's & boys' shoes	3,000	2.50	7,500	60	180,000	7	12,600
Children's shoes	3,000	2.50	7,500	60	180,000	7	12,600

Fig. 16. Rent schedule for hypothetical regional shopping center.

	Rentable Area (sq. ft.)	Guaranteed Rent		Estimated Stabilized Sales		Total Rent	
		Per Sq. Ft.	Total	Per Sq. Ft.	Total	Rate (%)	Total
Millinery	1,200	$3.00	$ 3,600	$50	$ 60,000	10	$ 6,000
Maternity	800	3.25	2,600	55	44,000	7	3,080
Lingerie	800	3.25	2,600	70	56,000	8	4,480
Hosiery	800	3.25	2,600	70	56,000	8	4,480
Teen shop	3,000	2.50	7,500	60	180,000	7	12,600
Bridal shop	1,200	3.25	3,900	55	66,000	8	5,280
Women's accessories	2,200	3.00	6,600	60	132,000	8	10,560
Furniture	27,000		56,000		1,255,000		59,775
Furniture	23,000	2.00	46,000	45	1,035,000	4½	46,575
China & glassware	4,000	2.50	10,000	55	220,000	6	13,200
Hardware	9,000	1.75	15,750	45	405,000	5	20,250
Drugs (chain)	12,000	1.90	22,800	65	780,000	3	23,400
Eating & drinking	25,000		62,250		1,625,000		100,620
Bakery & cafeteria	9,000	2.25	20,250	65	585,000	6	35,100
Fountain	800	3.00	2,400	65	52,000	7	3,640
Fountain (lunch)	4,000	2.25	9,000	65	260,000	7	18,200
Restaurant	6,000	2.50	15,000	65	390,000	6	23,400
Cafe	5,200	3.00	15,600	65	338,000	6	20,280
Other retail stores	43,000		123,675		2,438,250		164,955
Costume jewelry & handbags	2,500	3.50	8,750	70	175,000	7	12,250
Jewelry	3,000	3.50	10,500	75	225,000	6	13,500
Leather goods	1,500	3.00	4,500	45	67,500	8	5,400
Cosmetics	700	3.50	2,450	70	49,000	7	3,430
Fabrics	8,000	2.25	18,000	50	400,000	5	20,000

Fig. 16. Rent schedule for hypothetical regional shopping center (*continued*).

	Rentable Area (sq. ft.)	Guaranteed Rent		Estimated Stabilized Sales		Total Rent	
		Per Sq. Ft.	Total	Per Sq. Ft.	Total	Rate (%)	Total
Sporting goods	1,800	$3.00	$ 5,400	$55	$ 99,000	7	$ 6,930
Toys	3,600	2.50	9,000	55	198,000	6	11,880
Gifts	2,000	3.25	6,500	50	100,000	10	10,000
Hobby shop	1,200	3.25	3,900	45	54,000	10	5,400
Stationery & cards	4,500	3.25	14,625	50	225,000	7	15,750
Sewing machines	3,800	2.25	8,550	55	209,000	5	10,450
Florist	750	3.50	2,625	55	41,250	10	4,125
Cards & gifts	750	3.50	2,625	50	37,500	10	3,750
Imports	3,500	3.00	10,500	50	175,000	8	14,000
Cameras	1,600	3.50	5,600	80	128,000	8	10,240
Liquor	1,300	3.00	3,900	100	130,000	7	9,100
Music	2,500	2.50	6,250	50	125,000	7	8,750
Services	7,000		17,850		287,000		28,700
Optometrists	700	3.00	2,100	50	35,000	10	3,500
Slenderizing	2,500	2.50	6,250	40	100,000	10	10,000
Beauty	1,600	2.50	4,000	40	64,000	10	6,400
Barber	700	2.50	1,750	40	28,000	10	2,800
Shoe repair	1,500	2.50	3,750	40	60,000	10	6,000
Institutions	10,000		35,275				35,275
Savings & loan	2,700	3.25	8,775	Guaranteed Rent			8,775
Bank	5,500	4.00	22,000	Guaranteed Rent			22,000
Post office	1,800	2.50	4,500	Guaranteed Rent			4,500
Total project	500,000		$937,375		$30,579,250		$1,274,855

Source: Victor Gruen and Larry Smith. *Shopping Towns USA* (New York: Reinhold Publishing Corp., 1960. Pp. 138, 139.

Fig. 16. Rent schedule for hypothetical regional shopping center (*continued*).

INVESTMENT CRITERIA FOR SHOPPING CENTERS

A number of criteria have been developed which are useful as general guides in evaluating the investment quality of a shopping center. When these are supported by a careful market study, a successful center should result. These criteria are

1. An investor buying an existing shopping center will require 10–18 per cent on his cash investment.

2. The mortgagee will expect about 70 per cent of rental income to be derived from tenants having net worth over $1,000,000, and usually higher. The income from this portion of the rent roll must be sufficient to meet operating expenses, realty taxes, and debt charges of the mortgage desired. Thus, if a mortgage of $1,100,000 is wanted on a center having 100,000 square feet, income from premium tenants usually must meet the following charges:

Debt charges @ 9% =	$ 99,000
Operating charges =	30,000
Realty taxes =	30,000
Total of debt-service, operating, and realty taxes =	$159,000

The income from AA–A1 tenants must be about $160,000 on fixed minimum rentals, if the $1,100,000 mortgage is to be made. A mortgage of about $9–$11 per square foot of ground-floor area is usually obtainable under these circumstances. It can also be seen that, if 70,000 square feet of this center is leased to the prime tenants, their average rental will exceed $2 per square foot. It is true that the variety store or junior department store will be difficult to rent at this rate, but the apparel store, the shoe store, and even the supermarkets are now renting at these rates and higher, and others will follow.

3. Location should have future. More apartments and homes must be planned for the nearby area.

4. The mortgage should have at least ten years before maturity.

5. Secondary financing should be analyzed to determine if the investment is satisfactory without any of its features that may be more favorable than those currently obtainable in the junior financing market.

6. Rentals should be at levels that ensure the possibility of increases at expiration of the lease. If term of the lease is very long, percentage rent rate should give full potential to property earnings.

7. Real estate taxes should be checked to determine if any substantial increases will be forthcoming.

8. Physical inspection should be made to determine if major roof, paving, store-front, or other capital-investment costs must be made.

9. Inspection should reveal if sufficient parking is available and if any traffic hazards adversely affect the center.

10. A tour of each store should be made to determine the success of its operations. Counts of numbers of cars and of customers in stores, as well as conversations with merchants, will reveal information not found in financial statements.

11. A regional survey should be made to determine entry of competing centers, changes of road patterns, and general economic conditions.

Although most of this chapter refer to regional- and community-type centers, obviously, most centers are of the neighborhood type. Similar investment features are applicable, but at this point the investor must be cautioned against a center that doesn't have a prime supermarket chain as its major tenant. Without this tenancy, mortgage financing and liquidity of investment will always be major problems.

29

One-Tenant Realty

One of the most popular types of real estate investment is one in which a single, financially responsible tenant has signed a long-term lease for the use of an entire property. Such *one-tenant realty* presents minimum problems of property and investment management and is considered a most desirable type of real estate investment by almost all investors, particularly by pension funds, insurance companies, and similar institutional investors.

In the 1930's and 1940's, a single-tenant variety-chain property in a choice retail location would sell at a price that would yield as little as 4–5 per cent on cash investment. The reasons for the high price of these properties were

1. It was thought that central retail districts would grow rapidly and perhaps even faster than the cities in which they were located.
2. The high credit standing of the financially strong prime tenants, particularly variety chains, gave assurance of "trouble-free" income for the lease term.
3. It was believed rentals could be increased upon expiration of the leases because of expected improvements in business conditions.
4. Investors with sufficient funds and without realty knowledge bid higher than warranted for these high-credit, "trouble-free," "easy to value" investments.

It has only been during recent years that disillusionment with these investments has occurred. Only now are investors discovering that residential neighborhoods and the adjacent retail areas become obsolete and may not show increases in rents and values. Quite to the contrary, they have declined. In many such cases, investors have discovered that the rates of return were not sufficient to provide a "cushion" against error. Even if rentals did not decline, higher financing terms decreased the cash return and the resale value. Furthermore, after receiving a comparatively low rate of return for ten to twenty years, many owners found that they could not get more than a small portion of their original investment in a resale.

Nevertheless, it was this type of investment that encouraged most realty investors. Fortunately, today many professional investors have found methods of improving these investments, and institutional investors have special reasons to find them attractive.

RETAIL PROPERTIES

One-tenant retail properties are often most favored for investment, because they are expected to have both growth potential and a fixed minimum value. Furthermore, choice retail locations may have franchise value, which would mean that their location is adjacent to pedestrian or vehicular traffic and a high-volume sales potential. Franchise values may be created by restrictions on the ability of competing businesses to locate nearby, by the flow of local traffic, or by the flow of through traffic.

Franchise value may also be created when property is adjacent to a ball field, bus terminal, or subway station, because the traffic to these locations will produce varying volumes of business, depending upon the nature of the business. For example, a ladies' wear chain store will count the number of women passing a given location and a children's shop will consider the number of preschool children and the school registration in the trading area. The better the location, the easier the marketing procedures.

In other words, the market for well-located retail realty is strong because the realty has stability with a use potential which is attractive to many possible occupants. Investors, particularly, will favor this realty owing to the combination of prime location, high-credit tenancy, and little day-to-day management.

ROLE OF PERCENTAGE LEASES

Once a site has proven to be a valuable business location, the investor will want to work out some means by which he can share in the increasing business which the tenant enjoys because of the location. Furthermore, the investor will want to protect himself against rising costs which might occur because of inflationary business conditions or changes in the purchasing power of the dollar. On the other hand, the tenant will want to avoid having to pay high rental costs in periods when he is not enjoying high sales. Percentage leases represent an almost ideal solution to these problems, because they relate rental payments to the volume of business being done by the tenant. Usually the tenant is required to pay a minimum fixed rental plus an amount expressed as a percentage of all sales made in excess of a stipulated minimum. Percentage leases originated in the 1930's, when chain stores were seeking flexible rental schedules in return for giving long-term leases. Today, percentage leases have become an integral part of business practice.

Administration. The use of the percentage lease creates two main problems. First of all, the lease is somewhat difficult to administer, because the property owner either must have implicit faith in the willingness of the tenant to report sales accurately and completely or he must provide adequate controls against cheating. These controls include audited sales reports, numbered sales tickets, controlled cash registers, shopping services to spot-check reporting of sales, and numerous other devices, all of which involve time and expense. In general, chain stores tend to give more reliable sales reports, because they have such effective financial and personnel controls. Sometimes an independent shop owner in poor financial condition might be tempted to conceal some sales so as to "save" some rent.

The second problem with percentage leases is the difficulty in establishing a rental percentage appropriate to specific types of retail property. Most rates have resulted from duplicating past lease transactions, which were often based on the negotiating abilities of the owner and tenant. It is obvious that tenants usually have better information on their rent-paying ability than owners.

SETTING PERCENTAGE RATES

Basically, rates vary for different types of retail operations, on the basis of the following factors:

1. *Degree of contribution of real estate to sales.* It is obvious that the tenant operator of a public garage is actually "retailing" realty that he has obtained "wholesale"; therefore, the rental percentage is very high. At the other extreme, a supermarket sells low-priced foods, and each dollar's worth of merchandise occupies very little space and turns over quickly. The contribution of the realty to food sales is obviously much less than for the garage, and the rates used reflect this.

2. *Amount of markup.* The higher the markup, the greater the percentage which can be paid.

3. *Turnover rate.* Merchandise kept on the shelves for a short time will carry a lower markup but can produce a higher total sales volume.

Percentage Tables. Many real estate experts and professional societies have set up tables reflecting percentage sales rates in use in local areas. These tables are utilized quite widely but are often subject to modifications. A few years ago, one of the authors had to study a proper rate for a large parking lot operation with customer self-parking. Prospective operators had offered from 25 to 50 per cent, and percentage rent tables generally supported that range. After a careful study of expected parking income, the services which the operator had to furnish, and the expenses to be incurred by the operator, the rate was set at about 75 per cent. One of the largest parking-lot operators then agreed to pay this rental. If the first range of rates had been accepted, the owner would have received one-third to two-thirds of a fair rental.

FIXING MINIMUM RENTAL PAYMENTS AND LEASE CONDITIONS

Most percentage leases also provide for a fixed minimum rental. This minimum should be sufficient to pay all the charges against the realty, including interest and amortization on conventional financing. In addition, a small rate of return should also be included which corresponds to the return on a safe investment.

Provision should also be made that the tenant will not have competing stores close to the subject property. Conversely, sometimes the tenant will restrict the owner from leasing a nearby store to a directly competing tenant.

The prudent owner will insist that the store operate during all hours consistent with local business practices and that the operation be consistent with aggressive merchandising for the type of business involved.

INVESTMENT CONSIDERATIONS

Income-Tax Problems. One of the principal disadvantages, from an investor's viewpoint, of a one-tenant retail realty operating on a percentage lease is that the major portion of the investment is represented by the land; therefore, there is little to be depreciatd for income-tax purposes. This situation may be improved somewhat if the property is located in a suburban highway area where extensive improvements would be needed in order to have an attractive business property.

Investment Returns. Returns available on retail one-tenant realty have recently varied from about 7 to 12 per cent and more, with the variation related to the quality of the tenant, the term of the lease, the attractiveness of the realty, the degree of specialty of the tenancy, and the lack of responsibility for expenses on the part of the owner. These percentages may be improved if expenses can be shifted to the tenant.

Net Leases. The tenant could be required to pay all costs of property maintenance, heating, real estate taxes, and insurance so that the only expense payable by the owner would be his income taxes and mortgage payments. This type of lease is referred to as a "strictly net" lease or by the more emphatic real estate people as a "net, net, net" lease.

Other leases may require the owners to pay for fire insurance, structural and exterior repairs, and real estate taxes. Obviously, this type of lease does not give the owner as much assurance of a fixed income. Taxes and insurance rates may rise, and repairs may suddenly become necessary. An investor with this type of lease would want a higher return on his money. In some cases, the realty-tax provision will not be a burden to the owner, as a tax-stop clause will require the tenant to pay taxes in excess of a stated amount.

When a tax-stop clause is included, it must be studied carefully. It may provide that the tenant pay taxes in excess of those incurred after a particular year of the lease. If the building has just been completed, the tax liability of the owner may increase during those first years. Sometimes, the tax liability to the tenant may only be based on increases in the assessed value; other times, the liability will only occur if the tax rates increase. Obviously, the owner's protection is complete only if there is tenant liability for any change in tax payments because of a change in either the assessed value or the tax rate.

INDUSTRIAL PROPERTIES

Single-tenant industrial realty includes manufacturing plants, warehouses and other storage facilities, and terminal buildings. This type of realty is usually located at the fringe of, or a few miles distant from, a large community on major transportation arteries such as railroads, highways, rivers, canals, or bays and near sources of raw materials, markets, and manpower.

Risk Factor. Single-tenant industrial property is a somewhat more hazardous investment than prime retail realty, because the market for industrial realty is normally smaller with the buyer in the more advantageous role. Thus, when an industrial property is vacated, it usually is vacant for a longer period of time than a well-located retail property. One very interesting recent trend has been the conversion of some industrial buildings to retail uses when the market for industrial properties is weak. The ability to convert industrial property to the higher-grade retail use depends upon the property being in a strategic location near large population centers and with large areas for parking. Many discount stores and mill-outlet stores have prospered in quarters of this type.

Income Tax. Industrial properties usually have a large ratio of building value to land value; therefore, they are usually located on as cheap land as can be obtained. For this reason, the depreciation allowance for income-tax purposes is generous. Many affluent investors favor this type of investment owing to its tax advantages.

Investment Returns. Rates available to investors, as is true of retail properties, vary from as little as 7 to 12 per cent and more on equity, with the reasons for the variation related to the quality of tenancy, the length of the lease, whether the property is for general use or highly specialized use, and the number of expense items paid for by the tenant.

Typical Investors. Types of investors who favor this property are similar to those who favor retail one-tenant realty, and include insurance companies, estates, non-profit organizations, pension funds, foundations, and individual investors. Of these, insurance companies, non-profit organizations, estates, and pension funds will usually want a completely net income investment. Large investors, other than those mentioned, have included Yale University, the Knights of Columbus, General Electric Pension Fund, and Teachers Insurance and Annuity Society of America, among others.

GASOLINE STATIONS

One of the most interesting single-tenant investments is the gasoline station operated by a major oil company. This type of realty investment can be the best available when all circumstances are optimum. However, it is successful most often when arranged by highly skilled investors.

There are many types of gasoline-station occupancies. Some stations are owned or operated by independent dealers who merely purchase gasoline products from the oil company, which has no interest in, or responsibility to, the realty. This type of realty is not favored by investors, for the tenant usually has little financial standing and the oil company has not used its skills to determine the use of the realty.

The gasoline-station investment which is usually most interesting to realty investors is one in which the oil company is a direct tenant of the property owner. The oil company may then operate with its own employees or obtain a subtenant, but, in either event, it is liable for rent payments and it will have approved the location and the rental arrangements.

The lease usually calls for a flat payment of rent on a monthly basis and lease terms which usually vary from ten to twenty-five years. In many cases, these leases are completely net, with the tenant paying all realty taxes and operating charges. Other leases may require the owner to pay taxes, but often the tenant must pay taxes above those payable during the early years of the lease. The purpose of this is to have the owner pay taxes that are computable but to have the tenant pay taxes above that amount in order to assure the owner of a suitable rate of return.

In most leases, there is also an overage payment which requires the oil company to pay additional rental, usually one to two cents per gallon, if its gallonage sales exceed a stated amount. In some cases, there may also be a maximum on the overage rental that will be payable. This overage clause must not be confused with a percentage lease, because it gives the owner no protection against inflation, since it is based on units of sales, not on dollar sales. It is typically based only on gasoline sales and not on sales of tires, batteries, oil, accessories, refreshments, and repairs.

Highway locations are usually the most risky for the investor, because changes in the highway routes have often made a location valueless.

Prime gasoline-station investments are usually not those on highways, but are those in towns or just on the urban fringe. The largest corporations in the country are usually the tenants. If the location is in the line of growth, there can be a large capital appreciation due to the desirability of the location for more intensive land use at expiration of the lease. Thus, a good return is being earned with the best-credit tenants and capital-appreciation potential. Equally important are the low income-tax shelter and income-tax liability which occur because of the relatively high building-land ratio and the large amount of specialized structure and equipment involved.

MORTGAGE AND LEASE TERMS

Mortgage financing and liquidity of property toward lease expiration must be kept in mind. Usually, one-tenant investments can be mortgaged under favorable terms if the tenant is highly rated and the term of the lease is sufficiently long. Financial institutions usually shy away from single-purpose realty, so investments such as industrials and gas stations must normally have strong occupancy to secure prime mortgages. Many mortgages affecting one-tenant realty will require complete payout of the loan during the term of the lease. However, some will have an amortization schedule that will leave a "balloon" at the end of the mortgage. An example of the latter may be a fifteen-year mortgage on a gas station having a fifteen-year lease with a prime tenant. The mortgage may call for 9 per cent constant payments including interest of 5¾ per cent. This will require about eighteen years to be repaid, and, at the end of fifteen years, about 23 per cent of the loan will not have been amortized. This will have to be paid in one final payment to discharge the mortgage indebtedness at the expiration of its term.

Relationship of Investment Return and Lease Term. The market for one-tenant realty changes considerably toward the lease expiration. When the rent-paying liability of a prime tenant has been reduced to a term of five to ten years, most institutional investors have no interest in acquiring these investments. With each year's reduction in the lease, there will be fewer investors interested, and they seek higher rates of return owing to the risk of losing the tenant. When the lease is finally reduced to about three years, usually only speculators will be interested, and they will seek to buy the property under one or more of the following conditions:

1. They are confident that the tenant will require the realty for an additional term of years.
2. The tenant's rent is below the current market, and the speculator judges that a new tenant or the present one will pay a higher rent.
3. A property user gladly will pay a higher price in order to obtain occupancy of the realty, in the speculator's opinion.
4. The property can be bought at a price below its market value.

Naturally, if the original investor is skilled, he may hold the realty and take the risks of the speculator rather than sell to him.

DESIRABILITY AND HAZARDS OF ONE-TENANT REALTY

The lists following show both the desirability and hazards of one-tenant realty investments:

Factors favoring these investments, when well selected, are

1. Stability and security
2. Income-tax advantages if the investment is carefully prepared
3. Advantageous mortgage money available
4. Ease of management
5. When well planned, some inflation protection

Hazards facing investors in one-tenant investment are

1. Competition by uninformed buyers, with resulting low returns
2. Neighborhoods, areas, and roads which may lose value
3. Dependability of the tenant and conditions in the lease
4. Lack of, or poor, inflation hedge
5. At times, poor income-tax position

30

Land for Subdividing
and Developing

More fortunes have probably been made and lost in land subdividing and developing than in any other phase of real estate activities. In the early twenties, unwarranted enthusiasm about land value futures led to the laying out of miles of streets and sidewalks and the placing of street names for communities which were finally developed with homes in the late fifties. The plotting of large areas of raw land for future uses and the selling of these for "speculative investment" in anticipation of rapid population increases are still practiced today. The higher costs of developing land for immediate use and the difficulties of securing financing for this type of venture have slowed development until effective demand for the developments could be proved. The purpose of this chapter is to discuss the various types of analyses which should be made prior to subdividing or developing ventures.

ALTERNATIVE USES OF LAND

Every investor who anticipates the purchase of raw land faces three alternatives: (1) Do nothing to the land, hoping it will increase sufficiently to provide large profits without commensurate outlays for developing costs. (2) Subdivide the land into smaller parcels, perhaps adding streets. (3) Divide the land into parcels, add streets and utilities, and place some type of improvements in the sites. The rewards, risks, and costs differ in each instance.

Holding Land. The greatest risks are usually attached to buying and holding raw land, because profit potential is great only when the purchase is well ahead of the market. The sales price of the raw land must be high enough to return interest on any invested capital and borrowed money, and taxes and assessments. The return should equal what would have been earned in alternative forms of investment of equal risk.

Timing considerations are most important in holding raw land, since the costs previously mentioned can mount so rapidly that a rapid increase in land prices is necessary just to achieve a cost-recovery point. Price increases can be anticipated if careful analyses are made of the rate and direction of growth of adjacent urban centers. Primary attention to locational potential will pay higher returns than attention to site characteristics, primarily because good location can bear heavier development costs.

Subdividing Land. Stricter laws in the majority of the states require that subdividers invest more money than was required years ago. Typically, the subdivision must be approved and some utilities and streets installed. Sometimes rather extensive utility installations, paved streets, and sidewalks may be required. For these reasons, greater capital investments are required; the loss risk is, therefore, greater; and profits may not be proportionately more than in holding raw land. On the other hand, land with some utilities and streets planned or installed is more attractive to the typical buyer, who often has difficulty visualizing how raw land might look if subdivided.

Successful subdividing usually requires more complete and accurate market forecasts than do raw-land sales. Subdivisions must be placed on the market just slightly prior to the crest of the market prices so that sales move rapidly and investment recovery is assured. Subdivisions move quickly only when a good sales organization and a sound advertising and marketing plan have been developed. This, of course, raises the investment costs and reduces the return but assures a quicker return of the invested capital at a good profit rate.

Subdividing and Developing. Most of the profits from land sales are made before the improvements are constructed. Usually, a builder will have made his profits before he begins construction, or he will not make them, at least not at a very high rate. The costs of developing are very high, and sales are usually on a retail basis, so recovery of capital is sometimes slow.

Estimating the timing on a development is difficult because of the longer time period between land purchase and completed construction. Once market conditions are propitious for development, competition among subdividers becomes very keen and substantial profits are possible only from large-scale developments. The degree to which retail-property sales are dependent upon good mortgage financing usually means that profits and even the actual investment decisions are dependent almost exclusively on the securing of "take out," that is, consumer mortgage financing, financing while the development is still in the planning stage.

SUBDIVIDING AND DEVELOPING ANALYSIS

The types of analyses required in moving from raw land to finished development are presented in Fig. 17. Column 1 shows the steps in the sequence in which the analyses should be made. Column 2 lists the pre-

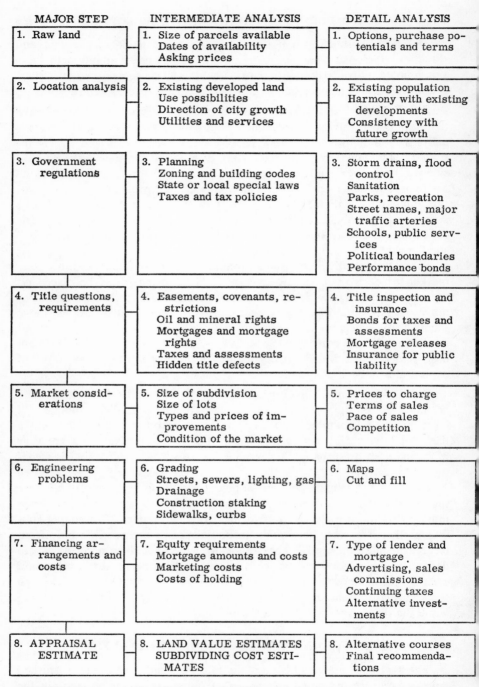

MAJOR STEP	INTERMEDIATE ANALYSIS	DETAIL ANALYSIS
1. Raw land	1. Size of parcels available Dates of availability Asking prices	1. Options, purchase potentials and terms
2. Location analysis	2. Existing developed land Use possibilities Direction of city growth Utilities and services	2. Existing population Harmony with existing developments Consistency with future growth
3. Government regulations	3. Planning Zoning and building codes State or local special laws Taxes and tax policies	3. Storm drains, flood control Sanitation Parks, recreation Street names, major traffic arteries Schools, public services Political boundaries Performance bonds
4. Title questions, requirements	4. Easements, covenants, restrictions Oil and mineral rights Mortgages and mortgage rights Taxes and assessments Hidden title defects	4. Title inspection and insurance Bonds for taxes and assessments Mortgage releases Insurance for public liability
5. Market considerations	5. Size of subdivision Size of lots Types and prices of improvements Condition of the market	5. Prices to charge Terms of sales Pace of sales Competition
6. Engineering problems	6. Grading Streets, sewers, lighting, gas Drainage Construction staking Sidewalks, curbs	6. Maps Cut and fill
7. Financing arrangements and costs	7. Equity requirements Mortgage amounts and costs Marketing costs Costs of holding	7. Type of lender and mortgage Advertising, sales commissions Continuing taxes Alternative investments
8. APPRAISAL ESTIMATE	8. LAND VALUE ESTIMATES SUBDIVIDING COST ESTIMATES	8. Alternative courses Final recommendations

Fig. 17. The process of analysis for subdivision of land (*When You Subdivide,* Title Insurance & Trust Co., Los Angeles, Calif.; *Successful Subdivisions,* Federal Housing Administration, Land Planning Bulletin 1, Washington, D.C.: Government Printing Office).

liminary analyses to be made. If the majority of these analyses indicate that the risks compared to the profit are too great, further analyses can be halted. If the intermediate analyses show a favorable potential, the detailed analysis listed in the third column should be made. No particular combination of these analyses will yield any type of magic formulas which will consistently predict what should be done. Rather, the analyst must determine what is to be achieved from the development being considered, the costs and risks of the development, and the profits to be made.

Raw Land. A careful study of raw-land prices is a necessary first step in development analysis. Prices should be reduced to a comparable unit figure, usually per acre; down payments and purchase terms should be compared; and consideration should be given only to land priced at or below the market. Often raw land can be purchased for a low down payment, with the seller encouraged to subordinate his interests to those of the mortgage lender who finances the construction. As the initial sales are made, first profit returns are used to pay off the seller. Few developers pay all cash for raw land, because they wish to retain a maximum amount of their finances for development needs.

Locational Analysis. Locational analysis should be based on all of the principles and precedents presented in the previous chapters on city and neighborhood analysis. The location will have many important effects on development, not only because it will influence the kinds of uses to which the property can or should be put, but also because adjacent uses in the same location will directly affect the use potential of the vacant sites. For example, an area of office buildings will usually require that vacant sites be developed with office buildings or facilities which can service the occupants of the offices. Highest use potentials will normally be found in locations in the direct line of city growth.

Urban-fringe locations usually present the greatest development problems, because they are so often inadequately served by utilities. A large subdivision, for example, may require greater water and sewage facilities than are available, so the subdivider may have to bear the entire costs of installing such facilities. These problems will rarely arise in developed urban areas, but such areas may not have a sufficient number of vacant, contiguous sites to attract any but the smallest developers.

Governmental Regulation. City planning is developing rapidly in the majority of American communities, so almost all development in urban areas must conform to planned land uses. For this reason, detailed analyses must be made of the requirements under zoning and building codes. Usually these analyses are supplemented with detailed, explicit statements of what is expected from the developer in the way of streets, sidewalks, curbing, street lighting, tying in with existing utilities and street patterns, drains, and security to insure that the developer does the work properly.

Important points which also need to be settled prior to the start of development are what taxes will be levied and in what amounts as the development moves along to the point of final sale.

Dealing with governmental regulations is sometimes complicated even further when the subdivider is attempting a single development which lies in more than one political subdivision. The potential for conflicting planning and building regulations is so great that such problems should be assiduously avoided by locating the entire development within one political subdivision.

Title Questions. Numerous rights may exist even in raw land, so title questions should be settled prior to the beginning of construction. For example, an important question to be settled, even prior to the purchase of land, is what private restrictions on use and construction have been placed in the deeds. Lenders will also demand certain priorities of rights as security for their loans, so releases and subordination of other rights may have to be secured. Provisions must also be made to pay any taxes or assessments which arise during the development period, in order that liens may be avoided. Search may also have to be instituted to determine whether there are any additional clouds, defects, or encumbrances, either recorded or not recorded, which might affect the title. Finally, steps must be taken to obtain proper liability insurance so that suits will not hold up development in the case of any personal injuries on the site.

The best subdivisions include in the deeds of sale certain protective covenants for the purpose of producing harmony in construction and protection of property values. For example, among the minimum covenants which the Federal Housing Administration has required are

1. Regulation of the manner in which each site may be improved and used
2. Control of type of architecture and size of dwellings (in terms of either size or price)
3. Amount of side yards between dwellings, and number of feet main dwelling must be set back from front lot line
4. Minimum square feet of lot per main dwelling unit
5. Prohibitions against uses, noises, odors, or other nuisances which might destroy property values
6. Restrictions against any types of temporary dwellings including trailers for any purpose except during construction
7. Reservations for utility easements
8. Provisions for covenants to be in force for a given number of years, for methods of changing covenants, and for enforcing them.

Market Considerations. Once the locational, legal, and title problems have been solved, consideration must be given to the most important element of all—the market. Failure to consider the market has probably caused financial disaster to more subdivisions than any other single factor. Normally, the market analysis should include all of the items mentioned in previous chapters on analysis of business and real estate trends. The purpose of the analysis is to determine how many lots should be included in the subdivision, the average size of the lots, the sizes and prices of buildings to be placed on the lots, and the terms on which the properties should be sold. This analysis provides the basis not only for planning the subdivision but also for planning the advertising and sales campaigns. Finally, if determination can be made of exact prices to be charged for each property, the down payments and mortgage payments required, the rate at which sales can be made, and what steps will have to be taken to meet sales efforts in competing subdivisions.

The need for a subdivision may be estimated roughly from a study of population increases, unsatisfied demand represented by prices not included in current construction, rate of sales of existing subdivisions, and inventories of unsold new dwellings. Prices can be set by examining family incomes, wage scales, and prices at which new and used homes are selling.

Engineering Problems. The engineering problems in a subdivision are very complex and, if not properly handled, can cause financial disaster. Subdividing within corporate city limits is usually closely inspected for compliance with requirements for grading, connections with existing streets, size and capacity of utilities, and sidewalks and curbs. Streets which must serve as main traffic arteries may have to be 54–60 feet wide, while little-used residential streets may narrow to less than one-half of these distances.

Grading presents a difficult problem in any subdivision and must be carefully planned and executed in order that all lots will drain to the streets and all streets will drain to the sewers. For this reason, very flat land may present as many grading problems as very hilly land. In some cities, much residential construction takes place in hilly areas where a great deal of leveling and filling takes place. This type of work requires considerable engineering skill and is usually closely supervised by governmental inspectors. Appraisers working in such subdivisions should always ask for soil-stability reports from reputable soil-engineering firms.

Streets, sidewalks, and lot lines are usually laid out almost at once by means of stakes. Once this is done, work can be begun simultaneously on all improvements. At this point, an appraiser may have to check the staking against the maps to make sure that plans are being followed. He cannot, of course, make a detailed, accurate check of the engineering work, only rough spot checks to observe general conformity.

Financing. Financing arrangements and costs for subdivisions can be as varied and complicated as those in any phase of the real estate business.

A typical arrangement might be for the builder to secure an option to purchase a vacant parcel, the option to be exercised in six months or sooner. The builder then finds a private investor who will provide funds for purchase of the land in return for participation in the profits. The builder then plans the subdivision and takes it to interested lenders. One lender may agree to furnish funds for the construction if he can have a first lien and be repaid as the sales are made. A second lender may agree to finance up to 80 per cent of each sale, provided his lien is a first lien. The proceeds from this second lien are then used to pay off the first loan. Often the buyers will be able to pay only 10 per cent down, which requires the builder to accept the remaining 10 per cent of the purchase price in the form of a second trust deed. The details might be something like the following:

1. Purchase price, 20 acres at $3,000 per acre, or total price of $60,000
2. Option to purchase of $6,000 to be exercised in ninety days
3. Participation in profits by private investor for a loan of $54,000, or $2,700 per acre
4. Land-development costs at $1,000 per acre
5. Homes to be built to cost $12,000 each (including land development), five homes per acre, or total cost of $1,200,000
6. Estimated sales price per home of $15,500, or total proceeds of $1,550,000
7. Construction loan of $1,200,000
8. Sales financing on sales mortgage of 80 per cent of sales price, or $1,240,000—used to pay off construction mortgage of $1,200,000
9. 10 per cent of sales price per home, or $1,550 cash, received from each buyer, or $7,750, for each acre; original land-purchase lender receives $5,400 per acre
10. Second mortgages at 7 per cent interest, equal to $1,550 per home, taken back by builder; total proceeds to builder:

$ 40,000	proceeds from mortgage financing in excess of amount needed to pay off construction loans
$ 47,000	proceeds from down payments in excess of proceeds paid to private land-purchase financier
$155,000	proceeds from 2d trust deeds taken back as part of purchase price
$242,000	

Costs of advertising and selling 6% of gross

$ 93,000	
$149,000	total profit
$ 1,490	profit per house.

This illustration indicates the types of financing needed in subdividing, that is, Funds

1. For land purchases
2. For development of sites and construction of homes
3. To aid sale of homes
4. To pay for advertising and sales promotion

The illustration typifies problems faced quite often by subdividers who must use one lender to finance construction and another to finance sales. It includes neither the costs of this type of financing nor other incidental costs in connection with construction, so final profits to the builder might easily be approximately $1,000 to $1,500 per house.

Places where costs might vary considerably are in the engineering, connection of utilities, paving, grading, and street lighting. Listed below are the average cost figures for a 20-acre subdivision of eighty-five lots, or 4¼ lots per acre, on which middle-priced homes are to be built. Sales price of the homes would be approximately $20,000, with lots selling for $5,200–$6,100, depending upon size and location, an average of $5,600 per lot.

Cost Item	Cost per Lot
Engineering	$ 125
Lot grading	100
Concrete paving	142
Curbs and gutters	138
Asphalt paving	295
Sidewalks	125
Water charges	84
Sewers and sewer connections	310
Street lighting	143
Street signs, misc. development costs	32
	$1,494
Maps and permit fees	53
Improvement bond	18
	$1,565
Land costs	2,500
	$4,065
Average sales price per lot	$5,600
Profit per lot	$1,535

APPRAISAL PROBLEMS

An appraiser faced with the problems of estimating the value of a subdivision that is being planned will find that lenders, engineering firms, and building and safety departments are good sources of information on types and amounts of costs to be used in estimating total costs. Usually, the appraiser must also consider the various ways in which parcels might be developed and the costs and returns of each alternative. From these calculations, he can develop recommendations about the highest and best use.

Appraisers should look for indications of any of the following, which have been found to be the chief causes of failure in subdividing:

1. Premature and unwarranted developments, usually due to inadequate market analysis
2. Inaccurate market and locational analysis, the results of which are mispriced homes, over- and underimproved sites, lagging sales, and costs in excess of sales income
3. Poor and inadequate public improvements, which reduce sales and adversely affect values because utilities services are inadequate, sewers do not drain, and, in other ways, living becomes difficult to the detriment of property values
4. Poor designing and engineering, because of which the entire subdivision will present a poor appearance so that sales will be slow
5. Financing at too high costs, requiring sales prices at above-market levels or resulting in loss of profits

31

Analysis of Physical Features of Buildings

ARCHITECTURAL TYPES

Investors should become acquainted with the physical qualities of buildings in order to make more intelligent decisions as to purchases and property management.

The physical makeup of any American community consists of a multitude of different building types, each providing a useful function. These building types may generally be classified as residential, commercial, industrial, institutional, and governmental. Each physical community is molded by economic, social, and political forces that have shaped the pattern of community growth and development. As the national economy has developed from its earliest colonial mercantile capitalism to industrial, financial, and cooperative capitalism, the introduction of new means of transportation, technology, and building materials has served to produce an ever changing architectural style and building type to serve the American people in the performance of their various daily functions.

If we were to trace the growth of American communities during the various periods corresponding to the development of the national economy, we would recognize definite building types, both functional and structural, characteristic of each era. The log cabin, the plantation house, the three-story brick house with mortised and tenoned frame construction are all associated with the early colonial pattern of our society. The period after the American Revolution saw the introduction of the urban row house, wooden factory buildings, governmental buildings, colleges, theaters, and merchants' exchanges. With the development of industrial capitalism, from 1825 on to just prior to the Civil War, came the development of balloon-frame construction, the southern mansion house, warehouses, banks, hotels, custom houses, etc. The first era of financial capitalism, covering the period just prior to the Civil War and ending about 1880, brought with it the development of wood and brick tenements, brownstone houses (in the east), department stores, commercial "blocks," and public schools. As the cities began to expand during the second period of financial capitalism, which brought with it the rise of the corporation, and lasted until the outbreak of World War I, new building types began to appear. These included the early skyscrapers, apartment houses, large town houses, steel-frame office buildings, steel-sash factories, railroad terminals, general hospitals, public libraries, and art and science museums. The period from World War I to the onset of the Great Depression saw the rise of the third stage of financial capitalism and the introduction of mass-production techniques. New building types that appeared in this era included tower-form skyscrapers, movie theaters, medical centers, garden apartments, gas stations, garages, and electric-power stations. The current phase of our economy, characterized by joint business and governmental enterprise in banking, farming, home financing, and scientific research, has seen the introduction of low-cost housing, factory-produced homes, motels, trailer homes, regional shopping centers, and one-story industrial plants.

ARCHITECTURAL STYLES

Concurrent with the introduction of new building types to meet developing needs, there has been a continuing change in architectural styles, particularly as applied to residences. The early colonial buildings were architectural carry-overs from the memory of mechanics, often rooted in medieval practices, and only later were influenced by English book designs, primarily Georgian in character. By adaptation of these designs to the materials available locally, there arose the various residence types that are generally classified as English colonial, Dutch colonial, and southern colonial. The English types were influenced by the woods of New England; the Dutch types, by the stone of New York and Pennsylvania; the southern, by the brick available in the southern colonies.

There followed in succession a variety of architectural styles beginning with the Greek revival (1820–1860), which indicated an interest in the Greek classic types. This was succeeded by the parvenu period (1860–1880), characterized by the erection of expensive architectural monstrosities by the generally uncultured newly rich of that period. Then came the Romanesque period (1880–1893), bringing with it the brownstone mansions—huge, heavy in style, with round-top windows and recessed round- and oval-top doors—of which many examples may still be seen in most of our cities. The Chicago World's Fair of 1893 ushered in the modern eclectic period, based on the philosophy of Louis Sullivan, who advocated a new American style that took as its guiding philosophy the proposition that the function of a building should follow its form. This philosophy also abhorred imitations of stone, brick, wood or other material, and demanded that all ornamentation be original and indigenous, not copies from European designs. At the time that this new philosophy was coming in, two new building materials, steel and concrete, were developed. These two materials revolutionized architecture and made possible the new multistory steel-skeleton office building, the high-rise apartment house, and many other familiar modern structures. The eclectic period is characterized by a taking of the best of several different types to form a superior functional combination. Modern residential construction has been characteristically an adaptation of the Cape Cod colonial, the California ranch, and Spanish types to present-day requirements.

INFLUENCE OF CONSTRUCTION METHODS

Concurrent with the development of style and style changes, American building has been influenced by the results of innovations in mechanical arts. These innovations have added to the more or less simple shelter of years ago a whole complex arrangement of mechanical systems designed to supply the occupants with all manner of services. They have also made possible new services and designs for commercial, industrial, and institutional buildings. As a result of the introduction of these new developments, the relative economic importance of the structure itself has been diminished, and the services and the equipment through which the services have been rendered have taken on more and more importance in the appraisal of buildings.

The problems facing the appraiser in property valuation now require that he have a sound working knowledge not only of basic construction but also of equipment systems.

The problems of reproduction cost, depreciation, operating costs, and market demand must be considered and solved on the basis of knowledge of these systems. As building-equipment costs continually increase to form a major portion of required investment, comprising in the case of modern office buildings some 35 per cent of the total cost, their effect on depreciation, operating costs, and rentals becomes more and more significant.

BUILDING CLASSIFICATION

Structural Classification. Types of construction, quality of materials, floor loads, allowable stresses, and all the other requirements relating to buildings are covered by building codes. Each community has its own building code to which the buildings in that community must conform, and appraisers should have some knowledge of the major requirements in the code

Building codes commonly classify buildings according to type of construction and according to use or occupancy. The most important factor in the classification according to type of construction is the resistance to fire exposure. The classification of buildings according to construction, as given by the National Board of Fire Underwriters, is as follows:

1. Fireproof construction
2. Semifireproof construction
3. Heavy timber construction
4. Ordinary construction
5. Frame construction

This classification may be considered as typical in most areas, and the categories may be defined in the following manner:

Fireproof construction is that in which the walls are of approved masonry or reinforced concrete and in which the structural members have fire-resistive ratings sufficient to withstand the hazard involved in the occupancy—but not less than a four-hour rating for bearing walls, fire walls, party walls, isolated piers, columns and wall supporting girders; a three-hour rating for walls and girders other than those already specified and for beams, floors, roofs, and floor fillings; and a two-hour rating for fire partitions

Semifireproof construction is similar to fireproof construction except that bearing walls, isolated piers and columns, and wall-supporting girders may have a three-hour rating instead of a four-hour rating, and exposed beams, floors, and floor fillings may have a two-hour rating instead of a three-hour rating.

Heavy timber construction is that in which the walls are of brick, concrete, or reinforced concrete, and in which the interior structural elements including posts, floors, and roof consist of heavy timbers with smooth flat surfaces assembled to avoid thin sections, sharp projections, and concealed or inaccessible spaces, and in which wall-supporting girders and structural members of steel or reinforced concrete, if used in lieu of timber construction, have a fire-resistive rating of not less than three-hours. Frequently this type of construction is known as mill construction or slow-burning construction.

Ordinary construction is that in which the exterior walls are of approved masonry or reinforced concrete, and in which the interior structural members are wholly or partly of wood of smaller dimension than required for heavy timber construction, or of steel or iron that is not protected as required for fireproof or semifireproof construction.

Frame construction is that in which the exterior or party walls are wholly or partly of wood. This type includes buildings with brick or stone veneer, stucco, or sheet metal over wood exterior walls.

No building is really fireproof. The fire-exposure conditions may be such as to cause damage to the highest type of construction, particularly if surrounding buildings are burning. The term *fire-resistive* is a more accurate description of the actual situation. The degree of resistance to fire hazard is determined by exposing samples of material or building members to a fire of specified intensity and, in most cases, to a fire-hose stream when the sampled material is in a heated condition. The fire ratings are then determined in accordance with the performance each material provides and are expressed in hours.

Buildings may also be classified structurally as bearing-wall construction or skeleton construction. In bearing-wall construction the loads are transmitted to the foundations by walls, while in skeleton construction all loads are transmitted to the foundations by a rigidly connected framework of steel or reinforced concrete beams, girders, trusses, and columns, with enclosing walls, partitions, and floors supported at each floor level by the structural frame.

Use Classification. Building codes also classify structures according to use. The most typical classifications are

1. Residential
2. Commercial
3. Industrial
4. Institutional
5. Governmental, or public

Residential buildings are those in which sleeping accommodations are provided. These include dwellings, tenements, multifamily apartments, hotels, rooming houses, dormitories, convents, studios, and clubhouses.

Commercial buildings are those occupied for the transaction of business; for the rendering of professional services; for the display, sale, or storage of merchandise; or for the supplying of food, drink, or other physical comforts; they generally include such buildings as office buildings, stores, markets, restaurants, and laboratories.

Industrial buildings are those used for the manufacture and storage of commodities and include factories, workshops, garages, warehouses, freight depots, and grain elevators among the most common types.

Institutional buildings are those in which persons are kept to receive medical, charitable, or other care and treatment, or in which persons are held or detained by reason of public or civic duty. This class includes, among others, hospitals, asylums, sanitariums, firehouses, police stations, and jails.

Governmental, or, more accurately, *public,* buildings are those in which people congregate for civic, political, educational, religious, social, or recreational purposes. This class includes courthouses, schools, colleges, libraries, museums, exhibition halls, lecture halls, churches, lodge rooms, dance halls, theaters, armories, and recreation piers.

STRUCTURAL ELEMENTS

The appraiser should have some knowledge of the elements that go into the construction of buildings and the materials of which they are composed. The structures of all buildings are made up of various combinations and forms of walls, columns, ties, beams, trusses, rigid frames, and arches. These elements, along with the foundations, floors, roof, outside walls, and utilities, comprise the major portions of all buildings and account for the major elements of dollar investment. The type and quality of the materials used, as well as the workmanship applied to putting these elements in place, have an important effect on not only the physical life but also the economic life of the building. The assembling of the various structural elements so that each may perform its functions is known as framing. One classification of buildings is on the basis of the functions of the walls. A building may be classed as wall bearing if the walls carry their share of the dead, live, and other loads. If, however, the loads including the weight of the walls are carried by the structural frame consisting of columns, beams, trusses, rigid frames, and arches, the building is classed as skeleton construction.

The various types of buildings generally have characteristic structural patterns. Frame construction is generally used for one- and two-family houses and not for larger buildings. Ordinary construction, while occasionally used for dwellings, is found most frequently in apartment houses, stores, and industrial buildings which do not need to be slow-burning or fireproof. Slow-burning construction is found most often in manufacturing plants and industrial buildings requiring a substantial form of construction which will offer considerable resistance to fire. Steel construction is extensively used on all types of buildings except small dwellings. Reinforced concrete may be used for nearly all classes of buildings where good construction is essential. For buildings up to fifteen to twenty stories in height, steel and reinforced concrete are equally competitive; for higher buildings, steel is better, owing to the greater speed in construction. Types of buildings commonly constructed of reinforced concrete include apartment houses, hotels, office buildings, schoolhouses, warehouses, and industrial buildings. Frequently buildings with a steel framework will have floors and roof of reinforced concrete.

BASIC PARTS OF A BUILDING

A brief discussion of the basic parts of a building is presented so that the appraiser may recognize and understand the function each plays in the complete structure.

Columns. Columns are the vertical members of a structural frame. They are called upon to transfer the floor and roof loads to the foundations. Columns are often called *posts,* especially when made of timber. The light, closely spaced, vertical members used in frame construction are called *studs.* Relatively slender blocks of masonry carrying loads and stresses are known as *piers.* Sometimes stone and brick columns are called *pillars,* which is a non-technical term synonymous with the term *pier.* Columns are usually made of timber, steel, reinforced concrete, or cast iron, and in some cases stone columns are used for ornamental purposes.

Beams and Girders. Beams and girders are structural members supported at one or more points along their length and designed to carry loads perpendicular to their length. When any distinction is made between beams and girders, the beam is the smaller member and may be supported by the girder. Many types of beams are used in building construction. Some of the more common are *lintels,* which are beams supporting the masonry and other loads over an opening in the wall; *joists,* which are closely spaced beams supporting a floor or ceiling; and *rafters,* which are closely spaced beams supporting the roof and running parallel to the slope of the roof. Beams may be constructed of wood, steel, or reinforced concrete. Stone may occasionally be used in lintels, but, owing to their low flexural strength, they are supported by steel lintels which do not show on the face of the building.

Trusses. Trusses are framed structures consisting of a group of triangles arranged in a single plane in such a manner that loads applied at the points of intersection of the members will cause only direct stresses in the members. Trusses may be built wholly of wood, of wood and steel rods combined, or of rolled-steel sections. Concrete is used to a limited extent but is not usually a suitable material for trusses.

Arches and Rigid Frames. Arches are usually constructed of wood, steel, or reinforced concrete. Their primary function is structural. They are used chiefly for the support of roofs covering large areas, such as those required on auditoriums, armories, field houses, gymnasiums, dance halls, garages, and exhibition buildings. Rigid frames are rapidly coming into use. The most common type of rigid frame consists of a roof girder or arch rigidly connected to the columns at its ends so that the three elements act together in resisting vertical and lateral loads.

Floors. The most common form of floor construction for non-fireproof buildings consists of wood joists supporting a 1-inch wood subfloor, and a matched wood finished floor, preferably with a layer of building paper or other material between the subfloor and the finished floor. A substitute for the matched finished floor might be title, terrazzo, or some type of asbestos tile. Other types of floors are heavy wood subfloors on steel beams, concrete slabs on light steel joists, reinforced concrete slabs sup-

ported by steel beams, and reinforced-concrete slabs supported by reinforced-concrete beams.

Roofs. Roofs of buildings are divided into various types, depending
upon the shape. *Flat* roofs are extensively used on all kinds of buildings.
Gable roofs slope in two directions and are widely used, especially on
residences. *Hip* roofs slope in four directions and are also widely used.
Gambrel roofs slope in two directions, but there is a break in the slope
on each side. The gambrel roof is used for residences because of the use
that can be made of the space under the roof. *Mansard* roofs slope in four
directions, but there is a break in each slope. *Saw-toothed* roofs are used
widely on industrial buildings because of the advantages they offer in light
and ventilation. An illustrated diagram of the various roof types will be
found in the Appendix.

There are many types of roof coverings, and some of the factors that
enter into the selection of a roofing material include slope of the roof,
durability, initial cost, maintenance cost, resistance to fire, weight, type of
roof construction, and appearance. Generally speaking, the longest-lasting
materials are clay tile, slate, copper, zinc, and lead. The shortest-lasting
include asphalt shingles and corrugated steel. In between are asbestos
shingles, cement tile, built-up roofing, and wood shingles. The most expensive roofing materials are clay tile, slate, sheet copper, and lead. The
low-priced materials include asphalt shingles, wood shingles, built-up roofing, and corrugated steel. Maintenance costs are lowest with built-up
roofing, copper, zinc, and lead, and are highest with wood shingles, corrugated steel, and tin sheets.

In general, for high-class buildings and residences with sloping roofs,
clay tile, slate, asbestos shingles, and sheet copper seem to be the most
suitable. Less expensive buildings will probably use asphalt or wood
shingles, small cement tiles, zinc, or tin. On the cheapest sort of buildings,
corrugated zinc or steel or prepared roofing will be found. For flat roofs,
built-up roofing is the most satisfactory.

Other Parts of a Building. The heating, plumbing, and electrical systems will be discussed under the next section, which deals with the effects
of design and construction on value. The other integral parts of the building, such as the stairs, windows, partitions, doors, etc., while important in
the whole picture of building construction, do not require discussion in this
volume.

EFFECTS OF DESIGN AND CONSTRUCTION ON VALUE

The investment value of various buildings is influenced by their income
potentialities and their probable resale value. Both of these factors are, in
turn, affected by the physical condition, functional utility, design, and lay-

out of the building. Each building in its class must be compared with buildings of similar age and style and with the typical modern building performing the same function.

As land costs, wage rates, and material prices have shown a steady postwar rise, there has been an attempt to devise new techniques and materials to hold costs down in relation to the amount of rent obtainable for new space. The development of new techniques, equipment, and material, in turn, has led to new architectural designs. Each advance in design, technology, and equipment that is reflected in the growing supply of commercial and apartment-house space acts either as a potential or an actual threat to the value of the pre-existing stock of space. Similarly, any breakthrough in technology that permits building costs to reverse their upward spiral will adversely affect the value of existing buildings.

The appraiser must keep informed of new trends in materials, design, and space requirements in order to make a meaningful analysis of the building. He must know the relationship between the existing materials, utilities, and equipment and operating costs and rentals. For example, many new office buildings are constructed with metal-panel (aluminum or stainless steel) or double plate-glass walls in place of the more familiar masonry cavity walls. From an aesthetic point of view, the new types of walls have greater appeal. However, their initial cost is greater, and operating costs for heating, maintenance, insurance, and real estate taxes also seem to be more than for masonry wall construction. In return for their increased operating costs, they provide greater amounts of rentable area, better lighting, and some savings in construction time.

What has been said about exterior walls applies also to the other components of the building: the frame, the interior structure and layout, the utilities. From the point of view of a builder embarking upon the construction of a new building, the prime consideration must be the use of materials, equipment, and layout which will produce the maximum returns for each dollar invested in costs. The consideration must not be the original cost of a specific material or piece of equipment but the ultimate cost. The ultimate cost would take into consideration those factors which tend to hold operating expenses to a minimum and guarantee full rentals over as long a period as possible. Good layout, sturdy materials, and efficient utility systems go a long way toward realizing these objectives.

From the point of view of an investor seeking to purchase an existing building, the objectives will be largely the same: smooth operation at minimum expense to realize maximum rentals. However, since the investor does not have any choice in the matter of types of materials, equipment, and design, he can only express his opinion by the price he is willing to pay for an existing property. In an area where the locational advantages are equal, the prices that can be obtained for various investment properties should reflect the positive or negative aspect of an existing building. Frequently, a few years' operating experience will show up any defects in design and construction that were not apparent at the time of construction. When they appear, the market will be quick to evaluate them.

Just as value comparisons can be made of similar buildings constructed in one period, so comparisons can also be made between similar functional types created during different periods. While the older buildings tend to lose value relative to the new owing to deterioration and obsolescence, not every building of one vintage will lose value in the same proportions. Well-designed, well-constructed, and well-maintained structures will have greater value than those that suffer from poor construction, maintenance, and design. The appraiser's function is to analyze the building in the light of its relative physical and functional soundness so as to be able to predict its future earning power in the light of existing competitive buildings and probable new technological improvements.

ANALYSIS OF APARTMENT HOUSES

Type and Design. Apartment houses may be classified according to construction types as fire-resistive, non-fire-resistive, and "fireproof." Most apartment houses six stories or less in height are of the non-fire-resistive type, while those over that height are usually classified as fire-resistive or "fireproof."

For six-story buildings, the cost of non-fire-resistive construction is generally figured at 5 to 10 per cent less than that of fire-resistive construction. But this is offset to some extent by the lower cost of insurance in the fire-resistive buildings and by the increased rentals obtainable from larger room sizes owing to the fact that 2-inch fire-resistive partitions are used instead of 5-inch plaster and wood stud partitions. Apartment houses of six stories or less are usually found in relatively inexpensive land permitting rentals that will cater to the middle-income populace.

Large modern apartment houses are usually built in the shape of an H, L, or V in order to obtain a degree of privacy as well as a maximum amount of light and air for each apartment. Apartments built upon rather small, but expensive, land are usually H-shaped to take advantage of the maximum coverage. Recently, two significant new designs have made their appearance. The first is the *tower design,* and the second is the *open-corridor design.*

The *tower design,* or *tower scheme,* is a name given to a plan type which is approximately square, with the rooms disposed around all four sides of a central service core. This type has made its appearance in Chicago and New York, a notable example being the Levitt House. This plan requires a high-rise apartment house but has a minimum of perimeter wall construction and has short utility runs, affording initial construction economies. It also provides for a relatively small public corridor space, with the attendant economies in operating expenses. In most cases, there are only four to six apartments per floor, providing cross-ventilation and two exposures per apartment, giving it a high livability rating. The main drawback is the initial high cost of elevators, which is usually two to two and one-half times higher than in the standard interior-corridor layout which provides ten to twelve apartments per floor.

The *open-corridor design* allows all apartments to be reached by means of outdoor corridors. The usual shape is long and thin. The outstanding advantage is improved livability derived from through ventilation and two exposures for each apartment. All rooms including bathrooms have outside light and ventilation. The inside corridor is eliminated entirely. The open-corridor plan eliminates the cost of mechanical ventilation for the bathrooms and kitchens. In addition, it does away with the objections usually voiced by tenants about inadequate light and ventilation in modern interior kitchens and baths, which became features of new apartment houses solely as space-saving and cost-cutting elements. Opposed to the advantages in this plan are considerations of snow removal for which provision must be made. This is usually done by the installation of electric heating cable in the floors of all open corridors. The open corridor must usually be one and one-half times the length of interior corridors in order to accommodate an economic number of apartments per floor. This requires additional stair construction, as most building codes limit the distance from apartment to stairs. Since all apartment doors open to the outside, the doors must be of the exterior type and weatherstripped. Finally, the long thin shape with its high perimeter to enclosed area is not basically an economic design, and in high-rise buildings extra costs for wind bracing must be assumed.

Most standard apartment houses suffer from a lack of amenities afforded by the newer design types. Except for those apartments built for the upper income bracket, the typical speculative builder is concerned with getting as many rental rooms in his building as possible. Kitchen, bath, and dining space are kept at a minimum, while the other rooms are planned to be as spacious as possible within the confines of the architectural plan. Since the amounts of mortgage loans and rental income depend a great deal on the number of rooms in the building, the temptation to substitute quantity for quality is generally irresistible.

Structure and Exterior. The relationship between initial cost economies, potential operating economies and basic structural components is well known to architects. The design must be consistent with the system of construction. For smaller multiple dwellings, up to six stories, the non-fire-resistive type of construction is dictated by lower initial costs and fair economy in maintenance, and in a highly competitive rental market this has been the predominant mode of construction.

The high-rise or luxury-type apartment houses are either of a steel-frame or reinforced-concrete-frame construction with what is known as "spattered" columns. New developments in high-rise construction, such as the two-column cantilever system, which permits the floor slabs to cantilever out from two instead of the usual four rows of columns, with the slabs supporting light-weight exterior walls, promise economies in construction and operating costs and permit better apartment arrangement. Other new construction systems are the lift-slab and box-frame systems, used mainly in Europe and Latin America, but beginning to attract the attention of American architects. Finally, there is a construction system that utilizes light steel framing. This system was used in the Levitt House and in some recent luxury-type apartment houses in New York City. The use of light steel has proved economic, especially in foundation costs.

Analysis of exterior walls, as we have already indicated, requires consideration not only of their initial costs but also of their insulation value and, thus, of the heating costs that will occur as a result of the type of wall used. The walls are usually of a masonry type or of a prefabricated metal or concrete type. Allied with the problem of the proper wall to use to keep heating costs as low as possible is the problem of window selection, as over 77 per cent of the heat loss in a room usually comes from the window glass and window-frame infiltration. New structural ideas that will incorporate proper insulation for the walls and windows, while initially costlier, should ultimately more than pay back their increased investment by savings in fuel costs.

Interior. The analysis of apartment interiors must consider the interior partitions, the floor, the ceiling and bathroom finishes, and the cubing heights. In each case, it will be found that the prime consideration in new construction has been initial cost economy. Partitions and floor slabs have been decreased in thickness, and ceiling heights have been steadily reduced to their legal minimum. Unfortunately, much of this has been accomplished at the expense of livability, which poses a threat to the future appeal of those apartments. Tenants frequently complain about noises that originate from adjoining apartments, noisy plumbing fixtures, and a closed-in feeling caused by low ceilings. In these respects, the well-constructed apartment houses of an older vintage seem more desirable but are usually more expensive to operate. The savings in heating and painting costs by use of low ceilings are obvious, but, in a truly competitive market, it remains to be seen if the new buildings will be able to compete, particularly if some relatively inexpensive method of soundproofing is developed.

Mechanical Equipment. In order to properly analyze an apartment building, the appraiser must be cognizant of the many new developments in central heating, air conditioning, plumbing, and electrical and elevator systems that have taken place in an effort to create a greater degree of service and appeal. As more and more services are added, the equipment necessary for their proper function has become a greater and greater part of the initial cost and operating expenses of the property. In addition, the introduction of a new service such as air conditioning serves as a strong incentive for attracting and keeping tenants at high rentals. It also serves to decrease the relative desirability of all non-air-conditioned apartments, for, as more and more of the air-conditioned units come onto the market, they will attract more and more tenants out of the older houses. Thus, the problems of building cost, functional depreciation, operating costs, relative desirability, and warranted rehabilitation costs are all bound up with the study of the mechanical systems.

HEATING. Heating systems may be classified, according to the mediums used to distribute the heat, into either warm-air, hot-water, or steam heating. The function of a heating system is to burn fuel, usually coal, oil, or gas, to produce heat which is conveyed by one of the mediums to the various parts of the building. The system includes the furnace or boiler plus all piping, valves, air vents, traps, radiators, and heat controls, the chimney, and the mechanical means of introducing fuel into the furnace. A heating system should be operated in as efficient a manner as possible in order to ensure the comfort and health of the tenants and to keep costs as low as possible. The appraiser is not expected to be a heating engineer, but, where he can determine from inspection and inquiry that the function of the system is not being performed properly, he must make adequate allowance in his appraisal.

The problem thus reduces itself to the proper installation of the original heating system, its maintenance, and its cost of operation. Frequently, a builder may select a system that requires a minimum of initial cost but involves higher yearly fuel costs. Such a system exists in some cities where a utility company will supply steam heat from a central plant via underground pipes to a building. This obviates the expense of installing a boiler and fuel-storage space, reduces repairs, and provides more basement space for other purposes. However, the fuel costs are higher than if a separate heating system were installed.

The proper evaluation of a heating system depends upon a comprehension of heating principles. Heat is a form of energy. It is important to measure it by some universal yardstick. That yardstick is the *BTU* (British thermal unit), defined as the heat energy necessary to raise the temperature of one pound of water 1° F. The BTU is used to determine the value of a pound of coal, a gallon of oil, or a cubic foot of gas. It offers a basis for comparison of the relative values of various fuels used in heating.

A building heated by steam has fuel fed into a boiler partly filled with water. The fuel burns and transfers its heat to the water in the boiler, thus generating steam. The steam travels through pipes into radiators in rooms throughout the building and then transfers its heat to the air in the various rooms. The air circulates throughout each room, thus creating the proper room temperature. In performing its work, the steam is condensed to water and returns to the boiler, to be reheated to steam. The process is continuous. If the condensed steam returns to the boiler through the pipe from which it came, the heating plant is termed a *one-pipe* system. If it returns through an entirely different pipe, installed for that purpose, the heating plant is termed a *two-pipe* system.

A principle in physics is put to use in heating with steam. A pound of water will rise in temperature 1° for every BTU it absorbs until it reaches its boiling point, at 212°. But it does not turn to steam until it has absorbed an additional 970 BTU's. Its temperature remains at 212°. When it has absorbed the additional BTU's, the water is transformed into a gas—steam. This amount of heat energy is called the *latent heat of evaporation*. When the process is reversed and the steam condenses to water, the 970 BTU's, which were originally absorbed to turn water into steam, are given up by the steam and made available for heating. Thus, the latent heat of evaporation becomes a major part of the heat value.

Boilers. In order for the system to function properly, the boiler, pipes, and radiators must be of just the proper capacity to accomplish its purpose. Boiler and radiator capacities are generally indicated in "square feet of radiation." There are a few rules of thumb for determining the size or capacity of radiators to be installed in rooms or of boilers to be installed. The size is measured in square feet of radiation for every 2 square feet of glass, plus 1 square foot for every 20 square feet of exposed wall, plus 1 square foot for every 200 cubic feet of space. The total will be the size of the radiator required, measured in square feet of radiation. For boilers, the total of all the radiation required in all rooms in the building, plus 25 per cent for heat loss caused by transmitting steam through the pipes, should give the approximate size of the boiler. Where the piping is insulated, the heat loss will drop to 10–15 per cent, giving a corresponding potential fuel saving. Another check to determine boiler size may be made by dividing the cubic contents of a building by 85. The result, in square feet of radiation, should approximate the proper size of the boiler.

The most important single element in the heating system is the furnace or boiler. Good efficiency depends on proper design. Most manufacturers prepare data sheets on their boilers so that given capacities and performances may be obtained and used for analytical purposes. Boilers are usually a cast-iron sectional or steel, designed for coal or oil, or a gas-fired design, for gas. Most cast-iron sectional types were originally designed for coal but are adaptable for conversion to oil. Such is the usual round boiler found in smaller houses, and, when converted to oil from coal, its efficiency is rather low. For larger buildings, the vertical section cast-iron boiler is used. The sections are assembled one behind the other, standing vertically, and the whole assembly is covered with either insulation or an insulated metal casing. These boilers are more efficient than the round type.

The steel-tube boiler is usually of the low-pressure fire type in which the combustion gases pass through tubes inserted in a cylindrical drum containing the water. The two principal types in use are the brick-set return tubular boiler and the portable steel firebox boiler. The brick-set type has a furnace of brick construction and is set in brick to the top of the drum; the steel firebox type has a furnace of steel-walled construction, the walls containing water. Coal-burning steel boilers are now almost invariably made with automatic stokers to feed the coal into the furnace.

Gas-fired boilers are of special construction in order to get every possible bit of heat into the water, since gas is usually a more expensive fuel. The design is usually that of a water-tube boiler with small, thickly nested copper tubes for the highest heat transfer.

One-Pipe System. The one-pipe gravity return steam-heating system is found in the majority of privately financed multiple dwellings of six stories or less in the eastern part of the United States. Other systems that may be found in use are the one- or two-pipe hot-water system, the two-pipe vacuum steam-heating system (used in most high-rise apartments), a one-pipe continuous-loop steam system developed by the Metropolitan Life Insurance Company for its housing projects, and a central steam system.

In the one-pipe system, the steam is conveyed from the boiler to the radiators by a series of pipes which also carry the condensed steam back to the boiler. Air in the system is eliminated by air valves located on each radiator near the top and upon the opposite end from the intake valves. In this type of system, the steam pipes slope downward toward the boiler from the farthest point so that the water may flow back to the furnace.

Two-Pipe System. In two-pipe systems, the condensed steam (water) is returned to the boiler by a separate set of pipes. Thermostatic traps are installed in the end of the radiator, opposite the intake valve. These traps allow water to pass but close when the radiator fills with steam. This allows the amount of steam entering the radiators to be controlled and is, thus, an improvement over the one-pipe system. In the one-pipe system, the supply valve must be kept either completely open or tightly closed; otherwise the radiator will fill with water, causing hammering, and will not heat. The two-pipe system is better adapted to larger buildings, and, while it costs more initially to install, it provides greater efficiency.

Vacuum System. The vacuum system is considered an improvement over the two-pipe system. In this method, a pump is installed upon the return apparatus near the boiler. It pumps the air out of the lines, creating and holding a vacuum in the system. Thus, little or no steam pressure is required on the furnace.

A hot-water system works either by gravity or by a pump which makes for quicker and more positive circulation. It is best suited to smaller buildings. In the gravity system, the water loses its density as it is warmed and replaces the cold water in the piping and radiators. The cold water, in turn, replaces the water in the boiler through circulation.

The central steam system, used primarily in large cities for commercial buildings, is sometimes found in apartment buildings close by the central business districts. Mains laid in the streets and alleys carry steam from a central steam-generating plant to the various buildings. This saves space for heating equipment and fuel storage and removes the problem of ash removal, firemen, and maintenance employees. The steam is forced at high temperature to the building's location, where connections are made to the heating system. As was previously pointed out, this system is usually the highest in fuel costs but very economic in installation costs.

AIR CONDITIONING. The development of air conditioning for apartment houses is a recent and significant factor. As more and more buildings come on the market with built-in air conditioning, the lack of such equipment in older buildings creates another form of obsolescence for these structures.

Air-conditioning systems are generally of two types, the central system and the individual built-in unit system. The central system is generally designed to perform both heating and cooling functions through a system of ducts, fans, filters, coils, compressors, and condensers. Finned copper radiators are generally used for the heating and cooling element. The only purposes of an air-conditioning system are to remove heat from the inhabited space and to dispose of it. Fans circulate a mixture of outside and recirculated air. All air passing through the system is cleaned by filters. Mechanical filters made of such materials as spun glass are coated with adhesive which catches and holds lint, dust, and dirt. Warm, humid air is drawn over a cooling coil. Heat always flows from a higher to a lower temperature level. Therefore, the coil, kept cold by a gaseous refrigerant such as Freon passing through it, absorbs heat from the air. As the air is cooled, excess moisture is condensed away from it and drained away. All this time, a compressor has been drawing Freon out of the cooling coil and compressing it, with all the heat "units" it has trapped, into a much smaller volume. This raises the temperature of the Freon so that heat may be discarded to water in the condenser. Water circulating through a water coil in the condenser absorbs the heat from the Freon and is either returned to a cooling tower or disposed of directly. This condensing process returns the Freon to a liquid state; in this form it flows back to the cooling coil to be allowed to capture and dispose of more heat "units" entering the room. In winter, a separate steam or hot-water coil in the system supplies heat where needed.

The central air-conditioning system is usually found in high-rental apartment buildings and is more costly to install than the individual built-in unit conditioner located under the windows. The built-in conditioners set flush with the exterior walls and arranged in a uniform pattern are aesthetically more desirable than the individual unit conditioners that extend beyond the exterior walls haphazardly. In addition, the built-in type permits full use of the window space. However, the built-in unit has its disavantages. While providing the air conditioning that is required for modern living, it also requires additional expense for fuel and repairs. A greater amount of heat is lost owing to the wall openings, and provision must be made for servicing the individual units. Service charges may run from $7 to $15 per unit per annum, depending on the kind of service and the frequency of filter changes required.

PLUMBING. An evaluation of the plumbing system of an apartment building involves consideration of aesthetic appeal and durability. The appeal of the kitchen and bathroom fixtures is significant. Items such as bathtubs, lavatories, kitchen sinks, and water closets, are very important in maintaining rental values. The appraiser must be familiar with the latest designs in these fixtures and must be able to pinpoint any functional obsolescence due to outmoded fixtures. Modernization of bathrooms and kitchens frequently provides high returns per dollar invested and goes a long way toward maintaining the value of the rented space.

The piping used in the building usually comprises a large part of the cost of the initial installation of the plumbing and heating systems. If the piping is durable and selected to suit its service requirements, it will eliminate the possibility of tenant complaints, future maintenance, and repair expenses. While brass piping is the most desirable from the point of view of ultimate cost, it is also the most expensive initially. Other serviceable materials are copper, black wrought iron, galvanized wrought iron, galvanized steel, and black steel, the initial costs generally decreasing in the order named. For hot-water and drinking-water lines, copper and brass are generally preferred, as corrosive action will shorten the life of pipes constucted with other materials.

The location of the pipes is another factor in aesthetic appeal and maintenance costs. For aesthetic reasons, there should be a minimum of exposed piping, but concealed piping may make repairs very expensive if wall plastering or floors must be torn out to make them accessible. For concealed piping, the most durable materials are used, while separate pipe shafts for risers afford the maximum concealment with ease of access in the event of needed repairs.

ELECTRICAL EQUIPMENT. A building will generally suffer in rental value whenever its electrical system fails to function properly or is incapable of meeting the latest trends in modern living. There is a trend toward indirect lighting and a greater number of outlets. In addition, the constantly increasing use of appliances such as air-conditioning units, television sets, and automatic toasters, requires more adequate wiring. The spreading use of color television and electrical cooking ranges will further require more efficient electrical systems, the lack of which in any building will be a handicap to these structures and is a source of future obsolescence.

In high-grade fireproof construction, the electrical systems are generally designed with oversize conduits to permit increasing the circuits or power loads that may be required in the future. In ordinary construction, the conduits will ordinarily be of a size sufficient to accommodate the circuits for which they were designed.

The former standards for lighting cabinets, featuring steel cabinets and a number of knife, snap, or tumbler switch cutouts with fuse protection, have given way to the modern cabinet in which the circuits are protected by circuit breakers instead of fuses, thus eliminating fuse-renewal trouble and expense. Similarly, the old snap switch and its successor, the tumbler-type switch, both noisy, have given way to the mercury-tube tumbler switch, a silent mechanism which has greater appeal.

Probably the greatest single source of tenant dissatisfaction is the insufficiency and/or improper placement of electrical service outlets in an apartment. The great use of floor lamps, radios, television sets, electric clocks, etc., has made this element of the electrical system most important. In addition, inadequate electrical outlets lead to overloading the circuits with unsightly extension wires and create a definite fire hazard.

ELEVATORS. Electric elevators have now replaced the old hydraulic types, which are considered obsolete. Further, the self-service type of elevator is now standard for most new buildings, regardless of size or rental level. Only in the highest luxury-type and cooperative apartment houses will the manually operated elevators still be found. In some new high-rise apartment houses, the passenger elevators will be self-service but the service elevator will be manually operated in order to afford protection and assistance to the tenants. Many of the older luxury-type apartments have converted from manual to self-service types in order to make savings in the wage bill. In many properties, these savings may spell the difference between profitable and unprofitable operation. In those cases where tenants complain of a diminution of services and lack of protection when a conversion is undertaken, another innovation has been introduced. This consists of a closed-circuit television system installed in the elevator, which provides a doorman with a view of the elevator as it proceeds from the lobby floor to its destination.

Inspection Procedure. In inspecting an apartment building, the appraiser must have a standard by which to measure the physical and functional adequacy of the property under appraisal. The inspection must be made in such form that estimates of maintenance and rehabilitation expenses, accrued depreciation, rental value, and possible economic life expectancies may be based on fact.

To accomplish the purpose of such an inspection, the appraiser must not only have an understanding of the basic construction data but must also have a planned method of procedure and an orderly system of recording his observed data.

The most logical way to plan the inspection is first to consider the type of building and then to plan the steps by which the inspection will take place. Having planned the steps, the appraiser should be equipped with a form on which he can record his observations. A typical form that has been tested and used is illustrated in Figure 18.

The form should be of fairly rigid thick paper that permits easy notation, and it should contain a printed check list of the items to be inspected. The use of such a form will remove the necessity of carrying a clipboard and has been found to be very practical. Other advantages of a printed form are that it serves as a reminder to the appraiser not to overlook any of the items that have a significant bearing upon the value of the property and that it provides him with a permanent record of the condition of the building, about which he may be required to testify at some future date.

OTHER INVESTMENT BUILDINGS

Just as with apartment-house properties, analyses of other types of investment property such as office buildings, garages, stores, and motels require some knowledge of the latest construction practices and the relationship between physical condition, functional utility, rental value, operating expenses, and current market value and trends. We will now proceed to comment briefly on some of the other investment types of property.

Office Buildings. The measure of efficiency of the services offered to the tenants in an office building is the ratio of net rentable area to gross area. The net rentable area of office space is generally considered to be the space between the outside wall and the corridor wall.

INSPECTION REPORT

(MULTIPLE DWELLING)

DATE: .... PROJECT: ....

INSPECTOR: .... PARCEL: .... BLOCK: .... LOT: ....

ADDRESS: ....

IMPROVEMENT: OLT   NLT   DWG   RMG HSE

    OTHER ....

    Stories .... (Basement................. Cellar.............)

    Construction .... Age ....

    Plot Size...

    Bldg Size...

EXTERIOR DESCRIPTION:

    FRONT:

    Facade (Material) ....

    Sash and Trim ....

    Cornice ....

    Fire Escapes ....

    Stoop ....

    Entrance Doors ....

    Entrance Location ....

    Store Fronts ....

    REAR & COURTS:

    Sash & Trim ....

    Fire Escapes ....

    Yard Surface ....

    Fences ....

PUBLIC SPACE:

	VESTIBULE	MAIN HALL	UPPER HALLS
Floors			
Wainscot			
Walls			
Ceilings			
Condition			
Mail Boxes			

APARTMENT DOORS: ....

STAIRS:

    Treads ....   Soffits ....

    Risers ....   Hand Rails ....

    Sides ....   Condition ....

ELEVATOR: ....

INCINERATOR: ....   DUMBWAITER: ....

Fig. 18. Inspection report for a multiple

The newer postwar office buildings have generally been constructed with an outside wall of metal or glass panels. These walls are thinner than the conventional masonry wall and thus increase the net rentable area. Stairs and elevators generally form a core, and current lighting and air-conditioning developments permit the distance from the outside wall to the corridor to be increased over prewar averages. The ratio of net rentable area to gross area has been increased to over 80 per cent as compared with 60–70 per cent for older office buildings or 70–80 per cent for those built in the 1920's.

SPRINKLER: .... FIRE ALARM: ....

ROOF: Access ....

    Type ....

    Condition ....

    Misc. ....

BASEMENT:

    Entry ....

    Full .... Part (Size) ....

    Clg Ht. ....Clg Finish ....

    Floors .... Walls ....

    Boiler Room ....

    Comml Space......................................

    Apts. ....

    Misc. ....

CELLAR (Sub-Base.) Entry ....

    Full .... Part (Size) ....

    Floors .... Walls .... Ceiling ...

    Boiler Rm. (Describe Above)

    Fuel Storage

HEATING:

    Central .... [Steam   Hot Water   Hot Air]

    Boiler ....

    .... Fuel ....

    Individual (Type) ....

HOT WATER:

    Central .... Individual .... None .....

    Boiler ....

    Fuel ....

    If Individual (Type) ....

PLUMBING: Brass .... Galv. .... Cond. ......

LAYOUT: (Designate Baths & Toilets)

    Basement ....

    1st Flr ....

    Upper Flrs ....

Total No: Stores .... Apts. .... Rooms ....

    Bathrooms .... Toilets ....

    Other Units ....

BATHROOMS/TOILETS:

    Floors .... Tub ....

    Wainscot .... Shower ....

    Walls .... Bowl ....

    Ceilings .... Other ....

        Cond ....

KITCHENS/KITCHENETTES:

    Floors .... Walls .... Ceilings ....

    Sink .... Wash Tub ....

    Bath Tub .... Gas Range ....

    Refrig .... Cabinets ....

    Tenants claim ownership of ....

    Cond. ....

APARTMENTS:

    Floors .... Walls .... Ceilings ....

    Cond. ....

GENERAL CONDITION OF BLDG. ....

SUPT. & SALARY: ....

TYPE OF TENANCY: ....

MISCELLANEOUS: ....

STORES & COMMERCIAL SPACE:

Space	Size	Tenant and Use	Rent, Lease, Remarks

dwelling (Sanders A. Kahn Associates, Inc.).

The services in the new buildings include air conditioning, fluorescent lighting, automatic or autotronic elevators, acoustic ceilings for soundproofing, adequate wiring for office machinery, and good exterior appeal for tenants.

The older buildings were generally constructed with 8-foot-wide corridors which served offices on either side. The distance from outside wall to corridor wall was generally 25–30 feet and lacked the air conditioning, automatic elevators, adequate wiring, and other features that can be found in the newer buildings.

One aspect of the ability to create a greater ratio of rentable area to gross area has been the greater rental income that has been realized and the ability to pay higher land prices in the face of increased construction costs. Another feature has been the practice of renting an entire floor or floors to large corporate tenants, with the tenant indicating the layout of the office space to the builder or making his own interior layout after renting a bare floor. This practice has further increased the rentable-area ratio for the builder.

Older buildings, in order to meet the competition afforded by the new structures, have undergone extensive modernization programs that have included installation of air conditioning, rewiring, and installation of autotronic elevators. Even some of the early postwar buildings have converted to autotronic elevator operation where they found the labor costs for elevator operation to be excessive. In one 1950 building with nine elevators, where the wage and operating cost exclusive of electric power came to over $80,000 annually, it was possible to convert to autotronic elevators at a cost of some $240,000 with a resultant wage saving of over $50,000 per annum.

In other cases, older buildings have been able to instal air-conditioning systems that have brought increased rentals from the tenants. The costs of air-conditioning systems will vary widely with the type installed. A good system, providing year-round cooling, heating, and ventilation, costs about $6 per square foot and can be amortized and operated over a ten-year period with an increase of about $1 per square foot in rentals. It has been found that tenants of the older buildings have been willing to pay the increased rentals for the new services, since, even at the increased rates, the rentals in the older buildings are still below the rates in the new ones.

In analyzing office buildings, the factors to be taken into consideration include, in addition to net-rentable-area ratios and services rendered to tenants, such items as corridor widths, ceiling heights, operating expenses directly attributable to exterior-wall construction, washroom facilities, electrical capacity, and labor costs. This last item is very significant, as approximately 60 per cent of the total operating expenses are attributable to labor costs.

Garages. Perhaps no other type of building has suffered as much from functional obsolescence in recent years as garage buildings. The earlier parking garages found in downtown locations were essentially multistory buildings with ramps and occasionally elevators. The bays were generally either 22 or 24 feet in width. The production of larger cars in recent years has severely decreased the capacity of these older buildings. In addition, ramps, elevators, and turning capacity have been found to be inadequate. Many garage owners have been forced either to turn away the larger cars or to charge premium rentals when they could accommodate them. The recent trend away from larger and larger cars to "compact" types may reverse the situation.

The modern garage may be either a ramp type or a mechanical type. Many variations of the mechanical type are in existence, all primarily concerned with reducing the initial investment and operating with minimum labor costs. To accomplish these purposes, the buildings are no longer inclosed or heated but, instead, generally consist of a series of platforms substituting wainscoting for exterior walls or brick or decorative metal.

Of the mechanical-type garages developed, perhaps the most popular is the "pigeonhole" type. In this garage a hydraulic elevator, supported either on the ground or from the roof, is able to move both horizontally and vertically. An incoming car can be carried to any available stall and may be moved off the elevator either by a dolly operated from a control mechanism on the elevator or by an attendant who will drive it in and out of its stall. These garages are generally multistory buildings; some have been constructed up to fourteen stores. Building costs will vary depending on design but will range from $1,500 to $2,500 per stall, excluding land cost, in most areas.

Another mechanical system, specially adapted to long, narrow lots but costing about $3,000 per car space, can be operated with only one attendant. The motorist drives into one or two parking stations on the ground floor and walks to the attendant's desk. Then the attendant removes a numbered key from a central control panel, which sets the elevator in motion. The elevator moves into position adjacent to the car, where a fork-lift conveyor is extended from the elevator and under the car's wheels. The conveyor picks up the car and moves it laterally into the elevtaor, which carries it to the space corresponding to the numbered key. On departure, the car is delivered by inserting the key into the control panel, causing the elevator to reverse its parking process.

The self-service ramp garage has two big advantages over the mechanical system—speed and lower initial investment cost. In this garage, cars can be discharged more than twice as fast as in the mechanical systems, and the construction cost per car space is about $1,200. The big disadvantage lies in the greater space per car needed in the ramp system—about 320 square feet against 250 square feet in the mechanical garages.

Retail Stores. Retail-store design, like that of most other commercial property, reveals a trend toward increasing the functional utility of the space inclosed within the building. Much of the impetus for better design and construction is a result of the rapid growth of chain stores within the past thirty years. Stores have tended to grow larger and larger to provide more selling and display space for the increasing variety of goods being offered to the public. While the older stores had columns or bearing walls spaced at 14-foot and 20-foot centers, the modern store uses long-span steel beams, usually 30 feet to 60 feet between columns. This allows flexibility in arrangement of dividing walls or display space. Improved electrical and heating systems permit the installation of air conditioning, fluorescent lighting, cooling systems, and other services that may be required.

Parking space for retail stores has come to play an extremely important role in determining the degree of obsolescence of retail-store properties. While location is still the most important factor of value in these properties, even the best location will suffer if people find it increasingly difficult to get to the stores. The shift from mass-transportation facilities to private-car transportation has aggravated the traffic and congestion problem of most cities, large or small. The development of suburban shopping centers during the past fifteen years, with parking provisions at ratios of 3 or 4 to 1 (3 or 4 feet of parking area for every foot of store area) is indicative not only of the shift of middle-class population from city to suburb but also of the increasing inconvenience of shopping in crowded downtown locations.

The comparison of old store buildings with new ones must consider not only the presence or absence of the latest design and service facilities but also the factors of parking and delivery access, which will affect the amount and cost of business available to a store and, hence, will ultimately determine the amount of rent that can be paid for the location.

Hotels and Motels. Hotels, in construction style, have many similarities with apartment and office buildings. The newer hotels have been of concrete-frame construction, sometimes cantilevered, with exterior walls of masonry, metal, or glass. Room ceilings have been lowered; more window space has been provided; and air conditioning with individual controls in each room has been installed. The ground-floor space has been increasingly devoted to profitable store and food facilities, with the main lobby moved one level above the street floor. The ballroom and other meeting rooms are designed to provide the greatest amount of flexibility to meet the needs of groups of varying sizes. As more and more travelers have taken to motels just outside city limits, hotels have emphasized their convention and other public facilities to a greater degree. Many older hotels within city limits have undertaken rehabilitation programs, not only in their rooms, providing air conditioning, etc., but also in their public facilities, to attract more and more public functions.

The cost and value of hotels are usually expressed on an over-all rental basis which includes the cost and value of all the other facilities found in the building. Construction costs of hotels will vary with size, design, and facilities offered. Small hotels (100–500 rooms) will range from $8,500 to $15,000 per room, while big hotels (over 500 rooms) will range from

$10,000 to $20,000 and up. The average annual occupancy ratio of small hotels is about 60 per cent while that of large hotels is about 70–75 per cent. In hotels where ratios are consistently falling below these averages, it may be a sign of obsolescence, improper improvement of the land or both.

Since most centrally located hotels have lost business to motels owing to inadequate parking facilities, there is a tendency either to acquire adjacent parking space or to construct motels which will adjoin the hotel, offering the customer the benefits of both motel convenience and hotel service. The most modern hotels will now provide parking garages within the hotel building in an effort to meet motel competition and to attract the traveler who desires to be in the heart of the city and have his car readily available.

The motels, which have come a long way from the tourist-cabin days, are interestingly enough evolving into full-scale hotels. The original idea of motels was to offer good rooms with minimum service, at reasonable rates, with maximum convenience of access and departure. The small motels containing 10–20 rooms have generally proven to be uneconomic. The trend is to larger multistory types either outside or in the fringes of the city limits, with restaurants and public meeting places. These new multistory motels are really indistinguishable from hotels but are built on cheaper land and do not have as easy access to the center of the city.

As with hotels, motel construction costs will vary. Small motels (10–60 rooms) will cost from $5,000 to $8,000 per room, while large motels (61–250 rooms) will range from $8,000 to $15,000 and up. Occupancy ratios average 70 per cent for the small units and 77 per cent for the large ones.

Real estate taxes tend to be higher on the big downtown hotels, as they are generally constructed on more valuable land. Operating costs in general tend to be higher per room in the large hotels and motels than in their smaller counterparts. In a study made by *Fortune* magazine,[1] from data assembled by Horwath and Horwath, hotel accountants and consultants, based on a nationwide sampling of 500 hotels, it was found that operating costs, exclusive of fixed charges, for small hotels averaged $1,370 per room per annum as against $1,895 for large hotels. The operating costs for small motels averaged $830 per room against $1,610 for large motels. These costs included payroll, housekeeping, administrative, advertising, utilities, and maintenance expenses.

In spite of the lower operating costs and lower initial investment for small hotels and motels, the larger buildings command higher rentals and ultimately provide a greater net return for their investors. It is probably for this reason that the trend is toward the construction of larger buildings, with the interesting development of hotels and motels becoming almost indistinguishable, as has already been indicated.

[1] *Fortune* (June 1959), p. 123.

CONCLUSION

In addition to the building types discussed in this chapter, other building types such as theaters, gas stations, factories, and truck terminals are all subject to some general observations. The comparison of buildings and building values must encompass not only original costs and designs but also ultimate costs, as reflected in operating expenses and stability of rental values. The degrees of functional and economic obsolescence of older structures must be measured by what is considered typical for modern buildings. The need for more and more space, with improved equipment and services, has led builders to different solutions for various types of buildings. Apartments, hotels, office buildings, motels, and garages have tended to develop vertical expansion as the solution, while stores and factories find it more efficient to develop along horizontal lines. New construction methods are constantly being experimented with in order to hold down initial costs and provide economic operation. Equipment such as air-conditioning, elevator, plumbing, power, and heating equipment, or its lack, has become more and more important in the determination of building values. The appraiser must continually be alert to all new economic and social developments that will ultimately translate themselves into new building designs to meet the needs and requirements they engender.

32

"Rule-of-Thumb" Investment Guides

There are many occasions when an investor or appraiser will want a relatively simple, easy-to-use method of establishing a value range for a property. The investor will use certain guides to select from a number of properties the particular ones about which he will want more detailed information and a more thorough analysis. The appraiser may use these guides to establish a range within which he will expect to find the final estimate of value which will be based on a more complete appraisal. Other uses of these guides include application to mass appraisals, for use when time for completion of the appraisal is short and to the testing of changes in the market value of properties.

CAUTION IN USE OF GUIDES

These guides must always be used with great care, because they rely on gross estimates which are usually applicable only in a general way to any particular property. The lack of similarity among properties—the variations due to location, quality of construction, and intensity of property use—the passage of time, and a variety of other factors will change not only the guides themselves but also their usefulness. For these reasons, the guides which have been developed from observations of particular types of properties and their uses should be applied only to similar properties and property uses. Even then, the final estimate should not be relied upon until it can be checked against a more thorough property analysis and valuation.

GROSS INCOME MULTIPLIERS

Among the most popular types of guides, the gross income multiplier is the best known and most frequently used. Not only is it simple to use, but a number of devices can be used to develop gross income estimates in cases where the detailed data needed for a complete appraisal might not be obtainable.

The gross income multiplier is simply a means of expressing the value of a property as a multiple of either the annual or the monthly gross income. Thus the expression "this property is worth five times the gross annual rent" means that the gross income is capitalized at twenty per cent (the multiplier, five divided into one). If the gross annual rent for such a property were $12,000, the value of the property would be $12,000 times five or $60,000. If a monthly gross rent and a comparable monthly multiplier were used, the value would be estimated at $1,000 ($12,000 divided by twelve months) multiplied by sixty (five times twelve months).

MULTIPLIER USED FOR COMPARABLE PROPERTIES

There is rarely a single multiplier that can be used consistently, even for the same type of properties; rather, it must be constantly recalculated from completed sales and current rental incomes. When a gross multiplier is used, it must always be treated as a rough approximation that has to be tempered by the knowledge and good judgment of an experienced appraiser or investor who must be fully aware of differences in markets, which will require either recalculation of the multiplier or tempered use of one currently favored.

The gross multiplier is an excellent additional guide in the income-capitalization approach to a value estimate. For example, assume that the problem is to establish a series of guides which will provide general clues to the value of a six-story, self-service-elevator apartment house located in a city of 300,000 in the northeastern part of the United States. The property can be mortgaged for two-thirds of its appraised value at a constant rate of 8 per cent for interest and amortization, and the typical investor will be satisfied with a 12 per cent return on his equity. The series of analyses could be made in this way:

Percentage of total market value absorbed by mortgage charges 5.33%
  (⅔ of the appraised value × 8%)
Percentage of total market value absorbed by owner's equity interest 4.00%
  (⅓ of the appraised value × 12%)
Real estate taxes 3.20%
  (Assessed value equal to 80% of market value × 4% tax rate)
Percentage of market value absorbed by operating costs 5.02%

Fuel	0.72
Labor	1.00
Insurance	0.30
Repairs and vacancies	2.50
Miscellaneous	0.50

Percentage of gross income absorbed by all charges 17.55%

If 17.5 per cent of the total value of the property represents the total income which must be produced to warrant the investment, gross income times a multiplier of 5.7 (1.00 ÷ 0.175) will give an estimate of value. This multiplier could then be applied to other properties having similar types of expenses. Any deviations from these ratios would require the calculation of a new multiplier. The danger of using this multiplier lies in the degree to which properties may differ in their income and expense experiences.

If a sufficient number of property operating histories can be developed, it may be possible to develop some useful general multipliers, and it may be possible to say that apartment houses of this general type should sell for approximately 5.7 times their gross annual incomes. In time, multipliers can be developed for a full range of representative property types.

ESTIMATING GROSS INCOME

Once properties have been grouped in categories which reflect common income, expenses, and use characteristics, gross income can also be related to other measures of values. For examples, gross income can be expressed as so much per apartment, per room, per square foot for apartment houses; or per front foot for stores; or per net square foot for office buildings. If an apartment house should produce $5 gross annual income per square foot, a 10,000-square-foot apartment house should yield $50,000 gross income, which multiplied by the gross annual multiplier of 5.7, gives an estimated price of $285,000.

NON-RESIDENTIAL INCOME

Other methods may also be used to estimate gross income for non-residential properties. For example, some supermarkets are known to pay 1–1.5 per cent of their sales for rent. Department stores will pay about 2–3.5 per cent of their sales for rent. Gasoline stations may pay 1.5¢ per gallon sold plus 2 per cent on sales of accessories. Motion-picture theaters may pay from 10 to 20 per cent of their gross admissions for rent. These and other standard rental percentages may be found in trade journals and a variety of other nationally and locally published sources. Since most published schedules are averages, care must be taken with their use, and, as in every other case in appraisal work, the actual local experience should govern.

PER ROOM OR PER SQUARE FOOT?

One of the difficulties encountered in the appraisal of some apartment houses is in finding a universally accepted definition of a room, which can produce a certain degree of fuzziness in estimating gross income for these properties. For example, several fairly new apartment houses in New York City were studied, and it was found that, by shifting the unit of valuation to rental per square foot instead of per room, it was possible to estimate within 5 per cent of actual gross income. The $3 per square foot which was developed proved very valuable as a guide and a tool for comparison.

On the other hand, in older apartment properties, where the room count was generally established and agreed upon, it was possible to use a standard rent per room in order to arrive at a reliable estimate.

FRONT-FOOT RETAIL VALUES

Retail-store properties lend themselves readily to a standard front-foot rental value in addition to percentage standards. The chief problem in using front-foot estimates is the varying depths of stores within similar neighborhoods; therefore, it is necessary to establish a front-foot rental for a store of standard depth. If 60 feet is considered the standard depth, the appraiser is obliged to make adjustments for stores of differing depths. One useful solution of this problem is to develop a scale on the basis of 5-foot variations. For every 5 feet in excess of the standard, perhaps a 5 per cent additional rent could be assigned to the space, and, for every 5 feet less of depth, some percentage allowance such as 3 per cent might be given. Once again, it must be emphasized that local conditions will govern the scale and that, if, on further examination, actual rentals produce different results, the actual rentals must, of course, govern.

Office buildings and lofts, as was previously indicated, will lend themselves to the development of guides on a square-foot basis after analysis of similar rentals for these types of properties. Garages and parking-lot rentals can be estimated on the basis of car capacity.

EXPENSE RATIOS

Expense can also be used to estimate gross income when standard percentage ratios can be developed. For example, it may be possible to obtain the expense estimates for a particular building belonging to a type which normally has total expenses equal to 50 per cent of gross income. If expenses for such a building were $12,000, the gross income would be $24,000. A series of recent studies of apartment investments in New York, Los Angeles, Chicago, and San Francisco showed that expenses do tend to average a consistent percentage of total expenses for certain types of properties.[1] These studies showed that new apartments usually had expenses equal to 25 per cent of gross income; apartments in mid-life, 50 per cent; and old properties, 75 per cent. The authors of this book found that older office buildings in New York usually required outlays of 60 per cent of gross income for all expenses. Similar relationships between total expenses and individual items that make up the expenses can be developed from an analysis of various types of properties. The income and expense guides that are obtained by the appraiser should be among the most important data in

[1] Fred E. Case, *Los Angeles: A History of Investment Experience, 1935–1954* (Los Angeles: University of California, Real Estate Research Program, 1961).

his files, subject to the oft repeated caution: "Keep the data current, lest the guides become misleading!"

CORRELATING COSTS AND INCOME

Equally important as the knowledge of current rentals and expenses is a knowledge of current costs. This is especially true where the appraisal of new buildings is involved. The costs of acqusition of land and buildings will be the major factor in establishing rental levels.

Clues to possible gross rentals for new properties can often be developed when the acquisition costs of the land and the construction costs of the buildings are known. For example, if total land and building costs for a new commercial property should equal $15.00 a square foot, if the investors expect an 8 per cent return on their costs, and if total operating costs will average 4 per cent of total costs, gross rentals annually must be at least 12 per cent of the $15.00 square-foot costs, or $1.80 per square foot. If rents in the market are below this figure, the appraiser and the investor know immediately that the property suffers from economic obsolescence and would not be a good investment.

BUILDING-SPACE GUIDES

One type of guide that is of help to appraisers is the building area needed for each unit of use. This can be readily seen from a study of the reality requirements for parking.

Parking. Automobile sizes range from about 6×16 feet (compact and foreign) to about $6\frac{1}{2} \times 20$ feet (larger American models). Although this knowledge is helpful, it certainly does not advise the realtor and appraiser of building parking requirements. The requirements will vary with the shape of the garage or parking field, the access into the parking area, and whether parking is done by an attendant or directly by the customer. If there is customer parking, the angle of the parking stalls will vary the area requirement.

From the table, we can now see that the 130 square feet that the average car covers in its parking space require in a parking structure from 225 to 360 square feet after consideration has been given to maneuvering of the car and to the person that will do this. A parking field requires somewhat less area, since building members and elevators and ramps are not involved.

Motels. In a similar fashion, an actual rental unit in a motel consisting of a sleeping room, bathroom, and closet may require from 200 to 320 square feet, depending on the market to which the motel caters, whether the unit is a single or double, and its location. However, the unit may be in a two-story structure with elevators, stairwells, corridors, linen closets, an elaborate lobby, and many public-function rooms. When these extras are included within the motel building, it may require from 300 to 375 square feet per unit.

Apartment Houses. One additional example is the apartment house. A moderate-rental garden apartment house may have the following room sizes:

Room	Dimensions	Area
Living room	12′ × 18′	186
Kitchen	9′ × 11′	99
Bedroom	10′ × 13′	130
Bedroom	10′ × 10′	100
Dining alcove	7′ × 9′	63
Bathroom	6′ × 7′	42
Closets (5)		100
Corridors and halls		40
		770 square feet

In many areas of the country, this is considered to be a four-and-one-half-room apartment. (The bathroom is considered a service area.) It can be seen that this apartment averages 171 square feet per room. However, the table indicates an average of 200–300 square feet for each room. This includes corridors, stairs, the lobby, and the utility core.

It is to be noted that the table shows three categories of apartment structures. Generally speaking, high-rise apartment houses require large building areas for many reasons. Usually, this type of apartment house has luxury units with very large individual room sizes and a generous amount of closets. In addition, proportionately large areas will have to be utilized for lobby, stairwell, elevators, corridors, and other utility areas. Therefore, high-rise apartments usually require 285–335 square feet. It can be seen that the minimum and maximum areas for this category exceed those for the garden and five- to seven-story categories.

Guides Not Accurate. Like all guides, this building-space guide must be used with extreme caution. The areas listed are considered typical for today's construction. In the 1920's, apartment room areas were much larger in almost all types of construction; therefore, buildings of that era will not fit the pattern shown in the table on page 417. Similarly, if automobile sizes increase, larger units will be required for aisle space and stalls in parking areas. The appraiser must use utmost care when using all the guides in this text, and with any others that he acquires.

Possibly the most difficult category to refine into a guide is the one covering office buildings. In a building catering to small-space users, it is possible that a unit of 800 square feet will be rented to a branch office of a national corporation. The area may consist of a large private office for the manager and an open area for his secretary, with a product showroom and a waiting room. This would mean that this area of 800 square feet serves two employees at a rate of 400 square feet per person. In addition, it normally requires 900–1,000 square feet of office building to provide 800 square feet of rentable area. The other space is required for corridors, elevators, stairwells, a utility room, and washrooms. Under this formula, 450–500 square feet would be required for each employee. This is an extreme example. The other extreme would be an entire-floor tenant with no showroom, a large proportion of clerical workers, and few executives. This type of operation may use an area of 80 square feet per employee within its space and requires 90–100 square feet of building area. Space guides for several classifications of realty development are offered in the following table, but the above precautions should be kept in mind in their usage.

BUILDING-SPACE AREA (*Above Basement*)

Type	Area (square feet)
Apartment house (per room)	
High rise (luxury)	285–335
Garden	200–300
Five to seven stories	265–310
Bowling alley (per lane)	750–900
Motel (per unit)	300–375
Hotel (per unit)	320–400
Hospital (per bed)	450–650
Nursing home (per bed)	175–450
Office building	
Per clerical worker (net)	65–90
Per executive (net)	125–250
20,000 square-foot, entire-floor tenant (per employee)	100–150
Parking garage (per parking space)	
Attended	225–275
Unattended	280–360
Parking field (per parking space)	
Attended	160–185
Unattended	285–310
Restaurant (per seat)	
Counter service	15–19
Table service	20–40
Diner (per seat)	15–25
Theater (per seat)	12–16

Bibliography—Part IV

BABCOCK, FREDERICK M. *Valuation of Real Estate.* New York: McGraw-Hill Book Co., Inc., 1932.

BANFIELD, EDWARD C., and MORTON GRODZINS. *Government and Housing in Metropolitan Areas.* New York: McGraw-Hill Book Co., Inc., 1958.

BEYER, GLENN H. *Housing: A Factual Analysis.* New York: The Macmillan Co., 1958.

CASE, FREDERICK E. *Real Estate.* Englewood Cliffs, N.J.: Allyn & Bacon, Inc., 1962.

COWGILL, CLINTON H. *Building for Investment.* New York: Reinhold Publishing Corp., 1949.

GRUEN, VICTOR, and LARRY SMITH. *Shopping Towns USA.* New York: Reinhold Publishing Corp., 1960.

HUSBAND, WILLIAM H., and FRANK R. ANDERSON. *Real Estate Analysis.* Homewood, Ill.: Richard D. Irwin Inc., 1960.

KETCHUM, MORRIS. *Shops and Stores.* New York: Reinhold Publishing Corp., 1948.

McCONAGLE, JAMES R. *Apartment House Rental, Investment, and Management.* Englewood Cliffs, N.J.: Prentice-Hall, Inc., 1937.

McMICHAEL, STANLEY L., and PAUL T. O'KEEFE. *How To Finance Real Estate* (2d ed.). Englewood Cliffs, N.J.: Prentice-Hall, Inc., 1953.

MAY, ARTHUR A. *The Valuation of Residential Real Estate* (2d ed.). Englewood Cliffs, N.J.: Prentice-Hall, Inc., 1953.

NATIONAL ASSOCIATION OF BUILDING OWNERS AND MANAGERS. Annual Experience Exchange Reports. Chicago: National Association of Building Owners and Managers.

NELSON, RICHARD L. *The Selection of Retail Locations.* New York: F. W. Dodge Corp., 1958.

RATCLIFF, RICHARD U. *Real Estate Analysis.* New York: McGraw-Hill Book Co., Inc., 1961.

ROBICHAUD, BERYL. *Selecting, Planning, and Managing Office Space.* New York: McGraw-Hill Book Co., Inc., 1958.

WEIMER, ARTHUR M., and HOMER HOYT. *Principles of Real Estate* (4th ed.). New York: The Ronald Press Co., 1960.

WINNICK, LOUIS. *Rental Housing: Opportunities for Private Investment.* New York: McGraw-Hill Book Co., Inc., 1958.

APPENDIXES

Roof Types

A

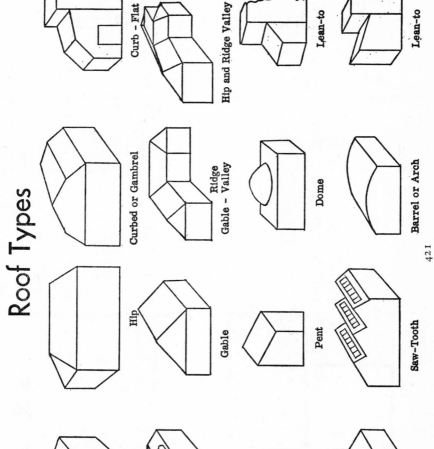

Hip Pyramid

Mansard with Dormers

Conical

Monitor

Hip

Gable

Pent

Saw-Tooth

Curbed or Gambrel

Ridge Gable – Valley

Dome

Barrel or Arch

Curb – Flat

Hip and Ridge Valley

Lean–to

Lean–to

B

Replacement-Cost Example—
One-Story Residence

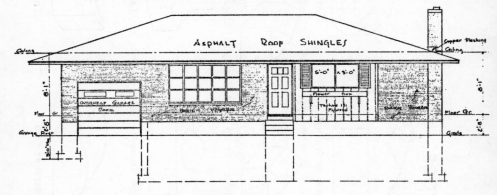

FRONT ELEVATION

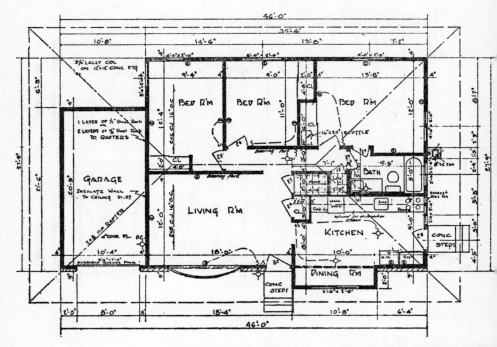

FLOOR PLAN

Marshall & Stevens Co.

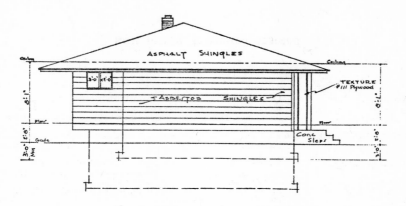

LEFT SIDE ELEVATION

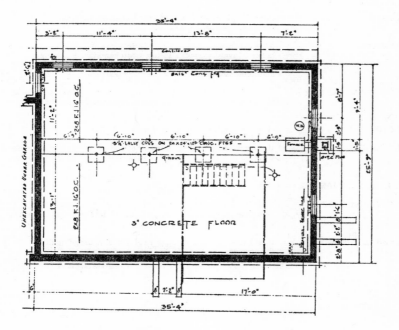

BASEMENT PLAN

Marshall & Stevens Co.

SUBJECT RESIDENCE DESCRIPTION

BASEMENT:	Unreinforced concrete walls approximately 5' below grade; waterproofing; no abnormal soil condition. 3" thick concrete floor, steel lally columns supporting wood floor structure above
STRUCTURAL FRAME:	All frame members are wood. Average workmanship and material.
EXTERIOR FINISH:	Asbestos shingles are primary finish. Front of residence has combination of brick veneer and plywood finish.
ROOF:	210 lb. asphalt shingles over 15 lb. felt on plywood sheathing. Metal gutters and leaders.
INTERIOR FINISH:	3/8" drywall, taped and spackled; wallpaper or paint finish throughout; ceramic tile wainscot at tub area in bath.
SASH & DOORS:	Natural finished hollow flush wood doors; solid wood and glass side door. Wood bow window at front elevation; balance sliding aluminum sash.
FLOORS:	Asphalt tile in kitchen; ceramic tile in bath; balance #1 oak over 1/2" plywood subfloor.
PLUMBING:	Five average quality fixtures as follows: 1 bathtub with shower head; 1 lavatory sink; 1 toilet; 1 kitchen sink; 1 hot water heater. Average faucets, valves and trim. One rough-in for automatic washer.
CABINETS & CLOSETS:	Adequate amount of kitchen cabinets, modern design, natural wood finish. Formica drainboard and splash. Sufficient wardrobe type bedroom closets and linen closet.
HEATING:	Gas fired forced warm air heater.
ELECTRICAL:	Romex wiring, average number of convenience outlets; ceiling fixtures in hall and kitchen; entrance door lights; front and side door chimes.
BUILT-IN APPLIANCES:	Gas oven and range; exhaust fan.
ATTACHED GARAGE:	Frame, asbestos shingle and brick veneer; concrete floor; sectional O.H. wood door; pull chain light. Roof and exterior finish conform to that of house.
GENERAL QUALITY:	Residence, basement and garage are of average quality throughout.

Marshall & Stevens Co.

SQUARE FOOT APPRAISAL FORM
for use with the RESIDENTIAL COST HANDBOOK

Appraisal for _____ Property owner _____

Address or legal description of property _____

Appraiser _____ Date of appraisal _____

1. Measure buildings and make sketch showing outside dimensions on reverse side of form.
2. From dimensions compute the necessary square foot areas of residence, basement, and garage. When determining the square foot area of residences having more than one story always use the total area of all floors above the basement.
3. List floor areas: Residence *1002 SQ. FT.* Basement *910 SQ. FT.* Porch *FRONT 12 SQ. FT.* Garage ☒ Carport ☐ *229 SQ. FT.* Other *PORCH, SIDE 12 SQ. FT.*
4. Note type of exterior wall *ASBESTOS SHINGLES*
5. Type of residence: One Story ☒ One and One Half Story ☐ Two Story ☐ Split Level ☐ Detached ☒ Semidetached ☐ End Row House ☐ Inside Row House ☐
6. From overall appearance indicate general quality: Fair ☐ Average ☒ Good ☐

APPRAISAL COMPUTATIONS

		PLUS	MINUS		
7. **Select residence basic sq. ft. cost** *$9.50*				16. Multiply residence sq. ft. area x line 15	9,519
8. Roofing. *ASPHALT SHINGLES* ...		—	—	17. Plumbing: Number of fixtures *FIVE*	–150
9. Floor . *HARDWOOD*		—	—	18. Built-in range and oven .. *GAS*	355
10. Interior finish *DRYWALL - PAINT & PAPER*		—	—	19. Dishwasher ... *NONE*	
11. Heating *FORCED AIR, GAS*		—	—	20. Garbage disposal .. *NONE*	
12. Cooling . *NONE*		—	—	21. Misc. *KITCHEN EXHAUST FAN.*	40
13. Misc:		—	—	22. *ROUGH-IN FOR AUTO. WASHER*	60
14. Total square foot adjustments		—	—	23. *EXTRA ROOF - SEE REVERSE SIDE*	118
15. **Adjusted sq. ft. cost:** Line 7 + and - line 14	*$9.50*			24. . . . . : . . .	

25. Multiply basement sq. ft. area *910 SQ. FT.* x adjusted unfinished basement cost *$1.36* — 1,238
26. Add for basement garage: Single ☐ Double ☐ .. *NONE* ....
27. Add for basement outside entrance. .. *NONE* ....
28. Basement interior finish: Sq. ft. area of finished rooms *NONE* x sq. ft. cost _____
29. Miscellaneous basement costs...
30. Porch: Type *OPEN WITH STEPS - FRONT* sq. ft. area *12 SQ. FT.* x sq. ft. cost *$4.90* — 59
31. Porch: Type *OPEN WITH STEPS - SIDE* sq. ft. area *12 SQ. FT.* x sq. ft. cost *$4.90* — 59
32. **Residence and basement subtotal:** Sum of lines 16 to 31 less deductions .... — 11,298
33. Garage ☒ Carport ☐ : Sq. ft. area *229 SQ. FT.* x sq. ft. cost *$3.87* .... — 886
34. Attached garage common wall deduction: Lineal ft. *21.5* x lineal ft. cost *$8.68* — –187
35. Garage miscellaneous ....
36. **Garage or carport subtotal:** Sum of lines 33 to 35 less deductions .... — 699
37. Subtotal of all building improvements: Sum of lines 32 and 36 .... — 11,997
38. **Current local cost of buildings:** Local multiplier *1.01* x line 37 .... — 12,117
39. Depreciation: Age *NEW* Condition *EXCELLENT* Deduction *NONE* % of line 38 ....
40. **Depreciated cost of building improvements:** Line 38 less line 39 .... — 12,117
41. Yard improvements cost: List, total, apply local multiplier, and depreciate on reverse side .... — 547
42. Landscaping cost: List and compute on reverse side .... — 204
43. Lot or land value .... — 3,000
44. **Total indicated value of land and improvements:** Sum of lines 40 to 43..................... — 15,868

Marshall & Stevens Co.

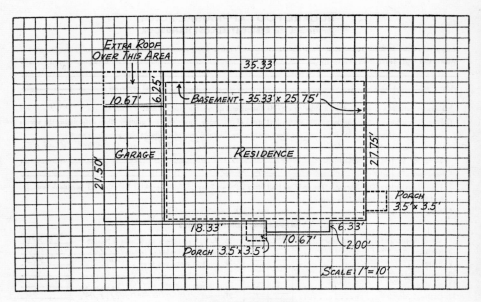

NOTES AND COMPUTATIONS

AREA COMPUTATIONS

RESIDENCE 27.75' × 35.33' =   980.41
                 2.00' × 10.67' =   21.34
                                  TOTAL 1001.75 SQ.FT.
BASEMENT 25.75' × 35.33' =   909.75 SQ.FT.
FRONT PORCH 3.5' × 3.5' =   12.25 SQ.FT.
REAR PORCH 3.5' × 3.5' =   12.25 SQ.FT.
ATT. GARAGE 10.67' × 21.50' =   229.40 SQ.FT.

GARAGE COMMON WALL . 21.5 LIN. FT.

YARD IMPROVEMENTS

CONCRETE FLATWORK ON 4" GRAVEL FILL:
DRIVEWAY RIBBONS 2.5' × 72.0' = 180 SQ.FT. × $.46 = $83.
WALKS   3.0' × 50.0' = 150 SQ.FT. × $.46 = 69.
APPROACH APRON 9.0' × 12.0' = 108 SQ.FT. × $.46 =   50.

CESSPOOLS, 2000 GAL. 2 EA. × $170. =   340.
                             SUBTOTAL $ 542.

        LOCAL MULTIPLIER   × 1.01
    YARD IMPROVEMENTS TOTAL $ 547.

LANDSCAPING

LAWN:
 SEED FRONT YARD – 3000 SQ.FT. × $.05 = $150.
 SMALL SHRUBS – 8 EA. × $3.00   = 24.
 LARGE SHRUBS – 3 EA. × $10.00   = 30.
        LANDSCAPING TOTAL $ 204.

ITEM NO.23

EXTRA RESIDENCE ROOF BEHIND GARAGE
(PORCH ROOF AND CEILING COSTS USED
FOR PRICING)
10.67' × 6.25' = 67 SQ.FT. × $1.76 = $118.00

Marshall & Stevens Co.

SEGREGATED COST APPRAISAL FORM

for use with the **RESIDENTIAL COST HANDBOOK**

1. Owner _____ Appraiser _____

2. Property Address _____

3. Quality _____ Type _____ Number of Stories _____ Date _____

	UNITS	QUALITY	QUANTITY	UNIT COST	LUMP SUM EXTENSION
4. Foundation *NONE - INCL. IN BASEMENT*	Square ft. of 1st floor area				
5. Basement *8" POURED CONCRETE WALLS*	Square ft. of basement	AVG.	910	1.97	1,793
6. Basement Finish *NONE*	Square ft. of finished area				
7. Exterior Wall *ASBESTOS SHINGLES*	Linear ft. of exterior wall	AVG.	130	14.86	1,932
8. Gable Wall *NONE - HIP ROOF*	Square ft. of gable wall				
9. Roof *ASPHALT SHINGLE*	Square ft. of 1st floor area	AVG.	1002	1.14	1,142
10. Dormers *NONE*	Linear ft. across front				
11. Floor *HARDWOOD*	Square ft. of floor area	AVG.	1002	1.17	1,172
12. Ceiling *PAINTED DRYWALL*	Square ft. of floor area	AVG.	1002	.30	301
13. Interior Construction *DETACHED, ONE STORY*	Square ft. of floor area	AVG.	1002	2.40	2,405
14. Stairways *NONE*	Each				
15. Heating and Cooling *HEATING-FORCED AIR, GAS*	Square ft. of floor area	AVG.	1002	.59	591
16. Electrical *ROMEX WIRING*	Square ft. of floor area	AVG.	1002	.33	331
17. Plumbing *FIVE FIXTURES*	Each	AVG.	5	150.00	750
18. Built-In Appliances *GAS RANGE & OVEN - EXHAUST FAN*	Each	AVG.	1	395.00	395
19. *ROUGH IN FOR AUTOMATIC WASHER*		AVG.	1	60.00	60
20. *EXTRA ROOF - SEE REVERSE SIDE FOR DETAIL*		AVG.	67	1.76	118
21. Fireplace *NONE*	Each				
22. Porches *FRONT - OPEN WITH STEPS*	Square ft. of porch area	AVG.	12	4.90	59
23. *PORCH, SIDE - OPEN WITH STEPS*		AVG.	12	4.90	59
24. Garage Foundation *FRAME - ASBESTOS*	Linear ft. of exterior wall	AVG.	43	1.89	81
25. Garage Exterior Wall *ASBESTOS SHINGLE*	Linear ft. of exterior wall	AVG.	43	6.79	292
26. Garage Floor *CONCRETE*	Square ft. of floor area	AVG.	229	.60	137
27. Garage Roof *ASPHALT SHINGLE*	Square ft. of floor area	AVG.	229	.83	190
28. Garage Ceiling *NONE*	Square ft. of floor area				
29. Carport *NONE*	Square ft. of floor area				
30. Basement Garage *NONE*	Lump Sum				

31. Subtotal of all building improvements **11,808**

32. Current local cost of buildings: local multiplier *1.01* x line 31 . . . . **11,926**

33. Depreciation: Age *NEW* Condition *EXCELLENT* Deduction *NONE* % of line 32 . . . .

34. Depreciated cost of building improvements: line 32 less line 33 . . . . **11,926**

35. Yard improvements cost: list, total, apply local multiplier and depreciate on reverse side **547**

36. Landscaping cost: list and compute on reverse side **204**

37. Lot or land value **3000**

38. **Total indicated value of land and improvements:** **15,677**

Marshall & Stevens Co.

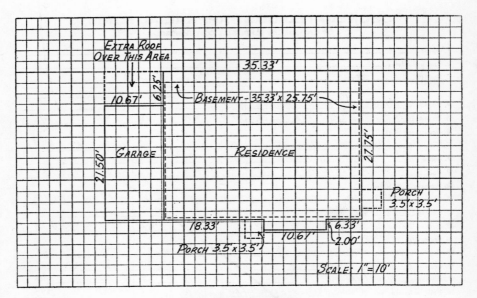

NOTES AND COMPUTATIONS

AREA COMPUTATIONS

RESIDENCE 27.75' x 35.33' =   980.41
        2.00 x 10.67' =   21.34
                   1001.75 Sq. Ft.
BASEMENT 25.75' x 35.33' =   909.75 Sq. Ft.
FRONT PORCH 3.5' x 3.5'   12.25 Sq. Ft.
REAR PORCH 3.5' x 3.5'   12.25 Sq. Ft.
ATT. GARAGE 10.67' x 21.50' =   229.40 Sq. Ft.

RESIDENCE PERIMETER

FRONT	18.33	LINEAR FEET
"	2.00	
"	10.67	
"	2.00	
"	6.33	
RIGHT SIDE	27.75	
REAR	35.33	
LEFT SIDE	27.75	
TOTAL	130.16	LINEAR FEET

GARAGE PERIMETER

FRONT	10.67	LINEAR FEET
LEFT SIDE	21.50	
REAR	10.67	
TOTAL	42.84	LINEAR FEET

YARD IMPROVEMENTS

CONCRETE FLATWORK ON 4" GRAVEL FILL:
DRIVEWAY RIBBONS 2.5' x 72.0' = 180 S.F. x $.46 = $83.
WALKS   3.0' x 50.0' = 150 S.F. x $.46 =   69.
APPROACH APRON 9.0' x 12.0' = 108 S.F. x $.46 =   50.

CESSPOOLS, 2000 GAL. 2 EA. x $170. =   340.
                     SUBTOTAL $ 542.
           LOCAL MULTIPLIER x 1.01
      YARD IMPROVEMENTS TOTAL $ 547.

LANDSCAPING

LAWN:
SEED FRONT YARD - 3000 SQ. FT. x $.05 = $150.
SMALL SHRUBS - 8 EA. x $ 3.00   =   24.
LARGE SHRUBS - 3 EA. x $10.00   =   30.
          LANDSCAPING TOTAL $ 204

ITEM No. 20

EXTRA RESIDENCE ROOF BEHIND GARAGE
(PORCH ROOF AND CEILING COSTS USED
FOR PRICING)
10.67' x 6.25' = 67 SQ. FT. x $1.76 = $118.00

Marshall & Stevens Co.

C

Rentable Floor Area

Single Tenancy Floors: The rentable area of a single tenancy floor shall be computed by measuring from *the inside surface* of the outer building wall *to the inside surface* of the opposite outer building wall.

Rentable area of a single tenancy floor *shall include* all area within the outside wall, *less building stairs, fire towers, elevator shafts, flues, vents, stacks, pipe shafts and vertical ducts, with their enclosing walls,* serving more than one floor.

Private stairs, private elevators, toilets, air conditioning rooms, fan rooms, air ducts, janitors' closets, slop sinks, electrical closets, telephone closets, with their enclosing walls, within and exclusively serving only that floor, shall be included in rentable area.

No deductions shall be made for columns and projections necessary to the building.

The area of air conditioning and fan rooms located on a rentable floor, serving more than the floor on which located, shall be apportioned and included as rentable area of the floors they serve.

Divided Floors: The rentable area of an individual office or a portion of a divided floor shall be computed by measuring from the inside surface of the outer building wall to the finished surface of the corridor side of corridor partition and from the center of the partitions that separate the premises from adjoining rentable area.

No deductions shall be made for columns and projections necessary to the building.

Building stairs, fire towers, elevator shafts, flues, vents, stacks, pipe shafts, vertical ducts, toilets, air conditioning rooms, fan rooms, air ducts, janitors' closets, slop sinks, electrical closets, telephone closets, with their enclosing walls, shall be excluded from rentable area.

Stores: The rentable area of a store shall be computed by measuring from the building line in the case of street frontages, and from the inside surface of other outer building walls to the finished surface of the corridor side of corridor partition and from the center of the partitions that separate the premises from adjoining rentable area.

No deductions shall be made for columns and projections necessary to the building.

Rentable area of a store shall include all area within the outside walls, less building stairs, fire towers, elevator shafts, flues, vents, stacks, pipe shafts, vertical ducts, with their enclosing walls if serving more than one floor.

Private stairs, private elevators, toilets, air conditioning rooms, fan rooms, air ducts, janitors' closets, slop sinks, electrical closets, telephone closets, with their enclosing walls, within and exclusively serving only that store, shall be included in rentable area.

No deductions shall be made for store vestibules inside the building line. No additions shall be made for bay windows extending outside the building line.

Basements: If the rentable area extends beyond the building line under the sidewalk, the area shall be computed by measuring from the curtain wall or finished surface of the retaining wall to the finished surface of the corridor side of corridor or other permanent partition, and from the center of the partitions that separate the premises from adjoining rentable area provided such partitions are not bearing walls.

If the rentable area is entirely inside the building line, the area shall be computed by measuring from the inside surface of the outer building wall to the finished surface of corridor side of corridor partition or to other permanent partition, and from the center of the partitions that separate the premises from adjoining rentable area, provided such partitions are not bearing walls.

No deductions shall be made for columns, projections or footings necessary to the building.

Rentable area of a basement shall include all area within the outside wall, less building stairs, fire towers, elevator shafts, flues, vents, stacks, pipe shafts and vertical ducts, with their enclosing walls serving more than one floor.

Private stairs, private elevators, toilets, air conditioning rooms, fan rooms, air ducts, janitors' closets, slop sinks, electrical closets, telephone closets, with their enclosing walls, within and exclusively serving only that basement, shall be included in rentable area.

Determining Rentable Areas in Computing Operating Costs: In computing operating costs on a square foot basis, the rentable area of an entire building shall be based on the method adopted for determining rentable area of entire floors. Rentable areas of stores and basements shall be included in the total rentable area of the building.

CUBIC CONTENT

The cubic content (cube or cubage) of a building is the actual cubic space enclosed within the outer surfaces of the outside or enclosing walls and contained between the outer surfaces of the roof and six inches below the finished surfaces of the lowest floors.

Interpretation: The above definition requires the cube of dormers, pent houses, vaults, pits, enclosed porches and other enclosed appendages to be included as part of the cube of the building. It does not include the cube of courts or light shafts, open at the top, or the cube of outside steps, cornices, parapets, or open porches or loggias.

ROOF VOLUMES

Gable: $W \, L \, H/2$

Mansard: $[(W \times L) + W' \times L')] \times H/2$

Gambrel: $W \, L \, H/2$ (to break of gable) plus $L \, H' \, (A + B)/2$
  or $^2W \, L \, H \times 2/3$

Pyramid: $W \, L \, H/3$

Building Quantity Units

Excavation: Cubic yards
Concrete: Cubic feet or yards
Brickwork: Thousand
Lumber: Thousand board feet (mbm)
Flooring: Square feet
Plaster: Square feet or yards
Concrete floors: Square feet
Roofing: Square feet or square (100 square feet)
Insulation: Square feet
Steel: Pounds or tons
Doors: Number
Windows: Number
Plumbing: Number of fixtures
Heating: Square feet of radiation
Electrical: Number of outlets and fixtures
Tile and Terrazzo: Square feet

D

Geometric Mensuration

Tables – Definitions

DECIMALS OF A FOOT FOR EACH 1/8 INCH

Inch	0"	1"	2"	3"	4"	5"	6"	7"	8"	9"	10"	11"
0	0	.083	.167	.250	.333	.417	.500	.583	.667	.750	.833	.917
1/8	.010	.094	.177	.260	.344	.427	.510	.594	.677	.760	.844	.927
1/4	.021	.104	.188	.271	.354	.438	.521	.604	.688	.771	.854	.938
3/8	.031	.115	.198	.281	.365	.448	.531	.615	.698	.781	.865	.948
1/2	.042	.125	.208	.292	.375	.458	.542	.625	.708	.792	.875	.958
5/8	.052	.135	.219	.302	.385	.469	.552	.635	.719	.802	.885	.969
3/4	.063	.146	.229	.313	.396	.479	.563	.646	.729	.813	.896	.979
7/8	.073	.156	.240	.323	.406	.490	.573	.656	.740	.823	.906	.990

SQUARE AND CUBIC MEASURE

144 sq. in. = 1 sq. ft.
9 sq. ft. = 1 sq. yd.
1 acre   = 43,560 sq. ft.

1,728 cu. in. = 1 cu. ft.
27 cu. ft. = 1 cu. yd.

12 lots, 25 × 100, in one acre with streets
17.424 lots, 25 × 100, in one acre without streets

1 rod = $5\frac{1}{2}$ yds. = $16\frac{1}{2}$ ft.

Circle

Area – Square of Radius × 3.1416
Circumference – Diameter × 3.1416
Area of a Sector – Length of arc × $\frac{1}{2}$ the radius

DEFINITIONS AND GEOMETRIC MENSURATION

Angle:

An Angle is a figure formed by two straight lines from a point. The point "O" is called the vertex.

O

A Right Angle is one formed by two lines which meet at an angle of 90 degrees.

432

An <u>Acute Angle</u> is an angle smaller than a right angle. (less than 90 degrees.)

An <u>Obtuse Angle</u> is an angle larger than a right angle but smaller than a straight angle. (greater than 90 degrees.)

A <u>Polygon</u> is a plane surface bounded by straight lines. The number of sides of the following polygons are: Triangle, 3; Quadrilateral, 4; Pentagon, 5; Hexagon, 6; Octagon, 8; Decagon, 10.

The <u>Perimeter</u> of a polygon is the sum of its sides.

A <u>Perpendicular</u> to a line is a line which makes a right angle with the given line.

<u>Triangle:</u>

A <u>Triangle</u> is a polygon of 3 sides.

An <u>Equilateral Triangle</u> is one in which all sides are equal.

A <u>Right Triangle</u> is one in which one angle is a right angle.

An <u>Isosceles Triangle</u> is one in which two sides are equal.

A <u>Scalene Triangle</u> is one in which no two sides are equal.

The <u>Area of a Triangle</u> is equal to $\frac{1}{2}$ the product of the base and altitude. $A = \frac{1}{2}ah$

Where A denotes the area and S $\frac{1}{2}$ the perimeter of $\triangle ABC$ then

$$A = \sqrt{S(s-a)(s-b)(s-c)}$$

The hypotenuse of a right triangle is the side opposite the right angle. (AC)

In a right triangle the sum of the squares on the arms is equivalent to the square on the hypotenuse.

$$AC^2 = BC^2 + BA^2$$

The square on an arm of a right triangle is equivalent to the difference between the squares on the hypotenuse and the other arm.

$$AB^2 = AC^2 - BC^2 \text{ and } BC^2 = AC^2 - AB^2$$

A <u>Trapezium</u> is a quadrilateral having no two sides parallel.

Trapezoid:

Area is equal to ½ the product of its altitude and the sum of its bases.

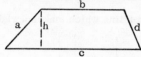

Area = ½h (b + c)

A <u>Trapezoid</u> is a quadrilateral having 2, and only 2, sides parallel.

A <u>Parallelogram</u> is a quadrilateral having its opposite sides parallel.

A <u>Rectangle</u> is a parallelogram whose angles are right angles.

A <u>Rhomboid</u> is a parallelogram whose angles are oblique.

A <u>Square</u> is an equilateral rectangle.

Rectangle

Area of a rectangle is equal to the product of its base and altitude.

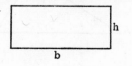

Rhombus is a parallelogram whose angles are oblique and whose sides are equal.

The altitude of a parallelogram or trapezoid is the perpendicular distance between the parallel sides.

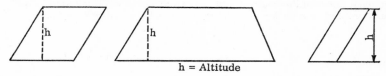

h = Altitude

Parallelogram

Area = product of its base and altitude.

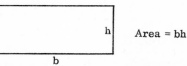

Area = bh

The altitude of a triangle is the perpendicular from any vertex to the opposite side (produced if necessary).

A proportion is a statement of the equality of two ratios, as $\frac{a}{b} = \frac{c}{d}$

$a : b = c : d$. (These are identical statements.)

The first and fourth terms of a proportion are called the <u>extremes</u> and the second and third, the <u>means</u>.

The product of the means is equal to the product of the extremes. ad = bc

A line parallel to one side of a triangle divides the other two sides proportionally. $EC : EA = BD : DA$

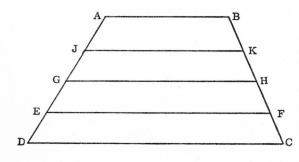

If 3 or more parallels intercept equal lengths on one transversal, they intercept equal lengths on every transversal.

If AB ∥ JK ∥ GH ∥ EF ∥ DC and $AJ = JG = GE = ED$

then $BK = KH = HF = FC$

To find the area of shapes other than squares, rectangles, or triangles, convert shape to series of these forms.

When the means of a proportion are equal, either mean is said to be the mean proportional between the first and last term.

In $a : b = b : c$ "b" is the mean proportional.

In a right triangle, the altitude upon the hypotenuse is the mean proportional between the segments of the hypotenuse and either arm is the mean proportional between the hypotenuse and the adjacent segment.

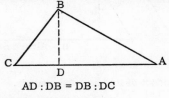

AD : DB = DB : DC

and   AD : AB = AB : AC

E

Methods of Area Computations

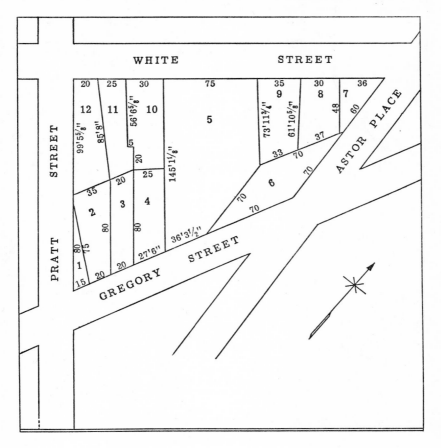

Area of Lot #1 = $\sqrt{S(S-A)(S-B)(S-C)}$ where A,B,&C are the sides $S = \frac{1}{2}(A + B + C)$.

Area = $\sqrt{(85)(5)(10)(70)}$ = 545 sq. ft.

Area of Lot #2: Construct a diagonal and erect perpendiculars as shown scale values.

Area = $\frac{1}{2}(89)(28 + 17)$ = 2,002 sq. ft.

Area of Lot #3: Construct perpendicular between parallel lines & scale.

Area = (18.18)(80) = 1,454 sq. ft.

Exact Area of Lots
1,2,&3 = (50)(80)
= 4,000 square feet.

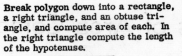

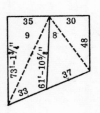

Break polygon down into a rectangle, a right triangle, and an obtuse triangle, and compute area of each. In the right triangle compute the length of the hypotenuse.

Hyp. = $\sqrt{(71.115)^2 + (75)^2} = 103.35$

Area of Obtuse Triangle

= $\sqrt{(104.82)(1.47)(68.53)(34.82)}$
Area = 606.37 sq. ft.

Area of Right Triangle

= $\frac{1}{2}(75)(71.115) = 2,666.81$

Area of Rectangle

= $(73.979)(75) = 5,548.425$

Total Area = 8,822 sq. ft.

Wherever possible, compute lengths of lines rather than scaled values.

Area of Triangle
= $\frac{1}{2}$(B)(H)
where B denotes the base and H the altitude.

Area of a rectangle = (A)(B) where A & B denote the lengths of sides.

Area of parallelogram = (A)(H) (opposite sides parallel) where A denotes the side and H the altitude.

Area of Lot 8. Break polygon down into a right triangle and an obtuse triangle. Compute length of hypotenuse.

Hyp. = $\sqrt{(30)^2 + (48)^2} = 56.604$

Area of Obtuse Triangle

= $\sqrt{(77.745)(15.860)(21.141)(40.745)}$
Area = 1,031 sq. ft.

Area of Right Triangle

= $\frac{1}{2}(30)(48) = 720$ sq. ft.
Total area = 1,751 sq. ft.
Compute area of Lot 9 similarly
Check areas by computing Lots 8 and 9 as one lot.
Area = $\frac{1}{2}(73.979 + 48)(65)$
Area = 3,963 sq. ft.

Do Lots 11 & 12 similarly.

Area of a trapezoid = $\frac{1}{2}$H(A + B) (four sides, two parallel) where A & B are the sides and H the altitude.

Area of any triangle =
S(S − A)(S − B)(S − C)
where S = $\frac{1}{2}$(A + B + C)
and A, B, & C denote the sides.

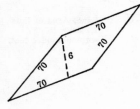

Area of Lot 6 Scale perpendicular to any side.
Area = (36)(70) = 2,520 sq. ft.

F   Land Appraisal

The valuation of land for tax purposes is accomplished by appraising large acreage parcels on a unit per acre basis; Platted areas are appraised on the basis of foot front values. In both instances the values used are the consequence of a constant study of land values based on sales, income derived from land, and a comparison of parcels to assure equitability, and uniformity.

The foot front method is the most commonly used of the two methods as land in Cuyahoga County is intensely used. This method is based on the observation that increases in value of land are not proportionate to an increase in the depth. For this reason depth percentage tables are always applied which successively decrease the value of the land as it proceeds from the street to the rear of the lot. For example: a lot that is 50 ft. wide and 100 ft. deep located on a street with a $100 foot front value would be priced at $5,000. The first 25 ft. is valued at $2395 and each successive foot decreases in value so that the last 25 ft. is valued at only $585.

The application of this factor is based upon the assumption that the land is in desirable condition with no topographical or other encumbrances. A field check of each parcel is made to correct any factor that will detract from the normal usefulness of the land.

The following tables and illustrations demonstrate how land values are computed for lots with regular and irregular shapes as well as a demonstration of the valuation of a lot with corner influence.

25 ft. — $585

25 ft. — $790

25 ft. — $1,230

25 ft. — $2,395

Street $100 unit value

Effect of depth influence upon the value of successive increments of land

Courtesy of John J. Carney, Auditor of Cuyahoga County, Ohio.

439

G

Land-Value Tables

Triangular Lot Table

Lot with BASE on street, compute as rectangle and apply Table.
Lot with APEX on street, reverse Table.

Depth of Perpendicular	% of Rectangle Value
10	
10 feet	50 %
20 "	55.5%
30 "	58 %
40 "	59 %
50 "	60 %
60 "	61 %
70 "	62 %
80 "	63 %
90 "	64 %
100 "	65 %
110 "	66 %
120 "	67 %
130 "	68 %
140 "	69 %
150 "	70 %
200 "	73.5%
250 "	77.5%
300 "	79 %
350 "	80 %
400 "	81 %
450 "	82 %
500 "	83 %
550 "	84 %
600 "	85 %

Corner Influence Percentage Table

Feet Deep	%	Feet Deep	%	Feet Deep	%	Feet Deep	%	Feet Deep	%
1	2.6	21	30.2	41	40.5	61	45.2	81	48.1
2	4.9	22	30.9	42	40.8	62	45.4	82	48.2
3	7.0	23	31.6	43	41.1	63	45.6	83	48.3
4	9.0	24	32.3	44	41.4	64	45.8	84	48.4
5	10.9	25	33.0	45	41.7	65	46.0	85	48.5
6	12.7	26	33.6	46	42.0	66	46.2	86	48.6
7	14.4	27	34.2	47	42.3	67	46.4	87	48.7
8	16.0	28	34.8	48	42.6	68	46.6	88	48.8
9	17.5	29	35.4	49	42.8	69	46.8	89	48.9
10	19.0	30	36.0	50	43.0	70	47.0	90	49.0
11	20.4	31	36.5	51	43.2	71	47.1	91	49.1
12	21.7	32	37.0	52	43.4	72	47.2	92	49.2
13	22.9	33	37.5	53	43.6	73	47.3	93	49.3
14	24.0	34	37.9	54	43.8	74	47.4	94	49.4
15	25.0	35	38.3	55	44.0	75	47.5	95	49.5
16	26.0	36	38.7	56	44.2	76	47.6	96	49.6
17	26.9	37	39.1	57	44.4	77	47.7	97	49.7
18	27.8	38	39.5	58	44.6	78	47.8	98	49.8
19	28.6	39	39.9	59	44.8	79	47.9	99	49.9
20	29.4	40	40.2	60	45.0	80	48.0	100	50.0

Courtesy of John J. Carney, Auditor of Cuyahoga County, Ohio.

Depth Percentage Table

CLEVELAND

For Lots From 1 to 700 Feet Deep

1	3.10%	51	73.25%	101	100.43%	151	115.19%	201	122.10%
2	6.10	2	74.00	2	100.85	2	115.38	2	122.20
3	9.00	3	74.75	3	101.27	3	115.57	3	122.30
4	11.75	4	75.50	4	101.70	4	115.76	4	122.40
5	14.35	5	76.20	5	102.08	5	115.95	5	122.50
6	16.75	6	76.90	6	102.48	6	116.12	210	122.95
7	19.05	7	77.55	7	102.88	7	116.29	15	123.38
8	21.20	8	78.20	8	103.25	8	116.46	20	123.80
9	23.20	9	78.85	9	103.62	9	116.62	30	124.60
10	25.00	60	79.50	110	104.00	160	116.80	240	125.35
1	26.70	1	80.14	1	104.36	1	116.96	50	126.05
2	28.36	2	80.77	2	104.72	2	117.13	60	126.75
3	29.99	3	81.38	3	105.08	3	117.30	70	127.40
4	31.61	4	82.00	4	105.43	4	117.47	80	128.05
5	33.22	5	82.61	5	105.78	5	117.64	90	128.65
6	34.82	6	83.21	6	106.13	6	117.79	300	129.25
7	36.41	7	83.82	7	106.47	7	117.94	10	129.80
8	37.97	8	84.42	8	106.81	8	118.09	20	130.35
9	39.50	9	85.01	9	107.15	9	118.24	30	130.90
20	41.00	70	85.60	120	107.50	170	118.40	340	131.40
1	42.50	1	86.15	1	107.80	1	118.54	50	131.90
2	43.96	2	86.70	2	108.11	2	118.70	60	132.40
3	45.30	3	87.24	3	108.43	3	118.85	70	132.85
4	46.61	4	87.78	4	108.75	4	119.00	80	133.30
5	47.90	5	88.30	5	109.05	5	119.14	90	133.75
6	49.17	6	88.82	6	109.35	6	119.28	400	134.20
7	50.40	7	89.35	7	109.65	7	119.41	10	134.60
8	51.61	8	89.87	8	109.93	8	119.54	20	135.00
9	52.81	9	90.39	9	110.21	9	119.67	30	135.40
30	54.00	80	90.90	130	110.50	180	119.80	440	135.80
1	55.05	1	91.40	1	110.76	1	119.92	50	136.15
2	56.10	2	91.89	2	111.02	2	120.05	60	136.50
3	57.15	3	92.38	3	111.28	3	120.18	70	136.85
4	58.20	4	92.86	4	111.55	4	120.31	80	137.20
5	59.25	5	93.33	5	111.80	5	120.43	90	137.55
6	60.25	6	93.80	6	112.05	6	120.55	500	137.85
7	61.25	7	94.27	7	112.28	7	120.66	10	138.15
8	62.20	8	94.73	8	112.52	8	120.77	20	138.45
9	63.10	9	95.17	9	112.76	9	120.88	30	138.75
40	64.00	90	95.60	140	113.00	190	121.00	540	139.05
1	64.95	1	96.04	1	113.22	1	121.10	50	139.30
2	65.90	2	96.50	2	113.43	2	121.21	60	139.55
3	66.75	3	96.95	3	113.64	3	121.32	70	139.80
4	67.60	4	97.40	4	113.85	4	121.43	80	140.05
5	68.45	5	97.85	5	114.05	5	121.53	600	140.55
6	69.30	6	98.30	6	114.25	6	121.62	20	140.95
7	70.10	7	98.74	7	114.45	7	121.71	40	141.35
8	70.90	8	99.17	8	114.64	8	121.80	60	141.75
9	71.70	9	99.58	9	114.82	9	121.90	80	142.05
50	72.50	100	100.00	150	115.00	200	122.00	700	142.35

Courtesy of John J. Carney, Auditor of Cuyahoga County, Ohio.

H Rectangular-Lot Computation

A Rectangular Lot

The value of a rectangular parcel with 45 feet frontage on a street with a $24 unit value and a depth of 120 feet is computed as follows:

1) 45 ft. x 107.50% (See depth percentage table opposite 120 feet) = 48.38 size factor

2) 48.38 size factor x $24 unit for street = $1,161 value of lot
Total for tax purposes = 1160
(all tax values are carried to the closest ten dollar amount)

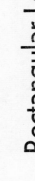

street $24 unit

45 feet

6

120 feet

The parcels below all have the same dimensions - 45 feet by 120. The $24 unit value applies to all these parcels. The land value is therefore the same for all parcels. This is illustrative of the results achieved by uniformity in appraising techniques.

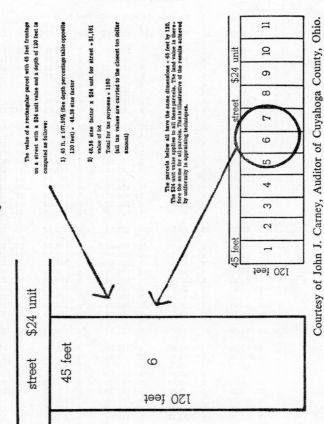

Courtesy of John J. Carney, Auditor of Cuyahoga County, Ohio.

442

Corner-Influence Computation

Lot With Full Corner Influence

Corner lots frequently have a value greater than lots with inside frontage. The reasons for this increased value are not difficult to recognize. Such lots for example have increased accessibility — more potential utilization of space for display purposes. Recognition of these facts has resulted in the development of corner influence tables to measure the increased value resulting from the benefits of corner locations. The corner influence is generally assumed not to extend beyond a distance of 100 feet from the street with the highest unit value. Commercial enterprises are most frequently benefited by such corner locations. Corner influence is not applied to residential properties.

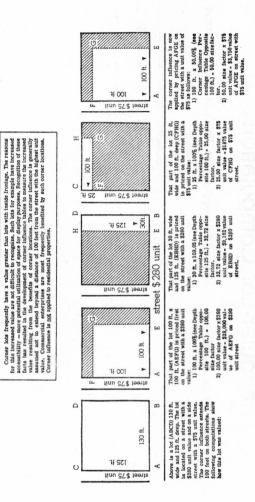

Above is a lot (ABCD) 130 ft. wide and 125 ft. deep. The lot is located on a street with a $280 unit value and on a side street with a $75 unit value. The corner influence extends 100 feet on both streets. The following computations show how this lot was valued:

That part of the lot 100 ft. x 100 ft. (AEFG) is priced first on the street with a $280 unit value:
1) 100 ft. x 100% (see Depth Percentage Table opposite 100 ft.) - 100.00 size factor
2) 100.00 size factor x $280 unit value - $28,000 value of AEFG on $280 unit street

That part of the lot 30 ft. wide and 125 ft. (EBHD) is priced on the street with a $280 unit value:
1) 30 ft. x 103.05 (see Depth Percentage Table opposite 125 ft.) - 32.72 size factor.
2) 32.72 size factor x $280 unit value - $9,162 value of EBHD on $280 unit street.

That part of the lot 25 ft. wide and 100 ft. deep (CFHG) is priced on the street with a $75 unit value:
1) 25 ft. x 100% (see Depth Percentage Table opposite 100 ft.) - 25.00 size factor.
2) 25.00 size factor x $75 unit value - $1875 value of CFHG on $75 unit street.

The corner influence is now applied by pricing AFGE on the street with a unit value of $75 as follows:
1) 100 ft. x 50.00% (see Corner Influence Table Opposite 100 ft.) - 50.00 size factor.
2) 50.00 size factor x $75 unit value - $3,750 value of AFGE on street with $75 unit value.

Value for tax purposes is the sum of these Computations as follows: AEFG $28,000 + EBHD $9,162 + CFHG $1,875 + AFGE $3,750 (Corner Influence) - $42,790 (All tax values are carried to the nearest ten dollar amount)

Triangular-Lot Computation

Triangular Lot With Apex On Street

Triangular Lot With Base On Street

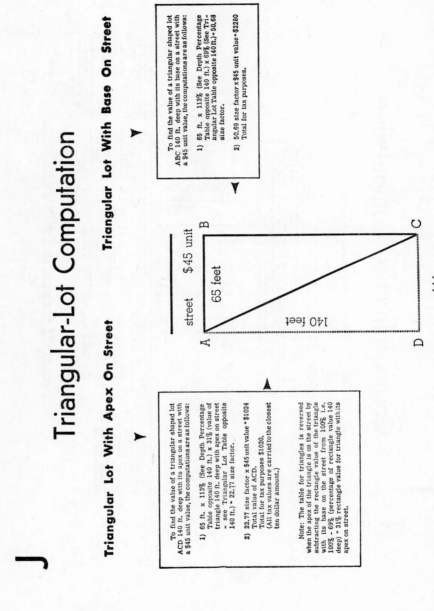

To find the value of a triangular shaped lot ACD 140 ft. deep with its apex on a street with a $45 unit value, the computations are as follows:

1) 65 ft. x 113% (See Depth Percentage Table opposite 140 ft.) x 31% (value of triangle 140 ft. deep with apex on street – see Triangular Lot Table opposite 140 ft.) = 22.77 size factor.

2) 22.77 size factor x $45 unit value = $1024
   Total value of ACD.
   Total for tax purposes $1020.
   (All tax values are carried to the closest ten dollar amount.)

Note: The table for triangles is reversed when the apex of the triangle is on the street by subtracting the rectangle value of the triangle with its base on the street from 100% i.e. 100% – 69% (percentage of rectangle value 140 deep) = 31% rectangle value for triangle with its apex on street.

To find the value of a triangular shaped lot ABC 140 ft. deep with its base on a street with a $45 unit value, the computations are as follows:

1) 65 ft. x 113% (See Depth Percentage Table opposite 140 ft.) x 69% (See Triangular Lot Table opposite 140 ft.) = 50.68 size factor.

2) 50.69 size factor x $45 unit value = $2280
   Total for tax purposes.

street $45 unit

65 feet

140 feet

A   B

C   D

444

K

Depth Tables

The following are tables for apportioning the value of front lots that are longer or shorter than 25 x 100 feet. These rules are helpful guides, but actual value in each instance much depends on the use to which such lots or parts of lots can be profitably put, their marketability for such use, and the usual factors of value. The tables are not strictly applicable to rear or inside land when the frontage is in different ownership.

Hoffman Rule

The first recognized rule for appraising lots of varying depths is credited to Judge Murray Hoffman in 1866 and is generally known as the Hoffman Rule. In his opinion the front half (50 feet deep) of a 100-foot deep lot is worth two-thirds its whole value. It was assumed, therefore, that the first 25 feet was worth two-thirds of 50 feet, 12½ feet two-thirds of 25 feet, and so on.

Hoffman-Neill Rule

The following table revising and elaborating on the Hoffman Rule was published in the Evening Mail by its real estate editor, the late Henry Harmon Neill.

Feet	P.C.	Feet	P.C.	Feet	P.C.	Feet	P.C.
1	06.76	26	45.48	51	67.45	76	85.14
2	10.14	27	46.50	52	68.22	77	85.79
3	12.86	28	47.51	53	68.99	78	86.44
4	15.20	29	48.50	54	69.75	79	87.09
5	17.32	30	49.47	55	70.51	80	87.73
6	19.29	31	50.42	56	71.26	81	88.37
7	21.12	32	51.36	57	72.01	82	89.01
8	22.82	33	52.29	58	72.75	83	89.64
9	24.43	34	53.21	59	73.48	84	90.27
10	25.98	35	54.12	60	74.20	85	90.90
11	27.48	36	55.01	61	74.92	86	91.53
12	28.93	37	55.89	62	75.63	87	92.16
13	30.33	38	56.76	63	76.34	88	92.78
14	31.68	39	57.63	64	77.04	89	93.40
15	32.98	40	58.49	65	77.74	90	94.01
16	34.24	41	59.34	66	78.43	91	94.62
17	35.47	42	60.18	67	79.12	92	95.23
18	36.67	43	61.02	68	79.81	93	95.83
19	37.84	44	61.85	69	80.49	94	96.43
20	38.99	45	62.67	70	81.17	95	97.03
21	40.12	46	63.48	71	81.85	96	97.63
22	41.23	47	64.29	72	82.51	97	98.23
23	42.32	48	65.09	73	83.17	98	98.82
24	43.49	49	65.88	74	83.83	99	99.41
25	44.44	50	66.67	75	84.49	100	100.00

Courtesy of the *Annual Diary and Manual of the Real Estate Board of New York, Inc.*

Davies Rule

(See preceding page for Hoffman Rule and Hoffman-Neill Rule and Depth Table)

The following depth table was prepared by William E. Davies based on the following formula:

$$Y = \sqrt{1.45\ (X + .0352)} - .226.\quad Y = \text{is the ratio sought.}\quad X = \frac{\text{is the depth of lot}}{100}$$

Depth	Ratio	Depth	Ratio	Depth	Ratio	Depth	Ratio
1	.030	51	.663	101	1.006	151	1.271
2	.057	52	.671	102	1.011	152	1.276
3	.081	53	.679	103	1.017	153	1.281
4	.104	54	.687	104	1.023	154	1.285
5	.125	55	.695	105	1.029	155	1.290
6	.146	56	.703	106	1.034	156	1.295
7	.165	57	.711	107	1.040	157	1.300
8	.183	58	.718	108	1.046	158	1.304
9	.200	59	.726	109	1.051	159	1.309
10	.217	60	.734	110	1.057	160	1.314
11	.233	61	.741	111	1.063	161	1.319
12	248	62	.749	112	1.068	162	1.323
13	263	63	.756	113	1.074	163	1.328
14	278	64	.763	114	1.080	164	1.333
15	.292	65	.771	115	1.085	165	1.337
16	.306	66	.778	116	1.090	166	1.342
17	.319	67	.785	117	1.096	167	1.346
18	.333	68	.792	118	1.101	168	1.351
19	.345	69	.799	119	1.107	169	1.356
20	.358	70	.806	120	1.112	170	1.360
21	.370	71	.813	121	1.118	171	1.365
22	.382	72	.820	122	1.123	172	1.369
23	.394	73	.827	123	1.128	173	1.374
24	406	74	.834	124	1.134	174	1.378
25	417	75	.841	125	1.139	175	1.383
26	428	76	.848	126	1.144	176	1.387
27	439	77	.855	127	1.150	177	1.392
28	450	78	.861	128	1.155	178	1.397
29	.461	79	.868	129	1.160	179	1.401
30	.471	80	.874	130	1.165	180	1.405
31	.481	81	.881	131	1.171	181	1.410
32	.492	82	.888	132	1.176	182	1.414
33	.502	83	.894	133	1.181	183	1.419
34	.512	84	.901	134	1.186	184	1.423
35	.521	85	.907	135	1.191	185	1.427
36	.531	86	.913	136	1.196	186	1.432
37	.541	87	.920	137	1.201	187	1.436
38	.550	88	.926	138	1.206	188	1.440
39	.559	89	.932	139	1.212	189	1.445
40	.568	90	.938	140	1.217	190	1.449
41	.577	91	.945	141	1.222	191	1.453
42	.586	92	.951	142	1.228	192	1.458
43	.595	93	.957	143	1.232	193	1.462
44	.604	94	.963	144	1.237	194	1.466
45	.613	95	.969	145	1.241	195	1.471
46	.621	96	.976	146	1.246	196	1.475
47	.630	97	.981	147	1.251	197	1.479
48	.638	98	.988	148	1.256	198	1.483
49	.647	99	.993	149	1.261	199	1.487
50	.655	100	1.000	150	1.266	200	1.492

Courtesy of the *Annual Diary and Manual of the Real Estate Board of New York, Inc.*

L

Level Constant Payment Plans (Monthly Payments)

Left table

TOTAL CONSTANT RATE	INTEREST RATE	PERCENT PAID OFF IN				FULL TERM
		5 Yrs	10 Yrs	15 Yrs	20 Yrs	
5½%	4 1/4%	7.0%	15.5%	26.2%	39.3%	35 YRS.- 0 MOS.
	4 1/2%	5.6%	12.6%	21.4%	32.3%	38 YRS.- 0 MOS.
6%	4 1/4%	9.7%	21.8%	36.6%	55.0%	29 YRS.- 1 MOS.
	4 1/2%	8.4%	18.9%	32.1%	48.5%	30 YRS.-11 MOS.
	4 3/4%	7.0%	16.0%	27.3%	41.6%	33 YRS.- 2 MOS.
	5 %	5.7%	12.9%	22.3%	34.3%	35 YRS.-11 MOS.
6½%	4 1/4%	12.5%	28.0%	47.1%	70.7%	25 YRS.- 1 MOS.
	4 1/2%	11.2%	25.2%	42.7%	64.7%	26 YRS.- 3 MOS.
	4 3/4%	9.9%	22.3%	38.2%	58.2%	27 YRS.- 9 MOS.
	5 %	8.5%	19.4%	33.4%	51.4%	29 YRS.- 6 MOS.
	5 1/4%	7.1%	16.4%	28.4%	44.1%	31 YRS.- 6 MOS.
	5 1/2%	5.7%	13.3%	23.2%	36.3%	34 YRS.- 2 MOS.
7%	4 1/4%	15.3%	34.2%	57.6%	86.5%	22 YRS.- 1 MOS.
	4 1/2%	14.0%	31.5%	53.4%	80.9%	23 YRS.- 0 MOS.
	4 3/4%	12.7%	28.7%	49.1%	74.9%	24 YRS.- 0 MOS.
	5 %	11.3%	25.9%	44.5%	68.5%	25 YRS.- 2 MOS.
	5 1/4%	10.0%	23.0%	39.8%	61.7%	26 YRS.- 6 MOS.
	5 1/2%	8.6%	19.9%	34.8%	54.5%	28 YRS.- 2 MOS.
	5 3/4%	7.2%	16.8%	29.7%	46.7%	30 YRS.- 1 MOS.
	6 %	5.8%	13.7%	24.2%	38.5%	32 YRS.- 7 MOS.
7¼%	4 1/4%	16.7%	37.3%	62.8%	94.3%	20 YRS.-10 MOS.
	4 1/2%	15.4%	34.6%	58.8%	88.9%	21 YRS.- 7 MOS.
	4 3/4%	14.1%	31.9%	54.5%	83.2%	22 YRS.- 6 MOS.
	5 %	12.8%	29.1%	50.1%	77.1%	23 YRS.- 6 MOS.
	5 1/4%	11.4%	26.2%	45.5%	70.5%	24 YRS.- 8 MOS.
	5 1/2%	10.0%	23.3%	40.7%	63.5%	25 YRS.-11 MOS.
	5 3/4%	8.7%	20.2%	35.6%	56.1%	27 YRS.- 6 MOS.
	6 %	7.3%	17.1%	30.3%	48.1%	29 YRS.- 5 MOS.
7½%	4 1/4%	18.1%	40.4%	68.0%		19 YRS.- 9 MOS.
	4 1/2%	16.8%	37.8%	64.1%	97.0%	20 YRS.- 5 MOS.
	4 3/4%	15.5%	35.1%	60.0%	91.5%	21 YRS.- 2 MOS.
	5 %	14.2%	32.4%	55.7%	85.6%	22 YRS.- 1 MOS.
	5 1/4%	12.8%	29.5%	51.2%	79.3%	23 YRS.- 0 MOS.
	5 1/2%	11.5%	26.6%	46.5%	72.6%	24 YRS.- 2 MOS.
	5 3/4%	10.1%	23.6%	41.5%	65.4%	25 YRS.- 5 MOS.
	6 %	8.7%	20.5%	36.4%	57.8%	26 YRS.-11 MOS.
	6 1/2%	5.9%	14.0%	25.3%	40.9%	31 YRS.- 1 MOS.
7¾%	4 1/4%	19.5%	43.5%	73.3%		18 YRS.- 9 MOS.
	4 1/2%	18.2%	40.9%	69.4%		19 YRS.- 5 MOS.
	4 3/4%	16.9%	38.3%	65.4%	99.8%	20 YRS.- 1 MOS.
	5 %	15.6%	35.6%	61.3%	94.2%	20 YRS.-10 MOS.
	5 1/4%	14.3%	32.8%	56.9%	88.1%	21 YRS.- 8 MOS.
	5 1/2%	12.9%	29.9%	52.3%	81.7%	22 YRS.- 7 MOS.
	5 3/4%	11.6%	26.9%	47.5%	74.8%	23 YRS.- 8 MOS.
	6 %	10.2%	23.9%	42.4%	67.4%	24 YRS.-11 MOS.
	6 1/2%	7.4%	17.5%	31.6%	51.1%	28 YRS.- 2 MOS.
8%	4 1/4%	20.9%	46.6%	78.5%		17 YRS.-11 MOS.
	4 1/2%	19.6%	44.1%	74.8%		18 YRS.- 5 MOS.
	4 3/4%	18.3%	41.5%	70.9%		19 YRS.- 1 MOS.
	5 %	17.0%	38.8%	66.8%		19 YRS.- 8 MOS.
	5 1/4%	15.7%	36.1%	62.5%	97.0%	20 YRS.- 5 MOS.
	5 1/2%	14.4%	33.2%	58.1%	90.8%	21 YRS.- 3 MOS.
	5 3/4%	13.0%	30.3%	53.4%	84.1%	22 YRS.- 2 MOS.
	6 %	11.6%	27.3%	48.5%	77.0%	23 YRS.- 2 MOS.
	6 1/2%	8.8%	21.1%	37.9%	61.3%	25 YRS.-10 MOS.
	7 %	6.0%	14.4%	26.4%	43.4%	29 YRS.-10 MOS.
8¼%	4 1/4%	22.2%	49.7%	83.7%		17 YRS.- 1 MOS.
	4 1/2%	21.0%	47.2%	80.1%		17 YRS.- 7 MOS.
	4 3/4%	19.7%	44.7%	76.4%		18 YRS.- 2 MOS.
	5 %	18.4%	42.1%	72.4%		18 YRS.- 9 MOS.
	5 1/4%	17.1%	39.3%	68.2%		19 YRS.- 4 MOS.
	5 1/2%	15.8%	36.6%	63.9%	99.8%	20 YRS.- 1 MOS.
	5 3/4%	14.4%	33.7%	59.3%	93.5%	20 YRS.-10 MOS.
	6 %	13.1%	30.7%	54.5%	86.6%	21 YRS.- 9 MOS.
	6 1/2%	10.3%	24.6%	44.3%	71.5%	24 YRS.- 0 MOS.
	7 %	7.5%	18.0%	33.0%	54.3%	27 YRS.- 1 MOS.
8½%	4 1/4%	23.6%	52.8%	89.0%		16 YRS.- 5 MOS.
	4 1/2%	22.4%	50.4%	85.5%		16 YRS.-11 MOS.
	4 3/4%	21.1%	47.9%	81.8%		17 YRS.- 4 MOS.
	5 %	19.8%	45.3%	78.0%		17 YRS.-10 MOS.
	5 1/4%	18.5%	42.6%	73.9%		18 YRS.- 5 MOS.
	5 1/2%	17.2%	39.9%	69.7%		19 YRS.- 0 MOS.
	5 3/4%	15.9%	37.1%	65.2%		19 YRS.- 9 MOS.
	6 %	14.5%	34.1%	60.6%	96.3%	20 YRS.- 6 MOS.
	6 1/2%	11.8%	28.1%	50.6%	81.7%	22 YRS.- 4 MOS.
	7 %	8.9%	21.6%	39.6%	65.1%	24 YRS.-11 MOS.
	7 1/2%	6.0%	14.8%	27.6%	46.1%	28 YRS.- 8 MOS.

Right table

TOTAL CONSTANT RATE	INTEREST RATE	PERCENT PAID OFF IN				FULL TERM
		5 Yrs	10 Yrs	15 Yrs	20 Yrs	
8¾%	4 1/4%	25.0%	56.0%	94.2%		15 YRS.- 9 MOS.
	4 1/2%	23.8%	53.5%	90.8%		16 YRS.- 1 MOS.
	4 3/4%	22.5%	51.1%	87.3%		16 YRS.- 7 MOS.
	5 %	21.3%	48.5%	83.5%		17 YRS.- 0 MOS.
	5 1/4%	20.0%	45.9%	79.6%		17 YRS.- 6 MOS.
	5 1/2%	18.7%	43.2%	75.5%		18 YRS.- 1 MOS.
	5 3/4%	17.3%	40.4%	71.2%		18 YRS.- 8 MOS.
	6 %	16.0%	37.6%	66.6%		19 YRS.- 5 MOS.
	6 1/2%	13.3%	31.6%	56.9%	92.0%	21 YRS.- 0 MOS.
	7 %	10.4%	25.2%	46.2%	76.0%	23 YRS.- 1 MOS.
9%	4 1/4%	26.4%	59.1%	99.4%		15 YRS.- 1 MOS.
	4 1/2%	25.2%	56.7%	96.2%		15 YRS.- 6 MOS.
	4 3/4%	23.9%	54.3%	92.7%		15 YRS.-10 MOS.
	5 %	22.7%	51.8%	89.1%		16 YRS.- 4 MOS.
	5 1/4%	21.4%	49.2%	85.3%		16 YRS.- 9 MOS.
	5 1/2%	20.1%	46.5%	81.3%		17 YRS.- 3 MOS.
	6 %	17.4%	41.0%	72.7%		18 YRS.- 5 MOS.
	6 1/2%	14.7%	35.1%	63.2%		19 YRS.-10 MOS.
	7 %	11.9%	28.8%	52.8%	86.8%	21 YRS.- 7 MOS.
	7 1/2%	9.1%	22.2%	41.4%	69.2%	24 YRS.- 0 MOS.
	8 %	6.1%	15.2%	28.8%	49.1%	27 YRS.- 7 MOS.
9½%	4 1/4%	29.2%	65.3%			14 YRS.- 0 MOS.
	4 1/2%	28.0%	63.0%			14 YRS.- 4 MOS.
	4 3/4%	26.7%	60.7%			14 YRS.- 8 MOS.
	5 %	25.5%	58.2%			15 YRS.- 0 MOS.
	5 1/4%	24.2%	55.7%	96.7%		15 YRS.- 5 MOS.
	5 1/2%	23.0%	53.2%	92.9%		15 YRS.-10 MOS.
	5 3/4%	21.7%	50.5%	89.0%		16 YRS.- 3 MOS.
	6 %	20.9%	47.8%	84.8%		16 YRS.- 9 MOS.
	6 1/2%	17.7%	42.1%	75.9%		17 YRS.-10 MOS.
	7 %	14.9%	36.1%	66.0%		19 YRS.- 2 MOS.
	7 1/2%	12.1%	29.7%	55.2%	92.3%	20 YRS.-11 MOS.
	8 %	9.2%	22.9%	43.3%	73.6%	23 YRS.- 2 MOS.
10%	4 1/4%	32.0%	71.5%			13 YRS.- 0 MOS.
	4 1/2%	30.8%	69.3%			13 YRS.- 4 MOS.
	4 3/4%	29.6%	67.0%			13 YRS.- 8 MOS.
	5 %	28.3%	64.7%			13 YRS.-11 MOS.
	5 1/4%	27.1%	62.3%			14 YRS.- 3 MOS.
	5 1/2%	25.8%	59.8%			14 YRS.- 7 MOS.
	5 3/4%	24.6%	57.3%			15 YRS.- 0 MOS.
	6 %	23.3%	54.6%	96.9%		15 YRS.- 4 MOS.
	6 1/2%	20.6%	49.1%	88.5%		16 YRS.- 3 MOS.
	7 %	17.9%	43.3%	79.2%		17 YRS.- 3 MOS.
	7 1/2%	15.1%	37.1%	69.0%		18 YRS.- 7 MOS.
	8 %	12.2%	30.5%	57.7%	98.2%	20 YRS.- 5 MOS.
10½%	4 1/4%	34.8%	77.7%			12 YRS.- 3 MOS.
	4 1/2%	33.6%	75.6%			12 YRS.- 6 MOS.
	4 3/4%	32.4%	73.4%			12 YRS.- 9 MOS.
	5 %	31.2%	71.2%			13 YRS.- 0 MOS.
	5 1/4%	29.9%	68.9%			13 YRS.- 3 MOS.
	5 1/2%	28.7%	66.5%			13 YRS.- 7 MOS.
	5 3/4%	27.4%	64.0%			13 YRS.-10 MOS.
	6 %	26.2%	61.5%			14 YRS.- 2 MOS.
	6 1/2%	23.6%	56.1%			14 YRS.-11 MOS.
	7 %	20.9%	50.5%	92.4%		15 YRS.- 9 MOS.
	7 1/2%	18.1%	44.5%	82.8%		16 YRS.-11 MOS.
	8 %	15.5%	38.1%	72.1%		18 YRS.- 0 MOS.
11%	4 1/4%	37.5%	83.9%			11 YRS.- 9 MOS.
	4 1/2%	36.4%	81.9%			11 YRS.-11 MOS.
	4 3/4%	35.2%	79.8%			12 YRS.- 0 MOS.
	5 %	34.0%	77.6%			12 YRS.- 2 MOS.
	5 1/4%	32.8%	75.4%			12 YRS.- 5 MOS.
	5 1/2%	31.6%	73.1%			12 YRS.- 8 MOS.
	5 3/4%	30.3%	70.7%			12 YRS.-11 MOS.
	6 %	29.1%	68.3%			13 YRS.- 3 MOS.
	6 1/2%	26.5%	63.2%			13 YRS.-10 MOS.
	7 %	23.9%	57.7%			14 YRS.- 6 MOS.
	7 1/2%	21.2%	51.9%	96.6%		15 YRS.- 4 MOS.
	8 %	18.4%	45.7%	86.5%		16 YRS.- 4 MOS.
11½%	4 1/4%	40.3%	90.1%			10 YRS.-11 MOS.
	4 1/2%	39.2%	88.0%			11 YRS.- 1 MOS.
	4 3/4%	38.0%	86.2%			11 YRS.- 3 MOS.
	5 %	36.8%	84.0%			11 YRS.- 5 MOS.
	5 1/4%	35.6%	82.0%			11 YRS.- 6 MOS.
	5 1/2%	34.4%	79.8%			11 YRS.-11 MOS.
	5 3/4%	33.2%	77.5%			12 YRS.- 1 MOS.
	6 %	32.0%	75.1%			12 YRS.- 4 MOS.
	6 1/2%	29.5%	70.2%			12 YRS.-11 MOS.
	7 %	26.8%	64.9%			13 YRS.- 6 MOS.
	7 1/2%	24.2%	59.3%			14 YRS.- 1 MOS.
	8 %	21.4%	53.4%			15 YRS.- 0 MOS.

Financial Publishing Co., Boston.

M

Compound Interest Tables

4%   **MONTHLY COMPOUND INTEREST TABLE**   **4%**

EFFECTIVE RATE = 1/3%   i = .00333333+

MONTHS	1 AMOUNT OF 1 AT COMPOUND INTEREST $s = (1+i)^n$	2 ACCUMULATION OF 1 PER PERIOD $s_{\overline{n}|} = \frac{s-1}{i}$	3 SINKING FUND FACTOR $\frac{1}{s_{\overline{n}|}} = \frac{i}{s-1}$	4 PRES. VALUE REVERSION OF 1 $v^n = \frac{1}{s}$	5 PRESENT VALUE ORD. ANNUITY 1 PER PERIOD $a_{\overline{n}|} = \frac{s-1}{si}$	6 INSTALMENT TO AMORTIZE 1 $\frac{1}{a_{\overline{n}|}} = \frac{si}{s-1}$	n MONTHS
1	1.003333	1.000000	1.000000	.996678	.996678	1.003333	1
2	1.006678	2.003333	.499168	.993367	1.990044	.502501	2
3	1.010033	3.010011	.332225	.990066	2.980111	.335558	3
4	1.013400	4.020044	.248753	.986777	3.966888	.252086	4
5	1.016778	5.033445	.198671	.983499	4.950386	.202004	5
6	1.020167	6.050223	.165283	.980231	5.930618	.168616	6
7	1.023568	7.070390	.141435	.976975	6.907592	.144768	7
8	1.026980	8.093958	.123549	.973729	7.881321	.126882	8
9	1.030403	9.120938	.109638	.970494	8.851815	.112971	9
10	1.033838	10.151341	.098509	.967270	9.819085	.101842	10
11	1.037284	11.185179	.089404	.964056	10.783141	.092737	11

YEARS

							MONTHS
1	1.040742	12.222463	.081817	.960853	11.743994	.085150	12
2	1.083143	24.942888	.040092	.923239	23.028251	.043425	24
3	1.127272	38.181562	.026191	.887097	33.870766	.029524	36
4	1.173199	51.959601	.019246	.852371	44.288834	.022579	48
5	1.220997	66.298978	.015083	.819003	54.299069	.018416	60
6	1.270742	81.222564	.012312	.786942	63.917437	.015645	72
7	1.322514	96.754159	.010335	.756136	73.159278	.013668	84
8	1.376395	112.918536	.008856	.726536	82.039332	.012189	96
9	1.432472	129.741474	.007708	.698094	90.571761	.011041	108
10	1.490833	147.249804	.006791	.670766	98.770175	.010124	120
11	1.551571	165.471451	.006043	.644508	106.647648	.009376	132
12	1.614785	184.435477	.005422	.619278	114.216745	.008755	144
13	1.680574	204.172125	.004898	.595035	121.489536	.008231	156
14	1.749043	224.712875	.004450	.571741	128.477623	.007783	168
15	1.820302	246.090487	.004064	.549360	135.192149	.007397	180
16	1.894464	268.339056	.003727	.527854	141.643824	.007060	192
17	1.971647	291.494066	.003431	.507190	147.842938	.006764	204
18	2.051975	315.592447	.003169	.487335	153.799377	.006502	216
19	2.135575	340.672633	.002935	.468258	159.522641	.006268	228
20	2.222582	366.774625	.002726	.449927	165.021859	.006059	240
21	2.313133	393.940051	.002538	.432314	170.305801	.005871	252
22	2.407374	422.212240	.002368	.415390	175.382894	.005701	264
23	2.505454	451.636280	.002214	.399129	180.261236	.005547	276
24	2.607530	482.259102	.002074	.383505	184.948607	.005407	288
25	2.713765	514.129545	.001945	.368492	189.452484	.005278	300
26	2.824328	547.298438	.001827	.354067	193.780049	.005160	312
27	2.939396	581.818684	.001719	.340206	197.938204	.005052	324
28	3.059151	617.745337	.001619	.326888	201.933581	.004952	336
29	3.183786	655.135698	.001526	.314091	205.772553	.004859	348
30	3.313498	694.049400	.001441	.301796	209.461241	.004774	360
31	3.448495	734.548506	.001361	.289982	213.005530	.004694	372
32	3.588992	776.697608	.001288	.278630	216.411072	.004621	384
33	3.735213	820.563929	.001219	.267722	219.683299	.004552	396
34	3.887391	866.217432	.001154	.257242	222.827429	.004487	408
35	4.045770	913.730929	.001094	.247172	225.848476	.004427	420
36	4.210601	963.180200	.001038	.237496	228.751260	.004371	432
37	4.382147	1014.644110	.000986	.228199	231.540409	.004319	444
38	4.560682	1068.204739	.000936	.219265	234.220373	.004269	456
39	4.746492	1123.947510	.000890	.210682	236.795425	.004223	468
40	4.939871	1181.961329	.000846	.202434	239.269672	.004179	480
41	5.141129	1242.338719	.000805	.194510	241.647061	.004138	492
42	5.350587	1305.175978	.000766	.186895	243.931383	.004099	504
43	5.568578	1370.573323	.000730	.179579	246.126282	.004063	516
44	5.795450	1438.635057	.000695	.172549	248.235257	.004028	528
45	6.031566	1509.469732	.000662	.165794	250.261674	.003995	540
46	6.277301	1583.190320	.000632	.159304	252.208762	.003965	552
47	6.533048	1659.914398	.000602	.153068	254.079629	.003935	564
48	6.799214	1739.764334	.000575	.147076	255.877258	.003908	576
49	7.076225	1822.867480	.000549	.141318	257.604516	.003882	588
50	7.364521	1909.356375	.000524	.135786	259.264157	.003857	600

Reprinted by permission, from *Ellwood's Tables for Real Estate Appraising and Financing* (Ridgewood, N.J.: published by the author, 1959).

4¼% MONTHLY COMPOUND INTEREST TABLE 4¼%

EFFECTIVE RATE = 17/48% i = .00354166+

MONTHS	1 AMOUNT OF 1 AT COMPOUND INTEREST $s=(1+i)^n$	2 ACCUMULATION OF 1 PER PERIOD $s_{\overline{n}|}=\frac{s-1}{i}$	3 SINKING FUND FACTOR $\frac{1}{s_{\overline{n}|}}=\frac{i}{s-1}$	4 PRES. VALUE REVERSION OF 1 $v^n=\frac{1}{s}$	5 PRESENT VALUE ORD. ANNUITY 1 PER PERIOD $a_{\overline{n}|}=\frac{s-1}{si}$	6 INSTALMENT TO AMORTIZE 1 $\frac{1}{a_{\overline{n}|}}=\frac{si}{s-1}$	n MONTHS
1	1.003542	1.000000	1.000000	.996471	.996471	1.003542	1
2	1.007096	2.003542	.499116	.992954	1.989425	.502658	2
3	1.010663	3.010638	.332156	.989450	2.978875	.335698	3
4	1.014242	4.021300	.248676	.985958	3.964833	.252218	4
5	1.017834	5.035542	.198588	.982478	4.947311	.202130	5
6	1.021439	6.053377	.165197	.979011	5.926322	.168739	6
7	1.025057	7.074816	.141346	.975556	6.901878	.144888	7
8	1.028687	8.099872	.123459	.972113	7.873991	.127001	8
9	1.032330	9.128559	.109546	.968682	8.842673	.113088	9
10	1.035986	10.160890	.098417	.965264	9.807936	.101959	10
11	1.039656	11.196876	.089311	.961857	10.769793	.092853	11

YEARS

							MONTHS
1	1.043338	12.236532	.081723	.958462	11.728256	.085265	12
2	1.088554	25.003367	.039995	.918650	22.969348	.043537	24
3	1.135729	38.323487	.026094	.880492	33.743513	.029636	36
4	1.184949	52.220871	.019149	.843918	44.070145	.022691	48
5	1.236302	66.720536	.014988	.808864	53.967834	.018530	60
6	1.289880	81.848584	.012218	.775266	63.454397	.015760	72
7	1.345781	97.632246	.010243	.743063	72.546911	.013785	84
8	1.404104	114.099936	.008764	.712198	81.261745	.012306	96
9	1.464955	131.281299	.007617	.682615	89.614585	.011159	108
10	1.528442	149.207262	.006702	.654261	97.620468	.010244	120
11	1.594682	167.910096	.005956	.627084	105.293807	.009498	132
12	1.663791	187.423468	.005336	.601037	112.648413	.008878	144
13	1.735896	207.782504	.004813	.576071	119.697527	.008355	156
14	1.811126	229.023855	.004366	.552143	126.453838	.007908	168
15	1.889616	251.185758	.003981	.529208	132.929509	.007523	180
16	1.971508	274.308107	.003646	.507226	139.136195	.007188	192
17	2.056949	298.432526	.003351	.486157	145.085071	.006893	204
18	2.146092	323.602442	.003090	.465963	150.786845	.006632	216
19	2.239099	349.863164	.002858	.446608	156.251781	.006400	228
20	2.336136	377.261967	.002651	.428057	161.489717	.006193	240
21	2.437379	405.848171	.002464	.410277	166.510082	.006006	252
22	2.543009	435.673235	.002295	.393235	171.321913	.005837	264
23	2.653218	466.790850	.002142	.376901	175.933872	.005684	276
24	2.768202	499.257031	.002003	.361245	180.354262	.005545	288
25	2.888170	533.130223	.001876	.346240	184.591039	.005418	300
26	3.013336	568.471401	.001759	.331858	188.651831	.005301	312
27	3.143927	605.344185	.001652	.318074	192.543948	.005194	324
28	3.280178	643.814952	.001553	.304862	196.274395	.005095	336
29	3.422333	683.952954	.001462	.292198	199.849889	.005004	348
30	3.570650	725.830445	.001378	.280061	203.276866	.004920	360
31	3.725393	769.522810	.001300	.268428	206.561494	.004842	372
32	3.886843	815.108704	.001227	.257278	209.709686	.004769	384
33	4.055290	862.670185	.001159	.246591	212.727111	.004701	396
34	4.231037	912.292873	.001096	.236349	215.619198	.004638	408
35	4.414401	964.066095	.001037	.226531	218.391156	.004579	420
36	4.605711	1018.083050	.000982	.217122	221.047973	.004524	432
37	4.805312	1074.440976	.000931	.208103	223.594432	.004473	444
38	5.013563	1133.241327	.000882	.199459	226.035118	.004424	456
39	5.230839	1194.589950	.000837	.191174	228.374424	.004379	468
40	5.457532	1258.597283	.000795	.183233	230.616560	.004337	480
41	5.694049	1325.378547	.000755	.175622	232.765564	.004297	492
42	5.940816	1395.053958	.000717	.168327	234.825303	.004259	504
43	6.198278	1467.748943	.000681	.161335	236.799485	.004223	516
44	6.466897	1543.594363	.000648	.154634	238.691665	.004190	528
45	6.747157	1622.726750	.000616	.148211	240.505248	.004158	540
46	7.039564	1705.288554	.000586	.142054	242.243500	.004128	552
47	7.344642	1791.428398	.000558	.136154	243.909548	.004100	564
48	7.662942	1881.301346	.000532	.130498	245.506393	.004074	576
49	7.995037	1975.069182	.000506	.125078	247.036909	.004048	588
50	8.341523	2072.900703	.000482	.119882	248.503851	.004024	600

Reprinted by permission, from *Ellwood's Tables for Real Estate Appraising and Financing* (Ridgewood, N.J.: published by the author, 1959).

4½% MONTHLY COMPOUND INTEREST TABLE 4½%

EFFECTIVE RATE = 3/8% i = .00375

MONTHS	1 AMOUNT OF I AT COMPOUND INTEREST $s=(1+i)^n$	2 ACCUMULATION OF I PER PERIOD $s_{\overline{n}}=\frac{s-1}{i}$	3 SINKING FUND FACTOR $\frac{1}{s_{\overline{n}}}=\frac{i}{s-1}$	4 PRES. VALUE REVERSION OF I $v^n=\frac{1}{s}$	5 PRESENT VALUE ORD. ANNUITY 1 PER PERIOD $a_{\overline{n}}=\frac{s-1}{si}$	6 INSTALMENT TO AMORTIZE I $\frac{1}{a_{\overline{n}}}=\frac{si}{s-1}$	n MONTHS
1	1.003750	1.000000	1.000000	.996264	.996264	1.003750	1
2	1.007514	2.003750	.499064	.992542	1.988806	.502814	2
3	1.011292	3.011264	.332086	.988834	2.977640	.335836	3
4	1.015085	4.022556	.248598	.985140	3.962779	.252348	4
5	1.018891	5.037641	.198506	.981459	4.944239	.202256	5
6	1.022712	6.056532	.165111	.977792	5.922031	.168861	6
7	1.026547	7.079244	.141258	.974139	6.896170	.145008	7
8	1.030397	8.105791	.123369	.970500	7.866670	.127119	8
9	1.034261	9.136188	.109455	.966874	8.833544	.113205	9
10	1.038139	10.170449	.098324	.963262	9.796806	.102074	10
11	1.042032	11.208588	.089217	.959663	10.756470	.092967	11
YEARS							
1	1.045940	12.250620	.081629	.956078	11.712548	.085379	12
2	1.093990	25.064031	.039898	.914085	22.910656	.043648	24
3	1.144248	38.466089	.025997	.873937	33.616921	.029747	36
4	1.196814	52.483834	.019053	.835551	43.852944	.022803	48
5	1.251796	67.145552	.014893	.798852	53.639380	.018643	60
6	1.309303	82.480827	.012124	.763765	62.995976	.015874	72
7	1.369452	98.520602	.010150	.730219	71.941611	.013900	84
8	1.432365	115.297241	.008673	.698146	80.494336	.012423	96
9	1.498167	132.844596	.007528	.667482	88.671407	.011278	108
10	1.566993	151.198074	.006614	.638165	96.489324	.010364	120
11	1.638980	170.394707	.005869	.610136	103.963863	.009619	132
12	1.714275	190.473230	.005250	.583337	111.110104	.009000	144
13	1.793028	211.474157	.004729	.557716	117.942468	.008479	156
14	1.875399	233.439862	.004284	.533220	124.474740	.008034	168
15	1.961555	256.414669	.003900	.509800	130.720101	.007650	180
16	2.051669	280.444934	.003566	.487408	136.691154	.007316	192
17	2.145922	305.579145	.003272	.466000	142.399945	.007022	204
18	2.244505	331.868017	.003013	.445533	147.857995	.006763	216
19	2.347617	359.364596	.002783	.425964	153.076316	.006533	228
20	2.455466	388.124363	.002576	.407255	158.065437	.006326	240
21	2.568270	418.205348	.002391	.389367	162.835426	.006141	252
22	2.686256	449.668249	.002224	.372265	167.395908	.005974	264
23	2.809662	482.576549	.002072	.355915	171.756084	.005822	276
24	2.938737	516.996652	.001934	.340282	175.924751	.005684	288
25	3.073743	552.998007	.001808	.325336	179.910323	.005558	300
26	3.214950	590.653259	.001693	.311047	183.720840	.005443	312
27	3.362644	630.038387	.001587	.297385	187.363991	.005337	324
28	3.517123	671.232860	.001490	.284323	190.847127	.005240	336
29	3.678699	714.319800	.001400	.271835	194.177277	.005150	348
30	3.847698	759.386147	.001317	.259896	197.361160	.005067	360
31	4.024461	806.522833	.001240	.248481	200.405200	.004990	372
32	4.209344	855.824971	.001168	.237567	203.315540	.004918	384
33	4.402720	907.392041	.001102	.227132	206.098052	.004852	396
34	4.604980	961.328092	.001040	.217156	208.758350	.004790	408
35	4.816532	1017.741957	.000983	.207618	211.301802	.004733	420
36	5.037803	1076.747464	.000929	.198499	213.733541	.004679	432
37	5.269239	1138.463674	.000878	.189781	216.058472	.004628	444
38	5.511307	1203.015116	.000831	.181445	218.281288	.004581	456
39	5.764495	1270.532040	.000787	.173476	220.406474	.004537	468
40	6.029315	1341.150680	.000746	.165856	222.438316	.004496	480
41	6.306301	1415.013527	.000707	.158572	224.380916	.004457	492
42	6.596011	1492.269621	.000670	.151607	226.238194	.004420	504
43	6.899031	1573.074847	.000636	.144948	228.013895	.004386	516
44	7.215971	1657.592250	.000603	.138581	229.711604	.004353	528
45	7.547471	1745.992368	.000573	.132495	231.334747	.004323	540
46	7.894201	1838.453572	.000544	.126675	232.886597	.004294	552
47	8.256859	1935.162427	.000517	.121111	234.370287	.004267	564
48	8.636178	2036.314071	.000491	.115792	235.788811	.004241	576
49	9.032922	2142.112603	.000467	.110706	237.145030	.004217	588
50	9.447893	2252.771501	.000444	.105844	238.441681	.004194	600

Reprinted by permission, from *Ellwood's Tables for Real Estate Appraising and Financing* (Ridgewood, N.J.: published by the author, 1959).

4 ¾% MONTHLY COMPOUND INTEREST TABLE 4 ¾%

EFFECTIVE RATE = 19/48% i = .00395833+

	1 AMOUNT OF 1 AT COMPOUND INTEREST $s = (1+i)^n$	2 ACCUMULATION OF 1 PER PERIOD $s_{\overline{n}|} = \frac{s-1}{i}$	3 SINKING FUND FACTOR $\frac{1}{s_{\overline{n}|}} = \frac{i}{s-1}$	4 PRES. VALUE REVERSION OF 1 $v^n = \frac{1}{s}$	5 PRESENT VALUE ORD. ANNUITY 1 PER PERIOD $a_{\overline{n}|} = \frac{s-1}{si}$	6 INSTALMENT TO AMORTIZE 1 $\frac{1}{a_{\overline{n}|}} = \frac{si}{s-1}$	n
MONTHS							MONTHS
1	1.003958	1.000000	1.000000	.996057	.996057	1.003958	1
2	1.007932	2.003958	.499012	.992130	1.988187	.502970	2
3	1.011922	3.011891	.332017	.988218	2.976406	.335975	3
4	1.015928	4.023813	.248521	.984322	3.960728	.252479	4
5	1.019949	5.039740	.198423	.980441	4.941169	.202381	5
6	1.023986	6.059689	.165025	.976576	5.917745	.168983	6
7	1.028040	7.083676	.141170	.972725	6.890470	.145128	7
8	1.032109	8.111715	.123278	.968890	7.859360	.127236	8
9	1.036194	9.143824	.109363	.965070	8.824430	.113321	9
10	1.040296	10.180018	.098232	.961265	9.785695	.102190	10
11	1.044414	11.220314	.089124	.957475	10.743170	.093082	11
YEARS							
1	1.048548	12.264728	.081535	.953700	11.696870	.085493	12
2	1.099453	25.124882	.039801	.909543	22.852173	.043759	24
3	1.152829	38.609370	.025900	.867432	33.490985	.029858	36
4	1.208796	52.748501	.018958	.827269	43.637218	.022916	48
5	1.267481	67.574057	.014799	.788967	53.313680	.018757	60
6	1.329014	83.119362	.012031	.752437	62.542120	.015989	72
7	1.393535	99.419359	.010058	.717600	71.343283	.014016	84
8	1.461188	116.510686	.008583	.684375	79.736951	.012541	96
9	1.532126	134.431761	.007439	.652688	87.741991	.011397	108
10	1.606507	153.222866	.006526	.622468	95.376397	.010484	120
11	1.684500	172.926240	.005783	.593648	102.657329	.009741	132
12	1.766279	193.586170	.005166	.566162	109.601153	.009124	144
13	1.852028	215.249097	.004646	.539949	116.223478	.008604	156
14	1.941940	237.963712	.004202	.514949	122.539188	.008160	168
15	2.036217	261.781074	.003820	.491107	128.562480	.007778	180
16	2.135071	286.754718	.003487	.468369	134.306892	.007445	192
17	2.238724	312.940780	.003195	.446683	139.785338	.007153	204
18	2.347409	340.398120	.002938	.426002	145.010132	.006896	216
19	2.461371	369.188455	.002709	.406278	149.993016	.006667	228
20	2.580865	399.376500	.002504	.387467	154.745193	.006462	240
21	2.706161	431.030111	.002320	.369527	159.277343	.006278	252
22	2.837539	464.220438	.002154	.352418	163.599655	.006112	264
23	2.975296	499.022084	.002004	.336101	167.721843	.005962	276
24	3.119740	535.513277	.001867	.320540	171.653173	.005825	288
25	3.271197	573.776040	.001743	.305699	175.402482	.005701	300
26	3.430006	613.896379	.001629	.291545	178.978197	.005587	312
27	3.596526	655.964475	.001524	.278046	182.388357	.005482	324
28	3.771130	700.074888	.001428	.265173	185.640626	.005386	336
29	3.954210	746.326768	.001340	.252895	188.742314	.005298	348
30	4.146179	794.824079	.001258	.241186	191.700394	.005216	360
31	4.347467	845.675832	.001182	.230019	194.521515	.005140	372
32	4.558527	898.996330	.001112	.219369	197.212017	.005070	384
33	4.779834	954.905425	.001047	.209212	199.777949	.005005	396
34	5.011885	1013.528788	.000987	.199526	202.225078	.004945	408
35	5.255201	1074.998191	.000930	.190288	204.558904	.004888	420
36	5.510330	1139.451803	.000878	.181477	206.784674	.004836	432
37	5.777845	1207.034501	.000828	.173075	208.907391	.004786	444
38	6.058347	1277.898197	.000783	.165062	210.931826	.004741	456
39	6.352467	1352.202174	.000740	.157419	212.862529	.004698	468
40	6.660866	1430.113452	.000699	.150131	214.703840	.004657	480
41	6.984237	1511.807158	.000661	.143180	216.459899	.004619	492
42	7.323307	1597.466920	.000626	.136550	218.134652	.004584	504
43	7.678838	1687.285282	.000593	.130228	219.731863	.004551	516
44	8.051629	1781.464135	.000561	.124198	221.255124	.004519	528
45	8.442518	1880.215172	.000532	.118448	222.707857	.004490	540
46	8.852385	1983.760362	.000504	.112964	224.093329	.004462	552
47	9.282149	2092.332452	.000478	.107734	225.414653	.004436	564
48	9.732778	2206.175487	.000453	.102746	226.674799	.004411	576
49	10.205284	2325.545360	.000430	.097988	227.876601	.004388	588
50	10.700729	2450.710388	.000408	.093452	229.022759	.004366	600

Reprinted by permission, from *Ellwood's Tables for Real Estate Appraising and Financing* (Ridgewood, N.J.: published by the author, 1959).

5%   MONTHLY COMPOUND INTEREST TABLE   5%

EFFECTIVE RATE = 5/12% $i = .004166666+$

MONTHS	1 AMOUNT OF 1 AT COMPOUND INTEREST $s=(1+i)^n$	2 ACCUMULATION OF 1 PER PERIOD $s_{\overline{n}|}=\frac{s-1}{i}$	3 SINKING FUND FACTOR $\frac{1}{s_{\overline{n}|}}=\frac{i}{s-1}$	4 PRES. VALUE REVERSION OF 1 $v^n=\frac{1}{s}$	5 PRESENT VALUE ORD. ANNUITY 1 PER PERIOD $a_{\overline{n}|}=\frac{s-1}{si}$	6 INSTALMENT TO AMORTIZE 1 $\frac{1}{a_{\overline{n}|}}=\frac{si}{s-1}$	n MONTHS
1	1.004167	1.000000	1.000000	.995851	.995851	1.004167	1
2	1.008351	2.004167	.498960	.991718	1.987569	.503127	2
3	1.012552	3.012517	.331948	.987603	2.975173	.336115	3
4	1.016771	4.025070	.248443	.983506	3.958678	.252610	4
5	1.021008	5.041841	.198340	.979425	4.938103	.202507	5
6	1.025262	6.062848	.164939	.975361	5.913463	.169106	6
7	1.029534	7.088110	.141081	.971313	6.884777	.145248	7
8	1.033824	8.117644	.123188	.967283	7.852060	.127355	8
9	1.038131	9.151467	.109272	.963269	8.815329	.113439	9
10	1.042457	10.189599	.098139	.959272	9.774602	.102306	10
11	1.046800	11.232055	.089031	.955292	10.729894	.093198	11
YEARS							
1	1.051162	12.278855	.081441	.951328	11.681222	.085608	12
2	1.104941	25.185921	.039705	.905025	22.793898	.043872	24
3	1.161472	38.753336	.025804	.860976	33.365701	.029971	36
4	1.220895	53.014885	.018863	.819071	43.422956	.023030	48
5	1.283359	68.006083	.014705	.779205	52.990706	.018872	60
6	1.349018	83.764259	.011938	.741280	62.092777	.016105	72
7	1.418036	100.328653	.009967	.705201	70.751835	.014134	84
8	1.490585	117.740513	.008493	.670877	78.989441	.012660	96
9	1.566847	136.043196	.007351	.638225	86.826108	.011518	108
10	1.647010	155.282280	.006440	.607161	94.281350	.010607	120
11	1.731274	175.505671	.005698	.577609	101.373733	.009865	132
12	1.819849	196.763730	.005082	.549496	108.120917	.009249	144
13	1.912956	219.109392	.004564	.522751	114.539704	.008731	156
14	2.010826	242.598300	.004122	.497308	120.646077	.008289	168
15	2.113704	267.288945	.003741	.473103	126.455243	.007908	180
16	2.221845	293.242810	.003410	.450076	131.981666	.007577	192
17	2.335519	320.524524	.003120	.428170	137.239108	.007287	204
18	2.455008	349.202023	.002864	.407331	142.240661	.007031	216
19	2.580611	379.346717	.002636	.387505	146.998780	.006803	228
20	2.712640	411.033670	.002433	.368645	151.525313	.006600	240
21	2.851424	444.341789	.002251	.350702	155.831531	.006418	252
22	2.997308	479.354014	.002086	.333633	159.928159	.006253	264
23	3.150656	516.157530	.001937	.317394	163.825396	.006104	276
24	3.311850	554.843985	.001802	.301946	167.532948	.005969	288
25	3.481290	595.509712	.001679	.287250	171.060047	.005846	300
26	3.659400	638.255975	.001567	.273269	174.415476	.005734	312
27	3.846622	683.189218	.001464	.259968	177.607590	.005631	324
28	4.043422	730.421330	.001369	.247315	180.644338	.005536	336
29	4.250291	780.069928	.001282	.235278	183.533282	.005449	348
30	4.467744	832.258641	.001202	.223827	186.281617	.005369	360
31	4.696323	887.117429	.001127	.212933	188.896185	.005294	372
32	4.936595	944.782896	.001058	.202569	191.383497	.005225	384
33	5.189161	1005.398638	.000995	.192709	193.749748	.005162	396
34	5.454648	1069.115596	.000935	.183330	196.000829	.005102	408
35	5.733719	1136.092435	.000880	.174407	198.142346	.005047	420
36	6.027066	1206.495936	.000829	.165918	200.179632	.004996	432
37	6.335423	1280.501414	.000781	.157843	202.117759	.004948	444
38	6.659555	1358.293153	.000736	.150160	203.961554	.004903	456
39	7.000270	1440.064865	.000694	.142852	205.715609	.004861	468
40	7.358417	1526.020172	.000655	.135899	207.384290	.004822	480
41	7.734888	1616.373117	.000619	.129284	208.971754	.004786	492
42	8.130620	1711.348689	.000584	.122992	210.481953	.004751	504
43	8.546598	1811.183392	.000552	.117006	211.918649	.004719	516
44	8.983858	1916.125828	.000522	.111311	213.285417	.004689	528
45	9.443489	2026.437318	.000493	.105893	214.585663	.004660	540
46	9.926636	2142.392554	.000467	.100739	215.822623	.004634	552
47	10.434501	2264.280279	.000442	.095836	216.999379	.004609	564
48	10.968350	2392.404012	.000418	.091171	218.118860	.004585	576
49	11.529512	2527.082798	.000396	.086734	219.183853	.004563	588
50	12.119383	2668.652007	.000375	.082512	220.197012	.004542	600

Reprinted by permission, from *Ellwood's Tables for Real Estate Appraising and Financing* (Ridgewood, N.J.: published by the author, 1959).

5 ¼ % MONTHLY COMPOUND INTEREST TABLE 5 ¼ %

EFFECTIVE RATE = 7/16% i = 004375

MONTHS	1 AMOUNT OF 1 AT COMPOUND INTEREST $s = (1+i)^n$	2 ACCUMULATION OF 1 PER PERIOD $s_{\overline{n}} = \frac{s-1}{i}$	3 SINKING FUND FACTOR $\frac{1}{s_{\overline{n}}} = \frac{i}{s-1}$	4 PRES. VALUE REVERSION OF 1 $v^n = \frac{1}{s}$	5 PRESENT VALUE ORD. ANNUITY 1 PER PERIOD $a_{\overline{n}} = \frac{s-1}{si}$	6 INSTALMENT TO AMORTIZE 1 $\frac{1}{a_{\overline{n}}} = \frac{si}{s-1}$	n MONTHS
1	1.004375	1.000000	1.000000	.995644	.995644	1.004375	1
2	1.008769	2.004375	.498909	.991307	1.986951	.503284	2
3	1.013183	3.013144	.331879	.986989	2.973940	.336254	3
4	1.017615	4.026327	.248365	.982690	3.956630	.252740	4
5	1.022067	5.043942	.198258	.978409	4.935039	.202633	5
6	1.026539	6.066009	.164853	.974147	5.909186	.169228	6
7	1.031030	7.092548	.140993	.969904	6.879090	.145368	7
8	1.035541	8.123578	.123098	.965679	7.844770	.127473	8
9	1.040071	9.159118	.109181	.961473	8.806242	.113556	9
10	1.044621	10.199190	.098047	.957285	9.763527	.102422	10
11 YEARS	1.049192	11.243811	.088938	.953115	10.716641	.093313	11
1	1.053782	12.293003	.081347	.948963	11.665604	.085722	12
2	1.110456	25.247146	.039608	.900531	22.735831	.043983	24
3	1.170179	38.897988	.025708	.854570	33.241067	.030083	36
4	1.233113	53.282998	.018768	.810956	43.210146	.023143	48
5	1.299432	68.441661	.014611	.769567	52.670433	.018986	60
6	1.369318	84.415585	.011846	.730290	61.647896	.016221	72
7	1.442963	101.248617	.009877	.693019	70.167175	.014252	84
8	1.520568	118.986962	.008404	.657649	78.251656	.012779	96
9	1.602347	137.679308	.007263	.624085	85.923530	.011638	108
10	1.688524	157.376963	.006354	.592233	93.203853	.010729	120
11	1.779336	178.133996	.005614	.562007	100.112611	.009989	132
12	1.875032	200.007381	.005000	.533324	106.668766	.009375	144
13	1.975875	223.057158	.004483	.506105	112.890314	.008858	156
14	2.082141	247.346595	.004043	.480275	118.794333	.008418	168
15	2.194123	272.942365	.003664	.455763	124.397029	.008039	180
16	2.312127	299.914723	.003334	.432502	129.713780	.007709	192
17	2.436477	328.337705	.003046	.410429	134.759180	.007421	204
18	2.567516	358.289329	.002791	.389482	139.547077	.007166	216
19	2.705602	389.851808	.002565	.369604	144.090615	.006940	228
20	2.851114	423.111776	.002363	.350740	148.402263	.006738	240
21	3.004452	458.160529	.002183	.332839	152.493859	.006558	252
22	3.166037	495.094269	.002020	.315852	156.376631	.006395	264
23	3.336313	534.014376	.001873	.299732	160.061238	.006248	276
24	3.515746	575.027679	.001739	.284435	163.557794	.006114	288
25	3.704830	618.246755	.001617	.269918	166.875896	.005992	300
26	3.904082	663.790235	.001507	.256142	170.242652	.005882	312
27	4.114051	711.783129	.001405	.243069	173.012705	.005780	324
28	4.335313	762.357171	.001312	.230664	175.848256	.005687	336
29	4.568474	815.651181	.001226	.218891	178.539090	.005601	348
30	4.814175	871.811443	.001147	.207720	181.092591	.005522	360
31	5.073090	930.992110	.001074	.197118	183.515769	.005449	372
32	5.345931	993.355624	.001007	.187058	185.815276	.005382	384
33	5.633445	1059.073167	.000944	.177511	187.997422	.005319	396
34	5.936422	1128.325123	.000886	.168452	190.068199	.005261	408
35	6.255694	1201.301579	.000832	.159854	192.033289	.005207	420
36	6.592137	1278.202847	.000782	.151696	193.898086	.005157	432
37	6.946675	1359.240011	.000736	.143954	195.667710	.005111	444
38	7.320280	1444.635506	.000692	.136607	197.347018	.005067	456
39	7.713979	1534.623732	.000652	.129635	198.940619	.005027	468
40	8.128851	1629.451694	.000614	.123019	200.452887	.004989	480
41	8.566036	1729.379683	.000578	.116740	201.887973	.004953	492
42	9.026734	1834.681988	.000545	.110782	203.249817	.004920	504
43	9.512208	1945.647649	.000514	.105128	204.542157	.004889	516
44	10.023793	2062.581254	.000485	.099763	205.768539	.004860	528
45	10.562891	2185.803768	.000457	.094671	206.932330	.004832	540
46	11.130984	2315.653421	.000432	.089839	208.036725	.004807	552
47	11.729629	2452.486634	.000408	.085254	209.084755	.004783	564
48	12.360471	2596.678995	.000385	.080903	210.079297	.004760	576
49	13.025240	2748.626293	.000364	.076774	211.023080	.004739	588
50	13.725762	2908.745604	.000344	.072856	211.918695	.004719	600

Reprinted by permission, from *Ellwood's Tables for Real Estate Appraising and Financing* (Ridgewood, N.J.: published by the author, 1959).

5 ½ %　　MONTHLY COMPOUND INTEREST TABLE　　5 ½ %

EFFECTIVE RATE = 11/24% $i = .00458333+$

MONTHS	1 AMOUNT OF 1 AT COMPOUND INTEREST $s = (1+i)^n$	2 ACCUMULATION OF 1 PER PERIOD $s_{\overline{n}} = \frac{s-1}{i}$	3 SINKING FUND FACTOR $\frac{1}{s_{\overline{n}}} = \frac{i}{s-1}$	4 PRES. VALUE REVERSION OF 1 $v^n = \frac{1}{s}$	5 PRESENT VALUE ORD. ANNUITY 1 PER PERIOD $a_{\overline{n}} = \frac{s-1}{si}$	6 INSTALMENT TO AMORTIZE 1 $\frac{1}{a_{\overline{n}}} = \frac{si}{s-1}$	n MONTHS
1	1.004583	1.000000	1.000000	.995438	.995438	1.004583	1
2	1.009188	2.004583	.498857	.990896	1.986334	.503440	2
3	1.013813	3.013771	.331810	.986375	2.972709	.336393	3
4	1.018460	4.027584	.248288	.981875	3.954583	.252871	4
5	1.023128	5.046044	.198175	.977395	4.931979	.202758	5
6	1.027817	6.069172	.164767	.972936	5.904914	.169350	6
7	1.032528	7.096989	.140905	.968497	6.873411	.145488	7
8	1.037260	8.129516	.123009	.964078	7.837489	.127592	8
9	1.042014	9.166777	.109090	.959680	8.797169	.113673	9
10	1.046790	10.208791	.097955	.955301	9.752470	.102538	10
11	1.051588	11.255581	.088845	.950943	10.703413	.093428	11
YEARS							
1	1.056408	12.307170	.081253	.946604	11.650017	.085836	12
2	1.115998	25.308560	.039512	.896059	22.677971	.044095	24
3	1.178949	39.043331	.025613	.848213	33.117077	.030196	36
4	1.245451	53.552852	.018673	.802922	42.998777	.023256	48
5	1.315704	68.880823	.014518	.760050	52.352835	.019101	60
6	1.389920	85.073412	.011755	.719466	61.207425	.016338	72
7	1.468322	102.179391	.009787	.681049	69.589216	.014370	84
8	1.551147	120.250281	.008316	.644684	77.523453	.012899	96
9	1.638644	139.340512	.007177	.610261	85.034035	.011760	108
10	1.731076	159.507582	.006269	.577675	92.143582	.010852	120
11	1.828723	180.812232	.005531	.546830	98.873509	.010114	132
12	1.931877	203.318633	.004918	.517631	105.244085	.009501	144
13	2.040850	227.094572	.004403	.489992	111.274498	.008986	156
14	2.155970	252.211660	.003965	.463828	116.982912	.008548	168
15	2.277584	278.745549	.003588	.439062	122.386520	.008171	180
16	2.406057	306.776159	.003260	.415618	127.501597	.007843	192
17	2.541778	336.387915	.002973	.393425	132.343550	.007556	204
18	2.685154	367.670007	.002720	.372418	136.926963	.007303	216
19	2.836618	400.716655	.002496	.352532	141.265640	.007079	228
20	2.996626	435.627393	.002296	.333709	145.372649	.006879	240
21	3.165659	472.507372	.002116	.315890	149.260361	.006699	252
22	3.344227	511.467671	.001955	.299023	152.940485	.006538	264
23	3.532867	552.625637	.001810	.283056	156.424106	.006393	276
24	3.732149	596.105236	.001678	.267942	159.721715	.006261	288
25	3.942672	642.037427	.001558	.253635	162.843246	.006141	300
26	4.165069	690.560553	.001448	.240092	165.798099	.006031	312
27	4.400012	741.820766	.001348	.227272	168.595176	.005931	324
28	4.648207	795.972457	.001256	.215137	171.242900	.005839	336
29	4.910402	853.178730	.001172	.203649	173.749246	.005755	348
30	5.187388	913.611886	.001095	.192775	176.121764	.005678	360
31	5.479997	977.453946	.001023	.182482	178.367599	.005606	372
32	5.789112	1044.897201	.000957	.172738	180.493516	.005540	384
33	6.115664	1116.144786	.000896	.163515	182.505917	.005479	396
34	6.460635	1191.411294	.000839	.154784	184.410864	.005422	408
35	6.825066	1270.923425	.000787	.146519	186.214095	.005370	420
36	7.210053	1354.920665	.000738	.138695	187.921041	.005321	432
37	7.616757	1443.656010	.000693	.131289	189.536843	.005276	444
38	8.046402	1537.396726	.000650	.124279	191.066367	.005233	456
39	8.500282	1636.425154	.000611	.117643	192.514222	.005194	468
40	8.979765	1741.039565	.000574	.111361	193.884766	.005157	480
41	9.486294	1851.555050	.000540	.105415	195.182130	.005123	492
42	10.021395	1968.304478	.000508	.099787	196.410219	.005091	504
43	10.586681	2091.639491	.000478	.094458	197.572734	.005061	516
44	11.183853	2221.931568	.000450	.089415	198.673155	.005033	528
45	11.814710	2359.573142	.000424	.084640	199.714856	.005007	540
46	12.481153	2504.978783	.000399	.080121	200.700917	.004982	552
47	13.185188	2658.586445	.000376	.075843	201.634325	.004959	564
48	13.928936	2820.858786	.000355	.071793	202.517894	.004938	576
49	14.714637	2992.284563	.000334	.067960	203.354284	.004917	588
50	15.544659	3173.380101	.000315	.064331	204.146013	.004898	600

Reprinted by permission, from *Ellwood's Tables for Real Estate Appraising and Financing* (Ridgewood, N.J.: published by the author, 1959).

5¾%   MONTHLY COMPOUND INTEREST TABLE   5¾%

EFFECTIVE RATE = 23/48% i = .00479166+

MONTHS	1 AMOUNT OF 1 AT COMPOUND INTEREST $s=(1+i)^n$	2 ACCUMULATION OF 1 PER PERIOD $s_{\overline{n}|}=\frac{s-1}{i}$	3 SINKING FUND FACTOR $\frac{1}{s_{\overline{n}|}}=\frac{i}{s-1}$	4 PRES. VALUE REVERSION OF 1 $v^n=\frac{1}{s}$	5 PRESENT VALUE ORD. ANNUITY 1 PER PERIOD $a_{\overline{n}|}=\frac{s-1}{si}$	6 INSTALMENT TO AMORTIZE 1 $\frac{1}{a_{\overline{n}|}}=\frac{si}{s-1}$	n MONTHS
1	1.004792	1.000000	1.000000	.995231	.995231	1.004792	1
2	1.009606	2.004792	.498805	.990485	1.985716	.503597	2
3	1.014444	3.014398	.331741	.985762	2.971478	.336533	3
4	1.019305	4.028842	.248210	.981061	3.952539	.253002	4
5	1.024189	5.048147	.198092	.976382	4.928921	.202884	5
6	1.029097	6.072336	.164681	.971726	5.900647	.169473	6
7	1.034028	7.101432	.140817	.967092	6.867739	.145609	7
8	1.038982	8.135460	.122919	.962480	7.830219	.127711	8
9	1.043961	9.174443	.108998	.957890	8.788110	.113790	9
10	1.048963	10.218403	.097863	.953322	9.741432	.102655	10
11 YEARS	1.053989	11.267367	.088752	.948776	10.690208	.093544	11
1	1.059040	12.321356	.081160	.944252	11.634460	.085952	12
2	1.121565	25.370163	.039416	.891611	22.620316	.044208	24
3	1.187782	39.189369	.025517	.841905	32.993728	.030309	36
4	1.257909	53.824459	.018579	.794970	42.788838	.023371	48
5	1.332176	69.323602	.014425	.750652	52.037886	.019217	60
6	1.410827	85.737812	.011663	.708804	60.771314	.016455	72
7	1.494122	103.121114	.009697	.669289	69.017867	.014489	84
8	1.582335	121.530724	.008228	.631978	76.804687	.013020	96
9	1.675755	141.027233	.007091	.596746	84.157405	.011883	108
10	1.774692	161.674813	.006185	.563478	91.100219	.010977	120
11	1.879469	183.541423	.005448	.532065	97.655982	.010240	132
12	1.990433	206.699034	.004838	.502403	103.846272	.009630	144
13	2.107948	231.223866	.004325	.474395	109.691463	.009117	156
14	2.232401	257.196640	.003888	.447948	115.210793	.008680	168
15	2.364201	284.702843	.003512	.422976	120.422429	.008304	180
16	2.503783	313.833007	.003186	.399396	125.343525	.007978	192
17	2.651606	344.683011	.002901	.377130	129.990277	.007693	204
18	2.808156	377.354394	.002650	.356106	134.377980	.007442	216
19	2.973950	411.954690	.002427	.336253	138.521075	.007219	228
20	3.149531	448.597782	.002229	.317508	142.433199	.007021	240
21	3.335479	487.404275	.002052	.299807	146.127228	.006844	252
22	3.532405	528.501898	.001892	.283093	149.615321	.006684	264
23	3.740958	572.025917	.001748	.267311	152.908958	.006540	276
24	3.961823	618.119587	.001618	.252409	156.018980	.006410	288
25	4.195728	666.934620	.001499	.238338	158.955623	.006291	300
26	4.443444	718.631683	.001392	.225051	161.728552	.006184	312
27	4.705784	773.380933	.001293	.212504	164.346895	.006085	324
28	4.983612	831.362569	.001203	.200658	166.819270	.005995	336
29	5.277844	892.767432	.001120	.189471	169.153813	.005912	348
30	5.589447	957.797627	.001044	.178909	171.358210	.005836	360
31	5.919447	1026.667193	.000974	.168935	173.439714	.005766	372
32	6.268930	1099.602808	.000909	.159517	175.405178	.005701	384
33	6.639047	1176.844529	.000850	.150624	177.261071	.005642	396
34	7.031015	1258.646588	.000795	.142227	179.013500	.005587	408
35	7.446125	1345.278226	.000743	.134298	180.668234	.005535	420
36	7.885743	1437.024583	.000696	.126811	182.230719	.005488	432
37	8.351316	1534.187628	.000652	.119742	183.706098	.005444	444
38	8.844376	1637.087164	.000611	.113066	185.099227	.005403	456
39	9.366547	1746.061870	.000573	.106763	186.414691	.005365	468
40	9.919546	1861.470425	.000537	.100811	187.656820	.005329	480
41	10.505194	1983.692682	.000504	.095191	188.829703	.005296	492
42	11.125419	2113.130920	.000473	.089884	189.937198	.005265	504
43	11.782262	2250.211170	.000444	.084873	190.982953	.005236	516
44	12.477885	2395.384615	.000417	.080142	191.970409	.005209	528
45	13.214577	2549.129076	.000392	.075674	192.902815	.005184	540
46	13.994763	2711.950584	.000369	.071455	193.783241	.005161	552
47	14.821012	2884.385046	.000347	.067472	194.614585	.005139	564
48	15.696042	3067.000010	.000326	.063710	195.399583	.005118	576
49	16.622733	3260.396530	.000307	.060159	196.140818	.005099	588
50	17.604137	3465.211149	.000289	.056805	196.840731	.005081	600

Reprinted by permission, from *Ellwood's Tables for Real Estate Appraising and Financing* (Ridgewood, N.J.: published by the author, 1959).

6% MONTHLY COMPOUND INTEREST TABLE 6%

EFFECTIVE RATE = 1/2% $i = .005$

MONTHS	1 AMOUNT OF 1 AT COMPOUND INTEREST $s = (1+i)^n$	2 ACCUMULATION OF 1 PER PERIOD $s_{\overline{n}} = \frac{s-1}{i}$	3 SINKING FUND FACTOR $\frac{1}{s_{\overline{n}}} = \frac{i}{s-1}$	4 PRES. VALUE REVERSION. OF 1 $v^n = \frac{1}{s}$	5 PRESENT VALUE ORD. ANNUITY 1 PER PERIOD $a_{\overline{n}} = \frac{s-1}{si}$	6 INSTALMENT TO AMORTIZE 1 $\frac{1}{a_{\overline{n}}} = \frac{si}{s-1}$	n MONTHS
1	1.005000	1.000000	1.000000	.995025	.995025	1.005000	1
2	1.010025	2.005000	.498753	.990075	1.985099	.503753	2
3	1.015075	3.015025	.331672	.985149	2.970248	.336672	3
4	1.020151	4.030100	.248133	.980248	3.950496	.253133	4
5	1.025251	5.050251	.198010	.975371	4.925866	.203010	5
6	1.030378	6.075502	.164595	.970518	5.896384	.169595	6
7	1.035529	7.105879	.140729	.965690	6.862074	.145729	7
8	1.040707	8.141409	.122829	.960885	7.822959	.127829	8
9	1.045911	9.182116	.108907	.956105	8.779064	.113907	9
10	1.051140	10.228026	.097771	.951348	9.730412	.102771	10
11	1.056396	11.279167	.088659	.946615	10.677027	.093659	11
YEARS							
1	1.061678	12.336562	.081066	.941905	11.618932	.086066	12
2	1.127160	25.431955	.039321	.887186	22.562866	.044321	24
3	1.196681	39.336105	.025422	.835645	32.871016	.030422	36
4	1.270489	54.097832	.018485	.787098	42.580318	.023485	48
5	1.348850	69.770031	.014333	.741372	51.725561	.019333	60
6	1.432044	86.408856	.011573	.698302	60.339514	.016573	72
7	1.520370	104.073927	.009609	.657735	68.453042	.014609	84
8	1.614143	122.828542	.008141	.619524	76.095218	.013141	96
9	1.713699	142.739900	.007006	.583533	83.293424	.012006	108
10	1.819397	163.879347	.006102	.549633	90.073453	.011102	120
11	1.931613	186.322629	.005367	.517702	96.459599	.010367	132
12	2.050751	210.150163	.004759	.487626	102.474743	.009759	144
13	2.177237	235.447328	.004247	.459298	108.140440	.009247	156
14	2.311524	262.304766	.003812	.432615	113.476990	.008812	168
15	2.454094	290.818713	.003439	.407482	118.503514	.008439	180
16	2.605457	321.091337	.003114	.383810	123.238025	.008114	192
17	2.766156	353.231110	.002831	.361513	127.697486	.007831	204
18	2.936766	387.353195	.002582	.340511	131.897876	.007582	216
19	3.117899	423.579854	.002361	.320729	135.854246	.007361	228
20	3.310204	462.040895	.002164	.302096	139.580771	.007164	240
21	3.514371	502.874129	.001989	.284546	143.090806	.006989	252
22	3.731129	546.225867	.001831	.268015	146.396926	.006831	264
23	3.961257	592.251446	.001688	.252445	149.510979	.006688	276
24	4.205579	641.115782	.001560	.237779	152.444121	.006560	288
25	4.464970	692.993963	.001443	.223966	155.206864	.006443	300
26	4.740359	748.071876	.001337	.210954	157.809106	.006337	312
27	5.032734	806.546875	.001240	.198699	160.260171	.006240	324
28	5.343142	868.628484	.001151	.187156	162.568843	.006151	336
29	5.672696	934.539150	.001070	.176283	164.743393	.006070	348
30	6.022575	1004.515043	.000996	.166042	166.791614	.005996	360
31	6.394034	1078.806895	.000927	.156396	168.720844	.005927	372
32	6.788405	1157.680906	.000864	.147310	170.537996	.005864	384
33	7.207098	1241.419694	.000806	.138752	172.249581	.005806	396
34	7.651617	1330.323306	.000752	.130691	173.861732	.005752	408
35	8.123551	1424.710299	.000702	.123099	175.380226	.005702	420
36	8.624594	1524.918875	.000656	.115947	176.810503	.005656	432
37	9.156540	1631.308097	.000613	.109212	178.157689	.005613	444
38	9.721296	1744.259174	.000573	.102867	179.426611	.005573	456
39	10.320884	1864.176825	.000536	.096891	180.621815	.005536	468
40	10.957454	1991.490735	.000502	.091262	181.747584	.005502	480
41	11.633285	2126.657088	.000470	.085960	182.807952	.005470	492
42	12.350801	2270.160207	.000440	.080966	183.806718	.005440	504
43	13.112571	2422.514283	.000413	.076263	184.747461	.005413	516
44	13.921326	2584.265226	.000387	.071832	185.633552	.005387	528
45	14.779963	2755.992612	.000363	.067659	186.468166	.005363	540
46	15.691559	2938.311769	.000340	.063729	187.254293	.005340	552
47	16.659380	3131.875972	.000319	.060026	187.994750	.005319	564
48	17.686894	3337.378791	.000300	.056539	188.692191	.005300	576
49	18.777783	3555.556574	.000281	.053254	189.349115	.005281	588
50	19.935955	3787.191086	.000264	.050161	189.967874	.005264	600

Reprinted by permission, from *Ellwood's Tables for Real Estate Appraising and Financing* (Ridgewood, N.J.: published by the author, 1959).

6 ¼ % MONTHLY COMPOUND INTEREST TABLE 6 ¼ %

EFFECTIVE RATE = 25/48% i = .00520833+

	1 AMOUNT OF 1 AT COMPOUND INTEREST $s=(1+i)^n$	2 ACCUMULATION OF 1 PER PERIOD $s_{\overline{n}}=\frac{s-1}{i}$	3 SINKING FUND FACTOR $\frac{1}{s_{\overline{n}}}=\frac{i}{s-1}$	4 PRES. VALUE REVERSION OF 1 $v^n=\frac{1}{s}$	5 PRESENT VALUE ORD. ANNUITY 1 PER PERIOD $a_{\overline{n}}=\frac{s-1}{si}$	6 INSTALMENT TO AMORTIZE 1 $\frac{1}{a_{\overline{n}}}=\frac{si}{s-1}$	n
MONTHS							MONTHS
1	1.005208	1.000000	1.000000	.994819	.994819	1.005208	1
2	1.010444	2.005208	.498701	.989664	1.984483	.503909	2
3	1.015707	3.015652	.331603	.984536	2.969019	.336811	3
4	1.020997	4.031359	.248055	.979435	3.948454	.253263	4
5	1.026314	5.052355	.197927	.974360	4.922815	.203135	5
6	1.031660	6.078670	.164510	.969312	5.892126	.169718	6
7	1.037033	7.110329	.140640	.964290	6.856416	.145848	7
8	1.042434	8.147362	.122739	.959293	7.815709	.127947	8
9	1.047864	9.189797	.108816	.954323	8.770032	.114024	9
10	1.053321	10.237660	.097679	.949378	9.719410	.102887	10
11	1.058807	11.290981	.088566	.944459	10.663869	.093774	11
YEARS							
1	1.064322	12.349788	.080973	.939565	11.603434	.086181	12
2	1.132781	25.493938	.039225	.882783	22.505621	.044433	24
3	1.205643	39.483542	.025327	.829433	32.748938	.030535	36
4	1.283193	54.372984	.018391	.779306	42.373205	.023599	48
5	1.365730	70.220141	.014241	.732029	51.415834	.019449	60
6	1.453576	87.086616	.011483	.687958	59.911975	.016691	72
7	1.547073	105.037974	.009520	.646382	67.894656	.014728	84
8	1.646583	124.143995	.008055	.607318	75.394907	.013263	96
9	1.752495	144.478951	.006921	.570615	82.441884	.012129	108
10	1.865218	166.121887	.006020	.536130	89.062980	.011228	120
11	1.985192	189.156937	.005287	.503730	95.283933	.010495	132
12	2.112884	213.673643	.004680	.473287	101.128925	.009888	144
13	2.248788	239.767308	.004171	.444684	106.620678	.009379	156
14	2.393434	267.539364	.003738	.417810	111.780540	.008946	168
15	2.547384	297.097770	.003366	.392560	116.628567	.008574	180
16	2.711237	328.557426	.003044	.368835	121.183606	.008252	192
17	2.885628	362.040624	.002762	.346545	125.463363	.007970	204
18	3.071237	397.677522	.002515	.325602	129.484476	.007723	216
19	3.268785	435.606650	.002296	.305924	133.262573	.007504	228
20	3.479039	475.975448	.002101	.287436	136.812344	.007309	240
21	3.702817	518.940841	.001927	.270065	140.147585	.007135	252
22	3.940989	564.669846	.001771	.253743	143.281263	.006979	264
23	4.194480	613.340223	.001630	.238409	146.225558	.006838	276
24	4.464277	665.141168	.001503	.224000	148.991916	.006711	288
25	4.751427	720.274043	.001388	.210463	151.591091	.006596	300
26	5.057048	778.953164	.001284	.197744	154.033185	.006492	312
27	5.382326	841.406633	.001188	.185793	156.327693	.006396	324
28	5.728527	907.877223	.001101	.174565	158.483533	.006309	336
29	6.096996	978.623321	.001022	.164015	160.509086	.006230	348
30	6.489166	1053.919937	.000949	.154103	162.412225	.006157	360
31	6.906561	1134.059768	.000882	.144790	164.200349	.006090	372
32	7.350804	1219.354338	.000820	.136040	165.880409	.006028	384
33	7.823621	1310.135209	.000763	.127818	167.458935	.005971	396
34	8.326850	1406.755271	.000711	.120093	168.942063	.005919	408
35	8.862448	1509.590111	.000662	.112836	170.335560	.005870	420
36	9.432497	1619.039473	.000618	.106016	171.644840	.005826	432
37	10.039213	1735.528818	.000576	.099609	172.874996	.005784	444
38	10.684953	1859.510969	.000538	.093590	174.030807	.005746	456
39	11.372228	1991.467876	.000502	.087934	175.116767	.005710	468
40	12.103711	2131.912491	.000469	.082619	176.137098	.005677	480
41	12.882243	2281.390758	.000438	.077626	177.095765	.005646	492
42	13.710853	2440.483739	.000410	.072935	177.996496	.005618	504
43	14.592760	2609.809869	.000383	.068527	178.842792	.005591	516
44	15.531392	2790.027363	.000358	.064386	179.637942	.005566	528
45	16.530400	2981.836773	.000335	.060495	180.385037	.005543	540
46	17.593665	3185.983712	.000314	.056839	181.086983	.005522	552
47	18.725322	3403.261753	.000294	.053404	181.746506	.005502	564
48	19.929768	3634.515512	.000275	.050176	182.366172	.005483	576
49	21.211687	3880.643931	.000258	.047144	182.948388	.005466	588
50	22.576061	4142.603778	.000241	.044295	183.495418	.005449	600

Reprinted by permission, from *Ellwood's Tables for Real Estate Appraising and Financing* (Ridgewood, N.J.: published by the author, 1959).

6 ½ % MONTHLY COMPOUND INTEREST TABLE 6 ½ %

EFFECTIVE RATE = 13/24% i = .00541666+

MONTHS	1 AMOUNT OF 1 AT COMPOUND INTEREST $s = (1+i)^n$	2 ACCUMULATION OF 1 PER PERIOD $s_{\overline{n}\|} = \frac{s-1}{i}$	3 SINKING FUND FACTOR $\frac{1}{s_{\overline{n}\|}} = \frac{i}{s-1}$	4 PRES. VALUE REVERSION OF 1 $v^n = \frac{1}{s}$	5 PRESENT VALUE ORD. ANNUITY 1 PER PERIOD $a_{\overline{n}\|} = \frac{s-1}{si}$	6 INSTALMENT TO AMORTIZE 1 $\frac{1}{a_{\overline{n}\|}} = \frac{si}{s-1}$	n MONTHS
1	1.005417	1.000000	1.000000	.994613	.994613	1.005417	1
2	1.010863	2.005417	.498649	.989254	1.983867	.504066	2
3	1.016338	3.016279	.331534	.983924	2.967791	.336951	3
4	1.021843	4.032618	.247978	.978624	3.946415	.253395	4
5	1.027378	5.054461	.197845	.973351	4.919766	.203262	5
6	1.032943	6.081839	.164424	.968107	5.887873	.169841	6
7	1.038538	7.114782	.140552	.962892	6.850765	.145969	7
8	1.044164	8.153321	.122649	.957704	7.808469	.128066	8
9	1.049820	9.197485	.108725	.952545	8.761014	.114142	9
10	1.055506	10.247304	.097587	.947413	9.708426	.103004	10
11	1.061224	11.302811	.088474	.942309	10.650735	.093891	11

YEARS

	1 AMOUNT OF 1 AT COMPOUND INTEREST	2 ACCUMULATION OF 1 PER PERIOD	3 SINKING FUND FACTOR	4 PRES. VALUE REVERSION OF 1	5 PRESENT VALUE ORD. ANNUITY 1 PER PERIOD	6 INSTALMENT TO AMORTIZE 1	n MONTHS
1	1.066972	12.364034	.080880	.937232	11.587967	.086297	12
2	1.138429	25.556111	.039130	.878404	22.448578	.044547	24
3	1.214672	39.631685	.025232	.823268	32.627489	.030649	36
4	1.296020	54.649927	.018298	.771593	42.167488	.023715	48
5	1.382817	70.673968	.014149	.723161	51.108680	.019566	60
6	1.475427	87.771168	.011393	.677770	59.488649	.016810	72
7	1.574239	106.013400	.009433	.635227	67.342623	.014850	84
8	1.679669	125.477348	.007970	.595355	74.703617	.013387	96
9	1.792160	146.244833	.006838	.557986	81.602576	.012255	108
10	1.912184	168.403155	.005938	.522962	88.068500	.011355	120
11	2.040246	192.045460	.005207	.490137	94.128569	.010624	132
12	2.176885	217.271135	.004603	.459372	99.808259	.010020	144
13	2.322675	244.186219	.004095	.430538	105.131446	.009512	156
14	2.478229	272.903857	.003664	.403514	110.120506	.009081	168
15	2.644201	303.544768	.003294	.378186	114.796412	.008711	180
16	2.821288	336.237757	.002974	.354448	119.178820	.008391	192
17	3.010235	371.120257	.002695	.332200	123.286152	.008112	204
18	3.211836	408.338902	.002449	.311348	127.135674	.007866	216
19	3.426938	448.050149	.002232	.291806	130.743570	.007649	228
20	3.656447	490.420932	.002039	.273490	134.125004	.007456	240
21	3.901326	535.629365	.001867	.256323	137.294192	.007284	252
22	4.162605	583.865490	.001713	.240234	140.264455	.007130	264
23	4.441382	635.332077	.001574	.225155	143.048281	.006991	276
24	4.738830	690.245477	.001449	.211023	145.657372	.006866	288
25	5.056198	748.836530	.001335	.197777	148.102694	.006752	300
26	5.394821	811.351534	.001233	.185363	150.394528	.006650	312
27	5.756122	878.053283	.001139	.173728	152.542508	.006556	324
28	6.141620	949.222172	.001053	.162823	154.555663	.006470	336
29	6.552936	1025.157374	.000975	.152603	156.442456	.006392	348
30	6.991798	1106.178096	.000904	.143025	158.210819	.006321	360
31	7.460052	1192.624927	.000838	.134047	159.868185	.006255	372
32	7.959665	1284.861262	.000778	.125633	161.421520	.006195	384
33	8.492739	1383.274835	.000723	.117748	162.877356	.006140	396
34	9.061513	1488.279347	.000672	.110357	164.241812	.006089	408
35	9.668380	1600.316206	.000625	.103430	165.520624	.006042	420
36	10.315889	1719.856381	.000581	.096938	166.719166	.005998	432
37	11.006763	1847.402383	.000541	.090853	167.842479	.005958	444
38	11.743906	1983.490377	.000504	.085151	168.895283	.005921	456
39	12.530417	2128.692436	.000470	.079806	169.882005	.005887	468
40	13.369603	2283.618946	.000438	.074797	170.806792	.005855	480
41	14.264990	2448.921171	.000408	.070102	171.673532	.005825	492
42	15.220343	2625.293993	.000381	.065702	172.485868	.005798	504
43	16.239677	2813.478829	.000355	.061578	173.247215	.005772	516
44	17.327278	3014.266752	.000332	.057712	173.960774	.005749	528
45	18.487718	3228.501814	.000310	.054090	174.629544	.005727	540
46	19.725875	3457.084595	.000289	.050695	175.256337	.005706	552
47	21.046953	3700.975989	.000270	.047513	175.843787	.005687	564
48	22.456507	3961.201241	.000252	.044531	176.394364	.005669	576
49	23.960461	4238.854260	.000236	.041735	176.910382	.005653	588
50	25.565137	4535.102216	.000221	.039116	177.394011	.005638	600

Reprinted by permission, from *Ellwood's Tables for Real Estate Appraising and Financing* (Ridgewood, N.J.: published by the author, 1959).

6¾% MONTHLY COMPOUND INTEREST TABLE 6¾%

EFFECTIVE RATE = 9/16% i = .005625

MONTHS	1 AMOUNT OF 1 AT COMPOUND INTEREST $s=(1+i)^n$	2 ACCUMULATION OF 1 PER PERIOD $s_{\overline{n}} = \frac{s-1}{i}$	3 SINKING FUND FACTOR $\frac{1}{s_{\overline{n}}} = \frac{i}{s-1}$	4 PRES. VALUE REVERSION OF 1 $v^n = \frac{1}{s}$	5 PRESENT VALUE ORD. ANNUITY 1 PER PERIOD $a_{\overline{n}} = \frac{s-1}{si}$	6 INSTALMENT TO AMORTIZE 1 $\frac{1}{a_{\overline{n}}} = \frac{si}{s-1}$	n MONTHS
1	1.005625	1.000000	1.000000	.994406	.994406	1.005625	1
2	1.011282	2.005625	.498598	.988844	1.983251	.504223	2
3	1.016970	3.016970	.331465	.983313	2.966564	.337090	3
4	1.022691	4.033877	.247900	.977813	3.944377	.253525	4
5	1.028443	5.056567	.197763	.972343	4.916720	.203388	5
6	1.034228	6.085010	.164338	.966905	5.883625	.169963	6
7	1.040046	7.119239	.140464	.961496	6.845121	.146089	7
8	1.045896	8.159284	.122560	.956118	7.801239	.128185	8
9	1.051779	9.205180	.108634	.950770	8.752009	.114259	9
10	1.057695	10.256960	.097495	.945452	9.697461	.103120	10
11	1.063645	11.314655	.088381	.940163	10.637624	.094006	11
YEARS 1	1.069628	12.378300	.080787	.934905	11.572529	.086412	12
2	1.144104	25.618475	.039034	.874046	22.391738	.044659	24
3	1.223766	39.780537	.025138	.817150	32.506666	.030763	36
4	1.308974	54.928673	.018205	.763957	41.963157	.023830	48
5	1.400115	71.131543	.014058	.714227	50.804074	.019683	60
6	1.497602	88.462585	.011304	.667734	59.069488	.016929	72
7	1.601877	107.000353	.009346	.624268	66.796860	.014971	84
8	1.713412	126.828866	.007885	.583631	74.021215	.013510	96
9	1.832714	148.037998	.006755	.545639	80.775298	.012380	108
10	1.960322	170.723878	.005857	.510120	87.089720	.011482	120
11	2.096815	194.989330	.005128	.476914	92.993102	.010753	132
12	2.242812	220.944334	.004526	.445869	98.512201	.010151	144
13	2.398974	248.706532	.004021	.416845	103.672031	.009646	156
14	2.566010	278.401755	.003592	.389710	108.495979	.009217	168
15	2.744676	310.164594	.003224	.364342	113.005911	.008849	180
16	2.935782	344.139015	.002906	.340625	117.222266	.008531	192
17	3.140194	380.479004	.002628	.318452	121.164156	.008253	204
18	3.358840	419.349272	.002385	.297722	124.849446	.008010	216
19	3.592709	460.925996	.002170	.278342	128.294841	.007795	228
20	3.842862	505.397622	.001979	.260223	131.515956	.007604	240
21	4.110432	552.965715	.001808	.243283	134.527391	.007433	252
22	4.396633	603.845877	.001656	.227447	137.342795	.007281	264
23	4.702762	658.268719	.001519	.212641	139.974930	.007144	276
24	5.030205	716.480912	.001396	.198799	142.435724	.007021	288
25	5.380448	778.746299	.001284	.185858	144.736331	.006909	300
26	5.755077	845.347097	.001183	.173760	146.887180	.006808	312
27	6.155792	916.585171	.001091	.162449	148.898018	.006716	324
28	6.584407	992.783405	.001007	.151874	150.777960	.006632	336
29	7.042865	1074.287164	.000931	.141988	152.535525	.006556	348
30	7.533245	1161.465863	.000861	.132745	154.178682	.006486	360
31	8.057770	1254.714634	.000797	.124104	155.714876	.006422	372
32	8.618816	1354.456125	.000738	.116025	157.151071	.006363	384
33	9.218926	1461.142410	.000684	.108473	158.493776	.006309	396
34	9.860821	1575.257041	.000635	.101411	159.749077	.006260	408
35	10.547409	1697.317238	.000589	.094810	160.922664	.006214	420
36	11.281804	1827.876235	.000547	.088638	162.019855	.006172	432
37	12.067333	1967.525785	.000508	.082868	163.045625	.006133	444
38	12.907556	2116.898846	.000472	.077474	164.004621	.006097	456
39	13.806282	2276.672444	.000439	.072431	164.901191	.006064	468
40	14.767585	2447.570748	.000409	.067716	165.739399	.006034	480
41	15.795822	2630.368349	.000380	.063308	166.523043	.006005	492
42	16.895652	2825.893769	.000354	.059187	167.255675	.005979	504
43	18.072062	3035.033221	.000329	.055334	167.940616	.005954	516
44	19.330382	3258.734622	.000307	.051732	168.580971	.005932	528
45	20.676317	3498.011889	.000286	.048365	169.179641	.005911	540
46	22.115966	3753.949539	.000266	.045216	169.739341	.005891	552
47	23.655855	4027.707599	.000248	.042273	170.262606	.005873	564
48	25.302964	4320.526868	.000231	.039521	170.751810	.005856	576
49	27.064757	4633.734539	.000216	.036948	171.209169	.005841	588
50	28.949220	4968.750213	.000201	.034543	171.636755	.005826	600

Reprinted by permission, from *Ellwood's Tables for Real Estate Appraising and Financing* (Ridgewood, N.J.: published by the author, 1959).

7%   MONTHLY COMPOUND INTEREST TABLE   7%

EFFECTIVE RATE = 7/12%   i = .00583333+

	1 AMOUNT OF 1 AT COMPOUND INTEREST $s = (1+i)^n$	2 ACCUMULATION OF 1 PER PERIOD $s_{\overline{n}} = \frac{s-1}{i}$	3 SINKING FUND FACTOR $\frac{1}{s_{\overline{n}}} = \frac{i}{s-1}$	4 PRES. VALUE REVERSION OF 1 $v^n = \frac{1}{s}$	5 PRESENT VALUE ORD. ANNUITY 1 PER PERIOD $a_{\overline{n}} = \frac{s-1}{si}$	6 INSTALMENT TO AMORTIZE 1 $\frac{1}{a_{\overline{n}}} = \frac{si}{s-1}$	n
MONTHS							**MONTHS**
1	1.005833	1.000000	1.000000	.994200	.994200	1.005833	1
2	1.011701	2.005833	.498546	.988435	1.982635	.504379	2
3	1.017602	3.017534	.331396	.982702	2.965337	.337229	3
4	1.023538	4.035136	.247823	.977003	3.942340	.253656	4
5	1.029509	5.058675	.197680	.971337	4.913677	.203513	5
6	1.035514	6.088184	.164253	.965704	5.879381	.170086	6
7	1.041555	7.123698	.140377	.960103	6.839484	.146210	7
8	1.047631	8.165253	.122470	.954535	7.794019	.128303	8
9	1.053742	9.212883	.108544	.948999	8.743018	.114377	9
10	1.059889	10.266625	.097403	.943495	9.686513	.103236	10
11	1.066071	11.326514	.088288	.938024	10.624537	.094006	11
YEARS							
1	1.072290	12.392585	.080693	.932583	11.557120	.086526	12
2	1.149806	25.681032	.038939	.869712	22.335099	.044772	24
3	1.232926	39.930101	.025044	.811079	32.386464	.030877	36
4	1.322054	55.209236	.018113	.756399	41.760201	.023946	48
5	1.417625	71.592902	.013968	.705405	50.501993	.019801	60
6	1.520106	89.160943	.011216	.657849	58.654444	.017049	72
7	1.629994	107.998981	.009259	.613499	66.257285	.015092	84
8	1.747826	128.198821	.007800	.572139	73.347569	.013633	96
9	1.874177	149.858909	.006673	.533568	79.959850	.012506	108
10	2.009661	173.084807	.005778	.497596	86.126354	.011611	120
11	2.154940	197.989707	.005051	.464050	91.877134	.010884	132
12	2.310721	224.694984	.004450	.432765	97.240216	.010283	144
13	2.477763	253.330788	.003947	.403590	102.241738	.009780	156
14	2.656881	284.036676	.003521	.376381	106.906075	.009354	168
15	2.848947	316.962296	.003155	.351007	111.255958	.008988	180
16	3.054897	352.268111	.002839	.327343	115.312587	.008672	192
17	3.275736	390.126186	.002563	.305275	119.095732	.008396	204
18	3.512539	430.721025	.002322	.284694	122.623831	.008155	216
19	3.766461	474.250468	.002109	.265501	125.914077	.007942	228
20	4.038739	520.926657	.001920	.247602	128.982507	.007753	240
21	4.330700	570.977073	.001751	.230910	131.844073	.007584	252
22	4.643766	624.645636	.001601	.215342	134.512723	.007434	264
23	4.979464	682.193905	.001466	.200825	137.001461	.007299	276
24	5.339430	743.902343	.001344	.187286	139.322418	.007177	288
25	5.725418	810.071688	.001234	.174660	141.486903	.007067	300
26	6.139309	881.024421	.001135	.162885	143.505467	.006968	312
27	6.583120	957.106332	.001045	.151904	145.387946	.006878	324
28	7.059015	1038.688211	.000963	.141663	147.143515	.006796	336
29	7.569311	1126.167651	.000888	.132112	148.780729	.006721	348
30	8.116497	1219.970986	.000820	.123206	150.307568	.006653	360
31	8.703240	1320.555373	.000757	.114900	151.731473	.006590	372
32	9.332398	1428.411012	.000700	.107154	153.059383	.006533	384
33	10.007037	1544.063544	.000648	.099930	154.297770	.006481	396
34	10.730447	1668.076607	.000599	.093193	155.452669	.006432	408
35	11.506152	1801.054585	.000555	.086910	156.529709	.006388	420
36	12.337932	1943.645551	.000514	.081051	157.534139	.006347	432
37	13.229842	2096.544429	.000477	.075587	158.470853	.006310	444
38	14.186229	2260.496380	.000442	.070491	159.344418	.006275	456
39	15.211752	2436.300430	.000410	.065739	160.159089	.006243	468
40	16.311411	2624.813370	.000381	.061307	160.918839	.006214	480
41	17.490564	2826.953925	.000354	.057174	161.627369	.006187	492
42	18.754959	3043.707236	.000329	.053319	162.288132	.006162	504
43	20.110756	3276.129663	.000305	.049725	162.904348	.006138	516
44	21.564564	3525.353925	.000284	.046372	163.479022	.006117	528
45	23.123469	3792.594629	.000264	.043246	164.014953	.006097	540
46	24.795066	4079.154185	.000245	.040331	164.514754	.006078	552
47	26.587503	4386.429154	.000228	.037612	164.980859	.006061	564
48	28.509516	4715.917056	.000212	.035076	165.415542	.006045	576
49	30.570471	5069.223664	.000197	.032711	165.820919	.006030	588
50	32.780413	5448.070836	.000184	.030506	166.198968	.006017	600

Reprinted by permission, from *Ellwood's Tables for Real Estate Appraising and Financing* (Ridgewood, N.J.: published by the author, 1959).

7½% MONTHLY COMPOUND INTEREST TABLE 7½%

EFFECTIVE RATE = 5/8% $i = .00625$

MONTHS	1 AMOUNT OF 1 AT COMPOUND INTEREST $s = (1+i)^n$	2 ACCUMULATION OF 1 PER PERIOD $s_{\overline{n}|} = \frac{s-1}{i}$	3 SINKING FUND FACTOR $\frac{1}{s_{\overline{n}|}} = \frac{i}{s-1}$	4 PRES. VALUE REVERSION OF 1 $v^n = \frac{1}{s}$	5 PRESENT VALUE ORD. ANNUITY 1 PER PERIOD $a_{\overline{n}|} = \frac{s-1}{si}$	6 INSTALMENT TO AMORTIZE 1 $\frac{1}{a_{\overline{n}|}} = \frac{si}{s-1}$	n MONTHS
1	1.006250	1.000000	1.000000	.993789	.993789	1.006250	1
2	1.012539	2.006250	.498442	.987616	1.981405	.504692	2
3	1.018867	3.018789	.331259	.981482	2.962887	.337509	3
4	1.025235	4.037656	.247668	.975386	3.938273	.253918	4
5	1.031643	5.062892	.197516	.969327	4.907600	.203766	5
6	1.038091	6.094535	.164081	.963307	5.870907	.170331	6
7	1.044579	7.132626	.140201	.957324	6.828231	.146451	7
8	1.051108	8.177205	.122291	.951377	7.779608	.128541	8
9	1.057677	9.228312	.108362	.945468	8.725076	.114612	9
10	1.064287	10.285989	.097220	.939596	9.664672	.103470	10
11	1.070939	11.350277	.088104	.933760	10.598432	.094354	11

YEARS

	1	2	3	4	5	6	n MONTHS
1	1.077633	12.421216	.080507	.927960	11.526392	.086757	12
2	1.161292	25.806723	.038750	.861110	22.222423	.045000	24
3	1.251446	40.231382	.024856	.799076	32.147913	.031106	36
4	1.348599	55.775864	.017929	.741510	41.358371	.024179	48
5	1.453294	72.527105	.013788	.688092	49.905308	.020038	60
6	1.566117	90.578789	.011040	.638522	57.836524	.017290	72
7	1.687699	110.031871	.009088	.592523	65.196376	.015338	84
8	1.818720	130.995147	.007634	.549837	72.026024	.013884	96
9	1.959912	153.585857	.006511	.510227	78.363665	.012761	108
10	2.112065	177.930342	.005620	.473470	84.244743	.011870	120
11	2.276030	204.164753	.004898	.439362	89.702148	.011148	132
12	2.452724	232.435809	.004302	.407710	94.766402	.010552	144
13	2.643135	262.901621	.003804	.378339	99.465827	.010054	156
14	2.848329	295.732572	.003381	.351083	103.826706	.009631	168
15	3.069452	331.112276	.003020	.325791	107.873427	.009270	180
16	3.307741	369.238599	.002708	.302321	111.628623	.008958	192
17	3.564530	410.324767	.002437	.280542	115.113294	.008687	204
18	3.841254	454.600560	.002200	.260332	118.346930	.008450	216
19	4.139460	502.313599	.001991	.241577	121.347616	.008241	228
20	4.460817	553.730725	.001806	.224174	124.132131	.008056	240
21	4.807122	609.139496	.001642	.208025	126.716051	.007892	252
22	5.180311	668.849794	.001495	.193039	129.113825	.007745	264
23	5.582472	733.195558	.001364	.179132	131.338864	.007614	276
24	6.015854	802.536650	.001246	.166227	133.403610	.007496	288
25	6.482880	877.260872	.001140	.154252	135.319613	.007390	300
26	6.986163	957.786129	.001044	.143140	137.097587	.007294	312
27	7.528517	1044.562771	.000957	.132828	138.747476	.007207	324
28	8.112976	1138.076110	.000879	.123259	140.278507	.007129	336
29	8.742807	1238.849131	.000807	.114380	141.699242	.007057	348
30	9.421534	1347.445425	.000742	.106140	143.017628	.006992	360
31	10.152952	1464.472331	.000683	.098494	144.241037	.006933	372
32	10.941152	1590.584340	.000629	.091398	145.376312	.006879	384
33	11.790542	1726.486752	.000579	.084814	146.429802	.006829	396
34	12.705873	1872.939621	.000534	.078704	147.407398	.006784	408
35	13.692263	2030.762007	.000492	.073034	148.314569	.006742	420
36	14.755228	2200.836555	.000454	.067773	149.156387	.006704	432
37	15.900715	2384.114432	.000419	.062890	149.937560	.006669	444
38	17.135129	2581.620647	.000387	.058360	150.662458	.006637	456
39	18.465374	2794.459783	.000358	.054155	151.335134	.006608	468
40	19.898889	3023.822175	.000331	.050254	151.959350	.006581	480
41	21.443691	3270.990564	.000306	.046634	152.538598	.006556	492
42	23.108420	3537.347278	.000283	.043274	153.076118	.006533	504
43	24.902387	3824.381956	.000261	.040157	153.574914	.006511	516
44	26.835624	4133.699883	.000242	.037264	154.037777	.006492	528
45	28.918944	4467.030963	.000224	.034579	154.467295	.006474	540
46	31.163996	4826.239402	.000207	.032088	154.865871	.006457	552
47	33.583338	5213.334125	.000192	.029777	155.235733	.006442	564
48	36.190500	5630.480018	.000178	.027632	155.578951	.006428	576
49	39.000063	6080.010030	.000164	.025641	155.897443	.006414	588
50	42.027739	6564.438226	.000152	.023794	156.192991	.006402	600

Reprinted by permission, from *Ellwood's Tables for Real Estate Appraising and Financing* (Ridgewood, N.J.: published by the author, 1959).

8% MONTHLY COMPOUND INTEREST TABLE 8%

EFFECTIVE RATE = 2/3%   i = .00666666+

MONTHS	1 AMOUNT OF 1 AT COMPOUND INTEREST $s = (1+i)^n$	2 ACCUMULATION OF 1 PER PERIOD $s_{\overline{n}} = \frac{s-1}{i}$	3 SINKING FUND FACTOR $\frac{1}{s_{\overline{n}}} = \frac{i}{s-1}$	4 PRES. VALUE REVERSION OF 1 $v^n = \frac{1}{s}$	5 PRESENT VALUE ORD. ANNUITY 1 PER PERIOD $a_{\overline{n}} = \frac{s-1}{si}$	6 INSTALMENT TO AMORTIZE 1 $\frac{1}{a_{\overline{n}}} = \frac{si}{s-1}$	n MONTHS
1	1.006667	1.000000	1.000000	.993377	.993377	1.006667	1
2	1.013378	2.006667	.498339	.986799	1.980176	.505006	2
3	1.020134	3.020044	.331121	.980264	2.960440	.337788	3
4	1.026935	4.040178	.247514	.973772`	3.934212	.254181	4
5	1.033781	5.067113	.197351	.967323	4.901535	.204018	5
6	1.040673	6.100893	.163910	.960917	5.862452	.170577	6
7	1.047610	7.141566	.140025	.954553	6.817005	.146692	7
8	1.054595	8.189176	.122112	.948232	7.765237	.128779	8
9	1.061625	9.243771	.108181	.941952	8.707189	.114848	9
10	1.068703	10.305396	.097037	.935714	9.642903	.103704	10
11	1.075827	11.374099	.087919	.929517	10.572420	.094586	11

YEARS

	1	2	3	4	5	6	n MONTHS
1	1.083000	12.449926	.080322	.923361	11.495782	.086989	12
2	1.172888	25.933190	.038561	.852596	22.110544	.045228	24
3	1.270237	40.535558	.024670	.787255	31.911805	.031337	36
4	1.375666	56.349915	.017746	.726921	40.961913	.024413	48
5	1.489846	73.476856	.013610	.671210	49.318433	.020277	60
6	1.613502	92.025325	.010867	.619770	57.034522	.017534	72
7	1.747422	112.113308	.008920	.572272	64.159261	.015587	84
8	1.892457	133.868583	.007470	.528414	70.737970	.014137	96
9	2.049530	157.429536	.006352	.487917	76.812497	.013019	108
10	2.219640	182.946036	.005466	.450523	82.421481	.012133	120`
11	2.403869	210.580392	.004749	.415996	87.600600	.011416	132
12	2.603389	240.508387	.004158	.384115	92.382799	.010825	144
13	2.819469	272.920391	.003664	.354677	96.798498	.010331	156
14	3.053484	308.022575	.003247	.327495	100.875783	.009914	168
15	3.306921	346.038223	.002890	.302396	104.640592	.009557	180
16	3.581394	387.209151	.002583	.279221	108.116871	.009250	192
17	3.878648	431.797246	.002316	.257822	111.326733	.008983	204
18	4.200574	480.086130	.002083	.238063	114.290596	.008750	216
19	4.549220	532.382969	.001878	.219818	117.027313	.008545	228
20	4.926803	589.020419	.001698	.202971	119.554291	.008365	240
21	5.335725	650.358749	.001538	.187416	121.887606	.008205	252
22	5.778588	716.788131	.001395	.173053	124.042099	.008062	264
23	6.258207	788.731119	.001268	.159790	126.031475	.007935	276
24	6.777636	866.645339	.001154	.147544	127.868388	.007821	288
25	7.340176	951.026401	.001051	.136237	129.564522	.007718	300
26	7.949407	1042.411050	.000959	.125796	131.130667	.007626	312
27	8.609204	1141.380579	.000876	.116155	132.576785	.007543	324
28	9.323764	1248.564531	.000801	.107253	133.912075	.007468	336
29	10.097631	1364.644698	.000733	.099033	135.145030	.007400	348
30	10.935730	1490.359462	.000671	.091443	136.283493	.007338	360
31	11.843390	1626.508488	.000615	.084435	137.334707	.007282	372
32	12.826386	1773.957818	.000564	.077964	138.305356	.007231	384
33	13.890969	1933.645368	.000517	.071989	139.201617	.007184	396
34	15.043913	2106.586907	.000475	.066472	140.029189	.007142	408
35	16.292550	2293.882508	.000436	.061378	140.793337	.007103	420
36	17.644824	2496.723552	.000401	.056674	141.498922	.007068	432
37	19.109335	2716.400303	.000368	.052330	142.150433	.007035	444
38	20.695401	2954.310116	.000338	.048320	142.752012	.007005	456
39	22.413109	3211.966325	.000311	.044617	143.307487	.006978	468
40	24.273386	3491.007874	.000286	.041197	143.820391	.006953	480
41	26.288065	3793.209733	.000264	.038040	144.293988	.006931	492
42	28.469961	4120.494198	.000243	.035125	144.731288	.006910	504
43	30.832954	4474.943112	.000223	.032433	145.135074	.006890	516
44	33.392074	4858.811111	.000206	.029947	145.507915	.006873	528
45	36.163600	5274.539965	.000190	.027652	145.852182	.006857	540
46	39.165161	5724.774109	.000175	.025533	146.170065	.006842	552
47	42.415850	6212.377465	.000161	.023576	146.463585	.006828	564
48	45.936345	6740.451660	.000148	.021769	146.734611	.006815	576
49	49.749039	7312.355752	.000137	.020101	146.984865	.006804	588
50	53.878184	7931.727602	.000126	.018560	147.215941	.006793	600

Reprinted by permission, from *Ellwood's Tables for Real Estate Appraising and Financing* (Ridgewood, N.J.: published by the author, 1959).

8½% MONTHLY COMPOUND INTEREST TABLE 8½%

EFFECTIVE RATE = 17/24% i = .00708333+

	1 AMOUNT OF 1 AT COMPOUND INTEREST $s = (1+i)^n$	2 ACCUMULATION OF 1 PER PERIOD $s_{\overline{n}|} = \frac{s-1}{i}$	3 SINKING FUND FACTOR $\frac{1}{s_{\overline{n}|}} = \frac{i}{s-1}$	4 PRES. VALUE REVERSION OF 1 $v^n = \frac{1}{s}$	5 PRESENT VALUE ORD. ANNUITY 1 PER PERIOD $a_{\overline{n}|} = \frac{s-1}{si}$	6 INSTALMENT TO AMORTIZE 1 $\frac{1}{a_{\overline{n}|}} = \frac{si}{s-1}$	n
MONTHS							MONTHS
1	1.007083	1.000000	1.000000	.992966	.992966	1.007083	1
2	1.014217	2.007083	.498235	.985982	1.978949	.505318	2
3	1.021401	3.021300	.330983	.979048	2.957996	.338066	3
4	1.028636	4.042701	.247359	.972161	3.930158	.254442	4
5	1.035922	5.071337	.197187	.965324	4.895482	.204270	5
6	1.043260	6.107259	.163740	.958534	5.854016	.170823	6
7	1.050650	7.150519	.139850	.951792	6.805808	.146933	7
8	1.058092	8.201168	.121934	.945098	7.750906	.129017	8
9	1.065586	9.259260	.108000	.938450	8.689356	.115083	9
10	1.073134	10.324846	.096854	.931850	9.621206	.103937	10
11	1.080736	11.397980	.087735	.925296	10.546501	.094818	11
YEARS							
1	1.088391	12.478716	.080136	.918788	11.465289	.087219	12
2	1.184595	26.060437	.038372	.844171	21.999453	.045455	24
3	1.289302	40.842659	.024484	.775613	31.678112	.031567	36
4	1.403265	56.931495	.017565	.712624	40.570744	.024648	48
5	1.527301	74.442437	.013433	.654750	48.741183	.020516	60
6	1.662300	93.501188	.010695	.601576	56.248080	.017778	72
7	1.809232	114.244559	.008753	.552721	63.145324	.015836	84
8	1.969152	136.821455	.007309	.507833	69.482425	.014392	96
9	2.143207	161.393943	.006196	.466590	75.304875	.013279	108
10	2.332647	188.138416	.005315	.428698	80.654470	.012398	120
11	2.538832	217.246857	.004603	.393882	85.569611	.011686	132
12	2.763242	248.928219	.004017	.361894	90.085581	.011100	144
13	3.007487	283.409926	.003528	.332504	94.234798	.010611	156
14	3.273321	320.939502	.003116	.305500	98.047047	.010199	168
15	3.562653	361.786352	.002764	.280690	101.549693	.009847	180
16	3.877559	406.243691	.002462	.257894	104.767882	.009545	192
17	4.220300	454.630655	.002200	.236950	107.724713	.009283	204
18	4.593337	507.294586	.001971	.217707	110.441412	.009054	216
19	4.999346	564.613530	.001771	.200026	112.937482	.008854	228
20	5.441243	626.998947	.001595	.183782	115.230840	.008678	240
21	5.922199	694.898668	.001439	.168856	117.337949	.008522	252
22	6.445667	768.800107	.001301	.155143	119.273934	.008384	264
23	7.015406	849.233760	.001178	.142543	121.052693	.008261	276
24	7.635504	936.777018	.001067	.130967	122.686994	.008150	288
25	8.310413	1032.058303	.000969	.120331	124.188570	.008052	300
26	9.044978	1135.761586	.000880	.110559	125.568200	.007963	312
27	9.844472	1248.631298	.000801	.101580	126.835786	.007884	324
28	10.714633	1371.477665	.000729	.093330	128.000428	.007812	336
29	11.661710	1505.182533	.000664	.085751	129.070487	.007747	348
30	12.692499	1650.705697	.000606	.078787	130.053644	.007689	360
31	13.814400	1809.091784	.000553	.072388	130.956956	.007636	372
32	15.035467	1981.477761	.000505	.066509	131.786908	.007588	384
33	16.364466	2169.101090	.000461	.061108	132.549457	.007544	396
34	17.810936	2373.308616	.000421	.056145	133.250078	.007504	408
35	19.385261	2595.566229	.000385	.051586	133.893800	.007468	420
36	21.098741	2837.469395	.000352	.047396	134.485244	.007435	432
37	22.963678	3100.754600	.000323	.043547	135.028655	.007406	444
38	24.993459	3387.311823	.000295	.040010	135.527934	.007378	456
39	27.202653	3699.198098	.000270	.036761	135.986666	.007353	468
40	29.607120	4038.652283	.000248	.033776	136.408143	.007331	480
41	32.224120	4408.111132	.000227	.031033	136.795390	.007310	492
42	35.072440	4810.226782	.000208	.028512	137.151189	.007291	504
43	38.172524	5247.885799	.000191	.026197	137.478092	.007274	516
44	41.546628	5724.229893	.000175	.024069	137.778446	.007258	528
45	45.218972	6242.678472	.000160	.022115	138.054408	.007243	540
46	49.215918	6806.953191	.000147	.020319	138.307959	.007230	552
47	53.566158	7421.104663	.000135	.018669	138.540918	.007218	564
48	58.300919	8089.541540	.000124	.017152	138.754957	.007207	576
49	63.454190	8817.062157	.000113	.015759	138.951614	.007196	588
50	69.062963	9608.888981	.000104	.014480	139.132301	.007187	600

Reprinted by permission, from *Ellwood's Tables for Real Estate Appraising and Financing* (Ridgewood, N.J.: published by the author, 1959).

5% ANNUAL COMPOUND INTEREST TABLE 5%

EFFECTIVE RATE = 5% i = .05

YEARS	1 AMOUNT OF 1 AT COMPOUND INTEREST $s = (1+i)^n$	2 ACCUMULATION OF 1 PER PERIOD $s_{\overline{n}|} = \frac{s-1}{i}$	3 SINKING FUND FACTOR $\frac{1}{s_{\overline{n}|}} = \frac{i}{s-1}$	4 PRES. VALUE REVERSION OF 1 $v^n = \frac{1}{s}$	5 PRESENT VALUE ORD. ANNUITY 1 PER PERIOD $a_{\overline{n}|} = \frac{s-1}{si}$	6 INSTALMENT TO AMORTIZE 1 $\frac{1}{a_{\overline{n}|}} = \frac{si}{s-1}$	n YEARS
1	1.050000	1.000000	1.000000	.952381	.952381	1.050000	1
2	1.102500	2.050000	.487805	.907029	1.859410	.537805	2
3	1.157625	3.152500	.317209	.863838	2.723248	.367209	3
4	1.215506	4.310125	.232012	.822702	3.545951	.282012	4
5	1.276282	5.525631	.180975	.783526	4.329477	.230975	5
6	1.340096	6.801913	.147017	.746215	5.075692	.197017	6
7	1.407100	8.142008	.122820	.710681	5.786373	.172820	7
8	1.477455	9.549109	.104722	.676839	6.463213	.154722	8
9	1.551328	11.026564	.090690	.644609	7.107822	.140690	9
10	1.628895	12.577893	.079505	.613913	7.721735	.129505	10
11	1.710339	14.206787	.070389	.584679	8.306414	.120389	11
12	1.795856	15.917127	.062825	.556837	8.863252	.112825	12
13	1.885649	17.712983	.056456	.530321	9.393573	.106456	13
14	1.979932	19.598632	.051024	.505068	9.898641	.101024	14
15	2.078928	21.578564	.046342	.481017	10.379658	.096342	15
16	2.182875	23.657492	.042270	.458112	10.837770	.092270	16
17	2.292018	25.840366	.038699	.436297	11.274066	.088699	17
18	2.406619	28.132385	.035546	.415521	11.689587	.085546	18
19	2.526950	30.539004	.032745	.395734	12.085321	.082745	19
20	2.653298	33.065954	.030243	.376889	12.462210	.080243	20
21	2.785963	35.719252	.027996	.358942	12.821153	.077996	21
22	2.925261	38.505214	.025971	.341850	13.163003	.075971	22
23	3.071524	41.430475	.024137	.325571	13.488574	.074137	23
24	3.225100	44.501999	.022471	.310068	13.798642	.072471	24
25	3.386355	47.727099	.020952	.295303	14.093945	.070952	25
26	3.555673	51.113454	.019564	.281241	14.375185	.069564	26
27	3.733456	54.669126	.018292	.267848	14.643034	.068292	27
28	3.920129	58.402583	.017123	.255094	14.898127	.067123	28
29	4.116136	62.322712	.016046	.242946	15.141074	.066046	29
30	4.321942	66.438848	.015051	.231377	15.372451	.065051	30
31	4.538039	70.760790	.014132	.220359	15.592811	.064132	31
32	4.764941	75.298829	.013280	.209866	15.802677	.063280	32
33	5.003189	80.063771	.012490	.199873	16.002549	.062490	33
34	5.253348	85.066959	.011755	.190355	16.192904	.061755	34
35	5.516015	90.320307	.011072	.181290	16.374194	.061072	35
36	5.791816	95.836323	.010434	.172657	16.546852	.060434	36
37	6.081407	101.628139	.009840	.164436	16.711287	.059840	37
38	6.385477	107.709546	.009284	.156605	16.867893	.059284	38
39	6.704751	114.095023	.008765	.149148	17.017041	.058765	39
40	7.039989	120.799774	.008278	.142046	17.159086	.058278	40
41	7.391988	127.839763	.007822	.135282	17.294368	.057822	41
42	7.761588	135.231751	.007395	.128840	17.423208	.057395	42
43	8.149667	142.993339	.006993	.122704	17.545912	.056993	43
44	8.557150	151.143006	.006616	.116861	17.662773	.056616	44
45	8.985008	159.700156	.006262	.111297	17.774070	.056262	45
46	9.434258	168.685164	.005928	.105997	17.880067	.055928	46
47	9.905971	178.119422	.005614	.100949	17.981016	.055614	47
48	10.401270	188.025393	.005318	.096142	18.077158	.055318	48
49	10.921333	198.426663	.005040	.091564	18.168722	.055040	49
50	11.467400	209.347996	.004777	.087204	18.255925	.054777	50
51	12.040770	220.815395	.004529	.083051	18.338977	.054529	51
52	12.642808	232.856165	.004294	.079096	18.418073	.054294	52
53	13.274949	245.498974	.004073	.075330	18.493403	.054073	53
54	13.938696	258.773922	.003864	.071743	18.565146	.053864	54
55	14.635631	272.712618	.003667	.068326	18.633472	.053667	55
56	15.367412	287.348249	.003480	.065073	18.698545	.053480	56
57	16.135783	302.715662	.003303	.061974	18.760519	.053303	57
58	16.942572	318.851445	.003136	.059023	18.819542	.053136	58
59	17.789701	335.794017	.002978	.056212	18.875754	.052978	59
60	18.679186	353.583718	.002828	.053536	18.929290	.052828	60

Reprinted by permission, from *Ellwood's Tables for Real Estate Appraising and Financing* (Ridgewood, N.J.: published by the author, 1959).

6%   ANNUAL COMPOUND INTEREST TABLE   6%

EFFECTIVE RATE = 6%   i = .06

YEARS	1 AMOUNT OF 1 AT COMPOUND INTEREST $s=(1+i)^n$	2 ACCUMULATION OF 1 PER PERIOD $s_{\overline{n}|}=\frac{s-1}{i}$	3 SINKING FUND FACTOR $\frac{1}{s_{\overline{n}|}}=\frac{i}{s-1}$	4 PRES. VALUE REVERSION OF 1 $v^n=\frac{1}{s}$	5 PRESENT VALUE ORD. ANNUITY 1 PER PERIOD $a_{\overline{n}|}=\frac{s-1}{si}$	6 INSTALMENT TO AMORTIZE 1 $\frac{1}{a_{\overline{n}|}}=\frac{si}{s-1}$	n YEARS
1	1.060000	1.000000	1.000000	.943396	.943396	1.060000	1
2	1.123600	2.060000	.485437	.889996	1.833393	.545437	2
3	1.191016	3.183600	.314110	.839619	2.673012	.374110	3
4	1.262477	4.374616	.228591	.792094	3.465106	.288591	4
5	1.338226	5.637093	.177396	.747258	4.212364	.237396	5
6	1.418519	6.975319	.143363	.704961	4.917324	.203363	6
7	1.503630	8.393838	.119135	.665057	5.582381	.179135	7
8	1.593848	9.897468	.101036	.627412	6.209794	.161036	8
9	1.689479	11.491316	.087022	.591898	6.801692	.147022	9
10	1.790848	13.180795	.075868	.558395	7.360087	.135868	10
11	1.898299	14.971643	.066793	.526788	7.886875	.126793	11
12	2.012196	16.869941	.059277	.496969	8.383844	.119277	12
13	2.132928	18.882138	.052960	.468839	8.852683	.112960	13
14	2.260904	21.015066	.047585	.442301	9.294984	.107585	14
15	2.396558	23.275970	.042963	.417265	9.712249	.102963	15
16	2.540352	25.672528	.038952	.393646	10.105895	.098952	16
17	2.692773	28.212880	.035445	.371364	10.477260	.095445	17
18	2.854339	30.905653	.032357	.350344	10.827603	.092357	18
19	3.025600	33.759992	.029621	.330513	11.158116	.089621	19
20	3.207135	36.785591	.027185	.311805	11.469921	.087185	20
21	3.399564	39.992727	.025005	.294155	11.764077	.085005	21
22	3.603537	43.392290	.023046	.277505	12.041582	.083046	22
23	3.819750	46.995828	.021278	.261797	12.303379	.081278	23
24	4.048935	50.815577	.019679	.246979	12.550358	.079679	24
25	4.291871	54.864512	.018227	.232999	12.783356	.078227	25
26	4.549383	59.156383	.016904	.219810	13.003166	.076904	26
27	4.822346	63.705766	.015697	.207368	13.210534	.075697	27
28	5.111687	68.528112	.014593	.195630	13.406164	.074593	28
29	5.418388	73.639798	.013580	.184557	13.590721	.073580	29
30	5.743491	79.058186	.012649	.174110	13.764831	.072649	30
31	6.088101	84.801677	.011792	.164255	13.929086	.071792	31
32	6.453387	90.889778	.011002	.154957	14.084043	.071002	32
33	6.840590	97.343165	.010273	.146186	14.230230	.070273	33
34	7.251025	104.183755	.009598	.137912	14.368141	.069598	34
35	7.686087	111.434780	.008974	.130105	14.498246	.068974	35
36	8.147252	119.120867	.008395	.122741	14.620987	.068395	36
37	8.636087	127.268119	.007857	.115793	14.736780	.067857	37
38	9.154252	135.904206	.007358	.109239	14.846019	.067358	38
39	9.703507	145.058458	.006894	.103056	14.949075	.066894	39
40	10.285718	154.761966	.006462	.097222	15.046297	.066462	40
41	10.902861	165.047684	.006059	.091719	15.138016	.066059	41
42	11.557033	175.950545	.005683	.086527	15.224543	.065683	42
43	12.250455	187.507577	.005333	.081630	15.306173	.065333	43
44	12.985482	199.758032	.005006	.077009	15.383182	.065006	44
45	13.764611	212.743514	.004700	.072650	15.455832	.064700	45
46	14.590487	226.508125	.004415	.068538	15.524370	.064415	46
47	15.465917	241.098612	.004148	.064658	15.589028	.064148	47
48	16.393872	256.564529	.003898	.060998	15.650027	.063898	48
49	17.377504	272.958401	.003664	.057546	15.707572	.063664	49
50	18.420154	290.335905	.003444	.054288	15.761861	.063444	50
51	19.525364	308.756059	.003239	.051215	15.813076	.063239	51
52	20.696885	328.281422	.003046	.048316	15.861393	.063046	52
53	21.938698	348.978308	.002866	.045582	15.906974	.062866	53
54	23.255020	370.917006	.002696	.043001	15.949976	.062696	54
55	24.650322	394.172027	.002537	.040567	15.990543	.062537	55
56	26.129341	418.822348	.002388	.038271	16.028814	.062388	56
57	27.697101	444.951689	.002247	.036105	16.064919	.062247	57
58	29.358927	472.648790	.002116	.034061	16.098980	.062116	58
59	31.120463	502.007718	.001992	.032133	16.131113	.061992	59
60	32.987691	533.128181	.001876	.030314	16.161428	.061876	60

Reprinted by permission, from *Ellwood's Tables for Real Estate Appraising and Financing* (Ridgewood, N.J.: published by the author, 1959).

7%   ANNUAL COMPOUND INTEREST TABLE   7%

EFFECTIVE RATE = 7% $i = .07$

YEARS	1 AMOUNT OF 1 AT COMPOUND INTEREST $s = (1+i)^n$	2 ACCUMULATION OF 1 PER PERIOD $s_{\overline{n}|} = \frac{s-1}{i}$	3 SINKING FUND FACTOR $\frac{1}{s_{\overline{n}|}} = \frac{i}{s-1}$	4 PRES. VALUE REVERSION OF 1 $v^n = \frac{1}{s}$	5 PRESENT VALUE ORD. ANNUITY 1 PER PERIOD $a_{\overline{n}|} = \frac{s-1}{si}$	6 INSTALMENT TO AMORTIZE 1 $\frac{1}{a_{\overline{n}|}} = \frac{si}{s-1}$	n YEARS
1	1.070000	1.000000	1.000000	.934579	.934579	1.070000	1
2	1.144900	2.070000	.483092	.873439	1.808018	.553092	2
3	1.225043	3.214900	.311052	.816298	2.624316	.381052	3
4	1.310796	4.439943	.225228	.762895	3.387211	.295228	4
5	1.402552	5.750739	.173891	.712986	4.100197	.243891	5
6	1.500730	7.153291	.139796	.666342	4.766540	.209796	6
7	1.605781	8.654021	.115553	.622750	5.389289	.185553	7
8	1.718186	10.259803	.097468	.582009	5.971299	.167468	8
9	1.838459	11.977989	.083486	.543934	6.515232	.153486	9
10	1.967151	13.816448	.072378	.508349	7.023582	.142378	10
11	2.104852	15.783599	.063357	.475093	7.498674	.133357	11
12	2.252192	17.888451	.055902	.444012	7.942686	.125902	12
13	2.409845	20.140643	.049651	.414964	8.357651	.119651	13
14	2.578534	22.550488	.044345	.387817	8.745468	.114345	14
15	2.759032	25.129022	.039795	.362446	9.107914	.109795	15
16	2.952164	27.888054	.035858	.338735	9.446649	.105858	16
17	3.158815	30.840217	.032425	.316574	9.763223	.102425	17
18	3.379932	33.999033	.029413	.295864	10.059087	.099413	18
19	3.616528	37.378965	.026753	.276508	10.335595	.096753	19
20	3.869684	40.995492	.024393	.258419	10.594014	.094393	20
21	4.140562	44.865177	.022289	.241513	10.835527	.092289	21
22	4.430402	49.005739	.020406	.225713	11.061241	.090406	22
23	4.740530	53.436141	.018714	.210947	11.272187	.088714	23
24	5.072367	58.176671	.017189	.197147	11.469334	.087189	24
25	5.427433	63.249038	.015811	.184249	11.653583	.085811	25
26	5.807353	68.676470	.014561	.172195	11.825779	.084561	26
27	6.213868	74.483823	.013426	.160930	11.986709	.083426	27
28	6.648838	80.697691	.012392	.150402	12.137111	.082392	28
29	7.114257	87.346529	.011449	.140563	12.277674	.081449	29
30	7.612255	94.460786	.010586	.131367	12.409041	.080586	30
31	8.145113	102.073041	.009797	.122773	12.531814	.079797	31
32	8.715271	110.218154	.009073	.114741	12.646555	.079073	32
33	9.325340	118.933425	.008408	.107235	12.753790	.078408	33
34	9.978114	128.258765	.007797	.100219	12.854009	.077797	34
35	10.676581	138.236878	.007234	.093663	12.947672	.077234	35
36	11.423942	148.913460	.006715	.087535	13.035208	.076715	36
37	12.223618	160.337402	.006237	.081809	13.117017	.076237	37
38	13.079271	172.561020	.005795	.076457	13.193473	.075795	38
39	13.994820	185.640292	.005387	.071455	13.264928	.075387	39
40	14.974458	199.635112	.005009	.066780	13.331709	.075009	40
41	16.022670	214.609570	.004660	.062412	13.394120	.074660	41
42	17.144257	230.632240	.004336	.058329	13.452449	.074336	42
43	18.344355	247.776496	.004036	.054513	13.506962	.074036	43
44	19.628460	266.120851	.003758	.050946	13.557908	.073758	44
45	21.002452	285.749311	.003500	.047613	13.605522	.073500	45
46	22.472623	306.751763	.003260	.044499	13.650020	.073260	46
47	24.045707	329.224386	.003037	.041587	13.691608	.073037	47
48	25.728907	353.270093	.002831	.038867	13.730474	.072831	48
49	27.529930	378.998999	.002639	.036324	13.766799	.072639	49
50	29.457025	406.528929	.002460	.033948	13.800746	.072460	50
51	31.519017	435.985955	.002294	.031727	13.832473	.072294	51
52	33.725348	467.504971	.002139	.029651	13.862124	.072139	52
53	36.086122	501.230319	.001995	.027711	13.889836	.071995	53
54	38.612151	537.316442	.001861	.025899	13.915735	.071861	54
55	41.315001	575.928593	.001736	.024204	13.939939	.071736	55
56	44.207052	617.243594	.001620	.022621	13.962560	.071620	56
57	47.301545	661.450646	.001512	.021141	13.983701	.071512	57
58	50.612653	708.752191	.001411	.019758	14.003459	.071411	58
59	54.155539	759.364844	.001317	.018465	14.021924	.071317	59
60	57.946427	813.520383	.001229	.017257	14.039181	.071229	60

Reprinted by permission, from *Ellwood's Tables for Real Estate Appraising and Financing* (Ridgewood, N.J.: published by the author, 1959).

8%   ANNUAL COMPOUND INTEREST TABLE   8%

EFFECTIVE RATE = 8% $i = .08$

YEARS	1 AMOUNT OF 1 AT COMPOUND INTEREST $s = (1+i)^n$	2 ACCUMULATION OF 1 PER PERIOD $s_{\overline{n}} = \frac{s-1}{i}$	3 SINKING FUND FACTOR $\frac{1}{s_{\overline{n}}} = \frac{i}{s-1}$	4 PRES. VALUE REVERSION OF 1 $v^n = \frac{1}{s}$	5 PRESENT VALUE ORD. ANNUITY 1 PER PERIOD $a_{\overline{n}} = \frac{s-1}{si}$	6 INSTALMENT TO AMORTIZE 1 $\frac{1}{a_{\overline{n}}} = \frac{si}{s-1}$	n YEARS
1	1.080000	1.000000	1.000000	.925926	.925926	1.080000	1
2	1.166400	2.080000	.480769	.857339	1.783265	.560769	2
3	1.259712	3.246400	.308034	.793832	2.577097	.388034	3
4	1.360489	4.506112	.221921	.735030	3.312127	.301921	4
5	1.469328	5.866601	.170456	.680583	3.992710	.250456	5
6	1.586874	7.335929	.136315	.630170	4.622880	.216315	6
7	1.713824	8.922803	.112072	.583490	5.206370	.192072	7
8	1.850930	10.636628	.094015	.540269	5.746639	.174015	8
9	1.999005	12.487558	.080080	.500249	6.246888	.160080	9
10	2.158925	14.486562	.069029	.463193	6.710081	.149029	10
11	2.331639	16.645487	.060076	.428883	7.138964	.140076	11
12	2.518170	18.977126	.052695	.397114	7.536078	.132695	12
13	2.719624	21.495297	.046522	.367698	7.903776	.126522	13
14	2.937194	24.214920	.041297	.340461	8.244237	.121297	14
15	3.172169	27.152114	.036830	.315242	8.559479	.116830	15
16	3.425943	30.324283	.032977	.291890	8.851369	.112977	16
17	3.700018	33.750226	.029629	.270269	9.121638	.109629	17
18	3.996019	37.450244	.026702	.250249	9.371887	.106702	18
19	4.315701	41.446263	.024128	.231712	9.603599	.104128	19
20	4.660957	45.761964	.021852	.214548	9.818147	.101852	20
21	5.033834	50.422921	.019832	.198656	10.016803	.099832	21
22	5.436540	55.456755	.018032	.183941	10.200744	.098032	22
23	5.871464	60.893296	.016422	.170315	10.371059	.096422	23
24	6.341181	66.764759	.014978	.157699	10.528758	.094978	24
25	6.848475	73.105940	.013679	.146018	10.674776	.093679	25
26	7.396353	79.954415	.012507	.135202	10.809978	.092507	26
27	7.988061	87.350768	.011448	.125187	10.935165	.091448	27
28	8.627106	95.338830	.010489	.115914	11.051078	.090489	28
29	9.317275	103.965936	.009619	.107328	11.158406	.089619	29
30	10.062657	113.283211	.008827	.099377	11.257783	.088827	30
31	10.867669	123.345868	.008107	.092016	11.349799	.088107	31
32	11.737083	134.213537	.007451	.085200	11.434999	.087451	32
33	12.676050	145.950620	.006852	.078889	11.513888	.086852	33
34	13.690134	158.626670	.006304	.073045	11.586934	.086304	34
35	14.785344	172.316804	.005803	.067635	11.654568	.085803	35
36	15.968172	187.102148	.005345	.062625	11.717193	.085345	36
37	17.245626	203.070320	.004924	.057986	11.775179	.084924	37
38	18.625276	220.315945	.004539	.053690	11.828869	.084539	38
39	20.115298	238.941221	.004185	.049713	11.878582	.084185	39
40	21.724521	259.056519	.003860	.046031	11.924613	.083860	40
41	23.462483	280.781040	.003561	.042621	11.967235	.083561	41
42	25.339482	304.243523	.003287	.039464	12.006699	.083287	42
43	27.366640	329.583005	.003034	.036541	12.043240	.083034	43
44	29.555972	356.949646	.002802	.033834	12.077074	.082802	44
45	31.920449	386.505617	.002587	.031328	12.108401	.082587	45
46	34.474085	418.426067	.002390	.029007	12.137409	.082390	46
47	37.232012	452.900152	.002208	.026859	12.164267	.082208	47
48	40.210573	490.132164	.002040	.024869	12.189136	.082040	48
49	43.427419	530.342737	.001886	.023027	12.212163	.081886	49
50	46.901613	573.770156	.001743	.021321	12.233485	.081743	50
51	50.653742	620.671769	.001611	.019742	12.253227	.081611	51
52	54.706041	671.325510	.001490	.018280	12.271506	.081490	52
53	59.082524	726.031551	.001377	.016925	12.288432	.081377	53
54	63.809126	785.114075	.001274	.015672	12.304103	.081274	54
55	68.913856	848.923201	.001178	.014511	12.318614	.081178	55
56	74.426965	917.837058	.001090	.013436	12.332050	.081090	56
57	80.381122	992.264022	.001008	.012441	12.344491	.081008	57
58	86.811612	1072.645144	.000932	.011519	12.356010	.080932	58
59	93.756540	1159.456755	.000862	.010666	12.366676	.080862	59
60	101.257064	1253.213296	.000798	.009876	12.376552	.080798	60

Reprinted by permission, from *Ellwood's Tables for Real Estate Appraising and Financing* (Ridgewood, N.J.: published by the author, 1959).

9%   ANNUAL COMPOUND INTEREST TABLE   9%

EFFECTIVE RATE = 9%   i = .09

YEARS	1 AMOUNT OF 1 AT COMPOUND INTEREST $s = (1+i)^n$	2 ACCUMULATION OF 1 PER PERIOD $s_{\overline{n}|} = \frac{s-1}{i}$	3 SINKING FUND FACTOR $\frac{1}{s_{\overline{n}|}} = \frac{i}{s-1}$	4 PRES. VALUE REVERSION OF 1 $v^n = \frac{1}{s}$	5 PRESENT VALUE ORD. ANNUITY 1 PER PERIOD $a_{\overline{n}|} = \frac{s-1}{si}$	6 INSTALMENT TO AMORTIZE 1 $\frac{1}{a_{\overline{n}|}} = \frac{si}{s-1}$	n YEARS
1	1.090000	1.000000	1.000000	.917431	.917431	1.090000	1
2	1.188100	2.090000	.478469	.841680	1.759111	.568469	2
3	1.295029	3.278100	.305055	.772183	2.531295	.395055	3
4	1.411582	4.573129	.218669	.708425	3.239720	.308669	4
5	1.538624	5.984711	.167092	.649931	3.889651	.257092	5
6	1.667100	7.523335	.132920	.596267	4.485919	.222920	6
7	1.828039	9.200435	.108691	.547034	5.032953	.198691	7
8	1.992563	11.028474	.090674	.501866	5.534819	.180674	8
9	2.171893	13.021036	.076799	.460428	5.995247	.166799	9
10	2.367364	15.192930	.065820	.422411	6.417658	.155820	10
11	2.580426	17.560293	.056947	.387533	6.805191	.146947	11
12	2.812665	20.140720	.049651	.355535	7.160725	.139651	12
13	3.065805	22.953385	.043567	.326179	7.486904	.133567	13
14	3.341727	26.019189	.038433	.299246	7.786150	.128433	14
15	3.642482	29.360916	.034059	.274538	8.060688	.124059	15
16	3.970306	33.003399	.030300	.251870	8.312558	.120300	16
17	4.327633	36.973705	.027046	.231073	8.543631	.117046	17
18	4.717120	41.301338	.024212	.211994	8.755625	.114212	18
19	5.141661	46.018458	.021730	.194490	8.950115	.111730	19
20	5.604411	51.160120	.019546	.178431	9.128546	.109546	20
21	6.108808	56.764530	.017617	.163698	9.292244	.107617	21
22	6.658600	62.873338	.015905	.150182	9.442425	.105905	22
23	7.257874	69.531939	.014382	.137781	9.580207	.104382	23
24	7.911083	76.789813	.013023	.126405	9.706612	.103023	24
25	8.623081	84.700896	.011806	.115968	9.822580	.101806	25
26	9.399158	93.323977	.010715	.106393	9.928972	.100715	26
27	10.245082	102.723135	.009735	.097608	10.026580	.099735	27
28	11.167140	112.968217	.008852	.089548	10.116128	.098852	28
29	12.172182	124.135356	.008056	.082155	10.198283	.098056	29
30	13.267678	136.307539	.007336	.075371	10.273654	.097336	30
31	14.461770	149.575217	.006686	.069148	10.342802	.096686	31
32	15.763329	164.036987	.006096	.063438	10.406240	.096096	32
33	17.182028	179.800315	.005562	.058200	10.464441	.095562	33
34	18.728411	196.982344	.005077	.053395	10.517835	.095077	34
35	20.413968	215.710755	.004636	.048986	10.566821	.094636	35
36	22.251225	236.124723	.004235	.044941	10.611763	.094235	36
37	24.253835	258.375948	.003870	.041231	10.652993	.093870	37
38	26.436680	282.629783	.003538	.037826	10.690820	.093538	38
39	28.815982	309.066463	.003236	.034703	10.725523	.093236	39
40	31.409420	337.882445	.002960	.031838	10.757360	.092960	40
41	34.236268	369.291865	.002708	.029209	10.786569	.092708	41
42	37.317532	403.528133	.002478	.026797	10.813366	.092478	42
43	40.676110	440.845665	.002268	.024584	10.837951	.092268	43
44	44.336960	481.521775	.002077	.022555	10.860505	.092077	44
45	48.327286	525.858735	.001902	.020692	10.881197	.091902	45
46	52.676742	574.186021	.001742	.018984	10.900181	.091742	46
47	57.417649	626.862762	.001595	.017416	10.917597	.091595	47
48	62.585237	684.280411	.001461	.015978	10.933575	.091461	48
49	68.217908	746.865648	.001339	.014659	10.948234	.091339	49
50	74.357520	815.083556	.001227	.013449	10.961683	.091227	50
51	81.049697	889.441077	.001124	.012338	10.974021	.091124	51
52	88.344170	970.490773	.001030	.011319	10.985340	.091030	52
53	96.295145	1058.834943	.000944	.010385	10.995725	.090944	53
54	104.961708	1155.130088	.000866	.009527	11.005252	.090866	54
55	114.408262	1260.091796	.000794	.008741	11.013993	.090794	55
56	124.705005	1374.500057	.000728	.008019	11.022012	.090728	56
57	135.928456	1499.205063	.000667	.007357	11.029369	.090667	57
58	148.162017	1635.133518	.000612	.006749	11.036118	.090612	58
59	161.496598	1783.295535	.000561	.006192	11.042310	.090561	59
60	176.031292	1944.792133	.000514	.005681	11.047991	.090514	60

Reprinted by permission, from *Ellwood's Tables for Real Estate Appraising and Financing* (Ridgewood, N.J.: published by the author, 1959).

9 ½ % ANNUAL COMPOUND INTEREST TABLE 9 ½ %

EFFECTIVE RATE = 9 1/2% i = .095

YEARS	1 AMOUNT OF 1 AT COMPOUND INTEREST $s = (1+i)^n$	2 ACCUMULATION OF 1 PER PERIOD $s_{\overline{n}|} = \frac{s-1}{i}$	3 SINKING FUND FACTOR $\frac{1}{s_{\overline{n}|}} = \frac{i}{s-1}$	4 PRES. VALUE REVERSION OF 1 $v^n = \frac{1}{s}$	5 PRESENT VALUE ORD. ANNUITY 1 PER PERIOD $a_{\overline{n}|} = \frac{s-1}{si}$	6 INSTALMENT TO AMORTIZE 1 $\frac{1}{a_{\overline{n}|}} = \frac{si}{s-1}$	n YEARS
1	1.095000	1.000000	1.000000	.913242	.913242	1.095000	1
2	1.199025	2.095000	.477327	.834011	1.747253	.572327	2
3	1.312932	3.294025	.303580	.761654	2.508907	.398580	3
4	1.437661	4.606957	.217063	.695574	3.204481	.312063	4
5	1.574239	6.044618	.165436	.635228	3.839709	.260436	5
6	1.723791	7.618857	.131253	.580117	4.419825	.226253	6
7	1.887552	9.342648	.107036	.529787	4.949612	.202036	7
8	2.066869	11.230200	.089046	.483824	5.433436	.184046	8
9	2.263222	13.297069	.075205	.441848	5.875284	.170205	9
10	2.478228	15.560291	.064266	.403514	6.278798	.159266	10
11	2.713659	18.038518	.055437	.368506	6.647304	.150437	11
12	2.971457	20.752178	.048188	.336535	6.983839	.143188	12
13	3.253745	23.723634	.042152	.307338	7.291178	.137152	13
14	3.562851	26.977380	.037068	.280674	7.571852	.132068	14
15	3.901322	30.540231	.032744	.256323	7.828175	.127744	15
16	4.271948	34.441553	.029035	.234085	8.062260	.124035	16
17	4.677783	38.713500	.025831	.213777	8.276037	.120831	17
18	5.122172	43.391283	.023046	.195230	8.471266	.118046	18
19	5.608778	48.513454	.020613	.178292	8.649558	.115613	19
20	6.141612	54.122233	.018477	.162824	8.812382	.113477	20
21	6.725065	60.263845	.016594	.148697	8.961080	.111594	21
22	7.363946	66.988910	.014928	.135797	9.096876	.109928	22
23	8.063521	74.352856	.013449	.124015	9.220892	.108449	23
24	8.829556	82.416378	.012134	.113256	9.334148	.107134	24
25	9.668364	91.245934	.010959	.103430	9.437578	.105959	25
26	10.586858	100.914297	.009909	.094457	9.532034	.104909	26
27	11.592610	111.501156	.008969	.086262	9.618296	.103969	27
28	12.693908	123.093766	.008124	.078778	9.697074	.103124	28
29	13.899829	135.787673	.007364	.071943	9.769018	.102364	29
30	15.220313	149.687502	.006681	.065702	9.834719	.101681	30
31	16.666242	164.907815	.006064	.060002	9.894721	.101064	31
32	18.249535	181.574057	.005507	.054796	9.949517	.100507	32
33	19.983241	199.823593	.005004	.050042	9.999559	.100004	33
34	21.881649	219.806834	.004549	.045700	10.045259	.099549	34
35	23.960406	241.688483	.004138	.041736	10.086995	.099138	35
36	26.236644	265.648889	.003764	.038115	10.125109	.098764	36
37	28.729126	291.885534	.003426	.034808	10.159917	.098426	37
38	31.458393	320.614659	.003119	.031788	10.191705	.098119	38
39	34.446940	352.073052	.002840	.029030	10.220735	.097840	39
40	37.719399	386.519992	.002587	.026512	10.247247	.097587	40
41	41.302742	424.239391	.002357	.024211	10.271458	.097357	41
42	45.226503	465.542133	.002148	.022111	10.293569	.097148	42
43	49.523020	510.768636	.001958	.020193	10.313762	.096958	43
44	54.227707	560.291656	.001785	.018441	10.332203	.096785	44
45	59.379340	614.519364	.001627	.016841	10.349043	.096627	45
46	65.020377	673.898703	.001484	.015380	10.364423	.096484	46
47	71.197313	738.919080	.001353	.014045	10.378469	.096353	47
48	77.961057	810.116393	.001234	.012827	10.391296	.096234	48
49	85.367358	888.077450	.001126	.011714	10.403010	.096126	49
50	93.477257	973.444808	.001027	.010698	10.413707	.096027	50
51	102.357596	1066.922065	.000937	.009770	10.423477	.095937	51
52	112.081568	1169.279661	.000855	.008922	10.432399	.095855	52
53	122.729317	1281.361229	.000780	.008148	10.440547	.095780	53
54	134.388602	1404.090545	.000712	.007441	10.447988	.095712	54
55	147.155519	1538.479147	.000650	.006796	10.454784	.095650	55
56	161.135293	1685.634666	.000593	.006206	10.460990	.095593	56
57	176.443146	1846.769959	.000541	.005668	10.466657	.095541	57
58	193.205245	2023.213105	.000494	.005176	10.471833	.095494	58
59	211.559743	2216.418351	.000451	.004727	10.476560	.095451	59
60	231.657919	2427.978094	.000412	.004317	10.480877	.095412	60

Reprinted by permission, from *Ellwood's Tables for Real Estate Appraising and Financing* (Ridgewood, N.J.: published by the author, 1959).

10% ANNUAL COMPOUND INTEREST TABLE 10%

EFFECTIVE RATE =10%   i =.10

YEARS	1 AMOUNT OF 1 AT COMPOUND INTEREST $s = (1+i)^n$	2 ACCUMULATION OF 1 PER PERIOD $s_{\overline{n}} = \frac{s-1}{i}$	3 SINKING FUND FACTOR $\frac{1}{s_{\overline{n}}} = \frac{i}{s-1}$	4 PRES. VALUE REVERSION OF 1 $v^n = \frac{1}{s}$	5 PRESENT VALUE ORD. ANNUITY 1 PER PERIOD $a_{\overline{n}} = \frac{s-1}{si}$	6 INSTALMENT TO AMORTIZE 1 $\frac{1}{a_{\overline{n}}} = \frac{si}{s-1}$	n YEARS
1	1.100000	1.000000	1.000000	.909091	.909091	1.100000	1
2	1.210000	2.100000	.476190	.826446	1.735537	.576190	2
3	1.331000	3.310000	.302115	.751315	2.486852	.402115	3
4	1.464100	4.641000	.215471	.683013	3.169865	.315471	4
5	1.610510	6.105100	.163797	.620921	3.790787	.263797	5
6	1.771561	7.715610	.129607	.564474	4.355261	.229607	6
7	1.948717	9.487171	.105405	.513158	4.868419	.205405	7
8	2.143589	11.435888	.087444	.466507	5.334926	.187444	8
9	2.357948	13.579477	.073641	.424098	5.759024	.173641	9
10	2.593742	15.937425	.062745	.385543	6.144567	.162745	10
11	2.853117	18.531167	.053963	.350494	6.495061	.153963	11
12	3.138428	21.384284	.046763	.318631	6.813692	.146763	12
13	3.452271	24.522712	.040779	.289664	7.103356	.140779	13
14	3.797498	27.974983	.035746	.263331	7.366687	.135746	14
15	4.177248	31.772482	.031474	.239392	7.606080	.131474	15
16	4.594973	35.949730	.027817	.217629	7.823709	.127817	16
17	5.054470	40.544703	.024664	.197845	8.021553	.124664	17
18	5.559917	45.599173	.021930	.179859	8.201412	.121930	18
19	6.115909	51.159090	.019547	.163508	8.364920	.119547	19
20	6.727500	57.274999	.017460	.148644	8.513564	.117460	20
21	7.400250	64.002499	.015624	.135131	8.648694	.115624	21
22	8.140275	71.402749	.014005	.122846	8.771540	.114005	22
23	8.954302	79.543024	.012572	.111678	8.883218	.112572	23
24	9.849733	88.497327	.011300	.101526	8.984744	.111300	24
25	10.834706	98.347059	.010168	.092296	9.077040	.110168	25
26	11.918177	109.181765	.009159	.083905	9.160945	.109159	26
27	13.109994	121.099942	.008258	.076278	9.237223	.108258	27
28	14.420994	134.209936	.007451	.069343	9.306567	.107451	28
29	15.863093	148.630930	.006728	.063039	9.369606	.106728	29
30	17.449402	164.494023	.006079	.057309	9.426914	.106079	30
31	19.194342	181.943425	.005496	.052099	9.479013	.105496	31
32	21.113777	201.137767	.004972	.047362	9.526376	.104972	32
33	23.225154	222.251544	.004499	.043057	9.569432	.104499	33
34	25.547670	245.476699	.004074	.039143	9.608575	.104074	34
35	28.102437	271.024368	.003690	.035584	9.644159	.103690	35
36	30.912681	299.126805	.003343	.032349	9.676508	.103343	36
37	34.003949	330.039486	.003030	.029408	9.705917	.103030	37
38	37.404343	364.043434	.002747	.026735	9.732651	.102747	38
39	41.144778	401.447778	.002491	.024304	9.756956	.102491	39
40	45.259256	442.592556	.002259	.022095	9.779051	.102259	40
41	49.785181	487.851811	.002050	.020086	9.799137	.102050	41
42	54.763699	537.636992	.001860	.018260	9.817397	.101860	42
43	60.240069	592.400692	.001688	.016600	9.833998	.101688	43
44	66.264076	652.640761	.001532	.015091	9.849089	.101532	44
45	72.890484	718.904837	.001391	.013719	9.862808	.101391	45
46	80.179532	791.795321	.001263	.012472	9.875280	.101263	46
47	88.197485	871.974853	.001147	.011338	9.886618	.101147	47
48	97.017234	960.172338	.001041	.010307	9.896926	.101041	48
49	106.718957	1057.189572	.000946	.009370	9.906296	.100946	49
50	117.390853	1163.908529	.000859	.008519	9.914814	.100859	50
51	129.129938	1281.299382	.000780	.007744	9.922559	.100780	51
52	142.042932	1410.429320	.000709	.007040	9.929599	.100709	52
53	156.247225	1552.472252	.000644	.006400	9.935999	.100644	53
54	171.871948	1708.719477	.000585	.005818	9.941817	.100585	54
55	189.059142	1880.591425	.000532	.005289	9.947106	.100532	55
56	207.965057	2069.650567	.000483	.004809	9.951915	.100483	56
57	228.761562	2277.615624	.000439	.004371	9.956286	.100439	57
58	251.637719	2506.377186	.000399	.003974	9.960260	.100399	58
59	276.801490	2758.014905	.000363	.003613	9.963873	.100363	59
60	304.481640	3034.816395	.000330	.003284	9.967157	.100330	60

Reprinted by permission, from *Ellwood's Tables for Real Estate Appraising and Financing* (Ridgewood, N.J.: published by the author, 1959).

11% ANNUAL COMPOUND INTEREST TABLE 11%

YEARS	1 AMOUNT OF 1 AT COMPOUND INTEREST $s=(1+i)^n$	2 ACCUMULATION OF 1 PER PERIOD $s_{\overline{n}}=\frac{s-1}{i}$	3 SINKING FUND FACTOR $\frac{1}{s_{\overline{n}}}=\frac{i}{s-1}$	4 PRES. VALUE REVERSION OF 1 $v^n=\frac{1}{s}$	5 PRESENT VALUE ORD. ANNUITY 1 PER PERIOD $a_{\overline{n}}=\frac{s-1}{si}$	6 INSTALMENT TO AMORTIZE 1 $\frac{1}{a_{\overline{n}}}=\frac{si}{s-1}$	n YEARS
1	1.110000	1.0000	1.000000	.900901	.900901	1.110000	1
2	1.232100	2.1100	.473933	.811622	1.712523	.583933	2
3	1.367631	3.3421	.299213	.731191	2.443714	.409213	3
4	1.518070	4.7097	.212326	.658731	3.102445	322326	4
5	1.685058	6.2278	.160570	.593451	3.695896	.270570	5
6	1.870414	7.9129	.126377	.534641	4.230537	.236377	6
7	2.076160	9.7833	.102215	.481658	4.712195	.212215	7
8	2.304538	11.8594	.084321	.433926	5.146121	.194321	8
9	2.558037	14.1640	.070602	.390925	5.537046	.180602	9
10	2.839421	16.7220	.059801	.352184	5.889230	.169801	10
11	3.151757	19.5614	.051121	.317283	6.206513	.161121	11
12	3.498450	22.7132	.044027	.285841	6.492354	.154027	12
13	3.883280	26.2116	.038151	.257514	6.749868	.148151	13
14	4.310441	30.0949	.033228	.231995	6.981863	.143228	14
15	4.784590	34.4054	.029065	.209004	7.190867	.139065	15
16	5.310895	39.1899	.025517	.188292	7.379159	.135517	16
17	5.895093	44.5008	.022472	.169633	7.548792	.132472	17
18	6.543553	50.3959	.019843	.152822	7.701614	.129843	18
19	7.263344	56.9395	.017563	.137678	7.839292	.127563	19
20	8.062312	64.2028	.015576	.124034	7.963326	.125576	20
21	8.949166	72.2651	.013838	.111742	8.075068	.123838	21
22	9.933574	81.2143	.012313	.100669	8.175737	.122313	22
23	11.026267	91.1479	.010971	.090693	8.266430	.120971	23
24	12.239156	102.1742	.009787	.081705	8.348135	.119787	24
25	13.585463	114.4133	.008740	.073608	8.421743	.118740	25
26	15.079864	127.9988	.007813	.066314	8.488057	.117813	26
27	16.738649	143.0786	.006989	.059742	8.547799	.116989	27
28	18.579900	159.8173	.006257	.053822	8.601621	.116257	28
29	20.623689	178.3972	.005605	.048488	8.650109	.115605	29
30	22.892295	199.0209	.005025	.043683	8.693791	.115025	30

Reprinted by permission, from *Ellwood's Tables for Real Estate Appraising and Financing* (Ridgewood, N.J.: published by the author, 1959).

12% ANNUAL COMPOUND INTEREST TABLE 12%

YEARS	1 AMOUNT OF 1 AT COMPOUND INTEREST $s = (1+i)^n$	2 ACCUMULATION OF 1 PER PERIOD $s_{\overline{n}|} = \frac{s-1}{i}$	3 SINKING FUND FACTOR $\frac{1}{s_{\overline{n}|}} = \frac{i}{s-1}$	4 PRES. VALUE REVERSION OF 1 $v^n = \frac{1}{s}$	5 PRESENT VALUE ORD. ANNUITY 1 PER PERIOD $a_{\overline{n}|} = \frac{s-1}{si}$	6 INSTALMENT TO AMORTIZE 1 $\frac{1}{a_{\overline{n}|}} = \frac{si}{s-1}$	n YEARS
1	1.120000	1.0000	1.000000	.892857	.892857	1.120000	1
2	1.254400	2.1200	.471698	.797194	1.690051	.591698	2
3	1.404928	3.3744	.296349	.711780	2.401831	.416349	3
4	1.573519	4.7793	.209234	.635518	3.037349	.329234	4
5	1.762341	6.3528	.157410	.567427	3.604776	.277410	5
6	1.973822	8.1152	.123226	.506631	4.111407	.243226	6
7	2.210681	10.0890	.099118	.452349	4.563756	.219118	7
8	2.475963	12.2997	.081302	.403883	4.967639	.201302	8
9	2.773079	14.7757	.067679	.360610	5.328249	.187679	9
10	3.105848	17.5487	.056984	.321973	5.650222	.176984	10
11	3.478550	20.6546	.048415	.287476	5.937698	.168415	11
12	3.895976	24.1331	.041437	.256675	6.194373	.161437	12
13	4.363493	28.0291	.035677	.229174	6.423547	.155677	13
14	4.887112	32.3926	.030871	.204620	6.628167	.150871	14
15	5.473565	37.2797	.026824	.182696	6.810863	.146824	15
16	6.130393	42.7533	.023390	.163122	6.973985	.143390	16
17	6.866040	48.8837	.020457	.145644	7.119629	.140457	17
18	7.689965	55.7497	.017937	.130040	7.249669	.137937	18
19	8.612761	63.4397	.015763	.116107	7.365776	.135763	19
20	9.646292	72.0524	.013879	.103667	7.469443	.133879	20
21	10.803847	81.6987	.012240	.092560	7.562003	.132240	21
22	12.100309	92.5026	.010811	.082643	7.644646	.130811	22
23	13.552346	104.6029	.009560	.073788	7.718434	.129560	23
24	15.178628	118.1552	.008463	.065882	7.784316	.128463	24
25	17.000063	133.3339	.007500	.058823	7.843139	.127500	25
26	19.040071	150.3339	.006652	.052521	7.895660	.126652	26
27	21.324879	169.3740	.005904	.046894	7.942554	.125904	27
28	23.883864	190.6989	.005244	.041869	7.984423	.125244	28
29	26.749928	214.5827	.004660	.037383	8.021806	.124660	29
30	29.959918	241.3327	.004144	.033378	8.055184	.124144	30

Reprinted by permission, from *Ellwood's Tables for Real Estate Appraising and Financing* (Ridgewood, N.J.: published by the author, 1959).

13% ANNUAL COMPOUND INTEREST TABLE 13%

YEARS	1 AMOUNT OF 1 AT COMPOUND INTEREST $s=(1+i)^n$	2 ACCUMULATION OF 1 PER PERIOD $s_{\overline{n}}=\frac{s-1}{i}$	3 SINKING FUND FACTOR $\frac{1}{s_{\overline{n}}}=\frac{i}{s-1}$	4 PRES. VALUE REVERSION OF 1 $v^n=\frac{1}{s}$	5 PRESENT VALUE ORD. ANNUITY 1 PER PERIOD $a_{\overline{n}}=\frac{s-1}{si}$	6 INSTALMENT TO AMORTIZE 1 $\frac{1}{a_{\overline{n}}}=\frac{si}{s-1}$	n YEARS
1	1.130000	1.0000	1.000000	.884956	.884956	1.130000	1
2	1.276900	2.1300	.469483	.783147	1.668103	.599483	2
3	1.442897	3.4069	.293522	.693050	2.361153	.423522	3
4	1.630474	4.8498	.206194	.613319	2.974472	.336194	4
5	1.842436	6.4803	.154314	.542760	3.517232	.284314	5
6	2.081952	8.3227	.120153	.480318	3.997550	.250153	6
7	2.352607	10.4047	.096111	.425060	4.422610	.226111	7
8	2.658446	12.7573	.078387	.376160	4.798770	.208387	8
9	3.004044	15.4157	.064869	.332885	5.131655	.194869	9
10	3.394570	18.4198	.054290	.294588	5.426243	.184290	10
11	3.835864	21.8143	.045841	.260697	5.686940	.175841	11
12	4.334526	25.6502	.038986	.230706	5.917646	.168986	12
13	4.898014	29.9847	.033350	.204164	6.121810	.163350	13
14	5.534756	34.8827	.028668	.180676	6.302486	.158668	14
15	6.254274	40.4175	.024742	.159891	6.462377	.154742	15
16	7.067330	46.6718	.021426	.141496	6.603873	.151426	16
17	7.986083	53.7391	.018608	.125218	6.729091	.148608	17
18	9.024274	61.7252	.016201	.110812	6.839903	.146201	18
19	10.197430	70.7494	.014134	.098064	6.937967	.144134	19
20	11.523096	80.9469	.012354	.086782	7.024749	.142354	20
21	13.021098	92.4700	.010814	.076798	7.101547	.140814	21
22	14.713841	105.4911	.009480	.067963	7.169510	.139480	22
23	16.626640	120.2049	.008319	.060144	7.229654	.138319	23
24	18.788103	136.8316	.007308	.053225	7.282679	.137308	24
25	21.230556	155.6197	.006426	.047102	7.329984	.136426	25
26	23.990528	176.8502	.005655	.041683	7.371664	.135655	26
27	27.109297	200.8407	.004979	.036888	7.408552	.134979	27
28	30.633506	227.9500	.004387	.032644	7.441196	.134387	28
29	34.615862	258.5835	.003867	.028888	7.470084	.133867	29
30	39.115924	293.1994	.003411	.025565	7.495653	.133411	30

Reprinted by permission, from *Ellwood's Tables for Real Estate Appraising and Financing* (Ridgewood, N.J.: published by the author, 1959).

14% ANNUAL COMPOUND INTEREST TABLE 14%

YEARS	1 AMOUNT OF 1 AT COMPOUND INTEREST $s = (1+i)^n$	2 ACCUMULATION OF 1 PER PERIOD $s_{\overline{n}|} = \frac{s-1}{i}$	3 SINKING FUND FACTOR $\frac{1}{s_{\overline{n}|}} = \frac{i}{s-1}$	4 PRES. VALUE REVERSION OF 1 $v^n = \frac{1}{s}$	5 PRESENT VALUE ORD. ANNUITY 1 PER PERIOD $a_{\overline{n}|} = \frac{s-1}{si}$	6 INSTALMENT TO AMORTIZE 1 $\frac{1}{a_{\overline{n}|}} = \frac{si}{s-1}$	n YEARS
1	1.140000	1.0000	1.000000	.877193.	.877193	1.140000	1
2	1.299600	2.1400	.467290	.769468	1.646661	.607290	2
3	1.481544	3.4396	.290731	.674971	2.321623	.430731	3
4	1.688960	4.9211	.203205	.592080	2.913712	.343205	4
5	1.925415	6.6101	.151284	.519368	3.433080	.291284	5
6	2.194973	8.5355	.117158	.455587	3.888667	.257158	6
7	2.502269	10.7305	.093192	.399637	4.288304	.233192	7
8	2.852586	13.2328	.075570	.350559	4.638863	.215570	8
9	3.251949	16.0853	.062168	.307508	4.946371	.202168	9
10	3.707221	19.3373	.051714	.269744	5.216115	.191714	10
11	4.226232	23.0445	.043394	.236617	5.452732	.183394	11
12	4.817905	27.2707	.036669	.207559	5.660291	.176669	12
13	5.492411	32.0887	.031164	.182069	5.842360	.171164	13
14	6.261349	37.5811	.026609	.159710	6.002070	.166609	14
15	7.137938	43.8424	.022809	.140096	6.142166	.162809	15
16	8.137249	50.9804	.019615	.122892	6.265058	.159615	16
17	9.276464	59.1176	.016915	.107800	6.372858	.156915	17
18	10.575169	68.3941	.014621	.094561	6.467419	.154621	18
19	12.055693	78.9692	.012663	.082948	6.550367	.152663	19
20	13.743490	91.0249	.010986	.072762	6.623129	.150986	20
21	15.667578	104.7684	.009545	.063826	6.686955	.149545	21
22	17.861039	120.4360	.008303	.055988	6.742943	.148303	22
23	20.361585	138.2970	.007231	.049112	6.792055	.147231	23
24	23.212207	158.6586	.006303	.043081	6.835136	.146303	24
25	26.461916	181.8708	.005498	.037790	6.872926	.145498	25
26	30.166584	208.3327	.004800	.033149	6.906075	.144800	26
27	34.389906	238.4993	.004193	.029078	6.935153	.144193	27
28	39.204492	272.8892	.003665	.025507	6.960660	.143665	28
29	44.693121	312.0937	.003204	.022375	6.983035	.143204	29
30	50.950158	356.7868	.002803	.019627	7.002662	.142803	30

Reprinted by permission, from *Ellwood's Tables for Real Estate Appraising and Financing* (Ridgewood, N.J.: published by the author, 1959).

15%   ANNUAL COMPOUND INTEREST TABLE   15%

YEARS	1 AMOUNT OF I AT COMPOUND INTEREST $s = (1+i)^n$	2 ACCUMULATION OF I PER PERIOD $s_{\overline{n}|} = \frac{s-1}{i}$	3 SINKING FUND FACTOR $\frac{1}{s_{\overline{n}|}} = \frac{i}{s-1}$	4 PRES. VALUE REVERSION OF I $v^n = \frac{1}{s}$	5 PRESENT VALUE ORD. ANNUITY 1 PER PERIOD $a_{\overline{n}|} = \frac{s-1}{si}$	6 INSTALMENT TO AMORTIZE I $\frac{1}{a_{\overline{n}|}} = \frac{si}{s-1}$	n YEARS
1	1.150000	1.0000	1.000000	.869565	.869565	1.150000	1
2	1.322500	2.1500	.465116	.756144	1.625709	.615116	2
3	1.520875	3.4725	.287976	.657516	2.283225	.437976	3
4	1.749006	4.9934	.200265	.571753	2.854978	.350265	4
5	2.011357	6.7424	.148315	.497177	3.352155	.298315	5
6	2.313061	8.7537	.114236	.432328	3.784483	.264236	6
7	2.660020	11.0668	.090360	.375937	4.160420	.240360	7
8	3.059023	13.7268	.072850	.326902	4.487322	.222850	8
9	3.517876	16.7858	.059574	.284262	4.771584	.209574	9
10	4.045558	20.3037	.049252	.247185	5.018769	.199252	10
11	4.652391	24.3493	.041068	.214943	5.233712	.191068	11
12	5.350250	29.0017	.034480	.186907	5.420619	.184480	12
13	6.152788	34.3519	.029110	.162528	5.583147	.179110	13
14	7.075706	40.5047	.024688	.141329	5.724476	.174688	14
15	8.137062	47.5804	.021017	.122894	5.847370	.171017	15
16	9.357621	55.7175	.017947	.106865	5.954235	.167947	16
17	10.761264	65.0751	.015366	.092926	6.047161	.165366	17
18	12.375454	75.8364	.013186	.080805	6.127966	.163186	18
19	14.231772	88.2118	.011336	.070265	6.198231	.161336	19
20	16.366537	102.4436	.009761	.061100	6.259331	.159761	20
21	18.821518	118.8101	.008416	.053131	6.312462	.158416	21
22	21.644746	137.6316	.007265	.046201	6.358663	.157265	22
23	24.891458	159.2764	.006278	.040174	6.398837	.156278	23
24	28.625176	184.1678	.005429	.034934	6.433771	.155429	24·
25	32.918953	212.7930	.004699	.030378	6.464149	.154699	25
26	37.856796	245.7120	.004069	.026415	6.490564	.154069	26
27	43.535315	283.5688	.003526	.022970	6.513534	.153526	27
28	50.065612	327.1041	.003010	.019974	6.535508	153010	28
29	57.575454	377.1697	.002651	.017369	6.550877	.152651	29
30	66.211772	434.7451	.002300	.015103	6.565980	.152300	30

Reprinted by permission, from *Ellwood's Tables for Real Estate Appraising and Financing* (Ridgewood, N.J.: published by the author, 1959).

APPENDIXES

16% ANNUAL COMPOUND INTEREST TABLE 16%

YEARS	1 AMOUNT OF 1 AT COMPOUND INTEREST $s = (1+i)^n$	2 ACCUMULATION OF 1 PER PERIOD $s_{\overline{n}|} = \dfrac{s-1}{i}$	3 SINKING FUND FACTOR $\dfrac{1}{s_{\overline{n}|}} = \dfrac{i}{s-1}$	4 PRES. VALUE REVERSION OF 1 $v^n = \dfrac{1}{s}$	5 PRESENT VALUE ORD. ANNUITY 1 PER PERIOD $a_{\overline{n}|} = \dfrac{s-1}{si}$	6 INSTALMENT TO AMORTIZE 1 $\dfrac{1}{a_{\overline{n}|}} = \dfrac{si}{s-1}$	n YEARS
1	1.160000	1.0000	1.000000	.862068	.862068	1.160000	1
2	1.345600	2.1600	.462963	.743163	1.605231	.622963	2
3	1.560896	3.5056	.285257	.640658	2.245889	.445257	3
4	1.810639	5.0665	.197375	.552291	2.798180	.357375	4
5	2.100342	6.8771	.145409	.476113	3.274293	.305409	5
6	2.436396	8.9775	.111390	.410442	3.684735	.271390	6
7	2.826220	11.4139	.087613	.353829	4.038564	.247613	7
8	3.278415	14.2401	.070224	.305025	4.343589	.230224	8
9	3.802961	17.5185	.057083	.262953	4.606542	.217083	9
10	4.411435	21.3215	.046901	.226684	4.833226	.206901	10
11	5.117265	25.7329	.038861	.195417	5.028643	.198861	11
12	5.936027	30.8502	.032415	.168463	5.197106	.192415	12
13	6.885792	36.7862	.027184	.145227	5.342333	.187184	13
14	7.987518	43.6720	.022898	.125195	5.467528	.182898	14
15	9.265521	51.6595	.019358	.107927	5.575455	.179358	15
16	10.748005	60.9250	.016414	.093041	5.668496	.176414	16
17	12.467685	71.6730	.013952	.080207	5.748703	.173952	17
18	14.462515	84.1407	.011885	.069144	5.817847	.171885	18
19	16.776517	98.6032	.010142	.059607	5.877454	.170142	19
20	19.460760	115.3797	.008667	.051385	5.928839	.168667	20
21	22.574482	134.8405	.007416	.044298	5.973137	.167416	21
22	26.186399	157.4150	.006353	.038188	6.011325	.166353	22
23	30.376223	183.6014	.005447	.032920	6.044245	.165447	23
24	35.236418	213.9776	.004673	.028380	6.072625	.164673	24
25	40.874245	249.2140	.004013	.024465	6.097090	.164013	25
26	47.414124	290.0883	.003447	.021091	6.118181	.163447	26
27	55.000384	337.5024	.002963	.018182	6.136363	.162963	27
28	63.800446	392.5028	.002548	.015674	6.152037	.162548	28
29	74.008517	456.3032	.002192	.013512	6.165549	.162192	29
30	85.849880	530.3117	.001886	.011648	6.177197	.161886	30

Reprinted by permission, from *Ellwood's Tables for Real Estate Appraising and Financing* (Ridgewood, N.J.: published by the author, 1959).

17%   **ANNUAL COMPOUND INTEREST TABLE**   **17%**

YEARS	1 AMOUNT OF I AT COMPOUND INTEREST $s = (1+i)^n$	2 ACCUMULATION OF I PER PERIOD $s_{\overline{n}|} = \frac{s-1}{i}$	3 SINKING FUND FACTOR $\frac{1}{s_{\overline{n}|}} = \frac{i}{s-1}$	4 PRES. VALUE REVERSION OF I $v^n = \frac{1}{s}$	5 PRESENT VALUE ORD. ANNUITY I PER PERIOD $a_{\overline{n}|} = \frac{s-1}{si}$	6 INSTALMENT TO AMORTIZE I $\frac{1}{a_{\overline{n}|}} = \frac{si}{s-1}$	n YEARS
1	1.170000	1.0000	1.000000	.854701	.854701	1.170000	1
2	1.368900	2.1700	.460829	730514	1.585215	.630829	2
3	1.601613	3.5389	.282573	.624371	2.209586	.452573	3
4	1.873887	5.1405	.194533	.533650	2.743236	.364533	4
5	2.192448	7.0144	.142564	.456111	3.199347	.312564	5
6	2.565164	9.2068	.108615	.389839	3.589186	.278615	6
7	3.001242	11.7720	.084947	.333195	3.922381	.254947	7
8	3.511453	14.7733	.067690	.284782	4.207163	.237690	8
9	4.108400	18.2847	.054690	.243404	4.450567	.224690	9
10	4.806828	22.3931	.044657	.208037	4.658604	.214657	10
11	5.623989	27.1999	.036765	.177810	4.836414	.206765	11
12	6.580067	32.8239	.030466	.151974	4.988388	.200466	12
13	7.698679	39.4040	.025378	.129892	5.118280	.195378	13
14	9.007454	47.1027	.021230	.111019	5.229299	.191230	14
15	10.538722	56.1101	.017822	.094888	5.324187	.187822	15
16	12.330304	66.6488	.015004	.081101	5.405288	.185004	16
17	14.426456	78.9792	.012662	.069317	5.474605	.182662	17
18	16.878954	93.4055	.010706	.059245	5.533850	.180706	18
19	19.748376	110.2846	.009067	.050637	5.584487	.179067	19
20	23.105599	130.0329	.007690	.043280	5.627767	.177690	20
21	27.033551	153.1385	.006530	.036991	5.664758	.176530	21
22	31.629255	180.1721	.005550	.031616	5.696374	.175550	22
23	37.006228	211.8013	.004721	.027022	5.723396	.174721	23
24	43.297287	248.8076	.004019	.023096	5.746492	.174019	24
25	50.657826	292.1049	.003423	.019740	5.766232	.173423	25
26	59.269657	342.7627	.002918	.016872	5.783104	.172918	26
27	69.345498	402.0323	.002487	.014421	5.797525	.172487	27
28	81.134233	471.3778	.002121	.012325	5.809850	.172121	28
29	94.927052	552.5121	.001810	.010534	5.820384	.171810	29
30	111.064651	647.4391	.001545	.009004	5.829388	.171545	30

Reprinted by permission, from *Ellwood's Tables for Real Estate Appraising and Financing* (Ridgewood, N.J.: published by the author, 1959).

18% ANNUAL COMPOUND INTEREST TABLE 18%

YEARS	1 AMOUNT OF 1 AT COMPOUND INTEREST $s=(1+i)^n$	2 ACCUMULATION OF 1 PER PERIOD $s_{\overline{n}|}=\frac{s-1}{i}$	3 SINKING FUND FACTOR $\frac{1}{s_{\overline{n}|}}=\frac{i}{s-1}$	4 PRES. VALUE REVERSION OF 1 $v^n=\frac{1}{s}$	5 PRESENT VALUE ORD. ANNUITY 1 PER PERIOD $a_{\overline{n}|}=\frac{s-1}{si}$	6 INSTALMENT TO AMORTIZE 1 $\frac{1}{a_{\overline{n}|}}=\frac{si}{s-1}$	n YEARS
1	1.180000	1.0000	1.000000	.847458	.847458	1.180000	1
2	1.392400	2.1800	.458715	.718184	1.565642	.638715	2
3	1.643032	3.5724	.279923	.608631	2.174273	.459923	3
4	1.938778	5.2154	.191738	.515789	2.690062	.371738	4
5	2.287758	7.1542	.139778	.437109	3.127171	.319778	5
6	2.699554	9.4420	.105910	.370432	3.497603	.285910	6
7	3.185474	12.1415	.082362	.313925	3.811528	.262362	7
8	3.758859	15.3270	.065243	.266038	4.077566	.245243	8
9	4.435454	19.0859	.052395	.225456	4.303022	.232395	9
10	5.233836	23.5213	.042515	.191064	4.494086	.222515	10
11	6.175926	28.7551	.034776	.161919	4.656005	.214776	11
12	7.287593	34.9311	.028628	.137220	4.793225	.208628	12
13	8.599360	42.2187	.023686	.116288	4.909513	.203686	13
14	10.147244	50.8180	.019678	.098549	5.008062	.199678	14
15	11.973748	60.9653	.016403	.083516	5.091578	.196403	15
16	14.129023	72.9390	.013710	.070776	5.162354	.193710	16
17	16.672247	87.0680	.011485	.059980	5.222334	.191485	17
18	19.673251	103.7403	.009639	.050830	5.273164	.189639	18
19	23.214437	123.4135	.008103	.043077	5.316241	.188103	19
20	27.393035	146.6280	.006820	.036506	5.352747	.186820	20
21	32.323782	174.0210	.005746	.030937	5.383684	.185746	21
22	38.142063	206.3448	.004846	.026218	5.409902	.184846	22
23	45.007634	244.4869	.004090	.022218	5.432120	.184090	23
24	53.109008	289.4945	.003454	.018829	5.450949	.183454	24
25	62.668629	342.6035	.002919	.015957	5.466906	.182919	25
26	73.948983	405.2721	.002467	.013523	5.480429	.182467	26
27	87.259799	479.2211	.002087	.011460	5.491889	.182087	27
28	102.966563	566.4809	.001765	.009712	5.501601	.181765	28
29	121.500545	669.4475	.001494	.008230	5.509831	.181494	29
30	143.370643	790.9480	.001264	.006975	5.516806	.181264	30

Reprinted by permission, from *Ellwood's Tables for Real Estate Appraising and Financing* (Ridgewood, N.J.: published by the author, 1959).

ANNUAL COMPOUND INTEREST TABLE

19% YEARS	1 AMOUNT OF 1 AT COMPOUND INTEREST $s = (1+i)^n$	2 ACCUMULATION OF 1 PER PERIOD $s_{\overline{n}} = \frac{s-1}{i}$	3 SINKING FUND FACTOR $\frac{1}{s_{\overline{n}}} = \frac{i}{s-1}$	4 PRES. VALUE REVERSION OF 1 $v^n = \frac{1}{s}$	5 PRESENT VALUE ORD. ANNUITY 1 PER PERIOD $a_{\overline{n}} = \frac{s-1}{si}$	6 INSTALMENT TO AMORTIZE 1 $\frac{1}{a_{\overline{n}}} = \frac{si}{s-1}$	19% n YEARS
1	1.190000	1.0000	1.000000	.840336	.840336	1.190000	1
2	1.416100	2.1900	.456621	.706165	1.546501	.646621	2
3	1.685159	3.6061	.277308	.593416	2.139917	.467308	3
4	2.005339	5.2913	.188991	.498669	2.638586	.378991	4
5	2.386354	7.2966	.137050	.419049	3.057635	.327050	5
6	2.839761	9.6830	.103274	.352142	3.409777	.293274	6
7	3.379315	12.5227	.079855	.295918	3.705695	.269855	7
8	4.021385	15.9020	.062885	.248671	3.954366	.252885	8
9	4.785449	19.9234	.050192	.208967	4.163333	.240192	9
10	5.694684	24.7089	.040471	.175602	4.338935	.230471	10
20%							**20%**
1	1.200000	1.0000	1.000000	.833333	.833333	1.200000	1
2	1.440000	2.2000	.454546	.694444	1.527777	.654546	2
3	1.728000	3.6400	.274725	.578704	2.106481	.474725	3
4	2.073600	5.3680	.186289	.482253	2.588734	.386289	4
5	2.488320	7.4416	.134380	.401878	2.990612	.334380	5
6	2.985984	9.9299	.100706	.334898	3.325510	.300706	6
7	3.583181	12.9159	.077424	.279082	3.604592	.277424	7
8	4.299817	16.4991	.060609	.232568	3.837160	.260609	8
9	5.159780	20.7989	.048079	.193807	4.030967	.248079	9
10	6.191736	25.9587	.038523	.161506	4.192473	.238523	10
21%							**21%**
1	1.210000	1.0000	1.000000	.826446	.826446	1.210000	1
2	1.464100	2.2100	.452489	.683013	1.509459	.662489	2
3	1.771561	3.6741	.272176	.564474	2.073933	.482176	3
4	2.143589	5.4457	.183633	.466507	2.540440	.393633	4
5	2.593742	7.5893	.131765	.385543	2.925983	.341765	5
6	3.138428	10.1830	.098203	.318631	3.244614	.308203	6
7	3.797498	13.3214	.075067	.263331	3.507945	.285067	7
8	4.594973	17.1189	.058415	.217629	3.725574	.268415	8
9	5.559917	21.7139	.046054	.179859	3.905433	.256054	9
10	6.727500	27.2738	.036665	.148644	4.054077	.246665	10
22%							**22%**
1	1.220000	1.0000	1.000000	.819672	.819672	1.220000	1
2	1.488400	2.2200	.450451	.671862	1.491534	.670451	2
3	1.815848	3.7084	.269658	.550707	2.042241	.489658	3
4	2.215335	5.5242	.181020	.451399	2.493640	.401020	4
5	2.702708	7.7396	.129206	.369999	2.863639	.349206	5
6	3.297304	10.4423	.095765	.303278	3.166917	.315765	6
7	4.022711	13.7396	.072782	.248589	3.415506	.292782	7
8	4.907707	17.7623	.056299	.203761	3.619267	.276299	8
9	5.987403	22.6700	.044111	.167017	3.786284	.264111	9
10	7.304632	28.6574	.034895	.136899	3.923183	.254895	10

Reprinted by permission, from *Ellwood's Tables for Real Estate Appraising and Financing* (Ridgewood, N.J.: published by the author, 1959).

ANNUAL COMPOUND INTEREST TABLE

23%	1 AMOUNT OF 1 AT COMPOUND INTEREST $s = (1+i)^n$	2 ACCUMULATION OF 1 PER PERIOD $s_{\overline{n}\|} = \frac{s-1}{i}$	3 SINKING FUND FACTOR $\frac{1}{s_{\overline{n}\|}} = \frac{i}{s-1}$	4 PRES. VALUE REVERSION OF 1 $v^n = \frac{1}{s}$	5 PRESENT VALUE ORD. ANNUITY 1 PER PERIOD $a_{\overline{n}\|} = \frac{s-1}{si}$	6 INSTALMENT TO AMORTIZE 1 $\frac{1}{a_{\overline{n}\|}} = \frac{si}{s-1}$	23% n
YEARS							YEARS
1	1.230000	1.0000	1.000000	.813008	.813008	1.230000	1
2	1.512900	2.2300	.448431	.660982	1.473990	.678431	2
3	1.860867	3.7429	.267173	.537384	2.011374	.497173	3
4	2.288866	5.6038	.178451	.436898	2.448272	408451	4
5	2.815306	7.8926	.126700	.355201	2.803473	.356700	5
6	3.462826	10.7079	.093389	.288781	3.092254	.323389	6
7	4.259276	14.1708	.070568	.234782	3.327036	.300568	7
8	5.238909	18.4300	.054259	.190879	3.517915	.284259	8
9	6.443859	23.6690	.042249	.155187	3.673102	.272249	9
10	7.925946	30.1128	.033208	.126168	3.799270	.263208	10
24%							**24%**
1	1.240000	1.0000	1.000000	.806452	.806452	1.240000	1
2	1.537600	2.2400	.446428	.650364	1.456816	.686428	2
3	1.906624	3.7776	.264718	.524487	1.981303	.504718	3
4	2.364214	5.6842	.175925	.422974	2.404277	.415925	4
5	2.931625	8.0484	.124248	.341108	2.745385	.364248	5
6	3.635215	10.9801	.091074	.275087	3.020472	.331074	6
7	4.507667	14.6153	.068422	.221844	3.242316	.308422	7
8	5.589507	19.1229	.052293	.178907	3.421223	.292293	8
9	6.930988	24.7125	.040465	.144280	3.565503	.280465	9
10	8.594425	31.6434	.031602	.116354	3 681857	.271602	10
25%							**25%**
1	1.250000	1.0000	1.000000	.800000	.800000	1.250000	1
2	1.562500	2.2500	.444444	.640000	1.440000	.694444	2
3	1.953125	3.8125	.262295	.512000	1.952000	.512295	3
4	2.441406	5.7656	.173442	.409600	2.361600	.423442	4
5	3.051758	8.2070	.121847	.327680	2.689280	.371847	5
6	3.814697	11.2588	.088819	.262144	2.951424	.338819	6
7	4.768372	15.0735	.066342	.209715	3.161139	.316342	7
8	5.960465	19.8419	.050399	.167772	3.328911	.300399	8
9	7.450581	25.8023	.038756	.134218	3.463129	.288756	9
10	9.313226	33.2529	.030073	.107374	3.570503	.280073	10
30%							**30%**
1	1.300000	1.0000	1.000000	.769231	.769231	1.300000	1
2	1.690000	2.3000	.434782	.591716	1.360947	.734782	2
3	2.197000	3.9900	.250627	.455166	1.816113	.550627	3
4	2.856100	6.1870	.161629	.350128	2.166241	.461629	4
5	3.712930	9.0431	.110582	.269329	2.435570	.410582	5
6	4.826809	12.7560	.078394	.207176	2.642746	.378394	6
7	6.274852	17.5828	.056874	.159366	2.802112	.356874	7
8	8.157307	23.8577	.041915	.122589	2.924701	.341915	8
9	10.604499	32.0150	.031235	.094300	3.019001	.331235	9
10	13.785849	42.6195	.023463	.072538	3.091539	.323463	10

Reprinted by permission, from *Ellwood's Tables for Real Estate Appraising and Financing* (Ridgewood, N.J.: published by the author, 1959).

Heating Systems

GRAVITY WARM-AIR HEATING SYSTEM

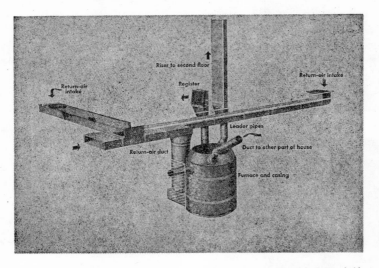

Air circulation in a gravity warm-air system results from the fact that heated air flows upward and cool air flows downward. Air is warmed as it comes into contact with heated surfaces of the furnace. As the air becomes warmer, it rises and flows through leader pipes (and risers if the house has more than one story) to the warm-air supply registers in the rooms. The cooler air in the rooms flows downward and is drawn through return-air intakes (usually located in first-floor rooms) to return-air ducts, and then to the space between the furnace and the furnace casing.

A gravity warm-air system:

● Is economical to install and is well suited to low-cost homes.

● Has no motors or electrical connections other than those required if controls or an automatic burner are used.

● Is simple to operate.

● Responds to rapid changes in outdoor temperatures.

● Is best adapted to a house with a compact floor plan since leader pipes and return-air ducts should be as short as possible.

● Requires a centrally located furnace, and either horizontal or inclined leader pipes. (The inclined pipes reduce the amount of usable basement head room.)

● Is not suitable for basementless houses or for heating basement rooms since the furnace must be below the level of the rooms to be heated.

● Permits air to be humidified.

Room Heating Units: Supply registers for gravity warm-air systems are usually installed in the baseboard on the inside walls or in the floor.
    Return-air intakes are placed in the floor near an outside wall, usually below windows.

Maintenance: Furnace must be inspected periodically.

Design and Installation: Use Manual 5, "Code and Manual for the Design and Installation of Gravity Warm-Air Heating Systems," published by the National Warm Air Heating and Air Conditioning Association.

University of Illinois Small Homes Council Circular G3.1

479

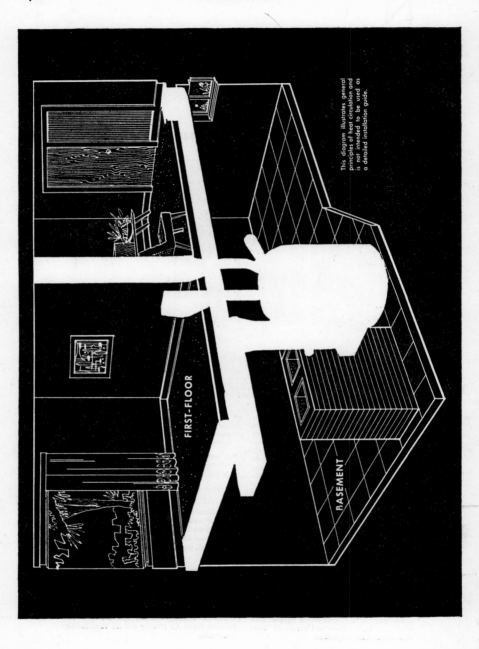

FIRST-FLOOR

BASEMENT

This diagram illustrates general principles of heat circulation and is not intended to be used as a detailed installation guide.

WARM-AIR PERIMETER-LOOP SYSTEM

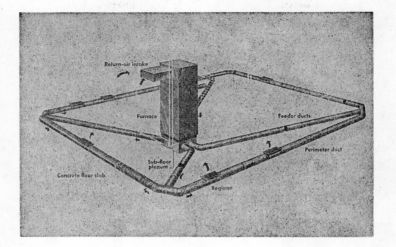

Perimeter-loop heating with a down-flow furnace is intended for basementless houses built on a concrete floor slab. The warm air from the furnace is circulated through a duct system which is embedded in the concrete slab. This duct system encircles the slab at its outer edge and is connected to the furnace by feeder ducts.

The warm air in the ducts is discharged into the room through outlets — either floor diffusers or baseboard diffusers placed on the outside walls, usually below windows. Air is taken back to the furnace through return-air intakes at locations either on an inside wall or in a hallway ceiling close to the furnace.

Several arrangements of perimeter ducts and feeder ducts are possible. These ducts can be of sheet metal, vitrified tile, concrete pipe or other precast forms.

A perimeter-loop heating system:

● Is designed to eliminate cold floors and retain all the advantages of a forced warm air heating system.

● Is economical to install.

● Needs very little floor area since a down-flow-type

furnace has been designed for basementless installations. These furnaces may be placed in closets, alcoves, or utility rooms, but provisions must be made to supply air to the furnace for combustion purposes.

● Requires a well-constructed concrete slab which is laid on suitable porous fill and which has a waterproof membrane and edge insulation.

● Is well adapted to conventional thermostatic controls.

● Can, through the use of filters and a humidifier, condition room air.

● Can be adapted to summer air conditioning with the addition of cooling equipment.

Maintenance: Motor and blower must be oiled, filters cleaned or replaced, and furnace inspected periodically.

Design and Installation: Use Manual 4, "Warm-Air Perimeter Heating" and Manual 6, "Adjusting Air Conditioning Systems for Maximum Comfort," published by the National Warm Air Heating and Air Conditioning Association.

University of Illinois Small Homes Council Circular G3.1

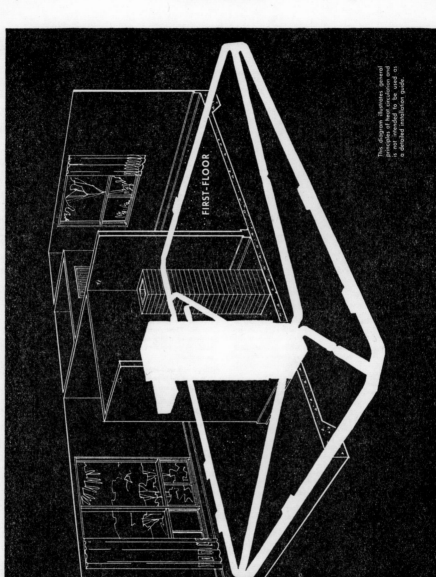

FIRST-FLOOR

This diagram illustrates general principles of heat circulation and is not intended to be used as a detailed installation guide.

FORCED WARM-AIR EXTENDED-PLENUM SYSTEM

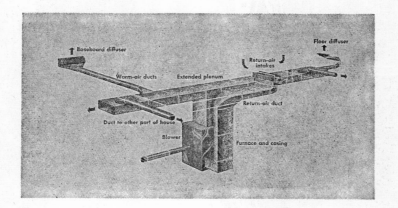

Air circulation in a forced warm-air system is maintained by a blower (fan) in the furnace. The air is warmed by the heated surfaces of the furnace and then distributed to the various rooms through supply ducts and supply outlets. The blower also draws the room air back to the furnace through the return-air intakes and return ducts to be reheated and filtered. After the room air has been heated and filtered it is redistributed to the rooms.

A forced warm-air system:

- Responds rapidly to changes in outdoor temperature.
- Is economical to install.
- Is adapted to basementless houses and large structures, and to the heating of basement rooms since air circulation is maintained by the blower.
- Requires less space for the furnace and ducts than a gravity system. The furnace does not need to be centrally located and all the ducts are smaller.
- Can through the use of filters and a humidifier condition room air.
- Can be adapted to summer air conditioning with the addition of cooling equipment.

- Can provide controlled outdoor ventilation through the duct system.

Room Heating Units: Adjustable registers and diffusers located on the outside wall at the floor level, preferably below windows, are recommended for heating. The supply outlets so installed will curtain the cold outside wall with warm air and will not discharge directly on the occupants.

For small houses a single central return-air intake may be sufficient. In larger structures multiple return-air intakes may be necessary. The return-air intakes are usually located on inside walls, or in the ceilings of hallways.

Maintenance: Motor and blower must be oiled, filters cleaned or replaced, and the furnace inspected periodically.

Design and Installation: Use Manual 4, "Warm-Air Perimeter Heating" and Manual 6, "Adjusting Air Conditioning Systems for Maximum Comfort," published by the National Warm Air Heating and Air Conditioning Association.

University of Illinois Small Homes Council Circular G3.1

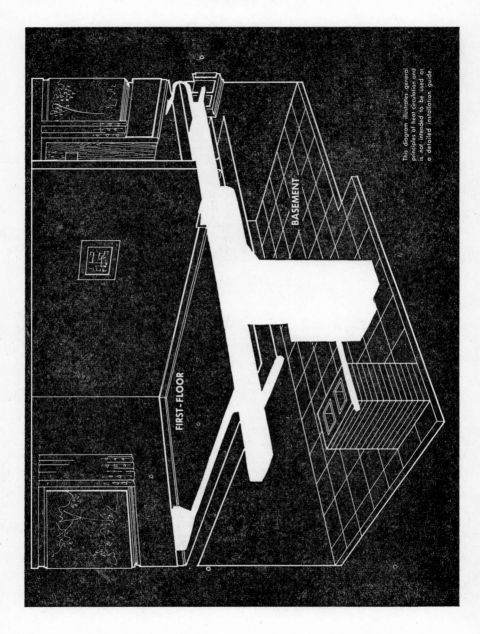

BASEMENT

FIRST-FLOOR

This diagram illustrates general principles of heat circulation and is not intended to be used as a detailed installation guide.

STEAM HEATING SYSTEM

In a steam system, the steam is generated in the boiler and rises to the room heating units. Here it condenses and forms water which is returned to the boiler.

Steam systems may be either one-pipe (shown above) or two-pipe.* The latter is not generally used for small homes because of its cost.

One-Pipe System

In the one-pipe steam system, the pipe which carries the steam to a radiator or convector also returns the condensed steam (water) to the boiler.

Since both steam and water are present in the single main, the pipes must be larger than those of other boiler systems and must be accurately pitched to avoid water pockets and "hammering" in the main.

A one-pipe steam system:

● Is simple and economical to install.

● Has no motors or electrical connections other than those required if controls or an automatic burner are used.

● Heats domestic water the year-round if heating coils are installed in the boiler, and an automatic fuel burner is used.

● Offers difficulty in control as radiator tempera-

ture cannot be varied. The radiator valve must be either entirely on or off in order to prevent the convectors or radiators from filling with water. (In the two-pipe system, the heat input rate to rooms can be controlled.)

● Is not recommended for basementless houses or for heating basement rooms since the boiler must be below the level of the room heating units.

Room Heating Units: Either radiators or convectors may be used. Baseboard units are not generally recommended for the one-pipe steam system; they may be used with the two-pipe.

Maintenance: The water level in the boiler should be checked regularly, as should the operation of boiler safety controls and the air vents on each radiator or convector.

Design and Installation: Use I-B-R Piping Guide No. 700, "Residential Heating Systems," and Installation Guide No. 800, "Hydronic Heating Systems," published by the Institute of Boiler and Radiator Manufacturers.

* In the two-pipe system (not illustrated), the steam rises through a supply main and risers to the room heating units. Air in the system and the condensed steam (water) are forced through thermostatic traps at the outlets of the radiators into the return main. An air eliminator in the return main expels the air through a vent and allows the water to return to the boiler.
The system can be adapted to basementless structures if a condensation pump or a vacuum pump is added.

University of Illinois Small Homes Council Circular G3.1

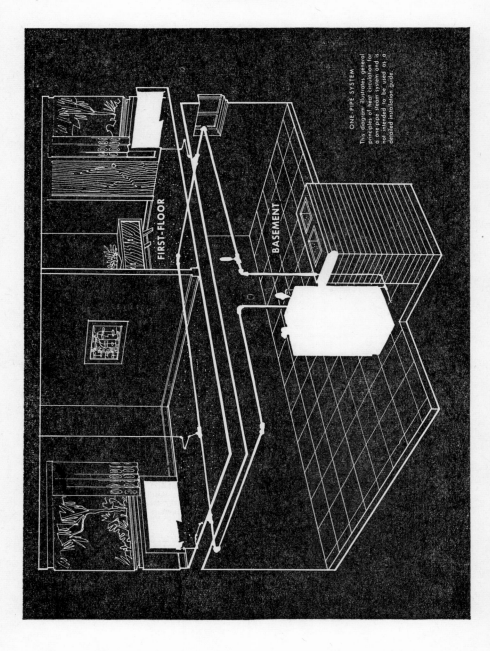

ONE-PIPE SYSTEM

This diagram illustrates general principles of heat circulation for a one-pipe steam system and is not intended to be used as a detailed installation guide.

FIRST-FLOOR

BASEMENT

GRAVITY HOT-WATER HEATING SYSTEM

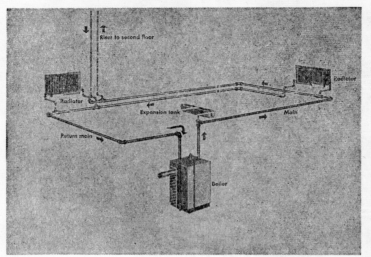

Circulation in a gravity hot-water system results from the fact that heated water flows to the top and cool water to the bottom of a container. Water is heated in the boiler and as it becomes warmer, it rises and flows out through supply pipes (mains and risers) to the room heating units (radiators, convectors or baseboards); the cooled water flows downward through the return pipes (risers and mains) to the bottom of the boiler.

This system may be operated either as a *closed* or as an *open* system.

In the closed, or pressure, system (shown above), the expansion tank is usually located near the boiler. As the heated water expands, the air in the tank is compressed. Since an increase in pressure raises the boiling point of the water, higher temperatures can be maintained in the closed system than in the open system without having steam form in the room heating units. These higher temperatures permit the use of smaller heating units than those needed for the open system.

In the open system, the expansion tank is located above the highest radiator, and the water is "open" or exposed to the air.

A gravity hot-water system:

- Is economical to install as it requires a minimum of special fittings or devices.

- Has no motors or electrical connections other than those required if controls or an automatic burner are used.

- Is not generally recommended for basementless houses or for the heating of basement rooms since the boiler should be at a lower level than the room heating units.

- Requires large supply and return mains in order to reduce friction since circulation of the water is by gravity action.

- Has a slower response to temperature changes than a forced hot-water system because of the larger amount of water retained in pipes and room heating units.

Room Heating Units: Radiators, baseboards or convectors may be used with this system.

Maintenance: Water pressure (altitude) in system must be checked, and room heating units vented regularly unless automatic air vents are used.

Design and Installation: The design and installation of this system should be the work of competent men experienced in gravity hot-water heating.

University of Illinois Small Homes Council Circular G3.1

BASEMENT

FIRST-FLOOR

This diagram illustrates general principles of heat circulation and is not intended to be used as a detailed installation guide.

FORCED HOT-WATER HEATING SYSTEM

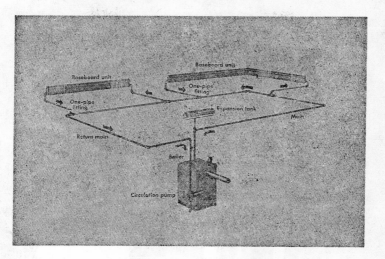

In a forced hot-water system, the water is heated in the boiler and is forced through the pipes (mains and risers) to the room heating units. The circulation of water is produced by the action of a circulating pump at the boiler. The pump is motor driven and requires electrical connections.

Two basic types of piping layout are common:

The one-pipe system (shown above) — This has a single pipe or main which supplies the heated water to the baseboard units (or convectors or radiators) and also returns the cooled water from the units to the boiler.

The two-pipe system — This system has two mains. The heated water is supplied to room heating units through a supply main, and the cooled water is returned to the boiler through a separate return main.

A forced hot-water system:

- Responds rapidly to changes in outside temperature. Temperature of the room heating unit can be varied in accordance with changing weather so that uniform room air temperatures are maintained.

- Can be used to heat domestic water the year-round when heating coils are installed with the boiler and an automatic fuel burner is used.

- Is adapted to basementless houses and to the heating of basement rooms. Circulation of water by means of the pump makes it possible to locate radiators, baseboard units or convectors either above or below the level of the boiler.

- Makes possible a large amount of usable basement space since small pipes can be used for the mains and risers. (The pump is capable of circulating water against high friction heads, making large pipes unnecessary.)

- May cost more to install than a gravity hot-water system due to the need for the circulating pump and, for one-pipe systems, special fittings. Frequently the reduction in pipe size results in lower labor and material costs which partially offset the cost of the pump and one-pipe fittings.

Room Heating Units: Radiators, convectors or baseboard units may be used.

Maintenance: Water pressure in system must be checked, motor oiled, and room heating units vented regularly unless automatic vents are used.

Design and Installation: For one-pipe systems which use radiators or convectors use I-B-R Piping Guide No. 700, "Residential Heating Systems," and Installation Guide No. 800, "Hydronic Heating Systems," published by the Institute of Boiler and Radiator Manufacturers.

University of Illinois Small Homes Council Circular G3.1

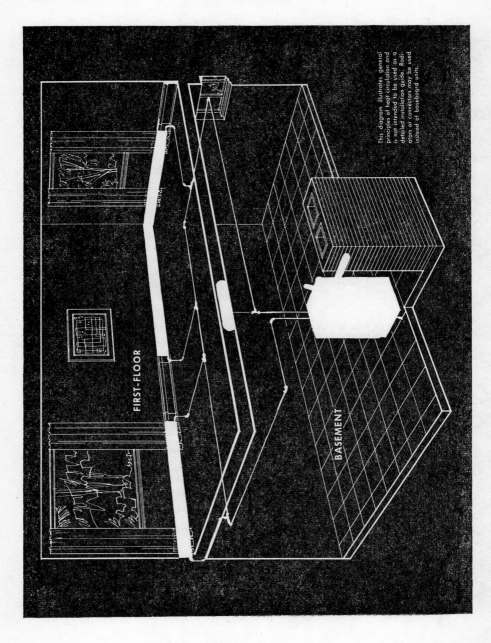

This diagram illustrates general principles of heat circulation and is not intended to be used as a detailed installation guide. Radiators or convectors may be used instead of baseboard units.

FIRST-FLOOR

BASEMENT

Index

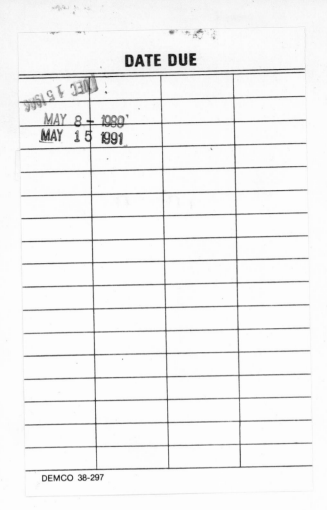